W9-CKJ-362

Subaru Automotive Repair Manual

by Mike Stubblefield and John H Haynes

Member of the Guild of Motoring Writers

Models covered:

2WD and 4WD Sedan, Hatchback,
Station Wagon, XT, Brat Pick-up and Loyale models
1980 through 1994

Does not include Justy, Legacy or XT6 models

(12A1 - 89003)
(681)

ABCDE
FGHIJ
KLMNO
PQRS

Haynes Publishing Group
Sparkford Nr Yeovil
Somerset BA22 7JJ England

Haynes North America, Inc
861 Lawrence Drive
Newbury Park
California 91320 USA

About this manual

Its purpose

The purpose of this manual is to help you get the best value from your vehicle. It can do so in several ways. It can help you decide what work must be done, even if you choose to have it done by a dealer service department or a repair shop; it provides information and procedures for routine maintenance and servicing; and it offers diagnostic and repair procedures to follow when trouble occurs.

We hope you use the manual to tackle the work yourself. For many simpler jobs, doing it yourself may be quicker than arranging an appointment to get the vehicle into a shop and making the trips to leave it and pick it up. More importantly, a lot of money can be saved by avoiding the expense the shop must pass on to you to cover its labor and overhead costs. An added benefit is the sense of satisfaction and accomplishment that you feel after doing the job yourself.

Using the manual

The manual is divided into Chapters. Each Chapter is divided into numbered Sections, which are headed in bold type between horizontal lines. Each Section consists of consecutively numbered paragraphs.

At the beginning of each numbered Section you will be referred to any illustrations which apply to the procedures in that Section. The reference numbers used in illustration captions pinpoint the pertinent Section and the Step within that Section. That is, illustration 3.2 means the illustration refers to Section 3 and Step (or paragraph) 2 within that Section.

Procedures, once described in the text, are not normally repeated. When it's necessary to refer to another Chapter, the reference will be given as Chapter and Section number. Cross references given without use of the word "Chapter" apply to Sections and/or paragraphs in the same Chapter. For example, "see Section 8" means in the same Chapter.

References to the left or right side of the vehicle assume you are sitting in the driver's seat, facing forward.

Even though we have prepared this manual with extreme care, neither the publisher nor the author can accept responsibility for any errors in, or omissions from, the information given.

NOTE

A **Note** provides information necessary to properly complete a procedure or information which will make the procedure easier to understand.

CAUTION

A **Caution** provides a special procedure or special steps which must be taken while completing the procedure where the Caution is found. Not heeding a Caution can result in damage to the assembly being worked on.

WARNING

A **Warning** provides a special procedure or special steps which must be taken while completing the procedure where the Warning is found. Not heeding a Warning can result in personal injury.

Acknowledgements

Technical writers who contributed to this project include Larry Holt, Rob Maddox, Jeff Kibler and Jay Storer. Wiring diagrams provided exclusively for Haynes North America, Inc. by Valley Forge Technical Communications.

A book in the Haynes Automotive Repair Manual Series

Printed in the U.S.A.

ISBN 1 56392 203 7

Library of Congress Catalog Card Number 95-80970

Contents

1991 Subaru Loyale Wagon

Introduction to the Subaru models in this manual

These Subarus are available in two-door and four door sedan, hatchback and station wagon models and have a conventional front engine/front-wheel drive layout on 2WD models.

All models covered by this manual are equipped with a 1.6L OHV engine, a 1.8L OHV engine or a 1.8L OHC engine. Early models are equipped with a carburetor while later models are equipped with throttle body or multi-port fuel injection systems.

Power from the engine is transferred through a five speed manual or four speed automatic transaxle via front independent driveaxles. On 4WD models, additional power is transferred to the rear of the vehicle through the driveshaft and into the rear differential which also utilizes independent rear driveaxles.

Suspension is independent in the front, utilizing coil springs with Mac Phearson struts and lower control arms to locate the knuckle assembly at each wheel. The rear suspension features either a torsion bar type or a coil over shock type.

The steering gear is a power assisted rack and pinion type that is mounted to the front of the engine crossmember with rubber insulators.

The brakes are disc at the front and drums at the rear, with power assist standard. Some later models are equipped with disc brakes in the rear, instead of drums.

Vehicle identification numbers

Modifications are a continuing and unpublicized process in vehicle manufacturing. Since spare parts lists and manuals are compiled on a numerical basis, the individual vehicle numbers are necessary to correctly identify the component required.

Vehicle Identification Number (VIN)

This very important identification num-ber is stamped on a plate attached to the dashboard inside the windshield on the driver's side of the vehicle and on the engine compartment firewall **(see illustrations)**. The VIN also appears on the Vehicle Certificate of Title and Registration. It contains information such as where and when the vehicle was manufactured, the model year and the body style.

VIN engine and model year codes

Two particularly important pieces of information found in the VIN are the engine code and the model year code. Counting from the left, the engine code letter designation is the 6th digit and the model year code letter designation is the 10th digit.

The VIN number is visible through the driver's side window . . .

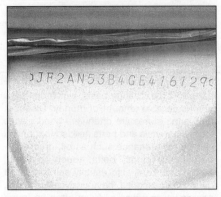

. . . and on the center of the firewall in the engine compartment

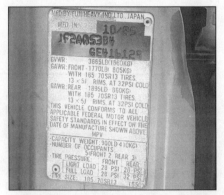

The vehicle certification label is affixed the to the driver's side door pillar

The engine identification number is stamped into the right side of the crankcase near the front

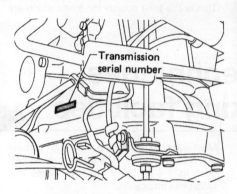

The transaxle identification tag is affixed to the top of the bellhousing

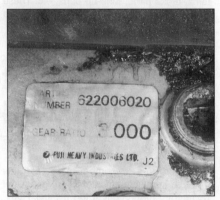

The rear differential identification tag is affixed to the differential cover

On the models covered by this manual the engine codes are:

2	1.6L
3	1.6L 4WD
4	1.8L
5	1.8L 4WD
7	1.8L 4WD with air suspension

On the models covered by this manual the model year codes are:

A	1980	J	1988
B	1981	K	1989
C	1982	L	1990
D	1983	M	1991
E	1984	N	1992
F	1985	P	1993
G	1986	R	1994
H	1987		

IMPORTANT VEHICLE INFORMATION

ENGINE FAMILY —
GFJ1.8T2HCP1 (109 CID)
EGR/AIV/TWC+EGS/OC
EVAPORATIVE
EMISSION FAMILY-LU

THIS VEHICLE CONFORMS TO U.S. EPA AND STATE OF CALIFORNIA REGULATIONS APPLICABLE TO 1986 MODEL YEAR NEW LIGHT-DUTY TRUCKS PROVIDED THAT THIS VEHICLE IS ONLY INTRODUCED INTO COMMERCE FOR SALE IN THE STATE OF CALIFORNIA.

ENGINE TUNE-UP SPECIFICATIONS AND ADJUSTMENTS	CATALYST
MAKE IDLE ADJUSTMENT WITH ENGINE AT NORMAL OPERATING TEMPERATURES AND LIGHTS OFF.	

IDLE SPEED	MANUAL: 700 ± 100 RPM IN NEUTRAL
	AUTOMATIC: 800 ± 100 RPM IN "N" OR "P" POSITION
IDLE MIXTURE	IDLE MIXTURE IS PRESET AT FACTORY AND SHOULD NOT BE ADJUSTED DURING ENGINE TUNE-UP.
IGNITION TIMING	MANUAL: 8° ± 2° BTDC AT 700 RPM — WITH VACUUM LINE DISCONNECTED FROM DISTRIBUTOR
	AUTOMATIC: 8° ± 2° BTDC AT 800 RPM
VALVE LASH	ADJUSTMENT DURING TUNE-UP IS NOT NECESSARY.

ABOVE TUNE-UP SPECIFICATIONS AND ADJUSTMENTS ARE APPLICABLE TO ANY ELEVATION.

FUJI HEAVY INDUSTRIES LTD. JAPAN   J9

The vehicle emissions label is affixed to the underside of the hood in the engine compartment

Vehicle Certification Label

The Vehicle Certification Label is attached to the driver's side door pillar **(see illustration)**. Information on this label includes the name of the manufacturer, the month and year of production, as well as the tire size and tire inflation information.

Engine identification number

Labels containing the engine code, engine number and build date can be found on the valve cover **(see illustration)**. The engine number is also stamped onto a machined pad on the external surface of the engine block.

Manual and Automatic transaxle identification number(s)

The transaxle ID number is stamped on a tag which is riveted to the top of the bell housing **(see illustration)**.

Rear differential (4WD) identification number

The rear differential ID number is stamped on a tag which is affixed to the differential cover **(see illustration)**.

Vehicle Emissions Control Information label

This label is found on the inside of the hood in the engine compartment **(see illustration)**. See Chapter 6 for more information on this label.

Buying parts

Replacement parts are available from many sources, which generally fall into one of two categories - authorized dealer parts departments and independent retail auto parts stores. Our advice concerning these parts is as follows:

Retail auto parts stores: Good auto parts stores will stock frequently needed components which wear out relatively fast, such as clutch components, exhaust systems, brake parts, tune-up parts, etc. These stores often supply new or reconditioned parts on an exchange basis, which can save a considerable amount of money. Discount auto parts stores are often very good places to buy materials and parts needed for general vehicle maintenance such as oil, grease, filters, spark plugs, belts, touch-up paint, bulbs, etc. They also usually sell tools and general accessories, have convenient hours, charge lower prices and can often be found not far from home.

Authorized dealer parts department: This is the best source for parts which are unique to the vehicle and not generally available elsewhere (such as major engine parts, transmission parts, trim pieces, etc.).

Warranty information: If the vehicle is still covered under warranty, be sure that any replacement parts purchased - regardless of the source - do not invalidate the warranty!

To be sure of obtaining the correct parts, have engine and chassis numbers available and, if possible, take the old parts along for positive identification.

Maintenance techniques, tools and working facilities

Maintenance techniques

There are a number of techniques involved in maintenance and repair that will be referred to throughout this manual. Application of these techniques will enable the home mechanic to be more efficient, better organized and capable of performing the various tasks properly, which will ensure that the repair job is thorough and complete.

Fasteners

Fasteners are nuts, bolts, studs and screws used to hold two or more parts together. There are a few things to keep in mind when working with fasteners. Almost all of them use a locking device of some type, either a lockwasher, locknut, locking tab or thread adhesive. All threaded fasteners should be clean and straight, with undamaged threads and undamaged corners on the hex head where the wrench fits. Develop the habit of replacing all damaged nuts and bolts with new ones. Special locknuts with nylon or fiber inserts can only be used once. If they are removed, they lose their locking ability and must be replaced with new ones.

Rusted nuts and bolts should be treated with a penetrating fluid to ease removal and prevent breakage. Some mechanics use turpentine in a spout-type oil can, which works quite well. After applying the rust penetrant, let it work for a few minutes before trying to loosen the nut or bolt. Badly rusted fasteners may have to be chiseled or sawed off or removed with a special nut breaker, available at tool stores.

If a bolt or stud breaks off in an assembly, it can be drilled and removed with a special tool commonly available for this purpose.

Most automotive machine shops can perform this task, as well as other repair procedures, such as the repair of threaded holes that have been stripped out.

Flat washers and lockwashers, when removed from an assembly, should always be replaced exactly as removed. Replace any damaged washers with new ones. Never use a lockwasher on any soft metal surface (such as aluminum), thin sheet metal or plastic.

Grade 1 or 2   Grade 5   Grade 8

Bolt strength marking (standard/SAE/USS; bottom - metric)

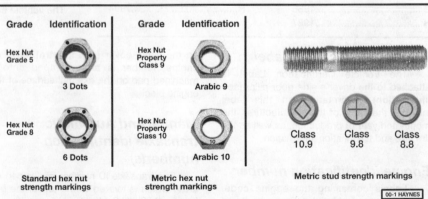

Grade	Identification	Grade	Identification
Hex Nut Grade 5	3 Dots	Hex Nut Property Class 9	Arabic 9
Hex Nut Grade 8	6 Dots	Hex Nut Property Class 10	Arabic 10

Standard hex nut strength markings

Metric hex nut strength markings

Class 10.9   Class 9.8   Class 8.8

Metric stud strength markings

00-1 HAYNES

Fastener sizes

For a number of reasons, automobile manufacturers are making wider and wider use of metric fasteners. Therefore, it is important to be able to tell the difference between standard (sometimes called U.S. or SAE) and metric hardware, since they cannot be interchanged.

All bolts, whether standard or metric, are sized according to diameter, thread pitch and length. For example, a standard 1/2 - 13 x 1 bolt is 1/2 inch in diameter, has 13 threads per inch and is 1 inch long. An M12 - 1.75 x 25 metric bolt is 12 mm in diameter, has a thread pitch of 1.75 mm (the distance between threads) and is 25 mm long. The two bolts are nearly identical, and easily confused, but they are not interchangeable.

In addition to the differences in diameter, thread pitch and length, metric and standard bolts can also be distinguished by examining the bolt heads. To begin with, the distance across the flats on a standard bolt head is measured in inches, while the same dimension on a metric bolt is sized in millimeters (the same is true for nuts). As a result, a standard wrench should not be used on a metric bolt and a metric wrench should not be used on a standard bolt. Also, most standard bolts have slashes radiating out from the center of the head to denote the grade or strength of the bolt, which is an indication of the amount of torque that can be applied to it. The greater the number of slashes, the greater the strength of the bolt. Grades 0 through 5 are commonly used on automobiles. Metric bolts have a property class (grade) number, rather than a slash, molded into their heads to indicate bolt strength. In this case, the higher the number, the stronger the bolt. Property class numbers 8.8, 9.8 and 10.9 are commonly used on automobiles.

Strength markings can also be used to distinguish standard hex nuts from metric hex nuts. Many standard nuts have dots stamped into one side, while metric nuts are marked with a number. The greater the number of dots, or the higher the number, the greater the strength of the nut.

Metric studs are also marked on their ends according to property class (grade). Larger studs are numbered (the same as metric bolts), while smaller studs carry a geometric code to denote grade.

It should be noted that many fasteners, especially Grades 0 through 2, have no distinguishing marks on them. When such is the case, the only way to determine whether it is standard or metric is to measure the thread pitch or compare it to a known fastener of the same size.

Standard fasteners are often referred to as SAE, as opposed to metric. However, it should be noted that SAE technically refers to a non-metric fine thread fastener only. Coarse thread non-metric fasteners are referred to as USS sizes.

Since fasteners of the same size (both standard and metric) may have different

Metric thread sizes	Ft-lbs	Nm
M-6	6 to 9	9 to 12
M-8	14 to 21	19 to 28
M-10	28 to 40	38 to 54
M-12	50 to 71	68 to 96
M-14	80 to 140	109 to 154

Pipe thread sizes		
1/8	5 to 8	7 to 10
1/4	12 to 18	17 to 24
3/8	22 to 33	30 to 44
1/2	25 to 35	34 to 47

U.S. thread sizes		
1/4 - 20	6 to 9	9 to 12
5/16 - 18	12 to 18	17 to 24
5/16 - 24	14 to 20	19 to 27
3/8 - 16	22 to 32	30 to 43
3/8 - 24	27 to 38	37 to 51
7/16 - 14	40 to 55	55 to 74
7/16 - 20	40 to 60	55 to 81
1/2 - 13	55 to 80	75 to 108

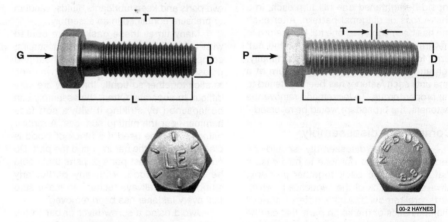

Standard (SAE and USS) bolt dimensions/grade marks

G Grade marks (bolt strength)
L Length (in inches)
T Thread pitch (number of threads per inch)
D Nominal diameter (in inches)

Metric bolt dimensions/grade marks

P Property class (bolt strength)
L Length (in millimeters)
T Thread pitch (distance between threads in millimeters)
D Diameter

strength ratings, be sure to reinstall any bolts, studs or nuts removed from your vehicle in their original locations. Also, when replacing a fastener with a new one, make sure that the new one has a strength rating equal to or greater than the original.

Tightening sequences and procedures

Most threaded fasteners should be tightened to a specific torque value (torque is the twisting force applied to a threaded component such as a nut or bolt). Overtightening the fastener can weaken it and cause it to break, while undertightening can cause it to eventually come loose. Bolts, screws and studs, depending on the material they are

made of and their thread diameters, have specific torque values, many of which are noted in the Specifications at the beginning of each Chapter. Be sure to follow the torque recommendations closely. For fasteners not assigned a specific torque, a general torque value chart is presented here as a guide. These torque values are for dry (unlubricated) fasteners threaded into steel or cast iron (not aluminum). As was previously mentioned, the size and grade of a fastener determine the amount of torque that can safely be applied to it. The figures listed here are approximate for Grade 2 and Grade 3 fasteners. Higher grades can tolerate higher torque values.

Fasteners laid out in a pattern, such as cylinder head bolts, oil pan bolts, differential cover bolts, etc., must be loosened or tight-

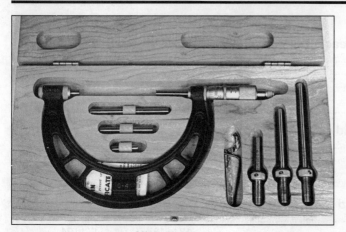

Micrometer set

Dial indicator set

ened in sequence to avoid warping the component. This sequence will normally be shown in the appropriate Chapter. If a specific pattern is not given, the following procedures can be used to prevent warping.

Initially, the bolts or nuts should be assembled finger-tight only. Next, they should be tightened one full turn each, in a criss-cross or diagonal pattern. After each one has been tightened one full turn, return to the first one and tighten them all one-half turn, following the same pattern. Finally, tighten each of them one-quarter turn at a time until each fastener has been tightened to the proper torque. To loosen and remove the fasteners, the procedure would be reversed.

Component disassembly

Component disassembly should be done with care and purpose to help ensure that the parts go back together properly. Always keep track of the sequence in which parts are removed. Make note of special characteristics or marks on parts that can be installed more than one way, such as a grooved thrust washer on a shaft. It is a good idea to lay the disassembled parts out on a clean surface in the order that they were removed. It may also be helpful to make sketches or take instant photos of components before removal.

When removing fasteners from a component, keep track of their locations. Sometimes threading a bolt back in a part, or putting the washers and nut back on a stud, can prevent mix-ups later. If nuts and bolts cannot be returned to their original locations, they should be kept in a compartmented box or a series of small boxes. A cupcake or muffin tin is ideal for this purpose, since each cavity can hold the bolts and nuts from a particular area (i.e. oil pan bolts, valve cover bolts, engine mount bolts, etc.). A pan of this type is especially helpful when working on assemblies with very small parts, such as the carburetor, alternator, valve train or interior dash and trim pieces. The cavities can be marked with paint or tape to identify the contents.

Whenever wiring looms, harnesses or connectors are separated, it is a good idea to identify the two halves with numbered pieces of masking tape so they can be easily reconnected.

Gasket sealing surfaces

Throughout any vehicle, gaskets are used to seal the mating surfaces between two parts and keep lubricants, fluids, vacuum or pressure contained in an assembly.

Many times these gaskets are coated with a liquid or paste-type gasket sealing compound before assembly. Age, heat and pressure can sometimes cause the two parts to stick together so tightly that they are very difficult to separate. Often, the assembly can be loosened by striking it with a soft-face hammer near the mating surfaces. A regular hammer can be used if a block of wood is placed between the hammer and the part. Do not hammer on cast parts or parts that could be easily damaged. With any particularly stubborn part, always recheck to make sure that every fastener has been removed.

Avoid using a screwdriver or bar to pry apart an assembly, as they can easily mar the gasket sealing surfaces of the parts, which must remain smooth. If prying is absolutely necessary, use an old broom handle, but keep in mind that extra clean up will be necessary if the wood splinters.

After the parts are separated, the old gasket must be carefully scraped off and the gasket surfaces cleaned. Stubborn gasket material can be soaked with rust penetrant or treated with a special chemical to soften it so it can be easily scraped off. A scraper can be fashioned from a piece of copper tubing by flattening and sharpening one end. Copper is recommended because it is usually softer than the surfaces to be scraped, which reduces the chance of gouging the part. Some gaskets can be removed with a wire brush, but regardless of the method used, the mating surfaces must be left clean and smooth. If for some reason the gasket surface is gouged, then a gasket sealer thick enough to fill scratches will have to be used during reassembly of the components. For most applications, a non-drying (or semi-drying) gasket sealer should be used.

Hose removal tips

Warning: *If the vehicle is equipped with air conditioning, do not disconnect any of the A/C hoses without first having the system depressurized by a dealer service department or a service station.*

Hose removal precautions closely parallel gasket removal precautions. Avoid scratching or gouging the surface that the hose mates against or the connection may leak. This is especially true for radiator hoses. Because of various chemical reactions, the rubber in hoses can bond itself to the metal spigot that the hose fits over. To remove a hose, first loosen the hose clamps that secure it to the spigot. Then, with slip-joint pliers, grab the hose at the clamp and rotate it around the spigot. Work it back and forth until it is completely free, then pull it off. Silicone or other lubricants will ease removal if they can be applied between the hose and the outside of the spigot. Apply the same lubricant to the inside of the hose and the outside of the spigot to simplify installation.

As a last resort (and if the hose is to be replaced with a new one anyway), the rubber can be slit with a knife and the hose peeled from the spigot. If this must be done, be careful that the metal connection is not damaged.

If a hose clamp is broken or damaged, do not reuse it. Wire-type clamps usually weaken with age, so it is a good idea to replace them with screw-type clamps whenever a hose is removed.

Tools

A selection of good tools is a basic requirement for anyone who plans to maintain and repair his or her own vehicle. For the owner who has few tools, the initial investment might seem high, but when compared to the spiraling costs of professional auto maintenance and repair, it is a wise one.

To help the owner decide which tools are needed to perform the tasks detailed in this manual, the following tool lists are offered: *Maintenance and minor repair, Repair/overhaul* and *Special*.

The newcomer to practical mechanics

Dial caliper

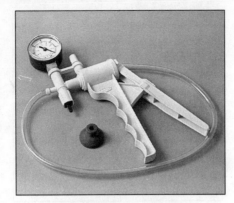

Hand-operated vacuum pump

Timing light

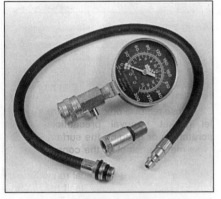

Compression gauge with spark plug
hole adapter

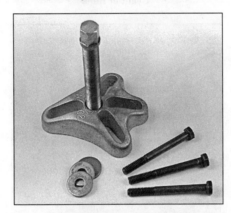

Damper/steering wheel puller

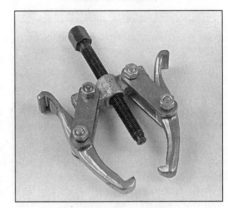

General purpose puller

Hydraulic lifter removal tool

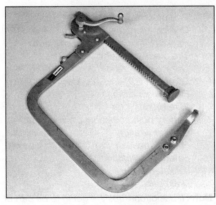

Valve spring compressor

Valve spring compressor

Ridge reamer

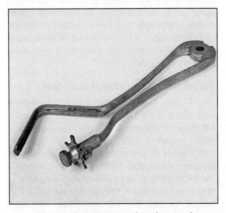

Piston ring groove cleaning tool

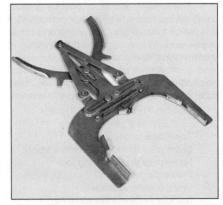

Ring removal/installation tool

Ring compressor

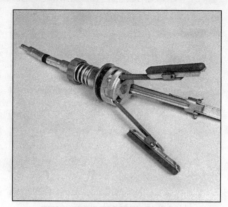

Cylinder hone

Brake hold-down spring tool

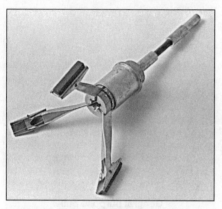

Brake cylinder hone

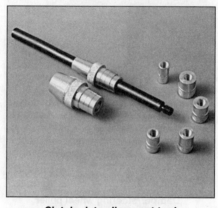

Clutch plate alignment tool

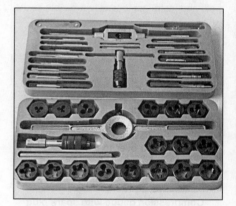

Tap and die set

should start off with the *maintenance and minor repair* tool kit, which is adequate for the simpler jobs performed on a vehicle. Then, as confidence and experience grow, the owner can tackle more difficult tasks, buying additional tools as they are needed. Eventually the basic kit will be expanded into the *repair and overhaul* tool set. Over a period of time, the experienced do-it-yourselfer will assemble a tool set complete enough for most repair and overhaul procedures and will add tools from the special category when it is felt that the expense is justified by the frequency of use.

Maintenance and minor repair tool kit

The tools in this list should be considered the minimum required for performance of routine maintenance, servicing and minor repair work. We recommend the purchase of combination wrenches (box-end and open-end combined in one wrench). While more expensive than open end wrenches, they offer the advantages of both types of wrench.

Combination wrench set (1/4-inch to
*   1 inch or 6 mm to 19 mm)*
Adjustable wrench, 8 inch
Spark plug wrench with rubber insert
Spark plug gap adjusting tool
Feeler gauge set
Brake bleeder wrench
Standard screwdriver (5/16-inch x
*   6 inch)*

Phillips screwdriver (No. 2 x 6 inch)
Combination pliers - 6 inch
Hacksaw and assortment of blades
Tire pressure gauge
Grease gun
Oil can
Fine emery cloth
Wire brush
Battery post and cable cleaning tool
Oil filter wrench
Funnel (medium size)
Safety goggles
Jackstands (2)
Drain pan

Note: *If basic tune-ups are going to be part of routine maintenance, it will be necessary to purchase a good quality stroboscopic timing light and combination tachometer/dwell meter. Although they are included in the list of special tools, it is mentioned here because they are absolutely necessary for tuning most vehicles properly.*

Repair and overhaul tool set

These tools are essential for anyone who plans to perform major repairs and are in addition to those in the maintenance and minor repair tool kit. Included is a comprehensive set of sockets which, though expensive, are invaluable because of their versatility, especially when various extensions and drives are available. We recommend the 1/2-inch drive over the 3/8-inch drive. Although the larger drive is bulky and more expensive,

it has the capacity of accepting a very wide range of large sockets. Ideally, however, the mechanic should have a 3/8-inch drive set and a 1/2-inch drive set.

Socket set(s)
Reversible ratchet
Extension - 10 inch
Universal joint
Torque wrench (same size drive as
*   sockets)*
Ball peen hammer - 8 ounce
Soft-face hammer (plastic/rubber)
Standard screwdriver (1/4-inch x 6 inch)
Standard screwdriver (stubby -
*   5/16-inch)*
Phillips screwdriver (No. 3 x 8 inch)
Phillips screwdriver (stubby - No. 2)
Pliers - vise grip
Pliers - lineman's
Pliers - needle nose
Pliers - snap-ring (internal and external)
Cold chisel - 1/2-inch
Scribe
Scraper (made from flattened copper
*   tubing)*
Centerpunch
Pin punches (1/16, 1/8, 3/16-inch)
Steel rule/straightedge - 12 inch
Allen wrench set (1/8 to 3/8-inch or
*   4 mm to 10 mm)*
A selection of files
Wire brush (large)
Jackstands (second set)
Jack (scissor or hydraulic type)

Note: *Another tool which is often useful is an electric drill with a chuck capacity of 3/8-inch and a set of good quality drill bits.*

Special tools

The tools in this list include those which are not used regularly, are expensive to buy, or which need to be used in accordance with their manufacturer's instructions. Unless these tools will be used frequently, it is not very economical to purchase many of them. A consideration would be to split the cost and use between yourself and a friend or friends. In addition, most of these tools can be obtained from a tool rental shop on a temporary basis.

This list primarily contains only those tools and instruments widely available to the public, and not those special tools produced by the vehicle manufacturer for distribution to dealer service departments. Occasionally, references to the manufacturer's special tools are included in the text of this manual. Generally, an alternative method of doing the job without the special tool is offered. However, sometimes there is no alternative to their use. Where this is the case, and the tool cannot be purchased or borrowed, the work should be turned over to the dealer service department or an automotive repair shop.

Valve spring compressor
Piston ring groove cleaning tool
Piston ring compressor
Piston ring installation tool
Cylinder compression gauge
Cylinder ridge reamer
Cylinder surfacing hone
Cylinder bore gauge
Micrometers and/or dial calipers
Hydraulic lifter removal tool
Balljoint separator
Universal-type puller
Impact screwdriver
Dial indicator set
Stroboscopic timing light (inductive pick-up)
Hand operated vacuum/pressure pump
Tachometer/dwell meter
Universal electrical multimeter
Cable hoist
Brake spring removal and installation tools
Floor jack

Buying tools

For the do-it-yourselfer who is just starting to get involved in vehicle maintenance and repair, there are a number of options available when purchasing tools. If maintenance and minor repair is the extent of the work to be done, the purchase of individual tools is satisfactory. If, on the other hand, extensive work is planned, it would be a good idea to purchase a modest tool set from one of the large retail chain stores. A set can usually be bought at a substantial savings over the individual tool prices, and they often come with a tool box. As additional tools are needed, add-on sets, individual tools and a larger tool box can be purchased to expand the tool selection. Building a tool set gradually allows the cost of the tools to be spread over a longer period of time and gives the mechanic the freedom to choose only those tools that will actually be used.

Tool stores will often be the only source of some of the special tools that are needed, but regardless of where tools are bought, try to avoid cheap ones, especially when buying screwdrivers and sockets, because they won't last very long. The expense involved in replacing cheap tools will eventually be greater than the initial cost of quality tools.

Care and maintenance of tools

Good tools are expensive, so it makes sense to treat them with respect. Keep them clean and in usable condition and store them properly when not in use. Always wipe off any dirt, grease or metal chips before putting them away. Never leave tools lying around in the work area. Upon completion of a job, always check closely under the hood for tools that may have been left there so they won't get lost during a test drive.

Some tools, such as screwdrivers, pliers, wrenches and sockets, can be hung on a panel mounted on the garage or workshop wall, while others should be kept in a tool box or tray. Measuring instruments, gauges, meters, etc. must be carefully stored where they cannot be damaged by weather or impact from other tools.

When tools are used with care and stored properly, they will last a very long time. Even with the best of care, though, tools will wear out if used frequently. When a tool is damaged or worn out, replace it. Subsequent jobs will be safer and more enjoyable if you do.

How to repair damaged threads

Sometimes, the internal threads of a nut or bolt hole can become stripped, usually from overtightening. Stripping threads is an all-too-common occurrence, especially when working with aluminum parts, because aluminum is so soft that it easily strips out.

Usually, external or internal threads are only partially stripped. After they've been cleaned up with a tap or die, they'll still work. Sometimes, however, threads are badly damaged. When this happens, you've got three choices:

1) *Drill and tap the hole to the next suitable oversize and install a larger diameter bolt, screw or stud.*
2) *Drill and tap the hole to accept a threaded plug, then drill and tap the plug to the original screw size. You can also buy a plug already threaded to the original size. Then you simply drill a hole to the specified size, then run the threaded plug into the hole with a bolt and jam nut. Once the plug is fully seated, remove the jam nut and bolt.*
3) *The third method uses a patented thread repair kit like Heli-Coil or Slimsert. These easy-to-use kits are designed to repair damaged threads in straight-through holes and blind holes. Both are available as kits which can handle a variety of sizes and thread patterns. Drill the hole, then tap it with the special included tap. Install the Heli-Coil and the hole is back to its original diameter and thread pitch.*

Regardless of which method you use, be sure to proceed calmly and carefully. A little impatience or carelessness during one of these relatively simple procedures can ruin your whole day's work and cost you a bundle if you wreck an expensive part.

Working facilities

Not to be overlooked when discussing tools is the workshop. If anything more than routine maintenance is to be carried out, some sort of suitable work area is essential.

It is understood, and appreciated, that many home mechanics do not have a good workshop or garage available, and end up removing an engine or doing major repairs outside. It is recommended, however, that the overhaul or repair be completed under the cover of a roof.

A clean, flat workbench or table of comfortable working height is an absolute necessity. The workbench should be equipped with a vise that has a jaw opening of at least four inches.

As mentioned previously, some clean, dry storage space is also required for tools, as well as the lubricants, fluids, cleaning solvents, etc. which soon become necessary.

Sometimes waste oil and fluids, drained from the engine or cooling system during normal maintenance or repairs, present a disposal problem. To avoid pouring them on the ground or into a sewage system, pour the used fluids into large containers, seal them with caps and take them to an authorized disposal site or recycling center. Plastic jugs, such as old antifreeze containers, are ideal for this purpose.

Always keep a supply of old newspapers and clean rags available. Old towels are excellent for mopping up spills. Many mechanics use rolls of paper towels for most work because they are readily available and disposable. To help keep the area under the vehicle clean, a large cardboard box can be cut open and flattened to protect the garage or shop floor.

Whenever working over a painted surface, such as when leaning over a fender to service something under the hood, always cover it with an old blanket or bedspread to protect the finish. Vinyl covered pads, made especially for this purpose, are available at auto parts stores.

Jacking and towing

Jacking

Warning: *The jack supplied with the vehicle should only be used for changing a tire or placing jackstands under the frame. Never work under the vehicle or start the engine while this jack is being used as the only means of support.*

The vehicle should be on level ground. Place the shift lever in Park, if you have an automatic, or Reverse if you have a manual transmission. Block the wheel diagonally opposite the wheel being changed. Set the parking brake.

Remove the spare tire and jack from stowage. Remove the wheel cover and trim ring (if so equipped) with the tapered end of the lug nut wrench by inserting and twisting the handle and then prying against the back of the wheel cover. Loosen the wheel lug nuts about 1/4-to-1/2 turn each.

Place the scissors-type jack under the side of the vehicle and adjust the jack height until it fits in the notch in the vertical rocker panel flange nearest the wheel to be changed. There is a front and rear jacking point on each side of the vehicle **(see illustration)**.

Turn the jack handle clockwise until the tire clears the ground. Remove the lug nuts and pull the wheel off. Replace it with the spare.

Install the lug nuts with the beveled edges facing in. Tighten them snugly. Don't attempt to tighten them completely until the vehicle is lowered or it could slip off the jack. Turn the jack handle counterclockwise to lower the vehicle. Remove the jack and tighten the lug nuts in a diagonal pattern.

Install the cover (and trim ring, if used) and be sure it's snapped into place all the way around.

Stow the tire, jack and wrench. Unblock the wheels.

Towing

Warning: *Before towing 1988 and later models equipped with an automatic transaxle, the vehicle must be placed in front wheel drive mode. This is done by inserting a spare fuse into the FWD connector inside the engine compartment* **(see illustration)**. *If this isn't done. damage to the transfer clutch may occur.*

The vehicle can be towed with all four wheels on the ground, as long as speeds do not exceed 20 mph and the distance is not over six miles.

For distances exceeding six miles, towing equipment specifically designed for this purpose must be used and should be attached to the main structural members of the vehicle, not the bumper or brackets.

While towing, the parking brake should be fully released and the transaxle should be in Neutral. The steering must be unlocked (ignition switch in the Off position). Remember that power steering and power brakes will not work with engine off and never use your tie-

Front jacking point - Place the jack so it engages the notch in the rocker panel

down tabs to tow another vehicle.

Safety is a major consideration when towing and all applicable state and local laws must be obeyed. A safety chain system must be used at all times. Remember that power steering and power brakes will not work with the engine off.

Rear jacking point - Place the jack so it engages the notch in the rocker panel

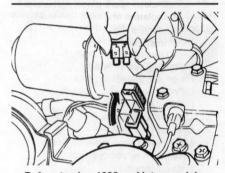

Before towing 1988 and later models, insert a fuse into the FWD connector to disable the 4WD circuit

Booster battery (jump) starting

Observe these precautions when using a booster battery to start a vehicle:

a) *Before connecting the booster battery, make sure the ignition switch is in the Off position.*

b) *Turn off the lights, heater and other electrical loads.*

c) *Your eyes should be shielded. Safety goggles are a good idea.*

d) *Make sure the booster battery is the same voltage as the dead one in the vehicle.*

e) *The two vehicles MUST NOT TOUCH each other!*

f) *Make sure the transaxle is in Neutral (manual) or Park (automatic).*

g) *If the booster battery is not a maintenance-free type, remove the vent caps and lay a cloth over the vent holes.*

Connect the red jumper cable to the positive (+) terminals of each battery **(see illustration)**.

Connect one end of the black jumper cable to the negative (-) terminal of the booster battery. The other end of this cable should be connected to a good ground on the vehicle to be started, such as a bolt or bracket on the body.

Start the engine using the booster battery, then, with the engine running at idle speed, disconnect the jumper cables in the reverse order of connection.

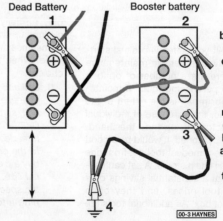

Make the booster battery cable connections in the numerical order shown (note that the negative cable of the booster battery is NOT attached to the negative terminal of the dead battery)

Automotive chemicals and lubricants

A number of automotive chemicals and lubricants are available for use during vehicle maintenance and repair. They include a wide variety of products ranging from cleaning solvents and degreasers to lubricants and protective sprays for rubber, plastic and vinyl.

Cleaners

Carburetor cleaner and choke cleaner is a strong solvent for gum, varnish and carbon. Most carburetor cleaners leave a dry-type lubricant film which will not harden or gum up. Because of this film it is not recommended for use on electrical components.

Brake system cleaner is used to remove grease and brake fluid from the brake system, where clean surfaces are absolutely necessary. It leaves no residue and often eliminates brake squeal caused by contaminants.

Electrical cleaner removes oxidation, corrosion and carbon deposits from electrical contacts, restoring full current flow. It can also be used to clean spark plugs, carburetor jets, voltage regulators and other parts where an oil-free surface is desired.

Demoisturants remove water and moisture from electrical components such as alternators, voltage regulators, electrical connectors and fuse blocks. They are non-conductive, non-corrosive and non-flammable.

Degreasers are heavy-duty solvents used to remove grease from the outside of the engine and from chassis components. They can be sprayed or brushed on and, depending on the type, are rinsed off either with water or solvent.

Lubricants

Motor oil is the lubricant formulated for use in engines. It normally contains a wide variety of additives to prevent corrosion and reduce foaming and wear. Motor oil comes in various weights (viscosity ratings) from 5 to 80. The recommended weight of the oil depends on the season, temperature and the demands on the engine. Light oil is used in cold climates and under light load conditions. Heavy oil is used in hot climates and where high loads are encountered. Multi-viscosity oils are designed to have characteristics of both light and heavy oils and are available in a number of weights from 5W-20 to 20W-50.

Gear oil is designed to be used in differentials, manual transmissions and other areas where high-temperature lubrication is required.

Chassis and wheel bearing grease is a heavy grease used where increased loads and friction are encountered, such as for wheel bearings, balljoints, tie-rod ends and universal joints.

High-temperature wheel bearing grease is designed to withstand the extreme temperatures encountered by wheel bearings in disc brake equipped vehicles. It usually contains molybdenum disulfide (moly), which is a dry-type lubricant.

White grease is a heavy grease for metal-to-metal applications where water is a problem. White grease stays soft under both low and high temperatures (usually from -100 to +190-degrees F), and will not wash off or dilute in the presence of water.

Assembly lube is a special extreme pressure lubricant, usually containing moly, used to lubricate high-load parts (such as main and rod bearings and cam lobes) for initial start-up of a new engine. The assembly lube lubricates the parts without being squeezed out or washed away until the engine oiling system begins to function.

Silicone lubricants are used to protect rubber, plastic, vinyl and nylon parts.

Graphite lubricants are used where oils cannot be used due to contamination problems, such as in locks. The dry graphite will lubricate metal parts while remaining uncontaminated by dirt, water, oil or acids. It is electrically conductive and will not foul electrical contacts in locks such as the ignition switch.

Moly penetrants loosen and lubricate frozen, rusted and corroded fasteners and prevent future rusting or freezing.

Heat-sink grease is a special electrically non-conductive grease that is used for mounting electronic ignition modules where it is essential that heat is transferred away from the module.

Sealants

RTV sealant is one of the most widely used gasket compounds. Made from silicone, RTV is air curing, it seals, bonds, waterproofs, fills surface irregularities, remains flexible, doesn't shrink, is relatively easy to remove, and is used as a supplementary sealer with almost all low and medium temperature gaskets.

Anaerobic sealant is much like RTV in that it can be used either to seal gaskets or to form gaskets by itself. It remains flexible, is solvent resistant and fills surface imperfections. The difference between an anaerobic sealant and an RTV-type sealant is in the curing. RTV cures when exposed to air, while an anaerobic sealant cures only in the absence of air. This means that an anaerobic sealant cures only after the assembly of parts, sealing them together.

Thread and pipe sealant is used for sealing hydraulic and pneumatic fittings and vacuum lines. It is usually made from a Teflon compound, and comes in a spray, a paint-on liquid and as a wrap-around tape.

Chemicals

Anti-seize compound prevents seizing, galling, cold welding, rust and corrosion in fasteners. High-temperature anti-seize, usually made with copper and graphite lubricants, is used for exhaust system and exhaust manifold bolts.

Anaerobic locking compounds are used to keep fasteners from vibrating or working loose and cure only after installation, in the absence of air. Medium strength locking compound is used for small nuts, bolts and screws that may be removed later. High-strength locking compound is for large nuts, bolts and studs which aren't removed on a regular basis.

Oil additives range from viscosity index improvers to chemical treatments that claim to reduce internal engine friction. It should be noted that most oil manufacturers caution against using additives with their oils.

Gas additives perform several functions, depending on their chemical makeup. They usually contain solvents that help dissolve gum and varnish that build up on carburetor, fuel injection and intake parts. They also serve to break down carbon deposits that form on the inside surfaces of the combustion chambers. Some additives contain upper cylinder lubricants for valves and piston rings, and others contain chemicals to remove condensation from the gas tank.

Miscellaneous

Brake fluid is specially formulated hydraulic fluid that can withstand the heat and pressure encountered in brake systems. Care must be taken so this fluid does not come in contact with painted surfaces or plastics. An opened container should always be resealed to prevent contamination by water or dirt.

Weatherstrip adhesive is used to bond weatherstripping around doors, windows and trunk lids. It is sometimes used to attach trim pieces.

Undercoating is a petroleum-based, tar-like substance that is designed to protect metal surfaces on the underside of the vehicle from corrosion. It also acts as a sound-deadening agent by insulating the bottom of the vehicle.

Waxes and polishes are used to help protect painted and plated surfaces from the weather. Different types of paint may require the use of different types of wax and polish. Some polishes utilize a chemical or abrasive cleaner to help remove the top layer of oxidized (dull) paint on older vehicles. In recent years many non-wax polishes that contain a wide variety of chemicals such as polymers and silicones have been introduced. These non-wax polishes are usually easier to apply and last longer than conventional waxes and polishes.

Conversion factors

Length (distance)
Inches (in)	X	25.4	= Millimetres (mm)	X 0.0394	= Inches (in)
Feet (ft)	X	0.305	= Metres (m)	X 3.281	= Feet (ft)
Miles	X	1.609	= Kilometres (km)	X 0.621	= Miles

Volume (capacity)
Cubic inches (cu in; in³)	X	16.387	= Cubic centimetres (cc; cm³)	X 0.061	= Cubic inches (cu in; in³)
Imperial pints (Imp pt)	X	0.568	= Litres (l)	X 1.76	= Imperial pints (Imp pt)
Imperial quarts (Imp qt)	X	1.137	= Litres (l)	X 0.88	= Imperial quarts (Imp qt)
Imperial quarts (Imp qt)	X	1.201	= US quarts (US qt)	X 0.833	= Imperial quarts (Imp qt)
US quarts (US qt)	X	0.946	= Litres (l)	X 1.057	= US quarts (US qt)
Imperial gallons (Imp gal)	X	4.546	= Litres (l)	X 0.22	= Imperial gallons (Imp gal)
Imperial gallons (Imp gal)	X	1.201	= US gallons (US gal)	X 0.833	= Imperial gallons (Imp gal)
US gallons (US gal)	X	3.785	= Litres (l)	X 0.264	= US gallons (US gal)

Mass (weight)
Ounces (oz)	X	28.35	= Grams (g)	X 0.035	= Ounces (oz)
Pounds (lb)	X	0.454	= Kilograms (kg)	X 2.205	= Pounds (lb)

Force
Ounces-force (ozf; oz)	X	0.278	= Newtons (N)	X 3.6	= Ounces-force (ozf; oz)
Pounds-force (lbf; lb)	X	4.448	= Newtons (N)	X 0.225	= Pounds-force (lbf; lb)
Newtons (N)	X	0.1	= Kilograms-force (kgf; kg)	X 9.81	= Newtons (N)

Pressure
Pounds-force per square inch (psi; lbf/in²; lb/in²)	X	0.070	= Kilograms-force per square centimetre (kgf/cm²; kg/cm²)	X 14.223	= Pounds-force per square inch (psi; lbf/in²; lb/in²)
Pounds-force per square inch (psi; lbf/in²; lb/in²)	X	0.068	= Atmospheres (atm)	X 14.696	= Pounds-force per square inch (psi; lbf/in²; lb/in²)
Pounds-force per square inch (psi; lbf/in²; lb/in²)	X	0.069	= Bars	X 14.5	= Pounds-force per square inch (psi; lbf/in²; lb/in²)
Pounds-force per square inch (psi; lbf/in²; lb/in²)	X	6.895	= Kilopascals (kPa)	X 0.145	= Pounds-force per square inch (psi; lbf/in²; lb/in²)
Kilopascals (kPa)	X	0.01	= Kilograms-force per square centimetre (kgf/cm²; kg/cm²)	X 98.1	= Kilopascals (kPa)

Torque (moment of force)
Pounds-force inches (lbf in; lb in)	X	1.152	= Kilograms-force centimetre (kgf cm; kg cm)	X 0.868	= Pounds-force inches (lbf in; lb in)
Pounds-force inches (lbf in; lb in)	X	0.113	= Newton metres (Nm)	X 8.85	= Pounds-force inches (lbf in; lb in)
Pounds-force inches (lbf in; lb in)	X	0.083	= Pounds-force feet (lbf ft; lb ft)	X 12	= Pounds-force inches (lbf in; lb in)
Pounds-force feet (lbf ft; lb ft)	X	0.138	= Kilograms-force metres (kgf m; kg m)	X 7.233	= Pounds-force feet (lbf ft; lb ft)
Pounds-force feet (lbf ft; lb ft)	X	1.356	= Newton metres (Nm)	X 0.738	= Pounds-force feet (lbf ft; lb ft)
Newton metres (Nm)	X	0.102	= Kilograms-force metres (kgf m; kg m)	X 9.804	= Newton metres (Nm)

Vacuum
Inches mercury (in. Hg)	X	3.377	= Kilopascals (kPa)	X 0.2961	= Inches mercury
Inches mercury (in. Hg)	X	25.4	= Millimeters mercury (mm Hg)	X 0.0394	= Inches mercury

Power
Horsepower (hp)	X	745.7	= Watts (W)	X 0.0013	= Horsepower (hp)

Velocity (speed)
Miles per hour (miles/hr; mph)	X	1.609	= Kilometres per hour (km/hr; kph)	X 0.621	= Miles per hour (miles/hr; mph)

Fuel consumption*
Miles per gallon, Imperial (mpg)	X	0.354	= Kilometres per litre (km/l)	X 2.825	= Miles per gallon, Imperial (mpg)
Miles per gallon, US (mpg)	X	0.425	= Kilometres per litre (km/l)	X 2.352	= Miles per gallon, US (mpg)

Temperature
Degrees Fahrenheit = (°C x 1.8) + 32   Degrees Celsius (Degrees Centigrade; °C) = (°F - 32) x 0.56

*It is common practice to convert from miles per gallon (mpg) to litres/100 kilometres (l/100km),
where mpg (Imperial) x l/100 km = 282 and mpg (US) x l/100 km = 235

Safety first!

Regardless of how enthusiastic you may be about getting on with the job at hand, take the time to ensure that your safety is not jeopardized. A moment's lack of attention can result in an accident, as can failure to observe certain simple safety precautions. The possibility of an accident will always exist, and the following points should not be considered a comprehensive list of all dangers. Rather, they are intended to make you aware of the risks and to encourage a safety conscious approach to all work you carry out on your vehicle.

Essential DOs and DON'Ts

DON'T rely on a jack when working under the vehicle. Always use approved jackstands to support the weight of the vehicle and place them under the recommended lift or support points.

DON'T attempt to loosen extremely tight fasteners (i.e. wheel lug nuts) while the vehicle is on a jack - it may fall.

DON'T start the engine without first making sure that the transmission is in Neutral (or Park where applicable) and the parking brake is set.

DON'T remove the radiator cap from a hot cooling system - let it cool or cover it with a cloth and release the pressure gradually.

DON'T attempt to drain the engine oil until you are sure it has cooled to the point that it will not burn you.

DON'T touch any part of the engine or exhaust system until it has cooled sufficiently to avoid burns.

DON'T siphon toxic liquids such as gasoline, antifreeze and brake fluid by mouth, or allow them to remain on your skin.

DON'T inhale brake lining dust - it is potentially hazardous (see *Asbestos* below).

DON'T allow spilled oil or grease to remain on the floor - wipe it up before someone slips on it.

DON'T use loose fitting wrenches or other tools which may slip and cause injury.

DON'T push on wrenches when loosening or tightening nuts or bolts. Always try to pull the wrench toward you. If the situation calls for pushing the wrench away, push with an open hand to avoid scraped knuckles if the wrench should slip.

DON'T attempt to lift a heavy component alone - get someone to help you.

DON'T rush or take unsafe shortcuts to finish a job.

DON'T allow children or animals in or around the vehicle while you are working on it.

DO wear eye protection when using power tools such as a drill, sander, bench grinder, etc. and when working under a vehicle.

DO keep loose clothing and long hair well out of the way of moving parts.

DO make sure that any hoist used has a safe working load rating adequate for the job.

DO get someone to check on you periodically when working alone on a vehicle.

DO carry out work in a logical sequence and make sure that everything is correctly assembled and tightened.

DO keep chemicals and fluids tightly capped and out of the reach of children and pets.

DO remember that your vehicle's safety affects that of yourself and others. If in doubt on any point, get professional advice.

Asbestos

Certain friction, insulating, sealing, and other products - such as brake linings, brake bands, clutch linings, torque converters, gaskets, etc. - may contain asbestos. Extreme care must be taken to avoid inhalation of dust from such products, since it is hazardous to health. If in doubt, assume that they do contain asbestos.

Fire

Remember at all times that gasoline is highly flammable. Never smoke or have any kind of open flame around when working on a vehicle. But the risk does not end there. A spark caused by an electrical short circuit, by two metal surfaces contacting each other, or even by static electricity built up in your body under certain conditions, can ignite gasoline vapors, which in a confined space are highly explosive. Do not, under any circumstances, use gasoline for cleaning parts. Use an approved safety solvent.

Always disconnect the battery ground (-) cable at the battery before working on any part of the fuel system or electrical system. Never risk spilling fuel on a hot engine or exhaust component. It is strongly recommended that a fire extinguisher suitable for use on fuel and electrical fires be kept handy in the garage or workshop at all times. Never try to extinguish a fuel or electrical fire with water.

Fumes

Certain fumes are highly toxic and can quickly cause unconsciousness and even death if inhaled to any extent. Gasoline vapor falls into this category, as do the vapors from some cleaning solvents. Any draining or pouring of such volatile fluids should be done in a well ventilated area.

When using cleaning fluids and solvents, read the instructions on the container carefully. Never use materials from unmarked containers.

Never run the engine in an enclosed space, such as a garage. Exhaust fumes contain carbon monoxide, which is extremely poisonous. If you need to run the engine, always do so in the open air, or at least have the rear of the vehicle outside the work area.

If you are fortunate enough to have the use of an inspection pit, never drain or pour gasoline and never run the engine while the vehicle is over the pit. The fumes, being heavier than air, will concentrate in the pit with possibly lethal results.

The battery

Never create a spark or allow a bare light bulb near a battery. They normally give off a certain amount of hydrogen gas, which is highly explosive.

Always disconnect the battery ground (-) cable at the battery before working on the fuel or electrical systems.

If possible, loosen the filler caps or cover when charging the battery from an external source (this does not apply to sealed or maintenance-free batteries). Do not charge at an excessive rate or the battery may burst.

Take care when adding water to a non maintenance-free battery and when carrying a battery. The electrolyte, even when diluted, is very corrosive and should not be allowed to contact clothing or skin.

Always wear eye protection when cleaning the battery to prevent the caustic deposits from entering your eyes.

Household current

When using an electric power tool, inspection light, etc., which operates on household current, always make sure that the tool is correctly connected to its plug and that, where necessary, it is properly grounded. Do not use such items in damp conditions and, again, do not create a spark or apply excessive heat in the vicinity of fuel or fuel vapor.

Secondary ignition system voltage

A severe electric shock can result from touching certain parts of the ignition system (such as the spark plug wires) when the engine is running or being cranked, particularly if components are damp or the insulation is defective. In the case of an electronic ignition system, the secondary system voltage is much higher and could prove fatal.

Troubleshooting

Contents

Engine

1 Engine will not rotate when attempting to start

1   Battery terminal connections loose or corroded (Chapter 1).
2   Battery discharged or faulty (Chapter 1).
3   Automatic transaxle not completely engaged in Park (Chapter 7) or clutch pedal not completely depressed (Chapter 8).
4   Broken, loose or disconnected wiring in the starting circuit (Chapters 5 and 12).
5   Starter motor pinion jammed in flywheel ring gear (Chapter 5).
6   Starter solenoid faulty (Chapter 5).
7   Starter motor faulty (Chapter 5).
8   Ignition switch faulty (Chapter 12).
9   Starter pinion or flywheel teeth worn or broken (Chapter 5).

2 Engine rotates but will not start

1   Fuel tank empty.
2   Battery discharged (engine rotates slowly) (Chapter 5).
3   Battery terminal connections loose or corroded (Chapter 1).
4   Leaking carburetor, fuel injector(s), faulty fuel pump, pressure regulator, etc. (Chapter 4).
5   Broken or stripped timing belt or chain (Chapter 2).
6   Ignition components damp or damaged (Chapter 5).
7   Worn, faulty or incorrectly gapped spark plugs (Chapter 1).
8   Broken, loose or disconnected wiring in the starting circuit (Chapter 5).
9   Loose distributor is changing ignition timing (Chapter 5).
10   Broken, loose or disconnected wires at the ignition coil or faulty coil (Chapter 5).

3 Engine hard to start when cold

1   Battery discharged or low (Chapter 1).
2   Malfunctioning fuel system (Chapter 4).
3   Faulty coolant temperature sensor or intake air temperature sensor (Chapter 6).
4   Injector(s) leaking (Chapter 4B).
5   Carburetor or choke problem (Chapter 4A).
6   Faulty ignition system (Chapter 5).

4 Engine hard to start when hot

1   Air filter clogged (Chapter 1).
2   Fuel not reaching the carburetor or fuel injection system (Chapter 4).
3   Corroded battery connections, especially ground (Chapter 1).
4   Faulty coolant temperature sensor or intake air temperature sensor (Chapter 6).
5   Carburetor or choke problem (Chapter 4A).

5 Starter motor noisy or excessively rough in engagement

1   Pinion or flywheel gear teeth worn or broken (Chapter 5).
2   Starter motor mounting bolts loose or missing (Chapter 5).

6 Engine starts but stops immediately

1   Loose or faulty electrical connections at distributor, coil or alternator (Chapter 5).
2   Insufficient fuel reaching the carburetor or fuel injector(s) (Chapters 1 and 4).
3   Vacuum leak at the gasket between the intake manifold/plenum and throttle body or carburetor (Chapters 1 and 4).
4   Idle speed incorrect (Chapter 1).

7 Oil puddle under engine

1   Oil pan gasket and/or oil pan drain bolt washer leaking (Chapter 2).
2   Oil pressure sending unit leaking (Chapter 2).
3   Cylinder head covers leaking (Chapter 2).
4   Engine oil seals leaking (Chapter 2).
5   Oil pump housing leaking (Chapter 2).

8 Engine lopes while idling or idles erratically

1   Vacuum leakage (Chapters 2 and 4).
2   Leaking EGR valve (Chapter 6).
3   Air filter clogged (Chapter 1).
4   Fuel pump not delivering sufficient fuel to the carburetor or fuel injection system (Chapter 4).
5   Leaking head gasket (Chapter 2).
6   Timing belt or chain and/or pulleys worn (Chapter 2).
7   Camshaft lobes worn (Chapter 2).

9 Engine misses at idle speed

1   Spark plugs worn or not gapped properly (Chapter 1).
2   Faulty spark plug wires (Chapter 1).
3   Vacuum leaks (Chapter 1).
4   Incorrect ignition timing (Chapter 1).
5   Uneven or low compression (Chapter 2).
6   Problem with the carburetor or fuel injection system (Chapter 4).

10 Engine misses throughout driving speed range

1   Fuel filter clogged and/or impurities in the fuel system (Chapter 1).
2   Low fuel output at the carburetor or injector(s) (Chapter 4).
3   Faulty or incorrectly gapped spark plugs (Chapter 1).
4   Incorrect ignition timing (Chapter 1).
5   Cracked distributor cap, disconnected distributor wires or damaged distributor components (Chapters 1 and 5).
6   Leaking spark plug wires (Chapters 1 or 5).
7   Faulty emission system components (Chapter 6).
8   Low or uneven cylinder compression pressures (Chapter 2).
9   Weak or faulty ignition system (Chapter 5).
10   Vacuum leak in fuel injection system, carburetor, intake manifold, air control valve or vacuum hoses (Chapter 4).

11 Engine stumbles on acceleration

1   Spark plugs fouled (Chapter 1).
2   Problem with fuel injection system or carburetor (Chapter 4).
3   Fuel filter clogged (Chapters 1 and 4).
4   Incorrect ignition timing (Chapter 1).
5   Intake manifold air leak (Chapters 2 and 4).
6   Problem with the emissions control system (Chapter 6).

12 Engine surges while holding accelerator steady

1   Intake air leak (Chapter 4).
2   Fuel pump or fuel pressure regulator faulty (Chapter 4).
3   Problem with carburetor or fuel injection system (Chapter 4).
4   Problem with the emissions control system (Chapter 6).

13 Engine stalls

1   Idle speed incorrect (Chapter 1).
2   Fuel filter clogged and/or water and impurities in the fuel system (Chapters 1 and 4).
3   Distributor components damp or damaged (Chapter 5).
4   Faulty emissions system components (Chapter 6).
5   Faulty or incorrectly gapped spark plugs (Chapter 1).
6   Faulty spark plug wires (Chapter 1).
7   Vacuum leak in the carburetor or fuel injection system, intake manifold or vacuum hoses (Chapters 2 and 4).
8   Valve clearances incorrectly set (Chapter 1).

14 Engine lacks power

1 Incorrect ignition timing (Chapter 5).
2 Excessive play in distributor shaft (Chapter 5).
3 Worn rotor, distributor cap, spark plug wires or faulty coil (Chapters 1 and 5).
4 Faulty or incorrectly gapped spark plugs (Chapter 1).
5 Problem with the carburetor or fuel injection system (Chapter 4).
6 Plugged air filter (Chapter 1).
7 Brakes binding (Chapter 9).
8 Automatic transaxle fluid level incorrect (Chapter 1).
9 Clutch slipping (Chapter 8).
10 Fuel filter clogged and/or impurities in the fuel system (Chapters 1 and 4).
11 Emission control system not functioning properly (Chapter 6).
12 Low or uneven cylinder compression pressures (Chapter 2).
13 Obstructed exhaust system (Chapter 4).

15 Engine backfires

1 Emission control system not functioning properly (Chapter 6).
2 Ignition timing incorrect (Chapter 1).
3 Faulty secondary ignition system (cracked spark plug insulator, faulty plug wires, distributor cap and/or rotor) (Chapters 1 and 5).
4 Problem with the carburetor or fuel injection system (Chapter 4).
5 Vacuum leak at fuel injector(s), intake manifold, air control valve or vacuum hoses (Chapters 2 and 4).
6 Valve clearances incorrectly set and/or valves sticking (Chapter 1).

16 Pinging or knocking engine sounds during acceleration or uphill

1 Incorrect grade of fuel.
2 Ignition timing incorrect (Chapter 1).
3 Carburetor or fuel injection system faulty (Chapter 4).
4 Improper or damaged spark plugs or wires (Chapter 1).
5 Worn or damaged distributor components (Chapter 5).
6 EGR valve not functioning (Chapter 6).
7 Vacuum leak (Chapters 2 and 4).

17 Engine runs with oil pressure light on

1 Low oil level (Chapter 1).
2 Idle rpm below specification (Chapter 1).
3 Short in wiring circuit (Chapter 12).
4 Faulty oil pressure sender (Chapter 2).
5 Worn engine bearings and/or oil pump (Chapter 2).

18 Engine diesels (continues to run) after switching off

1 Idle speed too high (Chapter 1).
2 Excessive engine operating temperature (Chapter 3).
3 Ignition timing in need of adjustment (Chapter 1).

Engine electrical system

19 Battery will not hold a charge

1 Alternator drivebelt defective or not adjusted properly (Chapter 1).
2 Battery electrolyte level low (Chapter 1).
3 Battery terminals loose or corroded (Chapter 1).
4 Alternator not charging properly (Chapter 5).
5 Loose, broken or faulty wiring in the charging circuit (Chapter 5).
6 Short in vehicle wiring (Chapter 12).
7 Internally defective battery (Chapters 1 and 5).

20 Alternator light fails to go out

1 Faulty alternator or charging circuit (Chapter 5).
2 Alternator drivebelt defective or out of adjustment (Chapter 1).
3 Alternator voltage regulator inoperative (Chapter 5).

21 Alternator light fails to come on when key is turned on

1 Warning light bulb defective (Chapter 12).
2 Fault in the printed circuit, dash wiring or bulb holder (Chapter 12).

Fuel system

22 Excessive fuel consumption

1 Dirty or clogged air filter element (Chapter 1).
2 Incorrectly set ignition timing (Chapter 5).
3 Emissions system not functioning properly (Chapter 6).
4 Carburetor or fuel injection system not functioning properly (Chapter 4).
5 Low tire pressure or incorrect tire size (Chapter 1).

23 Fuel leakage and/or fuel odor

1 Leaking fuel feed or return line (Chapters 1 and 4).
2 Tank overfilled.
3 Evaporative canister filter clogged (Chapters 1 and 6).
4 Problem with carburetor or fuel injection system (Chapter 4).

Cooling system

24 Overheating

1 Insufficient coolant in system (Chapter 1).
2 Water pump drivebelt defective or out of adjustment (Chapter 1).
3 Radiator core blocked or grille restricted (Chapter 3).
4 Thermostat faulty (Chapter 3).
5 Electric coolant fan inoperative or blades broken (Chapter 3).
6 Radiator cap not maintaining proper pressure (Chapter 3).
7 Ignition timing incorrect (Chapter 5).
8 Faulty cooling fan thermoswitch.
9 Faulty clutch on mechanical fan.

25 Overcooling

1 Faulty thermostat (Chapter 3).
2 Inaccurate temperature gauge sending unit (Chapter 3).
3 Faulty cooling fan thermoswitch.

26 External coolant leakage

1 Deteriorated/damaged hoses; loose clamps (Chapters 1 and 3).
2 Water pump defective (Chapter 3).
3 Leakage from radiator core or coolant reservoir bottle (Chapter 3).
4 Engine drain or water jacket core plugs leaking (Chapter 2).

27 Internal coolant leakage

1 Leaking cylinder head gasket (Chapter 2).
2 Cracked cylinder bore or cylinder head (Chapter 2).

28 Coolant loss

1 Too much coolant in system (Chapter 1).
2 Coolant boiling away because of overheating (Chapter 3).
3 Internal or external leakage (Chapter 3).
4 Faulty radiator cap (Chapter 3).

29 Poor coolant circulation

1 Inoperative water pump (Chapter 3).
2 Restriction in cooling system (Chapters 1 and 3).
3 Water pump drivebelt defective/out of adjustment (Chapter 1).
4 Thermostat sticking (Chapter 3).

Clutch

30 Fails to release (pedal pressed to the floor-shift lever does not move freely in and out of gear)

1 Improper free play adjustment (Chapter 1).
2 Clutch disc warped, bent or excessively damaged (Chapter 8).

31 Clutch slips (engine speed increase with no increase in vehicle speed)

1 Clutch cable in need of adjustment (Chapter 1).
2 Clutch disc oil soaked or facing worn. Remove disc (Chapter 8) and inspect.
3 Clutch disc not seated. It may take 30 or 40 normal starts for a new disc to seat.

32 Grabbing (chattering) on take-up

1 Oil on clutch disc. Remove disc (Chapter 8) and inspect. Correct any leakage source.
2 Worn or loose engine or transmission mounts. These units may move slightly when clutch is released. Inspect mounts and bolts.
3 Worn splines on clutch disc. Remove clutch components (Chapter 8) and inspect.
4 Warped pressure plate or flywheel. Remove clutch components and inspect.

33 Squeal or rumble with clutch fully engaged (pedal released).

1 Improper adjustment; no free play (Chapter 1).
2 Release bearing binding on transmission bearing retainer. Remove clutch components (Chapter 8) and check bearing. Remove any burrs or nicks, clean and relubricate before reinstallation.
3 Weak pedal return spring. Replace the spring.

34 Squeal or rumble with clutch fully disengaged (pedal depressed)

1 Worn, faulty or broken release bearing (Chapter 8).
2 Worn or broken pressure plate springs (or diaphragm fingers) (Chapter 8).

35 Clutch pedal stays on floor when disengaged

1 Bind in cable or release bearing. Inspect cable or remove clutch components as necessary.
2 Clutch pressure plate weak or broken. Remove and inspect clutch pressure plate (Chapter 8).

Manual transmission
Note: *All the Sections referred to here are contained within Chapter 7 unless noted.*

36 Noisy in Neutral with engine running

1 Mainshaft bearing worn.
2 Damaged pinion shaft bearing.

37 Noisy in all gears

1 Mainshaft bearing worn.
2 Damaged pinion shaft bearing.
3 Insufficient lubricant (see checking procedures in Chapter 1).

38 Noisy in one particular gear

1 Worn, damaged or chipped gear teeth for that particular gear.
2 Worn or damaged synchronizer for that particular gear.

39 Slips out of high gear

1 Transmission mounting bolts loose.
2 Shift mechanism not working freely.
3 Damaged pilot bearing.
4 Dirt between transmission housing and engine or misalignment of transmission.
5 Worn or improperly adjusted linkage.

40 Difficulty in engaging gears

1 Clutch not releasing (see clutch adjustment, Chapter 1).
2 Loose, damaged or maladjusted shift linkage. Make a thorough inspection, replacing parts as necessary. Adjust as described in Chapter 8.

41 Oil leakage

1 Excessive amount of lubricant in transmission (see Chapter 1 for correct checking procedures). Drain lubricant as required.
2 Drive axle oil seals defective.
3 Rear oil seal or speedometer oil seal in need of replacement.

Automatic transmission
Note: *Due to the complexity of the automatic transmission, it is difficult for the home mechanic to properly diagnose and service this component. For problems other than the following, the vehicle should be taken to a reputable mechanic.*

42 Fluid leakage

1 Automatic transmission fluid is a deep red color and fluid leaks should not be confused with engine oil which can easily be blown by air flow to the transmission.
2 To pinpoint a leak, first remove all built-up dirt and grime from around the transmission. Degreasing agents and/or steam cleaning will achieve this. With the underside clean, drive the vehicle at low speeds so that air flow will not blow the leak far from its source. Raise the vehicle and determine where the leak is coming from. Common areas of leakage are:

a) *Fluid pan: tighten mounting bolts and/or replace pan gasket as necessary (see Chapter 7)*
b) *Rear cover: tighten bolts and/or replace oil seal as necessary (Chapter 7)*
c) *Filler pipe: replace the rubber oil seal where pipe enters transmission case*
d) *Transmission fluid cooler lines: tighten connectors where lines enter transmission case and/or replace lines*
e) *Vent pipe: transmission over-filled and/or water in fluid (see checking procedures, Chapter 1)*
f) *Speedometer connector: replace the O-ring where speedometer cable enters transmission case*

43 General shift mechanism problems

Chapter 7 deals with checking and adjusting the shift linkage on automatic transmissions. Common problems which may be attributed to out-of-adjustment linkage are:

a) *Engine starting in gears other than P (Park) or N (Neutral)*
b) *Indicator pointing to a gear other than the one the transmission is actually in*
c) *Vehicle will not hold firm when in P (Park) position*

44   Transmission will not downshift with the accelerator pedal pressed to the floor

1   Disconnected or damaged vacuum hose between intake manifold and vacuum diaphragm on transmission.
2   Faulty vacuum control diaphragm.

45   Engine will start in gears other than P (Park) or N (Neutral)

Chapter 7 cleats with checking the Neutral switch used with automatic transmissions.

46   Transmission slips, shifts rough, is noisy or has no drive in forward or reverse gears

1   There are many probable causes for the above problems, but the home mechanic should concern himself only with one possibility: fluid level.
2   Before taking the vehicle to a repair shop, check the level of the fluid and condition of the fluid as described in Chapter 1. Correct fluid level as necessary or change the fluid and filter if needed. If problem persists, have a professional diagnose the probable cause.

Driveshaft (4WD vehicles)

47   Leakage of fluid at front of driveshaft

Defective transmission rear oil seal. See Chapter 7 for replacing procedures. While this is done, check the splined yoke for burrs or a rough condition which may be damaging the seal. If found, these can be dressed with crocus cloth or a fine whetstone.

48   Knock or clunk when the transmission is under initial load (just after transmission is put into gear)

1   Loose or disconnected rear suspension components. Check all mounting bolts and bushings (Chapters 1 and 11).
2   Loose driveshaft bolts. Inspect all bolts and nuts and tighten to the specified torque.
3   Worn or damaged universal joint bearings (Chapter 8).
4   Worn sleeve yoke and mainshaft splines (Chapter 8).

49   Metallic grating sound consistent with vehicle speed

Pronounced wear in the universal joint bearings. Replace bearings (Chapter 8).

50   Vibration

Note: *Before it can be assumed that the driveshaft is at fault, make sure the tires are perfectly balanced and perform the following test.*
1   Install a tachometer inside the vehicle to monitor engine speed as it is driven. Drive the vehicle and note the engine speed at which the vibration (roughness) is most pronounced. Now shift the transmission to a different gear and bring the engine speed to the same point.
2   If the vibration occurs at the same engine speed (rpm) regardless of which gear the transmission is in, the driveshaft is NOT at fault since the driveshaft speed varies.
3   If the vibration decreases or is eliminated when the transmission is in a different gear at the same engine speed, refer to the following probable causes.
4   Bent or dented driveshaft. Inspect and replace as necessary (Chapter 8).
5   Undercoating or built-up dirt, etc. on the driveshaft. Clean the shah thoroughly and test.
6   Worn universal joint bearings (Chapter 8).

Front differential

51   Gear noise when driving

If noise increases as vehicle speed increases, it may be due to insufficient gear. oil (Chapter 1), incorrect gear engagement or damaged gears. Remove the transmission/differential unit and have it checked and repaired by a Subaru dealer service department.

52   Gear noise when coasting

Damaged gears caused by bearings and shims that are worn or out of adjustment (see Section 48).

53   Bearing noise

Usually caused by cracked, broken or otherwise damaged bearings (see Section 48).

54   Noise when turning

Damaged or worn differential side gear, pinion gear or pinion shaft (see Section 48).

Rear differential (4WD vehicles)

55   Oil leakage

1   Worn or incorrectly installed pinion seal or axleshaft oil seal.
2   Scored or excessively worn sliding surface of companion flange.
3   Clogged air vent.
4   Loose side bearing retainer bolts or damaged O-ring (Chapter 8).
5   Loose rear cover attaching bolts or damaged gasket.
6   Loose oil fill or drain plug.

56   Noise when starting or shifting gears

1   Excessive gear backlash.
2   Insufficient bearing preload.
3   Loose drive pinion nut.
4   Loose side bearing retainer bolts (see Chapter 8).

57   Noise when turning

1   Damaged or worn side gears or bearings.
2   Broken or seized spider gear shaft.
3   Excessively worn side gear thrust washer.
4   Broken teeth on differential hypoid gears.

Driveaxles

58   Clicking noise in turns

Worn or damaged outboard CV joint. Check for cut or damaged: boots. Repair as necessary (Chapter 8).

59   Knock or clunk when accelerating after coasting

Worn or damaged inboard joint. Check for cut or damaged boots. Repair as necessary (Chapter 8).

60   Shudder or vibration during acceleration

1   Excessive joint angle. Check and cor-

rect as necessary (Chapter 8).
2   Worn or damaged inboard or outboard joints. Repair or replace as necessary (Chapter 8).
3   Sticking inboard joint assembly. Correct or replace as necessary (Chapter 8).

Brakes

Note: *Before assuming that a brake problem exists, make sure that the tires are in good condition and inflated properly (see Chapter 1), the front end alignment is correct (see Chapter 10) and that the vehicle is not loaded with weight in an unequal manner.*

61   Vehicle pulls to one side during braking

1   Defective, damaged or oil-contaminated disc pad on one side. Inspect as described in Chapter 1. Refer to Chapter 9 if replacement is required.
2   Excessive wear of brake pad material or disc on one side. Inspect and correct as necessary.
3   Loose or disconnected front suspension components. Inspect and tighten all bolts to the specified torque (Chapter 11).
4   Defective caliper assembly. Remove caliper and inspect for stuck piston or damage (Chapter 9).

62   Noise (high-pitched squeal without brake applied)

Front brake pads worn out. This noise comes from the wear sensor or pad backing plate rubbing against the disc. Replace pads with new ones immediately (Chapter 9).

63   Excessive brake pedal travel

1   Partial brake system failure. Inspect entire system (Chapter 1) and correct as required.
2   Insufficient fluid in master cylinder. Check (Chapter 1), add fluid and bleed system if necessary (Chapter 9).
3   Rear brakes not adjusting properly. Make a series of starts and stops while the vehicle is in Reverse. If this does not correct the situation, remove drums and inspect self-adjusters (Chapter 9).

64   Brake pedal feels spongy when depressed

1   Air in hydraulic lines. Bleed the brake system (Chapter 9).
2   Faulty flexible hoses. Inspect all system hoses and lines. Replace parts as necessary.
3   Master cylinder mount loose. Inspect

master cylinder bolts (nuts) and tighten to the specified torque.
4   Master cylinder faulty (Chapter 9).

65   Excessive effort required to stop vehicle

1   Power brake booster not operating properly (Chapter 9).
2   Excessively worn linings or pads. Inspect and replace if necessary (Chapter 1).
3   One or more caliper pistons (front wheels) or wheel cylinders (rear wheels) seized. Inspect and rebuild as required (Chapter 9).
4   Brake linings or pads contaminated with oil or grease. Inspect and replace as required (Chapter 1).
5   New pads or linings installed and not yet seated. It will take a while for the new material to seat against the drum (or rotor).

66   Pedal travels to floor with little resistance

Little or no fluid in the master cylinder reservoir (caused by leaking wheel cylinder(s), leaking caliper piston(s), loose, damaged or disconnected brake lines). Inspect entire system and correct as necessary.

67   Brake pedal pulsates during brake application

1   Wheel bearings not adjusted properly or in need of replacement (Chapter 1).
2   Caliper not sliding properly due to improper installation or obstructions. Remove and inspect (Chapter 9).
3   Rotor not within specifications. Remove the rotor (Chapter 9) and check for excessive lateral run-out and parallelism. Have the rotor machined or replace it with a new one.
4   Out-of-round rear brake drums. Remove the drums (Chapter 9) and have them machined, or replace them.

68   Hill-holder fails to hold

1   Incline of hill may be too gentle to activate holder.
2   Pressure holder valve in need of adjustment (Chapter 9).

Suspension and steering

69   Excessive tire wear (not specific to one area)

1   Incorrect tire pressures (Chapter 1).

2   Tires out of balance. Have professionally balanced.
3   Wheel damaged. Inspect and replace as necessary.
4   Suspension or steering components excessively worn (Chapter 1).

70   Excessive tire wear on outside edge

1   Inflation pressures not correct (Chapter 1).
2   Excessive speed on turns.
3   Front end alignment incorrect (excessive toe-in). Have professionally aligned (Chapter 11).
4   Suspension arm bent or twisted.

71   Excessive tire wear on inside edge

1   Inflation pressures incorrect (Chapter 1).
2   Front end alignment incorrect (toe-out). Have professionally aligned (Chapter 11).
3   Loose or damaged steering components (Chapter 1).

72   Tire tread worn in one place

1   Tires out of balance. Balance tires professionally.
2   Damaged or buckled wheel. Inspect and replace if necessary.
3   Defective tire.

73   General vibration at highway speeds

1   Out-of-balance front wheels or tires. Have them professionally balanced.
2   Front or rear wheel bearings loose or worn. Check (Chapter 1) and replace as necessary (Chapter 11).
3   Defective tire or wheel. Have them checked and replaced if necessary.

74   Noise whether coasting or in drive

1   Road noise. No corrective procedures available.
2   Tire noise. Inspect tires and tire pressures (Chapter 1).
3   Front wheel bearings loose, worn or damaged. Check (Chapter 1) and replace-if necessary (Chapter 11).
4   Lack of lubrication in the balljoints or tie-rod ends (Chapter 1).
5   Damaged shock absorbers or mounts (Chapter 1).
6   Loose road wheel lug nuts. Check and tighten as necessary (Chapter 11).

75 Vehicle pulls to one side

1 Tire pressures uneven (Chapter 1).
2 Defective tire (Chapter 1).
3 Excessive wear in suspension or steering components (Chapter 1).
4 Front end in need of alignment (Chapter 11).
5 Front brakes dragging. Inspect brakes as described in Chapter 1.

76 Shimmy, shake or vibration

1 Tire or wheel out of balance or out of round. Have professionally balanced.
2 Loose or worn wheel bearings (Chapter 1). Replace as necessary (Chapter 11).
3 Shock absorbers and/or suspension components worn or damaged (Chapter 11).

77 Excessive pitching and/or rolling around corners or during braking

1 Defective shock absorbers. Replace as a set (Chapter 11).
2 Broken or weak coil springs and/or suspension components. Inspect as described in Chapter 11.

78 Excessively stiff steering

1 Lack of fluid in power steering fluid reservoir (Chapter 1).
2 Incorrect tire pressures (Chapter 1).
3 Lack of lubrication at balljoints (Chapter 1).
4 Front end out of alignment.
5 Rack and pinion out of adjustment or lacking lubrication.

79 Excessive play in steering

1 Loose wheel bearings (Chapter 1).
2 Excessive wear in suspension or steering components (Chapter 1).
3 Rack and pinion out of adjustment (Chapter 11).

80 Lack of power assistance

1 Steering pump drivebelt faulty, broken or not adjusted properly (Chapter 1).
2 Fluid level low (Chapter 1).
3 Hoses or lines restricting the flow. Inspect and replace parts as necessary.
4 Air in power steering system. Bleed system (Chapter 11).

Chapter 1
Tune-up and routine maintenance

Contents

1

Specifications

Recommended lubricants and fluids

Note: *Listed here are manufacturer recommendations at the time this manual was written. Manufactures occasionally upgrade their fluid and lubricant specifications, so check with your local auto parts store for current recommendations*

Engine oil	
Type	API grade SE or SF energy conserving oil
Viscosity	SEE ACCOMPANYING CHART
Coolant	Ethylene glycol based anti-freeze

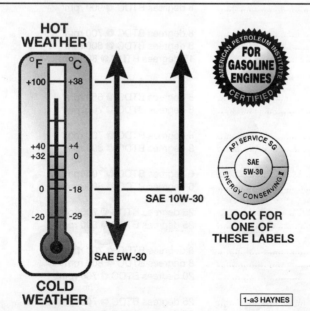

Engine oil viscosity chart - for best fuel economy and cold starting, select the lowest SAE viscosity grade for the expected temperature range

LOOK FOR ONE OF THESE LABELS

1-a3 HAYNES

Recommended lubricants and fluids (continued)

Brake fluid	DOT 3 or 4
Power steering fluid	DEXRON II ATF
Automatic transaxle fluid	DEXRON II ATF
Manual transaxle lubricant	API GL-5 SAE 80W-90 gear oil
Differential lubricant	API GL-5 SAE 80W-90 gear oil*
Chassis grease	NLGI no. 2 lithium base chassis grease

Limited slip differential add friction modifier (Subaru part no. 003304300 or equivalent) when oil is changed.

Capacities*   Quarts (liters)

Engine oil (with filter change)
    1600 OHV engine .... 3.7 qt (3.5 liters)
    1800 OHV and OHC engines .... 4.2 qt (4.0 liters)
Cooling system
    1600 OHV engine .... 5.6 qt (5.3 liters)
    1800 OHV and OHC engines .... 5.8 qt (5.5 liters)
Automatic transaxle (drain and refill)
    All except 4WD models with 4-speed .... 4.2 qt (4.0 liters)
    4WD 4-speed models .... 7.2 qt (6.8 liters)
Manual transaxle (drain and refill)
    1600 OHV engine .... 2.7 qt (2.6 liters)
    1800 OHV and OHC engines .... 3.5 qt (3.3 liters)
    1800 OHV and OHC engines (with full time 4WD) .... 3.7 qt (3.5 liters)
Differential
    Front differential (vehicles equipped with automatic transaxle)......... 2.3 pts (1.1 liters)
    Rear differential (4WD vehicles) .... 1.7 pts (0.8 liters)

All capacities approximate. Add as necessary to bring to appropriate level.

Ignition system

Spark plug type
    1980 .... NGK BPR6ES or equivalent
    1981 through 1984 (All models) .... NGK BPR6ES-11 or equivalent
Spark plug gap
    1980 .... 0.028 to 0.035 in (0.7 to 0.9 mm)
    1981 through 1994 .... 0.039 to 0.043 in (1.0 to 1.1 mm)

Distributor ignition points

Breaker point gap .... 0.018 to 0.022 in (0.45 to 0.55 mm)
Dwell angle .... 49 degrees to 55 degrees

Ignition timing and idle speed*

1980
    All models (except California)... 8 degrees BTDC @ 800 rpm*
    California models .... 8 degrees BTDC @ 900 rpm*
1981 through 1984
    Manual transaxle .... 8 degrees BTDC @ 700 rpm*
    Automatic transaxle .... 8 degrees BTDC @ 800 rpm*
    All turbo models .... 15 degrees BTDC @ 800 rpm*
1985
    DL models
        4-speed manual transaxle .... 6 degrees BTDC @ 650 rpm*
        5-speed manual transaxle .... 8 degrees BTDC @ 700 rpm*
    GL models
        Manual transaxle... 8 degrees BTDC @ 700 rpm*
        Automatic transaxle .... 8 degrees BTDC @ 800 rpm*
    GL-10 models
        Manual transaxle... 6 degrees BTDC @ 700 rpm*
        Automatic transaxle .... 6 degrees BTDC @ 800 rpm*
    All turbo models
        Manual transaxle... 25 degrees BTDC @ 700 rpm*
        Automatic transaxle .... 25 degrees BTDC @ 800 rpm*
1986
    Manual transaxle .... 8 degrees BTDC @ 700 rpm*
    Automatic transaxle .... 8 degrees BTDC @ 800 rpm*
    SPFI .... 20 degrees BTDC @ 700 rpm*
    All turbo models
        Manual transaxle... 25 degrees BTDC @ 700 rpm*
        Automatic transaxle .... 25 degrees BTDC @ 800 rpm*

1987 through 1989
    All carbureted models .... 8 degrees BTDC @ 700 rpm*
    SPFI .... 20 degrees BTDC @ 700 rpm*
    MPFI
        Manual transaxle .... 20 degrees BTDC @ 700 rpm**
        Automatic transaxle .... 20 degrees BTDC @ 800 rpm**
1990 through 1994
    All models .... 20 degrees BTDC @ 700 rpm*
    All turbo models .... 20 degrees BTDC @ 800 rpm**

Note: *Use the information printed on the Vehicle Emissions Control Information label, if different than the Specifications listed here.*
  With the distributor vacuum line disconnected and plugged.
  **With the test mode connector connected and the idle switch in the ON position.*

Firing order and distributor rotation

All engines
    Firing order 1-3-2-4
    Distributor rotation .... Counterclockwise

Valve clearance (engine cold)

Intake .... 0.010 in (0.25 mm)
Exhaust .... 0.014 in (0.35 mm)

Brakes

Disc brake pad lining thickness (minimum) .... 1/16-in (1.5 mm)
Drum brake shoe lining thickness (minimum) .... 1/16-in (1.5 mm)
Parking brake adjustment
    Drum brake .... 3 to 4 clicks
    Disc brake .... 3 to 4 clicks

Suspension and steering

Steering wheel freeplay limit .... 0.98 in (25 mm)
Balljoint allowable movement .... 0.0 in (0.0 mm)

Torque specifications

	Ft-lbs
Automatic transaxle drain plug	18
Manual transaxle drain plug	33
Front differential drain plug (automatic transaxle)	18
Engine oil drain plug	18
Spark plugs	15
Front drive hub castle nut	145
Wheel lug nuts	72

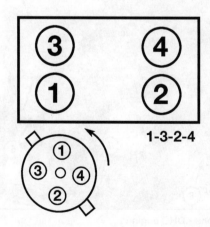

1-3-2-4

Cylinder location and distributor rotation diagram - OHV engines

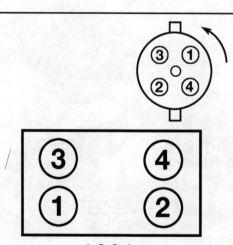

1-3-2-4

Cylinder location and distributor rotation diagram - OHC engines

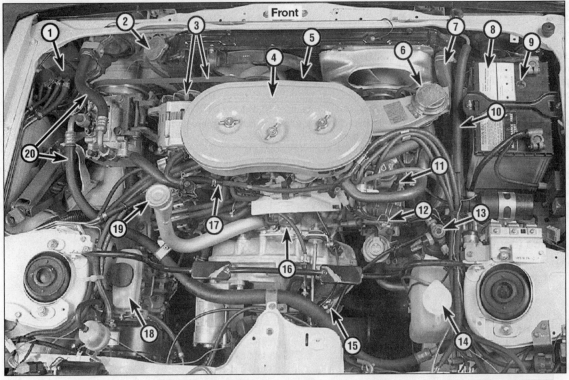

Engine compartment component locations - OHV engine

1	ECS canister	8	Battery	15	Manual transmission and
2	Radiator cap	9	Built-in hydrometer {not all models)		differential oil level dipstick
3	Drivebelts	10	Air conditioner line	16	EGR valve
4	Air cleaner housing	11	Spark plug wire(s))	17	Purge check valve
5	Distributor (under air cleaner)	12	Engine oil level dipstick	18	Brake fluid reservoir
6	Hot air intake system baffle motor	13	Air conditioning system sight glass	19	Oil filler cap and tub
7	Upper radiator hose	14	Windshield washer fluid reservoir	20	Air conditioner hose

Engine compartment component locations - OHC engine

1	Manual transaxle fluid dipstick (not visible) and front differential fluid dipstick on vehicles equipped with automatic transaxles	4	Automatic transaxle fluid dipstick (not visible)	9	Power steering fluid reservoir
		5	Engine coolant reservoir	10	Engine oil dipstick
		6	Battery	11	Evaporative emissions canister
2	Air filter housing	7	Radiator cap	12	Windshield washer fluid reservoir
3	Brake fluid reservoir	8	Engine drivebelts	13	Engine oil filler cap

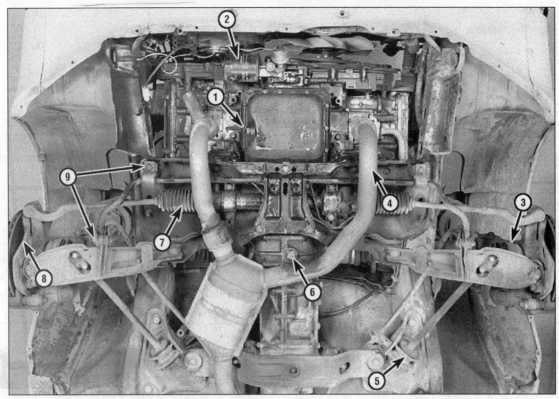

Typical engine compartment underside component locations

1	Engine oil drain plug	4	Exhaust pipe	7	Steering gear
2	Oil filter	5	Strut rod bushing	8	Brake disc
3	Front driveaxle	6	Manual transaxle drain plug	9	Sway bar bushing

Typical rear underside component locations

1 Muffler
2 Rear Differential drain plug
3 Rear Differential
4 Rear driveaxle
5 Fuel filter
6 Driveshaft
7 Control arm bushing

1 Subaru maintenance schedule

Every 250 miles or weekly, whichever comes first

Check the engine oil level (Section 4)
Check the engine coolant level (Section 4)
Check the windshield washer fluid level (Section 4)
Check the brake fluid level (Section 4)
Check the tires and tire pressures (Section 5)

Every 3000 miles or 3 months, whichever comes first

All items listed above, plus . . .
Check the automatic transaxle fluid level (Section 6)
Check the power steering fluid level (Section 7)
Change the engine oil and filter (Section 8)

Every 7500 miles or 6 months, whichever comes first

Check and service the battery (Section 9)
Check the cooling system (Section 10)
Inspect and replace, if necessary, all underhood hoses (Section 11)
Inspect and replace, if necessary, the windshield wiper blades (Section 12)
Rotate the tires (Section 13)
Inspect the suspension and steering components (Section 14)
Inspect the exhaust system (Section 15)
Check the manual transaxle lubricant (Section 16)
Check the rear differential lubricant level (Section 17)
Check the seat belts (Section 18)

Every 15,000 miles or 12 months, whichever comes first

All items listed above, plus . . .
Check the brakes (Section 19)
Inspect the fuel system (Section 20)
Replace the fuel filter (Section 21)
Check the engine drivebelts (Section 22)
Check and adjust if necessary, the valve clearance (OHV engines) (Section 23)
Check the EGR valve (Section 24)
Check the carburetor choke operation (Section 25)
Inspect and replace the ignition points, if equipped (Section 26)

Inspect the spark plug wires, distributor cap and rotor (Section 27)
Replace the spark plugs (Section 28)
Check the idle speed adjustment (Section 29)
Check the ignition timing (Section 30)
Check the clutch cable and hill holder adjustment (Chapter 8)
Check the timing belt tension (OHC engines) (Chapter 2B)

Every 30,000 miles or 24 months, whichever comes first

All items listed above, plus . . .
Replace the air filter and PCV filter (Section 31)*
Check the Positive Crankcase Ventilation (PCV) system (Section 32)
Inspect the evaporative emissions control system (Section 33)
Service the cooling system (drain, flush and refill) (Section 34)
Change the brake fluid (Section 35)
Change the automatic transaxle fluid and filter (Section 36)**
Change the manual transaxle lubricant (Section 37)
Change the rear differential lubricant (Section 38)

Every 60,000 miles

Inspect and repack the front wheel bearings (Section 39)
Inspect and repack the rear wheel bearings (Chapter 8)
Replace the timing belt (OHC engines) (Chapter 2B)

This item is affected by "severe" operating conditions, as described below. If the vehicle is operated under severe conditions, perform all maintenance indicated with an asterisk (*) at 7500 mile/six-month intervals. Severe conditions exist if you mainly operate the vehicle . . .
in dusty areas
towing a trailer
idling for extended periods and/or driving at low speeds when outside temperatures remain below freezing
and most trips are less than four miles long

**If operated under one or more of the following conditions, change the automatic transaxle fluid every 15,000 miles:*
in heavy city traffic where the outside temperature regularly reaches 90-degrees F or higher
in hilly or mountainous terrain
frequent trailer pulling

2   Introduction

This Chapter is designed to help the home mechanic maintain the Subaru for peak performance, economy, safety and long life.

On the following pages is a master maintenance schedule, followed by Sections dealing specifically with each item on the schedule. Visual checks, adjustments, component replacement and other helpful items are included. Refer to the accompanying illustrations of the engine compartment and the underside of the vehicle for the location of various components.

Servicing your Subaru in accordance with the mileage/time maintenance schedule and the following Sections will provide it with a planned maintenance program that should result in a long and reliable service life. This is a comprehensive plan, so maintaining some items but not others at the specified service intervals will not produce the same results.

As you service your vehicle, you will discover that many of the procedures can, and should, be grouped together because of the nature of the particular procedure you're performing or because of the close proximity of two otherwise unrelated components to one another.

For example, if the vehicle is raised for any reason, you should inspect the exhaust, suspension, steering and fuel systems while you're under the vehicle. When you're rotating the tires, it makes good sense to check the brakes and wheel bearings since the wheels are already removed.

Finally, let's suppose you have to borrow or rent a torque wrench. Even if you only need to tighten the spark plugs, you might as well check the torque of as many critical fasteners as time allows.

The first step of this maintenance program is to prepare yourself before the actual work begins. Read through all Sections pertinent to the procedures you're planning to do, then make a list of and gather together all the parts and tools you will need to do the job. If it looks as if you might run into problems during a particular segment of some procedure, seek advice from your local parts man or dealer service department.

3   Tune-up general information

The term tune-up is used in this manual to represent a combination of individual operations rather than one specific procedure.

If, from the time the vehicle is new, the routine maintenance schedule is followed closely and frequent checks are made of fluid levels and high wear items, as suggested throughout this manual, the engine will be kept in relatively good running condition and the need for additional work will be minimized.

More likely than not, however, there will be times when the engine is running poorly due to lack of regular maintenance. This is even more likely if a used vehicle, which has not received regular and frequent maintenance checks, is purchased. In such cases, an engine tune-up will be needed outside of the regular routine maintenance intervals.

The first step in any tune-up or diagnostic procedure to help correct a poor running engine is a cylinder compression check. A compression check (see Chapter 2C) will help determine the condition of internal engine components and should be used as a guide for tune-up and repair procedures. If, for instance, the compression check indicates serious internal engine wear, a conventional tune-up won't improve the performance of the engine and would be a waste of time and money. Because of its importance, the compression check should be done by someone with the right equipment and the knowledge to use it properly.

The following procedures are those most often needed to bring a generally poor running engine back into a proper state of tune.

Minor tune-up

Check all engine related fluids (Section 4)
Clean, inspect and test the battery (Section 9)
Check the cooling system (Section 10)
Check all underhood hoses (Section 11)
Check and adjust the drivebelts (Section 22)
Check and adjust the valve clearances (OHV engines) (Section 23)
Replace the ignition points, if equipped (Section 26)
Inspect the spark plug wires, distributor cap and rotor (Section 27)
Replace the spark plugs (Section 28)
Check and adjust the idle speed (Section 29)
Check and adjust the ignition timing (Section 30)
Check the air filter and the PCV filter (Section 31)
Check the PCV valve (Section 32)

Major tune-up

All items listed under Minor tune-up, plus . . .
Check the fuel system (Section 20)
Replace the fuel filter (Section 21)
Check the EGR system (Section 24)
Replace the distributor cap, rotor and spark plug wires (Section 27)
Replace the air filter and the PCV filter (Section 31)
Replace the PCV valve (Section 32)
Check the ignition system (Chapter 5)
Check the charging system (Chapter 5)

4   Fluid level checks (every 250 miles or weekly)

1

Note: *The following are fluid level checks to be done on a 250 mile or weekly basis. Additional fluid level checks can be found in specific maintenance procedures which follow. Regardless of intervals, be alert to fluid leaks under the vehicle which would indicate a fault to be corrected immediately.*

1   Fluids are an essential part of the lubrication, cooling, brake and windshield washer systems. Because the fluids gradually become depleted and/or contaminated during normal operation of the vehicle, they must be periodically replenished. See *Recommended lubricants and fluids* at the beginning of this Chapter before adding fluid to any of the following components. **Note:** *The vehicle must be on level ground when fluid levels are checked.*

Engine oil

Refer to illustrations 4.2a, 4.2b, 4.4 and 4.6

2   The engine oil level is checked with a dipstick that extends through a tube and into the oil pan at the bottom of the engine **(see illustrations)**.

3   The oil level should be checked before the vehicle has been driven, or about 15 minutes after the engine has been shut off. If the oil is checked immediately after driving the vehicle, some of the oil will remain in the upper engine components, resulting in an

4.2a The engine oil dipstick (arrow) on OHV engines is located on the right side of the engine

4.2b On OHC engines the oil dipstick (arrow) is located at the front of the engine

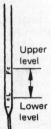

4.4 The oil level must be maintained between the marks at all times - it takes one quart of oil to raise the level from the LOW mark to the FULL mark

Upper
level

Lower
level

4.6 Oil is added to the engine after removing the twist off cap (arrow) located on the oil filler tube (OHC engine shown)

4.8 On 1984 and earlier models, coolant can be added to the cooling system after removing the radiator cap

inaccurate reading on the dipstick.

4   Pull the dipstick out of the tube and wipe all the oil from the end with a clean rag or paper towel. Insert the clean dipstick all the way back into the tube, then pull it out again. Note the oil at the end of the dipstick. Add oil as necessary to keep the level between the ADD and FULL marks on the dipstick **(see illustration)**.

5   Do not overfill the engine by adding too much oil since this may result in oil-fouled spark plugs, oil leaks or oil seal failures.

6   Oil is added to the engine after removing the threaded cap from the oil filler tube **(see illustration)**. A funnel may help to reduce spills.

7   Checking the oil level is an important preventive maintenance step. A consistently low oil level indicates oil leakage through damaged seals, defective gaskets or past worn rings or valve guides. If the oil looks milky or has water droplets in it, the cylinder head gasket(s) may be blown or the head(s) or block may be cracked. The engine should be checked immediately. The condition of the oil should also be checked. Whenever you check the oil level, slide your thumb and index finger up the dipstick before wiping off the oil. If you see small dirt or metal particles clinging to the dipstick, the oil should be changed (see Section 8).

Engine coolant

Refer to illustrations 4.8 and 4.9
Warning 1: *Do not allow antifreeze to come in contact with your skin or painted surfaces*

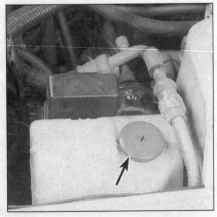

4.9 On 1985 and later models, coolant can be added to the cooling system after removing the cap from the coolant reservoir

of the vehicle. Flush contaminated areas immediately with plenty of water. Don't store new coolant or leave old coolant lying around where it's accessible to children or pets – they're attracted by its sweet smell. Ingestion of even a small amount of coolant can be fatal! Wipe up garage floor and drip pan spills immediately. Keep antifreeze containers covered and repair cooling system leaks as soon as they're noticed.

Warning 2: DO NOT remove the radiator cap or the coolant recovery cap while the cooling system is hot as escaping steam could cause serious injury.

8   On early model vehicles (1984 and earlier) the coolant level should be checked by removing the radiator cap **(see illustration)**. Wait until the engine has completely cooled, then wrap a thick cloth around the cap and turn it to its first stop. If any steam escapes from the cap, allow the engine to cool further, then remove the cap and check the level in the radiator.

9   Later model vehicles (1985 and later) are equipped with a pressurized coolant recovery system. A white coolant reservoir which is located by the radiator in the engine compartment is connected by a hose to the base of the coolant filler cap **(see illustration)**. If the coolant gets too hot during engine operation, coolant can escape through a pressurized filler cap, then through a connecting hose into the reservoir. As the engine cools, the coolant is automatically drawn back into the cooling system to maintain the correct level.

10   The coolant level should be checked regularly. On early models the coolant level should be just below the base of the filler neck. On later models the coolant level should be between the FULL and LOW lines on the reservoir tank. The level will vary with the temperature of the engine. When the engine is cold, the coolant level should be at or slightly above the LOW mark on the tank. Once the engine has warmed up, the level should be at or near the FULL mark. If it isn't, allow the fluid in the tank to cool, then remove the cap from the reservoir and add coolant to bring the level up to the FULL line.

11   Use only ethylene/glycol type coolant and water in the mixture ratio recommended by your owner's manual. Do not use supplemental inhibitor additives. If only a small amount of coolant is required to bring the system up to the proper level, water can be used. However, repeated additions of water will dilute the recommended antifreeze and water solution. In order to maintain the proper ratio of antifreeze and water, it is advisable to top up the coolant level with the correct mixture. Refer to your owner's manual for the recommended ratio.

12   If the coolant level drops within a short time after replenishment, there may be a leak in the system. Inspect the radiator, hoses, engine coolant filler cap, drain plugs and water pump. If no leak is evident, have the radiator cap pressure tested by your dealer.

Warning: *Never remove the radiator cap or the coolant recovery reservoir cap when the engine is running or has just been shut down, because the cooling system is hot. Escaping steam and scalding liquid could cause serious injury.*

13   If it is necessary to open the radiator cap on later models, wait until the system has cooled completely, then wrap a thick cloth around the cap and turn it to the first stop. If any steam escapes, wait until the system has cooled further, then remove the cap.

14   When checking the coolant level, always note its condition. It should be relatively clear. If it is brown or rust colored, the system should be drained, flushed and refilled. Even if the coolant appears to be normal, the corrosion inhibitors wear out with use, so it must be replaced at the specified intervals.

15   Do not allow antifreeze to come in contact with your skin or painted surfaces of the vehicle. Flush contacted areas immediately with plenty of water.

Brake fluid

Refer to illustration 4.17

16   The brake fluid level is checked by looking through the plastic reservoir mounted on the master cylinder. The master cylinder is mounted on the front of the power booster

4.17 The fluid level inside the brake reservoir can easily be checked by observing the level from the outside - fluid can be added to the reservoir after unscrewing the cap (later model shown)

4.24a On early models, the windshield washer fluid reservoir (arrow) is mounted to right strut tower in the engine compartment

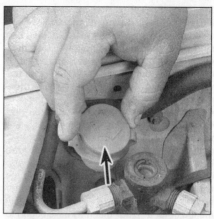

4.24b On later models, the windshield washer fluid reservoir (arrow) is located at right front of the engine compartment

unit in the driver's side) rear corner of the engine compartment.

17   The fluid level should be between the MAX and MIN lines on the side of the reservoir **(see illustration)**.

18   If the fluid level is low, wipe the top of the reservoir and the cap with a clean rag to prevent contamination of the system as the cap is unscrewed.

19   Add only the specified brake fluid to the reservoir (refer to *Recommended lubricants and fluids* at the front of this Chapter or your owner's manual). Mixing different types of brake fluid can damage the system. Fill the reservoir to the MAX line. **Warning:** *Brake fluid can harm your eyes and damage painted surfaces, so use extreme caution when handling or pouring it. Do not use brake fluid that has been standing open or is more than one year old. Brake fluid absorbs moisture from the air, which can cause a dangerous loss of braking effectiveness.*

20   While the reservoir cap is off, check the master cylinder reservoir for contamination. If rust deposits, dirt particles or water droplets are present, the system should be drained and refilled by a dealer service department or repair shop.

21   After filling the reservoir to the proper level, make sure the cap is seated to prevent fluid leakage and/or contamination.

22   The fluid level in the master cylinder will drop slightly as the brake shoes or pads at each wheel wear down during normal operation. If the brake fluid level drops consistently, check the entire system for leaks immediately. Examine all brake lines, hoses and connections, along with the calipers, wheel cylinders and master cylinder (see Section 19).

23   When checking the fluid level, if you discover one or both reservoirs empty or nearly empty, the brake system should be bled (see Chapter 9).

Windshield washer fluid

Refer to illustrations 4.24a and 4.24b

24   Fluid for the windshield washer system is stored in a plastic reservoir located on the

right side of the engine compartment **(see illustrations)**.

25   In milder climates, plain water can be used in the reservoir, but it should be kept no more than 2/3 full to allow for expansion if the water freezes. In colder climates, use windshield washer system antifreeze, available at any auto parts store, to lower the freezing point of the fluid. Mix the antifreeze with water in accordance with the manufacturer's directions on the container. **Caution:** *Do not use cooling system antifreeze - it will damage the vehicle's paint.*

Battery electrolyte

Refer to illustration 4.26

26   Most vehicles covered by this manual are equipped with a battery which is permanently sealed (except for vent holes) and has no filler caps. Water does not have to be added to these batteries at any time; however, if a maintenance-Type battery has been installed on the vehicle since it was new, remove all the cell caps on top of the battery **(see illustration)**. If the electrolyte level is low, add distilled water until the level is above the plates. There is usually a split-ring indicator in each cell to help you judge when enough water has been added. Add water until the electrolyte level is just up to the bottom of the split ring indicator. **Caution:** *Overfilling the cells may cause electrolyte to spill over during periods of heavy charging, causing corrosion or damage.*

5   Tire and tire pressure checks (every 250 miles or weekly)

Refer to illustrations 5.2, 5.3, 5.4a, 5.4b and 5.8

1   Periodic inspection of the tires may spare you the inconvenience of being stranded with a flat tire. It can also provide you with vital information regarding possible problems in the steering and suspension systems before major damage occurs.

4.26 On maintenance type batteries the cell caps have to be removed to check the water level in the battery - if the level is to low, add distilled water only

2   The original tires on this vehicle are equipped with 1/2-inch wear bands that will appear when tread depth reaches 1/16-inch, but they don't appear until the tires are worn out. Tread wear can be monitored with a simple, inexpensive device known as a tread depth indicator **(see illustration)**.

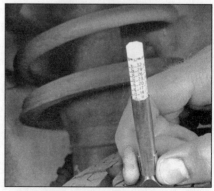

5.2 Use a tire tread depth gauge to monitor tire wear - they are available at auto parts stores and service stations and cost very little

3   Note any abnormal tread wear **(see illustration)**. Tread pattern irregularities such as cupping, flat spots and more wear on one side than the other are indications of front end alignment and/or balance problems. If any of these conditions are noted, take the vehicle to a tire shop or service station to correct the problem.

4   Look closely for cuts, punctures and embedded nails or tacks. Sometimes a tire will hold air pressure for a short time or leak down very slowly after a nail has embedded itself in the tread. If a slow leak persists, check the valve stem core to make sure it's tight **(see illustration)**. Examine the tread for an object that may have embedded itself in the tire or for a "plug" that may have begun to leak (radial tire punctures are repaired with a rubber plug that's installed in the hole). If a puncture is suspected, it can be easily verified by spraying a solution of soapy water onto the puncture area **(see illustration)**. The soapy solution will bubble if there's a leak. Unless the puncture is unusually large, a tire shop or service station can usually repair the tire.

5   Carefully inspect the inner sidewall of each tire for evidence of brake fluid leakage. If you see any, inspect the brakes immediately.

6   Correct air pressure adds miles to the lifespan of the tires, improves mileage and enhances overall ride quality. Tire pressure cannot be accurately estimated by looking at a tire, especially if it's a radial. A tire pressure gauge is essential. Keep an accurate gauge in the vehicle. The pressure gauges attached to the nozzles of air hoses at gas stations are often inaccurate.

7   Always check tire pressure when the tires are cold. Cold, in this case, means the vehicle has not been driven over a mile in the three hours preceding a tire pressure check. A pressure rise of four to eight pounds is not uncommon once the tires are warm.

8   Unscrew the valve cap protruding from the wheel or hubcap and push the gauge firmly onto the valve stem **(see illustration)**. Note the reading on the gauge and compare the figure to the recommended tire pressure shown on the placard on the driver's side door pillar. Be sure to reinstall the valve cap to keep dirt and moisture out of the valve stem mechanism. Check all four tires and, if necessary, add enough air to bring them up to the recommended pressure.

9   Don't forget to keep the spare tire inflated to the specified pressure (consult your owner's manual). Note that the air pressure specified for the compact spare is significantly higher than the pressure of the regular tires.

6   Automatic transaxle fluid level check (every 3000 miles or 3 months)

Refer to illustrations 6.4 and 6.6

1   The level of the automatic transaxle fluid should be carefully maintained. Low fluid level can lead to slipping or loss of drive, while overfilling can cause foaming, loss of fluid and transaxle damage.

2   The transaxle fluid level should only be checked when the transaxle is hot (at its normal operating temperature). If the vehicle has just been driven over 10 miles (15 miles in a frigid climate), and the fluid temperature is 160 to 175-degrees F, the transaxle is hot. **Caution:** *If the vehicle has just been driven for a long time at high speed or in city traffic in hot weather, or if it has been pulling a trailer, an accurate fluid level reading cannot be obtained. Allow the fluid to cool down for about 30 minutes.*

3   If the vehicle has not been driven, park the vehicle on level ground, set the parking brake, then start the engine and bring it to operating temperature. While the engine is idling, depress the brake pedal and move the selector lever through all the gear ranges, beginning and ending in Park.

UNDERINFLATION

CUPPING

Cupping may be caused by:

- Underinflation and/or mechanical irregularities such as out-of-balance condition of wheel and/or tire, and bent or damaged wheel.
- Loose or worn steering tie-rod or steering idler arm.
- Loose, damaged or worn front suspension parts.

OVERINFLATION

INCORRECT TOE-IN OR EXTREME CAMBER

FEATHERING DUE TO MISALIGNMENT

5.3 This chart will help you determine the condition of the tires, the probable cause(s) of abnormal wear and the corrective action necessary

5.4a If a tire loses air on a steady basis, check the valve core first to make sure it's snug (special inexpensive wrenches are commonly available at auto parts stores)

5.4b If the valve core is tight, raise the corner of the vehicle with the low tire and spray a soapy water solution onto the tread as the tire is turned slowly - leaks will cause small bubbles to appear

5.8 To extend the life of the tires, check the air pressure at least once a week with an accurate gauge (don't forget the spare)

6.4 The automatic transaxle fluid dipstick (arrow) is located on the left side of the engine compartment

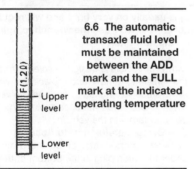

6.6 The automatic transaxle fluid level must be maintained between the ADD mark and the FULL mark at the indicated operating temperature

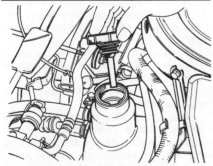

7.2a On Early models (without turbocharger) the power steering fluid reservoir is integral with the pump body - turn the cap counterclockwise to remove it

4   With the engine still idling, remove the dipstick from its tube **(see illustration)**. Check the level of the fluid on the dipstick and note its condition.

5   Wipe the fluid from the dipstick with a clean rag and reinsert it back into the filler tube until the cap seats.

6   Pull the dipstick out again and note the fluid level. If the transaxle is cold, the level should be in the COLD or COOL range on the dipstick. If it is hot, the fluid level should be in the HOT range. If the level is at the low side of either range, add the specified automatic transaxle fluid through the dipstick tube with a funnel **(see illustration)**.

7   Add just enough of the recommended fluid to fill the transaxle to the proper level. It takes about one pint to raise the level from the low mark to the high mark when the fluid is hot, so add the fluid a little at a time and keep checking the level until it is correct.

8   The condition of the fluid should also be checked along with the level. If the fluid at the end of the dipstick is black or a dark reddish

7.2b Later models are equipped with a remote power steering fluid reservoir which is located at the front of the engine compartment - turn the cap counterclockwise to remove it

brown color, or if it emits a burned smell, the fluid should be changed (see Section 36). If you are in doubt about the condition of the fluid, purchase some new fluid and compare the two for color and smell.

7   Power steering fluid level check (every 3000 miles or 3 months)

Refer to illustrations 7.2a, 7.2b and 7.6

1   Unlike manual steering, the power steering system relies on fluid which may, over a period of time, require replenishing.

2   The fluid reservoir for the power steering pump on early models is located on the pump body at the front of the engine. Later models are equipped with a remote fluid reservoir which is mounted on top of the engine in front of the air filter housing **(see illustrations)**.

3   For the check, the front wheels should be pointed straight ahead and the engine should be off.

4   Use a clean rag to wipe off the reservoir cap and the area around the cap. This will help prevent any foreign matter from entering the reservoir during the check.

5   Twist off the cap and determine the temperature of the fluid at the end of the dipstick with your finger.

6   Wipe off the fluid with a clean rag, rein-

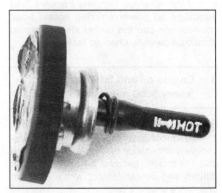

7.6 The marks on the dipstick indicate the safe fluid range

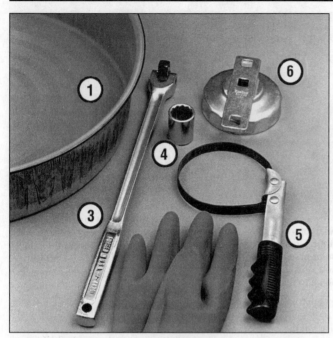

8.2 These tools are required when changing the engine oil and filter

1   **Drain pan** - It should be fairly shallow in depth, but wide to prevent spills
2   **Rubber gloves** - When removing the drain plug and filter, you will get oil on your hands (the gloves will prevent burns)
3   **Breaker bar** - Sometimes the oil drain plug is tight, and a long breaker bar is needed to loosen it
4   **Socket** - To be used with the breaker bar or a ratchet (must be the correct size to fit the drain plug)
5   **Filter wrench** - This is a metal band-type wrench, which requires clearance around the filter to be effective
6   **Filter wrench** - This type fits on the bottom of the filter and can be turned with a ratchet or breaker bar (different size wrenches are available for different types of filters)

8.7 The engine oil drain plug is located on the bottom of the oil pan - it is usually very tight, so use the proper size box end wrench or socket to avoid rounding it off

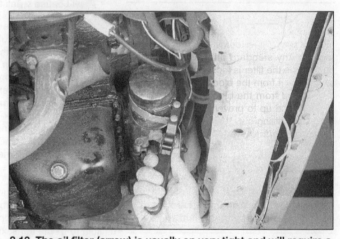

8.13 The oil filter (arrow) is usually on very tight and will require a special wrench for removal - DO NOT use the wrench to tighten the new filter!

sert the dipstick, then withdraw it and read the fluid level. The fluid should be at the proper level, depending on whether it was checked hot or cold **(see illustration)**. Never allow the fluid level to drop below the lower mark on the dipstick.
7   If additional fluid is required, pour the specified type directly into the reservoir, using a funnel to prevent spills.
8   If the reservoir requires frequent fluid additions, all power steering hoses, hose connections and the power steering pump should be carefully checked for leaks.

8   Engine oil and filter change (every 3000 miles or 3 months)

Refer to illustrations 8.2, 8.7, 8.13 and 8.15
1   Frequent oil changes are the best preventive maintenance the home mechanic can give the engine, because aging oil becomes diluted and contaminated, which leads to premature engine wear.
2   Make sure that you have all the necessary tools before you begin this procedure

(see illustration). You should also have plenty of rags or newspapers handy for mopping up any spills.
3   Access to the underside of the vehicle is greatly improved if the vehicle can be lifted on a hoist, driven onto ramps or supported by jackstands.
4   If this is your first oil change, get under the vehicle and familiarize yourself with the location of the oil drain plug. The engine and exhaust components will be warm during the actual work, so try to anticipate any potential problems before the engine and accessories are hot.
5   Park the vehicle on a level spot. Start the engine and allow it to reach its normal operating temperature (the needle on the temperature gauge should be at least above the bottom mark). Warm oil and contaminates will flow out more easily. Turn off the engine when it's warmed up. Remove the filler cap in the valve cover.
6   Raise the vehicle and support it on jackstands. **Warning:** *To avoid personal injury, never get beneath the vehicle when it is supported by only by a jack. The jack provided*

with your vehicle is designed solely for raising the vehicle to remove and replace the wheels. Always use jackstands to support the vehicle when it becomes necessary to place your body underneath the vehicle.
7   Being careful not to touch the hot exhaust components, place the drain pan under the drain plug in the bottom of the pan and remove the plug **(see illustration)**. You may want to wear gloves while unscrewing the plug the final few turns if the engine is really hot.
8   Allow the old oil to drain into the pan. It may be necessary to move the pan farther under the engine as the oil flow slows to a trickle. Inspect the old oil for the presence of metal shavings and chips.
9   After all the oil has drained, wipe off the drain plug with a clean rag. Even minute metal particles clinging to the plug would immediately contaminate the new oil.
10   Clean the area around the drain plug opening, reinstall the plug and tighten it securely, but do not strip the threads.
11   Move the drain pan into position under the oil filter.

8.15 Lubricate the oil filter gasket with clean engine oil before installing the filter on the engine

9.6a Battery terminal corrosion usually appears as light, fluffy powder

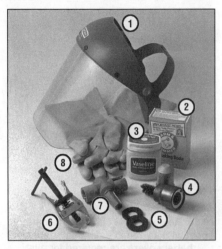

9.1 Tools and materials required for battery maintenance

12   Remove all tools, rags, etc. from under the vehicle, being careful not to spill the oil in the drain pan, then lower the vehicle.

13   Loosen the oil filter **(see illustration)** by turning it counterclockwise with the filter wrench. Any standard filter wrench should work. Once the filter is loose, use your hands to unscrew it from the block. Just as the filter is detached from the block, immediately tilt the open end up to prevent the oil inside the filter from spilling out. **Warning:** *The engine exhaust manifold may still be hot, so be careful.*

14   With a clean rag, wipe off the mounting surface on the block. If a residue of old oil is allowed to remain, it will smoke when the block is heated up. It will also prevent the new filter from seating properly. Also make sure that the none of the old gasket remains stuck to the mounting surface. It can be removed with a scraper if necessary.

15   Compare the old filter with the new one to make sure they are the same type. Smear some engine oil on the rubber gasket of the new filter and screw it into place **(see illustration)**. Because over-tightening the filter will damage the gasket, do not use a filter wrench to tighten the filter. Tighten it by hand until the gasket contacts the seating surface. Then seat the filter by giving it an additional 3/4-turn.

16   Add new oil to the engine through the oil filler cap in the valve cover. Use a spout or funnel to prevent oil from spilling onto the top of the engine. Pour three quarts of fresh oil into the engine. Wait a few minutes to allow the oil to drain into the pan, then check the level on the oil dipstick (see Section 4 if necessary). If the oil level is at or near the H mark, install the filler cap hand tight, start the engine and allow the new oil to circulate.

17   Allow the engine to run for about a minute. While the engine is running, look under the vehicle and check for leaks at the oil pan drain plug and around the oil filter. If either is leaking, stop the engine and tighten the plug or filter slightly.

18   Wait a few minutes to allow the oil to trickle down into the pan, then recheck the level on the dipstick and, if necessary, add

enough oil to bring the level to the H mark.

19   During the first few trips after an oil change, make it a point to check frequently for leaks and proper oil level.

20   The old oil drained from the engine cannot be reused in its present state and should be discarded. Oil reclamation centers, auto repair shops and gas stations will normally accept the oil, which can be recycled. After the oil has cooled, it can be drained into a suitable container (capped plastic jugs, topped bottles, milk cartons, etc.) for transport to one of these disposal sites.

9   Battery check, maintenance and charging (every 7500 miles or 6 months)

Refer to illustrations 9.1, 9.6a, 9.6b, 9.7a and 9.7b

Warning: *Certain precautions must be followed when checking and servicing the battery. Hydrogen gas, which is highly flammable, is always present in the battery cells, so keep lighted tobacco and all other open flames and sparks away from the battery. The electrolyte inside the battery is actually dilute sulfuric acid, which will cause injury if splashed on your skin or in your eyes. It will also ruin clothes and painted surfaces. When removing the battery cables, always detach the negative cable first and hook it up last!*

Maintenance

1   A routine preventive maintenance program for the battery in your vehicle is the only way to ensure quick and reliable starts. But before performing any battery maintenance, make sure that you have the proper equipment necessary to work safely around the battery **(see illustration)**.

2   There are also several precautions that should be taken whenever battery maintenance is performed. Before servicing the battery, always turn the engine and all accessories off and disconnect the cable from the negative terminal of the battery.

3   The battery produces hydrogen gas, which is both flammable and explosive. Never create a spark, smoke or light a match

1   Face shield/safety goggles - When removing corrosion with a brush, the acidic particles can easily fly up into your eyes

2   Baking soda - A solution of baking soda and water can be used to neutralize corrosion

3   Petroleum jelly - A layer of this on the battery posts will help prevent corrosion

4   Battery post/cable cleaner - This wire brush cleaning tool will remove all traces of corrosion from the battery posts and cable clamps

5   Treated felt washers - Placing one of these on each post, directly under the cable clamps, will help prevent corrosion

6   Puller - Sometimes the cable clamps are very difficult to pull off the posts, even after the nut/bolt has been completely loosened. This tool pulls the clamp straight up and off the post without damage

7   Battery post/cable cleaner - Here is another cleaning tool which is a slightly different version of Number 4 above, but it does the same thing

8   Rubber gloves - Another safety item to consider when servicing the battery; remember that's acid inside the battery!

around the battery. Always charge the battery in a ventilated area.

4   Electrolyte contains poisonous and corrosive sulfuric acid. Do not allow it to get in your eyes, on your skin or on your clothes. Never ingest it. Wear protective safety glasses when working near the battery. Keep children away from the battery.

5   Note the external condition of the battery. If the positive terminal and cable clamp on your vehicle's battery is equipped with a rubber protector, make sure that it's not torn or damaged. It should completely cover the terminal. Look for any corroded or loose connections, cracks in the case or cover or loose hold-down clamps. Also check the entire length of each cable for cracks and frayed conductors.

6   If corrosion, which looks like white, fluffy

9.6b Removing the cable from a battery post with a wrench - sometimes special battery pliers are required for this procedure if corrosion has caused deterioration of the nut hex (always remove the ground cable first and hook it up last!)

9.7a When cleaning the cable clamps, all corrosion must be removed (the inside of the clamp is tapered to match the taper on the post, so don't remove too much material)

9.7b Regardless of the type of tool used on the battery posts, a clean, shiny surface should be the end result

deposits **(see illustration)** is evident, particularly around the terminals, the battery should be removed for cleaning. Loosen the cable clamp bolts with a wrench, being careful to remove the ground cable first, and slide them off the terminals **(see illustration)**. Then disconnect the hold-down clamp bolt and nut, remove the clamp and lift the battery from the engine compartment.

7   Clean the cable clamps thoroughly with a battery brush or a terminal cleaner and a solution of warm water and baking soda **(see illustration)**. Wash the terminals and the top of the battery case with the same solution but make sure that the solution doesn't get into the battery. When cleaning the cables, terminals and battery top, wear safety goggles and rubber gloves to prevent any solution from coming in contact with your eyes or hands. Wear old clothes too - even diluted, sulfuric acid splashed onto clothes will burn holes in them. If the terminals have been extensively corroded, clean them up with a terminal cleaner **(see illustration)**. Thoroughly wash all cleaned areas with plain water.

8   Make sure that the battery tray is in good condition and the hold-down clamp bolts are tight. If the battery is removed from the tray, make sure no parts remain in the bottom of the tray when the battery is reinstalled. When reinstalling the hold-down clamp bolts, do not overtighten them.

9   Any metal parts of the vehicle damaged by corrosion should be covered with a zinc-based primer, then painted.

10   Information on removing and installing the battery can be found in Chapter 5. Information on jump starting can be found at the front of this manual. For more detailed battery checking procedures, refer to the *Haynes Automotive Electrical Manual*.

Charging

Warning: *When batteries are being charged, hydrogen gas, which is very explosive and*

flammable, is produced. Do not smoke or allow open flames near a battery. Wear eye protection when near the battery during charging. Also, make sure the charger is unplugged before connecting or disconnecting the battery from the charger.
Note: *The manufacturer recommends the battery be removed from the vehicle for charging because the gas that escapes during this procedure can damage the paint. Fast charging with the battery cables connected can result in damage to the electrical system.*

11   Slow-rate charging is the best way to restore a battery that's discharged to the point where it will not start the engine. It's also a good way to maintain the battery charge in a vehicle that's only driven a few miles between starts. Maintaining the battery charge is particularly important in the winter when the battery must work harder to start the engine and electrical accessories that drain the battery are in greater use.

12   It's best to use a one or two-amp battery charger (sometimes called a "trickle" charger). They are the safest and put the least strain on the battery. They are also the least expensive. For a faster charge, you can use a higher amperage charger, but don't use one rated more than 1/10th the amp/hour rating of the battery. Rapid boost charges that claim to restore the power of the battery in one to two hours are hardest on the battery and can damage batteries not in good condition. This type of charging should only be used in emergency situations.

13   The average time necessary to charge a battery should be listed in the instructions that come with the charger. As a general rule, a trickle charger will charge a battery in 12 to 16 hours.

14   Remove all the cell caps (if equipped) and cover the holes with a clean cloth to prevent spattering electrolyte. Disconnect the negative battery cable and hook the battery charger cable clamps up to the battery posts (positive to positive, negative to negative), then plug in the charger. Make sure it is set at

12-volts if it has a selector switch.

15   If you're using a charger with a rate higher than two amps, check the battery regularly during charging to make sure it doesn't overheat. If you're using a trickle charger, you can safely let the battery charge overnight after you've checked it regularly for the first couple of hours.

16   If the battery has removable cell caps, measure the specific gravity with a hydrometer every hour during the last few hours of the charging cycle. Hydrometers are available inexpensively from auto parts stores - follow the instructions that come with the hydrometer. Consider the battery charged when there's no change in the specific gravity reading for two hours and the electrolyte in the cells is gassing (bubbling) freely. The specific gravity reading from each cell should be very close to the others. If not, the battery probably has a bad cell(s).

17   Some batteries with sealed tops have built-in hydrometers on the top that indicate the state of charge by the color displayed in the hydrometer window. Normally, a bright-colored hydrometer indicates a full charge and a dark hydrometer indicates the battery still needs charging.

18   If the battery has a sealed top and no built-in hydrometer, you can hook up a voltmeter across the battery terminals to check the charge. A fully charged battery should read 12.6 volts or higher after the surface charge has been removed.

19   Further information on the battery and jump starting can be found in Chapter 5 and at the front of this manual.

10   Cooling system check (every 7500 miles or 6 months)

Refer to illustration 10.4

1   Many major engine failures can be attributed to a faulty cooling system. If the vehicle is equipped with an automatic transaxle, the cooling system also cools the transaxle fluid and thus plays an important role in prolonging transaxle life.

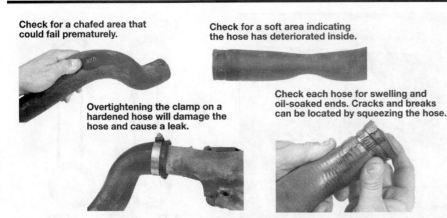

Check for a chafed area that could fail prematurely.

Overtightening the clamp on a hardened hose will damage the hose and cause a leak.

Check for a soft area indicating the hose has deteriorated inside.

Check each hose for swelling and oil-soaked ends. Cracks and breaks can be located by squeezing the hose.

10.4 Hoses, like drivebelts, have a habit of failing at the worst possible time - to prevent the inconvenience of a blown radiator or heater hose, inspect them carefully as shown here

2   The cooling system should be checked with the engine cold. Do this before the vehicle is driven for the day or after it has been shut off for at least three hours.

3   Remove the radiator cap by turning it to the left until it reaches a stop. If you hear a hissing sound (indicating there is still pressure in the system), wait until this stops. Now press down on the cap with the palm of your hand and continue turning to the left until the cap can be removed. Thoroughly clean the cap, inside and out, with clean water. Also clean the filler neck on the radiator. All traces of corrosion should be removed. The coolant inside the radiator should be relatively transparent. If it is rust colored, the system should be drained and refilled (see Section 34). If the coolant level is not up to the top, add additional antifreeze/coolant mixture (see Section 4).

4   Carefully check the large upper and lower radiator hoses along with the smaller diameter heater hoses which run from the engine to the firewall. Inspect each hose along its entire length, replacing any hose which is cracked, swollen or shows signs of deterioration. Cracks may become more apparent if the hose is squeezed **(see illustration)**. Regardless of condition, it's a good idea to replace hoses with new ones every two years.

5   Make sure all hose connections are tight. A leak in the cooling system will usually show up as white or rust colored deposits on the areas adjoining the leak. If wire-type clamps are used at the ends of the hoses, it may be a good idea to replace them with more secure screw-type clamps.

6   Use compressed air or a soft brush to remove bugs, leaves, etc. from the front of the radiator or air conditioning condenser. Be careful not to damage the delicate cooling fins or cut yourself on them.

7   Every other inspection, or at the first indication of cooling system problems, have the cap and system pressure tested. If you don't have a pressure tester, most gas stations and repair shops will do this for a minimal charge.

11   Underhood hose check and replacement (every 7500 miles or 6 months)

General

1   **Warning:** *Replacement of air conditioning hoses must be left to a dealer service department or air conditioning shop that has the equipment to depressurize the system safely. Never remove air conditioning components or hoses until the system has been depressurized.*

2   High temperatures in the engine compartment can cause the deterioration of the rubber and plastic hoses used for engine, accessory and emission systems operation. Periodic inspection should be made for cracks, loose clamps, material hardening and leaks. Information specific to the cooling system hoses can be found in Section 10.

3   Some, but not all, hoses are secured to the fittings with clamps. Where clamps are used, check to be sure they haven't lost their tension, allowing the hose to leak. If clamps aren't used, make sure the hose has not expanded and/or hardened where it slips over the fitting, allowing it to leak.

Vacuum hoses

4   It's quite common for vacuum hoses, especially those in the emissions system, to be color coded or identified by colored stripes molded into them. Various systems require hoses with different wall thickness, collapse resistance and temperature resistance. When replacing hoses, be sure the new ones are made of the same material.

5   Often the only effective way to check a hose is to remove it completely from the vehicle. If more than one hose is removed, be sure to label the hoses and fittings to ensure correct installation.

6   When checking vacuum hoses, be sure to include any plastic T-fittings in the check. Inspect the fittings for cracks and the hose where it fits over the fitting for distortion, which could cause leakage.

7   A small piece of vacuum hose (1/4-inch inside diameter) can be used as a stethoscope to detect vacuum leaks. Hold one end of the hose to your ear and probe around vacuum hoses and fittings, listening for the "hissing" sound characteristic of a vacuum leak. **Warning:** *When probing with the vacuum hose stethoscope, be very careful not to come into contact with moving engine components such as the drivebelt, cooling fan, etc.*

Fuel hose

Warning: *There are certain precautions which must be taken when inspecting or servicing fuel system components. Work in a well ventilated area and do not allow open flames (cigarettes, appliance pilot lights, etc.) or bare light bulbs near the work area. Mop up any spills immediately and do not store fuel soaked rags where they could ignite.*

8   Check all rubber fuel lines for deterioration and chafing. Check especially for cracks in areas where the hose bends and just before fittings, such as where a hose attaches to the fuel filter.

9   Only high quality fuel line should be used for fuel line replacement. Never, under any circumstances, use unreinforced vacuum line, clear plastic tubing or water hose for fuel lines.

10   Spring-type clamps are commonly used on fuel lines. These clamps often lose their tension over a period of time, and can be "sprung" during removal. Replace all spring-type clamps with screw clamps whenever a hose is replaced.

Metal lines

11   Sections of metal line are often used in the fuel system. Check carefully to be sure the line has not been bent or crimped and that cracks have not started in the line.

12   If a section of metal fuel line must be replaced, only seamless steel tubing should be used, since copper and aluminum tubing don't have the strength necessary to withstand normal engine vibration.

13   Check the metal brake lines where they enter the master cylinder and brake proportioning unit (if used) for cracks in the lines or loose fittings. Any sign of brake fluid leakage calls for an immediate thorough inspection of the brake system.

12   Wiper blade inspection and replacement (every 7500 miles or 6 months)

Refer to illustrations 12.3 and 12.5

1   The windshield wiper and blade assembly should be inspected periodically for damage, loose components and cracked or worn blade elements.

2   Road film can build up on the wiper blades and affect their efficiency, so they should be washed regularly with a mild detergent solution.

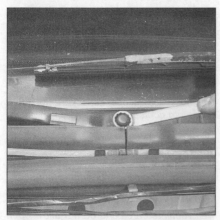

12.3 Pry off the trim cap and check the tightness of the wiper arm retaining nut

3   The action of the wiping mechanism can loosen bolts, nuts and fasteners, so they should be checked and tightened, as necessary **(see illustration)**, at the same time the wiper blades are checked.
4   If the wiper blade elements are cracked, worn or warped, or no longer clean adequately, they should be replaced with new ones.
5   Use needle-nose pliers to compress the blade element retaining tab, then slide the element out of the frame and discard it **(see illustration)**.
6   Installation is the reverse of removal.

13   Tire rotation (every 7500 miles or 6 months)

Refer to illustration 13.2
1   The tires should be rotated at the specified intervals and whenever uneven wear is noticed. Since the vehicle will be raised and the tires removed anyway, check the brakes (see Section 19) at this time.
2   Radial tires must be rotated in a specific pattern **(see illustration)**.

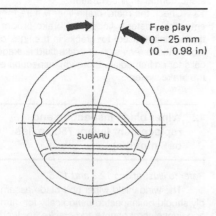

14.1 Steering wheel freeplay is the amount of travel between an initial steering input and the point at which the front wheels begin to turn (indicated by a slight resistance)

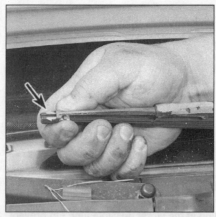

12.5 Use needle-nose pliers to compress the wiper element retaining tabs (arrow) then slide the element out - slide the new element in and lock the retaining tabs of the wiper element onto the fingers of the wiper arm

3   Refer to the information in *Jacking and towing* at the front of this manual for the proper procedures to follow when raising the vehicle and changing a tire. If the brakes are to be checked, do not apply the parking brake as stated. Make sure the tires are blocked to prevent the vehicle from rolling.
4   Preferably, the entire vehicle should be raised at the same time. This can be done on a hoist or by jacking up each corner and then lowering the vehicle onto jackstands placed under the frame rails. Always use four jackstands and make sure the vehicle is firmly supported.
5   After rotation, check and adjust the tire pressures as necessary and be sure to check the lug nut tightness.
6   For further information on the wheels and tires, refer to Chapter 10.

14   Suspension and steering check (every 7500 miles or 6 months)

Refer to illustrations 14.1, 14.6a, 14.6b and 14.9
Note: *For detailed illustrations of the steering and suspension components, refer to Chapter 10.*

With the wheels on the ground

1   With the vehicle stopped and the front wheels pointed straight ahead, rock the steering wheel gently back and forth. If freeplay **(see illustration)** is excessive, a front wheel bearing, main shaft yoke, intermediate shaft yoke, lower arm balljoint or steering system joint is worn or the steering gear is out of adjustment or broken. Refer to Chapter 10 for the appropriate repair procedure.
2   Other symptoms, such as excessive vehicle body movement over rough roads, swaying (leaning) around corners and binding as the steering wheel is turned, may indicate

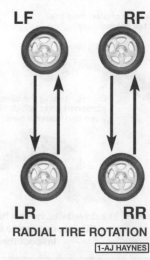

13.2 Tire rotation diagram for radial tires

faulty steering and/or suspension components.
3   Check the shock absorbers by pushing down and releasing the vehicle several times at each corner. If the vehicle does not come back to a level position within one or two bounces, the shocks/struts are worn and must be replaced. When bouncing the vehicle up and down, listen for squeaks and noises from the suspension components.

Under the vehicle

4   Raise the vehicle with a floor jack and support it securely on jackstands. See *jacking and towing* at the front of this book for proper jacking points.
5   Check the tires for irregular wear patterns and proper inflation. See Section 5 in this Chapter for information regarding tire wear.
6   Inspect the universal joint between the steering shaft and the steering gear housing. Check the steering gear housing for grease leakage. Make sure that the dust seals and boots are not damaged and that the boot clamps are not loose **(see illustration)**. Check the steering linkage for looseness or

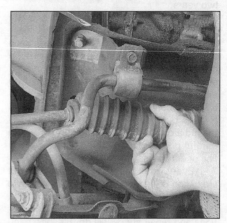

14.6a Check the steering gear dust boots for cracks and leaking steering fluid

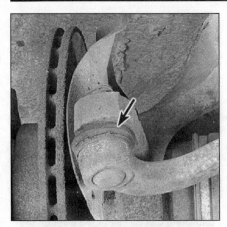

14.6b Inspect the suspension for deteriorated rubber bushings and torn grease seals (arrow)

14.9 Check the driveaxle boot (arrow) for cracks and/or leaking grease

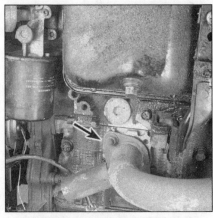

15.2a Check the exhaust pipes and connections (arrow) for signs of leakage and corrosion

damage. Check the tie-rod ends for excessive play. Look for loose bolts, broken or disconnected parts and deteriorated rubber bushings on all suspension and steering components **(see illustration)**. While an assistant turns the steering wheel from side to side, check the steering components for free movement, chafing and binding. If the steering components do not seem to be reacting with the movement of the steering wheel, try to determine where the slack is located.

7   Check the balljoints moving each lower arm up and down with a pry bar to ensure that its balljoint has no play. If any balljoint does have play, replace it. See Chapter 10 for the front balljoint replacement procedure.

8   Inspect the balljoint boots for damage and leaking grease. Replace the balljoints with new ones if they are damaged (see Chapter 10).

9   Inspect the front and rear driveaxle boots on 4WD models for tears and cracks as well as loose clamps **(see illustration)**. If there is any evidence of cracks or leaking lubricant, they must be replaced as described in Chapter 8. Oil and grease can cause the boot material to deteriorate prematurely, so it's a good idea to wash the boots with soap and water.

10   Check the wheel bearings. Do this by spinning the front wheels. Listen for any abnormal noises and watch to make sure the wheel spins true (doesn't wobble). Grab the top and bottom of the tire and pull in-and-out on it. Notice any movement which would indicate a loose wheel bearing assembly. If the bearings are suspect, they should be checked and repacked refer to Section 39 for more information.

11   Inspect the driveshaft on 4WD vehicles for worn U-joints and for excessive play in the slip yoke and spline area (see Chapter 8).

12   Check the transaxle and differentials for evidence of fluid leakage.

15   Exhaust system check (every 7500 miles or 6 months)

Refer to illustrations 15.2a and 15.2b

1   With the engine cold (at least three hours after the vehicle has been driven), check the complete exhaust system from the cylinder head to the end of the tailpipe. Be careful around the catalytic converter (if equipped), which may be hot even after three hours. The inspection should be done with

the vehicle on a hoist to permit unrestricted access. If a hoist isn't available, raise the vehicle and support it securely on jackstands.

2   Check the exhaust pipes and connections for signs of leakage and/or corrosion indicating a potential failure. Make sure that all brackets and hangers are in good condition and tight **(see illustrations)**.

3   Inspect the underside of the body for holes, corrosion, open seams, etc. which may allow exhaust gasses to enter the passenger compartment. Seal all body openings with silicone sealant or body putty.

4   Rattles and other noises can often be traced to the exhaust system, especially the hangers, mounts and heat shields. Try to move the pipes, mufflers and catalytic converter. If the components can come in contact with the body or suspension parts, secure the exhaust system with new brackets and hangers.

16   Manual transaxle/front differential lubricant level check (every 7500 miles or 6 months)

Refer to illustrations 16.1 and 16.2

Note: *Vehicles equipped with a manual transaxle have an integral front differential (meaning they share the same lubricant). Vehicles equipped with an automatic transaxle have a non-integral front differential (meaning they DO NOT share the same lubricant). The dipstick for the manual transaxle and the front differential on automatic transaxle equipped vehicles is approximately in the same position in the engine compartment and the lubricant level checking procedure is the same.*

1   The manual transaxle has a dipstick that extends through a tube and into the transaxle **(see illustration)**.

2   Pull the dipstick out of the tube and wipe all the lubricant from the end with a clean rag or paper towel. Insert the clean dipstick all the way back into the tube, then pull it out again. Note the lubricant at the end of

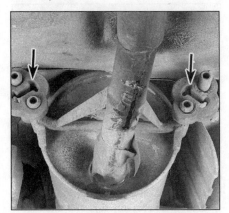

15.2b Check the exhaust system rubber hangers for cracks and damage (arrows)

16.1 The manual transaxle/front differential dipstick is located on the right side of the engine compartment

1

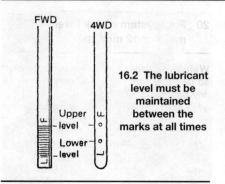

16.2 The lubricant level must be maintained between the marks at all times

17.2 The rear differential fill plug (A) and drain plug (B) are located on the differential cover - use your finger as a dipstick to check the lubricant level

19.5 With the wheels removed, the brake pad lining can be inspected through the caliper window (arrow) and at each end of the caliper

the dipstick. Add lubricant as necessary to keep the level between the ADD and FULL marks on the dipstick **(see illustration)**.

3   Lubricant is added to the transaxle through the dipstick tube. A funnel may help to reduce spills. Do not overfill the transaxle since this may result in lubricant leaks or lubricant seal failures.

4   Reinstall the dipstick and close the hood.

17   Differential lubricant level check (every 7500 miles or 6 months)

Refer to illustration 17.2

Note: *At the specified interval, the lubricant level in the front differential should be checked on vehicles equipped with automatic transaxles. Follow the procedures outlined in Section 16.*

1   The rear differential has a check/fill plug which must be removed to check the lubricant level. If the vehicle must be raised to gain access to the plug, be sure to support it safely on jackstands - DO NOT crawl under the vehicle when it's supported only by the jack.

2   Remove the oil check/fill plug from the back of the rear differential **(see illustration)**. On some models a tag is located in the area of the plug which gives information regarding lubricant type, particularly on models equipped with a limited-slip differential.

3   Use a finger to reach inside the housing to determine the lubricant level. The oil level should be at the bottom of the plug opening. If it isn't, use a hand pump (available at auto parts stores) to add the specified lubricant until it just starts to run out of the opening.

4   Install the plug and tighten it securely.

18   Seat belt check (every 7500 miles or 6 months)

1   Check the seat belts, buckles, latch plates and guide loops for any obvious damage or signs of wear.

2   Make sure the seat belt reminder light comes on when the key is turned on.

3   The seat belts are designed to lock up during a sudden stop or impact, yet allow free movement during normal driving. The

retractors should hold the belt against your chest while driving and rewind the belt when the buckle is unlatched.

4   If any of the above checks reveal problems with the seat belt system, replace parts as necessary.

19   Brake system check (every 15,000 miles or 12 months)

Warning: *The dust created by the brake system may contain asbestos, which is harmful to your health. Never blow it out with compressed air and don't inhale any of it. An approved filtering mask should be worn when working on the brakes. Do not, under any circumstances, use petroleum-based solvents to clean brake parts. Use brake system cleaner only! Try to use non-asbestos replacement parts whenever possible.*

Note: *For detailed photographs of the brake system, refer to Chapter 9.*

1   In addition to the specified intervals, the brakes should be inspected every time the wheels are removed or whenever a defect is suspected. Any of the following symptoms could indicate a potential brake system defect: The vehicle pulls to one side when the brake pedal is depressed; the brakes make squealing or dragging noises when applied; brake pedal travel is excessive; the pedal pulsates; brake fluid leaks, usually onto the inside of the tire or wheel.

2   Loosen the wheel lug nuts.

3   Raise the vehicle and place it securely on jackstands.

4   Remove the wheels (see *Jacking and towing* at the front of this book, or your owner's manual, if necessary).

Disc brakes

Refer to illustrations 19.5 and 19.10

5   There are two pads (an outer and an inner) in each caliper. The pads are visible through inspection holes in each caliper **(see illustration)**.

6   Check the pad thickness by looking at each end of the caliper and through the inspection hole in the caliper body. If the lining material is less than the thickness listed in this Chapter's Specifications, replace the pads. **Note:** *Keep in mind that the lining material is riveted or bonded to a metal backing plate and the metal portion is not included in this measurement.*

7   If it is difficult to determine the exact thickness of the remaining pad material by the above method, or if you are at all concerned about the condition of the pads, remove the caliper(s), then remove the pads from the calipers for further inspection (refer to Chapter 9).

8   Once the pads are removed from the calipers, clean them with brake cleaner and re-measure them with a ruler or a vernier caliper.

9   Measure the disc thickness with a micrometer to make sure that it still has service life remaining. If any disc is thinner than the specified minimum thickness, replace it (refer to Chapter 9). Even if the disc has service life remaining, check its condition. Look for scoring, gouging and burned spots. If these conditions exist, remove the disc and have it resurfaced (see Chapter 9).

10   Before installing the wheels, check all

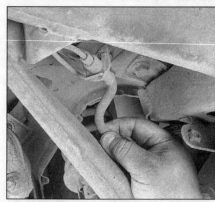

19.10 Check for any sign of brake fluid leakage at the line fittings and the brake hoses

19.12 If the lining is bonded to the brake shoe, measure the lining thickness from the outer surface to the metal shoe, as shown here; if the lining is riveted to the shoe, measure from the lining outer surface to the rivet head

19.14 Check for fluid leakage at both ends of the wheel cylinder dust covers (arrow)

brake lines and hoses for damage, wear, deformation, cracks, corrosion, leakage, bends and twists, particularly in the vicinity of the rubber hoses at the calipers **(see illustration)**. Check the clamps for tightness and the connections for leakage. Make sure that all hoses and lines are clear of sharp edges, moving parts and the exhaust system. If any of the above conditions are noted, repair, reroute or replace the lines and/or fittings as necessary (see Chapter 9).

Drum brakes

Refer to illustrations 19.12 and 19.14
11   Refer to Chapter 9 and remove the rear brake drums.
12   Note the thickness of the lining material on the rear brake shoes **(see illustration)** and look for signs of contamination by brake fluid and grease. If the lining material is within 1/16-inch of the recessed rivets or metal shoes, replace the brake shoes with new ones. The shoes should also be replaced if they are cracked, glazed (shiny lining surfaces) or contaminated with brake fluid or grease. See Chapter 9 for the replacement procedure.
13   Check the shoe return and hold-down springs and the adjusting mechanism to make sure they're installed correctly and in good condition. Deteriorated or distorted springs, if not replaced, could allow the linings to drag and wear prematurely.
14   Check the wheel cylinders for leakage by carefully peeling back the rubber boots **(see illustration)**. If brake fluid is noted behind the boots, the wheel cylinders must be replaced (see Chapter 9).
15   Check the drums for cracks, score marks, deep scratches and hard spots, which will appear as small discolored areas. If imperfections cannot be removed with emery cloth, the drums must be resurfaced by an automotive machine shop (see Chapter 9 for more detailed information).

16   Refer to Chapter 9 and install the brake drums.
17   Install the wheels and snug the wheel lug nuts finger tight.
18   Remove the jackstands and lower the vehicle.
19   Tighten the wheel lug nuts to the torque listed in this Chapter's Specifications.

Brake booster check

20   Sit in the driver's seat and perform the following sequence of tests.
21   With the engine stopped, depress the brake pedal several times - the travel distance should not change.
22   With the brake fully depressed, start the engine - the pedal should move down a little when the engine starts.
23   Depress the brake, stop the engine and hold the pedal in for about 30 seconds - the pedal should neither sink nor rise.
24   Restart the engine, run it for about a minute and turn it off. Then firmly depress the brake several times - the pedal travel should decrease with each application.
25   If your brakes do not operate as described above when the preceding tests are performed, the brake booster is either in need of repair or has failed. Refer to Chapter 9 for the removal procedure.

Parking brake

26   Slowly pull up on the parking brake and count the number of clicks you hear until the handle is up as far as it will go. The adjustment should be within the specified number of clicks listed in this Chapter's Specifications. If you hear more or fewer clicks, it's time to adjust the parking brake (refer to Chapter 9).
27   An alternative method of checking the parking brake is to park the vehicle on a steep hill with the parking brake set and the transaxle in Neutral (be sure to stay in the vehicle during this check!). If the parking brake cannot prevent the vehicle from rolling, it is in need of adjustment (see Chapter 9).

20   Fuel system check (every 15,000 miles or 12 months)

Warning: *Gasoline is extremely flammable, so take extra precautions when you work on any part of the fuel system. Don't smoke or allow open flames or bare light bulbs near the work area, and don't work in a garage where a natural gas-type appliance (such as a water heater or clothes dryer) with a pilot light is present. Since gasoline is carcinogenic, wear latex gloves when there's a possibility of being exposed to fuel, and, if you spill any fuel on your skin, rinse it off immediately with soap and water. Mop up any spills immediately and do not store fuel-soaked rags where they could ignite. The fuel system is under constant pressure, so, if any fuel lines are to be disconnected, the fuel pressure in the system must be relieved first (see Chapter 4 for more information). When you perform any kind of work on the fuel system, wear safety glasses and have a Class B type fire extinguisher on hand.*

1   The fuel system is most easily checked with the vehicle raised on a hoist so the components underneath the vehicle are readily visible and accessible.
2   If the smell of gasoline is noticed while driving or after the vehicle has been in the sun, the system should be thoroughly inspected immediately.
3   Remove the gas tank cap and check for damage, corrosion and an unbroken sealing imprint on the gasket. Replace the cap with a new one if necessary.
4   With the vehicle raised and safely supported, inspect the gas tank and filler neck for punctures, cracks and other damage. The connection between the filler neck and the tank is particularly critical. Sometimes a rubber filler neck will leak because of loose clamps or deteriorated rubber. These are problems a home mechanic can usually rectify. **Warning:** *Do not, under any circumstances, try to repair a fuel tank (except rubber components). A welding torch or any open flame can easily cause fuel vapors inside the tank to explode.*
5   Carefully check all rubber hoses and metal lines leading away from the fuel tank. Check for loose connections, deteriorated hoses, crimped lines and other damage. Follow the lines to the front of the vehicle, carefully inspecting them all the way to the carburetor or fuel injection system. Repair or replace damaged sections as necessary.
6   If a fuel odor is still evident after the inspection, refer to Chapter 6 and check the EVAP system.

21   Fuel filter replacement (every 15,000 miles or 12 months)

Refer to illustrations 21.2a and 21.2b
Warning 1: *Gasoline is extremely flammable, so take extra precautions when you work on any part of the fuel system. Don't smoke or*

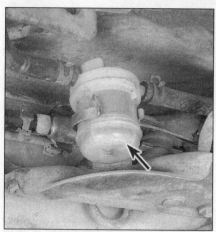

21.2a Depending on the model year of the vehicle, the fuel filter is located under the vehicle on the right side . . .

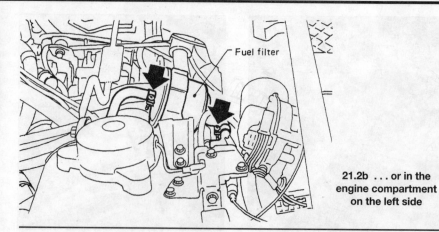

Fuel filter

21.2b . . . or in the engine compartment on the left side

allow open flames or bare light bulbs near the work area, and don't work in a garage where a natural gas-type appliance (such as a water heater or clothes dryer) with a pilot light is present. Since gasoline is carcinogenic, wear latex gloves when there's a possibility of being exposed to fuel, and, if you spill any

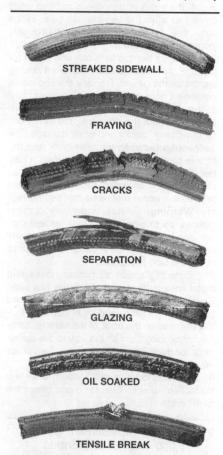

STREAKED SIDEWALL

FRAYING

CRACKS

SEPARATION

GLAZING

OIL SOAKED

TENSILE BREAK

22.3 Here are some of the more common problems associated with V-drivebelts (check the belts very carefully to prevent an untimely breakdown)

fuel on your skin, rinse it off immediately with soap and water. Mop up any spills immediately and do not store fuel-soaked rags where they could ignite. When you perform any kind of work on the fuel system, wear safety glasses and have a Class B Type fire extinguisher on hand.

Warning 2: *On fuel injected models refer to Chapter 4 and depressurize the fuel system before removing the filter!*

1   This job should be done with the engine cold (after sitting at least three hours). Place a metal container, rags or newspapers under the filter to catch spilled fuel.

2   The fuel filter is located under the vehicle, near the gas tank or in the engine compartment **(see illustrations)**. If the vehicle must be raised to change the filter, be sure to support it safely on jackstands!

3   To replace the filter, release the clamps and slide them down the hoses, past the fittings on the filter.

4   Carefully twist and pull on the hoses to separate them from the filter. If the hoses are in bad shape, now would be a good time to replace them with new ones. Slide off the old clamps and install new ones.

5   Pull the filter out of the clip and install the new one, then hook up the hoses and reposition the clamps. Note that the arrow on the filter must point in the direction of fuel flow (toward the engine). Start the engine and check carefully for leaks at the filter hose connections.

22 Drivebelt check, adjustment and replacement (every 15,000 miles or 12 months)

Check

Refer to illustrations 22.3 and 22.4

1   The drivebelts, or V-belts as they are sometimes called, are located at the front of the engine and play an important role in the overall operation of the vehicle and its components. Due to their function and material make-up, the belts are prone to failure after a period of time and should be inspected and adjusted periodically to prevent major engine damage.

2   The number of belts used on a particular vehicle depends on the accessories installed. Drivebelts are used to turn the alternator, power steering pump, water pump and air conditioning compressor. Depending on the pulley arrangement, more than one of these components may be driven by a single belt.

3   With the engine off, open the hood and locate the various belts at the front of the engine. Using your fingers (and a flashlight, if necessary), move along the belts checking for cracks and separation of the belt plies. Also check for fraying and glazing, which gives the belt a shiny appearance **(see illustration)**. Both sides of each belt should be inspected, which means you will have to twist the belt to check the underside.

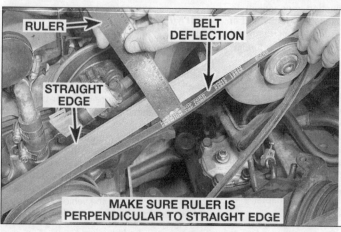

RULER

BELT DEFLECTION

STRAIGHT EDGE

MAKE SURE RULER IS PERPENDICULAR TO STRAIGHT EDGE

22.4 Measuring drivebelt deflection with a straightedge and ruler

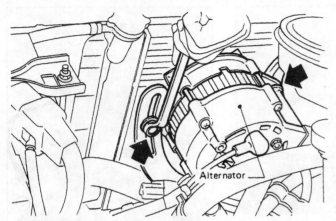

22.6a Loosen the lock bolt and the adjustment bolt (arrows) to adjust the alternator belt

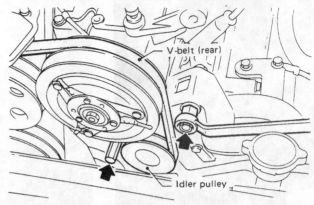

22.6b On models equipped air conditioning loosen the idler pulley bolts (arrows) to adjust the air conditioning compressor belt

4   The tension of each belt is checked by pushing on the belt at a distance halfway between the pulleys. Push firmly with your thumb and see how much the belt moves (deflects) **(see illustration)**. As rule of thumb, if the distance from pulley center-to-pulley center is between 7 and 11 inches, the belt should deflect 1/4-inch. If the belt travels between pulleys spaced 12 to 16 inches apart, the belt should deflect 1/2-inch for a V-belt or 1/4-inch for a serpentine belt.

Adjustment

Refer to illustration 22.6a and 22.6b

5   If it is necessary to adjust the belt tension, either to make the belt tighter or looser, it is done by moving the belt-driven accessory on the bracket.

6   For each belt on the engine there will be one component with an adjusting bolt and a pivot bolt. These bolts must be loosened slightly to enable you to move the component **(see illustrations)**.

7   After the two bolts have been loosened, move the component away from the engine to tighten the belt or toward the engine to loosen the belt. Hold the accessory in position and check the belt tension. If it is correct, tighten the two bolts until just snug, then recheck the tension. If the tension is all right, tighten the bolts.

8   It will be necessary to use some sort of prybar to move the accessory while the belt is adjusted. If this must be done to gain the proper leverage, be very careful not to damage the component being moved or the part being pried against.

Replacement

9   To replace a belt, follow the above procedures for drivebelt adjustment but slip the belt off the pulleys and remove it. Since belts tend to wear out more or less at the same time, it's a good idea to replace all of them at the same time. Mark each belt and the corresponding pulley grooves so the replacement belts can be installed properly.

10   Take the old belts with you when purchasing new ones in order to make a direct

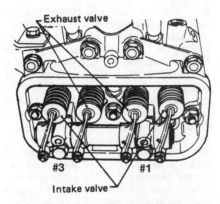

23.3 With the no. 1 piston at TDC on the compression stroke, check and adjust the clearance of the intake and exhaust valves on the no. 1 cylinder

comparison for length, width and design.

11   Adjust the belts as described earlier in this Section.

23 Valve clearance check and adjustment (OHV engines) (every 15,000 miles or 12 months)

Refer to illustrations 23.3 and 23.4

Note: *The manufacturer recommends adjusting the valve clearance at the specified interval only if the valve train is making excessive noise.*

1   To check and adjust the valve clearances, the engine must be cold with the coolant temperature between 68 and 104 degrees F (20 and 40 degrees C).

2   Refer to Chapter 2A and remove the valve cover, then use the rotor and timing marks, to position the number one piston at TDC on the compression stroke (see Chapter 2A). **Note:** *Verify TDC for the number one piston by observing that both valves are closed and the rocker arms are loose.*

3   With the crankshaft at number one TDC, measure the clearance of the intake and exhaust valves on the number one cylinder

23.4 Loosen the locknut and turn the adjusting screw until the feeler gauge slips between the valve stem tip and rocker arm with a slight amount of drag, then follow the firing order sequence to bring the remaining cylinders to their TDC position and adjust the valves for each of the remaining cylinders

(see illustration). Insert a feeler gauge of the specified thickness (see this Chapter's Specifications) between the valve stem tip and the rocker arm. The feeler gauge should slip between the valve stem tip and rocker arm with a slight amount of drag.

4   If the clearance is incorrect (too loose or too tight), loosen the locknut and turn the adjusting screw slowly until you can feel a slight drag on the feeler gauge as you withdraw it from between the valve stem tip and the rocker arm **(see illustration)**.

5   Once the clearance is adjusted, hold the adjusting screw with a screwdriver (to keep it from turning) and tighten the locknut to the torque listed in this Chapter's Specifications. Recheck the clearance to make sure it hasn't changed after tightening the locknut.

6   The valves in the remaining cylinders can now be checked. It is essential to adjust cylinder 3 next, followed by 2 and finally 4 (follow the firing order sequence). Before checking clearances, bring each cylinder (in order) to TDC by turning the crankshaft 180 degrees in a clockwise direction. Verify TDC by checking that the distributor rotor is pointing to the appropriate cylinder number you previously made on the distributor body.

24.2 The diaphragm in the EGR valve (which can be reached through the holes in the underside of the valve) should move easily with finger pressure

25.3 The carburetor choke plate (arrow) is visible after removing the air cleaner top plate

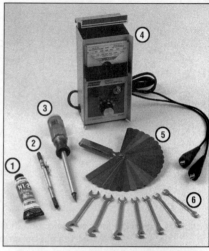

26.1 Tools and materials needed for ignition point replacement and dwell angle adjustment

7   If necessary, repeat the adjustment procedure described in Steps 3, 4 and 5 until all the valves are adjusted to specifications.

8   Install the valve covers (use new gaskets) and tighten the mounting bolts evenly and securely.

9   Install the distributor cap and spark plugs, then hook up the spark plug wires and the various hoses and vacuum lines (if removed).

10   Start the engine and check for oil leakage between the valve covers and the cylinder heads.

24   Exhaust Gas Recirculation (EGR) system check (every 15,000 miles or 12 months)

Refer to illustration 24.2

1   The EGR valve is usually located on the intake manifold. Most of the time when a problem develops in this emissions system, it's due to a stuck or corroded EGR valve.

2   With the engine cold, to prevent burns, push on the EGR valve diaphragm. Using moderate pressure, you should be able to push the diaphragm up into the housing **(see illustration)**.

3   If the diaphragm doesn't move or is hard to move, replace the EGR valve with a new one. If in doubt about the condition of the valve, compare the free movement of your EGR valve with a new valve.

4   Refer to Chapter 6 for more information on the EGR system.

25   Carburetor choke check (every 15,000 miles or 12 months)

Refer to illustration 25.3

1   The choke operates when the engine is cold, and thus this check can only be performed before the vehicle has been started for the day.

2   Open the hood and remove the top plate of the air cleaner assembly. If any vacuum hoses must be disconnected, make sure you tag the hoses for reinstallation in their original positions. Place the top plate and wing nut aside, out of the way of moving engine components.

3   Look at the center of the air cleaner housing. You will notice a flat plate (arrow) at the carburetor opening **(see illustration)**.

4   Press the accelerator pedal to the floor. The plate should close completely. Start the engine while you watch the plate at the carburetor. **Warning:** *Do not position your face directly over the carburetor, as the engine could backfire, causing serious burns.* When the engine starts, the choke plate should open slightly.

5   Allow the engine to continue running at an idle speed. As the engine warms up to operating temperature, the plate should slowly open, allowing more cold air to enter through the top of the carburetor.

6   After a few minutes, the choke plate should be fully open to the vertical position. Press quickly on the accelerator to make sure the fast idle cam disengages.

7   You will notice that the engine speed corresponds with the plate opening. With the plate fully closed, the engine should run at a fast idle speed. As the plate opens and the throttle is moved to disengage the fast idle cam, the engine speed will decrease.

26   Ignition point check, replacement and adjustment (every 15,000 miles or 12 months)

Refer to illustrations 26.1, 26.2 and 26.7
Note: *Some early models may be equipped with ignition points.*

Check and replacement

1   The ignition points must be replaced at regular intervals on vehicles not equipped with electronic ignition. Occasionally the rubbing block will wear enough to require adjust-

1   **Distributor cam lube** - *Sometimes this special lubricant comes with the new points; however, it's a good idea to buy a tube and have it on hand*

2   **Screw starter** - *This tool has special claws which hold the screw securely as it's started, which helps prevent accidental dropping of the screw*

3   **Magnetic screwdriver** - *Serves the same purpose as 2 above. If you don't have one of these special screwdrivers, you risk dropping the point mounting screws down into the distributor body*

4   **Dwell meter** - *A dwell meter is the only accurate way to determine the point setting (gap). Connect the meter according to the instructions supplied with it.*

5   **Blade-type feeler gauges** - *These are required to set the initial point gap (space between the points when they are open)*

6   **Ignition wrenches** - *These special wrenches are made to work within the tight confines of the distributor. Specifically, they are needed to loosen the nut/bolt which secures the leads to the points*

ment of the points. It's also possible to clean and dress them with a fine file, but replacement is recommended since they are relatively accessible and very inexpensive. Several special tools are required for this procedure **(see illustration)**.

2   After removing the distributor cap and rotor (see Section 27), the ignition points are plainly visible. They can be examined by gently prying them open to reveal the condition of the contact surfaces **(see illustration)**. If they're rough, pitted, covered with oil or burned, they should be replaced, along with the condenser. **Caution:** *This procedure requires the removal of small screws which can easily fall down into the distributor. To retrieve them, the distributor would have to be removed and disassembled. Use a mag-*

26.2 Although it is possible to restore ignition points that are pitted, burned and corroded (as shown here), they should be replaced

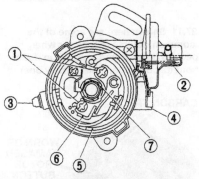

26.7 Ignition point mounting details

1   Contact point set screw
2   Vacuum controller
3   Primary terminal
4   Condenser
5   Contact breaker plate
6   Contact breaker set
7   Distributor cam
8   Cap
9   Rotor

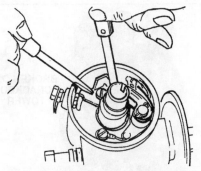

26.17 Turn the distributor shaft until the rubbing block is resting on one of the cam lobes (which will open the points) - the point gap/dwell angle can now be adjusted by inserting a screwdriver into the slot between the breaker plate and the point base - twist the screwdriver until the desired point gap/dwell angle is achieved

netic or spring-loaded screwdriver and be extra careful.

3   If not already done, remove the distributor cap.

4   Position the cap (with the spark plug wires still attached) out of the way. Use a length of wire to hold it out of the way, if necessary.

5   Remove the rotor, by grasping the rotor with one hand and pulling straight up on the rotor to remove it.

6   Note how the wires in the distributor are routed, then disconnect the primary wire leads from the points. The wires may be attached with a small nut (which should be loosened, but not removed), a small screw or by a spring-loaded terminal.

7   Loosen the screws which secure the ignition points to the breaker plate **(see illustration)**, but don't completely remove the screws (most ignition point sets have slots at these locations). Slide the points out of the distributor.

8   Disconnect the primary wire lead at the contact point set or the distributor body terminal connection. This wire may be attached with a small nut (which should be loosened, but not removed) or a small screw.

9   Disconnect the condenser wire from the distributor body. The condenser can now be removed from the side of the distributor. Loosen the mounting strap screw and slide the condenser out of the bracket, or completely remove the condenser and strap, depending on the exact mounting arrangement.

10   Before installing the new points and condenser, clean the breaker plate and the cam on the distributor shaft to remove all dirt, dust and oil.

11   Apply a small amount of distributor cam lube (usually supplied with the new points, but also available separately) to the cam lobes.

12   Position the new condenser and tighten the mounting strap screw securely.

13   Slide the new point set into place and make sure the protrusions on the breaker

plate fit into the holes in the point base (to properly position the point set), then tighten the screws securely.

14   Connect the primary wire lead to the new point assembly or the distributor body terminal. Make sure the lead is positioned the same as it was during removal.

Adjustment

Refer to illustration 26.17

15   Although the final dwell angle will be adjusted later, make the initial gap adjustment now, which will allow the engine to be started.

16   Make sure that the point rubbing block is resting on one of the high points of the cam. If it isn't, rotate the crankshaft with a breaker bar and socket attached to the large bolt that holds the vibration damper in place.

17   With the rubbing block on a cam high point (points open), insert a 0.018 inch (0.45 mm)gauge between the contact surfaces. Insert a screwdriver into the slot between the breaker plate and the point base to adjust the gap. The gap is correct when a slight amount of drag is felt as the feeler gauge is withdrawn **(see illustration)**.

18   Inspect and install the rotor and distributor cap as described in Section 27.

19   Whenever new ignition points are installed or the original points are cleaned, the dwell angle must be checked and adjusted. Precise adjustment of the dwell angle requires an instrument called a dwell meter. Combination tach/dwell meters are commonly available at reasonable cost from auto parts stores.

20   If a dwell meter is not available, the initial adjustment described above will be sufficient until a competent automotive repair facility can adjust the dwell angle for you.

21   Hook the dwell meter up following the manufacturer's instructions.

22   Start the engine and allow it to run at

idle until normal operating temperature is reached (the engine must be warm to obtain an accurate reading). Record the dwell reading on the meter. If the reading is not within specifications it will need to be adjusted.

23   Dwell angle specifications can be found in this Chapter's Specifications and on the VECI label or tune-up decal in the engine compartment. If there's a discrepancy between the two, assume the VECI label or tune-up decal is correct.

24   If the dwell angle is incorrect, readjust the point gap as described above in Step 17 **(see illustration 26.17)**. Repeat this process until the meter reading is as specified. **Note:** *Opening the point gap will decrease the dwell reading while closing the point gap will increase the dwell reading.*

27   Spark plug wire, distributor cap and rotor check and replacement (every 15,000 miles or 12 months)

Refer to illustrations 27.11 and 27.12

1   The spark plug wires should be checked whenever new spark plugs are installed.

2   Begin this procedure by making a visual check of the spark plug wires while the engine is running. In a darkened garage (make sure there is adequate ventilation) start the engine and observe each plug wire. Be careful not to come into contact with any moving engine parts. If there is a break in the wire, you will see arcing or a small spark at the damaged area. If arcing is noticed, make a note to obtain new wires, then allow the engine to cool and check the distributor cap and rotor.

3   The spark plug wires should be inspected one at a time to prevent mixing up the order, which is essential for proper engine operation. Each original plug wire should be numbered to help identify its location. If the number is illegible, a piece of tape can be marked with the correct number and wrapped around the plug wire.

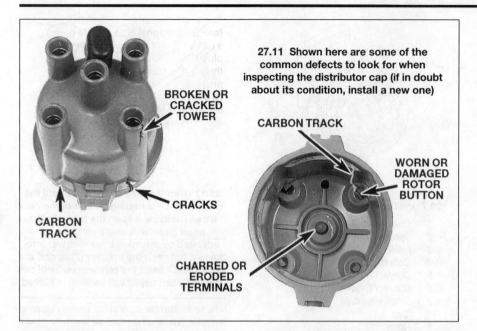

27.11 Shown here are some of the common defects to look for when inspecting the distributor cap (if in doubt about its condition, install a new one)

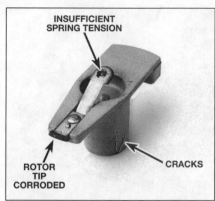

27.12 The ignition rotor should be checked for wear and corrosion as indicated here (if in doubt about its condition, buy a new one)

28   Spark plug replacement (every 15,000 miles or 12 months)

Refer to illustrations 28.1, 28.4a and 28.4b

1   Spark plug replacement requires a spark plug socket which fits onto a ratchet wrench. This socket is lined with a rubber grommet to protect the porcelain insulator of the spark plug and to hold the plug while you insert it into the spark plug hole. You will also need a wire-type feeler gauge to check and adjust the spark plug gap and a torque wrench to tighten the new plugs to the specified torque **(see illustration)**.

2   If you are replacing the plugs, purchase the new plugs, adjust them to the proper gap and then replace each plug one at a time. **Note:** *When buying new spark plugs, it's essential that you obtain the correct plugs for your specific vehicle. This information can be found in the Specifications Section at the beginning of this Chapter, on the Vehicle Emissions Control Information (VECI) label located on the underside of the hood or in the owner's manual. If these sources specify different plugs, purchase the spark plug type specified on the VECI label because that information is provided specifically for your engine.*

3   Inspect each of the new plugs for defects. If there are any signs of cracks in the porcelain insulator of a plug, don't use it.

4   Check the electrode gaps of the new plugs. Check the gap by inserting the wire gauge of the proper thickness between the electrodes at the tip of the plug **(see illustration)**. The gap between the electrodes should be identical to that listed in this Chapter's Specifications or on the VECI label. If the gap is incorrect, use the notched adjuster on the feeler gauge body to bend the curved side electrode slightly **(see illustration)**.

5   If the side electrode is not exactly over the center electrode, use the notched adjuster to align them. **Caution:** *If the gap of a new plug must be adjusted, bend only the base of the ground electrode - do not touch the tip.*

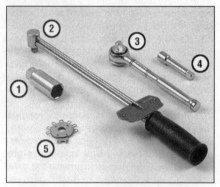

28.1   Tools required for changing spark plugs

1   **Spark plug socket** - *This will have special padding inside to protect the spark plug's porcelain insulator*
2   **Torque wrench** - *Although not mandatory, using this tool is the best way to ensure the plugs are tightened properly*
3   **Ratchet** - *Standard hand tool to fit the spark plug socket*
4   **Extension** - *Depending on model and accessories, you may need special extensions and universal joints to reach one or more of the plugs*
5   **Spark plug gap gauge** - *This gauge for checking the gap comes in a variety of styles. Make sure the gap for your engine is included*

4   Disconnect the plug wire from the spark plug. A removal tool can be used for this purpose or you can grasp the rubber boot, twist the boot half a turn and pull the boot free. Do not pull on the wire itself.

5   Check inside the boot for corrosion, which will look like a white crusty powder.

6   Push the wire and boot back onto the end of the spark plug. It should fit tightly onto the end of the plug. If it doesn't, remove the wire and use pliers to carefully crimp the metal connector inside the wire boot until the fit is snug.

7   Using a clean rag, wipe the entire length of the wire to remove built-up dirt and grease. Once the wire is clean, check for burns, cracks and other damage. Do not bend the wire sharply, because the conductor might break.

8   Remove the rubber boot (if equipped) and disconnect the wire from the distributor. Again, pull only on the rubber boot. Check for corrosion and a tight fit. Replace the wire in the distributor.

9   Inspect the remaining spark plug wires, making sure that each one is securely fastened at the distributor and spark plug when the check is complete.

10   If new spark plug wires are required, purchase a set for your specific engine model. Remove and replace the wires one at a time to avoid mix-ups in the firing order.

11   Detach the distributor cap by loosening the retaining screws, latches or clasps. Look inside it for cracks, carbon tracks and worn, burned or loose contacts **(see illustration)**.

12   Pull the rotor off the distributor shaft and examine it for cracks and carbon tracks **(see illustration)**. Replace the cap and rotor if any damage or defects are noted.

13   It is common practice to install a new cap and rotor whenever new spark plug wires are installed, but if you wish to continue using the old cap, check the resistance between the spark plug wires and the cap first. If the indicated resistance is more than the maximum value listed in this Chapter's Specifications, replace the cap and/or wires.

14   When installing a new cap, remove the wires from the old cap one at a time and attach them to the new cap in the exact same location. **Note:** *If an accidental mix-up occurs, refer to the firing order Specifications at the beginning of this Chapter.*

28.4a Spark plug manufacturers recommend using a wire type gauge when checking the gap - if the wire does not slide between the electrodes with a slight drag, adjustment is required

28.4b To change the gap, bend the *side* electrode only, as indicated by the arrows, and be very careful not to crack or chip the porcelain insulator surrounding the center electrode

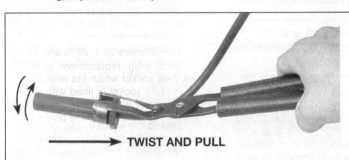

28.6 Using a spark plug boot puller tool like this one will make the job of removing the spark plug boots much easier

TWIST AND PULL

Removal

Refer to illustrations 28.6 and 28.8

6   To prevent the possibility of mixing up spark plug wires, work on one spark plug at a time. Remove the wire and boot from one spark plug. Grasp the boot - not the cable - then give it a half twisting motion and pull straight up **(see illustration)**.

7   If compressed air is available, blow any dirt or foreign material away from the spark plug area before proceeding (a common bicycle pump will also work).

8   Remove the spark plug **(see illustration)**.

9   Whether you are replacing the plugs at this time or intend to reuse the old plugs, compare each old spark plug with the chart shown on the inside back cover of this manual to determine the overall running condition of the engine.

Installation

Refer to illustrations 28.10a and 28.10b

10   Prior to installation, apply a coat of anti-seize compound to the plug threads. It's often difficult to insert spark plugs into their holes without cross-threading them. To avoid this possibility, fit a short piece of 3/8-inch ID

rubber hose over the end of the spark plug **(see illustrations)**. The flexible hose acts as a universal joint to help align the plug with the plug hole. Should the plug begin to cross-thread, the hose will slip on the spark plug, preventing thread damage. Tighten the plug to the torque listed in this Chapter's Specifications.

11   Attach the plug wire to the new spark plug, again using a twisting motion on the boot until it is firmly seated on the end of the spark plug.

12   Follow the above procedure for the remaining spark plugs, replacing them one at a time to prevent mixing up the spark plug wires.

29 Idle speed check and adjustment (every 15,000 miles or 12 months)

Refer to illustration 29.4
Note: *This Section pertains to carbureted models only. For models equipped with fuel injection, see Chapter 4 Part B.*

1   Engine idle speed is the speed at which the engine operates when no accelerator pedal pressure is applied. The idle speed is critical to the performance of the engine as well as many engine sub-systems.

2   Make sure the parking brake is firmly set and the wheels blocked to prevent the vehicle from rolling. This is especially true if the specifications require the transaxle to be in Drive. An assistant inside the vehicle pressing on the brake pedal is the safest method.

3   A hand-held tachometer must be used when adjusting idle speed to get an accurate reading. The exact hook-up for these meters varies with the manufacturer, so follow the particular directions included with the instrument.

4   For most applications, the idle speed is set by turning an adjustment screw which is located next to the throttle lever **(see illustration)**. This screw changes the amount the throttle plate is held open by the throttle linkage. The screw may be on the linkage itself or on the carburetor body.

28.8 Use a socket wrench with a long extension to unscrew the spark plugs

28.10a Apply a thin coat of anti-seize compound to the spark plug threads

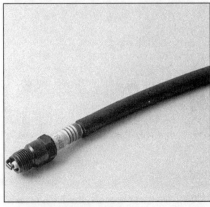

28.10b A length of 3/8-inch ID rubber hose will save time and prevent damaged threads when installing the spark plugs

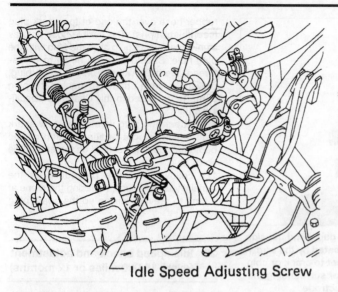

Idle Speed Adjusting Screw

29.4 The curb idle speed can be adjusted by turning the idle speed screw (arrow) located at the base of the carburetor by the throttle lever

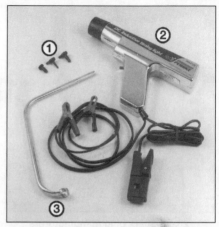

30.3 Tools needed to check and adjust the ignition timing

1   *Vacuum plugs - Vacuum hoses will, in most cases, have to be disconnected and plugged. Molded plugs in various shapes and sizes are available for this*
2   *Inductive pick -up timing light - Flashes a bright, concentrated beam of light when the number one spark plug fires. Connect the leads according to the instructions supplied with the light*
3   *Distributor wrench - On some models, the hold-down bolt for the distributor is difficult to reach and turn with conventional wrenches or sockets. A special wrench like this must be used*

5   For all applications, the engine must be completely warmed-up to operating temperature, which will automatically render the choke and fast idle inoperative.
6   Once you have located the idle screw, experiment with different length screwdrivers until the adjustment can be easily made without coming into contact with hot or moving engine components.
7   If the air cleaner is removed, the vacuum hose to the snorkel should be plugged.
8   Since the manufacturer recommended many different adjustment procedures over the time period covered by this manual, it would be impractical to cover all types in this Section. Most models have a tune-up decal or Vehicle Emission Control Information (VECI) label located in the engine compartment with instructions for setting idle speed. If no VECI label is found refer to the Specifications Section at the beginning of this Chapter and to the adjustment procedures specified in Chapter 4.

30   Ignition timing check and adjustment (every 15,000 miles or 12 months)

Refer to illustrations 30.3, 30.6a, 30.6b and 30.6c
Note: *It is imperative that the procedures included on the tune-up or Vehicle Emissions Control Information (VECI) label be followed when adjusting the ignition timing. The label will include all information concerning preliminary steps to be performed before adjusting the timing, as well as the timing specifications. If no VECI label is found refer to the specifications chart at the beginning of this Chapter.*
1   At the specified intervals, the ignition timing should be checked and adjusted.
2   Various procedures (depending on the model of the vehicle) must be performed to disable the distributor or computer advance mechanism before attempting to check the timing. Locate the Tune-up or VECI label under the hood and read through and perform all preliminary instructions concerning ignition timing. If no VECI label is found refer to the Specifications Section at the beginning

of this Chapter.
3   Before attempting to check the timing some special tools will be needed for this procedure **(see illustration)**.
4   Check that the idle speed is as specified (see Section 29).
5   Connect a timing light in accordance with the manufacturer's instructions. Generally, the light will be connected to power and ground sources and to the number one spark plug wire (refer to the cylinder location diagram in this Chapter's Specifications).
6   Locate the timing marks on the engine **(see illustrations)**. Clean them off with sol-

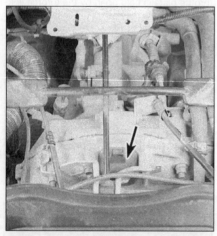

30.6a On most models, the timing mark can be observed after removing the spare tire and the window cover (arrow) on the flywheel housing

30.6b Each mark on the flywheel represents 2 degrees of ignition timing

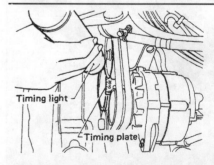

30.6c On models equipped with a turbocharger, the ignition timing indicator is located at the front of the engine by the crankshaft pulley

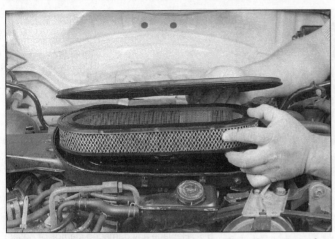

31.5a After setting the top cover aside, the filter element can be lifted out of the housing

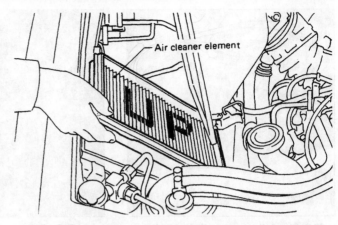

31.5b On fuel injected models, the first step in removing the air filter is detaching the clips on the housing - always position the new filter as indicated above

vent if necessary so you can see the numbers or marks and small grooves.

7　Use chalk or paint to mark the groove in the crankshaft pulley.

8　Mark the timing tab in accordance with the number of degrees called for on the VECI label or the tune-up label in the engine compartment.

9　Make sure timing light is clear of all moving engine components, then start the engine and warm it up to normal operating temperature.

10　Aim the flashing timing light at the timing mark by the crankshaft pulley, again being careful not to come in contact with moving parts. The marks should appear to be stationary. If the marks are in alignment, the timing is correct.

11　If the notch on the flywheel or crankshaft pulley (turbo models) is not aligned with the correct mark on the timing tab, loosen the distributor hold-down bolt and rotate the distributor until the notch is aligned with the correct timing mark.

12　Retighten the hold-down bolt and recheck the timing.

13　Turn off the engine and disconnect the timing light. Reconnect the vacuum advance hose, if removed, and any other components which were disconnected.

31　Air filter and PCV filter check and replacement (every 30,000 miles or 24 months)

Refer to illustrations 31.5a, 31.5b and 31.8

1　At the specified intervals, the air filter should be replaced with a new one. A thorough preventive maintenance schedule would also require the filter to be inspected between filter changes.

2　On carbureted models, the air filter housing is mounted on top of the carburetor in the engine compartment.

3　On fuel injected models, the air filter housing is located on the right side of the engine compartment.

4　Remove the wing nut(s) and the cover retaining clips. Then detach all hoses that would interfere with the removal of the air cleaner cover from the air cleaner housing. While the top cover is off, be careful not to drop anything down into the carburetor or air cleaner assembly.

5　Lift the air filter element out of the housing **(see illustrations)** and wipe out the inside of the air cleaner housing with a clean rag.

6　Inspect the outer surface of the filter ele-

ment. If it is dirty, replace it. If it is only moderately dusty, it can be reused by blowing it clean from the back to the front surface with compressed air. Because it is a pleated paper type filter, it cannot be washed or oiled. If it cannot be cleaned satisfactorily with compressed air, discard and replace it. **Caution:** *Never drive the vehicle with the air cleaner removed. Excessive engine wear could result and backfiring could even cause a fire under the hood.*

7　Place the new filter in the air cleaner housing, making sure it seats properly.

8　On carbureted models it will also be necessary to replace the PCV filter at the specified intervals **(see illustration)**.

9　Installation of the cover is the reverse of removal.

32　Positive Crankcase Ventilation (PCV) valve check and replacement (every 30,000 miles or 24 months)

Refer to illustration 32.1

1　The PCV valve is located in the intake manifold **(see illustration)**.

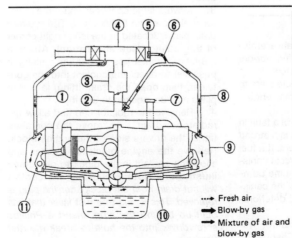

31.8 On carbureted models the PCV filter must also be replaced

32.1 PCV valve mounting details (OHV engine shown, all other engines similar)

1　*Connecting hose*
2　*PCV hose*
3　*Carburetor*
4　*Air cleaner*
5　*Air filter*
6　*Connecting hose*
7　*Oil filler cap (sealed)*
8　*Connecting hose*
9　*Rocker cover on #2 - #4 side*
10　*Crankcase*
9　*Rocker cover on #1 - #3 side*

----> Fresh air
➡ Blow-by gas
➡ Mixture of air and blow-by gas

33.2 Check the evaporative emissions control canister (arrow) and the hose connections for cracks and damage

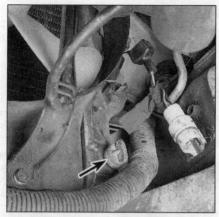

34.3 Radiator drain location (arrow)

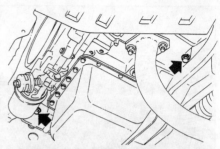

34.4 Engine block drain locations (arrows)

2   With the engine idling at normal operating temperature, pull the valve (with hose attached) from the intake manifold.

3   Place your finger over the valve opening or hose. If there's no vacuum, check for a plugged hose, manifold port, or the valve itself. Replace any plugged or deteriorated hoses.

4   Turn off the engine and shake the PCV valve, listening for a rattle. If the valve doesn't rattle, replace it with a new one.

5   To replace the valve, pull it from the end of the hose, noting its installed position.

6   When purchasing a replacement PCV valve, make sure it's for your particular vehicle and engine size. Compare the old valve with the new one to make sure they're the same.

7   Push the valve into the end of the hose until it's seated.

8   Inspect all rubber hoses and grommets for damage and hardening. Replace them, if necessary.

9   Press the PCV valve and hose securely into position.

33   Evaporative emissions control system check (every 30,000 miles or 24 months)

Refer to illustration 33.2

1   The function of the evaporative emissions control system is to draw fuel vapors from the gas tank and fuel system, store them in a charcoal canister and route them to the intake manifold during normal engine operation.

2   The most common symptom of a fault in the evaporative emissions system is a strong fuel odor in the engine compartment. If a fuel odor is detected, inspect the charcoal canister, located in the front of the engine compartment **(see illustration)**. Check the canister and all hoses for damage and deterioration.

3   The evaporative emissions control system is explained in more detail in Chapter 6.

34   Cooling system servicing (draining, flushing and refilling) (every 30,000 miles or 24 months)

Refer to illustrations 34.3 and 34.4
Warning: *Do not allow antifreeze to come in contact with your skin or painted surfaces of the vehicle. Rinse off spills immediately with plenty of water. Antifreeze is highly toxic if ingested. Never leave antifreeze lying around in an open container or in puddles on the floor; children and pets are attracted by it's sweet smell and may drink it. Check with local authorities about disposing of used antifreeze. Many communities have collection centers which will see that antifreeze is disposed of safely.*

1   Periodically, the cooling system should be drained, flushed and refilled to replenish the antifreeze mixture and prevent formation of rust and corrosion, which can impair the performance of the cooling system and cause engine damage. When the cooling system is serviced, all hoses and the radiator cap should be checked and replaced if necessary.

2   Apply the parking brake and block the wheels. **Warning:** *If the vehicle has just been driven, wait several hours to allow the engine to cool down before beginning this procedure.*

3   Move a large container under the radiator drain to catch the coolant. The radiator drain plug is located at the lower right corner of the radiator **(see illustration)**. Attach a 3/8-inch diameter hose to the drain fitting (if possible) to direct the coolant into the container, then open the drain fitting) (a pair of pliers may be required to turn it).

4   Remove the radiator cap and allow the radiator to drain, then, move the container under the drivers side of the engine block. Remove the engine block drain plugs and allow the coolant in the block to drain **(see illustration)**. **Note:** *Frequently, the coolant will not drain from the block after the plug is removed. This is due to a rust layer that has built up behind the plug. Insert a Phillips screwdriver into the hole to break the rust barrier.*

5   While the coolant is draining, check the condition of the radiator hoses, heater hoses and clamps (refer to Section 10 if necessary).

6   Replace any damaged clamps or hoses.

7   Once the system is completely drained, flush the radiator with fresh water from a garden hose until it runs clear at the drain. The flushing action of the water will remove sediments from the radiator but will not remove rust and scale from the engine and cooling tube surfaces.

8   These deposits can be removed with a chemical cleaner. Follow the procedure outlined in the manufacturer's instructions. If the radiator is severely corroded, damaged or leaking, it should be removed (see Chapter 3) and taken to a radiator repair shop.

9   Remove the fusible link case and the overflow hose from the coolant reservoir and flush the reservoir with clean water, then reconnect the hose.

10   Close and tighten the radiator drain fitting. Install and tighten the block drain plug.

11   Place the heater temperature control in the maximum heat position.

12   Slowly add new coolant (a 50/50 mixture of water and antifreeze) to the radiator until it's full. Add coolant to the reservoir up to the lower mark.

13   Leave the radiator cap off and run the engine in a well-ventilated area until the thermostat opens (coolant will begin flowing through the radiator and the upper radiator hose will become hot).

14   Turn the engine off and let it cool. Add more coolant mixture to bring the level back up to the lip on the radiator filler neck.

15   Squeeze the upper radiator hose to expel air, then add more coolant mixture if necessary. Replace the radiator cap.

16   Start the engine, allow it to reach normal operating temperature and check for leaks.

35   Brake fluid change (every 30,000 miles or 24 months)

Warning: *Brake fluid can harm your eyes and damage painted surfaces, so use extreme caution when handling or pouring it. Do not use brake fluid that has been standing open or is more than one year old. Brake fluid absorbs moisture from the air. Excess moisture can cause a dangerous loss of braking effectiveness.*

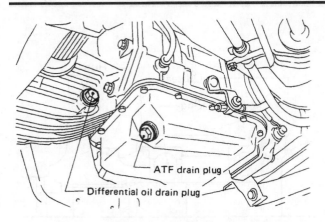

36.7 On automatic transaxles, the drain plug is located on the bottom of the fluid pan

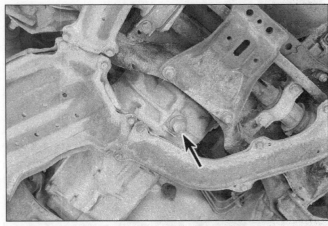

37.3 On manual transaxles, the drain plug (arrow) is located on the bottom of the transaxle case

1   At the specified intervals, the brake fluid should be drained and replaced. Since the brake fluid may drip or splash when pouring it, place plenty of rags around the master cylinder to protect any surrounding painted surfaces.

2   Before beginning work, purchase the specified brake fluid (see *Recommended lubricants and fluids* at the beginning of this Chapter).

3   Remove the cap from the master cylinder reservoir.

4   Using a hand suction pump or similar device, withdraw the fluid from the master cylinder reservoir.

5   Add new fluid to the master cylinder until it rises to the base of the filler neck.

6   Bleed the brake system as described in Chapter 9 at all four brakes until new and uncontaminated fluid expels from the bleeder screw. Be sure to maintain the fluid level in the master cylinder as you perform the bleeding process. If you allow the master cylinder to run dry, air will enter the system.

7   Refill the master cylinder with fluid and check the operation of the brakes. The pedal should feel solid when depressed , with no sponginess. **Warning:** *Do not operate the vehicle if you are in doubt about the effectiveness of the brake system.*

36 Automatic transaxle fluid change (every 30,000 miles or 24 months)

Refer to illustration 36.7

1   At the specified time intervals, the automatic transaxle fluid should be drained and replaced.

2   Before beginning work, purchase the specified transmission fluid (see *Recommended fluids and lubricants, and Capacities* at the beginning of this Chapter).

3   Other tools necessary for this job include jackstands to support the vehicle in a raised position, a wrench, a drain pan capable of holding at least eight quarts, newspapers and clean rags.

4   The fluid should be drained after the vehicle has been driven and brought to operating temperature. Hot fluid is more effective than cold fluid at removing built up sediment. **Warning:** *Fluid temperature can exceed 350-degrees F in a hot transaxle. Wear protective gloves.*

5   Raise the vehicle and place it on jackstands.

6   Move the necessary equipment under the vehicle, being careful not to touch any of the hot exhaust components.

7   Place the drain pan under the drain plug in the transaxle housing or fluid pan and remove the drain plug **(see illustration)**. Be sure the drain pan is in position, as fluid will come out with some force. Once the fluid is drained, reinstall the drain plug securely.

8   Lower the vehicle.

9   With the engine off, add new fluid to the transaxle through the dipstick tube. Use a funnel to prevent spills. It is best to add a little fluid at a time, continually checking the level with the dipstick (see Section 6). Allow the fluid time to drain into the pan.

10   Start the engine and shift the selector into all positions from Park through Low then shift into Park and apply the parking brake.

11   With the engine idling, check the fluid level. Add fluid up to the lower level on the dipstick.

37 Manual transaxle lubricant change (every 30,000 miles or 24 months)

Refer to illustration 37.3

1   Raise the vehicle and support it securely on jackstands.

2   Move a drain pan, rags, newspapers and wrenches under the transaxle.

3   Remove the transaxle drain plug at the bottom of the case and allow the lubricant to drain into the pan **(see illustration)**.

4   After the lubricant has drained completely, reinstall the plug and tighten it securely.

5   Fill the transaxle with the recommended lubricant as described in Section 16.

6   Lower the vehicle.

7   Drive the vehicle for a short distance, then check the drain plug for leakage.

38 Differential lubricant change (every 30,000 miles or 24 months)

Note: *The following procedure is used for the rear differential as well as the front differential on vehicles equipped automatic transaxles.*

1   Drive the vehicle for several miles to warm up the differential oil, then raise the vehicle and support it securely on jackstands.

2   Move a drain pan, rags, newspapers and the proper tools under the vehicle.

3   With the drain pan under the differential, use a socket and ratchet to loosen the drain plug. It's the lower of the two plugs **(see illustration 17.2** for the rear differential drain plug location and **illustration 36.7** for the front differential drain plug location on vehicles equipped automatic transaxles).

4   Once loosened, carefully unscrew it with your fingers until you can remove it from the case.

5   Allow all of the oil to drain into the pan, then replace the drain plug and tighten it securely.

6   Feel with your hands along the bottom of the drain pan for any metal bits that may have come out with the oil. If there are any, it's a sign of excessive wear, indicating that the internal components should be carefully inspected in the near future.

7   Remove the rear differential check/fill plug (see Section 17). Using a hand pump, syringe or funnel, fill the differential with the correct amount and grade of oil (see the Specifications) until the level is just at the bottom of the plug hole.

8   Reinstall the plug and tighten it securely.

9   On vehicles equipped automatic transaxles, fill the front differential with the recommended lubricant as described in Section 16.

10   Lower the vehicle. Check for leaks at the drain plug after the first few miles of driving.

1

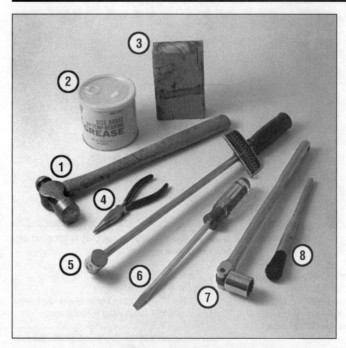

39.1 Tools and materials needed for front wheel bearing maintenance

1   **Hammer** - A common hammer will do just fine
2   **Grease** - High-temperature grease that is formulated specially for front wheel bearings should be used
3   **Wood block** - If you have a scrap piece of 2x4, it can be used to drive the new seal into the hub
4   **Needle-nose pliers** - Used to straighten and remove the cotter pin in the spindle
5   **Torque wrench** - This is very important in this procedure; if the bearing is too tight, the wheel won't turn freely - if it's too loose, the wheel will "wobble" on the spindle. Either way, it could mean extensive damage
6   **Screwdriver** - Used to remove the seal from the hub (a long screwdriver is preferred)
7   **Socket/breaker bar** - Needed to loosen the nut on the spindle if it's extremely tight
8   **Brush** - Together with some clean solvent, this will be used to remove old grease from the hub and spindle

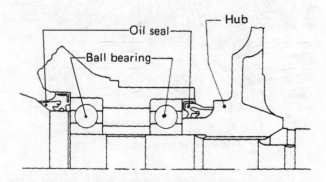

39.8 Use a screwdriver or seal removal tool to pry out the outer grease seal

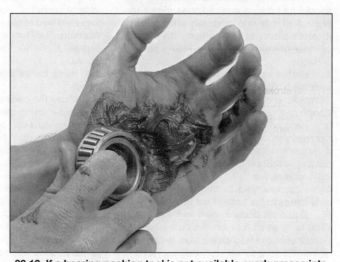

39.13 If a bearing packing tool is not available, work grease into the bearing rollers by pressing it against the palm of your hand (tapered roller bearing shown, ball bearing type similar)

39   Wheel bearings check and repack (every 30,000 miles or 24 months)

Check

Refer to illustrations 39.1, 39.8 and 39.13

1   In most cases the wheel bearings will not need servicing until the brake shoes or pads are changed. However, the bearings should be checked whenever the vehicle is raised for any reason and repacked at the recommended maintenance interval. Several items, including a torque wrench and special grease, are required for this procedure **(see illustration)**.

2   With the vehicle securely supported on jackstands, spin each wheel and check for noise, rolling resistance and freeplay.

3   Grasp the top of each tire with one hand and the bottom with the other. Move the wheel in and out on the spindle. If there's any noticeable movement, the bearings should be checked and then repacked with grease, or replaced if necessary. Further preliminary inspection of the front wheel bearings can be accomplished by following Steps 4 through 9.

4   Remove the wheel.

5   Remove the disc brake caliper (see Chapter 9) and hang it out of the way on a piece of wire.

6   Remove the brake disc assembly (see Chapter 9).

7   Remove the cotter pin, castle nut and drive hub as described in the driveaxle removal Section in Chapter 8.

8   Use a screwdriver or a seal puller tool to pry the outer seal out of the steering knuckle **(see illustration)**. Note how the seal is installed.

9   Inspect the bearing. If only a small amount of grease remains, the inner and outer bearing should be removed and repacked.

Repack

10   Refer to the appropriate Section in Chapter 10 and remove the wheel bearings.

11   Use solvent to remove all traces of the old grease from the bearings, hub and steering knuckle. A small brush may prove helpful; however make sure no bristles from the brush embed themselves inside the bearing rollers. Allow the parts to air dry.

12   Carefully inspect the bearings for cracks, heat discoloration, worn rollers, etc. Check the steering knuckle for wear and damage.

13   Use only high-temperature front wheel bearing grease to pack the bearings. Inexpensive bearing packing tools are available at automotive parts stores, but not entirely necessary. If one is not available, pack the grease by hand completely into the bearings, forcing it between the ball bearings **(see illustration)**.

14   Refer to the appropriate Section in Chapter 10 and install the wheel bearings.

Chapter 2 Part A
Overhead valve (OHV) engines

Contents

2A

Specifications

General

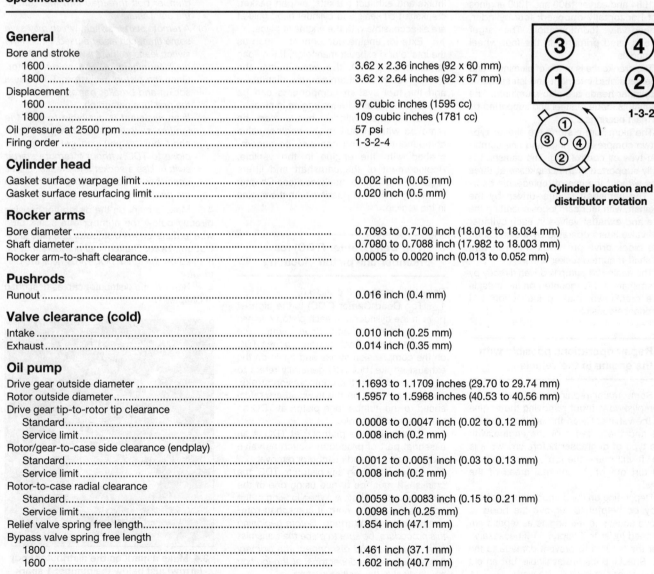

1-3-2-4

Cylinder location and distributor rotation

Bore and stroke
1600	3.62 x 2.36 inches (92 x 60 mm)
1800	3.62 x 2.64 inches (92 x 67 mm)

Displacement
1600	97 cubic inches (1595 cc)
1800	109 cubic inches (1781 cc)
Oil pressure at 2500 rpm	57 psi
Firing order	1-3-2-4

Cylinder head

Gasket surface warpage limit	0.002 inch (0.05 mm)
Gasket surface resurfacing limit	0.020 inch (0.5 mm)

Rocker arms

Bore diameter	0.7093 to 0.7100 inch (18.016 to 18.034 mm)
Shaft diameter	0.7080 to 0.7088 inch (17.982 to 18.003 mm)
Rocker arm-to-shaft clearance	0.0005 to 0.0020 inch (0.013 to 0.052 mm)

Pushrods

Runout	0.016 inch (0.4 mm)

Valve clearance (cold)

Intake	0.010 inch (0.25 mm)
Exhaust	0.014 inch (0.35 mm)

Oil pump

Drive gear outside diameter	1.1693 to 1.1709 inches (29.70 to 29.74 mm)
Rotor outside diameter	1.5957 to 1.5968 inches (40.53 to 40.56 mm)

Drive gear tip-to-rotor tip clearance
Standard	0.0008 to 0.0047 inch (0.02 to 0.12 mm)
Service limit	0.008 inch (0.2 mm)

Rotor/gear-to-case side clearance (endplay)
Standard	0.0012 to 0.0051 inch (0.03 to 0.13 mm)
Service limit	0.008 inch (0.2 mm)

Rotor-to-case radial clearance
Standard	0.0059 to 0.0083 inch (0.15 to 0.21 mm)
Service limit	0.0098 inch (0.25 mm)
Relief valve spring free length	1.854 inch (47.1 mm)

Bypass valve spring free length
1800	1.461 inch (37.1 mm)
1600	1.602 inch (40.7 mm)

Torque specifications

Ft-lbs (unless otherwise specified)

Oil pressure sending unit	16 to 20
Engine mount-to-crossmember nut	14 to 25
Front exhaust pipe-to-engine	18 to 25
Oil strainer mounting bolt	17 to 20
Cylinder head bolts/nuts **(see illustration 8.13)**	
Bolts 1 through 9	
Step 1	22
Step 2	43
Step 3	47
Bolts 10 and 11 (6 mm bolts)	96 in-lbs
Flywheel/driveplate housing-to-engine bolts	14 to 20
Oil pan bolts	40 to 48 in-lbs
Flywheel-to-crankshaft bolts	30 to 33
Driveplate-to-crankshaft bolts	36 to 39
Crankshaft pulley bolt	55
Intake manifold bolts	13 to 16

1   General information

1984 and earlier 1600 and 1800 engines are of horizontally opposed, four cylinder, overhead-valve configuration. The larger engine is used primarily in the four-wheel drive models.

The crankcase is made of aluminum and can be separated into right and left sections. The cylinder heads are also aluminum. The crankshaft is made of steel and supported by three main bearings.

The aluminum pistons are slipper type with two compression rings and one combination-type oil control ring. The camshaft is directly supported in the crankcase at three places *without* the use of replaceable bearings. The camshaft is gear-driven by the crankshaft, with four cam lobes operating the intake and exhaust valves in each cylinder head. Valve lifters operated by the camshaft in the block drive pushrods which in turn drive shaft-mounted rocker arms.

The engine oil pump is driven directly by the camshaft and is mounted on the outside of the crankcase, making inspection and maintenance possible.

2   Repair operations possible with the engine in the vehicle

Some major repair operations can be accomplished without removing the engine from the vehicle. Clean the engine compartment and the exterior of the engine with some type of degreaser before any work is done. It will make the job easier and help keep dirt out of the internal areas of the engine.

Depending on the components involved, it may be helpful to remove the hood to improve access to the engine as repairs are performed (refer to Chapter 11 if necessary). Cover the fenders to prevent damage to the paint. Special pads are available, but an old bedspread or blanket will also work.

If vacuum, exhaust, oil or coolant leaks develop, indicating a need for gasket or seal replacement, the repairs can generally be made with the engine in the vehicle. The intake and exhaust gaskets, oil pan gasket, crankshaft oil seals and cylinder head gasket are all accessible with the engine in place.

Exterior engine components, such as the intake and exhaust manifolds, the oil pan (and the oil pump), the water pump, the starter motor, the alternator, the distributor and the fuel system components can be removed for repair with the engine in place.

Since the cylinder heads can be removed without pulling the engine, valve component servicing can also be accomplished with the engine in the vehicle. Replacement of the camshaft and lifters requires splitting the crankcase (see Chapter 2, Part C) and is not possible with the engine in the vehicle.

3   Top Dead Center (TDC) for number one piston - locating

Refer to illustrations 3.4 and 3.6

1   Top Dead Center (TDC) is the highest point in the cylinder that each piston reaches as it travels up and down when the crankshaft turns. Each piston reaches TDC on the compression stroke and again on the exhaust stroke, but TDC generally refers to piston position on the compression stroke. The timing marks on the flywheel are referenced to the number one piston at TDC on the compression stroke.

2   Positioning the piston(s) at TDC is an essential part of procedures such as valve seal replacement and distributor removal.

3   In order to bring any piston to TDC, the crankshaft must be turned using one of the methods outlined below. When looking at the front of the engine, normal crankshaft rotation is clockwise. **Warning:** *Before beginning this procedure, be sure to place the transmission in Neutral and disconnect the primary (low voltage) wire connector(s) at the ignition coil to disable the ignition system.*

a) *The preferred method is to turn the crankshaft with a large socket and breaker bar attached to the vibration damper bolt threaded into the front of the crankshaft.*

b) *A remote starter switch, which may save some time, can also be used. Attach the switch leads to the S (switch) and B (battery) terminals on the starter motor. Once the piston is close to TDC, use a socket and breaker bar as described in the previous paragraph.*

c) *If an assistant is available to turn the ignition switch to the Start position in short bursts, you can get the piston close to TDC without a remote starter switch. Use a socket and breaker bar as described in paragraph a) to complete the procedure.*

4   Make a mark on the distributor housing directly below the number one spark plug wire terminal on the distributor cap **(see illustration)**. **Note:** *The terminal numbers may be marked on the spark plug wires near the distributor.*

5   Remove the distributor cap as described in Chapter 1.

3.4 Make a mark on the distributor body (arrow) just below the number 1 spark plug wire terminal

3.6 At the top of the bellhousing, there is an access hole where you can see the ignition timing marks

4.1 Disconnect the PCV hose from the fitting on each valve cover (arrow) and remove the valve cover mounting bolts

5.6 Disconnect and tag the hoses connected to the intake manifold/carburetor

2A

6   Turn the crankshaft (see paragraph 3 above) until the 0 mark on the flywheel is aligned with the pointer on the bellhousing **(see illustration)**. **Note:** *There are two sets of marks on the flywheel. One set is a group of three lines used for valve timing only, the ignition timing marks used for TDC setting is a scale of marks with numbers from 10 to 0 to 20. The left 10 mark is accompanied by an "A", representing After TDC, while the rest of the numbers are grouped with a "B" for Before TDC. Do not confuse the valve and ignition timing marks.*

7   The rotor should now be pointing directly at the mark on the distributor housing **(see illustration 3.4)**. If it isn't, the piston may be at TDC on the exhaust stroke.

8   To get the piston to TDC on the compression stroke, turn the crankshaft one complete turn (360-degrees) clockwise. The rotor should now be pointing at the mark. When the rotor is pointing at the number one spark plug wire terminal in the distributor cap (which is indicated by the mark on the housing) and the flywheel ignition timing marks are aligned, the number one piston is at TDC on the compression stroke.

9   After the number one piston has been positioned at TDC on the compression stroke, TDC for any of the remaining cylinders can be located by turning the crankshaft 180-degrees at a time and following the firing order (refer to the Specifications).

4   Valve covers - removal and installation

Removal

Refer to illustration 4.1

1   Disconnect the PCV hoses from each valve cover **(see illustration)**.

2   Remove the valve cover bolts.

3   Tap the edge of the valve cover with a plastic or wooden mallet to break the gasket seal and pull the valve cover off. **Note:** *If the valve cover will not break loose, slip a flexible putty knife between the cylinder head and*

valve cover to break the seal. Don't pry at the valve cover-to-cylinder head joint, as damage to the sealing surface and cover flange will result and oil leaks will develop.

Installation

4   The mating surfaces of each cylinder head and valve cover must be perfectly clean when the valve covers are installed. Use a gasket scraper to remove all traces of sealant or old gasket, then wipe the mating surfaces with a cloth saturated with lacquer thinner or acetone. If there is sealant or oil on the mating surfaces when the valve cover is installed, oil leaks may develop.

5   Make sure any threaded holes are clean. Run a tap into them to remove corrosion and restore damaged threads.

6   Apply a bead of sealant to the gasket edge of the valve covers and install the new gasket to the flange.

7   Carefully position the valve cover on the cylinder head and install the nuts/bolts.

8   Tighten the bolts in three steps to the torque listed in this Chapter's Specifications. **Caution:** *DON'T over-tighten the valve cover bolts.*

9   The remaining installation steps are the reverse of removal.

10   Start the engine and check carefully for oil leaks as the engine warms up.

5   Intake manifold - removal and installation

Removal

Refer to illustrations 5.6 and 5.21

1   In order to remove the intake manifold from the engine, a number of components have to be disconnected. First, drain the cooling system (see Chapter 1).

2   Disconnect the cables from the battery (negative first, then positive).

3   Remove the spare tire and support bracket.

4   On carbureted models, disconnect all of

the hoses and wires from the air cleaner assembly (see Chapter 4A).

5   On carbureted models, remove the air cleaner assembly. On fuel-injected models, detach the air intake duct from the throttle body. **Note:** *Plug the carburetor or throttle body opening to prevent dirt from entering.*

6   On carbureted models, disconnect the fuel delivery and return hoses from the carburetor **(see illustration)**. On fuel-injected models remove the fuel-rail (see Chapter 4B).

7   On carbureted models, disconnect the vacuum hose, the carburetor vent hose and the purge hose from the evaporation pipe. On fuel-injected models, mark the hoses and detach the vacuum pipe assembly from the right-side cylinder head. **Note:** *Tag all of the hoses and wires with masking tape to help identify their location during reassembly.*

8   Disconnect the brake booster vacuum hose from the intake manifold.

9   Disconnect the kick-down solenoid vacuum hose from the vacuum pipe (automatic transmission).

10   Disconnect the spark plug wires from the plugs and the high-tension wire leading to the distributor cap from the ignition coil (see Chapter 5).

11   Disconnect the accelerator cable from the carburetor (see Chapter 4).

12   Disconnect the coolant hose to the thermostat housing from the top of the radiator (see Chapter 3).

13   Disconnect the thermoswitch electrical connector.

14   Remove the carburetor protector on the back side of the carburetor (if applicable).

15   Disconnect the vacuum hose and the lead wire from the distributor.

16   Remove the EGR valve pipe cover and disconnect the pipe from the EGR valve (see Chapter 6).

17   Disconnect the ASV pipe from the air suction valve (see Chapter 6).

18   Disconnect the oil pressure switch/gauge and the thermoswitch electrical connectors.

19   Disconnect the hose from the PCV valve.

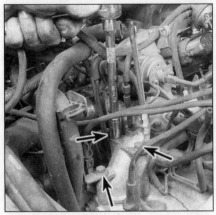

5.21 Remove the intake manifold mounting bolts and mark them as to their location - there are different length bolts

20 Disconnect the coolant bypass hoses and the heater hose from the intake manifold.
21 Remove the intake manifold mounting bolts **(see illustration)** and carefully lift the manifold off the engine. There are different lengths of intake manifold bolts, mark them as to their location. **Note:** *As you lift the intake manifold, check for any hoses or wires that may still be connected.*

Installation

22 Carefully place the intake manifold on the engine and bolt it into place with the mounting bolts. Clean the threads of the bolts with a wire brush before installation and tighten the bolts to the torque listed in this Chapter's Specifications.
23 Attach the hose assembly to the PCV valve.
24 Install the oil fill tube and bracket on the engine.
25 Attach the EGR supply tube to the EGR valve.
26 Connect the vacuum sensing line to the air injection system air suction valve. Install the two flexible hoses and the holder.
27 Attach the rubber hose and the air supply tube to the air injection system air suction valve.

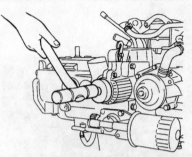

6.7 Use a large-diameter socket to tap the new crankshaft seal in squarely

28 Reconnect the right hand valve cover vent hose.
29 Connect the coolant transfer hose (from the thermostat housing) to the fitting directly below the carburetor.
30 Always use new gaskets when installing the intake manifold. **Note:** *Make sure that both the cylinder head and intake manifold mounting surfaces are thoroughly clean.*
31 Check all vacuum and other hoses for cracks and damage at this time. Replace them with new ones if necessary.
32 When installing the accelerator cable, make the cable adjustments by referring to Chapter 1.

6 Crankshaft front oil seal - replacement

Refer to illustration 6.7
1 Disconnect the negative battery cable.
2 Refer to Chapter 3 and remove the engine cooling fan and radiator, then refer to Chapter 1 and remove the drive belt(s).
3 Remove the large crankshaft pulley bolt with a socket and breaker bar. To keep the crankshaft from turning, have an assistant wedge a large screwdriver against the ring gear teeth, through the timing mark access hole **(see illustration 3.6)**.
4 Pry the front pulley from the crankshaft by using two screwdrivers behind opposite sides of the pulley, exerting equal force.

7.3 Remove the rocker arm assembly bolts

7.2 Back off the valve adjusting screws before loosening the rocker arm assembly bolts

5 Carefully pry the seal out of the crankcase with a seal puller or a large screwdriver. **Caution:** *Be careful not to scratch, gouge or distort the area that the seal fits into or an oil leak will develop.* **Note:** *An alternative method if you don't have a seal puller is to drill two 1/8-inch holes in the seal, being careful not to hit the seal housing or crankshaft. Screw two self-tapping screws into the holes and pull on them, alternating side to side, with a slide-hammer or self-locking pliers.*
6 Clean the bore to remove any old seal material and corrosion. Position the new seal in the bore with the seal lip (usually the side with the spring) facing IN (toward the engine). A small amount of oil applied to the outer edge of the new seal will make installation easier - but don't overdo it!
7 Drive the seal into the bore with a large socket and hammer until it's completely seated **(see illustration)**. Select a socket that's the same outside diameter as the seal and make sure the new seal is pressed into place until it bottoms against the flange, to the same depth as the original seal.
8 Reinstall the crankshaft pulley. Use a brass hammer to tap it on squarely, then use the large pulley bolt to draw it in the rest of the way. Tighten it to the torque listed in this Chapter's Specifications.
9 The remainder of installation is the reverse of the removal process.

7 Rocker arms, shafts and pushrods - removal, inspection and installation

Removal

Refer to Illustrations 7.2, 7.3 and 7.4
1 Refer to Section 4 for removal of the valve covers.
2 Back off the rocker arm adjustment screws before loosening the rocker arm assembly bolts **(see illustration)**.
3 Loosen all of the rocker assembly mounting bolts evenly **(see illustration)**, then pull off the assembly.

7.4 Rocker arm shaft components

1 Rocker arm assembly (right-hand)
2 Snap-ring
3 Nut
4 Washer
5 Valve adjusting screw
6 Shaft spring washer
7 Shaft supporter
8 Rocker arm
9 Rocker shaft spacer
10 Rocker arm shaft
11 Rocker arm
12 Rocker arm assembly (left-hand)
13 Rocker arm assembly (right-hand
14 Rocker shaft spacer
15 Rocker arm shaft
16 Rocker arm assembly (left-hand
17 Rocker arm
18 Rocker arm
19 Lock washer (only for hydraulic valve lifter)

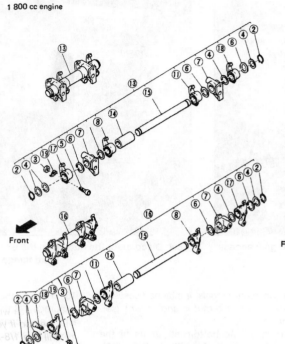

1 800 cc engine

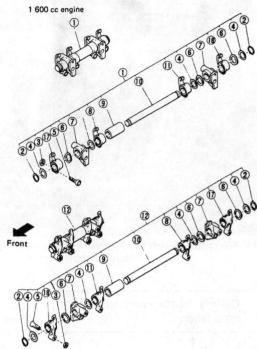

1 600 cc engine

2A

4   Keep track of the rocker arm positions, since they must be returned to the same locations **(see illustration)**. Store each set of rocker components separately in a marked plastic bag to ensure that they're reinstalled in their original locations.

5   Remove the pushrods and store them separately to make sure they don't get mixed up during installation. Label them so they can be reinstalled in their original locations.

Inspection

Refer to illustrations 7.6 and 7.7
Note: *Pay special attention to the installed direction of the rocker arm shaft, the position of the spring washers, the difference between the rocker arms and the R mark on the right-hand spacer.*

6   Remove the snap-ring and slide the parts off the shaft, taking care not to mix them up, so they can be reinstalled in the same order **(see illustration)**. **Note:** *Disassemble only one rocker shaft assembly at a time, using the other one as a reference guide.*

7   Examine the rocker arm shaft and bushings for wear **(see illustration)**. If the rocker arm surface that contacts the valve stem is worn considerably, replace the rocker arm with a new one. If it is worn slightly in a stepped shape it can be corrected on a valve refacing machine. If the rocker arm bushing has to be replaced it requires special tools and should be left to a dealership service department or an automotive machine shop. Check the adjuster buckets and the pushrod ends for wear.

8   Oil the parts and reassemble them on their respective shafts in the original order.

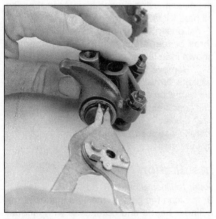

7.6 Remove the snap-ring from the end of the rocker assembly and slide the parts off the shaft

9   Check each rocker arm for wear, cracks and other damage, especially where the pushrods and valve stems contact the rocker arm.

10   Check the pivot seat in each rocker arm and the pivot faces. Look for galling, stress cracks and unusual wear patterns. If the rocker arms are worn or damaged, replace them with new ones and install new shafts as well.

11   Make sure the hole at the pushrod end of each rocker arm is open.

12   Inspect the pushrods for cracks and excessive wear at the ends. Roll each pushrod across a piece of plate glass to see if it's bent (if it wobbles, it's bent).

Installation

13   Lubricate the lower end of each pushrod

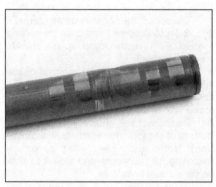

7.7 Look for scoring or abnormal wear on the rocker shaft - smooth, shiny spots do not necessarily indicate a worn shaft

with clean engine oil or engine assembly lube and install them in their original locations. Make sure each pushrod seats completely in the lifter socket.

14   Apply engine assembly lube to the ends of the valve stems, the upper ends of the pushrods and to the pivot faces to prevent damage to the mating surfaces on initial start-up.

15   Install and tighten the rocker arm bolts to the cylinder head bolt torque listed in this Chapter's Specifications. As the bolts are tightened, make sure the pushrods seat properly in the rocker arm adjusters, and that the rocker arm adjusters are backed off.

16   Refer to Chapter 1 for valve adjustment procedure.

17   Refer to Section 4 and install the valve covers.

18   Start the engine, listen for unusual valve train noses and check for oil leaks at the valve cover gaskets.

8.2 The splash shields (arrows) must be removed to gain access to the underside of the engine

8.4 Disconnect the nuts from the exhaust pipes at the cylinder head flange

8   Cylinder heads - removal and installation

Removal

Refer to Illustrations 8.2, 8.4, 8.7a and 8.7b

1   Disconnect the negative battery cable.

2   Refer to Chapter 1 and drain the cooling system. Remove the lower splash shields **(see illustration)**.

3   Refer to Chapter 1 for removal of the spark plugs, Section 4 for removal of the valve covers, and Section 7 for removal of the rocker arm assemblies and pushrods.

4   Disconnect the exhaust pipes from the bottom of the cylinder heads **(see illustration)**. **Note:** *Apply penetrating oil before beginning the procedure, and allow it to soak on the exhaust bolts/nuts.*

5   Refer to Section 5 and remove the intake manifold. Remove any hoses or brackets bolted to the cylinder heads, and on models with air-conditioning , remove the compressor bracket from the left cylinder head.

Note: *On some models, it may be necessary to remove the alternator and mount (see Chapter 5).*

6   Remove the bottom stud/nuts of the front engine mounts **(see illustration 13.6)**, and raise the engine with a floorjack under the oil pan, using a wood block to protect the oil pan.

7   Loosen the cylinder head nuts/bolts in three or four steps following the sequence shown **(see illustrations)**.

8   Remove the cylinder heads and the old gaskets. **Note:** *The block and cylinder heads are aluminum. Do not pry between the cylinder heads and the crankcase, as damage to the gasket sealing surfaces may result. Instead use a soft-faced hammer to tap the cylinder heads and break the gasket seal.*

Installation

Refer to Illustration 8.13

9   Clean the gasket mating surfaces of the cylinder heads and crankcase with lacquer thinner or acetone (they must be clean and oil-free).

10   Refer to the cylinder head gasket manufacturer's instructions and if necessary, apply a thin, even coat of the recommended gasket sealant to both sides of the new head gasket then lay it in place.

11   Install the cylinder head and lubricate the stud threads with engine oil. Install the nuts and tighten them finger-tight.

12   Slip the pushrods into place, then install the rocker arm assemblies. Make sure the pushrods are seated in the lifters and the adjuster buckets. Install the bolts and tighten them finger-tight.

13   Tighten the cylinder head nuts and bolts to the torque listed in this Chapter's Specifications. Follow the tightening sequence and work up to the final torque in three steps **(see illustration)**. **Note:** *After tightening all cylinder head bolts/nuts to the proper torque, recheck the torque on the nut at the center of each cylinder head (number 1 in the illustration) to make sure it is still at the specified torque.*

14   Repeat the procedure for the remaining cylinder head.

8.7a When loosening the cylinder head bolts, be sure to follow the correct sequence

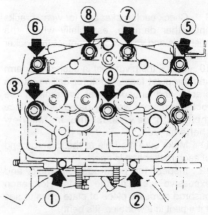

8.7b Cylinder head bolt/nut *loosening* sequence

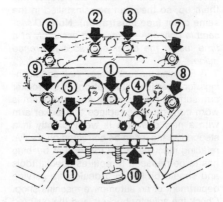

8.13 Cylinder head bolt/nut tightening sequence

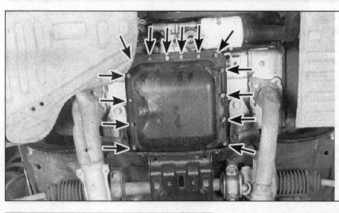

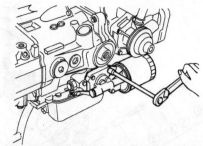

9.3 Remove the oil pan bolts (arrows)

10.4 Remove the three bolts (arrows) and remove the oil pump from the block, with or without the oil filter

9   Oil pan - removal and installation

Removal

Refer to illustration 9.3

1   Disconnect the negative battery cable. Raise the vehicle and support it securely on jackstands (see Chapter 1).
2   Drain the engine oil and remove the oil filter (see Chapter 1).
3   Remove the bolts securing the oil pan to the engine **(see illustration)**.
4   Tap on the pan with a soft-faced hammer to break the gasket seal. and lower the oil pan from the engine. A thin putty knife can be inserted between the pan and the block to break the gasket seal, but the block is aluminum, so do not use screwdriver or other

sharp tool at the pan/block interface. **Caution:** *Before using force on the oil pan, be sure all the bolts have been removed.*

Installation

5   Using a gasket scraper, scrape off all traces of the old gasket from the engine and the oil pan. Be especially careful not to nick or gouge the gasket sealing surfaces of the crankcase (they are made of aluminum and are quite soft).
6   Clean the oil pan with solvent and dry it thoroughly. Check the gasket sealing surfaces for distortion. If the oil pan is distorted at the bolt-hole areas, straighten the flange by supporting it from below on a 1x4 wood block and tapping the bolt holes with the rounded end of a ball-peen hammer. Wipe the gasket surfaces clean with a rag soaked

in lacquer thinner or acetone.
7   Remove the oil strainer mounting bolt, then carefully tap the strainer mounting flange to remove it from the crankcase hole. *Do not remove the bracket from the strainer.*
8   Use a new O-ring when installing the strainer and tap only on the mounting flange to seat the pipe in the crankcase hole. Install the bolt and tighten it to the torque listed in this Chapter's Specifications.
9   Before installing the oil pan, apply a thin coat of RTV-type gasket sealer to the crankcase gasket sealing surfaces. Lay a new oil pan gasket in place and carefully apply a coat of gasket sealer to the exposed side of the gasket.
10   Gently lay the oil pan in place (do not disturb the gasket) and install the bolts. Start with the bolts closest to the center of the pan and tighten them in a criss-cross pattern to the torque listed in this Chapter's Specifications. *Do not overtighten them or leakage may occur.*

10   Oil pump - removal, inspection and installation

Removal

Refer to illustration 10.4

1   The oil pump is located on the bottom-front of the engine. It is easily accessible from underneath the vehicle.
2   Remove the engine oil drain plug by referring to Chapter 1 and completely drain the oil from the engine.
3   Raise the front of the vehicle and place it on jackstands.
4   Disconnect the electrical connector at the oil pressure sending unit and remove the oil pump from the engine by removing the mounting bolts **(see illustration)**. **Note:** *Be prepared for some oil to spill at this time. You can remove the oil filter from the pump before or after the pump is removed from the engine.*

Inspection

Refer to illustrations 10.5a, 10.5b, 10.11, 10.12 and 10.13

5   Remove the filter and disassemble the oil pump, using the illustrations as a guide **(see illustrations)**.

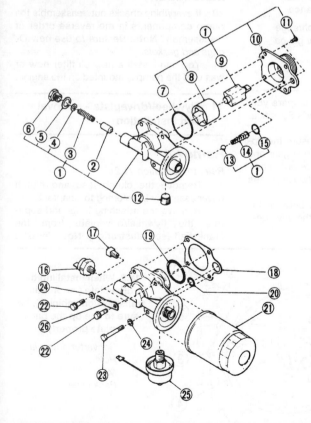

10.5a Oil pump components - 1800cc engine

1   Oil pump assembly
2   Oil relief valve
3   Relief valve spring
4   Washer
5   Washer
6   Plug
7   O-ring
8   Oil pump rotor
9   Oil pump drive gear
10   Oil pump body holder
11   Pan head screw
12   Plug (models without pressure gauge)
13   Ball
14   Bypass valve spring
15   O-ring
16   Oil pressure switch (models without pressure gauge)
17   Plug (models with pressure gauge)
18   Oil pump body gasket
19   O-ring
20   O-ring
21   Oil filter
22   Bolt
23   Bolt
24   Washer
25   Oil pressure sender (models with gauge)
26   Stay

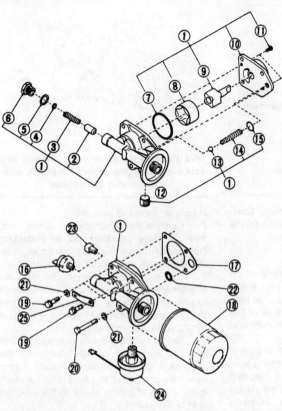

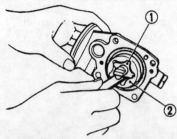

10.5b Oil pump components - 1600 cc engine

1   Oil pump assembly
2   Oil relief valve
3   Relief valve spring
4   Washer
5   Washer
6   Plug
7   O-ring
8   Oil pump rotor
9   Oil pump drive gear
10 Oil pump body holder
11 Pan head screw
12 Plug (models without pressure gauge)
13 Ball
14 Bypass valve spring
15 O-ring
16 Oil pressure switch (models without pressure gauge)
17 Oil pump body gasket
18 Oil filter
19 Bolt
20 Bolt
21 Washer
22 O-ring
23 Plug (models with pressure gauge)
24 Oil pressure sender (models with pressure gauge)
25 Stay

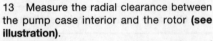

10.11 Checking drive gear-to-rotor tip clearance with a feeler gauge

1   Drive gear   2   Rotor

13   Measure the radial clearance between the pump case interior and the rotor (see illustration).
14   Carefully check the interior surface of the pump case and the exterior surfaces of the drive gear and the rotor for score marks and damage.
15   Check the relief valve for seat condition and damage.
16   Check both valve springs for damage and deterioration.
17   Check the pump shaft hole in the pump holder for wear and the holder surface for cracks and damage.
18   Check the pump case for clogged oil passages, case cracks and damage.
19   If your measurements are not within those listed in this Chapter's specifications or if there is damage to any of the components, replace the pump with a new one.

Installation

20   If everything checks out, reassemble the pump components in the reverse order of disassembly. **Note:** *Be sure to use new O-rings and gaskets.*
21   You can install a new oil filter now or wait until the pump is mounted on the engine.

11   Flywheel/driveplate - removal and installation

Removal

Refer to Illustration 11.2

1   Remove the clutch disc and clutch cover assembly by referring to Chapter 8.
2   Remove the attaching bolts and separate the flywheel/driveplate from the crankshaft (see illustration). **Note:** *Insert a*

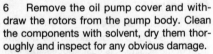

10.12 Measuring rotor-to-case and gear-to-case clearance

1   Straightedge
2   Feeler gauge

6   Remove the oil pump cover and withdraw the rotors from the pump body. Clean the components with solvent, dry them thoroughly and inspect for any obvious damage.
7   Remove the O-ring, the bypass valve spring and the ball from the pump.
8   Remove the oil pressure sending unit/switch and plugs from the pump.
9   Now, remove the relief valve plug, the washers, the spring and the relief valve from the pump body.
10   Measure the outside diameter of the

drive gear and the rotor and compare your measurements with this Chapter's Specifications.
11   Using a feeler gauge, measure the tip-to-tip clearance between the drive gear and the rotor. **Note:** *To do this, place both components back into the pump housing (see illustration).*
12   Measure the side clearance between the pump case face, the rotor and the drive gear (see illustration).

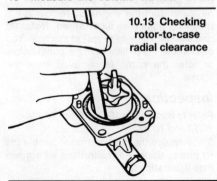

10.13 Checking rotor-to-case radial clearance

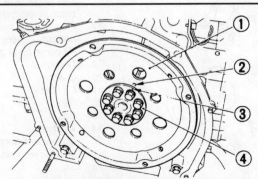

11.2 When installing the driveplate (automatic transmission vehicles), be sure to line up the back plate properly

1   Converter drive plate
2   Hole
3   Mark
4   Back plate

2A

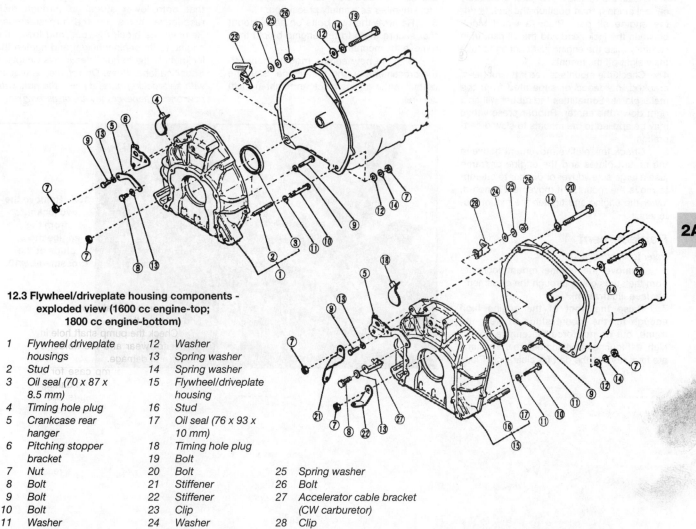

12.3 Flywheel/driveplate housing components - exploded view (1600 cc engine-top; 1800 cc engine-bottom)

1	Flywheel driveplate housings	12	Washer
2	Stud	13	Spring washer
3	Oil seal (70 x 87 x 8.5 mm)	14	Spring washer
4	Timing hole plug	15	Flywheel/driveplate housing
5	Crankcase rear hanger	16	Stud
6	Pitching stopper bracket	17	Oil seal (76 x 93 x 10 mm)
7	Nut	18	Timing hole plug
8	Bolt	19	Bolt
9	Bolt	20	Bolt	25	Spring washer
10	Bolt	21	Stiffener	26	Bolt
11	Washer	22	Stiffener	27	Accelerator cable bracket (CW carburetor)
		23	Clip	28	Clip
		24	Washer		

large screwdriver, pry bar or alignment punch through the timing mark hole in the housing and one of the holes in the flywheel/driveplate to keep it from turning as the bolts are loosened.

3   Remove the O-ring installed between the flywheel or driveplate and the crankshaft.

Installation

4   Attach the O-ring to the end of the crankshaft.

5   Apply thread locking compound to the bolt threads. Hold the flywheel/driveplate in position and install the bolts in the end of the crankshaft. On automatic transmission models, align the small hole in the driveplate with the mark on the backplate before installing the bolts. Note: *The flywheel/driveplate can only be installed in one position, since the bolt holes are not equally spaced. If the bolt holes don't line up, rotate the flywheel relative to the crankshaft until they all line up.*

6   While holding the flywheel/driveplate so that it doesn't turn, tighten the bolts (using a criss-cross pattern) to the torque listed in this Chapter's Specifications.

7   Install the clutch disc and clutch cover assembly as described in Chapter 8.

12   Rear main oil seal - replacement

Refer to illustration 12.3

1   Refer to Chapter 8 for removal of the transmission and clutch assembly.

2   Refer to Section 11 for removal of the flywheel.

3   Remove the bolts holding the flywheel housing (bellhousing) to the back of the engine block **(see illustration on following page)**.

4   Noting which direction it was installed, drive the old seal from the bellhousing with a socket or hammer and punch.

5   Clean the bore of the bellhousing and make sure the seal-mounting surface is free of burrs.

6   Lubricate the new seal's inner lip with white grease, and the outer diameter with clean engine oil.

7   With the bellhousing on a flat, hard sur-

face, drive the new seal in place squarely with a seal-driver, large socket, or section of pipe the right diameter. Drive the seal to the depth that the original was installed.

8   The remainder of assembly is the reverse of the disassembly process. **Note:** *Clean the back of the bellhousing's mounting surface and coat it with a thin film of RTV sealant prior to installation on the block.*

13   Engine mounts - check and replacement

Check

1   Engine mounts seldom require attention, but broken or deteriorated mounts should be replaced immediately or the added strain placed on the driveline components may cause damage.

2   During the check, the engine must be raised slightly to remove the weight from the mounts. Disconnect the negative battery cable from the battery.

3   Raise the vehicle and support it securely on jackstands, then position the jack under the engine oil pan. Place a wood block between the jack head and the oil pan, then carefully raise the engine just enough to take the weight off the mounts.

4   Check the mounts to see if the rubber is cracked, hardened or separated from the metal plates. Sometimes the rubber will split right down the center. Rubber preservative may be applied to the mounts to slow deterioration.

5   Check for relative movement between the mount plates and the engine or frame (use a large screwdriver or pry bar to attempt to move the mounts). If movement is noted, lower the engine and tighten the mount fasteners.

Replacement

Refer to illustration 13.6

6   Remove the engine mount locknuts from the studs going through the crossmember **(see illustration)**.

7   Raise the front of the engine high enough for the mount studs to clear the frame, but do not force the engine up too high. If it touches anything before the mounts are free, remove the part for clearance. Place a block of wood between the oil pan and crossmember as a safety precaution.

8   Remove the two bolts on each mount that secure them to the engine block, then remove the mounts.

9   Slip the new engine mounts between the crossmember and the engine. Start the bolts into the engine block and tighten them securely.

10   Lower the engine slowly, making sure that both lower studs go through their respective holes in the crossmember. Remove the block of wood and lower the engine to its original height and tighten the locknuts to the torque listed in this Chapter's Specifications. **Note:** *On vehicles equipped with self-locking nuts, replace the nuts with new ones whenever they are disassembled.*

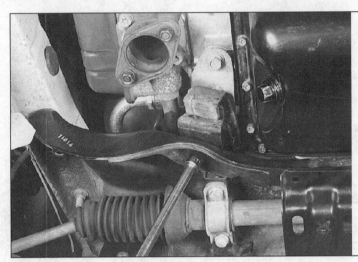

13.6 Remove the two locknuts from the engine mount studs at the crossmember10.

Chapter 2 Part B
Overhead camshaft (OHC) engine

Contents

Specifications

General

Bore and stroke	3.62 x 2.64 inches (92 x 67 mm)
Displacement	109 cubic inches (1781 cc)
Oil pressure	
2000 rpm	14 to 26 psi (98 to 177 kPa)
4000 rpm	34 to 46 psi (235 to 314 kPa)
Firing order	1-3-2-4

Cylinder location and distributor rotation

1-3-2-4

Cylinder head

Gasket surface warpage limit	0.002 inch (0.05 mm)
Gasket surface resurfacing limit	0.012 inch (0.3 mm)

Hydraulic lash adjusters

Diameter	0.842 to 0.843 inch (21.380 to 21.393 mm)
Tappet bore diameter	0.844 to 0.846 inch (21.413 to 21.470 mm)
Tappet-to-bore clearance	
Standard	0.0008 to 0.0035 inch (0.02 to 0.09 mm)
Service limit	0.0039 inch 0.10 mm

Camshafts

Lobe height	
Carbureted models	
DL 4-S	1.540 to 1.544 inches (39.10 to 39.20 mm)
All others	1.562 to 1.566 inches (39.64 to 39.74 mm)
MPFI	
Non-turbo	1.566 to 1.570 inches (39.75 to 39.85 mm)
Turbo	1.562 to 1.566 inches (39.64 to 39.74 mm)
Service limit (all)	0.006 inch (0.15 mm)
Journal diameters	
Front	1.4960 to 1.4964 inches (37.964 to 37.980 mm)
Center	1.9095 to 1.910 inches (48.464 to 48.480 mm)
Rear	
1987 and earlier	1.4960 to 1.4964 inches (37.964 to 37.980 mm)
1988 and later	1.8898 to 1.8904 inches (47.964 to 47.980 mm)
Journal bores (in camshaft housing)	
Front	1.4972 to 1.4979 inches (38.000 to 38.018 mm)
Center	1.9109 to 1.9116 inches (48.500 to 48.518 mm)
Rear	1.8912 to 1.8919 inches (48.000 to 48.018 mm)
Distributor journal (left camshaft)	1.5366 to 1.5373 inches (39.000 to 39.018 mm)
Thrust clearance	0.0012 to 0.0102 inches (0.030 to 0.260 mm)
Journal oil Clearance	
Standard	0.0008 to 0.0021 inch (0.020 to 0.054 mm)
Limit	0.0027 inch (0.070 mm)

Oil pump

Rotor outer diameter	
Inner rotor	1.4035 to 1.4055 inches (35.65 to 35.70 mm)
Outer rotor	1.9665 to 1.9685 inches (49.95 to 50.00 mm)
Rotor height (inner and outer rotors)	
Marking "A"	0.5468 to 0.5476 inch (13.89 to 13.91 mm)
Marking "B"	0.5472 to 0.5480 inch (13.90 to 13.92 mm)
Marking "C"	0.5476 to 0.5484 inch (13.91 to 13.93 mm)
Rotor housing depth	0.8646 to 0.8677 inch (21.96 to 22.04 inch)
Inner rotor-to-cover side clearance (endplay)	
Standard	0.0020 to 0.0063 inch (0.05 to 0.16 mm)
Limit	0.0071 inch (0.18 mm)
Outer rotor-to-pump housing clearance	
Standard	0.0039 to 0.0071 inch (0.10 to 0.18 mm)
Limit	0.0087 inch (0.22 mm)

Torque specifications

	Ft-lb (unless otherwise specified)
Oil pressure sending unit	16 to 20
Oil pump mounting bolts	13 to 15
Engine mount-to-crossmember nut	14 to 25
Front exhaust pipe-to-engine	18 to 22
Oil strainer mounting bolt	17 to 20
Cylinder head bolts	
Step 1	22
Step 2	43
Step 3	47
Camshaft housing mounting bolts	13 to 15
Camshaft housing oil relief pipe bolt	17 to 20
Camshaft seal retainer/support	80 to 97 in-lbs
Camshaft cover bolts	37 to 50 in-lbs
Camshaft sprocket bolts	80 to 97 in-lbs
Flywheel/driveplate housing-to-engine bolts	25 to 30
Oil pan bolts	40 to 48 in-lbs
Flywheel/driveplate-to-crankshaft bolts	51 to 55
Crankshaft pulley bolt	66 to 79
Intake manifold bolts	14 to 16
Timing belt cover bolts	40 to 48 in-lbs
Timing belt idler sprocket bolt	29 to 35
Timing belt tensioner adjusting and pivot bolts	13 to 15

1   General information

The 1800 overhead-cam (OHC) engine is a horizontally-opposed, four cylinder configuration, similar in many respects to the overhead-valve engines (see Part A of this Chapter), but with two camshafts, one mounted in a support plate on each cylinder head, directly operating the valves by rockers (no pushrods) dampened by hydraulic lash adjusters. The camshafts can be removed without separating the crankcase halves, as is necessary on the pushrod engines.

The crankcase is made of aluminum and can be separated into right and left sections. The cylinder heads are also aluminum while the crankshaft is made of steel and supported by three main bearings. The aluminum pistons are the slipper type with two compression rings and one combination-type oil control ring.

The engine oil pump, water pump and camshaft sprockets are all driven directly by two replaceable rubber timing belts.

2   Repair operations possible with the engine in the vehicle

Some major repair operations can be accomplished without removing the engine from the vehicle.

Clean the engine compartment and the exterior of the engine with some type of degreaser before any work is done. It will make the job easier and help keep dirt out of the internal areas of the engine.

Depending on the components involved, it may be helpful to remove the hood to improve access to the engine as repairs are performed (refer to Chapter 11 if necessary). Cover the fenders to prevent damage to the paint. Special pads are available, but an old bedspread or blanket will also work.

If vacuum, exhaust, oil or coolant leaks develop, indicating a need for gasket or seal replacement, the repairs can generally be made with the engine in the vehicle. The intake and exhaust gaskets, oil pan gasket, crankshaft oil seals and cylinder head gasket are all accessible with the engine in place. However, cylinder head gasket replacement is easier with the engine out of the chassis.

Exterior engine components, such as the intake and exhaust, the oil pan (and the oil pump), the water pump, the starter motor, the alternator, the distributor and the fuel system components can be removed for repair with the engine in place.

Since the cylinder heads can be removed without pulling the engine (although this is difficult), valve component servicing can also be accomplished with the engine in the vehicle. Replacement of the camshafts, rockers and lifters can be accomplished with the engine in the chassis.

3   Top Dead Center (TDC) for number one piston - locating

This procedure is essentially the same as that for the OHV (pushrod) engines. Refer to Part A of this Chapter.

4   Intake manifold - removal and installation

Removal

Refer to illustrations 4.3, 4.8, 4.15, 4.16, 4.19a and 4.19b

1   On fuel injected models, relieve the fuel pressure (see Chapter 4B).

2   Disconnect the cable from the negative battery terminal. Drain the cooling system (see Chapter 1).

4.3 Remove the bolt on each side (arrow indicates right side) and remove the spare tire support

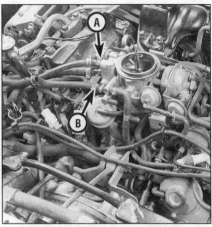

4.8 Disconnect and tag the hoses connected to the intake manifold/carburetor - (A) is the fuel delivery hose, (B) is the fuel return hose

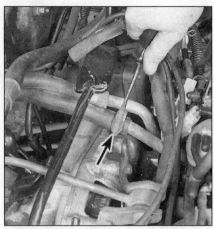

4.15 Above the flywheel housing, disconnect the coolant hose (arrow)

3   Remove the spare tire and support bracket **(see illustration)**.

4   Disconnect all of the hoses and wires from the air cleaner assembly (see Chapter 6).

5   Remove the air cleaner assembly and air intake ducts. **Note:** *Plug the carburetor or throttle body opening to prevent dirt from entering the carburetor or throttle body throat.*

6   Remove the alternator (see Chapter 5).

7   Remove the air-conditioning compressor and its mount (see Chapter 3). Lay the compressor aside without disconnecting the refrigerant lines. **Warning:** *The air conditioning system is under high pressure. DO NOT loosen any fittings unless the system has been discharged. Air conditioning refrigerant should be properly discharged into an approved container at a dealer service department or an automotive air-conditioning repair facility. Always wear eye protection when disconnecting air conditioning system fittings.*

8   Disconnect the fuel delivery and return hoses from the carburetor, throttle body or fuel rail **(see illustration)**. **Note:** *Disconnect only those hoses which need to be disconnected for manifold removal. There are many other vacuum hoses that can remain attached to the carburetor, throttle body and manifold. See chapter 4B for more information on fuel injected models.*

9   Disconnect the vacuum hose, the carburetor vent hose and the purge hose from the evaporation pipe. **Note:** *Tag all of the hoses and wires with masking tape to help identify their location during reassembly.*

10   Disconnect the brake booster vacuum hose from the intake manifold.

11   Disconnect the kick-down solenoid vacuum hose from the vacuum pipe (automatic transmission models).

12   Disconnect the spark plug wires from the plugs and the high-tension wire leading to the distributor cap from the ignition coil (see Chapter 5).

13   Disconnect the accelerator cable from the carburetor or throttle body (see Chapter 4).

14   Disconnect the coolant hose to the thermostat housing from the top of the radiator (see Chapter 3).

15   Disconnect the coolant hose from the intake manifold to the firewall **(see illustration)**. Place a rag under the connection to catch any coolant left in the hose.

16   Remove the two bolts holding the EGR pipe to the right-rear of the intake manifold **(see illustration)**.

17   Disconnect the ASV pipe from the air suction valve (see Chapter 6).

18   Disconnect the hose from the PCV valve.

19   Remove the intake manifold mounting bolts **(see illustrations)** and carefully lift the manifold off of the engine with the carburetor, throttle body or fuel injectors attached. There are more than one length of intake bolts, mark them as to their location. **Note:** *As you lift the manifold, check for any hoses or wires that may still be connected.*

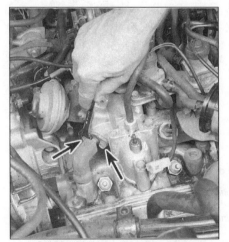

4.16 Remove the two bolts (arrows) holding the EGR pipe to the intake manifold

4.19a Remove the left-side intake manifold mounting bolts (arrows), and mark them as to their locations, (there are different lengths), then . . .

4.19b . . . remove the three mounting bolts on the right side (arrows) - the air cleaner bracket is under the rearmost bolt (carbureted model shown)

4.20 Use a gasket scraper to clean the manifold mounting surface, then use a small vacuum to suck up any debris

5.2 The valve timing marks are three lines (without numbers or letters) - align the center line with the pointer (arrows)

5.8 Use a long breaker bar and socket to remove the crankshaft pulley nut (radiator and condenser removed for clarity)

5.11a Remove the bolts holding the outer timing belt covers - three of the bolts (arrows) holding the left-side cover are shown

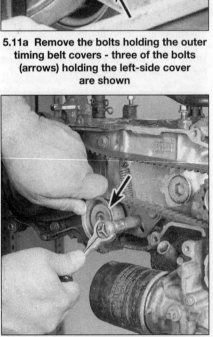

5.12 Loosen the right belt tensioner (arrow) then retighten the bolt with the tensioner pushed away from the belt

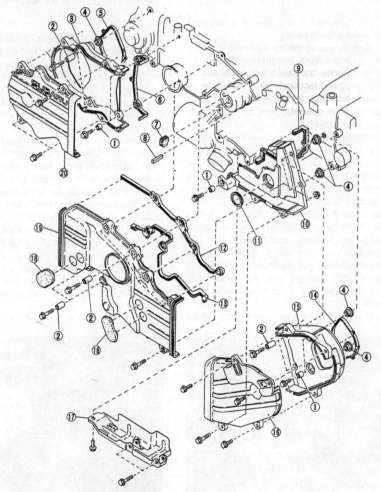

5.11b Exploded view of timing belt covers

1 Spacer	8 Water pump seal	15 Left inner belt cover
2 Spacer	9 Seal	16 Left outer belt cover
3 Right inner belt cover	10 Center inner belt cover	17 Lower-center belt cover plate
4 Plastic cover bolt insert	11 Seal	18 Belt cover plug
5 Seal	12 Seal	19 Center outer belt cover
6 Seal	13 Seal	
7 Seal	14 Seal	20 Right outer belt cover

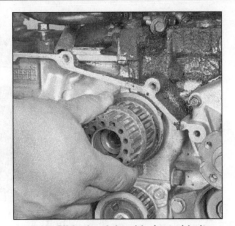

5.14 Position the left-side timing belt's tensioner away from the belt (slack position)

5.15 Slide the right-side (outer) belt sprocket off the crankshaft

5.17 If the inner crankshaft timing belt sprocket doesn't slip off, use two screwdrivers behind it to lever it off

2B

Installation

Refer to illustration 4.20

20   Scrape away any traces of sealant or old gasket materials from the intake manifold mounting surfaces and clean the gasket surface with a rag and lacquer thinner **(see illustration)**. **Note:** *When installing the manifold, always use new gaskets, and do not use sealant on the gaskets.*

21   Carefully place the intake manifold on the engine and bolt it into place with the mounting bolts, tightening them evenly to the torque listed this Chapter's Specifications. Clean the threads of the bolts with a wire brush before installation.

22   Attach the hose assembly to the PCV valve.

23   Install the oil fill tube and bracket on the engine.

24   Attach the EGR supply tube to the manifold.

25   Connect the wiring connectors and labeled vacuum and fuel hoses. **Note:** *Check all vacuum and other hoses for cracks and damage at this time. Replace them with new ones if necessary.*

26   Connect the coolant transfer hose and the radiator hose at the thermostat housing.

27   Connect the accelerator cable and adjust it, if necessary.

28   Refill the cooling system. When starting the engine, check carefully for coolant, fuel or vacuum leaks.

5   Timing belts and sprockets - removal, inspection and replacement

Removal

Refer to illustrations 5.2, 5.8, 5.11a, 5.11b, 5.12, 5.14, 5.15, 5.17, 5.18 and 5.19

1   Disconnect the cable from the negative battery terminal.

2   Turn the crankshaft until the center of the three valve timing marks on the flywheel is aligned with the timing pointer on the bell-housing **(see illustration)**. **Caution:** *Make sure you are using the valve timing marks as shown, NOT the ignition timing marks shown in Section 3.*

3   Refer to Chapter 1 and remove the alternator drivebelt.

4   Refer to Chapter 4 and remove the air cleaner assembly.

5   Refer to Chapter 3 and remove the air-conditioning compressor and bracket, **without** disconnecting the refrigerant lines. Set the compressor assembly aside. **Warning:** *The air conditioning system is under high pressure. DO NOT loosen any fittings unless the system has been discharged. Air conditioning refrigerant should be properly discharged into an approved container at a dealer service department or an automotive air-conditioning repair facility. Always wear eye protection when disconnecting air conditioning system fittings.*

6   Refer to Chapter 3 and remove the engine cooling fan(s) and shroud.

7   Remove the starter motor (see Chapter 5) and wedge a large screwdriver or prybar in the ring gear teeth of the flywheel to hold the crankshaft stationary (have an assistant hold the screwdriver or prybar in the flywheel).

8   Use a breaker bar and socket to remove the bolt from the crankshaft pulley **(see illustration)**. The crankshaft pulley should come off by hand, if not, use a screwdriver on either side of it to lever it off evenly.

9   Refer to Chapter 3 and remove the bolts and the water pump pulley.

10   Remove the oil level dipstick, then unbolt and remove the dipstick tube.

11   Remove the outer belt covers **(see illustrations)**. There are two side covers and one central cover.

12   Loosen the bolt on the right-side timing belt tensioner and release the tension **(see illustration)**. Move the tensioner away from the belt and temporarily retighten the bolt to hold the tensioner in this position. **Note:** *Right and left side designations are determined as if you were sitting in the vehicle*

5.18 Remove the single bolt (arrow) and remove the idler pulley

looking forward - the right side is the passenger side and the left side is the driver's side.

13   Slip the right-side timing belt off the engine. If the belt is not being replaced with a new one, mark the belt to indicate the direction of rotation.

14   Loosen the tensioner for the left-side timing belt as in Step 12 **(see illustration)**.

15   Slide the right-side timing belt sprocket from the crankshaft **(see illustration)**, then remove the left-side timing belt. If the belt is not being replaced with a new one, mark the belt to indicate the direction of rotation.

16   If only the timing belts are to be replaced, go to the Inspection and Installation Steps. If the sprockets are to be replaced, continue with the following Steps.

17   Remove the inner sprocket (for the left-side belt) from the crankshaft. If it doesn't slip off, use two screwdrivers behind it to evenly lever it off **(see illustration)**.

18   Remove the bolts and the left and right timing belt tensioners. Remove the bolt holding the timing belt idler pulley **(see illustration)**.

19   While keeping the camshaft sprocket timing mark aligned with the mark on the inner cover, remove the sprocket bolts, while hold-

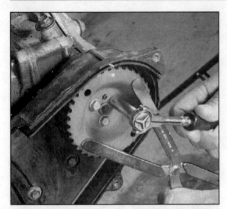

5.19 Use a two-pin spanner to hold the camshaft sprocket while removing the three sprocket bolts

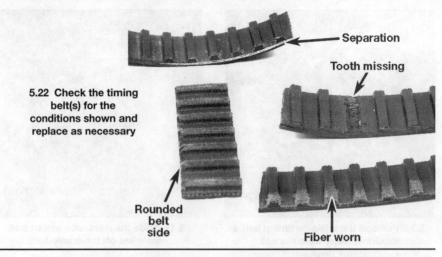

5.22 Check the timing belt(s) for the conditions shown and replace as necessary

ing the sprocket with an adjustable two-pin spanner **(see illustration)**. Remove both camshaft sprockets and mark them LH (left) and RH (right).

Inspection

Refer to illustration 5.22, 5.23 and 5.24
Caution: *Do not bend, twist or turn the timing belt inside out. Do not allow it to come in contact with oil, coolant or fuel. Do not use timing belt tension to keep the camshaft or crankshaft from turning when installing the sprocket bolt(s). Do not turn the crankshaft or camshaft more than a few degrees (necessary for tooth alignment) while the timing belt is removed.*
20   Rotate each tensioner pulley by hand and move it side-to-side to detect roughness and excessive play. Replace them if they don't turn smoothly or if play is noted.
21   If the timing belt was broken during engine operation, the belt may have been fouled by debris or may have been damaged by a defective component in the area of the timing belt; check for belt material in the teeth of the sprockets. Any defective parts or debris in the sprockets must be cleaned out of all the sprockets before installing the new belt or the belt will not mesh properly when installed. **Note:** *If one of the timing sprockets is dam-*

aged or worn, replace the sprockets as a set.
22   If the belt teeth are cracked or pulled off **(see illustration)**, the oil pump or camshaft(s) may have seized.
23   If there is noticeable wear or cracks in the belt **(see illustration)**, check to see if there are nicks or burrs on the sprockets.
24   If there is wear or damage on only one side of the belt **(see illustration)**, check the belt guide and the alignment of all sprockets. Also check the oil seals at the front of the engine and replace them if they are leaking.
25   Replace the timing belt with a new one if obvious wear or damage is noted or if it is the least bit questionable. Correct any problems which contributed to belt failure prior to belt installation. **Note:** *We recommend replacing the belt whenever it is removed, since belt failure can lead to expensive engine damage.*

Installation

Refer to illustrations 5.33 and 5.35
Note: *If the inner timing belt covers were removed from the engine (only necessary if the cylinder heads had been removed or the engine was to be overhauled, continue as below. If the inner covers were not removed, proceed to Step 30.*
26   Attach the belt cover seals to the cylinder block, where fitted **(see illustration 5.11b)**.

27   Attach the seals and belt cover mounts to the center inner belt cover, then install the assembly on the cylinder block.
28   Attach the seals and belt cover mounts to left inner belt cover and install the assembly on the cylinder head and camshaft case.
29   Attach the seals and belt cover mounts to right inner belt cover, then install the assembly on the cylinder head and camshaft case.
30   Install the camshaft sprockets **(see illustration 5.19)**. Tighten the bolts in three steps to the torque listed in this Chapter's Specifications.
31   If the idler sprocket had been removed, reinstall it **(see illustration 5.18)**.
32   Reinstall both tensioners with their springs, and tighten them temporarily in the position away from the belts **(see illustration 5.14)**.
33   Install the inner crankshaft sprocket onto the crankshaft (the inner crankshaft sprocket is the one without the dowel pin). Make sure the crankshaft timing marks at the flywheel are still aligned **(see illustration 5.2)**. Align the left camshaft sprocket timing mark with the notch in the inner cover and install the left-side timing belt **(see illustration)**. **Note:** *When installing the belt, wrap the belt around the crankshaft sprocket, oil pump sprocket, idler sprocket and camshaft sprocket in order. Keep the belt tight along the bottom and the slack under the tensioner.*
34   Loosen the left-side tensioner bolts until the tensioner applies pressure to the belt. Press the belt in-and-out to ensure the tensioner is operating smoothly. Using a torque wrench on one of the camshaft sprocket bolts, apply 18 ft-lbs of torque in a counterclockwise direction, then fully tighten the bolts on the tensioner while holding pressure on the sprocket. Tighten the slotted tensioner adjusting bolt first, then the pivot bolt. Make sure that the crankshaft (flywheel) and camshaft timing marks are properly aligned. Now rotate the engine one full turn (360-degrees) clockwise, aligning the crankshaft (flywheel) marks again **(see illustration5.2)**.
35   Install the outer crankshaft sprocket. Align the right camshaft sprocket timing mark

5.33 Left-hand timing belt installed with camshaft sprocket mark aligned with the notch in the inner cover (arrows)

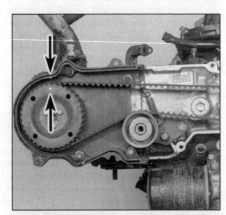

5.35 Right-hand timing belt installed with marks (arrows) aligned

6.3 Pry the seal (arrow) out with a seal-puller or screwdriver with the end taped to prevent scratching the crankshaft surface

6.5 Use a large-diameter socket to tap the new crankshaft seal in squarely

7.2 Remove the two bolts (arrows) and pull off the camshaft seal retainer (inner belt cover removed for clarity)

with the notch in the inner cover and then install the right-side timing belt **(see illustration)**. Keep the belt tight along the top and the slack over the tensioner.

36   Loosen the right-side tensioner bolts until the tensioner applies pressure to the belt. Press the belt in-and-out to ensure the tensioner is operating smoothly. Using a torque wrench on one of the camshaft sprocket bolts, apply 18 ft-lbs of torque in a counterclockwise direction, then fully tighten the bolts on the tensioner while holding pressure on the sprocket. Tighten the slotted tensioner adjusting bolt first, then the pivot bolt.

37   Install the timing belt covers and crankshaft pulley.

38   The remainder of installation is the reverse of the removal procedure.

6   Crankshaft front oil seal - replacement

Refer to illustrations 6.3 and 6.5

1   Disconnect the negative battery cable.

2   Refer to Section 5 and remove the timing belts and crankshaft sprockets.

3   Carefully pry the seal out of the cover

with a seal puller or a large screwdriver **(see illustration)**. **Caution:** *Be careful not to scratch, gouge or distort the area that the seal fits into or an oil leak will develop.* **Note:** *An alternative method if you don't have a seal puller is to drill two 1/8-inch holes in the seal, being careful not to hit the seal housing or crankshaft. Screw two self-tapping screws into the holes and pull on them, alternating side to side, with a slide-hammer or self-locking pliers on the screws.*

4   Clean the bore to remove any old seal material and corrosion. Position the new seal in the bore with the seal lip (usually the side with the spring) facing IN (toward the engine). A small amount of oil applied to the outer edge of the new seal will make installation easier - but don't overdo it!

5   Drive the seal into the bore with a large socket and hammer until it's completely seated **(see illustration)**. Select a socket that's the same outside diameter as the seal and make sure the new seal is pressed into place until it bottoms against the cover flange, to the same depth as the original seal.

6   Refer to Section 5 for installation of the sprockets and timing belts.

7   The remainder of installation is the reverse of the removal process.

7   Camshaft seals - Replacement

Refer to illustrations 7.2, 7.3, 7.4 and 7.5

1   Refer to Section 5 and remove the timing belts and camshaft sprockets.

2   Unbolt the camshaft seal retainer from the cylinder housing **(see illustration)**. **Note:** *It is not necessary to remove the camshaft cover, camshaft housing or inner timing covers.*

3   Pull the retainer from the engine. Use a seal puller to pry the old seal from the retainer **(see illustration)**.

4   Support the seal retainer on a block of hard wood, then tap the new seal into the retainer with a hammer and another block of wood **(see illustration)**. **Note:** *Drive the seal in squarely and only to the same depth as the original seal was installed.*

5   Before reinstalling the camshaft seal and retainer to the engine, remove the old O-ring from the back side **(see illustration)**. Clean the O-ring groove and install a new O-ring, lightly lubricated with clean engine oil.

6   The remainder of the procedure is the reverse of the disassembly process.

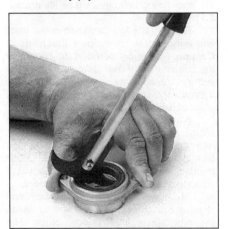

7.3 Use a seal-puller to remove the seal from the retainer

7.4 Drive the new seal in with a hammer and wood block

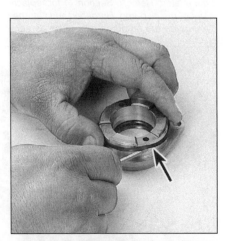

7.5 Remove the old O-ring (arrow) from the seal retainer and install a new one

8.3 Remove the bolts (arrows indicate four on the LH inner cover) and the inner belt covers

8.4 Remove the camshaft cover bolts (arrows)

8.5a Unbolt the EGR pipe (arrow) at the cylinder head . . .

8.5b . . . and at the EGR valve (arrow)

8.5c On the left side, unbolt the ground strap (A) and the water pipe bracket (B)

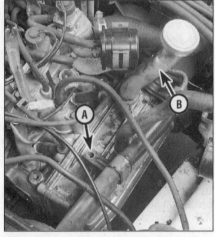

8.5d On the right side, remove the bolt at the air-conditioning hose bracket (A) and remove the oil filler tube (B)

8   Camshafts, rockers and lash adjusters - removal, inspection and installation

Note: *Valve train noise may develop on a high mileage engine. The fault is not generally the lash adjusters, even though the noise is valve-train related. Refer to Section 11 for replacement of the oil pump. Hardened and flattened O-rings on the oil pump can cause an aera-* *tion of the oil that creates valvetrain noise. Either the pump can be replaced with a new unit, or just the seals can be replaced if the pump is in good condition. This should elimi- nate the valvetrain noise.*

Removal

Refer to Illustrations 8.3, 8.4, 8.5a, 8.5b, 8.5c, 8.5d, 8.6, 8.7 and 8.8

1   Refer to Section 5 and remove the tim- ing belts.

8.6 Remove the eight bolts (arrows) and the camshaft housing

2   Refer to Chapter 5 and remove the dis- tributor. Refer to Chapter 1 to drain the cool- ing system, then refer to Chapter 3 and remove the lower pipe/hose from the water pump.

3   Remove the bolts **(see illustration)** and the inner timing belt covers **(see illustration 5.11b)**.

4   Remove the five camshaft cover bolts and remove the covers **(see illustration)**. **Caution:** *Do not pry between the cover and the camshaft housing. Both are aluminum and the sealing surfaces could be damaged. If the cover is stuck, tap the edge with a small block of hardwood and a hammer.*

5   When working on the left side of the engine, remove the EGR pipe and the bracket retaining the ground cable and coolant pipe **(see illustrations)**. On the right side, Unbolt the oil filler tube and the air-conditioning (if equipped) hose bracket **(see illustration)**.

6   Remove the camshaft housing bolts and remove the camshaft and housing as an assembly **(see illustration)**. **Note:** *The camshaft support/seal retainer may remain on the camshaft housing.*

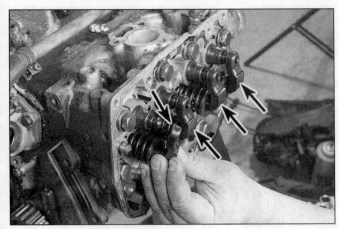

8.7 Remove the rocker arms (arrows)

8.8 Remove the lash adjusters (arrows) - keep the lash adjusters organized so they can be returned to their original locations

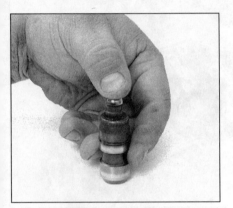

8.10 Test each lash adjuster by depressing the plunger by hand

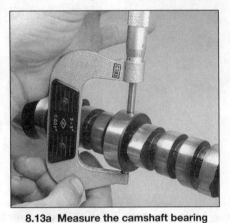

8.13a Measure the camshaft bearing journal diameter

8.13b Measure the camshaft lobe at its greatest dimension . . .

7   Remove the rocker arms **(see illustration)**. Keep the rocker arms organized so they can be returned to their original locations.

8   Remove the hydraulic lash adjusters **(see illustration)**. Keep the lash adjusters organized so they can be returned to their original locations. **Caution:** *Do not use pliers to remove the lash adjusters. If they are varnished and can't be removed easily, spray some carburetor cleaner around their bores and let it soak. The lash adjusters should come out by hand.*

9   The camshaft can be removed from the housing after removing the seal retainer (see Section 7). **Caution:** *Withdraw the camshaft carefully from the housing, so that the lobes do not nick the journal holes in the housing. There are no camshaft bearings to replace, the camshaft rides in the bores of the housing.*

Inspection

Refer to illustrations 8.10, 8.13a, 8.13b, 8.13c, 8.14 and 8.15

10   Check each lash adjuster for signs of wear. Put each adjuster in a pan of oil and push the plunger to "pump up" the hydraulic piston. Stand the lash adjuster on the bench after this treatment and depress the plunger by hand. If it depresses more than 0.5 mm,

the adjuster should be replaced **(see illustration)**.

11   Check the pivot seat in each rocker arm and the pivot faces. Look for galling, stress cracks and unusual wear patterns. If the rocker arms are worn or damaged, replace them with new ones.

12   Visually examine the camshaft lobes, journals, bearing caps, pivot points and metal-to-metal contact areas. Check for score marks, pitting and evidence of overheating (blue, discolored areas). If wear is

excessive or damage is evident, the component will have to be replaced. Also check the front of the camshaft for wear where the seal rides.

13   Using a micrometer, measure camshaft journal diameter and lobe height **(see illustrations)**, and compare your measurements to this Chapter's Specifications. If the lobe height is less than the minimum allowable, the camshaft is worn and must be replaced.

14   Measure the inside diameter of each camshaft journal bore **(see illustration)**. If the

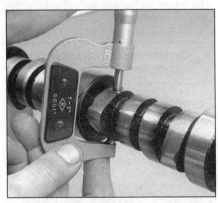

8.13c . . . and subtract the camshaft lobe diameter at its smallest dimension to obtain the lobe lift specification

8.14 Measure the inside diameter of the journal bores in the camshaft housing

8.15 Relief valve assembly

A   Banjo bolt
B   Oil relief pipe assembly
C   Relief spring
D   Relief valve

8.16 Install the camshaft carefully into the housing to avoid nicking the journal bores with the lobes

8.17 Coat the rocker arms with engine assembly lubricant to hold them in position until the camshaft housing can be installed

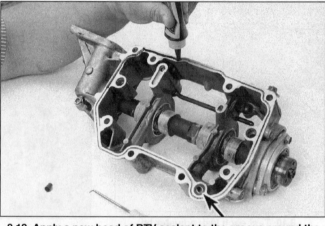

8.18 Apply a new bead of RTV sealant to the groove around the bottom of the camshaft housing and a new O-ring (arrow) around the oil passage

oil clearance (bore diameter less the camshaft journal diameter) is greater than the Specifications, the camshaft and housing must be replaced.

15 Remove the oil relief valve pipe and assembly from the camshaft housing, clean the parts thoroughly and examine the components for any signs of wear or damage **(see illustration)**.

Installation

Refer to illustrations 8.16, 8.17 and 8.18

16 Lubricate the camshaft journals and lobes with moly-based grease or engine assembly lubricant and install it carefully into the camshaft housing **(see illustration)**, then install the camshaft retainer with a new seal and O-ring (see Section 7).

17 Lubricate the lash adjusters with clean engine oil and install them in their respective bores. Install the rocker arms with a coat of moly-based grease or engine assembly lubricant (where they contact the lash adjusters) to hold them in place **(see illustration)**.

18 Clean out the groove on the cylinder-head side of the camshaft housing to remove any old sealant, then apply a new bead of RTV sealant in the groove and a new O-ring around the oil passage **(see illustration)**. Apply lubricant to the camshaft surfaces of

the rocker arms also.

19 Install the camshaft housing (with the dowel in the camshaft pointing straight up at 12 o'clock) to the cylinder head while the sealant is still wet and tighten the bolts to the torque listed in this Chapter's Specifications.

20 The remainder of the installation is the reverse of the disassembly process. **Note:** *Be sure to use new gaskets on the camshaft covers.*

21 Start the engine, listen for unusual valve train noses and check for oil leaks at the valve cover gaskets.

---

9   Cylinder heads- removal and installation

Removal

Refer to Illustrations 9.4 and 9.7

1 Disconnect the negative battery cable.

2 Drain the cooling system and remove the spark plugs (see Chapter 1). Remove the lower splash shields (see Chapter 2, Part A).

3 Remove the timing belts and inner and outer timing belt covers (see Section 5). Remove the camshaft covers, camshaft/camshaft housing assemblies, rocker arms and hydraulic lash adjusters (see Section 8).

4 Disconnect the exhaust pipes from the cylinder heads **(see illustration)**. **Note:** *Apply penetrating oil before beginning the procedure, and allow it to soak-in on the exhaust bolts/nuts.*

5 Refer to Section 4 and remove the intake manifold. Remove any hoses or brackets bolted to the cylinder heads, and on models equipped with air-conditioning, remove the compressor bracket from the left cylinder head. **Note:** *On some models, it may be necessary to remove the alternator and mount (see Chapter 5).*

6 Remove the bottom stud/nuts of the front engine mounts (see Section 14), and raise the engine with a floorjack under the oil pan, using a block of wood to protect the oil pan.

7 On the left side, disconnect the EGR tube as described in Section 4, and also unbolt the EGR bracket from the top-rear of the cylinder head **(see illustration)**.

8 Loosen the cylinder head nuts/bolts in three or four steps.

9 Remove the cylinder heads and the old gaskets. **Note:** *The block and cylinder heads are aluminum. Do not pry between the cylinder heads and the crankcase, as damage to the gasket sealing surfaces may result. Instead use a soft-faced hammer to tap the*

9.4 Disconnect the nuts (arrows) from the exhaust pipes at the cylinder head flange

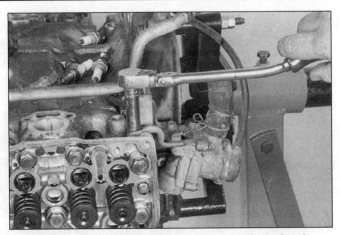

9.7 Unbolt the EGR bracket from the left cylinder head

2B

9.11 Be careful not to gouge the aluminum surfaces of the cylinder head or block when removing the old gasket material

cylinder heads and break the gasket seal.
10   Cylinder head disassembly and inspection procedures are covered in detail in Chapter 2, Part C.

Installation

Refer to Illustrations 9.11, 9.12 and 9.13
11   Clean the gasket mating surfaces of the

9.12 Place the new head gasket over the dowels (arrows) in the block - look for markings on the gaskets to indicate TOP or FRONT

cylinder heads and crankcase **(see illustration)** with lacquer thinner or acetone (they must be clean and oil-free).
12   Refer to the cylinder head gasket manufacturers instructions and if necessary, apply a thin, even coat of the recommended gasket sealant to both sides of the new head gasket then lay it in place **(see illustration)**.

13   Install the cylinder head(s). Lubricate the bolt threads with engine oil, then install them and tighten in three steps to Specifications, according to the recommended sequence **(see illustration)**.
14   Repeat the procedure for the remaining head.

10   Oil pan - removal and installation

Removal

Refer to illustrations 10.4 and 10.6
1   Disconnect the negative battery cable. Raise the vehicle and support it securely on jackstands (see Chapter 1).
2   Drain the engine oil and remove the oil filter (see Chapter 1).
3   Refer to Section 14 and remove the nuts from the engine mount studs at the chassis, then raise the engine two inches with an overhead engine-lift fixture or crane.
4   Remove the bolts securing the oil pan to the engine **(see illustration)**.
5   Tap on the pan with a soft-faced hammer to break the gasket seal. and lower the oil pan off the engine. A thin putty knife can

9.13 Cylinder head bolt/nut tightening sequence

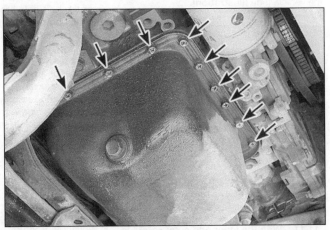

10.4 Remove the oil pan bolts (arrows, not all bolts are visible in this view)

10.6 Unbolt the oil pump pickup tube bracket (arrow) and swivel the pickup slightly to allow the oil pan to drop all the way out

11.5 Remove the five bolts (arrows) and remove the oil pump from the block, with or without the oil filter

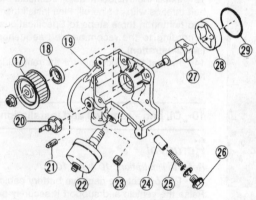

11.6 Oil pump components

17 *Oil pump sprocket*
18 *Oil pump shaft seal*
19 *Oil pump body*
20 *Oil pressure switch*
21 *Plug (models without oil pressure switch)*
22 *Oil pressure sending unit*
23 *Plug (models without oil pressure gauge)*
24 *Oil pressure relief valve*
25 *Oil pressure relief valve spring*
26 *Relief valve plug*
27 *Inner rotor*
28 *Outer rotor*
29 *O-ring seal*

be inserted between the pan and the block to break the gasket seal, but the block is aluminum, so do not use screwdriver or other sharp tool at the pan/block interface. **Caution:** *Before using force on the oil pan, be sure all the bolts have been removed.*
6   The oil pan will only drop down just so far before there is interference with the oil pump pickup tube. Unbolt the pickup tube from the block and remove the oil pan from the vehicle **(see illustration)**.

11.11a With the inner and outer rotors in place, measure the height of the rotors, then . . .

Installation

7   Using a gasket scraper, scrape off all traces of the old gasket from the engine and the oil pan. Be especially careful not to nick or gouge the gasket sealing surfaces of the crankcases (they are made of aluminum and are quite soft}.
8   Clean the oil pan with solvent and dry it thoroughly. Check the gasket sealing surfaces for distortion. If the oil pan is distorted at the bolt-hole areas, straighten the flange by supporting it from below on a wood block and tapping the bolt holes with the rounded end of a ball-peen hammer. Wipe the gasket surfaces clean with a rag soaked in lacquer thinner or acetone.
9   Use a new O-ring when installing the pickup and tap only on the mounting flange to seat the pipe in the crankcase hole. Do not tighten the pickup bracket yet.
10   Before installing the oil pan, apply a thin coat of RTV-type gasket sealer to the crankcase gasket sealing surfaces. Lay a new oil pan gasket in place and carefully apply a coat of gasket sealer to the exposed side of the gasket.
11   Gently lay the oil pan in place under the engine and on the "shelf" of the crossmember (do not disturb the gasket) and complete the installation of the pickup tube. Lift the pan

to the block and install all of the bolts finger-tight. Start with the bolts closest to the center of the pan and tighten them to the torque listed in this Chapter's Specifications using a crisscross pattern. *Do not overtighten them or leakage may occur.*
12   The remainder of installation is the reverse of the removal process. After refilling with fresh oil and installing a new filter, start the engine and watch for oil leaks.

11 Oil pump - removal, inspection and installation

Note: *Valve train noise may develop on a high mileage engine. The fault is not generally the lash adjusters, even though the noise is valvetrain related. Refer to Section 11 for replacement of the oil pump. Hardened and flattened O-rings on the oil pump can cause an aeration of the oil that creates valvetrain noise. Either the pump can be replaced with a new unit, or just the seals can be replaced if the pump is in good condition. This should eliminate the valvetrain noise.*

Removal

Refer to illustration 11.5
1   The oil pump is located on the bottom-front of the engine. It is accessible from underneath the vehicle.
2   Refer to Chapter 1 and drain the engine oil. Remove the oil filter.
3   Raise the front of the vehicle and place it on jackstands.
4   Refer to Section 5 for removal of the timing belt covers and timing belts.
5   Disconnect the electrical connector at the oil pressure sending unit. Remove the mounting bolts and the oil pump **(see illustration)**. Place a drain pan under the oil pump to catch the oil that will be spilled as the pump is removed. **Note:** *There are small cutouts in the front flange of the oil pump sprocket that allow the use of a socket and extension when removing the three oil pump mounting bolts nearest the sprocket.*

Inspection

Refer to illustrations 11.6, 11.11a and 11.11b
6   Disassemble the oil pump, using the illustration as a guide **(see illustration)**. To remove the sprocket, cover the teeth with rags and grip it with a pair of large adjustable pliers while removing the nut from the shaft.
7   Clean the components with solvent, dry them thoroughly and inspect for any obvious damage.
8   Remove the relief valve plug, the washers, the spring and the relief valve from the pump body **(see illustration 11.6)**.
9   Measure the outside diameter of the inner (measure the shaft diameter) and outer rotors and compare your measurements with this Chapter's Specifications.
10   Using a feeler gauge, measure the clearance between the outer rotor and the pump cavity in the block. If the clearance is too

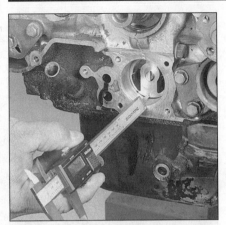

11.11b . . . compare that measurement with the depth of the cavity in the block

11.16 Always install a new pump seal and O-rings (arrows) when installing an oil pump

12.2 Hold a pry bar against two clutch cover bolts while removing the flywheel bolts with a breaker bar

great, obtain new rotors.

11   Check the housing-to-block clearance by measuring the height of the pump body with the rotors in place **(see illustration)**, then measure the depth of the cavity in the block **(see illustration)**. The difference in the two measurements is the clearance.

12   Carefully check the interior surface of the pump housing and the exterior surfaces of the rotors for score marks and damage.

13   Check the relief valve for seat condition and damage.

14   Check the pump housing for clogged oil passages, case cracks and damage.

15   If the specifications are not met or if there is damage to any of the components, replace the pump with a new one.

Installation

Refer to illustration 11.16

16   Reassemble the oil pump components in the reverse order of disassembly. **Note:** *Be sure to use new O-rings and a new shaft seal* **(see illustration)**. *The new shaft seal should be installed into the front of the pump before attaching the sprocket to the pump shaft.*

17   The remainder of installation is the reverse of the removal procedure. **Note:** *Apply a thin coating of RTV sealant to the split lines in the engine crankcase where the oil pump bolts cover them, and coat all the pump components with engine oil before reinstalling the pump.*

18   Refill the engine with fresh oil and install a new filter. Start the engine and observe for proper oil pressure, leaks, or valve train noise.

12   Flywheel/driveplate- removal and installation

Removal

Refer to Illustration 12.2

1   Remove the clutch disc and clutch cover assembly (see Chapter 8).

2   Remove the attaching bolts and separate the flywheel/driveplate from the crankshaft **(see illustration)**. **Note:** *Insert a*

large screwdriver. pry bar or alignment punch through the timing mark hole in the housing and one of the holes in the driveplate to keep it from turning as the bolts are loosened. On manual-transmission models, use a prybar against two clutch cover bolts.

Installation

3   On driveplates (automatic transmission), a secondary reinforcing ring is between the bolts and the driveplate. On manual-transmission models, a pilot bearing assembly will be pressed into the center of the flywheel. Replace it with a new one if a new clutch is being installed (see Chapter 8).

4   Apply liquid gasket sealer to the bolt threads. Hold the flywheel/driveplate in position and install the bolts in the end of the crankshaft. On automatic-transmission models, align the small hole in the driveplate with the mark on the backplate before installing the bolts. **Note:** *The flywheel/driveplate can only be installed in one position, since the bolt holes are not equally spaced. If the bolt holes don't line up, rotate the flywheel relative to the crankshaft until they all line up.*

5   While holding the flywheel/driveplate so that it doesn't turn, tighten the bolts (using a crisscross pattern) to the specified torque.

13.3 Use a seal-remover tool to pry the old rear seal from the back of the block

6   Install the clutch disc and clutch cover assembly as described in Chapter 8.

13   Rear main oil seal - replacement

Refer to illustration 13.3 and 13.6

1   Refer to Chapters 7 and 8 for removal of the transaxle and clutch assembly.

2   Refer to Section 12 for removal of the flywheel or driveplate.

3   Pry the rear main oil seal from the back of the block with a screwdriver or a seal-remover tool, making sure not to nick the crankshaft seal surface with the tool **(see illustration)**.

4   Clean the bore of the block of dirt and make sure the seal-mounting surface is free of burrs.

5   Lubricate the new seal's inner lip with multi-purpose grease, and the outer diameter with clean engine oil.

6   Drive the new seal in place squarely with a seal-driver, large socket, or section of pipe that's the same diameter as the seal. Drive the seal to the depth that the original was installed **(see illustration)**.

7   The remainder of assembly is the reverse of the disassembly process.

13.6 Drive the new seal in squarely with a socket, or tap in evenly all around with a flat punch

14 Engine mounts - check and replacement

Check

1   Engine mounts seldom require attention, but broken or deteriorated mounts should be replaced immediately or the added strain placed on the driveline components may cause damage.

2   During the check, the engine must be raised slightly to remove the weight from the mounts. Disconnect the negative battery cable from the battery.

3   Raise the vehicle and support it securely on jackstands, then position the jack under the engine oil pan. Place a wood block between the jack head and the oil pan, then carefully raise the engine just enough to take the weight off the mounts.

4   Check the mounts to see if the rubber is cracked, hardened or separated from the metal plates. Sometimes the rubber will split right down the center. Rubber preservative may be applied to the mounts to slow deterioration.

5   Check for relative movement between the mount plates and the engine or frame (use a large screwdriver or pry bar to attempt to move the mounts). If movement is noted, lower the engine and tighten the mount fasteners.

Replacement

Refer to illustrations 14.6

6   Remove the engine mount locknuts from the studs going through the crossmember **(see illustration)**.

7   Raise the front of the engine high enough for the mount studs to clear the frame, but do not force the engine up too high. If it touches anything before the mounts are free, remove the part for clearance.

8   Remove the two bolts on each mount that secure them to the engine block, then remove the mounts.

9   Slip the new engine mounts between the crossmember and the engine. Start the bolts into the engine block and tighten them to Specifications.

10   Lower the engine slowly, making sure that both lower studs go through their respective holes in the crossmember. Remove the block of wood and lower the engine to its original height and tighten the locknuts securely. **Note:** *On vehicles equipped with self-locking nuts and bolts, replace the nuts with new ones whenever they are disassembled.*

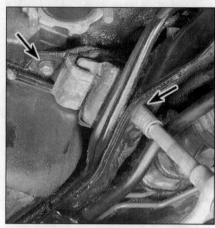

14.6 Remove the locknut (lower arrow) from the engine mount stud at the crossmember - upper arrow indicates one of the mount-to-block bolts, the other is towards the rear of the crossmember

Chapter 2 Part C
General engine overhaul procedures

Contents

Specifications

Overhead valve (OHV) engines

General

Bore and stroke	
1600 cc	3.62 x 2.36 in (92 x 60 mm)
1800 cc	3.62 x 2.64 in (92 x 67 mm)
Displacement	
1600 cc engine	97 cu inches (1595 cc)
1800 cc engine	109 cu inches (1781 cc)
Oil pressure at 2500 engine rpm	57 psi
Valve clearances	See Chapter 1

Cylinder head

Valve seat angle	45°
Valve seat width	
Intake	0.028 to 0.051 inch (0.7 to 1.3 mm)
Exhaust	0.039 to 0.071 inch (1.0 to 1.8 mm)
Valve guide bore diameter	0.3152 to 0.3158 inch (8.000 to 8.015 mm)
Valve guide protrusion (1980 through 1982)	
Intake	0.6895 to 0.7092 inch (17.5 to 18.0 mm)
Exhaust	0.8865 to 0.9062 inch (22.5 to 23.0 mm)
Valve guide protrusion (1983 only)	
Intake	0.6895 to 0.7289 inch (17.5 to 18.5 mm)
Exhaust	0.8865 to 0.9259 inch (22.5 to 23.5 mm)

Overhead valve (OHV) engines (continued)

Valves

Valve face angle..	45°
Margin width (standard)	
Intake...	0.059 inch (1.5 mm)
Exhaust..	0.051 inch (1.3 mm)
Margin width (service limit)	
Intake...	0.0394 inch (1.0 mm)
Exhaust..	0.315 inch (0.8 mm)
Stem diameter	
Intake...	0.3132 to 0.3138 inch (7.950 to 7.965 mm)
Exhaust..	0.3134 to 0.3136 inch (7.945 to 7.960 mm)
Valve stem-to-guide clearance (standard)	
Intake...	0.0013 to 0.0025 inch (0.035 to 0.065 mm)
Exhaust..	0.0016 to 0.0028 inch (0.040 to 0.070 mm)
Valve stem-to-guide clearance (service limit)............................	0.006 inch (0.15 mm)

Valve springs

Free length	
Inner spring	1.922 inches (48.8 mm)
Outer spring	1.785 inches (45.3 mm)
Out-of-square limit	0.0788 inch (2.0 mm)

Valve lifters

Lifter diameter...	0.8253 to 0.8262 inch (20.949 to 20.970 mm)
Lifter bore diameter	0.8274 to 0.8282 inch (21.000 to 21.021 mm)
Lifter-to-bore clearance	
Standard...	0.0011 to 0.0028 inch (0.030 to 0.072 mm)
Service limit	0.0039 inch (0.100 mm)

Cylinder bores

Diameter	3.6242 to 3.6253 inches (91.985 to 92.015 mm)
Taper limit	0.0012 inch (0.05 mm)
Out-of-round limit	0.0012 inch (0.05 mm)
Maximum increase in diameter (boring and honing)	0.0197 inch (0.5 mm)
Maximum difference in diameter between cylinders................	0.0012 inch (0.05 mm)
Cylinder-to-piston clearance	
Standard...	0.0004 to 0.0016 inch (0.01 to 0.04 mm)
Service limit	0.0024 inch (0.06 mm)

Pistons and rings

Piston diameter (std.)...	3.6232 to 3.6244 inches (91.960 to 91.990 mm)
Piston pin diameter..	0.8271 to 0.8274 inch (20.992 to 21.000 mm)
Piston pin bore diameter	0.8273 to 0.8277 inch (20.999 to 21.009 mm)
Piston pin-to-bore clearance...	0.0001 to 0.0004 inch (0.004 to 0.010 mm)
Piston ring end gap	
Top and second rings, standard	0.0087 to 0.0138 inch (0.20 to 0.35 mm)
Top and second rings, limit	
1980	0.0138 inch (0.35 mm)
1981 to 1987	0.0591 inch (1.5 mm)
Oil ring side rails	0.008 to 0.035 inch (0.20 to 0.9 mm)
Piston ring-to-groove clearance	
Top ring	
Standard	0.0016 to 0.0032 inch (0.04 to 0.08 mm)
Service limit..	0.006 inch (0.15 mm)
Second ring	
Standard	0.0012 to 0.0026 inch (0.03 to 0.07 mm)
Service limit..	0.006 inch (0.15 mm)
Oil ring	0

Connecting rods

Side clearance	
Standard	0.0028 to 0.0130 inch 0.07 to 0.33 mm)
Service limit	0.0157 inch (0.4 mm)
Piston pin bushing bore diameter	
1980 to 1982	0.8274 to 0.8298 inch (21.000 to 21.061 mm)
1983 to 1987	0.8274 to 0.8280 inch (21.000 to 21.016 mm)
Piston pin-to-rod bore clearance	
1980 and 1981	0.000 to 0.0016 inch (0.001 to 0.0417 mm)
1982 to 1987	0.0002 to 0.0004 inch (0.004 to 0.010 mm)

Crankshaft and bearings

Main bearing journal diameter (std.)

    1800 cc engine .... 2.1652 to 2.1658 inches (54.955 to 54.970 mm)

    1600 cc engine

        Front/rear journals .... 1.9683 to 1.9688 inches (49.957 to 49.970 mm)

        Center journal .... 1.9688 to 1.9693 inches (49.970 to 49.982 mm)

Connecting rod bearing journal diameter (std.) .... 1.7728 to 1.7734 inches (44.995 to 45.010 mm)

Bearing journal taper limit .... 0.0027 inch (0.07 mm)

Bearing journal out-of-round limit .... 0.0012 (0.03 mm)

bearing journal regrind limit .... 0.001 inch (0.25 mm)

Crankshaft runout limit .... 0.0014 inch (0.035 mm)

Crankshaft endplay

    Standard

        1980 and 1981 .... 0.0016 to 0.0054 inch (0.040 to 0.137 mm)

        1982 to 1987 .... 0.0004 to 0.0037 inch (0.010 to 0.095 mm)

    Service limit .... 0.012 inch (0.3 mm)

Main bearing oil clearance

    Standard (1800 cc engine)

        Center bearing .... 0.0004 to 0.0010 inch (0.010 to 0.025 mm)

        Front/rear bearings .... 0.0004 to 0.0012 inch (0.010 to 0.030 mm)

    Standard (1600 cc engine)

        Center bearing .... 0.0004 to 0.0012 inch (0.010 to 0.030 mm)

        Front/rear bearings .... 0.0004 to 0.0014 inch (0.010 to 0.035 mm)

    Service limit

        Center bearing .... 0.0017 inch (0.045 mm)

        Front/rear bearings .... 0.0022 inch (0.055 mm)

Connecting rod bearing oil clearance

    Standard .... 0.0008 to 0.0028 inch (0.020 to 0.070 mm)

    Service limit .... 0.004 inch (0.10 mm)

Camshaft

Runout limit .... 0.002 inch (0.05 mm)

Thrust clearance

    Standard .... 0.0008 to 0.0035 inch (0.020 to 0.090 mm)

    Service limit .... 0.008 inch (0.2 mm)

Cam lobe height

    Standard .... 1.283 to 1.287 inches (32.57 to 32.67 mm)

    Wear limit .... 0.006 inch (0.15 mm)

Camshaft bearing journal diameter

    Front/center journals

        1800 cc engine .... 1.2592 to 1.2598 inches (31.959 to 31.975 mm)

        1600 cc engine .... 1.0227 to 1.0234 inches (25.959 to 25.975 mm)

    Rear journal .... 1.4157 to 1.4163 inches (35.959 to 35.975 mm)

Camshaft bearing bore diameter (in crankcase)

    Front/center bores

        1800 cc engine .... 1.2598 to 1.2605 inches (32.00 to 32.018 mm)

        1600 cc engine .... 1.0236 to 1.0243 inches (26.00 to 26.018 mm)

    Rear bore .... 1.4173 to 1.4180 inches (36.00 to 36.018 mm)

Camshaft bearing oil clearance

    Standard .... 0.0010 to 0.0023 inch (0.025 to 0.059 mm)

    Service limit .... 0.0039 inch (0.100 mm)

Camshaft gear axial runout limit .... 0.0098 inch (0.25 mm)

Camshaft gear-to-crankshaft gear backlash

    Standard .... 0.0004 to 0.0020 inch (0.010 to 0.050 mm)

    Service limit .... 0.0039 inch (0.10 mm)

Crankcase

Mating surface warpage limit .... 0.002 inch (0.05 mm)

Stud protrusion from crankcase surface

    1600 cc engine .... 3.563 to 3.642 inches (90.5 to 92.5 mm)

    1800 cc engine .... 3.602 to 3.681 inches (91.5 to 93.5 mm)

Torque specifications

Ft lbs (unless otherwise indicated)

Oil pressure sensing unit .... 16 to 20

Engine-to-transmission bolts .... 34 to 40

Engine mount-to-crossmember nut .... 15 to 24

Front exhaust pipe-to-engine .... 18 to 25

Pitching stopper nut .... 89 to 160 in-lbs

Connecting rod nut .... 29 to 31

2C

Overhead valve (OHV) engines (continued)

Crankcase bolts and nuts

6 mm	40 to 44 in-lbs
8 mm	17 to 20
10 mm	29 to 35
Crankcase service hole plugs..	46 to 56
Oil strainer mounting bolt	17 to 20
Large crankcase studs	18 to 32

Overhead cam (OHC) engines

General

Bore and stroke	3.62 x 2.64 inches (92 x 67 mm)
Displacement..	1800 cc (1781 cc)
Oil pressure at 2500 rpm	57 psi

Cylinder head

Valve seat angle..	45°
Valve seat width	
Intake...	0. 0 to 0.071 inch (1.2 to 1.8 mm)
Exhaust...	0.059 to 0.079 inch (1.5 to 2.0 mm)
Valve guide bore diameter..	0.2758 to 0.2763 inch (7.000 to 7.015 mm)
Valve guide protrusion..	0.6895 to 0.7289 inch (17.5 to 18.5 mm)

Valves

Valve face angle..	45°
Margin width	
Standard..	0.051 inch (1.3 mm)
Limit...	0.0315 inch (0.8 mm)
Stem diameter	
Intake...	0.2738 to 0.2744 inch (6.950 to 6.965 mm)
Exhaust...	0.2736 to 0.2742 inch (6.945 to 6.960 mm)
Valve stem-to-guide clearance (standard)	
Intake...	0.0013 to 0.0025 inch (0.035 to 0.065 mm)
Exhaust...	0.0016 to 0.0028 inch (0.040 to 0.070 mm)
Valve stem-to-guide clearance (service limit).......................	0.006 inch (0.15 mm)

Valve springs

Free length	
Inner spring	1.982 inches (50.3 mm)
Outer spring	2.037 inches (51.7 mm)
Tension at height	
Inner spring	
19.8 to 22.7 pounds	@ 1.516 inches (38.5 mm)
45.2 to 51.8 pounds	@ 1.122 inches (28.5 mm)
Outer spring	
1985	
39.9 to 45.9 pounds	@ 1.634 inches (41.5 mm)
100.5 to 115.5 pounds	@ 1.240 inches (31.5 mm)
1986 and later	
45.6 to 53.6 pounds	@ 1.634 inches (41.5 mm)
112 to 129 pounds	@ 1.240 inches (31.5 mm)
Out-of-square limit	0.087 inch (2.2 mm)

Cylinder bores

Diameter	3.6242 to 3.6253 inches (91.985 to 92.015 mm)
Taper limit..	0.0012 inch (0.05 mm)
Out-of-round limit	0.0012 inch (0.05 mm)
Maximum increase in diameter (boring and honing)	0.0197 inch (0.5 mm)
Maximum difference in diameter between cylinders..............	0.0012 inch (0.05 mm)
Cylinder-to-piston clearance	
Standard	
1985	0.0004 to 0.0016 inch (0.010 to 0.040 mm)
1986 to 1994	0.0006 to 0.0014 inch (0.015 to 0.035 mm)
Service limit...	0.0024 inch (0.06 mm)

Pistons and rings

Piston diameter (std.)	
1985	3.6232 to 3.6244 inches (91.960 to 91.990 mm)
1986 to 1994	3.6209 to 3.6213 inches (91.970 to 91.980 mm)
Piston pin diameter	0.8265 to 0.8268 inch (20.994 to 21.000 mm)
Piston pin bore diameter	0.8273 to 0.8277 inch (20.999 to 21.009 mm)
Piston pin-to-piston bore clearance	0.0004 to 0.00059 inch (0.001 to 0.015 mm)
Piston ring end gap	
Top and second rings	
Standard	0.0087 to 0.0138 inch (0.20 to 0.35 mm)
Limit	0.0591 inch (1.5 mm)
Oil ring side rails	0.0118 to 0.0355 inch (0.3 to 0.9 mm)
Piston ring-to-groove clearance	
Top ring	
Standard	0.0016 to 0.0032 inch (0.04 to 0.08 mm)
Service limit	0.006 inch (0.15 mm)
Second ring	
Standard	0.0012 to 0.0026 inch (0.03 to 0.07 mm)
Service limit	0.006 inch (0.15 mm)
Oil ring	0

Connecting rods

Side clearance	
Standard	0.0028 to 0.0130 inch 0.07 to 0.33 mm)
Service limit	0.0157 inch (0.4 mm)
Piston pin bushing bore diameter	0.8274 to 0.8280 inch (21.000 to 21.016 mm)
Piston pin-to-rod bore clearance	0 to 0.0009 inch (0 to 0.022 mm)

Crankshaft and bearings

Main bearing journal diameter (std.)	
Front journal	2.1653 to 2.1659 inches (54.957 to 54.972 mm)
Center journal	2.16518 to 2.16581 inches (54.954 to 54.970 mm)
Rear journal	2.16523 to 2.16581 inches (54.955 to 54.970 mm)
Connecting rod bearing journal diameter (std.)	1.7728 to 1.7734 inches (44.995 to 45.010 mm)
Bearing journal taper limit	0.0027 inch (0.07 mm)
Bearing journal out-of-round limit	0.0012 (0.03 mm)
bearing journal regrind limit	0.001 inch (0.25 mm)
Crankshaft endplay	0.0004 to 0.0037 inch (0.010 to 0.095 mm)
Service limit	0.012 inch (0.3 mm)
Main bearing oil clearance	
Standard	
Center bearing	0.0003 to 0.0011 inch (0.008 to 0.027 mm)
Front/rear bearings	0.0001 to 0.0014 inch (0.003 to 0.036 mm)
Service limit	
Center bearing	0.0018 inch (0.045 mm)
Front/rear bearings	0.0022 inch (0.055 mm)
Connecting rod bearing oil clearance	
Standard	0.0004 to 0.0.0021 inch (0.010 to 0.054 mm)
Service limit	0.0039 inch (0.10 mm)

Torque specifications

	Ft lbs (unless otherwise indicated)
Oil pressure sending unit	16 to 20
Engine-to-transmission bolts	34 to 40
Engine mount-to-crossmember nut	15 to 24
Front exhaust pipe-to-engine nuts	18 to 25
Pitching stopper nut	89 to 160 in-lbs
Connecting rod nut	29 to 31
Crankcase bolts and nuts	
6 mm	40 to 44 in-lbs
8 mm	17 to 20
10 mm	29 to 35
Crankcase service hole plugs	46 to 56
Oil strainer mounting bolt	17 to 20

2C

2.4a The oil pressure sending unit (arrow) is located on the oil pump assembly

2.4b Remove the oil pressure sending unit and attach an oil pressure gauge - be sure the fittings you use have the same thread as the sender

1 General information

Included in this portion of Chapter 2 are the general overhaul procedures for the cylinder head(s) and internal engine components.

The information ranges from advice concerning preparation for an overhaul and the purchase of replacement parts to detailed, step-by-step procedures covering removal and installation of internal engine components and the inspection of parts.

The following Sections have been written based on the assumption that the engine has been removed from the vehicle. For information concerning in-vehicle engine repair, as well as removal and installation of the external components necessary for the overhaul, see Parts A and B of this Chapter and Section 6 of this Part.

The Specifications included in this Part are only those necessary for the inspection and overhaul procedures which follow. Refer to Parts A and B for additional Specifications.

2 Engine overhaul - general information

Refer to illustrations 2.4a and 2.4b

It is not always easy to determine when, or if, an engine should be completely overhauled, as a number of factors must be considered.

High mileage is not necessarily an indication that an overhaul is needed, while low mileage does not preclude the need for an overhaul. Frequency of servicing is probably the most important consideration. An engine that has had regular and frequent oil and filter changes, as well as other required maintenance, will most likely give many thousands of miles of reliable service. Conversely, a neglected engine may require an overhaul very early in its life.

Excessive oil consumption is an indication that piston rings and/or valve guides are in need of attention. Make sure that oil leaks are not responsible before deciding that the

rings and/or guides are bad. Test the cylinder compression (see Section 3) or have a leak down test performed by an experienced tune-up mechanic to determine the extent of the work required.

If the engine is making obvious knocking or rumbling noises, the connecting rod and/or main bearings are probably at fault. To accurately test oil pressure, temporarily connect a mechanical oil pressure gauge in place of the oil pressure sending unit **(see illustrations)**. Compare the reading to the pressure listed in this Chapter's Specifications. If the pressure is extremely low, the bearings and/or oil pump are probably worn out.

Loss of power, rough running, excessive valve train noise and high fuel consumption rates may also point to the need for an overhaul, especially if they are all present at the same time. If a complete tune-up does not remedy the situation, major mechanical work is the only solution.

An engine overhaul involves restoring the internal parts to the specifications of a new engine. During an overhaul, the piston rings are replaced and the cylinder walls are reconditioned (rebored and/or honed). If a rebore is done, new pistons are required. The main bearings, connecting rod bearings and camshaft bearings are generally replaced with new ones and, if necessary, the crankshaft may be reground to restore the journals. Generally, the valves are serviced as well, since they are usually in less-than-perfect condition at this point. While the engine is being overhauled, other components, such as the distributor, starter and alternator, can be rebuilt as well. The end result should be a like-new engine that will give many trouble free miles. **Note:** *Critical cooling system components such as the hoses, the drivebelts, the thermostat and the water pump MUST be replaced with new parts when an engine is overhauled. The radiator should be checked carefully to ensure that it isn't clogged or leaking. Some engine rebuilding shops will not honor their engine warranty unless you have had the radiator replaced or profession-*

ally cleaned. If in doubt, replace it with a new one. Also, we do not recommend overhauling the oil pump - always install a new one when an engine is rebuilt.

Before beginning the engine overhaul, read through the entire procedure to familiarize yourself with the scope and requirements of the job. Overhauling an engine is not difficult, but it is time consuming. Plan on the vehicle being tied up for a minimum of two weeks, especially if parts must be taken to an automotive machine shop for repair or reconditioning. Check on availability of parts and make sure that any necessary special tools and equipment are obtained in advance. Most work can be done with typical hand tools, although a number of precision measuring tools are required for inspecting parts to determine if they must be replaced. Often an automotive machine shop will handle the inspection of parts and offer advice concerning reconditioning and replacement. **Note:** *Always wait until the engine has been completely disassembled and all components, especially the engine block, have been inspected before deciding what service and repair operations must be performed by an automotive machine shop. Since the block's condition will be the major factor to consider when determining whether to overhaul the original engine or buy a rebuilt one, never purchase parts or have machine work done on other components until the block has been thoroughly inspected. As a general rule, time is the primary cost of an overhaul, so it does not pay to install worn or substandard parts.*

As a final note, to ensure maximum life and minimum trouble from a rebuilt engine, everything must be assembled with care in a spotlessly clean environment.

3 Cylinder compression check

Refer to illustration 3.6

1   A compression check will tell you what mechanical condition the upper end (pistons, rings, valves, head gaskets) of your engine is in. Specifically, it can tell you if the compression is down due to leakage caused by worn piston rings, defective valves and seats or a blown head gasket. **Note:** *The engine must be at normal operating temperature for this check and the battery must be fully charged.*

2   Begin by cleaning the area around the spark plugs before you remove them (compressed air works best for this). This will prevent dirt from getting into the cylinders as the compression check is being done.

3   Remove all of the spark plugs from the engine (see Chapter 1).

4   Block the throttle wide open.

5   Disconnect the primary wires from the coil(s).

6   With the compression gauge in the number one spark plug hole, crank the engine over at least four compression strokes and watch the gauge **(see illustration)**. The

compression should build up quickly in a healthy engine. Low compression on the first stroke, followed by gradually increasing pressure on successive strokes, indicates worn piston rings. A low compression reading on the first stroke, which does not build up during successive strokes, indicates leaking valves or a blown head gasket (a cracked head could also be the cause). Record the highest gauge reading obtained.

7   Repeat the procedure for the remaining cylinders and compare the results to the Specifications.

8   Add some engine oil (about three squirts from a plunger-type oil can) to each cylinder, through the spark plug hole, and repeat the test.

9   If the compression increases after the oil is added, the piston rings are definitely worn. If the compression does not increase significantly, the leakage is occurring at the valves or head gasket. Leakage past the valves may be caused by burned valve seats and/or faces or warped, cracked or bent valves.

10   If two adjacent cylinders have equally low compression, there is a strong possibility that the head gasket between them is blown. The appearance of coolant in the combustion chambers or the crankcase would verify this condition.

11   If the compression is unusually high, the combustion chambers are probably coated with carbon deposits. If that is the case, the cylinder heads should be removed and decarbonized.

12   If compression is way down or varies greatly between cylinders, it would be a good idea to have a leak-down test performed by an automotive repair shop. This test will pinpoint exactly where the leakage is occurring and how severe it is.

4   Vacuum gauge diagnostic checks

Refer to illustration 4.4

A vacuum gauge provides valuable information about what is going on in the engine at a low-cost. You can check for worn rings or cylinder walls, leaking head or intake manifold gaskets, incorrect carburetor adjustments, restricted exhaust, stuck or burned valves, weak valve springs, improper ignition or valve timing and ignition problems.

Unfortunately, vacuum gauge readings are easy to misinterpret, so they should be used in conjunction with other tests to confirm the diagnosis.

Both the absolute readings and the rate of needle movement are important for accurate interpretation. Most gauges measure vacuum in inches of mercury (in-Hg). The following references to vacuum assume the diagnosis is being performed at sea level. As elevation increases (or atmospheric pressure decreases), the reading will decrease. For every 1,000 foot increase in elevation above approximately 2000 feet, the gauge readings will decrease about one inch of mercury.

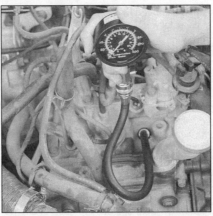

3.6 A compression gauge with a threaded fitting for the spark plug hole is preferred over the type that requires hand pressure to maintain the seal - be sure to open the throttle valve as far as possible during the compression check

Connect the vacuum gauge directly to intake manifold vacuum, not to ported (throttle body) vacuum **(see illustration)**. Be sure no hoses are left disconnected during the test or false readings will result.

Before you begin the test, allow the engine to warm up completely. Block the wheels and set the parking brake. With the transmission in Park, start the engine and allow it to run at normal idle speed. **Warning:** *Carefully inspect the fan blades for cracks or damage before starting the engine. Keep your hands and the vacuum gauge clear of the fan and do not stand in front of the vehicle or in line with the fan when the engine is running.*

Read the vacuum gauge; an average, healthy engine should normally produce about 17 to 22 inches of vacuum with a fairly steady needle. Refer to the following vacuum gauge readings and what they indicate about the engine's condition.

1   A low steady reading usually indicates a leaking gasket between the intake manifold and cylinder head(s) or throttle body, a leaky vacuum hose, late ignition timing or incorrect camshaft timing. Check ignition timing with a timing light and eliminate all other possible causes, utilizing the tests provided in this Chapter before you remove the timing chain cover to check the timing marks.

2   If the reading is three to eight inches below normal and it fluctuates at that low reading, suspect an intake manifold gasket leak at an intake port or a faulty fuel injector.

3   If the needle has regular drops of about two-to-four inches at a steady rate, the valves are probably leaking. Perform a compression check or leak-down test to confirm this.

4   An irregular drop or down-flick of the needle can be caused by a sticking valve or an ignition misfire. Perform a compression check or leak-down test and read the spark plugs.

5   A rapid vibration of about four in.-Hg vibration at idle combined with exhaust

4.4 An inexpensive vacuum gauge can tell a lot about the tune and general condition of an engine - test it before beginning an overhaul

smoke indicates worn valve guides. Perform a leak-down test to confirm this. If the rapid vibration occurs with an increase in engine speed, check for a leaking intake manifold gasket or head gasket, weak valve springs, burned valves or ignition misfire.

6   A slight fluctuation, say one inch up and down, may mean ignition problems. Check all the usual tune-up items and, if necessary, run the engine on an ignition analyzer.

7   If there is a large fluctuation, perform a compression or leak-down test to look for a weak or dead cylinder or a blown head gasket.

8   If the needle moves slowly through a wide range, check for a clogged PCV system, incorrect idle fuel mixture, carburetor/throttle body or intake manifold gasket leaks.

9   Check for a slow return after revving the engine by quickly snapping the throttle open until the engine reaches about 2,500 rpm and let it shut. Normally the reading should drop to near zero, rise above normal idle reading (about 5 in.-Hg over) and then return to the previous idle reading. If the vacuum returns slowly and doesn't peak when the throttle is snapped shut, the rings may be worn. If there is a long delay, look for a restricted exhaust system (often the muffler or catalytic converter). An easy way to check this is to temporarily disconnect the exhaust ahead of the suspected part and redo the test.

5   Engine removal - methods and precautions

If you have decided that an engine must be removed for overhaul or major repair work, several preliminary steps should be taken.

Locating a suitable work area is extremely important. A shop is, of course, the most desirable place to work. Adequate work space, along with storage space for the vehicle, will be needed. If a shop or garage is not available, at the very least a flat, level, clean

2C

6.16 Unbolt the pitching stopper rod (arrow) at the bellhousing

work surface made of concrete or asphalt is required.

Cleaning the engine compartment and engine before beginning the removal procedure will help keep tools clean and organized.

An engine hoist or A-frame will be needed. Make sure that the equipment is rated in excess of the combined weight of the engine and its accessories. Safety is of primary importance, considering the potential hazards involved in lifting the engine out of the vehicle.

If the engine is being removed by a novice, a helper should be available. Advice and aid from someone more experienced would also be helpful. There are many instances when one person cannot simultaneously perform all of the operations required when lifting the engine out of the vehicle.

Plan the operation ahead of time. Arrange for or obtain all of the tools and equipment you will need prior to beginning the job. Some of the equipment necessary to perform engine removal and installation safely and with relative ease are (in addition to an engine hoist) a heavy duty floor jack, complete sets of wrenches and sockets as described in the front of this manual, wooden blocks and plenty of rags and cleaning solvent for mopping up spilled oil, coolant and gasoline. If the hoist is to be rented, make sure that you arrange for it in advance and perform beforehand all of the operations possible without it. This will save you money and time.

Plan for the vehicle to be out of use for a considerable amount of time. A machine shop will be required to perform some of the work which the do-it-yourselfer cannot accomplish due to a lack of special equipment. These shops often have a busy schedule, so it would be wise to consult them before removing the engine in order to accurately estimate the amount of time required to rebuild or repair components that may need work.

Always use extreme caution when removing and installing the engine. Serious injury can result from careless actions. Plan ahead, take your time and a job of this

nature, although major, can be accomplished successfully.

---

6   Engine- removal

Refer to illustrations 6.16 and 6.26
Note: *The engine must be removed as a separate unit with the transmission left in place in the vehicle. Do not attempt to remove the transmission with the engine.*

1   Before starting this procedure. some method of lifting the engine must be devised. Ideally, a small crane mounted on wheels should be rented or borrowed. These are readily available and easy to use. An alternative would be to suspend a chain fall or cable hoist from the garage rafters or a framework fabricated from large timbers. ' Regardless of which type of hoist support is utilized, it must be strong enough to support the full weight of the engine. Do not take chances or cut corners here, as serious injury and damage to the engine and vehicle could result.

2   The following sequence of operations does not necessarily need to be performed in the order given. It is, rather, a checklist of everything that must be disconnected or removed before the engine can be lifted out of the vehicle. It is very important that all linkages, electrical wiring, hoses and cables be removed or disconnected before attempting to lift the engine clear of the vehicle, so double-check everything thoroughly. **Caution:** *If the vehicle is equipped with air conditioning have the system discharged and the refrigerant recovered by an automotive air conditioning shop. Do not attempt to do this at home as serious injury or damage could result.*

3   Scribe (or mark with paint) the location of the hood hinge brackets on the hood (to ensure proper alignment of the hood during reinstallation). Loosen and remove the bolts attaching the hood to the brackets and lift the hood carefully away from the vehicle (with the help of an assistant).

4   Remove the splash shields from the underside of the engine.

5   Remove the spare tire and support bracket.

6   Disconnect both cables from the battery (negative first, then positive).

7   Refer to Chapter 1 and drain the entire cooling system (including the engine), then remove the lower radiator hose.

8   Unplug the automatic transmission cooling fan connector (if applicable).

9   Disconnect the hoses and wiring from the air cleaner and remove the air cleaner assembly. **Note:** *Plug the carburetor opening to keep dirt out.*

10   Refer to Chapter 3 and remove the engine cooling fans, radiator, radiator hoses, and the air conditioner compressor (if equipped).

11   Refer to Chapter 5 and remove the alternator and mount, then the starter motor.

12   Remove the ground cable from the top-front of the left cylinder head.

6.26 Raise the engine enough to clear the engine mounts from the crossmember, then pull the engine forward to separate it from the transmission

13   Refer to Chapter 5 and remove the distributor and spark plug wires.

14   Refer to Part A or B of this Chapter and remove the intake manifold, tagging all of the vacuum, fuel and electrical connectors for ease of reassembly. **Note:** *Refer to Chapter 4 first for the procedure to relieve the fuel system pressure on fuel-injected models.*

15   Disconnect the heater hoses at the bellhousing/transmission parting line.

16   Remove the engine pitching stopper rod **(see illustration)**. Remove the spark plug wire bracket from the top front of the engine so the chain does not damage it as the engine is removed.

17   If vehicle is equipped with power steering, refer to Chapter 10 and remove the power steering pump. Remove the pump bracket as well.

18   Raise the front of the vehicle and support it on jackstands. Block the rear wheels to keep the vehicle from rolling.

19   Refer to Chapter 4 and disconnect the electrical lead from the oxygen sensor (not all models), then detach the front exhaust pipe from the head pipe flanges on each cylinder head.

20   If equipped with an automatic transaxle, refer to Chapter 7B for removing the converter-to-driveplate fasteners.

21   Remove the two upper engine-to-transmission mounting bolts and loosen the two lower engine-to-transmission mounting nuts.

22   Refer to Part A or B of this Chapter and remove the front engine mount retaining nuts.

23   Attach the engine hoist chain or cables to the engine lifting hooks, then support the transmission with a hydraulic floor jack.

24   Take the slack out of the hoist chain or cables, then remove the two lower engine-to-transmission mounting nuts.

25   Before proceeding, make sure that all wires, hoses, lines and brackets have been disconnected.

26   Very carefully lift the engine until the front engine mount studs clear the crossmember, then slowly move the engine forward and up **(see illustration)**. Be very care-

ful not to allow the engine to strike or catch on the engine compartment components or the body as it is being removed.

27 With the engine clear of the vehicle, lower it to the shop floor and remove the flywheel/driveplate (see Part A or Part B of this Chapter), then remove the flywheel housing (see Part A or B of this Chapter).

28 Because of the unusual design of the Subaru engine, it may be more desirable to disassemble the engine on a large, suitably-strong workbench, rather than on a traditional engine stand. It is difficult to separate the crankcase halves on a stand, and when stripped of the exterior parts, the engine is light enough to maneuver around on the bench by hand.

7 Engine rebuilding alternatives

The do-it-yourselfer is faced with a number of options when performing an engine overhaul. The decision to replace the engine block, piston/connecting rod assemblies and crankshaft depends on a number of factors, with the number one consideration being the condition of the block. Other considerations are cost, access to machine shop facilities, parts availability, time required to complete the project and the extent of prior mechanical experience on the part of the do-it-yourselfer.

Some of the rebuilding alternatives include:

Individual parts - If the inspection procedures reveal that the engine block and most engine components are in reusable condition, purchasing individual parts may be the most economical alternative. The block, crankshaft and piston/connecting rod assemblies should all be inspected carefully. Even if the block shows little wear, the cylinder bores should be surface-honed.

Crankshaft kit - This rebuild package consists of a reground crankshaft and a matched set of pistons and connecting rods. Piston rings and the necessary bearings will be included in the kit. These kits are commonly available for standard cylinder bores, as well as for engine blocks which have been bored to a regular oversize.

Short block - A short block consists of an engine block with a crankshaft and piston/connecting rod assemblies already installed. All new bearings are incorporated and all clearances will be correct. The existing cylinder heads, camshafts, valve train components and external parts can be bolted to the short block with little or no machine shop work necessary. In the case of pushrod engines, a new or reground camshaft and lifters will already be installed in the block.

Long block - A long block consists of a short block plus an oil pump, oil pan, cylinder heads, valve covers, camshaft and valve train components, timing sprockets, and timing belts and covers on OHC models. All components are installed with new bearings, seals

and gaskets incorporated throughout. The installation of manifolds and external parts is all that is necessary.

Give careful thought to which alternative is best for you and discuss the situation with local automotive machine shops, auto parts dealers or parts store countermen before ordering or purchasing replacement parts.

8 Engine overhaul - disassembly sequence

Refer to illustrations 8.1a, 8.1b, 8.1c and 8.1d

1 To completely disassemble the engine, remove the following items in the order given:

Pushrod engines

Engine external components
Flywheel/driveplate and housing
Oil pump
Oil pan
Oil strainer/pick-up tube
Cylinder head and valve train components
Pistons
Separate the crankcases
Crankshaft and connecting rods
Camshaft and valve lifters

Overhead cam (OHC) engines

Engine external components
Flywheel/driveplate and housing
Oil pump

2C

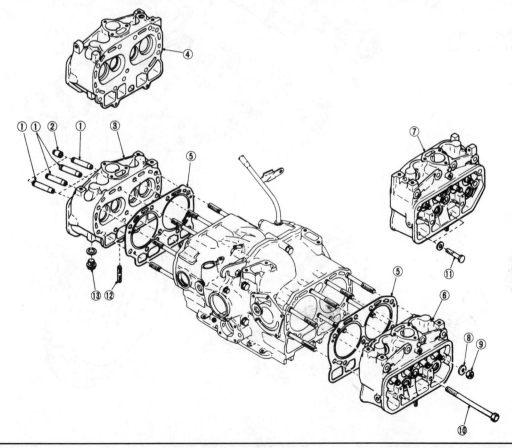

8.1a Exploded view - cylinder head/block (OHV engines)

1 Valve guide
2 Oil seal
3 Cylinder head (1600 engine)
4 cylinder head (1800 engine)
5 Head gasket
6 Cylinder head (1600 engine)
7 Cylinder head (1800 engine)
8 Washer
9 Nut
10 Bolt (11 x 34 mm)
11 Bolt (6 x 16 mm)
12 Stud
13 Plug and washer

1 800 cc engine

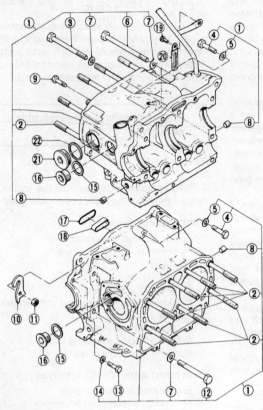

8.1b Crankcase components - exploded view (OHV engines)

1	Crankcase assembly	13	Bolt
2	Stud bolt	14	Washer
3	Bolt (10 x 108 x 28 mm)	15	Gasket (26.2 x 31.5 x 1 mm)
4	Bolt	16	Crankcase plug
5	Washer	17	Crankcase O-ring
6	Bolt (10 x 145 x 18 mm)	18	Backup ring
7	Washer	19	Bolt and washer (6 x 13 x
8	Main gallery plug		13 mm)
9	Bolt	20	Clip
10	Crankcase front hanger	21	Crankcase plug
11	Nut	22	Gasket (36.2 x 44 x 1 mm)
12	Bolt (10 x 70 x 28 mm)		

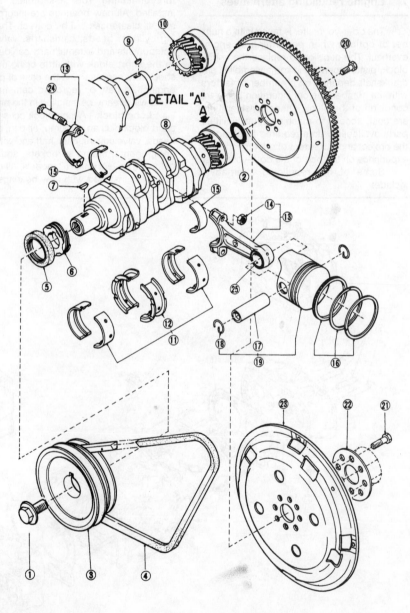

DETAIL "A"

8.1c Crankshaft, bearings, connecting rods, pistons and flywheel/driveplate components - exploded view

1   Bolt
2   O-ring
3   Crankshaft pulley
4   Drivebelt
5   Front oil seal
6   Distributor drive gear
7   Woodruff key
8   Crankshaft
9   Woodruff key
10 Crankshaft gear
11 Crankshaft main bearing set
12 Center (thrust) bearing set
13 Connecting rod and cap
14 Nut
15 Connecting rod bearing set
16 Piston ring set
17 Piston pin
18 Circlip
19 Piston components
20 Bolt (MT)
21 Bolt (AT)
22 Converter back plate (AT)
23 Converter driveplate (AT)
24 Connecting rod bolt
25 Connecting rod bushing

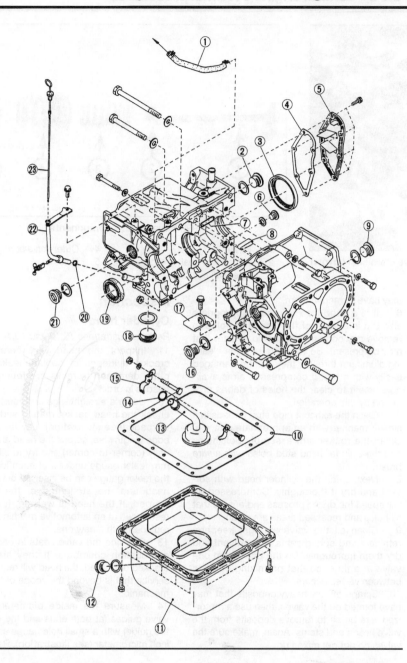

8.1d Crankcase components - exploded view (OHC engines)

1   Water bypass hose
2   Service hole plug
3   Rear oil seal
4   Oil separator cover gasket
5   Oil separator cover
6   Main gallery plug
7   Cylinder block O-ring
8   Backup ring
9   Service hole plug
10 Oil pan gasket
11 Oil pan
12 Oil drain plug
13 Oil strainer
14 O-ring
15 Oil strainer tray
16 Service hole plug
17 Front engine hanger
18 Cylinder block plug
19 Front oil seal
20 O-ring
21 Service hole plug
22 Oil dipstick tube
23 Oil level dipstick

2C

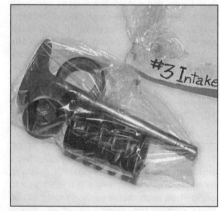

9.2 A small plastic bag, with an appropriate label, can be used to store the valve train components so they can be kept together and reinstalled in the original position

9.3a Use a clamp-type valve spring compressor to compress the spring just enough to remove the keepers with a magnet

Oil pan
Oil strainer/pick-up tube
Camshaft covers
Timing belts and sprockets
Camshafts and camshaft housings
Rocker arms and lash adjusters
Cylinder heads
Pistons
Separate the crankcases
Crankshaft and connecting rods

9 Cylinder head - disassembly

Refer to illustrations 9.2, 9.3a, 9.3b and 9.4

1   Cylinder head disassembly involves removal of the intake and exhaust valves and their related components.

2   Before the valves are removed, arrange to label and store them, along with their related components, so they can be kept separate and reinstalled in the same valve guides they were removed from. Use a separate plastic bag for the components for each valve, including the rocker arm, lifter or lash adjuster, valve, spring, retainer, seal and keepers **(see illustration)**.

3   Compress the valve spring on the first valve with a spring compressor, then remove the keepers and the retainer from the valve assembly **(see illustration)**. Carefully release the valve spring compressor and remove the springs, the seal, the spring seat and the valve from the head **(see illustration)**. If the valve binds in the guide (won't pull through), push it back into the head and deburr the area around the keeper groove with a fine file or whetstone.

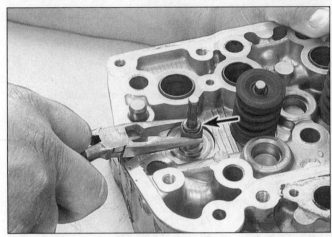

9.3b Pliers can be used to remove the old valve stem seal (arrow) from the guide

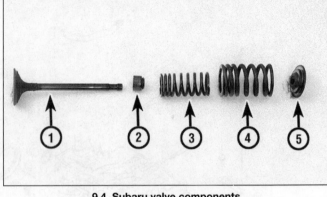

9.4 Subaru valve components

1   Valve
2   Valve stem seal
3   Inner valve spring
4   Outer valve spring
5   Retainer

4   Repeat the procedure for the remaining valves. Remember to keep all the parts for each valve in order so they can be reinstalled in the same locations. Use a marked plastic bag for each valve assembly **(see illustration)**.

5   Once the valves have been removed and safely stored, the head should be thoroughly cleaned and inspected. If a complete engine overhaul is being done, finish the engine disassembly procedures before beginning the cylinder head cleaning and inspection process.

10 Cylinder head- cleaning and inspection

1   Thorough cleaning of the cylinder head and related valve train components, followed by a detailed inspection, will enable you to decide how much valve service work must be done during the engine overhaul. **Note:** *Decarbonizing chemicals are available and may prove very useful when cleaning cylinder heads and valve train components. They are very caustic and should be used with caution. Be sure to follow the directions on the container.*

Cleaning

2   Scrape away any traces of old gasket material and sealing compound from the head gasket, the intake manifold and the exhaust pipe sealing surfaces. Work slowly and do not nick or gouge the soft aluminum of the head.

3   Carefully scrape all carbon deposits out of the combustion chamber areas. A hand-held wire brush or a piece of fine emery cloth can be used once the majority of deposits have been scraped away. Do not use a wire brush mounted in a drill motor, as the head material is soft and can be eroded away by the wire brush.

4   Remove any scale that may be built up around the coolant passages.

5   Run a stiff wire brush through the oil holes to remove any sludge deposits that

may have formed in them.

6   It is a good idea to run an appropriate size tap into each of the threaded holes to remove any corrosion or thread sealant that may be present. Be very careful when cleaning aluminum threads; they can be damaged easily with a tap. If compressed air is available, use it to clear the holes of debris produced by this operation.

7   Clean the exhaust pipe stud threads in a similar manner with an appropriate size die. Clean the rocker arm assembly bolt holes and the cylinder head stud holes with a wire brush.

8   Next, clean the cylinder head with solvent and dry it thoroughly. Compressed air will speed the drying process and ensure that all holes and recessed areas are clean.

9   Clean all the valve springs, keepers, retainers and spring seats with solvent and dry them thoroughly. Do the parts from one valve at a time, so that no mixing of parts between valves occurs.

10   Scrape off any heavy deposits that may have formed on the valves, then use a motorized wire brush to remove deposits from the valve heads and stems. Again, make sure the valves do not get mixed up.

Inspection

Cylinder head

Refer to illustrations 10.12 and 10.14

11   Inspect the head very carefully for cracks, evidence of coolant leakage and other damage. If cracks are found, a new head is in order.

12   Using a straightedge and feeler gauge, check the head gasket mating surfaces for warpage **(see illustration)**. Lay the straightedge lengthwise, across the head and diagonally (corner-to-corner) and try to slip a 0.05 mm feeler gauge under it at each location. If the feeler gauge can be inserted between the head and the straightedge, the head is warped. If the head is warped, it must be resurfaced at an automotive machine shop or replaced with a new one.

13   Examine the valve seats in each of the combustion chambers. If they are pitted, cracked or burned, the head will require valve service that is beyond the scope of the home mechanic.

14   Measure the inside diameters of the valve guides (at both ends and the center of the guide) with a small hole gauge and 0-to-1 inch micrometer **(see illustration)**. Record the

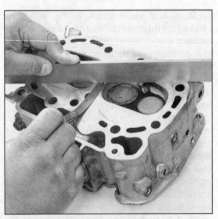

10.12 Check the flatness of the cylinder head's gasket surface with a straightedge and feeler gauges

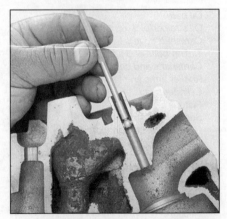

10.14 Use a small-hole gauge inside the valve guide to check diameter at the top, middle and bottom of the guide

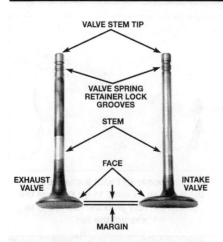

10.15 Check for valve wear at the points shown here

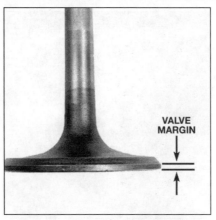

10.16 The margin width on each valve must be as specified (if no margin exists, the valve cannot be reused)

10.18a Measure the free length of each valve spring with a dial or vernier caliper

measurements for future reference. These measurements, along with the valve stem diameter measurements, will enable you to compute the valve stem-to-guide clearance. This clearance, when compared to the Specifications, will be one factor that will determine the extent of the valve service work required. The guides are measured at the ends and at the center to determine if they are worn in a bell-mouth pattern (more wear at the ends). If they are, guide reconditioning or replacement is an absolute must.

Valves

Refer to illustrations 10.15 and 10.16

15 Carefully inspect each valve face for cracks, pits and burned spots **(see illustration)**. Check the valve stem and neck for cracks. Rotate the valve and check for any obvious indication that it is bent. Check the end of the stem for pits and excessive wear. The presence of any of the above conditions indicates a need for valve service by a professional.

16 Measure the width of the valve margin (on each valve) and compare it to the Specifications **(see illustration)**. Any valve with a margin narrower than specified will have to be replaced with a new one.

17 Measure the valve stem diameter. By subtracting the stem diameter from the valve guide diameter, the valve stem-to-guide clearance is obtained. Compare the results to the Specifications. If the stem-to-guide clearance is greater than specified, the guides will have to be reconditioned or replaced and new valves may have to be installed, depending on the condition of the old ones.

Valve components

Refer to illustrations 10.18a and 10.18b

18 Check each valve spring for wear (on the ends) and pits. Measure the free length and compare it to the Specifications **(see illustrations)**. Any springs that are shorter than specified have sagged and should not be reused. Stand the spring on a flat surface and check it for squareness. Have the vehicle

spring tension checked by an automotive machine shop.

19 Check the spring retainers and keepers for obvious wear and cracks. Any questionable parts should not be reused, as extensive damage will occur in the event of failure during engine operation.

11 Valves - servicing

1 Because of the complex nature of the job and the special tools and equipment required, servicing of the valves, the valve seats and the valve guides (commonly known as a 'valve job') is best left to a professional.

2 The home mechanic can remove and disassemble the head, do the initial cleaning and inspection, then reassemble and deliver the head to a dealer service department or a reputable automotive machine shop for the actual valve servicing.

3 The dealer service department, or automotive machine shop, will remove the valves and springs, recondition or replace the valves and valve seats, recondition or replace the valve guides, check and replace the valve

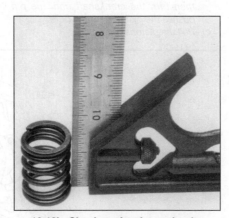

10.18b Check each valve spring for squareness; if it is bent it should be replaced

springs, retainers and keepers (as necessary), replace the valve seals with new ones, reassemble the valve components and make sure the installed spring height is correct. The cylinder head gasket surface will also be resurfaced if it is warped.

4 After the valve job has been performed by a professional, the head will be in like-new condition. When the head is returned, be sure to clean it again, very thoroughly (before installation on the engine), to remove any metal particles and abrasive grit that may still be present from the valve service or head resurfacing operations. Use compressed air, if available, to blow out all the oil holes and passages.

12 Cylinder head- reassembly

Refer to illustration 12.2

1 Regardless of whether or not the heads were sent to an automotive machine shop for valve servicing, make sure they are clean before beginning reassembly. If the heads were sent out for valve servicing, the valves and related components will already be in place.

2 Install new seals on the valve guides. Lubricate the outside of the guides and press the seals over them, with an appropriate-size

12.2 Use a hammer and a deep socket to install the valve guide seals

2C

13.2 Remove the four access plugs (arrow indicates one) that allow piston pin removal

13.3 Reach through the access hole with long pliers to squeeze and pull out the piston pin circlip

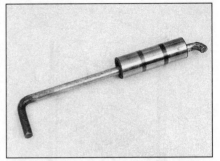

13.4a A heavy rod with a sharp bend in the end can be used to go through the piston pin and grab the rear edge to extract the pin

deep socket, until the tops of the seals are just seated fully **(see illustration)**. Be careful not to cock or deform the seals as they are installed or they may not contact the valve stems properly.

3   Next, install the valves (taking care not to damage the new seals), the springs, the retainers and the keepers. **Note:** *The springs must be installed with the paint mark next to the retainer and the tightly wound coil end next to the head. Coat the valve stems with clean multi-purpose grease (or engine assembly lube) before slipping them into the guides. When compressing the springs with the valve spring compressor, do not let the retainers contact the valve guide seals.*

4   Repeat the procedure for the remaining head.

5   Support the heads (one at a time) on wood blocks so the valves cannot contact the workbench top and very gently tap each of the valve stem ends with a soft-faced hammer. This will help seat the keepers in their grooves.

13   Pistons- removal

Refer to illustrations 13.2, 13.3, 13.4a, 13.4b
Note: *Check for the presence of a wear ridge at the top of each cylinder. If a ridge has formed, it must be machined out before the pistons are removed. Special ridge reaming tools are available at tool and auto parts stores (follow the directions supplied with the tool).*

1   Temporarily install the crankshaft pulley bolt in the crankshaft front end so you can turn the crankshaft.

2   Remove the crankcase plugs from the four service holes with an Allen wrench for access to the piston pin circlips **(see illustration)**. **Note:** *These plugs may be difficult to remove. Soak them first with penetrating oil. If you have to hit the Allen wrench with a hammer, make sure the wrench is fully into the plug to avoid rounding off the hexagonal opening.*

3   To remove the piston pin circlips from a piston, position that piston at bottom dead center by turning the crankshaft, then insert needle-nose pliers through the service holes and remove the circlips **(see illustration)**. **Note:** *Use a small penlight flashlight to see that the circlip is positioned directly at the access hole. You may have to make small movements of the crankshaft to align the piston just right.*

4   Remove the piston pins, using a length of heavy rod with the end bent over to pull the pins out through the   service hole **(see illustrations)**.

5   Keep the pistons and pins together and mark the pistons so they can be reinstalled in their original locations.

6   Leave the pistons in the bores until the crankcases are separated, then push them out.

7   The pistons can be removed without separating the crankcases as follows:

a)   *Turn the crankshaft very slowly until the connecting rods push the pistons out slightly.*
b)   *Insert the piston pins (clean and oil them first for easy installation) into the connecting rods (through the service holes), then turn the crankshaft until the pin pushes the piston from the bore.*
c)   *Pull the pistons out.*

13.4b If the pins are varnished from high mileage, you may have to use a slide hammer or hit the bent end of your homemade tool to force the pin out

14   Separating the crankcases

Refer to illustrations 14.3, 14.4, 14.5, 14.6a, 14.6b, 14.6c and 14.6d

1   In order to separate the crankcases, the oil pan, cylinder heads, pistons and flywheel/driveplate housing must be removed first.

2   Remove the bolt securing the oil dipstick tube and pitching stopper bracket. Remove the stiffener mounting bolts (4WD vehicles only).

3   On OHV engines, use a dial indicator set-up to check the backlash between the

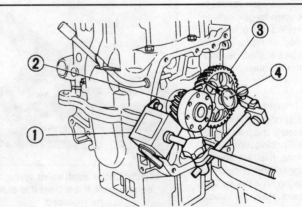

14.3 Checking backlash between the crankshaft and camshaft gears (pushrod engines)

1   *Magnetic base*
2   *Crankshaft gear*
3   *Camshaft gear*
4   *Dial indicator*

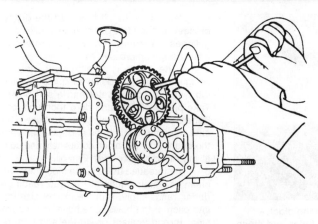

14.4 Removing the cam plate mounting bolts

14.5 Hold the lifters in position with wire before separating the crankcase sections

14.6a On the bottom side of the engine, remove the three bolts/nuts (arrows), including the one holding the oil pickup tube (OHC crankcase shown, OHV similar except pushrod cases have long cylinder head studs on each side)

14.6b At the rear of the crankcase, remove the three bolts (arrows)

2C

camshaft and crankshaft gears **(see illustration)**. If it is greater than specified, have the gears replaced with new ones at an automotive machine shop after the crankshaft and camshaft are removed.

4   On OHV engines, bend back the lock-plate tabs, then work through the holes in the gear to remove the cam plate mounting bolts **(see illustration)**.

5   On OHV engines, use sections of rubber hose or soft wire **(see illustration)** to hold the lifters in position.

6   On all engines, position the engine on a workbench with the left side (cylinders two and four) facing down, then remove the nuts and bolts holding the crankcase sections together **(see illustrations)**.

7   Pull the camshaft to the rear as far as

14.6c At the front of the engine, remove these three case bolts (arrows)

14.6d At the top of the engine, there will be two bolts (A) that are only on the right side - the bolts shown at B are on both sides

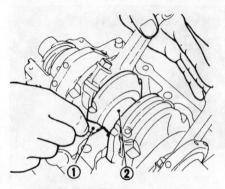

15.2 Checking crankshaft end play

1. Feeler gauge
2. Center main bearing journal

possible, then pull straight up on the right crankcase to separate the two sections. You may have to tap the right crankcase section with a soft-faced hammer to break the gasket seal. Once the case is apart, the crankshaft, rods and camshaft will remain in the left case.

15 Crankshaft and connecting rods - removal

Refer to illustration 15.2

1   Separate the crankcases (Section 14) and remove the front crankshaft oil seal.
2   Before lifting out the crankshaft/connecting rod assembly, check the crankshaft end play. Gently pry or push the crankshaft all the way to the rear of the engine **(see illustration)**. Slip feeler gauges between the crankshaft and the thrust face of the center main bearing to determine the clearance (which is equivalent to crankshaft end play). If the end play is greater than the specified limit, new main bearings *must* be installed when the engine is reassembled.
3   Carefully lift out the crankshaft and store it where it will not fall or get damaged.
4   Remove the main bearings from the cases and store them in containers marked 'front/left', 'front/right', etc. so they can be reinstalled in their original locations (if they are reused).
5   Main bearing inspection is covered in Section 22.

16 Camshaft and lifters- removal (OHV engines)

1   Separate the crankcases (Section 14) and remove the crankshaft/connecting rod assembly (Section 15).
2   Carefully lift out the camshaft and gear and store it where it will not fall or get damaged.
3   Remove the wires or pieces of rubber hose holding the lifters in place, then slip the lifters out of their bores. Store them in paper bags or cardboard boxes marked 'No 1 cylinder intake', 'No 1 cylinder exhaust', etc. so

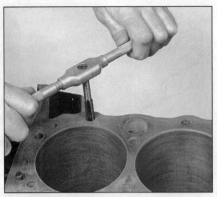

17.6 All bolt holes in the block - particularly the head bolt holes and those that hold the case halves together - should be cleaned and restored with a tap (be sure to remove debris from the holes after this is done)

they will be reinstalled in their original locations.

17 Engine block - cleaning

Refer to illustrations 17.6

1   Using a gasket scraper, remove all traces of gasket material from the engine block. Be very careful not to nick or gouge the gasket sealing surfaces.
2   Remove all of the threaded oil gallery plugs from the block. The plugs are usually very tight - they may have to be drilled out and the holes re-tapped. Use new plugs when the engine is reassembled.
3   If the engine is extremely dirty it should be taken to an automotive machine shop to be steam cleaned or hot tanked.
4   After the block is returned, clean all oil holes and oil galleries one more time. Brushes specifically designed for this purpose are available at most auto parts stores. Flush the passages with warm water until the water runs clear, dry the block thoroughly and wipe all machined surfaces with a light, rust preventive oil. If you have access to

compressed air, use it to speed the drying process and to blow out all the oil holes and galleries. **Warning:** *Wear eye protection when using compressed air!*
5   If the block isn't extremely dirty or sludged up, you can do an adequate cleaning job with hot soapy water and a stiff brush. Take plenty of time and do a thorough job. Regardless of the cleaning method used, be sure to clean all oil holes and galleries very thoroughly, dry the block completely and coat all machined surfaces with light oil.
6   The threaded holes in the block must be clean to ensure accurate torque readings during reassembly. Run the proper size tap into each of the holes to remove rust, corrosion, thread sealant or sludge and restore damaged threads **(see illustration)**. If possible, use compressed air to clear the holes of debris produced by this operation. Now is a good time to clean the threads on the head bolts and the main bearing cap bolts as well.
7   Apply non-hardening sealant (such as Permatex no. 2 or Teflon pipe sealant) to the new oil gallery plugs and thread them into the holes in the block. Make sure they're tightened securely.
8   If the engine isn't going to be reassembled right away, cover it with a large plastic trash bag to keep it clean.

18 Engine block - inspection

Refer to illustrations 18.4a, 18.4b and 18.4c

1   Before the block is inspected, it should be cleaned as described in Section 17.
2   Visually check the block for cracks, rust and corrosion. Look for stripped threads in the threaded holes. It's also a good idea to have the block checked for hidden cracks by an automotive machine shop that has the special equipment to do this type of work. If defects are found, have the block repaired, if possible, or replaced.
3   Check the cylinder bores for scuffing and scoring.
4   Check the cylinders for taper and out-of-round conditions as follows **(see illustrations):**

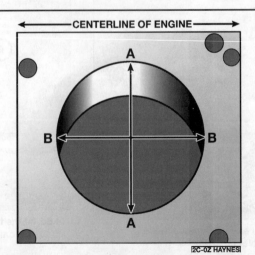

18.4a Measure the diameter of each cylinder at a right angle to the engine centerline (A), and parallel to engine centerline (B) - out-of-round is the difference between A and B; taper is the difference between A and B at the top of the cylinder and A and B at the bottom of the cylinder

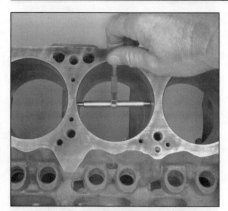

18.4b The ability to "feel" when the telescoping gauge is at the correct point will be developed over time, so work slowly and repeat the check until you're satisfied the bore measurement is accurate

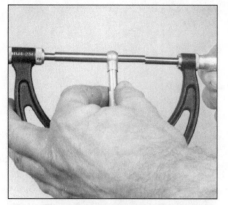

18.4c The gauge is then measured with a micrometer to determine the bore size

19.2a A "bottle brush" hone will produce better results if you've never honed cylinders before

5   Measure the diameter of each cylinder at the top (just under the ridge area), center and bottom of the cylinder bore, parallel to the crankshaft axis.

6   Next measure each cylinder's diameter at the same three locations perpendicular to the crankshaft axis.

7   The taper of the cylinder is the difference between the bore diameter at the top of the cylinder and the diameter at the bottom. The out-of-round specification of the cylinder bore is the difference between the parallel and perpendicular readings. Compare your results to those listed in this Chapter's Specifications.

8   Repeat the procedure for the remaining pistons and cylinders.

9   If the cylinder walls are badly scuffed or scored, or if they're out-of-round or tapered beyond the limits given in this Chapter's Specifications, have the engine block rebored and honed at an automotive machine shop. If a rebore is done, oversize pistons and rings will be required.

10   If the cylinders are in reasonably good condition and not worn to the outside of the limits, and if the piston-to-cylinder clearances can be maintained properly, then they don't have to be rebored. Honing is all that's necessary (see Section 19).

19 Cylinder honing

Refer to illustrations 19.2a and 19.2b

1   Prior to engine reassembly, the cylinder bores must be honed so the new piston rings will seat correctly and provide the best possible combustion chamber seal. **Note:** *If you don't have the tools or don't want to tackle the honing operation, most automotive machine shops will do it for a reasonable fee.*

2   Two types of cylinder hones are commonly available - the flex hone or "bottle brush" type and the more traditional surfacing hone with spring-loaded stones. Both will do the job, but for the less experienced mechanic the "bottle brush" hone will proba-

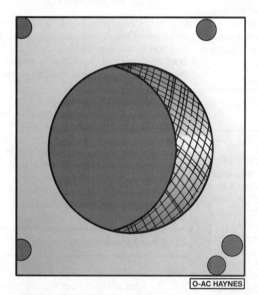

19.2b The cylinder hone should leave a smooth, crosshatch pattern with the lines intersecting at approximately a 60-degree angle

bly be easier to use. You'll also need some kerosene or honing oil, rags and an electric drill motor. Proceed as follows:

a) *Mount the hone in the drill motor, compress the stones and slip it into the first cylinder* (**see illustration**). *Be sure to wear safety goggles or a face shield!*

b) *Lubricate the cylinder with plenty of honing oil, turn on the drill and move the hone up-and-down in the cylinder at a pace that will produce a fine crosshatch pattern on the cylinder walls. Ideally, the crosshatch lines should intersect at approximately a 60-degree angle* (**see illustration**). *Be sure to use plenty of lubricant and don't take off any more material than is absolutely necessary to produce the desired finish.* **Note:** *Piston ring manufacturers may specify a smaller crosshatch angle than the traditional 60-degrees - read and follow any instructions included with the new rings.*

c) *Don't withdraw the hone from the cylinder while it's running. Instead, shut off the drill and continue moving the hone up-and-down in the cylinder until it*

comes to a complete stop, then compress the stones and withdraw the hone. If you're using a "bottle brush" type hone, stop the drill motor, then turn the chuck in the normal direction of rotation while withdrawing the hone from the cylinder.

d) *Wipe the oil out of the cylinder and repeat the procedure for the remaining cylinders.*

3   After the honing job is complete, chamfer the top edges of the cylinder bores with a small file so the rings won't catch when the pistons are installed. Be very careful not to nick the cylinder walls with the end of the file.

4   The entire engine block must be washed again very thoroughly with warm, soapy water to remove all traces of the abrasive grit produced during the honing operation. **Note:** *The bores can be considered clean when a lint-free white cloth - dampened with clean engine oil - used to wipe them out doesn't pick-up any more honing residue, which will show up as gray areas on the cloth. Be sure to run a brush through all oil holes and galleries and flush them with running water.*

2C

20.1 Checking the connecting rod side clearance

5   After rinsing, dry the block and apply a coat of light rust preventive oil to all machined surfaces. Wrap the block in a plastic trash bag to keep it clean and set it aside until reassembly.

20   Connecting rods and bearings - removal and inspection

Refer to illustration 20.1

1   Before removing the connecting rods from the crankshaft, check the side clearance with a feeler gauge **(see illustration)**. If the side clearance is greater than specified, new connecting rods will be required for engine reassembly.

2   If the rods and caps are not numbered, use a center punch and hammer and carefully mark the connecting rods and caps so they can be reinstalled in the same position on the same crankshaft journal. Mark the rod and cap at the front of the crankshaft with one dot, the second rod and cap with two dots and so on (both the rods and caps must be marked since they are going to be separated). Loosen the cap bolts on one connect-

21.5 Measure the diameter of each crankshaft journal (mains and rods) at several points to detect taper and out-of-round conditions

21.1 The oil holes should be chamfered so sharp edges don't gouge or scratch the new bearings

ing rod in three steps, carefully lift off the cap and bearing insert, then carefully remove the rod and remaining bearing insert from the crankshaft journal. Temporarily reassemble the rod, the bearing and the cap to prevent mixing up parts.

3   Repeat the procedure for the remaining connecting rods. Be very careful not to nick or scratch the crankshaft journals with the rod bolts.

4   Without mixing them up, clean the parts with solvent and dry them thoroughly. Make sure the oil holes are clear.

5   Refer to Section 25 for the connecting rod inspection procedures.

21   Crankshaft - inspection

Refer to illustrations 21.1, 21.2, 21.5 and 21.7

1   Remove all burrs from the crankshaft oil holes with a stone, file or scraper **(see illustration)**.

2   Clean the crankshaft with solvent and dry it with compressed air (if available). Be sure to clean the oil holes with a stiff brush **(see illustration)** and flush them with solvent.

21.7 If the seals have worn grooves in the crankshaft journals, or if the seal contact surfaces are nicked or scratched, the new seals will leak

21.2 Use a wire or stiff plastic bristle brush to clean the oil passages in the crankshaft

3   Check the main and connecting rod bearing journals for uneven wear, scoring, pits and cracks.

4   Check the rest of the crankshaft for cracks and other damage. It should be magnafluxed to reveal hidden cracks - an automotive machine shop will handle the procedure.

5   Using a micrometer, measure the diameter of the main and connecting rod journals and compare the results to this Chapter's Specifications **(see illustration)**. By measuring the diameter at a number of points around each journal's circumference, you'll be able to determine whether or not the journal is out-of-round. Take the measurement at each end of the journal, near the crank throws, to determine if the journal is tapered.

6   If the crankshaft journals are damaged, tapered, out-of-round or worn beyond the limits given in the Specifications, have the crankshaft reground by an automotive machine shop. Be sure to use the correct size bearing inserts if the crankshaft is reconditioned.

7   Check the oil seal journals at each end of the crankshaft for wear and damage. If the seal has worn a groove in the journal, or if it's nicked or scratched **(see illustration)**, the new seal may leak when the engine is reassembled. In some cases, an automotive machine shop may be able to repair the journal by pressing on a thin sleeve. If repair isn't feasible, a new or different crankshaft should be installed.

8   Refer to Section 22 and examine the main and rod bearing inserts.

22   Main and connecting rod bearings- inspection

Refer to illustration 22.1

1   Even though the main and connecting rod bearings should be replaced with new ones during the engine overhaul, the old bearings should be retained for close examination, as they may reveal valuable informa-

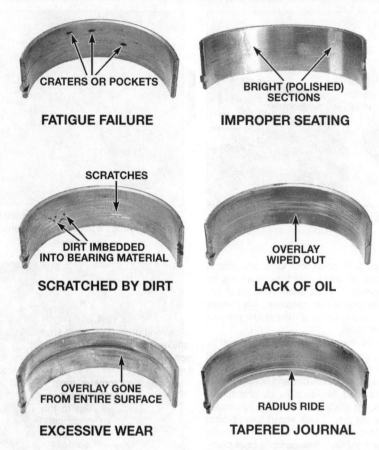

22.1 Typical bearing failures

tion about the condition of the engine **(see illustration)**.

2 Bearing failure occurs mainly because of lack of lubrication, the presence of dirt or other foreign particles, overloading the engine and/or corrosion. Regardless of the cause of bearing failure, it must be corrected before the engine is reassembled to prevent it from happening again.

3 When examining the bearings, remove them from the engine block, the connecting rods and the rod caps and lay them out on a clean surface in the same general position as their location in the engine. This will enable you to match any noted bearing problems with the corresponding crankshaft journal.

4 Dirt and other foreign particles get into the engine in a variety of ways. It may be left in the engine during assembly, or it may pass through filters or breathers. It may get into the oil, and from there into the bearings. Metal chips from machining operations and normal engine wear are often present. Abrasives are sometimes left in engine components after reconditioning, especially when parts are not thoroughly cleaned using the proper cleaning methods. Whatever the source, these foreign objects often end up embedded in the soft bearing material and are easily recognized. Large particles will not embed in the bearing and will score or gouge the bearing and shaft. The best prevention for this cause of bearing

failure is to clean all parts thoroughly and keep everything spotlessly-clean during engine assembly. Frequent and regular changes of engine oil, and oil filters, is also recommended.

5 Lack of lubrication (or lubrication breakdown) has a number of interrelated causes. Excessive heat (which thins the oil), overloading (which squeezes the oil from the bearing face) and oil leakage or throw-off (from excessive bearing clearances, worn oil pumps or high engine speeds) all contribute to lubrication breakdown. Blocked oil passages, which usually are the result of misaligned oil holes in a bearing shell, will also oil-starve a bearing and destroy it. When lack of lubrication is the cause of bearing failure, the bearing material is wiped or extruded from the steel backing of the bearing. Temperatures may increase to the point where the steel backing turns blue from overheating.

6 Driving habits can have a definite effect on bearing life. Too little throttle for the gear being used (or 'lugging' the engine) puts very high loads on bearings, which tends to squeeze out the oil film. These loads cause the bearings to flex, which produces fine cracks in the bearing face (fatigue failure). Eventually the bearing material will loosen in pieces and tear away from the steel backing. Short-trip driving leads to corrosion of bearings, as insufficient engine heat is produced to drive off the condensed water and corro-

sive gases produced. These products collect in the engine oil, forming acid and sludge. As the oil is carried to the engine bearings the acid attacks and corrodes the bearing material.

7 Incorrect bearing installation during engine assembly will lead to bearing failure as well. Tight-fitting bearings, which leave insufficient bearing oil clearance, result in oil starvation. Dirt or foreign particles trapped behind a bearing insert result in high spots on the bearing which lead to failure.

23 Engine overhaul - reassembly sequence

1 To assemble the engine, remove the following items in the order given:

Overhead valve (OHV) engines

Camshaft and valve lifters
Crankshaft and connecting rods
Join the crankcase halves
Pistons
Cylinder head and valve train components
Oil strainer/pick-up tube
Oil pump
Oil pan
Flywheel/driveplate and housing
Engine external components

Overhead-cam engines

Engine external components
Crankshaft and connecting rods
Join the crankcase halves
Pistons
Cylinder heads
Rocker arms and lash adjusters
Camshafts and camshaft housings
Timing belts and sprockets
Camshaft covers
Oil pump
Oil strainer/pick-up tube
Oil pan
Flywheel/driveplate and housing

24 Pistons - inspection

Refer to illustrations 24.4a, 24.4b, 24.10 and 24.11

1 Before the inspection process can be carried out, the pistons must be cleaned and the old piston rings removed from the pistons.

2 Using a piston ring installation tool, carefully remove the rings from the pistons. Do not nick or gouge the pistons in the process.

3 Scrape all traces of carbon from the top (or crown} of the piston. A hand-held wire brush or a piece of fine emery cloth can be used once the majority of the deposits have been scraped away. do not, under any circumstances, use a wire brush mounted in a drill motor to remove deposits from the pistons. The piston material is soft and will be eroded away by the wire brush.

2C

24.4a The piston ring grooves can be cleaned with a special tool, as shown here . . .

24.4b . . . or a section of a broken ring

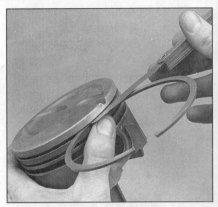

24.10 Check the ring side clearance with a feeler gauge at several points around the groove

4   Use a piston-ring-groove cleaning tool to remove any carbon deposits from the ring grooves. If a tool is not available, a piece-broken off the old ring will do the job **(see illustrations)**. Be very careful to remove only the carbon deposits. Do not remove any metal and do not nick or scratch the sides of the ring grooves.

5   Once the deposits have been removed, clean the pistons with solvent and dry them thoroughly. Make sure that the oil return slots in the back sides of the oil ring grooves are clear.

6   If the pistons are not damaged or worn excessively, and if the cylinders are not rebored, new pistons will not be necessary. Normal piston wear appears as even vertical wear on the piston thrust surfaces and slight looseness of the top ring in its groove. New piston rings, on the other hand, should always be used when an engine is rebuilt.

7   Carefully inspect each piston for cracks around the skirt, at the pin bosses and at the ring lands.

8   Look for scoring and scuffing (on the thrust faces of the skirt), holes (in the piston crown) and burned areas (at the edge of the crown). If the skirts are scored or scuffed, the engine may have been suffering from overheating and/or abnormal combustion, which caused excessively high operating temperatures. The cooling and lubrication systems should be checked thoroughly. A hole in the piston crown, an extreme to be sure, is an indication that abnormal combustion (preignition) was occurring. Burned areas at the edge of the piston crown are usually evidence of spark knock (detonation). If any of the above problems exist, the causes must be corrected or the damage will occur again.

9   Corrosion of the piston (evidenced by pitting) indicates that coolant is leaking into the combustion chambers and/or the crankcase. Again, the cause must be corrected or the problem may persist in the rebuilt engine.

10   Measure the piston ring-to-groove clearances by laying a new piston ring in each ring groove and slipping a feeler gauge in beside it **(see illustration)**. Check the

clearance at three or four locations around the groove. Be sure to use the correct ring for each groove; they are different. If the clearances are greater than specified, new pistons will have to be used and the cylinder rebored to accept them.

11   Check the piston-to-bore clearances by measuring the cylinder bores (see Section 24) and the piston diameter **(see illustration)**. Make sure that the pistons and bores are correctly matched. Measure the pistons across the skirt, on the thrust faces (at 90-degree angle to the piston pin), about 1 in up from the bottom of the skirt. Subtract the piston diameter from the corresponding bore diameter to obtain the clearance. If *any* are greater than specified, the cylinders will have to be rebored and new pistons and rings installed.

12   Measure the piston pin outside diameter and the pin bore inside diameter. Subtract the two measurements to obtain the piston-to-piston pin clearance. If it is greater than specified, new pistons and possibly new pins must be installed.

---

25 Connecting rods and bearings - installation and oil clearance check

---

Refer to illustrations 25.3 and 25.5

1   Once the crankshaft and rods have been cleaned and inspected and the decision has been made concerning bearing replacement, the connecting rods can be reinstalled on the crankshaft. **Note:** *If new bearings are being used, check the oil clearances before final installation of the connecting rods. If the clearances are within the specified limits, proceed with the installation. Never assume that the clearances are correct even though new bearings are involved.*

2   Make sure the bearing faces and backs are perfectly clean, then fit them to the rod and cap. The tab on each bearing must be engaged in the recess in the cap or rod.

3   Clean the number one rod journal on the crankshaft, then slip the number one rod into place. Make sure the mark on the rod is fac-

24.11 Measure the piston diameter at a 90-degree angle to the piston pin and in line with it

ing the front of the crankshaft **(see illustration)**.

4   Apply a length of Plastigage to the crankshaft journal, just off center. Gently install the rod cap in place, without turning the rod on the journal. Make sure the mating mark on the cap is on the same side as the mark on the connecting rod. Torque the rod bolts.

5   Remove the rod bolts without allowing the rod to turn on the journal, then remove the cap. Examine the Plastigage and compare its width to the scale on the Plastigage

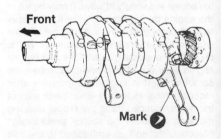

25.3 The connecting rods must be installed with the mark facing the front of the crankshaft

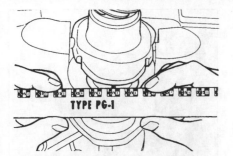

25.5 Compare the width of the crushed Plastigage to the scale printed on the container to obtain the connecting rod bearing oil clearance

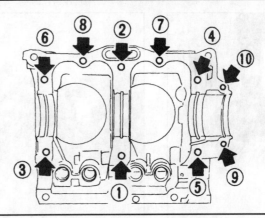

26.7 Crankcase bolt tightening sequence

package (see illustration). If the clearance is within Specifications, proceed with checking the other three rods.

6 If the rod clearances are all within Specifications, lubricate both halves of the bearings of rod number 1 with moly-based assembly lube, and install the rod bolts and tighten them to the specified torque, working up to it in three steps.

7 Repeat the procedure for the remaining rods: do not mix up the rods and caps and do not install the rods backwards.

8 After the connecting rods have been installed, rotate them by hand and check for any obvious binding.

9 As a final step, the connecting rod big end side clearances must be rechecked. Slide each connecting rod to one side of the journal and slip a feeler gauge between the side of each connecting rod and the crankshaft throw. Be sure to compare the measured clearances to the Specifications to make sure they are correct.

26 Crankshaft and main bearings - installation and oil clearance check

Refer to illustrations 26.7, 26.9, 26.12, 26.13, 26.14, 26.15 and 26.16

1 Before installation of the crankshaft, the main bearing oil clearances must be

checked. **Note:** *On pushrod engines, the camshaft bearing oil clearances should be checked at the same time.*

2 Position the left crankcase section on a workbench with the bearing saddles facing up. Wipe the main bearing surfaces of the crankcases with a clean lint-free cloth. They must be kept spotlessly clean.

3 Clean the back sides of the main bearing inserts and lay one bearing half in each main bearing saddle in the crankcase on the workbench and the other bearing half from each set in the corresponding location in the remaining crankcase section. Make sure the tab on the bearing insert fits into the recess in the crankcase. Do not hammer the bearings into place and do not nick or gouge the bearing faces. No lubrication should be used at this time.

4 Clean the faces of the bearings in the crankcases and the crankshaft main bearing journals with a clean, lint-free cloth. Once you are certain that the crankshaft is clean, carefully lay it in position in the crankcase section on the workbench.

5 Trim three pieces of type HPG-1 Plastigage so that they are slightly shorter than the width of the main bearings and place one piece on each crankshaft main bearing journal, parallel with the journal axis. On pushrod engines, lay a piece of Plastigage in the camshaft journal bores and lay the clean camshaft in place.

6 Clean the faces of the bearings in the

right crankcase, then carefully lay it in position. Do not disturb the Plastigage.

7 Install the crankcase bolts. Following the sequence shown in the accompanying illustration, tighten them in three steps to the specified torque (see illustration). Do not rotate the crankshaft at any time during this operation.

8 Remove the bolts and carefully lift off the right crankcase section. Do not disturb the Plastigage or rotate the crankshaft.

9 Compare the width of the crushed Plastigage on each journal to the scale printed on the Plastigage container to obtain the main bearing oil clearances (see illustration). Check the Specifications to make sure they are correct. On pushrod engines, check the Plastigage on the camshaft journals and compare it to Specifications for camshaft-to-case clearance.

10 If the clearance is not correct. double-check to make sure that you have the right size bearing inserts. Also, recheck the crankshaft main bearing journal diameters and make sure that no dirt or oil was between the bearing inserts and the main bearing caps or the block when the clearance was measured.

11 Be sure to remove all traces of the Plastigage from the bearing faces and/or journals. To prevent damage to the bearing surfaces, use a wood or plastic tool.

12 Carefully lift the crankshaft out of the case. Clean the bearing faces, then apply a

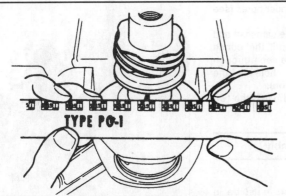

26.9 Compare the width of the crushed Plastigage to the scale on the package to determine the main bearing oil clearance

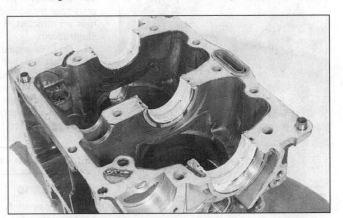

26.12 Apply moly-based assembly lube to the main bearing inserts before final assembly

26.13 Measuring camshaft thrust clearance with a feeler gauge

26.14 Installing the distributor drive gear onto the crankshaft (OHV engines)

26.15 Lay the lubed crankshaft/rods assembly into the bearings in the left case, aiming the two lower rods into their cylinders - when the right case is installed, the other two rods must be aligned with their cylinders

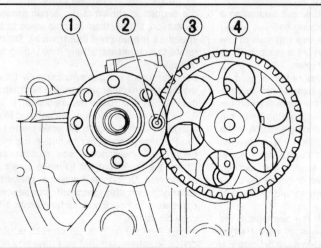

26.16 Correct camshaft gear-to-crankshaft gear mesh (OHV engines)

1   Crankshaft gear
2   Hole with large chamfer
3   Punch mark
4   Camshaft gear

thin layer of clean, high-quality multi-purpose grease or engine assembly lube (preferably one containing molybdenum disulfide) to each of the bearing faces in both crankcase sections **(see illustration)**. Be sure to coat the thrust bearing faces as well.

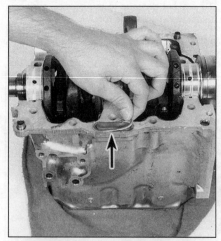

27.6 Install a new O-ring (arrow) in the left case, and make sure the metal O-ring guide is in place

13   On OHV engines, install the camshaft and lifters before final installation of the crankshaft. Check the clearance between the camshaft and the camshaft thrust plate with a feeler gauge before final installation in the case **(see illustration)**.
14   On OHV engines, install the Woodruff key and distributor drive gear at the front of the crankshaft **(see illustration)** (if they were removed).
15   Carefully lay the crankshaft in the left crankcase section. Make sure the connecting rods are directed into the cylinder bores **(see illustration)**.
16   On OHV engines, turn the camshaft and crankshaft independently until the punch mark in the cam gear can be seen through the large chamfered bolt hole in the crankshaft gear **(see illustration)**.
17   Refer to Section 27 and rejoin the two crankcase sections.

27   Crankcase - reassembly

OHV engine

1   The camshaft and lifters must be in position before the crankcases are rejoined.
2   Make sure the camshaft bearing oil

clearance (Section 26) has been checked before final installation of the camshaft and rejoining of the crankcases.
3   Lubricate the lifters with engine assembly lube or molybdenum disulfide grease, then slip them into the bores and retain them with wire or pieces of rubber hose.
4   Lubricate the camshaft bearing journals and lobes, then position the camshaft in the left crankcase section (the one containing cylinders numbered two and four). Align the camshaft gear and crankshaft gears **(see illustration 26.16)**.

All engines

Refer to illustrations 27.6, 27.7a, 27.7b, and 27.9

5   Clean the block mating surfaces with lacquer thinner or acetone (they must be clean and oil-free).
6   Install the O-ring and backup ring **(see illustration)** in the left crankcase section.
7   Apply a thin layer of liquid gasket sealer (Fuji Bond C or equivalent) to the crankcase mating surfaces **(see illustrations)**.

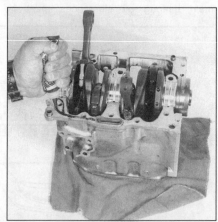

27.7a Apply a bead of the correct sealant to the face of the left case . . .

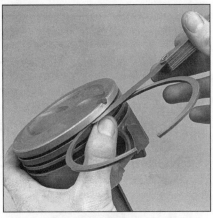

27.7b ... in this pattern to ensure proper sealing of the crankcase

Apply liquid packing along this line.

27.9 Tighten the four flywheel-housing-to-case bolts (arrows) evenly in a criss-cross pattern

28.3 Measuring piston ring-to-groove clearance with a feeler gauge

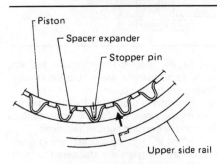

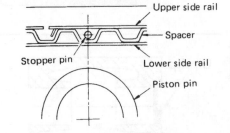

28.4 Checking piston ring end gap with a feeler gauge

28.11a Installation details for Nippon oil rings

Piston
Spacer expander
Stopper pin
Upper side rail

28.11b Installation details for *Riken* oil rings

Upper side rail
Spacer
Stopper pin
Lower side rail
Piston pin

2C

8   Carefully lower the right crankcase section into position on the left crankcase and install the nuts and bolts. Tighten them to the specified torque in three steps. Be sure to use the sequence shown in the accompanying illustration.

9   Install a new oil seal in the flywheel driveplate housing, then lubricate the seal lip with engine oil. Apply liquid gasket sealer to the mating surfaces and attach the housing to the crankcase. Tighten the bolts in a criss-cross pattern to the specified torque**(see illustration).**

10   Install a new front oil seal. Lubricate the outer edge and carefully drive it in with a hammer and block of wood until it is flush with the crankcase (see Part A or B of this Chapter).

11   Lubricate the seal lip, then install the crankshaft pulley (pushrod engines). Do not tighten the pulley bolt until the flywheel/driveplate is in place.

12   The remainder of the procedure is basically the reverse of the separation procedure.

28   Piston rings - installation

Refer to illustrations 28.3, 28.4, 28.11a, 28.11b and 28.16

1   Before installing the new piston rings, the ring end gaps and clearances must be checked.

2   Lay out the pistons and the new ring

sets so the rings will be matched with the same piston and cylinder during the end gap measurement and engine reassembly.

3   Insert one ring at a time into its groove on the piston, and measure its clearance to the groove with feeler gauges, and compare to Specifications **(see illustration).**

4   Insert the top (number one) ring into the first cylinder and square it up with the cylinder walls by pushing it in with the top of the piston. The ring should be near the bottom of the cylinder at the lower limit of ring travel. To measure the end gap, slip a feeler gauge between the ends of the ring **(see illustration).** Compare the measurement to Specifications.

5   If the gap is larger or smaller than specified, double-check to make sure that you have the correct rings before proceeding.

6   If the gap is too small, it must be enlarged or the ring ends may come in contact with each other during engine operation, which can cause serious damage to the engine. The end gap can be increased by filing the ring ends very carefully with a fine file. Mount the file in a vise equipped with soft jaws, slip the ring over the file so that the ends contact the file face and slowly move the ring to remove material from the ends. When performing this operation, file only from the outside in.

7   Excess end gap is not critical unless it is greater than 1.50 mm. Again, double-check to make sure you have the correct rings for

your engine. Use a fine file or whetstone to remove any burrs on the rings left from the filing procedure.

8   Repeat the procedure for each ring that will be installed in the first cylinder and for each ring in the remaining cylinders. Remember to keep rings, pistons and cylinders matched up.

9   Once the ring end gaps have been checked/corrected, the rings can be installed on the pistons.

10   The oil control ring (lowest one on the piston) is installed first. It is composed of three separate components. Slip the oil ring spacer into the groove with the end gap approximately 180° from the stopper pin. Install the upper side rail. Do not use a piston ring installation tool on the oil ring side rails, as they may be damaged. Instead, place one end of the upper oil rail into the groove between the spacer and the ring land, hold it firmly in place and slide a finger around the piston while pushing the rail into the groove (above the spacer). Next, install the lower side rail in the same manner below the spacer.

11   After the three oil ring components have been installed, check to make sure that the upper and lower rail end gaps are positioned exactly as shown **(see illustrations).**

12   The number two (middle) ring is installed next. It can be readily distinguished from the top ring by its cross section shape, lack of chrome plating on the face and the fact that it is thicker than the top ring. Follow the

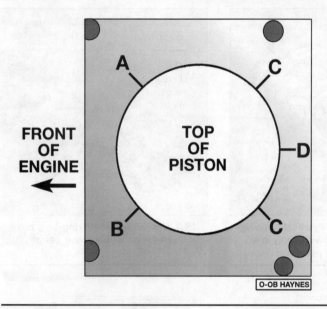

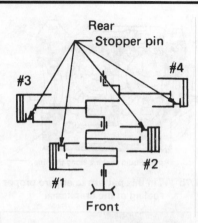

28.16 Ring end gap positions - Align the oil ring spacer gap at D, the oil ring side rails at C (one inch either side of the pin centerline), and the compression rings at A and B, one inch either side of the pin centerline

29.2a The oil ring spacer stopper pins must face in when the pistons are installed

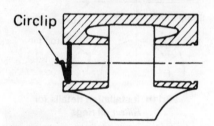

29.2b The circlip pigtail must point toward the top of the piston

instructions with the piston ring package for identification and proper orientation of the new rings.

13   Use a piston ring installation tool and *make sure that the identification mark is facing up,* then fit the ring into the middle groove on the piston. Do not expand the ring any more than is necessary to slide it over the piston.

14   Finally, install the number one (top) ring in the same manner. *Make sure the identifying mark is facing up.*

15   Repeat the procedure for the remaining pistons and rings. Be careful not to confuse the number one and number two rings.

16   When all rings on a piston are in place, make sure the gaps are staggered properly **(see illustration)**.

29   Pistons - installation

Refer to illustrations 29.2a, 29.2b, 29.5 and 29.6

1   Position the engine on a workbench with the left side (cylinders two and four) facing down.

2   Install the inner circlip (stopper pin side of the piston) in the number two (2) piston pin hole groove. Rotate the circlip until the circlip pigtail points toward the top of the piston **(see illustrations)**.

3   Make sure the ring end gaps are positioned correctly, then lubricate the skirt and rings with clean engine oil. Install a piston ring compressor on the piston. Leave the skirt protruding about 3 mm to guide the piston into the cylinder. The rings must be compressed as far as possible.

4   Carefully turn the crankshaft until the number two (2) connecting rod is at bottom dead center. At this point the rod should be as close to vertical as possible.

5   Gently guide the piston skirt into the number two (2) cylinder. Make sure the stopper pin is facing away from the service hole. Tap the exposed edge of the ring compressor so that it is contacting the crankcase around its entire circumference. **Note:** *The word TOP on the piston must face up as it is installed* **(see illustration)**.

6   Carefully tap on the top of the piston with a soft-faced hammer **(see illustration)**. The piston rings may try to pop out of the ring compressor just before entering the cylinder bore, so keep some pressure on the ring compressor. Work slowly, and if any resistance is felt as the piston rings enter the cylinder, stop immediately. Find out what is

29.5 The word UP or TOP must face up as the piston is installed

29.6 Gently tap the piston into the bore while maintaining hand pressure to keep the ring compressor against the block - stop if resistance is felt

hanging up and fix it before proceeding. Do not, for any reason, force the piston into the cylinder, as you will break a ring and/or the piston.

7 Push the piston in until the service hole, the piston pin bore and the small end of the connecting rod are all aligned. **Note:** *You may need to fish a length of coat-hanger wire into the service hole to lift the rod into position.*

8 Lubricate the pin with clean engine oil, then slip it through the service hole into the piston and connecting rod. If resistance is felt, do not force the pin. Instead, check to make sure the pin bore and connecting rod are aligned.

9 Install the outer circlip in the pin hole groove and rotate it until the pigtail points toward the top of the piston.

10 Repeat the procedure for the number four (4) piston.

11 Turn the engine upside-down (cylinders one and three should be facing down) and repeat the procedure for pistons one and three.

12 Make sure the aluminum washers are in place, then apply gasket sealer to the threads and install the service hole plugs in the front of the crankcase. Tighten them to the specified torque.

30 Engine - installation

1 Apply grease to the splines of the transmission mainshaft (manual transmission equipped vehicles only).

2 Slowly and carefully raise the engine with the hoist and then lower it into the engine compartment while you tip the rear of the engine down towards the transmission.

3 Align the engine crankshaft with the transmission mainshaft.

4 Attach the engine to the transmission as follows:

Manual transmission

a) *Turn the crankshaft pulley until the mainshaft is aligned with the clutch disc at the splines.*

Automatic transmission

b) *Jack the vehicle up until the front wheels are slightly off the ground.*

c) *Turn the crankshaft pulley until one mounting bolt hole in the converter driveplate is centered in the timing mark hole.*

d) *Turn the crankshaft until the mounting holes are aligned and then install the mounting bolt. Do this for each of the mounting bolts, but do not tighten the bolts until they are all installed.* **Note:** *Be careful not to drop the bolts into the converter housing.*

5 Now, attach the engine to the transmission by installing the upper and then the lower engine-to-transmission mounting bolts.

6 Make sure that the engine is properly aligned with the transmission, do not use the tightening of the bolts to align them. Tighten the bolts to the specified torque.

7 Lower the jack supporting the transmission and remove it from under the vehicle. Position the engine rubber mounts in place.

8 Lower the engine completely and remove the hoist from the area.

9 Raise the vehicle sufficiently to work underneath it and support it with jackstands.

10 Securely tighten all of the engine mounting nuts and bolts according to the Torque specifications.

11 Install the front exhaust pipe by referring to Chapter 4.

12 Now, lower the vehicle and install the engine pitching stopper as follows:

a) *Attach the pitching stopper rod to the bracket on the engine, then tighten it at the body end.*

b) *Tighten the rear nut on the pitching stopper so that 0.8 to 1.2 mm clearance is maintained between the rubber cushion and the washer.*

c) *Attach a wrench to the rear nut on the engine side of the pitching stopper to prevent it from turning and tighten the front nut securely.*

13 Attach the clutch cable (manual transmission) to the clutch release lever and adjust it by referring to Chapter 1.

14 The remainder of the installation is the reverse of the removal process.

15 Inspect the whole engine compartment and make sure that there are no hoses or wires that were missed and not hooked up.

16 Make sure that all mounting hardware is tight.

17 Refer to Chapter 1 and adjust the engine drivebelts.

18 Refer to Chapter 1 and fill the engine and transmission with the correct quantity and type of lubrication called for in the Specifications.

19 Make sure that the radiator is filled with new coolant.

31 Initial start-up and break-in after overhaul

1 Once the engine has been properly installed in the vehicle, double-check the engine oil and coolant levels.

2 With the spark plugs out of the engine and the coil high-tension lead grounded to the engine block, crank the engine over until oil pressure registers on the gauge.

3 Install the spark plugs, hook up the plug wires and the coil high-tension lead.

4 Start the engine. It may take a few moments, but the engine should start without a great deal of effort.

5 As soon as the engine starts, it should be set at a fast idle (to ensure proper oil circulation) and allowed to warm up to normal operating temperature. While the engine is warming up, make a thorough check for oil and coolant leaks.

6 After the engine reaches normal operating temperature, let it run for about 10 minutes then shut it off. On pushrod engines, after it has cooled down completely, remove the rocker arm covers, retorque the head nuts and check the valve clearances.

7 Recheck the engine oil and coolant levels. Also, check the ignition timing and the engine idle speed (refer to Chapter 1) and make any necessary adjustments.

8 Drive the vehicle to an area with no traffic, accelerate sharply from 30 to 50 mph, then allow the vehicle to slow to 30 mph with the throttle closed. Repeat the procedure 10 or 12 times. This will load the piston rings and cause them to seat properly against the cylinder walls. Check again for oil and coolant leaks.

9 Drive the vehicle gently for the first 500 miles (no sustained high speeds) and keep a constant check on the oil level. It is not unusual for an engine to use oil during the break-in period.

10 At approximately 500 to 600 miles, change the oil and filter and recheck the valve clearances (pushrod engines).

11 For the next few hundred miles, drive the vehicle normally. Do not pamper it or abuse it.

12 After 2000 miles, change the oil and filter again and consider the engine fully broken in.

2C

Notes

Chapter 3
Cooling, heating and air conditioning systems

Contents

Specifications

Capacity
1600 cc	5.3 US quarts (5.0L)
1800 cc	5.8 US quarts (5.5L)
Coolant type	50/50 mixture of non-phosphate ethylene glycol antifreeze

Thermostat
Opening temperature	188 to 193 degrees F (86.5 to 89.5 degrees C)
Fully open temperature	212 degrees F (100 degrees C)

Radiator pressure cap
Specified cap pressure	11.3 to 14.2 psi (78 to 98 kPa)
Test pressure.......................	10 psi (69 kPa)
Thermoswitch operation temperature	199 to 207 degrees F (93 to 97 degrees C)

Torque specifications
Ft-lbs (unless otherwise indicated)
Water pump-to-engine bolts	12 to 18
Water pump pulley to hub	80 to 93 in-lbs
Transmission oil line fitting-to-radiator	106 to 160 in-lbs
Fan shroud-to-radiator (electric fan).......................	88 to 160 in-lbs
Fan shroud-to-radiator (mechanical fan)	49 to 84 in-lbs
Fan clutch to mechanical fan nuts	49 to 84 in-lbs
Thermostat housing bolts	18 to 26
Radiator mounting bolts	88 to 160 in-lbs
Condenser mounting bolts	49 to 84 in-lbs
Compressor mounting bolts	18 to 26

1 General information

On all models, a cross-flow type radiator equipped with an electric-motor-driven fan is employed. With this system, cooling ability at idling speed, and warm-up characteristics, are improved. On models with air conditioning, a second fan, either electric or an engine-driven mechanical fan with clutch, is used in addition to the main cooling fan.

The radiator cooling fan is mounted in a housing/shroud at the engine side of the radiator. It is designed to come on when the engine reaches a certain temperature, and shut off again when the engine cools down some, thereby keeping the engine in the desired operating-temperature range. The range is controlled by a thermoswitch mounted on the radiator.

The system is pressurized by a spring-loaded radiator cap, which, by maintaining pressure, increases the boiling point of the coolant. If the coolant temperature goes above this increased boiling point, the extra pressure in the system forces the radiator cap valve off its seat and exposes the overflow pipe or hose. The overflow pipe/hose leads to a coolant recovery system. This consists of a plastic reservoir, mounted to the left side of the radiator, into which the coolant that normally escapes due to expansion is retained. When the engine cools, the excess

2.4 An inexpensive hydrometer can be used to test the condition of your coolant

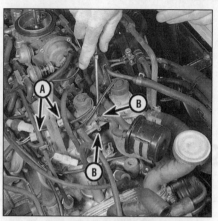

3.11a On models with these emissions solenoids, disconnect the electrical connectors (A) and the vacuum lines (B)

3.11b Remove the two screws per solenoid (arrows indicate three seen here)

coolant is drawn back into the radiator by the vacuum created as the system cools, maintaining the system at full capacity. This is a continuous process and provided the level in the reservoir is correctly maintained, it is not necessary to add coolant to the radiator.

On models equipped with an automatic transmission. an oil cooler is built into the radiator to cool the automatic transmission fluid. Heated oil circulating through the torque converter returns to the oil cooler and is cooled by the coolant, thus maintaining the oil at an adequate temperature.

The heating system works by directing air through the heater core, which is like a small radiator mounted behind the dash. Hot engine coolant heats the core, over which air passes to the interior of the vehicle by a system of ducts. Temperature is controlled by mixing heated air with fresh air, using a system of flapper doors in the ducts, and a heater blower motor.

Air conditioning is an optional accessory, consisting of an evaporator core located under the dash, a condenser in front of the radiator, an accumulator/drier in the engine compartment and a belt-driven compressor mounted at the front of the engine. **Warning:** *If an air conditioning unit is installed, do not attempt to service any of the air conditioning components without having the refrigerant discharged and recovered by an air conditioning shop or your dealer. If accidentally discharged, refrigerant can cause severe burns and may also result in damage to the air conditioning system.*

2 Antifreeze - general information

Refer to illustration 2.4
Warning: *Do not allow antifreeze to come in contact with your skin or painted surfaces of the vehicle. Rinse off spills immediately with plenty of water. Antifreeze is highly toxic if ingested. Never leave antifreeze lying around in an open container or in puddles on the floor; children and pets are attracted by it's sweet smell and may drink it. Check with local*

authorities about disposing of used antifreeze. Many communities have collection centers which will see that antifreeze is disposed of safely. Never dump used antifreeze on the ground or pour it into drains.
Note: *Non-toxic antifreeze is now manufactured and available at local auto parts stores, but even these types should be disposed of properly.*

The cooling system should be filled with a water/ethylene glycol based antifreeze solution which will prevent freezing down to at least -20-degrees F (even lower in cold climates). It also provides protection against corrosion and increases the coolant boiling point. The engines in the covered vehicles have aluminum block and heads. The manufacturer recommends that only coolant designated as safe for aluminum engine components be used.

The cooling system should be drained, flushed and refilled at least every other year (see Chapter 1). The use of antifreeze solutions for periods of longer than two years is likely to cause damage and encourage the formation of rust and scale in the system.

Before adding antifreeze to the system, check all hose connections. Antifreeze can leak through very minute openings.

The exact mixture of antifreeze to water which you should use depends on the relative weather conditions. The mixture should contain at least 50-percent antifreeze, but should never contain more than 70-percent antifreeze. Consult the mixture ratio chart on the container before adding coolant. Hydrometers are available at most auto parts stores to test the coolant **(see illustration)**. Use antifreeze which meets specifications for engines with aluminum heads and blocks.

3 Thermostat - check and replacement

1   The thermostat is located at the right side of the intake manifold. The thermostat allows for quick warm-ups and governs the

normal operating temperature of the engine.
2   If the thermostat is functioning properly, the temperature gauge should rise to the normal operating temperature quickly and then stay there, only rising above the normal position occasionally when the engine gets unusually hot. If the engine does not rise to normal operating temperature quickly, or if it overheats, the thermostat should be removed and checked or replaced.

Check

3   Before condemning the thermostat, check the coolant level, drivebelt tension and temperature gauge (or light) operation.
4   If the engine takes a long time to warm up, the thermostat is probably stuck open. Replace the thermostat.
5   If the engine runs hot, check the temperature of the upper radiator hose. If the hose isn't hot, the thermostat is probably stuck shut. Replace the thermostat.
6   If the upper radiator hose is hot, it means the coolant is circulating and the thermostat is open. Refer to the *Troubleshooting* Section for the cause of overheating.
7   If an engine has been overheated, you may find damage such as leaking head gaskets, scuffed pistons and warped or cracked cylinder heads.

Replacement

Refer to illustrations 3.11a, 3.11b, 3.12, 3.13 and 3.20
8   The engine must be cool when removal is performed.
9   Place a suitable container under the radiator and drain some of the coolant into the container by opening the radiator drain valve (see Chapter 1).
10   Loosen and slide back the hose clamp, then pull the upper radiator hose off the thermostat housing cover.
11   On models with emissions-required solenoid valves (Hitachi carburetor-equipped), tag and disconnect the vacuum lines and electrical connectors to the two solenoids **(see illustration)**, then unbolt the

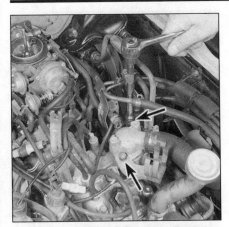

3.12 Remove the two thermostat housing bolts (arrows)

3.13 Note the direction the thermostat (arrow) was installed

3.20 Scrape the housing and cover of any old gasket material, but vacuum up any debris that falls into the open housing

solenoids from the top of the thermostat housing **(see illustration)**.

12 Remove the bolts and lift off the housing cover. You may have to tap the cover with a soft-faced hammer to break the gasket seal **(see illustration)**.

13 After the cover has been removed, note how the thermostat is installed and lift it out. If it is open when it is removed, it is defective and must be replaced with a new one **(see illustration)**.

14 To check the thermostat, submerge it in a container of water along with a thermometer. The thermostat should be suspended so it does not touch the container.

15 Gradually heat the water in the container with a hotplate or stove and check the temperature when the thermostat first starts to open.

16 Continue heating the water and check the temperature when the thermostat is fully open.

17 Lift the fully open thermostat out of the water and allow it to cool.

18 Compare the opening temperature and the fully open temperature to the Specifications.

19 If these Specifications are not met, or if the thermostat does not open while the water

is heated, replace it with a new one.

20 Scrape all traces of the old gasket from the thermostat housing and cover **(see illustration)**. Do not nick or gouge the gasket sealing surfaces.

21 To install the thermostat, lay it in place in the housing with the proper end facing up. Each thermostat has a breather, which must face out. Examine yours carefully before installing it. Make sure that the thermostat flange is properly seated in the recessed area of the housing. **Note:** *Check the construction of your radiator before ordering the thermostat. Models with aluminum radiators require a multi-stage thermostat.*

22 Apply a thin, even layer of RTV-type gasket sealer to both sides of a new gasket and lay it in place on the housing.

23 Next, carefully position the housing cover, install the bolts and tighten them securely.

24 Slip the upper radiator hose onto the housing cover spigot, install the hose clamp and tighten it securely.

25 Refill the radiator with coolant. Start the engine and check for leaks around the thermostat housing and the upper radiator hose.

---

4   Cooling fans, relay and clutch - check, removal and installation

Mechanical fan

Warning: *Keep hands, tools and clothing away from the fan when the engine is running. To avoid injury or damage DO NOT operate the engine with a damaged fan. Do not attempt to repair fan blades - replace a damaged fan with a new one.*

Check

Warning: *In order to check the fan clutch, the engine will need to be at operating temperature, so while going through checks, be careful that the engine is NOT started while the checks are being performed. Severe personal injury can result!*

1   Symptoms of failure of the fan clutch are continuous noisy operation, looseness, vibra-

tion and evidence of silicone fluid leaks.

2   Rock the fan back and forth by hand to check for excessive bearing play.

3   With the engine cold, turn the blades by hand. The fan should turn freely.

4   Visually inspect for substantial fluid leakage from the fan clutch assembly, a deformed bimetallic spring or grease leakage from the cooling fan bearing. If any of these conditions exist, replace the fan clutch.

5   When the engine is warmed up, turn off the ignition switch and disconnect the cable from the negative battery terminal. Turn the fan by hand. Some resistance should be felt. If the fan turns easily, replace the fan clutch.

Replacement

Refer to illustrations 4.7 and 4.8

6   Disconnect the battery cable at the negative battery terminal.

7   With an open or box wrench, reach between the fan and the water pump to remove the four bolts holding the fan assembly and water pump pulley to the water pump **(see illustration)**.

8   The fan clutch can be unbolted from the fan blade assembly for replacement **(see illustration)**. **Caution:** *To prevent silicone*

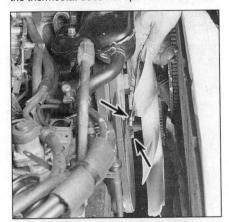

4.7 Remove the four bolts (arrows indicate two) holding the mechanical fan to the water pump (electric fan and shroud removed here for clarity)

4.8 Remove the three bolts (arrows) holding the clutch unit to the mechanical fan blade assembly

3

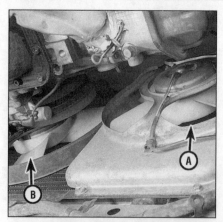

4.10 A 1982 pushrod model seen from below shows the two cooling fans, the right fan (A) is the main engine cooling fan, while the fan to the left (B) is the auxiliary fan operated when the air conditioning is on

4.11 Disconnect the fan's electrical plug (B) from the connector to the wiring harness (A), then apply battery voltage and ground to the two terminals to check fan operation

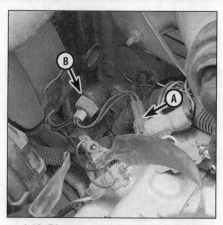

4.16 Disconnect the thermoswitch's harness plug (A), then unscrew the thermoswitch (B) from the radiator

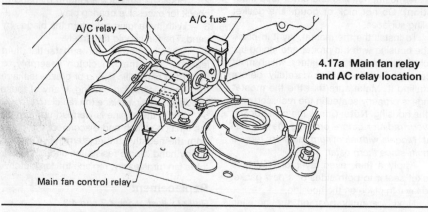

4.17a Main fan relay and AC relay location

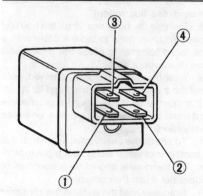

4.17b Test the fan relay for continuity - there should be 80 ohms resistance between terminals 3 and 4 and no resistance between 1 and 2

fluid from draining from the clutch assembly into the fan drive bearing and ruining the lubricant, DON'T place the drive unit in a position with the rear of the shaft pointing down. Store the fan in its upright position if possible.

9   Installation is the reverse of removal. Tighten the fan clutch-to-fan blade bolts and the fan assembly-to-drive hub nut to the torque listed in this Chapter's Specifications.

Electric cooling fans

Check

Refer to illustrations 4.10, 4.11, 4.16, 4.17a and 4.17b

10   All vehicles have a thermostatically-controlled fan and motor assembly which is actuated by a thermoswitch installed in the radiator. Vehicles with air conditioning have an additional fan and motor assembly installed behind the core of the transmission oil cooler **(see illustration)**. If the engine overheats because the cooling fan(s) fail to operate, check the motor as described in this Section.

11   To check the fan motor for proper operation, unplug the electrical connector and attach jumper wires to the two terminals in the connector half attached to the motor **(see illustration)**. **Caution:** *Make sure the jumper wires are not contacting each other.*

12   Connect the opposite ends of the jumper wires to the battery posts and see if the fan operates. **Caution:** *Keep your hands and the wires away from the cooling fan.*

13   If the fan fails to operate, replace the fan motor. If the motor operates, look for the fan problem in the rest of the circuit. Check the fan fuse (see Chapter 12).

14   Check the ground wire attached between the radiator and the chassis. If this wire is not well-grounded, the fan will not operate.

15   If the fan is still not operating with the harness connected, disconnect the connector and probe the positive side. If the engine is hot (thermoswitch activated) there should be battery voltage at the connector. If not, check the fan relay mounted near the ignition coil in the engine compartment.

16   Test the fan thermoswitch. Refer to Chapter 1 and drain the cooling system, then disconnect the wiring connector at the thermoswitch and unscrew the thermoswitch from the radiator **(see illustration)**.

17   Test the thermoswitch in a container of water heated on a stove, in the same manner in which the thermostat was checked in Section 3. With an ohmmeter attached to the terminals of the wiring connector, note the temperature at which the terminals exhibit continuity and compare this to Specifications. If

the fuse, fan, ground wire and thermoswitch are all good, check the fan relay **(see illustrations)**.

Removal and installation

Refer to illustrations 4.19a, 4.19b, 4.20 and 4.21

18   Disconnect the fan motor electrical connector.

19   Remove the fan motor shroud (with

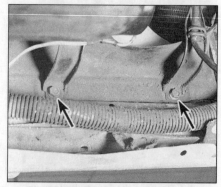

4.19a From below, remove the two fan shroud bolts (arrows) from the bottom of the radiator, then . . .

4.19b ... the two bolts (arrows) at the top of the radiator and pull out the fan assembly

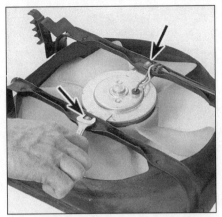

4.20 Unclip the fan's wiring harness from the shroud, then remove the two screws (arrows) holding the fan to the shroud

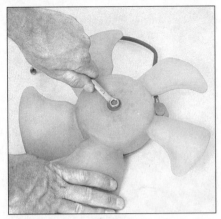

4.21 Remove the nut holding the fan to the motor

3

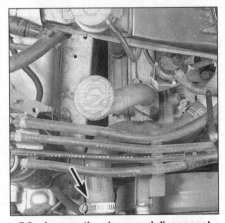

5.3a Loosen the clamp and disconnect the upper radiator hose (arrow)

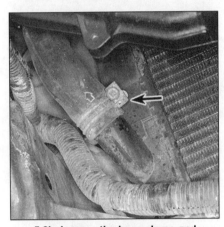

5.3b Loosen the hose clamp and disconnect the lower radiator hose (arrow)

5.7 Remove the two bolts (arrows) from the radiator support and pull the radiator up and out of the vehicle

motor attached) from the radiator frame **(see illustrations)**.

20 Remove the fan motor mounting bolts from the shroud and then remove the fan motor along with the fan **(see illustration)**.

21 If the motor is not working, replace it with a new one. Remove the fan from the old motor and attach it to the new motor with the fan mounting nut **(see illustration)**.

22 Install the motor on the fan shroud and the shroud on the radiator frame.

23 Connect the electrical connector to the motor and make sure that all of the mounting hardware is tight.

5   Radiator and coolant recovery tank - removal and installation

Radiator

Refer to illustrations 5.3a, 5.3b and 5.7

1   Drain the coolant out of the radiator by referring to Chapter 1.

2   Disconnect the negative battery cable.

3   Disconnect the radiator hoses by loosening the hose clamps **(see illustrations)**.

4   On vehicles with automatic transmis-

sions, disconnect the hoses from the oil cooler in the radiator. **Note:** *Be prepared to catch any transmission fluid that may run out of these hoses when they are disconnected.*

5   Disconnect the fan motor wiring connector, the thermoswitch wire and the radiator ground wire (see Section 4).

6   Remove the cooling fan and shroud

5.11 Pull the electrical box (arrow) up and out of the pocket on the recovery tank

from the radiator (Section 4). **Note:** *Vehicles with air conditioning also have an additional fan assembly to remove.*

7   Remove the radiator mounting bolts and remove the radiator by lifting it up and out of the engine compartment **(see illustration)**. Radiator service and repair should be left to a reputable radiator shop.

8   Install the radiator in the engine compartment with its mounting bolts and tighten them securely. **Note:** *The bottom of the radiator sits in two rubber bushings on the body. Make sure the bushings are in place before tightening the upper radiator mounting bolts.*

9   Run the engine until it is warm, while checking for leaks around each of the coolant hose attaching points. Allow the engine to cool completely before checking the coolant level again.

Coolant recovery tank

Refer to illustrations 5.11 and 5.12

10   Disconnect the cable from the negative battery terminal.

11   Drain the cooling system as described in Chapter 1, then remove the electrical junction/fusible link box from its pocket on the coolant recovery tank **(see illustration)**.

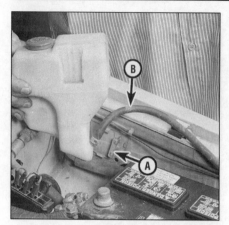

5.12 On most models, the recovery tank can be pulled straight up out of its bracket (A), then disconnect the hose (B) from the radiator

6.3 If there's coolant leaking from the weep hole (arrow) the water pump should be replaced

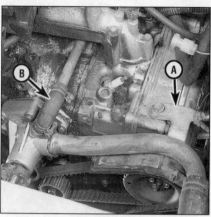

7.4 Remove the bolt (A) holding the radiator pipe to the water pump (OHC), then disconnect the bypass hose (B)

12   Pull the reservoir straight up and out of its bracket on the fenderwell **(see illustration). Note:** *Some models may have one or two bolts attaching it to the fenderwell.*
13   Prior to installation make sure the reservoir is clean and free of debris which could be drawn into the radiator (wash inside it with soapy water and a long brush if necessary). It will be easier to read the coolant level if the tank is cleaned.
14   Installation is the reverse of removal.

6   Water pump - check

Refer to illustration 6.3
1   Water pump failure can cause overheating and serious damage to the engine. There are three ways to check the operation of the water pump while it's installed on the engine. If any one of the three following quick checks indicates water pump problems, it should be replaced immediately.

7.5 Remove the water pump bolts (arrows), then break the gasket seal with a soft hammer - the water pipe (OHC shown) or hose must be removed first to remove the bolt shown here with a wrench on it

2   Start the engine and warm it up to normal operating temperature. Squeeze the upper radiator hose. If the water pump is working properly, you should feel a pressure surge as the hose is released. **Warning:** *Keep your hands away from the fan!*
3   A seal protects the water pump impeller shaft bearing from contamination by engine coolant. If this seal fails, a weep hole in the water pump snout will leak coolant **(see illustration)** (an inspection mirror can be used to look at the underside of the pump if the hole isn't on top). If the weep hole is leaking, shaft bearing failure will follow. Replace the water pump immediately. **Note:** *A small amount of gray discoloration is normal. A wet area or heavy brown deposits indicate the pump seal has failed.*
4   Besides contamination by coolant after a seal failure, the water pump impeller shaft bearing can also prematurely wear out. If a noise is coming from the water pump during engine operation, the shaft bearing has failed - replace the water pump immediately. **Note:** *Do not confuse drivebelt noise with bearing noise. Loose or glazed drivebelts may emit a high-pitched squealing noise.*
5   To identify excessive bearing wear before the bearing actually fails, grasp the water pump pulley (with drivebelt removed) and try to force it up-and-down or from side-to-side. If the pulley can be moved either horizontally or vertically, the bearing is nearing the end of its service life. Replace the water pump.

7   Water pump - replacement

Refer to illustrations 7.4, 7.5, 7.6, 7.7, 7.8 and 7.10
1   To replace the water pump, first drain the coolant out of the radiator by referring to the appropriate Section in Chapter 1.
2   Loosen the four bolts or nuts holding the water pump pulley to the water pump. Refer to Section 4 for models with a mechanical fan bolted to the water pump pulley. **Note:** *On*

some models, the pulley is retained by nuts and there is a cap plate over the front of the pulley. Do not misplace the plate.
3   Release the tension and remove the pump drivebelt (see Chapter 1). Do this after loosening the pulley bolts, as the belt helps hold the pulley while the bolts/nuts are loosened.
4   Disconnect the radiator outlet hose and the bypass hose from the water pump **(see illustration). Note:** *On OHV engines, the radiator hose is clamped to the water pump, while on OHC engines, it is a metal pipe bolted to the water pump and sealed with an O-ring. The pipe must be unbolted from the left camshaft housing in order to pull it out of the pump.*
5   Remove the bolts, then separate the water pump and gasket from the engine **(see illustration).** You may have to tap the pump gently with a soft-faced hammer to break the gasket seal. **Note:** *On OHC engines, the center timing belt outer cover must be removed first to access all the water pump bolts (see Chapter 2, Part B).*
6   Scrape all traces of the old gasket and gasket sealer off of the engine. Do not nick or gouge the gasket sealing surfaces **(see illustration).**

7.6 Scrape the gasket area on pump and block, then clean with thinner

7.7 Coat the pump with RTV sealant, then attach the gasket and line up the holes - apply a second thin coat of sealant on the engine side of the gasket

7.8 On OHC engines, insert the two rubber side sealing strips (arrows) as the pump is installed - it's too hard to slip them in after the pump is bolted down

7.10 Install a new O-ring on the OHC radiator pipe before installation

7   Coat both sides of a new gasket with RTV-type gasket sealer, then install the new pump **(see illustration)**. Be sure to line up the bolt holes in the pump body and the gasket before placing the pump in position on the engine.

8   On OHC engines, the water pump is part of the "sealing" of the timing belt area. On either side of the pump, there are grooves into which rubber strips are inserted that fit between the pump and bosses on the block **(see illustration)**. Insert these strips (lubricated) as the pump is installed.

9   Install the pump mounting bolts and tighten them evenly and securely.

10   Attach the hoses to the pump and tighten the hose clamps securely. On OHC engines, install a new O-ring (lubricated with antifreeze) on the water pipe before installing it **(see illustration)**.

11   Install the pump drivebelt and make the proper adjustments by referring to the appropriate Section in Chapter 1.

12   Refill the cooling system with coolant, start the engine and check for leaks and abnormal noises.

8   Coolant temperature sending unit - check and replacement

Warning: *Wait until the engine is completely cool before beginning this procedure.*

Check

1   The coolant temperature indicator system is composed of a temperature gauge mounted in the dash and a coolant temperature sending unit mounted on the engine at the right side of the intake manifold (see Chapter 4A). Some vehicles have more than one sending unit, but only one is used for the indicator system and the other is used to send engine temperature information to the computer.

2   If an overheating indication occurs, check the coolant level in the system. Make sure the wiring between the gauge and the

sending unit is secure and all fuses are intact.

3   To test the temperature sender, disconnect the electrical connector at the sender and connect an ohmmeter between the sender's terminal and an engine ground. When the engine is at ambient temperature (122 degrees F) resistance should be 130 to 170 ohms. As the engine warms up, the sender's resistance should drop, and at full operating temperature (212 degrees F) should read between 25 to 30 ohms.

Replacement

4   If the sending unit must be replaced, disconnect the electrical connector and simply unscrew the sensor from the engine and install the replacement. **Caution:** *The sending unit is made up of metal and plastic and is fragile. Use care when removing not to crack the unit.* Use sealant on the threads. Make sure the engine is cool before removing the defective sending unit. There will be some coolant loss as the unit is removed, so be prepared to catch it. Check the coolant level after the replacement unit has been installed.

9   Heater and air conditioning blower motor and circuit - check and component replacement

Check

Refer to illustration 9.4

1   Check the fuse and all connections in the circuit for looseness and corrosion. Make sure the battery is fully charged.

2   With the transmission in Park and the parking brake securely set, turn the ignition switch to the run position. It isn't necessary to start the vehicle.

3   Switch the heater controls to FLOOR and the blower speed to HI. Listen at the ducts to hear if the blower is operating. If it is, then switch the blower speed to LO and listen again. Try all the speeds.

4   If the blower motor does not operate,

disconnect the electrical connector at the blower motor, turn the ignition key On (engine not running) and check for battery voltage on the green/white wire terminal **(see illustration)**. If battery voltage is not present, there is a problem in the ignition feed circuit.

5   If battery voltage is present, reconnect the terminal to the blower motor and back-probe the blue wire with a jumper wire connected to ground **(see illustration 9.4)**. If the motor still does not operate, the motor is faulty. If the motor operated with the ground jumper in place, check the ground circuit to the blower connector.

6   If the motor is good, but doesn't operate at any speed, the heater/air conditioning control switch is probably faulty. Remove the control assembly (see Section 11) and check for continuity through the switch in each position.

7   If the blower motor operates at High speed, but not at one or more of the lower speeds, check the blower motor resistor, located under the instrument panel on the passenger side.

8   Disconnect the electrical connector

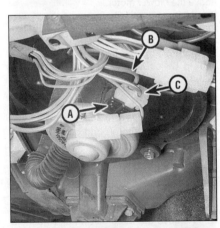

9.4 Disconnect the blower motor connector (A) and probe the power side wire (C) - with the connector back in place, backprobe the ground (B) side (glove box and trim panel shown removed for clarity)

3

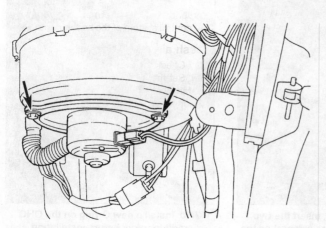

9.13 Disconnect the electrical connector, then remove the three mounting screws (arrows indicate two seen in this view)

9.14 Blower motor components:

| A | Motor | B | Fan | C | Fan retaining nut |

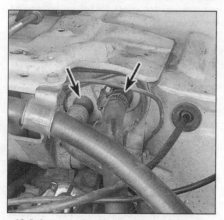

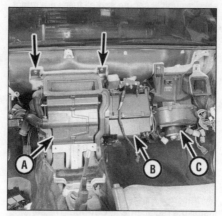

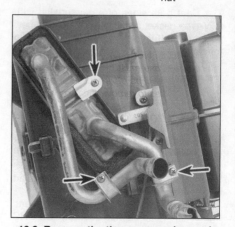

10.3 Loosen the clamps and pull off the heater hoses (arrows) from the heater core tubes where they protrude at the firewall

10.8 Heater/air conditioning components include the heater core case (A), the evaporator core case (B) and the blower housing (C) - remove the two bolts (upper arrows) to pull out the heater core case

10.9 Remove the three screws (arrows) and the retaining clamps holding the core in the case

from the blower motor resistor and withdraw the resistor from the pocket in the housing above the blower motor.

9   Using a continuity tester on the blower motor resistor, check between each input terminal (from the blower speed switch side) to the output terminal (to the blower). There should be continuity. If not, replace the resistor.

Removal

Refer to illustrations 9.13 and 9.14

10   Disconnect the ground cable from the battery.

11   Refer to Chapter 11 and remove the parcel shelf, the glove box and the lower trim panel.

12   Disconnect the electrical connector from the blower motor.

13   Remove the three screws and washers and remove the blower assembly from the vehicle **(see illustration)**. **Note:** *On some models, disconnect the vent hose before pulling the motor out, and on some early models, the fresh air duct may have to be removed first to access the blower motor.*

14   The motor may be replaced by removing the nut holding the fan to the motor **(see illustration)**.

15   The installation is basically the reverse of the removal procedure. **Note:** *If a vehicle has high mileage, a faulty blower can be caused by an accumulation of debris inside the blower housing. If debris is present, clean it out and retest the blower motor for proper operation before replacing it with a new one.*

10   Heater core - removal and installation

Warning: *The air conditioning system is under high pressure. DO NOT loosen any fittings or remove any components until after the system has been discharged. Air conditioning refrigerant should be properly discharged into an EPA-approved container at a dealer service department or an automotive air conditioning facility. Always wear eye protection when disconnecting air conditioning system fittings.*

Removal

Refer to illustrations 10.3, 10.8 and 10.9

1   Disconnect the ground cable from the battery.

2   Remove the radiator drain plug and drain the coolant from the radiator.

3   Disconnect both the inlet and the outlet hoses from the heater pipes at the firewall **(see illustration)**.

4   Remove the heater hose grommet from the firewall.

5   Refer to Chapter 11 and remove the dashboard, center console and the instrument panel from the vehicle.

6   Detach the heater duct between the heater unit and the blower assembly.

7   Remove both of the defroster nozzles.

8   Remove the bolts on the upper part of the heater unit, lift the heater unit and pull it to the rear of the vehicle **(see illustration)**. **Note:** *Keep some shop towels on the vehicle's floor to protect the carpeting from spilled coolant. If the coolant spills on any painted surfaces, wash it off immediately or it could cause discolorations.*

9   Remove the screws holding the three

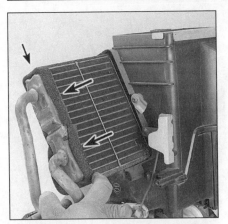

10.10 Make sure that the foam sealing material (arrows) is in place when installing the new heater core into the case

clamps over the heater core pipes on the fire-wall side of the heater core case **(see illustration)**. Pull the heater core straight out of the housing. **Note:** *On some early models, the heater case must be split to take out the core. Pry the clips off the case and separate the two halves to remove the heater core.*

Installation

Refer to illustration 10.10

10   Slide the new heater core into the case, making sure that the sealing foam is in place **(see illustration)**. **Note:** *Because of the labor involved in accessing the heater core, it does-n't pay to have a leaking core repaired. Replace a leaking core (you can have it pressure-tested at a radiator shop) with a new one.*

11   Install the heater unit in the vehicle.

12   Install the defroster nozzles and ducts.

13   Refer to Chapter 11 and reinstall the instrument panel and console. Connect the wires, cables and vacuum hoses discon-nected for removal.

14   Install the heater hose grommet in the firewall.

15   Connect both the inlet and the outlet hoses to the heater pipe. If either hose is hardened or split at the end, replace the heater hoses with new ones.

16   Fill the radiator with coolant and con-nect the ground cable to the battery.

17   Start the vehicle and operate the heater controls. Check for any leakage around the hose connections.

11   Air conditioning and heater control assembly - check, removal and installation

Note: *Models up to 1984 have heating/air conditioning control functions operated by cables, while later models have vacuum con-trols with servo vacuum motors at the various ducting doors or "shutters."*

Cable controls

Mode lever

1   Start the engine and set the temperature control dial to the Cold position. Set the fresh air ventilation control lever to the Off position.

2   With the fan switch on the fourth step, and the mode lever in the AC position (if applicable), outside air should be directed into the compartment only through the center and side air ducts.

3   If air is directed through the lower outlet or the defroster nozzle, the mode lever should be adjusted until the air directed through these ports is at a minimum.

4   With the fan switch on the fourth step and the mode lever in the Heat position, out-side air should be directed into the compart-ment only through the lower air ducts and the defroster nozzle.

5   If air is directed through the center or side outlets, the mode lever should be adjusted until the air directed through these ports is at a minimum.

6   With the fan switch on the fourth step and the mode lever in the Def position, out-side air should be directed into the compart-ment only through the defroster nozzle.

7   If air is directed through the lower, cen-ter or side outlets, the mode lever should be adjusted until the air directed through these ports is at a minimum.

Temperature control dial

8   To check the temperature control dial, check for correct outlet air temperature. Start the engine and let it warm up for 10 minutes. Set the fresh air ventilation lever to the Off position.

9   Set the mode lever to the Heat position, the fan switch at the first step and the tem-perature control dial to the Cold position.

10   Measure the air temperature coming out of the lower outlet of the heater unit with a thermometer. Hold the thermometer in place for a few minutes; the temperature should not vary more than 5 degrees from the outside temperature.

11   If the temperature variance is more than 5 degrees, adjust the control system of the heater control valve.

12   Set the mode lever to the Def position, the fan switch at the fourth step and the tem-perature control dial to the Hot position.

13   Measure the air temperature coming out of the defroster nozzle with a thermometer. Hold the thermometer in place for a few min-utes and check the reading. Defroster nozzle temperature directly corresponds with the outside temperature in that the warmer the temperature outside of the vehicle, the warmer the defroster nozzle temperature. The following example will illustrate this and will also give you something to shoot for as far as the correct temperature.

Outside air	Defroster nozzle air
-4°F (-20°C)	122°F (50°C) or more
32°F (0°C)	140°F (60°C) or more

14   If your temperature readings do not cor-respond with the information given, adjust the control system of the heater control valve.

Fresh air ventilation lever

15   Check the ventilation lever for air leak-age. Set the mode lever to the Circ position, the fan switch in the Off position and the ven-tilation lever to the Off position.

16   Outside air should be directed through the center outlet only. If air is directed through any other outlet around the console, the ventilation lever should be adjusted until the air directed through these ports is at a minimum.

Adjustment

Refer to illustrations 11.17, 11.18, 11.19, 11.20, 11.21 and 11.22

17   To connect the mode lever cable, set the mode lever to the Circ position. Set the mode lever linkage at the heater unit to the Circ position by pulling up and back **(see illustration)**.

18   After connecting the mode lever cable to lever B, connect the cable to the cable clamp while pulling the cable up and back. Maintain the specified distance **(see illustration)**.

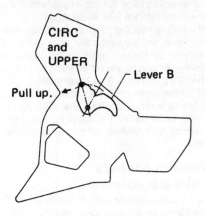

11.17 Mode Control lever setting

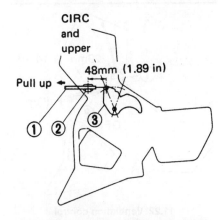

11.18 Mode control cable connection

1	*Cable*	*3 Lever B*
2	*Clamp*	

3

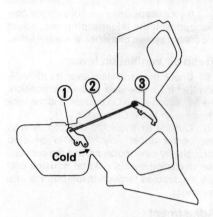

11.19 Temperature control lever setting

1	Lever E	3	Lever A
2	Rod		

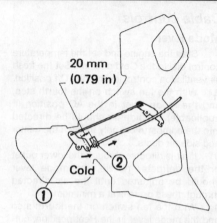

11.20 Temperature control cable connection

1	Lever E	2	Clamp

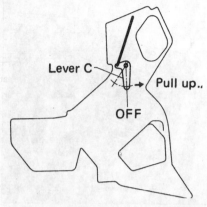

11.21 Ventilation control lever setting

19   To connect the temperature control cable, set the temperature control dial to the Cold position. Set the temperature control linkage at the heater to the Cold position by pulling the E lever up **(see illustration)**.
20   After connecting the temperature control cable to lever E, connect the cable to the clamp while pulling the cable up. Maintain the specified distance **(see illustration)**.
21   To connect the fresh air ventilation control cable, set the ventilation lever to the off position. Set the ventilation control linkage at the heater unit to the off position by pulling lever C up and back **(see illustration)**.
22   After connecting the ventilation control cable to lever C, connect the cable to the clamp while pulling the cable up and back. Maintain the specified distance **(see illustration)**.

Vacuum controls

Refer to illustration 11.23
23   On models with vacuum controls, check the operation of all modes with the engine running. If there are problems with the function in any one mode, check the vacuum

servo motor for that function **(see illustration)**.
24   Disconnect the vacuum hose (coming from the controls) and attach a hand-held vacuum pump. Slowly apply vacuum and watch the operation of the motor and the lever it operates. If the vacuum motor is responding properly but the door function doesn't go all the way, adjust the rod attached to the door, while the vacuum is still applied by the pump.
25   If the servos check out properly, but don't respond to the controls, check the hose coming from the controls to that servo for full vacuum by attaching a vacuum gauge while the engine is running. If there is insufficient or no vacuum, trace the main vacuum source. Go along the hose from the intake manifold to the vacuum reservoir tank behind the right shock tower, checking for manifold vacuum at the tank end of the hose.
26   If the vacuum is good at the tank, check for good vacuum in the line from the tank to the control assembly. You'll have to pull the controls out of the dash to check this end with a vacuum gauge.

27   If there is good vacuum there and one or more of the controls are not responding, check for a leak or restriction in the vacuum lines from the control assembly to the servos.

Removal, all types

Refer to illustrations 11.30 and 11.31
28   Disconnect the ground cable from the battery.
29   Remove the instrument panel trim panel (see Chapter 11). On some models, the knobs on the heating/air conditioning controls must be pried off before removing the trim panel.
30   Remove the heater control panel from the instrument panel **(see illustration)**. Two small plastic tabs must be pried from the corners of the control to expose the two mounting screws.
31   On cable systems, disconnect the cables for the temperature control, the mode control and the center ventilation control from the heater unit. On vacuum systems, disconnect the electrical wiring and the vacuum hoses **(see illustration)**. **Note:** *Mark the vacuum lines before disconnecting them.*

Installation

32   To install the heater controls, follow the removal procedure in reverse. **Note:** *Connect the cables before installing the heater control panel in the instrument panel.*

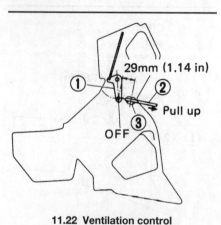

11.22 Ventilation control cable connection

1	Lever C	3	Clamp
2	Cable		

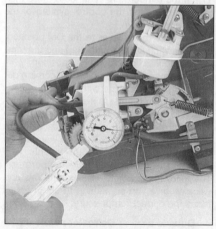

11.23 The operation of vacuum servo motors can be checked with a hand-held vacuum pump

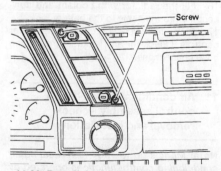

11.30 Pry off the knobs, remove the trim panel and remove the screws holding the heating/air conditioning controls (arrow)

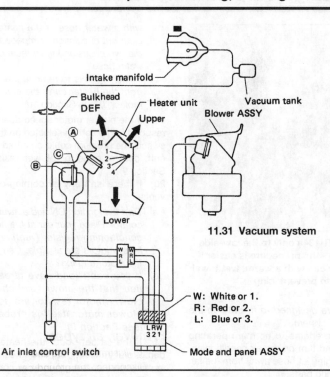

11.31 Vacuum system

W: White or 1.
R: Red or 2.
L: Blue or 3.

Air inlet control switch

Mode and panel ASSY

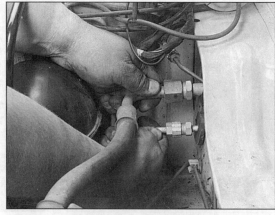

12.6 Feel the two refrigerant pipes at the firewall with the system running

12.7 Insert a thermometer into one of the center dash air outlets to check the effectiveness of your air conditioning system

12 Air conditioning and heating system - check and maintenance

Warning: *The air conditioning system is under high pressure. DO NOT loosen any fittings or remove any components until after the system has been discharged. Air conditioning refrigerant should be properly discharged into an approved container at a dealer service department or an automotive air conditioning repair facility. Always wear eye protection when disconnecting air conditioning system fittings.*

1   The following maintenance steps should be performed on a regular basis to ensure that the air conditioner continues to operate at peak efficiency.

a) *Check the tension of the drivebelt and adjust if necessary (see Chapter 1).*
b) *Check the condition of the hoses. Look for cracks, hardening and deterioration.* **Warning:** *Do not replace air conditioning hoses until the system has been discharged by a dealer or air conditioning shop.*
c) *Check the fins of the condenser for leaves, bugs and other foreign material. A soft brush and compressed air can be used to remove them.*
d) *Check the wire harness for correct routing, broken wires, damaged insulation, etc. Make sure the harness connections are clean and tight.*
e) *Maintain the correct refrigerant charge.*

2   The system should be run for about 10 minutes at least once a month. This is particularly important during the winter months because long-term non-use can cause hardening of the internal seals.

3   Because of the complexity of the air conditioning system and the special equipment required to effectively work on it, accurate troubleshooting of the system should be left to a professional technician. One probable cause for poor cooling that can be determined by the home mechanic is low refrigerant charge. Should the system lose its cooling ability, the following procedure will help you pinpoint the cause.

Check

Refer to illustrations 12.6 and 12.7

4   Warm the engine up to normal operating temperature.

5   Place the air conditioning temperature selector at the coldest setting and put the blower at the highest setting. Open the doors (to make sure the air conditioning system doesn't cycle off as soon as it cools the passenger compartment).

6   After the system reaches operating temperature, feel the two pipes connected to the evaporator at the firewall **(see illustration)**.

7   The pipe (thinner tubing) leading from the condenser outlet to the evaporator should be cold, and the evaporator outlet line (the thicker tubing that leads back to the compressor) should be slightly colder (3 to 10 degrees F). If the evaporator outlet is considerably warmer than the inlet, the system needs a charge. Insert a thermometer in the center air distribution duct **(see illustration)** while operating the air conditioning system - the temperature of the output air should be 35 to 40 degrees F below the ambient air temperature (down to approximately 40 degrees F). If the ambient (outside) air temperature is very high, say 110 degrees F, the duct air temperature may be as high as 60 degrees F, but generally the air conditioning

is 35 to 40 degrees F cooler than the ambient air. If the air isn't as cold as it used to be, the system probably needs a charge. Further inspection or testing of the system is beyond the scope of the home mechanic and should be left to a professional. **Note:** *Most R-12 systems have a sight glass on top of the receiver/drier. When the system is running, check the glass. A steady stream of bubbles or foam indicates the system is low on refrigerant.*

Adding refrigerant

Refer to illustrations 12.9, 12.12

8   Most models covered by this manual use refrigerant R-12, which was replaced by the environmentally-friendly R-134a beginning with 1994 models (only on selected models). When recharging or replacing air conditioning components, use only refrigerant, refrigerant oil and seals compatible with the system in your vehicle. The seals and compressor oil used with older, conventional R-12 refrigerant are not compatible with the components in the R-134a system. If in doubt about which refrigerant you have, look for labels on the air conditioning system. Only the R-134a systems have light-blue labels

3

12.9 A basic charging kit for R-134a systems is available at most auto parts stores - it must say R-134a (not R-12) and so must the 12-ounce can of refrigerant

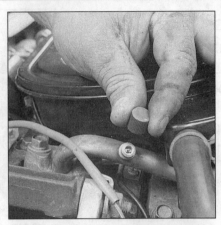

12.12 Add R-134a only to the low-side port (arrow) - the procedure is easier if you wrap the can with a warm, wet towel to prevent icing

marked R-134a. **Note:** *Your local auto parts dealer has kits available for some 1990 to 1994 models that will convert the air-conditioning system to accept R-134a refrigerant. If a kit is available for your specific vehicle, have your system's R-12 refrigerant discharged and recovered by an air-conditioning shop, install the kit components according the to the manufacturer's instructions, then charge the system with R-134a refrigerant. Cooling performance after the conversion may not be as efficient as with the old refrigerant, but the new refrigerant is friendlier to the environment and much less expensive to replace should a leak develop.*

9   Refrigerant cans of R-12 are no longer available for home use. Have an R-12 system charged at an air conditioning shop or dealership, or convert it to R-134a if possible. However, R-134a is available in cans and you can buy a charging kit for home use at an auto parts store. A charging kit includes a 12-ounce can of R-134a refrigerant, a tap valve and a short section of hose that can be attached between the tap valve and the system low side service valve **(see illustration)**. Because one can of refrigerant may not be sufficient to bring the system charge up to the proper level, it's a good idea to buy a couple of additional cans. Try to find at least one can that contains red refrigerant dye. If the system is leaking, the red dye will leak out with the refrigerant and help you pinpoint the location of the leak.

10   Connect the charging kit by following the manufacturer's instructions.

11   Back off the valve handle on the charging kit and screw the kit onto the refrigerant can, making sure first that the O-ring or rubber seal inside the threaded portion of the kit is in place. **Warning:** *Wear protective eye wear when dealing with pressurized refrigerant cans.*

12   Remove the dust cap from the low-side charging port and attach the quick-connect fitting on the kit hose **(see illustration)**. **Warning:** *DO NOT hook the charging kit hose to the system high side! The fittings on the*

charging kit are designed to fit **only** on the low side of the system.

13   Warm the engine to normal operating temperature and turn on the air conditioning. Keep the charging kit hose away from the fan and other moving parts.

14   Turn the valve handle on the kit until the stem pierces the can, then back the handle out to release the refrigerant. You should be able to hear the rush of gas. Add refrigerant to the low side of the system until both the outlet and the evaporator inlet pipe feel about the same temperature. Allow stabilization time between each addition. **Warning:** *Never add more than two cans of refrigerant to the system.* The can may tend to frost up, slowing the procedure. Wet a shop towel with hot water and wrap it around the bottom of the can to keep it from frosting.

15   Put your thermometer back in the center register and check that the output air is getting colder.

16   When the can is empty, turn the valve handle to the closed position and release the connection from the low-side port. Replace the dust cap.

17   Remove the charging kit from the can and store the kit for future use with the piercing valve in the UP position, to prevent inadvertently piercing the can on the next use.

Heating systems

18   If the air coming out of the heater vents isn't hot, the problem could stem from any of the following causes:

a) *The thermostat is stuck open, preventing the engine coolant from warming up enough to carry heat to the heater core. Replace the thermostat (see Section 3).*

b) *A heater hose is blocked, preventing the flow of coolant through the heater core. Feel both heater hoses at the firewall. They should be hot. If one of them is cold, there is an obstruction in one of the hoses or in the heater core, or the heater control valve is shut. Detach the hoses and back flush the heater core*

with a water hose. If the heater core is clear but circulation is impeded, remove the two hoses and flush them out with a water hose.

c) *If flushing fails to remove the blockage from the heater core, the core must be replaced. (see Section 10).*

19   If the blower motor speed does not correspond to the setting selected on the blower switch, the problem could be a bad fuse, circuit, control panel or blower resistor (see Section 9).

20   If there isn't any air coming out of the vents:

a) *Turn the ignition ON and activate the fan control. Place your ear at the heating/air conditioning register (vent) and listen. Most motors are audible. Can you hear the motor running?*

b) *If you can't (and have already verified that the blower switch and the blower motor resistor are good), the blower motor itself is probably bad (see Section 9).*

21   If the carpet under the heater core is damp, or if antifreeze vapor or steam is coming through the vents, the heater core is leaking. Remove it (see Section 10) and install a new unit (most radiator shops will not repair a leaking heater core).

22   Inspect the drain hose from the heater/evaporator assembly at the right-center of the firewall, make sure it is not clogged. If there is a humid mist coming from the system ducts, this hose may be plugged with leaves or road debris.

Eliminating air conditioning odors

23   Unpleasant odors that often develop in air conditioning systems are caused by the growth of a bacteria, usually on the surface of the evaporator core. The warm, humid environment there is a perfect breeding ground for mildew to develop.

24   The evaporator core on most vehicles is difficult to access, and factory dealerships have a lengthy, expensive process for eliminating the fungus by opening up the evaporator case and using a powerful disinfectant and rinse on the core until the fungus is gone. You can service your own system at home, but it takes something much stronger than basic household germ-killers or deodorizers.

25   Aerosol disinfectants for automotive air conditioning systems are available in most auto parts stores, but remember when shopping for them that the most effective treatments are also the most expensive. The basic procedure for using these sprays is to start by running the system in the RECIRC mode for ten minutes with the blower on its highest speed. Use the highest heat mode to dry out the system and keep the compressor from engaging by disconnecting the wiring connector at the compressor (see Section 14).

26   The disinfectant can usually comes with a long spray hose. Pry off the front clips on

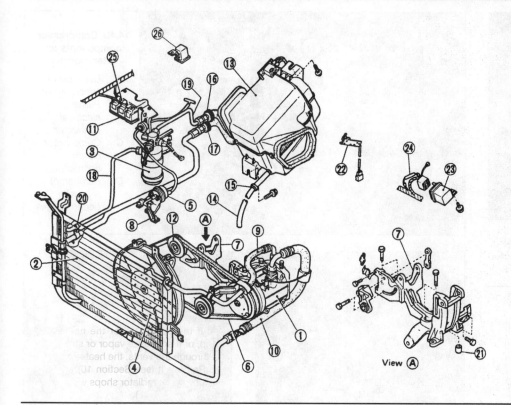

1	Compressor
2	Condenser
3	Receiver/drier
4	Condenser cooling fan
5	Actuator
6	Belt
7	Compressor bracket
8	Lever
9	Pipe and hose
10	Pipe and hose
11	Relay
12	Tension pulley
13	Evaporator
14	Drain hose
15	Grommet
16	Grommet
17	Grommet
18	Pipe
19	Pipe
20	Clamp
21	Spacer
22	Micro switch
23	Relay
24	Fuse
25	Fuse
26	Relay

View **(A)**

3

the evaporator case, open the two halves enough to insert the nozzle and spray, according to the manufacturer's recommendations. Try to cover the whole surface of the evaporator core, by aiming the spray up, down and sideways. Follow the manufacturer's recommendations for the length of spray and waiting time between applications.
27 Once the evaporator has been cleaned, the best way to prevent the mildew from coming back again is to make sure your evaporator housing drain tube is clear, and to run your system with heat and RECIRC for a few minutes after a long continuous usage of the air conditioning on a hot, humid day.

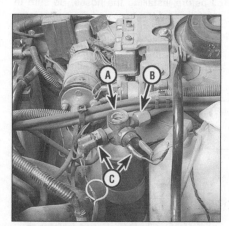

13.1b Receiver/drier in an early model vehicle - (A) is the sight glass, (B) is one of the two refrigerant lines (the other is behind in this photo), and (C) are the electrical connectors

13 Air conditioning receiver/dryer-removal and installation

Refer to illustrations 13.1a, 13.1b and 13.1c
Warning: *The air conditioning system is under high pressure. DO NOT loosen any fittings or remove any components until after the system has been discharged. Air conditioning refrigerant should be properly discharged into an approved container at a dealer service department or an automotive air conditioning repair facility. Always wear eye protection when disconnecting air conditioning system fittings.*
1   The receiver/dryer, which acts as a filter and reservoir for the refrigerant, is the canister-shaped object mounted on the passenger-side fender well in the engine compartment **(see illustrations)**.
2   Before removing the receiver/dryer, the system must be discharged by an air conditioning technician.
3   Detach the windshield washer tank from its mounting bracket and place it to the side.
4   Disconnect the wiring from the low-pressure switch.
5   Remove both tubes from the receiver/dryer **(see illustration 13.1c)**.
6   Loosen the clamp and pull up on the receiver/dryer to remove it from its mount.
7   When installing the receiver/dryer, lubricate the inside surfaces of the tubes and the outside of the fittings with refrigerant oil. Be sure the tubes are properly installed and securely tightened. If installing a new receiver/dryer, drain the refrigerant oil from

the old receiver drier into a measured container. Put that amount of new oil into the new receiver/drier.

14 Air conditioning compressor - removal and installation

Refer to illustrations 14.4a, 14.4b, 14.6a, 14.6b, 14.6c, 14.6d and 14.9
Warning: *The air conditioning system is under high pressure. DO NOT loosen any fittings or remove any components until after the system has been discharged. Air conditioning refrigerant should be properly dis-*

13.1c On later models, the electrical connectors are on the lines, not the receiver/drier - always use backup wrenches when disconnecting lines at the receiver/drier

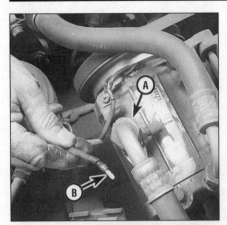

14.4a On early-model compressors, the refrigerant lines are secured by large fittings (A) - (B) is the electrical connector for the clutch

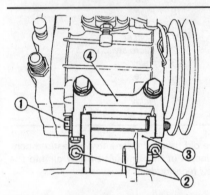

14.6a Compressor mounts and hardware, early models

1 Upper bolt
2 Bracket bolts
3 Compressors/bracket
4 Bracket (upper)

charged into an approved container at a dealer service department or an automotive air conditioning repair facility. Always wear eye protection when disconnecting air conditioning system fittings.

1   The air conditioning compressor is mounted at the front of the engine on the left side and is driven by a belt from the crankshaft **(see illustration 13.1a).**

14.6d . . . remove the adjuster bolt (arrow) below the compressor

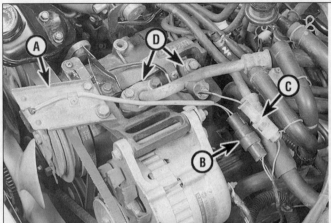

14.4b Compressor components on later models:

A Compressor speed pulser
B Pulser electrical connector
C Compressor clutch connector
D Refrigerant lines with bolted flanges

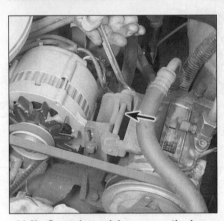

14.6b On early models, remove the long bolt (arrow) holding the upper compressor mount to the alternator mount

2   Before removing the compressor, the system must be discharged by an air conditioning technician.
3   Loosen the drivebelt tensioner pulley and slip the drivebelt off the compressor clutch pulley (see Chapter 1). On later models, the alternator must be removed before removing the compressor (see Chapter 5).
4   Disconnect the refrigerant lines from the compressor **(see illustrations).** **Note:** *Early models have the lines connected with large fittings, while on later models, the lines are bolted to the compressor with flanges.*
5   Unplug the air conditioning compressor clutch electrical connectors **(see illustrations 14.4a and 14.4b).**

14.6c On later models, remove the rear bolt(s) (arrow) holding the compressor to the bracket (alternator shown removed), then . . .

6   Remove the bolts attaching the compressor to the brackets and the compressor can be lifted out of the vehicle **(see illustrations).**
7   Installation is basically the reverse of removal. Lubricate the inside of the hoses and the outside of the fittings with refrigerant oil before installing the hoses. Be sure to carefully seat the hoses on the compressor fittings and install the hose clamps securely. On later models with flanged hoses, replace the O-rings (between the flanges and the compressor body) when reinstalling the hoses.

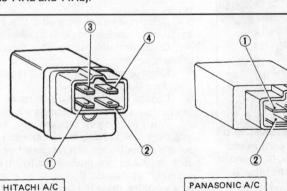

14.9 Check the air conditioning relay (either Hitachi or Panasonic) for continuity and resistance

HITACHI A/C   PANASONIC A/C

14.11 Check the pulser clearance (arrow) with feeler gauges - it should be 3 mm (0.012-inch)

15.4 Disconnect the refrigerant lines (arrows) at the condenser

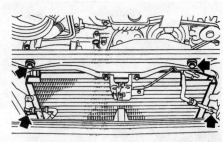

15.5 Remove the upper and lower condenser mounting bolts (arrows)

3

8   The belt must be correctly tensioned for proper air conditioning operation. When installing a new compressor, drain the oil from the old compressor into a measured container. Drain the oil out of the new compressor and install only that amount of new oil as was recovered from the old unit. **Note:** *When a new compressor is installed, a new receiver/drier should also be installed.*

9   If the compressor doesn't operate, even when the system is charged, check the air conditioning fuse and relay. There are both Hitachi and Panasonic systems, with slightly different pin arrangements on their relays **(see illustration)**. In both systems, there should be no continuity between terminals 1 and 2, and 80 ohms (90 on the Panasonic) between terminals 3 and 4. If not, replace the relay.

Compressor pulser

Refer to illustration 14.11

10   Most models have a compressor pulser mounted just above and in front of the clutch. The pulser (sensor) picks up a signal as the clutch rotates. The system amplifies that signal and compares the speed of the compres-

16.5 Use backup wrenches when disconnecting the refrigerant lines (arrows) at the firewall

sor (when the clutch is engaged) with the engine's speed. If the compressor clutch is turning too slow in relation to the engine (if the belt isn't properly tensioned, for instance), the system shuts off the compressor.

11   If your compressor seems to shut off soon after engaging, the pulser system may be at fault. First make sure that there is correct clearance between the metal blades on the front of the clutch and the sensor **(see illustration)**. Adjust the mounting of the sensor to achieve 3 mm (0.012-inch) clearance.

12   Locate the air conditioning relay in the relay group on the passenger side of the firewall **(see illustration 4.17a)**. Ground the red/black wire on the relay with a jumper wire to ground. If the compressor now stays on, the problem is most likely the pulser system. See your local dealer for further diagnosis of the pulser system.

15 Air conditioning condenser- removal and installation

Warning: *The air conditioning system is under high pressure. DO NOT loosen any fittings or remove any components until after the system has been discharged. Air conditioning refrigerant should be properly discharged into an approved container at a dealer service department or an automotive air conditioning repair facility. Always wear eye protection when disconnecting air conditioning system fittings.*

Refer to illustrations 15.4 and 15.5

1   The air conditioning condenser is mounted in front of the radiator **(see illustration 13.1a)**.

2   Before removing the condenser. the system must be discharged by an air conditioning technician.

3   Remove the grille (by referring to Chapter 11) and the lower stay.

4   Disconnect the refrigerant lines at the condenser, using backup wrenches to avoid damage to the fittings or lines **(see illustration)**.

5   Remove the bolts attaching the condenser to the radiator **(see illustration)**. Carefully lift the condenser out of the vehicle; do not bend the cooling fins or coil.

6   Loosen the hose clamps and remove the hoses from the condenser.

7   Installation is the reverse of removal. When installing the hoses, lubricate the inside surfaces of the hoses and the outside of the fittings with refrigerant oil. Be sure to install the hoses on the condenser before mounting the condenser in the vehicle. Support the hose fittings against a solid surface, such as a workbench, when pushing the hoses onto them. This will prevent bending of the fittings or the coils, which could cause leaks. Be sure to locate the clamps properly and tighten them securely. When installing a new condenser, drain the oil from the old condenser into a measured container. Install that amount of new oil into the new condenser. **Note:** *When a new condenser is installed, a new receiver/drier should also be installed.*

16 Air conditioning evaporator and expansion valve- removal and installation

Refer to illustrations 16.5, 16.7 and 16.9

Warning: *The air conditioning system is under high pressure. DO NOT loosen any fittings or remove any components until after the system has been discharged. Air conditioning refrigerant should be properly discharged into an approved container at a dealer service department or an automotive air conditioning repair facility. Always wear eye protection when disconnecting air conditioning system fittings.*

1   The air conditioning evaporator is combined with the heater assembly and is mounted under the passenger side of the vehicle instrument panel **(see illustration 13.1a)**.

2   Before removing the evaporator, the system must be discharged by an air conditioning technician.

3   Disconnect the negative terminal of the battery.

4   Refer to Chapter 11 for removal of the dashboard and center console.

5   Disconnect the discharge and suction pipes from the evaporator pipes at the firewall **(see illustration)**. Remove the grommets from the pipes.

6   Remove the large clamps at either side

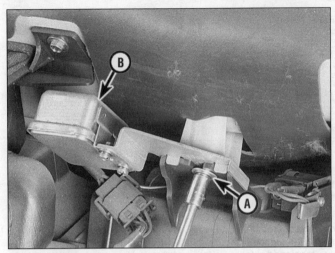

16.7 Remove the evaporator case mounting bolt (A), which also retains the pulser amplifier (B) - move the pulser amplifier and its wires out of the way

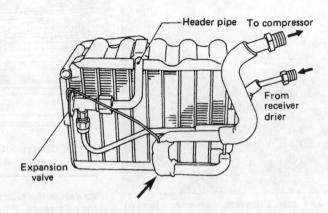

16.9 To remove the expansion valve from the evaporator core, disconnect the two fittings and pull away the stick packing (arrow) holding the probe to the pipe from the compressor

of the evaporator case that connect it to the heater core case and blower motor case.

7   Remove the mounting bolt at the top of the evaporator case (see illustration).

8   Disconnect the wiring to the evaporator housing and remove the housing.

9   Remove the clips holding the two halves of the evaporator case and separate the halves to remove the evaporator core and expansion valve (see illustration).

10   Installation is basically the reverse of removal. Be sure to position the plastic ducts before slipping the evaporator into place. When installing the tubes, lubricate the inside surfaces and the outside of the fittings with refrigerant oil. The pipes must be positioned properly and tightened securely. Do not forget to install the drain pipe. **Note:** If the evap-

orator fins are clogged with debris, blow through the core with compressed air to clean it before installation.

11   When installing a new evaporator, drain the oil from the old evaporator into a measured container. Install only that amount of new oil into the new evaporator. **Note:** When a new evaporator is installed, a new receiver/drier should also be installed.

Chapter 4 Part A Fuel and exhaust systems - carbureted models

Contents

Specifications

Fuel pressure

All carbureted engines	2 to 8 psi
Fuel-injected engines	
TBI fuel injection systems	
Fuel system pressure (at idle)	17.5 to 24 psi
Fuel pump hold pressure	20 psi
Fuel system hold pressure (after 5 minutes)	10 psi
MPFI fuel-injection systems	
Fuel system pressure (at idle)	
Vacuum hose attached to regulator	26 to 32 psi
Vacuum hose detached from regulator	30 to 36
Fuel pump pressure (maximum)	65 psi
Fuel pump hold pressure	30 psi
Fuel system hold pressure (after 5 minutes)	30 psi

Carburetor adjustment specifications (Hitachi carburetors only)

Fast idle opening (refer to illustration 14.3)

1980 models	
California with manual transmission	
G1 clearance	0.0516 in (1.31 mm)
Opening angle	17 degrees
California with automatic transmission	
G1 clearance	0.0602 in (1.53 mm)
Opening angle	19 degrees
49 States and Canada with manual transmission	
G1 clearance	0.0413 in (1.05 mm)
Opening angle	14 degrees
49 States and Canada with automatic transmission	
G1 clearance	0.0602 in (1.53 mm)
Opening angle	19 degrees
1981 models	
1600 cc engines	
G1 clearance	0.0460 in (1.17 mm)
Opening angle	17 degrees
1800 cc engines	
G1 clearance	0.0540 in (1.38 mm)
Opening angle	19 degrees
1982 and 1983 models	
1600 cc engines	
G1 clearance	0.0390 in (0.98 mm)
Opening angle	15 degrees
1800 cc engines with manual transmission	
G1 clearance	0.0480 in (1.22 mm)
Opening angle	17.5 degrees

4A

Carburetor adjustment specifications (Hitachi carburetors only) (continued)

1800 cc engines with automatic transmission
- G1 clearance .... 0.0520 in (1.33 mm)
- Opening angle .... 18.5 degrees

1984 and 1985 models

California and 49 States with 2WD manual transmission
- G1 clearance .... 0.0472 in (1.21 mm)
- Opening angle .... 15.5 degrees

California and 49 States with 2WD automatic transmission
- G1 clearance .... 0.0587 in (1.49 mm)
- Opening angle .... 18 degrees

49 States and Canada with 4WD manual transmission
- G1 clearance .... 0.0524 in (1.33 mm)
- Opening angle .... 17 degrees

49 States and Canada with 4WD automatic transmission
- G1 clearance .... 0.0571 in (1.45 mm)
- Opening angle .... 18 degrees

Secondary throttle valve (refer to illustration 14.6)

1980 models

California models
- G2 clearance .... 0.236 in (6.0 mm)
- Opening angle .... 47 degrees

49 States and Canada models
- G2 clearance .... 0.236 in (6.0 mm)
- Opening angle .... 47 degrees

1981 through 1983 models
- G2 clearance .... 0.236 in (6.0 mm)
- Opening angle .... 49 degrees

1984 and 1985 models

49 States and California with 2WD
- G2 clearance .... 0.2752 in (7.00 mm)
- Opening angle .... 50 degrees

49 States and Canada with 4WD
- G2 clearance .... 0.2713 in (6.89 mm)
- Opening angle .... 50 degrees

1 General information

The fuel system on all carbureted models consists of a fuel tank, an electrically operated fuel pump and a carburetor. A combination of metal and rubber fuel hoses is used to connect these components.

The electric assist choke system consists of a thermostatic spring (bimetal), a cover (choke assembly),a choke pull off diaphragm assembly, a choke valve (in carburetor venturi), a heater and vacuum lines from the intake manifold. As the heater warms, it causes the spring to pull the choke plate open within 1 to 1-1/2 minutes. Manifold vacuum is routed to the diaphragm chamber which in turn pulls the choke open to prevent over-choke. As the engine warms and the bimetal is heated, the choke valve will slowly open.

The carburetor is either a Hitachi or Carter/Weber two-barrel type, depending on engine displacement and year of production. The easiest way to distinguish these two carburetors is by the throttle lever. If the throttle lever and accelerator cable assembly is located on the right side (passenger's side) of the carburetor body, it is Hitachi. If the throttle lever and accelerator assembly is located on the left side (driver's side), it is Carter/Weber. Some models are equipped with electronic feedback carburetors. These carburetors are linked with a variety of sensors and output actuators to help control the emissions output.

Early carburetor models for both Hitachi and Carter/Weber were non-electronic, but later models of both designs have electronic controls for fuel efficiency and lower emissions; these are referred to as *feedback* carburetors, since mixture control at the carburetor is regulated according to feedback from a sensor that monitors the oxygen content of the exhaust. An on-board computer interprets this signal from the oxygen sensor to determine if the air/fuel ratio is too rich or too lean. The computer then sends signals to duty solenoids and actuators on the carburetor to alter the air/fuel ratio as necessary to produce a nearly ideal mixture for the current operating conditions. For more information on feedback systems, see Section 17.

These models are equipped with electric fuel pumps. The fuel pumps are different sizes, shapes and are located in various places depending on the year and model. Early models (1980 through 1983) are located in the engine compartment near the strut tower. Later models (1984 through 1994) are located near the rear of the vehicle under the chassis next to the fuel tank. Some fuel pumps are square shaped (early) while most others are cylindrical shaped.

The fuel vapor separator filters fuel vapors released from the fuel tank on their way to the evaporation system (EVAP). The vapor separator is a regular maintenance item that should be serviced regularly. The vapor separator is located in the corner of the engine compartment (early models up to 1981) or behind the rear fender (1982 and later). Early fuel vapor separators are distinguished by the third fuel line from the top of the canister.

The fuel system is interrelated with the emissions control systems on all vehicles produced for sale in the United States. Components of the emissions control systems are described in Chapter 6.

2 Fuel pressure relief

Refer to illustrations 2.1
Warning: *Gasoline is extremely flammable, so take extra precautions when you work on any part of the fuel system. Don't smoke or allow open flames or bare light bulbs near the work area, and don't work in a garage where a natural gas-type appliance (such as a water heater or a clothes dryer) with a pilot light is present. Since gasoline is carcinogenic, wear latex gloves when there's a possibility of being exposed to fuel, and, if you spill any fuel on your skin, rinse it off immediately with*

2.1 Location of the fuel pump fuse on a 1984 model

3.1 Typical fuel pump location on later models (arrow)

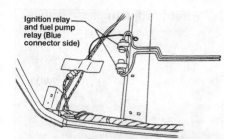

3.2 The fuel pump relay is located under the front driver's seat on early turbocharged models

soap and water. Mop up any spills immediately and do not store fuel-soaked rags where they could ignite. The fuel system is under constant pressure, so, if any fuel lines are to be disconnected, the fuel pressure in the system must be relieved first. When you perform any kind of work on the fuel system, wear safety glasses and have a Class B type fire extinguisher on hand.

Note: *After the fuel pressure has been relieved. it's a good idea to lay a shop towel over any fuel connection to be disassembled, to absorb the residual fuel that may leak out when servicing the fuel system.*

1   Remove the fuel pump fuse from the fuse panel **(see illustration)**. **Note:** *If the fuel pump cover is not clearly labeled, consult the owner's manual or dealer parts department for additional information for your year and model fuel pump fuse location.*

2   Start the engine and allow it to run until it stops. Disconnect the cable from the negative terminal of the battery before working on the fuel system.

3   The fuel system pressure is now relieved. When you're finished working on the fuel system, simply install the fuel pump fuse back into the fuse panel and connect the negative cable to the battery.

4   It is a good idea to double-check by relieving the fuel pressure directly at the fuel filter using a shop rag to catch fuel that might spill out (see Chapter 1).

---

3   Fuel pump/fuel pressure check

Warning: *Gasoline is extremely flammable, so take extra precautions when you work on any part of the fuel system. Don't smoke or allow open flames or bare light bulbs near the work area, and don't work in a garage where a natural gas-type appliance (such as a water heater or a clothes dryer) with a pilot light is present. Since gasoline is carcinogenic, wear latex gloves when there's a possibility of being exposed to fuel, and, if you spill any fuel on your skin, rinse it off immediately with soap and water. Mop up any spills immediately and do not store fuel-soaked rags where they could ignite. When you perform any kind of work on the fuel system, wear safety*

glasses and have a Class B type fire extinguisher on hand.

Note 1: *It is a good idea to check the fuel pump and lines for any obvious damage or fuel leakage. Also check all hoses from the tank to the pump, particularly the suction hoses at the fuel tank and pump which, if they have cracked or collapsed, may not allow fuel to the fuel pump.*

Note 2: *The fuel pumps are different sizes, shapes and are located in various places depending on the year and model. Early models (1980 through 1983) are located in the engine compartment near the strut tower. Later models are located near the rear of the vehicle under the chassis. Some fuel pumps are square shaped while most others are cylindrical shaped.*

Note 3: *The fuel vapor separator acts as a vapor filter for the evaporation system (EVAP). The vapor separator is located in the corner of the engine compartment (early models up to 1981) or behind the rear fender (1982 and later). Early fuel vapor separators are distinguished by the third fuel line from the top of the canister. Change both the fuel filter and separator as part of the normal maintenance. Refer to Chapter 6 for additional information.*

Preliminary inspection

Refer to illustrations 3.1, 3.2, 3.3 and 3.4

1   Should the fuel system fail to deliver the proper amount of fuel, or any fuel at all, inspect it as follows. First, locate the fuel pump in the corner of the engine compartment (1980 and 1981 models) or near the fuel tank attached to the underside of the body (later models) **(see illustration)**. Have an assistant turn the ignition key ON (engine not

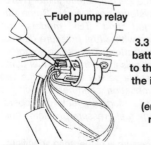

3.3 Check for battery voltage to the relay with the ignition key ON (engine not running)

running) while you listen close to the fuel pump. You should hear a whirring sound that lasts for a couple of seconds.

2   If you don't hear anything, check the fuel pump fuse (see Section 2). If the fuse is blown, replace it and see if it blows again. If it does, trace the fuel pump circuit for a short. If it isn't blown, check the fuel pump relay (if so equipped). **Note:** *Only MPFI and TBI fuel systems are equipped with a fuel pump relay. On most models, the relay is located under the passenger's side dash. On some early turbocharged models (1984 and earlier) the relay is located under the driver's front seat* **(see illustration)**.

3   Remove the relay and check for battery voltage to the fuel pump relay connector **(see illustration)**. If there is battery voltage present, test the relay (see Section 12). **Note:** *Carbureted models are not equipped with a fuel pump relay. Check the fuel pump fuse and the fuel pump circuit for problems in the event that battery voltage is not reaching the fuel pump. Refer to the wiring diagrams at the end of Chapter 12 for additional information.*

4   If battery voltage is present, remove the fuel pump harness connector and check for battery voltage to the fuel pump with the ignition key ON (engine not running). **(see illustration)**. If there is no voltage, check the fuel pump circuit. If there is voltage present, replace the pump (see Section 4). **Warning:** *It will often be necessary to raise the vehicle and secure it on jackstands to access the fuel pump. Be sure the vehicle is safely supported.*

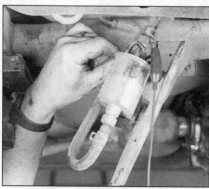

3.4 Check for battery voltage to the fuel pump directly at the fuel pump. Backprobe the harness connector using a pin or paper clip

4A

3.6a Install a fuel pressure gauge between the carburetor and the inlet fuel line using a T-fitting

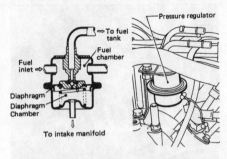

3.6b Be sure to attach the fuel pressure gauge to the fuel inlet line when checking the fuel pressure (MPFI system)

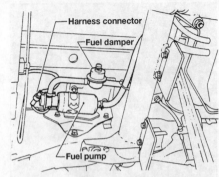

3.15 Location of the fuel pressure damper

Operating pressure check

Refer to illustrations 3.6a and 3.6b

5   Relieve the fuel system pressure (see Section 2). Detach the cable from the negative battery terminal.

6   Disconnect the inlet fuel line from the carburetor **(see illustration)**, throttle body on TBI systems or the fuel rail on MPFI systems **(see illustration)** and install a T-fitting. Connect a fuel pressure gauge to the T-fitting with a section of fuel hose that is no longer than six inches.

7   Attach the cable to the negative battery terminal. Start the engine and allow it to idle. Note the fuel pressure and compare it with the pressure listed in the Specifications.

8   If the pressure is not as listed in the Specifications, refer to Steps 13 and 14. On MPFI systems, confirm that the fuel pressure rises considerably when the vacuum hose at the bottom of the regulator is detached. If it doesn't, replace the regulator. **Note 1:** *Although the carbureted engines are not equipped with a fuel pressure regulator, it is a good idea to check fuel pressure at idle, high rpm and under load (pinch the return line [see step 12]). This will give some kind of indication that the fuel pump is performing throughout the driving range. If pressure drops off considerably at high rpm, the fuel pump may be weak or there may be a fuel line restriction to the carburetor.* **Note 2:** *Although the fuel pressure regulator is housed within the throttle body unit on TBI systems, it is a good idea to check the fuel pressure at high rpm and under load (pinch the return line [see Step 12]). Fuel pressure should increase slightly as rpm is increased and then increase more when the return line is pinched and fuel is prevented from returning back to the fuel tank.*

MPFI systems only

9   Disconnect the vacuum hose from the fuel pressure regulator and hook up a hand-held vacuum pump to the port on the fuel pressure regulator.

10   Read the fuel pressure gauge with vacuum applied to the pressure regulator and also with no vacuum applied. The fuel pressure should decrease as vacuum increases (and increase as vacuum decreases). Compare your readings with the values listed in the Specifications.

11   Reconnect the vacuum hose to the regulator and check the fuel pressure at idle, comparing your reading with the value listed in the Specifications. Disconnect the vacuum hose and watch the gauge - the pressure should jump up considerably as soon as the hose is disconnected. If it doesn't, check for a vacuum signal to the fuel pressure regulator (see Step 15).

12   If the fuel pressure is low, pinch the fuel return line shut and watch the gauge. If the pressure doesn't rise, the fuel pump is defective or there is a restriction in the fuel feed line. If the pressure rises sharply, replace the pressure regulator. **Caution:** *Perform this check for only 10 to 20 seconds to prevent damage to the fuel pump and the lines.*

13   If the fuel pressure is too high, turn the engine off. Disconnect the fuel return line and blow through it to check for a blockage. If there is no blockage, replace the fuel pressure regulator.

14   Connect a vacuum gauge to the pressure regulator vacuum hose. Start the engine and check for vacuum. If there isn't vacuum present, check for a clogged hose or vacuum port. If the amount of vacuum is adequate, replace the fuel pressure regulator.

All systems

Refer to illustration 3.15

15   If the system fuel pressure is less than specified:

a) *Inspect the system for a fuel leak. Repair any leaks and recheck the fuel pressure.*

b) *If the fuel pressure is still low, replace the fuel filter (it may be clogged) and recheck the fuel pressure.*

c) *If the pressure is still low, check the fuel pump output pressure (see below) and/or the fuel pressure regulator (TBI or MPFI systems only).* **Note:** *Some turbocharged and TBI models are equipped with a fuel pressure damper (see illustration). This device smoothes pressure pulsations from the fuel pump to prevent large spurts of gasoline into the combustion chamber. Check the damper for clogging, leaks and operation if the fuel pressure problems continue.*

16   If the pressure is higher than specified:

a) *Check the fuel return line for an obstruction.*

b) *Replace the fuel pressure regulator (TBI or MPFI systems only).*

17   Turn the ignition switch to Off, wait five minutes and recheck the pressure on the gauge. Compare the reading with the hold pressure listed in the Specifications. If the hold pressure is less than specified:

a) *The fuel lines may be leaking.*

b) *The fuel pressure regulator (TBI or MPFI systems only) may be allowing the fuel pressure to bleed through to the return line*

c) *A fuel injector (or injectors) may be leaking (TBI or MPFI systems only).*

d) *The fuel pump may be defective.*

Fuel pump output pressure check

Warning: *For this test it is necessary to use a fuel pressure gauge with a bleeder valve in order to relieve the fuel pressure after the test is completed (the normal procedure for pressure relief will not work because the gauge is connected directly to the fuel pump).*

18   Relieve the system fuel pressure (see Section 2).

19   Detach the cable from the negative battery terminal.

20   Attach a fuel pressure gauge directly to the fuel feed line at the fuel tank.

21   Attach the cable to the negative battery terminal.

22   Using a jumper wire from the battery, disconnect the fuel pump electrical connector and apply battery voltage to the fuel pump.

23   Note the pressure reading on the gauge and compare the reading to the value listed in the Specifications.

24   If the indicated pressure is less than specified, inspect the fuel line for leaks between the pump and gauge. If no leaks are found, replace the fuel pump.

25   Remove the jumper wire and wait five minutes. Note the reading on the gauge and compare it to the hold pressure listed in the Specifications. If the hold pressure is less than specified, check the fuel line between the pump and gauge for leaks. If no leaks are found, replace the fuel pump.

26   Open the bleeder valve on the gauge

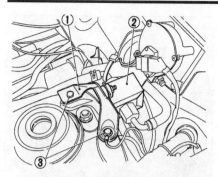

4.3 On early models, the fuel pump is in the engine compartment

1	Fuel pump	2	Fuel pump
	bracket	3	Bolts

and allow the pressurized fuel drain into an approved fuel container. Remove the gauge and reconnect the fuel line.

4 Fuel pump and fuel vapor separator - removal and installation

Warning: *Gasoline is extremely flammable, so take extra precautions when you work on any part of the fuel system. Don't smoke or allow open flames or bare light bulbs near the work area, and don't work in a garage where a natural gas-type appliance (such as a water heater or a clothes dryer) with a pilot light is present. Since gasoline is carcinogenic, wear latex gloves when there's a possibility of being exposed to fuel, and, if you spill any fuel on your skin, rinse it off immediately with soap and water. Mop up any spills immediately and do not store fuel-soaked rags where they could ignite. When you perform any kind of work on the fuel system, wear safety glasses and have a Class B type fire extinguisher on hand.*

Note: *The fuel vapor separator acts as a vapor filter for the evaporation system (EVAP). The vapor separator is located in the corner of the engine compartment (early models up to 1981) or behind the rear fender (1982 and later). Early fuel vapor separators are distinguished by the third fuel line from the top of the canister. Change both the fuel filter and separator as part of the normal maintenance. Refer to Chapter 6 for additional information.*

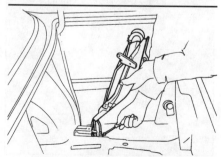

4.21 Remove the fuel vapor separator as an assembly (late model shown)

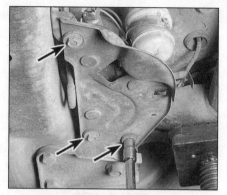

4.9 Remove the fuel pump bracket assembly bolts (arrows)

Fuel pump

Engine compartment mounted fuel pumps

Refer to illustration 4.3

1   The fuel pump is located near the top, rear of the strut tower on the driver's side. Relieve the fuel pressure (see Section 2).
2   Loosen the fuel line hose clamps and remove the fuel lines from the fuel pump.
3   Remove the mounting bolts from the fuel pump and lift the assembly from the engine compartment **(see illustration)**.
4   Before installation, remove the ground strap from the old fuel pump and install it onto the new fuel pump on the identical terminal designation.
5   Install the new fuel pump into the engine compartment. Be sure the ground strap is clean and there is no corrosion around the metal where the mounting bolt is attached . Clean the area with a wire brush if necessary.
6   Install the fuel lines onto the fuel pump.
7   Run the engine and check for leaks.

Chassis-mounted fuel pumps

Refer to illustrations 4.9 and 4.10

8   The fuel pump is located under the vehicle near the fuel tank. Relieve the fuel pressure (see Section 2).
9   Remove the mounting bolts that retain the bracket assembly and drop the fuel pump/fuel filter assembly down without removing any fuel lines **(see illustration)**.

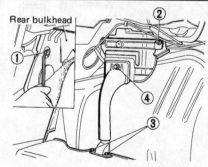

4.26 Fuel vapor separator assembly on sedans

1	Screw A	3	Screws C
2	Nut B	4	Screw D

4.10 Once the assembly has been lowered, remove the fuel pump bolt and slide the pump out of the collar

10   Remove the fuel pump mounting bolt **(see illustration)** and separate the fuel pump from the protection plate. Allow the assembly to drop but do not damage the fuel lines.
11   Place rags under the fuel pump to catch any gasoline which may be spilled during removal.
12   Carefully unscrew the fuel line clamps and detach the lines from the pump.
13   Remove the fuel pump.
14   Attach the lines to the pump and tighten the fuel line clamps.
15   Installation is the reverse of removal.
16   Run the engine and check for leaks.

4A

Fuel vapor separator

Refer to illustration 4.21

17   The vapor separator is located in the left, rear section of the engine compartment on early models or behind the trim panel in the trunk on later models.
18   On early models, disconnect the fuel lines and hoses from the fuel separator and remove the assembly from the engine compartment.

Station wagons

19   On late model station wagons, remove the right, trim panel from the trunk or rear seat area (see Chapter 11).
20   Disconnect the breather hoses from the fuel separator assembly **(see illustration 7.3)**.
21   Disconnect the fuel separator evaporation hose and remove the separator as an assembly **(see illustration)**.
22   Place the fuel separator on the bench and remove the remaining hoses.
23   Installation is the reverse of removal.

Sedans

Refer to illustrations 4.26 and 4.29

24   On late model sedans, remove the rear seat (see Chapter 11).
25   Remove the fuel separator mounting screw from behind the bulkhead.
26   Remove the fuel separator cover mounting bolts and nuts from inside the seating area **(see illustration)**.
27   Disconnect the breather hoses from the floor.

28   Remove the protective cover from the assembly.

29   Remove the fuel separator mounting band **(see illustration)**.

30   Installation is the reverse of removal.

5   Fuel lines and fittings - repair and replacement

Warning: *Gasoline is extremely flammable, so take extra precautions when you work on any part of the fuel system. Don't smoke or allow open flames or bare light bulbs near the work area, and don't work in a garage where a natural gas-type appliance (such as a water heater or a clothes dryer) with a pilot light is present. Since gasoline is carcinogenic, wear latex gloves when there's a possibility of being exposed to fuel, and, if you spill any fuel on your skin, rinse it off immediately with soap and water. Mop up any spills immediately and do not store fuel-soaked rags where they could ignite. When you perform any kind of work on the fuel system, wear safety glasses and have a Class B type fire extinguisher on hand.*

Inspection

Refer to illustrations 5.2

1   Once in a while, you will have to raise the vehicle to service or replace some component (an exhaust pipe hanger, for example). Whenever you work under the vehicle, always inspect the fuel lines and fittings for possible damage or deterioration.

2   Check all hoses and pipes for cracks, kinks, deformation or obstructions **(see illustration)**.

3   Make sure all hose and pipe clips attach their associated hoses or pipes securely to the underside of the vehicle.

4   Verify all hose clamps attaching rubber hoses to metal fuel lines or pipes are snug enough to assure a tight fit between the hoses and the metal pipes.

Replacement

5   If you must replace any damaged sections, use hoses approved for use in fuel systems or pipes made from steel only (it's best

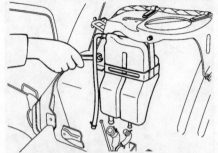

4.29 Remove the bracket bolts and separate the bracket from the fuel vapor separator

to use an original-type pipe from a dealer that's already flared and pre-bent). Do not install substitutes constructed from inferior or inappropriate material, as this could result in a fuel leak and a fire.

6   Always, before detaching or disassembling any part of the fuel line system, note the routing of all hoses and pipes and the orientation of all clamps and clips to assure that replacement sections are installed in exactly the same manner.

7   Before detaching any part of the fuel system, be sure to relieve the fuel tank pressure by removing the fuel filler cap.

8   Always use new hose clamps after loosening or removing them.

9   While you're under the vehicle, it's a good idea to check the following related components:

a) *Check the condition of the fuel filter - make sure that it's not clogged or damaged (see Chapter 1).*

b) *Inspect the evaporative emission control (EVAP) system. Verify that all hoses are attached and in good condition (see Chapter 6).*

6   Fuel level sending unit - check and replacement

Warning: *Gasoline is extremely flammable, so take extra precautions when you work on any part of the fuel system. Don't smoke or*

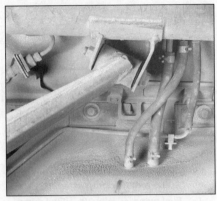

5.2 Check all the fuel lines and vapor hoses for cracks and damage

allow open flames or bare light bulbs near the work area, and don't work in a garage where a natural gas-type appliance (such as a water heater or a clothes dryer) with a pilot light is present. Since gasoline is carcinogenic, wear latex gloves when there's a possibility of being exposed to fuel, and, if you spill any fuel on your skin, rinse it off immediately with soap and water. Mop up any spills immediately and do not store fuel-soaked rags where they could ignite. When you perform any kind of work on the fuel system, wear safety glasses and have a Class B type fire extinguisher on hand.

Check

Refer to illustrations 6.3, 6.4a, 6.4b and 6.6

1   Before performing any tests on the fuel level sending unit, completely fill the tank with fuel.

2   Raise the vehicle and support it securely with jackstands.

3   Remove the carpet from the trunk area to expose the fuel level sending unit access cover **(see illustration)**.

4   Position the ohmmeter probes into the electrical connector **(see illustrations)** and check the resistance.

5   With the fuel tank completely full, the resistance should be 95 ohms. With the fuel tank empty, the resistance of the sending unit should be 7.0 ohms.

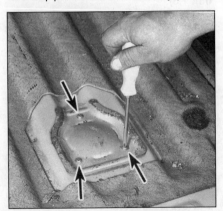

6.3 Remove the fuel level sending unit access cover screws (arrows)

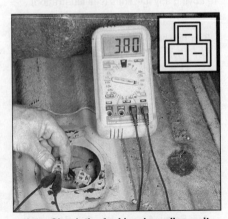

6.4a Check the fuel level sending unit resistance with an ohmmeter

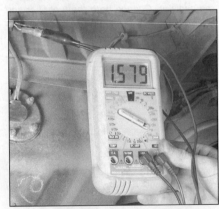

6.4b Checking the fuel level sending unit resistance on side mounted units

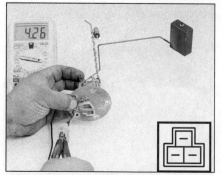

6.6 Probe the terminals of the sending unit and manually move the float from empty to full and observe the change in resistance. The transition should be smooth without "dead spots" or "damaged areas"

6 If the readings are incorrect, replace the sending unit. **Note:** *A more accurate check of the sending unit can be made by removing it (fuel level sending unit or assembly) from the fuel tank and checking its resistance while manually operating the float arm* **(see illustration)**.

7 If the readings are incorrect, replace the sending unit.

Replacement

Refer to illustrations 6.9 and 6.11

8 Remove the carpet from the trunk area

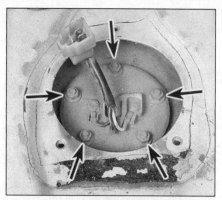

6.9 Remove the mounting nuts (arrows) from the fuel level sending unit assembly

to expose the fuel level sending unit access cover **(see illustration 6.3)**.

9 Remove the access cover nuts **(see illustration)** and separate the cover from the fuel tank. The hole is small and removal will require small hands or two screwdrivers acting as pry bars.

10 If the rubber sealing gasket is damaged while lifting the access cover off the fuel tank, replace it with a new part.

11 Lift the sending unit from the tank **(see illustration)**. Carefully angle the sending unit out of the opening without damaging the fuel level float located at the bottom of the assembly.

12 Installation is the reverse of removal.

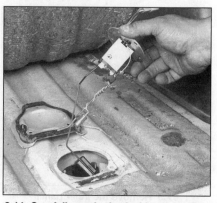

6.11 Carefully angle the fuel level sending unit from the fuel tank without damaging the float

7 Fuel tank - removal and installation

Refer to illustrations 7.3, 7.5, 7.6, 7.7a, 7.7b and 7.10

Warning: *Gasoline is extremely flammable, so take extra precautions when you work on any part of the fuel system. Don't smoke or allow open flames or bare light bulbs near the work area, and don't work in a garage where a natural gas-type appliance (such as a water heater or a clothes dryer) with a pilot light is present. Since gasoline is carcinogenic, wear latex gloves when there's a possibility of*

4A

7.3 Exploded view of a typical fuel tank and lines

1	Fuel tank	33	Fuel pump bracket	43	Purge hose
2	Fuel level sending unit	34	Cushion	44	Check valve
3	Gasket	35	Spacer	45	Purge hose
4	Filler pipe	36	Fuel filter	46	Hose clamp
5	Protector	37	Holder	47	Vacuum hose
6	Packing	38	Fuel delivery hose	48	Hose
7	Packing	39	Hose	49	Hose
8	Fuel filler cap	40	Fuel delivery hose	50	Hose
9	Fuel separator	41	Evaporation pipe	51	Hose
10	Separator bracket		complete	52	Hose
12	Air vent hose	42	Evaporation tube	53	Canister
13	Fuel filler hose				
14	Fuel vapor separator hose				
15	Fuel vapor separator hose				
16	Fuel vapor separator hose				
17	Hose				
18	Hose				
19	Hose				
20	Tube				
21	Fuel delivery hose				
22	Fuel return pipe				
23	Fuel delivery pipe				
24	Air breather pipe				
25	2-way valve				
26	Fuel delivery hose				
27	Hose				
28	Hose				
29	Hose				
30	Fuel delivery pipe		54	Canister bracket	58	Hose clamp bracket
31	Evaporation pipe		55	Hose clamp	59	Fuel return pipe
32	Fuel pump		56	Hose	60	Separator pipe hose
			57	Hose clamp	61	Air breather pipe

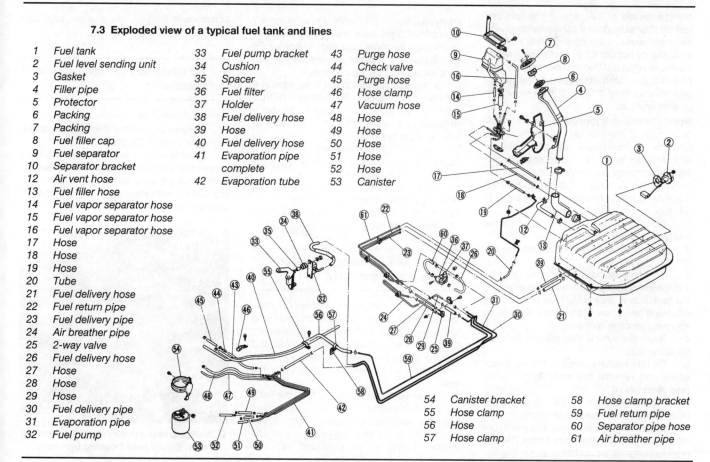

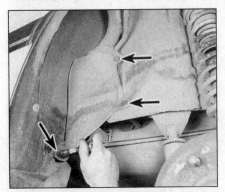

7.5 Remove the inner panel mounting screws

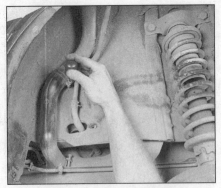

7.6 Remove the fuel filler tube mounting clamp

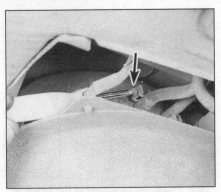

7.7a Remove the hose clamp (arrow) directly at the fuel tank

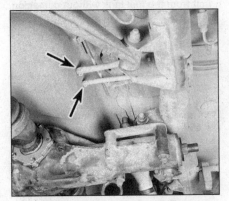

7.7b Remove the vent lines (arrows) at the back of the fuel tank

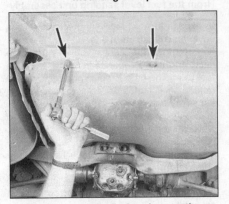

7.10 Remove the fuel tank mounting bolts (arrows)

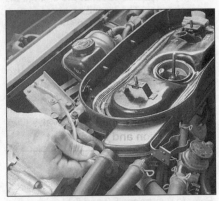

9.2a Disconnect the air hoses from the air filter assembly

being exposed to fuel, and, if you spill any fuel on your skin, rinse it off immediately with soap and water. Mop up any spills immediately and do not store fuel-soaked rags where they could ignite. When you perform any kind of work on the fuel system, wear safety glasses and have a Class B type fire extinguisher on hand.

Note: *The following procedure is much easier to perform if the fuel tank is empty. Some tanks have a drain plug for this purpose. If the tank does not have a drain plug, drain the fuel into an approved fuel container using a commercially available siphoning kit (NEVER start a siphoning action by mouth) or wait until the fuel tank is nearly empty, if possible.*

1   Remove the fuel tank filler cap to relieve fuel tank pressure.
2   Detach the cable from the negative terminal of the battery.
3   If the tank still has fuel in it, you can drain it at the fuel feed line after raising the vehicle. If the tank has a drain plug **(see illustration)** remove it and allow the fuel to collect in an approved gasoline container.
4   Raise the vehicle and place it securely on jackstands.
5   On late models, remove the right rear wheel and remove the inner fender panel **(see illustration)**.
6   Disconnect the fuel filler tube from the body of the vehicle **(see illustration)**.
7   Disconnect the fuel lines and the vapor return line **(see illustrations)**. **Note:** *The fuel feed and return lines and the vapor return line*

are three different diameters, so reattachment is simplified. If you have any doubts, however, clearly label the three lines and the fittings. Be sure to plug the hoses to prevent leakage and contamination of the fuel system.

8   If there is still fuel in the tank, siphon it out from the fuel inlet. Remember - NEVER start the siphoning action by mouth! Use a siphoning kit, which can be purchased at most auto parts stores.
9   Support the fuel tank with a floor jack. Position a wood block between the jack head and the fuel tank to protect the tank.
10   Remove the bolts that retain the fuel tank to the chassis **(see illustration)**.
11   Remove the tank from the vehicle.
12   Installation is the reverse of removal.

8   Fuel tank cleaning and repair - general information

1   All repairs to the fuel tank or filler neck should be carried out by a professional who has experience in this critical and potentially dangerous work. Even after cleaning and flushing of the fuel system, explosive fumes can remain and ignite during repair of the tank.
2   If the fuel tank is removed from the vehicle, it should not be placed in an area where sparks or open flames could ignite the fumes coming out of the tank. Be especially careful inside garages where a natural gas-type

appliance is located, because the pilot light could cause an explosion.

9   Air filter housing - removal and installation

Refer to illustrations 9.2a and 9.2b
1   Remove the air filter element from the air filter housing (see Chapter 1).
2   Disconnect any vacuum hose, electrical connectors and mounting bolts **(see illustrations)** that are attached to the housing and mark them with paint or marked pieces of tape for reassembly purposes.

9.2b Remove the mounting bolts (arrows) from the air filter housing brackets

10.1 Loosen the cable nuts and separate the accelerator cable from the bracket

10.2 Detach the accelerator cable end from the throttle lever by rotating the cable through the slot

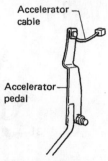

10.4 Detach the cable end from the accelerator pedal arm

3   Lift the air filter housing from the engine compartment.
4   Installation is the reverse of removal.

10   Accelerator cable - removal, installation and adjustment

Removal

Refer to illustrations 10.1, 10.2 and 10.4
1   Remove the accelerator cable from the mounting bracket **(see illustration)**.
2   Rotate the throttle valve and remove the cable end from the recess **(see illustration)**.
3   Detach the screws and the clips retaining the lower instrument trim panel on the driver's side and remove the trim piece (see Chapter 11).
4   Pull the cable end out and then up from the accelerator pedal recess **(see illustration)**.
5   To disconnect the cable at the firewall, push the cable assembly through the firewall from inside the passenger compartment.

Installation

6   Installation is the reverse of removal.
Note: *To prevent possible interference, flexible components (hoses, wires, etc.) must not be routed within two inches of moving parts, unless routing is controlled.*
7   Operate the accelerator pedal and check for any binding condition by completely opening and closing the throttle.
8   If necessary, at the engine compartment side of the firewall, apply sealant around the accelerator cable to prevent water from entering the passenger compartment.

Adjustment

9   The cable housing can be adjusted to allow for freeplay in the cable. Loosen the cable bracket screw **(see illustration 10.1)** and move the cable housing up or down to allow for more or less cable freeplay (slack). The throttle valve should be able to completely close (idle) without hindrance.

11   Carburetor - diagnosis and overhaul

Warning: *Gasoline is extremely flammable, so take extra precautions when you work on any part of the fuel system. Don't smoke or allow open flames or bare light bulbs near the work area, and don't work in a garage where a natural gas-type appliance (such as a water heater or a clothes dryer) with a pilot light is present. Since gasoline is carcinogenic, wear latex gloves when there's a possibility of being exposed to fuel, and, if you spill any fuel on your skin, rinse it off immediately with soap and water. Mop up any spills immediately and do not store fuel-soaked rags where they could ignite. When you perform any kind of work on the fuel system, wear safety glasses and have a Class B type fire extinguisher on hand.*

Diagnosis

1   A thorough road test and check of carburetor adjustments should be done before any major carburetor service. Specifications for some adjustments are listed on the *Vehicle Emissions Control Information* (VECI) label found in the engine compartment.
2   Carburetor problems usually show up as flooding, hard starting, stalling, severe backfiring and poor acceleration. A carburetor that's leaking fuel and/or covered with wet looking deposits definitely needs attention.
3   Some performance complaints directed at the carburetor are actually a result of loose, out-of-adjustment or malfunctioning engine or electrical components. Others develop when vacuum hoses leak, are disconnected or are incorrectly routed. The proper approach to analyzing carburetor problems should include the following items:

a) *Inspect all vacuum hoses and actuators for leaks and correct installation (see Chapters 1 and 6).*
b) *Tighten the intake manifold and carburetor mounting nuts/bolts evenly and securely.*
c) *Perform a compression test and vacuum test (see Chapter 2C).*

d) *Clean or replace the spark plugs as necessary (see Chapter 1).*
e) *Check the spark plug wires (see Chapter 1).*
f) *Inspect the ignition primary wires.*
g) *Check the ignition timing (follow the instructions printed on the Emissions Control Information label).*
h) *Check the fuel pump pressure/volume (see Section 2).*
i) *Check the heat control valve in the air filter assembly for proper operation (see Chapter 1).*
j) *Check/replace the air filter element (see Chapter 1).*
k) *Check the PCV system (see Chapter 6).*
l) *Check/replace the fuel filter (see Chapter 1). Also, the strainer in the tank could be restricted.*
m) *Check for a plugged exhaust system.*
n) *Check EGR valve operation (see Chapter 6).*
o) *Check the choke - it should be completely open at normal engine operating temperature (see Chapter 1).*
p) *Check for fuel leaks and kinked or dented fuel lines (see Chapters 1 and 4)*
q) *Check accelerator pump operation with the engine off (remove the air filter assembly cover and operate the throttle as you look into the carburetor throat - you should see a stream of gasoline enter the carburetor).*
r) *Check for incorrect fuel or bad gasoline.*
s) *Check the valve clearances (if applicable) and camshaft lobe lift (see Chapters 1 and 2)*
t) *Have a dealer service department or repair shop check the electronic engine and carburetor controls.*

4   Diagnosing carburetor problems may require that the engine be started and run with the air filter assembly off. While running the engine without the air filter assembly, backfires are possible. This situation is likely to occur if the carburetor is malfunctioning, but just the removal of the air filter assembly can lean the fuel/air mixture enough to produce an engine backfire. **Warning:** *Do not position any part of your body, especially your face, directly over the carburetor during inspection and servicing procedures. Wear eye protection!*

4A

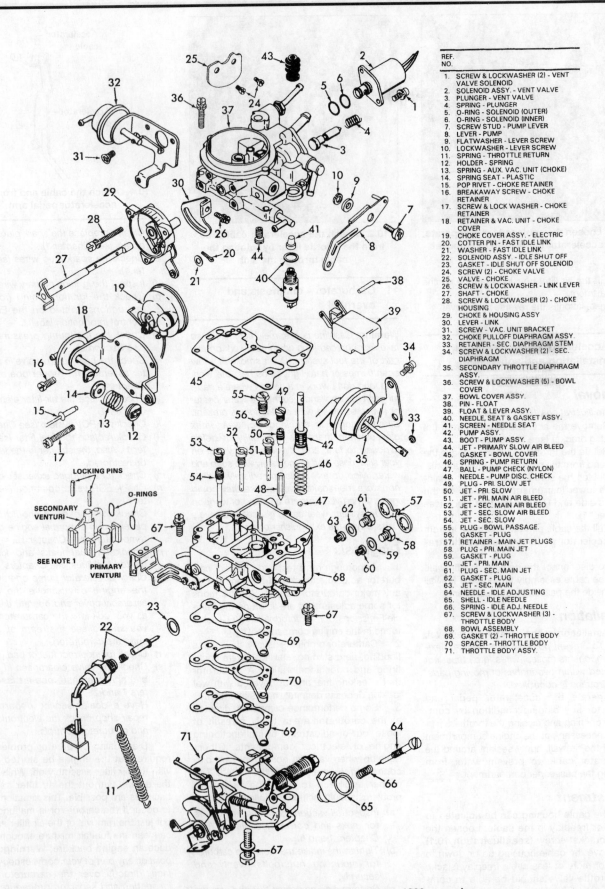

REF. NO.

1. SCREW & LOCKWASHER (2) - VENT VALVE SOLENOID
2. SOLENOID ASSY. - VENT VALVE
3. PLUNGER - VENT VALVE
4. SPRING - PLUNGER
5. O-RING - SOLENOID (OUTER)
6. O-RING - SOLENOID (INNER)
7. SCREW STUD - PUMP LEVER
8. LEVER - PUMP
9. FLATWASHER - LEVER SCREW
10. LOCKWASHER - LEVER SCREW
11. SPRING - THROTTLE RETURN
12. HOLDER - SPRING
13. SPRING - AUX. VAC. UNIT (CHOKE)
14. SPRING SEAT - PLASTIC
15. POP RIVET - CHOKE RETAINER
16. BREAKAWAY SCREW - CHOKE RETAINER
17. SCREW & LOCK WASHER - CHOKE RETAINER
18. RETAINER & VAC. UNIT - CHOKE COVER
19. CHOKE COVER ASSY. - ELECTRIC
20. COTTER PIN - FAST IDLE LINK
21. WASHER - FAST IDLE LINK
22. SOLENOID ASSY. - IDLE SHUT OFF
23. GASKET - IDLE SHUT OFF SOLENOID
24. SCREW (2) - CHOKE VALVE
25. VALVE - CHOKE
26. SCREW & LOCKWASHER - LINK LEVER
27. SHAFT - CHOKE
28. SCREW & LOCKWASHER (2) - CHOKE HOUSING
29. CHOKE & HOUSING ASSY.
30. LEVER - LINK
31. SCREW - VAC. UNIT BRACKET
32. CHOKE PULLOFF DIAPHRAGM ASSY.
33. RETAINER - SEC. DIAPHRAGM STEM
34. SCREW & LOCKWASHER (2) - SEC. DIAPHRAGM
35. SECONDARY THROTTLE DIAPHRAGM ASSY.
36. SCREW & LOCKWASHER (5) - BOWL COVER
37. BOWL COVER ASSY.
38. PIN - FLOAT
39. FLOAT & LEVER ASSY.
40. NEEDLE, SEAT & GASKET ASSY.
41. SCREEN - NEEDLE SEAT
42. PUMP ASSY.
43. BOOT - PUMP ASSY.
44. JET - PRIMARY SLOW AIR BLEED
45. GASKET - BOWL COVER
46. SPRING - PUMP RETURN
47. BALL - PUMP CHECK (NYLON)
48. NEEDLE - PUMP DISC. CHECK
49. PLUG - PRI. SLOW JET
50. JET - PRI. SLOW
51. JET - PRI. MAIN AIR BLEED
52. JET - SEC. MAIN AIR BLEED
53. JET - SEC. SLOW AIR BLEED
54. JET - SEC. SLOW
55. PLUG - BOWL PASSAGE
56. GASKET - PLUG
57. RETAINER - MAIN JET PLUGS
58. PLUG - PRI. MAIN JET
59. GASKET - PLUG
60. JET - PRI. MAIN
61. PLUG - SEC. MAIN JET
62. GASKET - PLUG
63. JET - SEC. MAIN
64. NEEDLE - IDLE ADJUSTING
65. SHELL - IDLE NEEDLE
66. SPRING - IDLE ADJ. NEEDLE
67. SCREW & LOCKWASHER (3) - THROTTLE BODY
68. BOWL ASSEMBLY
69. GASKET (2) - THROTTLE BODY
70. SPACER - THROTTLE BODY
71. THROTTLE BODY ASSY.

LOCKING PINS

SECONDARY VENTURI

O-RINGS

PRIMARY VENTURI

SEE NOTE 1

11.7a Exploded view a typical Hitachi carburetor on an 1800 cc engine

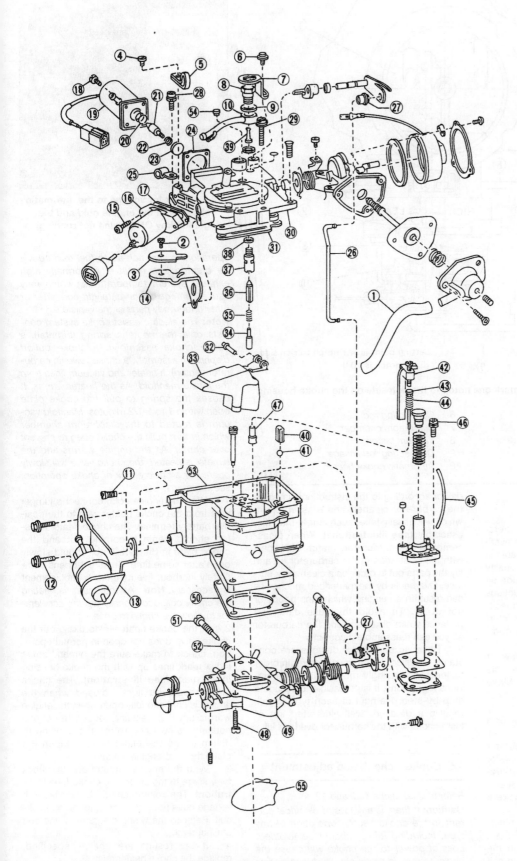

11.7b Exploded view of a typical Carter/Weber carburetor

1   Choke vacuum hose
2   Fuel line clamp screw (outer)
3   Fuel line clamp (outer)
4   Fuel line clamp screw (inner)
5   Fuel line clamp (inner)
6   Banjo lock screw
7   Banjo lock
8   Banjo fuel bolt
9   Banjo gasket
10 Banjo fuel line
11 Fuel line bracket attaching screw
12 Idle stop solenoid attaching screw
13 Idle stop solenoid
14 Fuel line bracket
15 Feedback solenoid attaching screw
16 Feedback solenoid
17 Feedback solenoid gasket
18 Bowl vent solenoid attaching screw
19 Bowl vent solenoid
20 Bowl vent armature spring
21 Bowl vent armature
22 Bowl vent armature spring retainer
23 Bowl vent valve
24 Bowl vent gasket
25 Wire support(s)
26 Connector rod
27 Connector rod bushing
28 Air horn attaching screw (short)
29 Air horn attaching screw (long)
30 Air horn
31 Air horn gasket
32 Float hinge pin
33 Float
34 Fuel inlet needle pin
35 Fuel inlet needle pin spring
36 Fuel inlet needle
37 Fuel inlet needle seat
38 Fuel inlet needle seat gasket
39 Fuel inlet filter
40 Pump discharge weight
41 Pump discharge check ball
42 Lifter link
43 Metering rod
44 Metering rod spring
45 Pump delivery hose
46 Pump assembly attaching screw
47 Main jet
48 Flange attaching screws
49 Flange
50 Flange gasket
51 Idle mixture adjusting screw
52 Idle mixture screw spring
53 Main body
54 Metering rod adjustment hole plug
55 Flange O-ring

4A

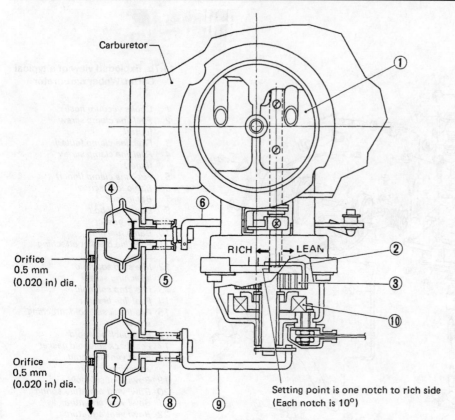

12.2 Align the bimetal cover index mark one notch to the rich side on the choke housing

1	*Choke valve*	6	*Connecting rod*
2	*Choke lever*	7	*Diaphragm chamber*
3	*Bimetal*	8	*Vacuum piston*
4	*Diaphragm chamber*	9	*Connecting rod linkage*
5	*Vacuum piston*	10	*Automatic choke heater*

12.3 Check for voltage to the automatic choke with the engine cold and the ignition key ON (engine not running)

Overhaul

Refer to illustrations 11.7a and 11.7b

5   Once it's determined that the carburetor needs an overhaul, several options are available. If you're going to attempt to overhaul the carburetor yourself, first obtain a good-quality carburetor rebuild kit (which will include all necessary gaskets, internal parts, instructions and a parts list). You'll also need some special solvent and a means of blowing out the internal passages of the carburetor with compressed air.

6   An alternative is to obtain a new or rebuilt carburetor. They are readily available from dealers and auto parts stores. Make absolutely sure the exchange carburetor is identical to the original. A tag is usually attached to the top of the carburetor or a number is stamped on the float bowl. It will help determine the exact type of carburetor you have. When obtaining a rebuilt carburetor or a rebuild kit, make sure the kit or carburetor matches your application exactly. Seemingly insignificant differences can make a large difference in engine performance.

7   If you choose to overhaul your own carburetor, allow enough time to disassemble it carefully, soak the necessary parts in the cleaning solvent (usually for at least one-half day or according to the instructions listed on the carburetor cleaner) and reassemble it, which will usually take much longer than disassembly **(see illustrations)**. When disassembling the carburetor, match each part with the illustration in the carburetor kit and lay the parts out in order on a clean work surface. Overhauls by inexperienced mechanics can result in an engine which runs poorly or not at all. To avoid this, use care and patience when disassembling the carburetor so you can reassemble it correctly.

8   Because carburetor designs are constantly modified by the manufacturer in order to meet increasingly more stringent emissions regulations, it isn't feasible to include a step-by-step overhaul of each type. You'll receive a detailed, well illustrated set of instructions with the carburetor overhaul kit.

12 Choke - check and adjustment

Refer to illustrations 12.2 and 12.3
Caution: *If there is any loss of electrical current to the choke heater, operation of any type, including idling, should be avoided. Loss of power to the choke will cause the choke to remain partly closed during engine* operation. A very rich air-to-fuel mixture will be created and result in abnormally high exhaust system temperatures, which may cause damage to the catalytic converter or other underbody parts of the vehicle.
Note: *The electric assist choke system consists of a thermostatic spring (bimetal), a cover (choke assembly), a choke pulloff diaphragm assembly, a choke valve (in carburetor venturi), a heater and vacuum lines from the intake manifold. As the heater warms, it causes the spring to pull the choke plate open within 1 to 1-1/2 minutes. Manifold vacuum is routed to the diaphragm chamber which in turn pulls the choke open to prevent over-choke. As the engine warms and the bimetal is heated, the choke valve will slowly open. For a basic check of choke operation, see Chapter 1.*

1   With the engine cold, connect a jumper wire from the choke heater wire to the positive battery terminal. The choke heater housing should begin becoming hot and the choke plate in the carburetor should slowly open after some time. Be sure it opens completely in about five minutes or replacement is necessary. **Note:** *As the heater is heating the choke coil, occasionally tap the accelerator to allow the choke to open.*

2   If the choke heater tests okay, but the choke valve does not open in normal operation, check to make sure the bimetal cover index mark lines up with the choke housing index mark **(see illustration)**. The choke plate should be lightly closed when the engine is cold and fully open when the engine warms up. If necessary, loosen the choke housing screws and rotate the housing to richen (close the plate) or lean (open the plate) the cold-engine mixture.

3   With the engine running at idle, check for voltage to the automatic choke **(see illustration)**. The voltage should be available. If voltage does not exist, check for an open circuit. Refer to the wiring diagrams at the end of Chapter 12.

4   If the results are not as specified, replace the choke heater relay.

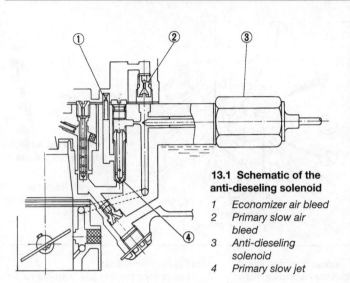

13.1 Schematic of the anti-dieseling solenoid

1. *Economizer air bleed*
2. *Primary slow air bleed*
3. *Anti-dieseling solenoid*
4. *Primary slow jet*

13.2 Check for voltage to the anti-dieseling solenoid harness connector

13 Anti-dieseling solenoid valve - check and replacement

Check

Refer to illustration 13.1 and 13.2

1 The anti-dieseling solenoid prevents excess engine idle and surges after the ignition switch has been turned off **(see illustration)**. The solenoid extends a plunger into the idle circuit within the carburetor when the ignition is turned OFF, immediately shutting off fuel to the idle circuit.

2 Turn the ignition key ON (engine not running) and using a voltmeter, check for battery voltage at the anti-dieseling solenoid **(see illustration)**. There should be approximately 12 volts.

3 Touch the electrical connector to the solenoid and listen for a distinct "click" from the solenoid. If necessary, remove the solenoid from the carburetor and watch the solenoid plunger move as voltage is applied. If there is no movement from the plunger, replace it with a new part.

Replacement

4 Disconnect the electrical connector from the anti-dieseling solenoid.

5 Remove the solenoid from the carburetor **(see illustration 11.7a and 11.7b)** using an open end wrench.

6 Installation is the reverse of removal.

14 Carburetor adjustments

Note: *These carburetor adjustments are strictly in-vehicle adjustments. During overhaul, refer to the instructions included in the overhaul kit for complete procedures and any additional adjustments that are required.*

Fast idle opening (Hitachi carburetors)

Refer to illustration 14.3

1 The fast idle opening is a critical carburetor adjustment directly involved with cold-running conditions and choke enrichment during cranking. The choke unloader is a mechanical device that partially opens the choke valve at wide open throttle to eliminate choke enrichment during hard acceleration.

2 Engines which have been stalled or flooded by excessive choke enrichment can be cleared by the use of the choke unloader. With the throttle valve at wide open throttle, the choke plate should be slightly open to allow a sufficient amount of intake air into the carburetor venturi.

3 Keep the choke valve fully closed. Make sure the top of the cam adjusting lever is resting on the highest step of the fast idle cam. Measure the clearance (G1) **(see illustration)**. Compare to the Specifications listed in this Chapter.

4 To adjust the fast idle opening, turn the fast idle adjusting screw until the correct clearance at G1 is obtained.

Secondary throttle valve (Hitachi carburetors)

Refer to illustrations 14.6

5 The primary and secondary throttle valves are interlocked so that the secondary valve starts to open when the primary valve is opened to a certain degree. This can be visualized by moving the throttle and observing the secondary valve open after the primary

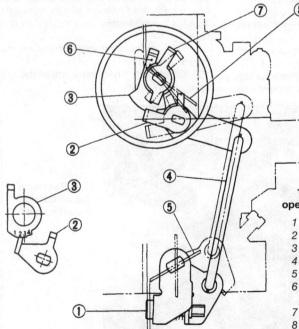

14.3 Details of the fast idle opening adjustment components

1. *Fast idle adjusting screw*
2. *Cam adjusting lever*
3. *Fast idle cam*
4. *Cam connecting rod*
5. *Throttle valve*
6. *Bend this pawl to adjust choke valve opening angle*
7. *Choke lever*
8. *Choke valve*

4A

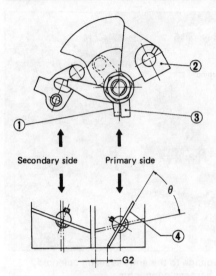

**14.6 Secondary throttle valve
adjustment details**

1	*Adjust plate*
2	*Throttle lever*
3	*Return plate*
4	*Primary throttle valve*

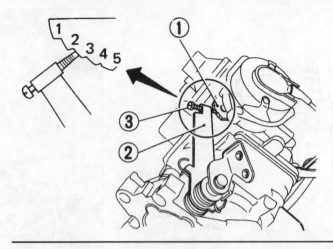

**14.10 Fast idle
adjustment details**

1	*Cam*
2	*Fast idle lever*
3	*Fast idle adjusting
screw*

throttle valve has reached approximately a 60 degree angle.

6   Measure the opened angle of the primary valve and the G2 clearance **(see illustration)**. Compare the measurement to the Specifications listed in this Chapter.

7   To adjust the secondary throttle valve, adjust the plate until the G2 clearance is as Specified.

Fast idle speed (Carter/Weber carburetors)

Refer to illustration 14.10

8   Warm the engine to normal operating temperatures and observe that the choke has fully opened. Install a tachometer according to the manufacturer's instructions.

9   Make sure the automatic choke housing cover index mark is opposite the center mark on the carburetor body.

10   Position the fast idle speed screw onto the third step on the fast idle cam **(see illustration)**. Start the engine and monitor the engine rpm. Adjust the fast idle to 2,000 rpm. Turn the fast idle cam adjusting screw IN to increase the rpm or OUT to decrease the rpm. **Note:** *Make sure the fast idle speed adjusting screw remains positioned onto the third step of the cam. during the procedure.*

11   Adjust the engine idle speed (see Chapter 1).

15 Carburetor - removal and installation

Warning: *Gasoline is extremely flammable, so take extra precautions when you work on any part of the fuel system. Don't smoke or allow open flames or bare light bulbs near the* work area, and don't work in a garage where *a natural gas-type appliance (such as a water heater or a clothes dryer) with a pilot light is present. Since gasoline is carcinogenic, wear latex gloves when there's a possibility of being exposed to fuel, and, if you spill any fuel on your skin, rinse it off immediately with soap and water. Mop up any spills immediately and do not store fuel-soaked rags where they could ignite. When you perform any kind of work on the fuel system, wear safety glasses and have a Class B type fire extinguisher on hand.*

Removal

Refer to illustration 15.9

1   Relieve the fuel pressure (see Section 2).

2   Remove the air filter housing from the carburetor (see Section 9). Be sure to label all vacuum hoses attached to the air filter housing.

3   Disconnect the accelerator cable from the throttle valve (see Section 10).

4   If the vehicle is equipped with cruise control, disconnect the cable from the throttle valve.

5   Clearly label all vacuum hoses and fittings, then disconnect the hoses.

6   Drain the coolant from the radiator (see Chapter 1) and disconnect the coolant lines from the intake manifold.

7   Disconnect the fuel line from the carburetor.

8   Label the wires and terminals, then unplug all the electrical connectors.

9   Remove the mounting fasteners **(see illustration)** and detach the carburetor from the intake manifold. Remove the carburetor mounting gasket. Stuff a rag into the intake manifold openings.

Installation

10   Use a gasket scraper to remove all traces of gasket material and sealant from the intake manifold (and the carburetor, if it's being reinstalled), then remove the shop rag from the manifold openings. Clean the mating surfaces with lacquer thinner or acetone.

11   Place a new gasket on the intake manifold.

12   Position the carburetor on the gasket and install the mounting fasteners.

13   To prevent carburetor distortion or damage, tighten the fasteners to approximately 16 ft-lbs in a criss-cross pattern, 1/4-turn at a time.

14   The remaining installation steps are the reverse of removal.

15   Check and, if necessary, adjust the idle speed (see Chapter 1).

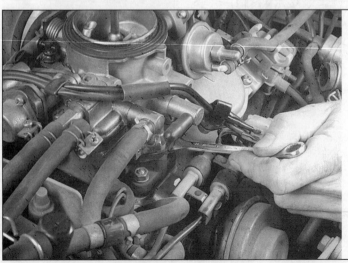

**15.9 Removing
the carburetor
mounting nuts**

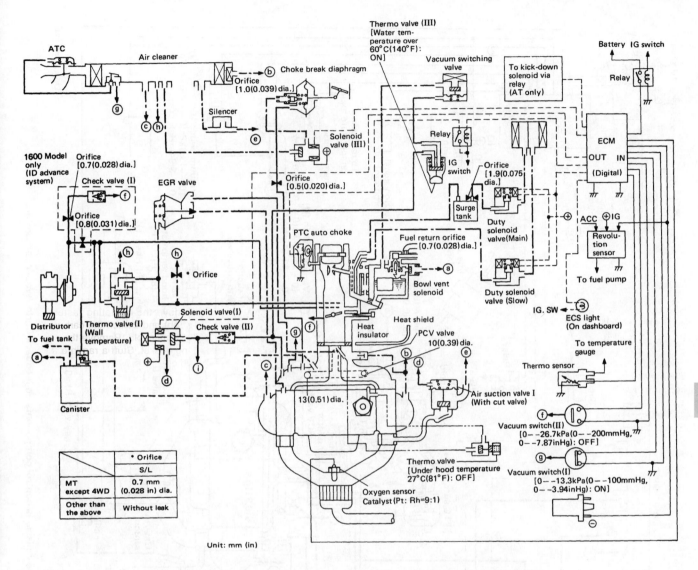

16.1a Schematic of the emissions control components on feedback Hitachi carburetors

16   If the vehicle is equipped with an automatic transaxle, refer to Chapter 7B for the kickdown solenoid adjustment procedure.
17   Start the engine and check carefully for fuel leaks.

16   Electronic feedback carburetor systems - general information

Refer to illustrations 16.1a, 16.1b, 16.1c and 16.1d

1   The electronically-controlled carburetor (ECC) emission system or most commonly called the electronic feedback carburetor system relies on an electronic signal, which is generated by an exhaust gas oxygen sensor, to control a variety of devices and keep emissions within limits **(see illustrations)**. The system works in conjunction with a three-way

catalyst to control the levels of carbon monoxide, hydrocarbons and oxides of nitrogen. The feedback carburetor system also works in conjunction with the computer. The two systems share certain sensors and output actuators; therefore, diagnosing the feedback carburetor system will require a thorough check of all the feedback carburetor components (refer to Chapter 6 for additional information).
2   The system operates in two modes: open loop and closed loop. When the engine is cold, the air/fuel mixture is controlled by the computer in accordance with a program designed in at the time of production. The air/fuel mixture during open loop mode will be richer to allow for proper engine warm-up. When the engine is at operating temperature, the system operates in closed loop and the air/fuel mixture is varied depending on the information supplied by the exhaust gas oxygen sensor.

3   Here is a list of the various sensors and output actuators involved with these feedback carburetor systems:

High Altitude Compensator
Thermosensor
Oxygen sensor
Vacuum switching solenoids (duty solenoids)
Computer
Vacuum sensor and vacuum switches
Air temperature sensor

4   Hitachi feedback carburetors are equipped with two duty solenoids mounted on the intake manifold. Carter/Weber feedback carburetors are equipped with a single duty solenoid that is mounted on the carburetor body.
5   Refer to Section 17 and also Chapter 6 for the diagnostic checks for the feedback carburetor system components.

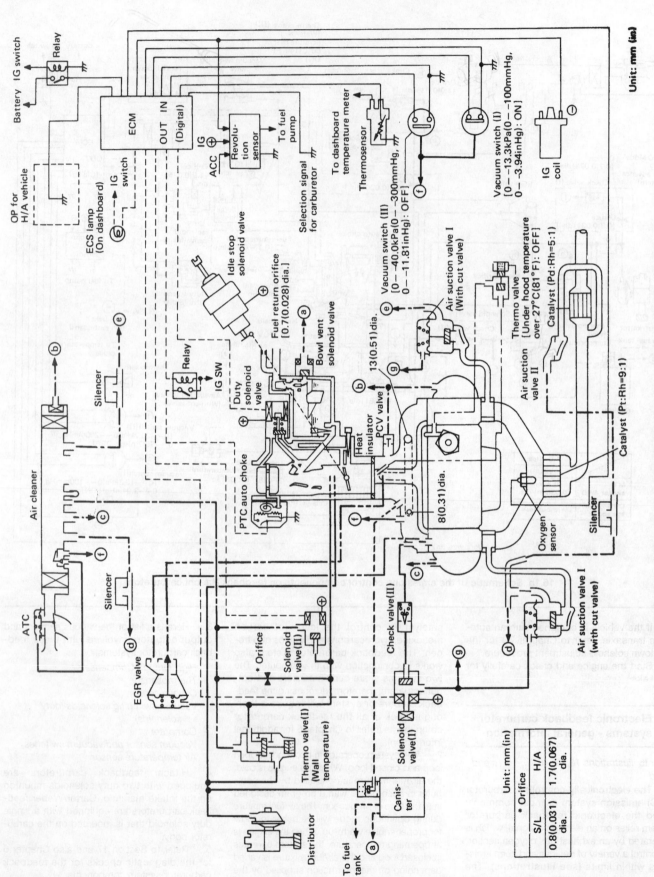

16.1b Schematic of the emissions control components on feedback Carter/Weber carburetors

4A

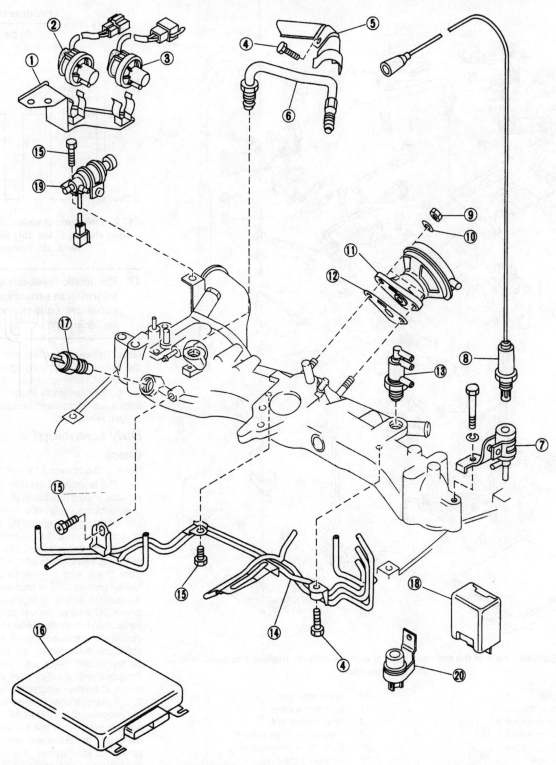

16.1c Exploded view of the emission control components on engines equipped with Carter/Weber carburetors

1	Bracket	8	Oxygen sensor	15	Bolt and washer
2	Vacuum switch 1	9	Nut	16	Electronic control module
3	Vacuum switch 2	10	Washer	17	Thermosensor
4	Bolt and washer	11	EGR valve	18	Revolution sensor
5	EGR pipe cover	12	Gasket	19	Solenoid valve I
6	EGR pipe	13	Thermo vacuum valve I	20	Ignition relay
7	Solenoid valve II	14	Vacuum pipe CP		

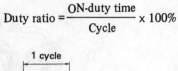

$$\text{Duty ratio} = \frac{\text{ON-duty time}}{\text{Cycle}} \times 100\%$$

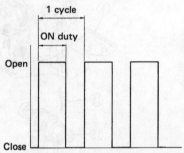

17.2 Schematic diagram of the opening and closing of the duty solenoids on feedback systems

17 Electronic feedback carburetor information sensors and output actuators - check and replacement

Note: *This section covers only a select few of the output actuators incorporated onto the carburetor. Refer to Chapter 6, Section 11 for additional information on the information sensors such as coolant temperature sensor, oxygen sensor, etc.*

Duty solenoid(s)

Check

Refer to illustrations 17.2 and 17.3

1   The function of the duty solenoid(s) is to provide limited regulation of the air/fuel ratio of a feedback carburetor in response to the electronic signals sent by the computer. This is accomplished by metering intake air through the duty solenoid into the high speed or low speed circuits of the carburetor and from there into the venturi, allowing the fuel/air mixture ratio to change. By controlling the duration of this voltage signal, the ratio of power ON-time versus the power OFF-time is called the duty cycle. **Note:** *Hitachi feedback carburetors are equipped with two duty solenoids mounted on the intake manifold. Carter/Weber feedback carburetors are equipped with a single duty solenoid that is mounted on the carburetor body.*

2   A dwell meter is used to measure the duty cycle (ON Time/OFF Time) of the solenoid(s). Install the probes of the dwell meter into the diagnostic terminal of the test connector located near the strut tower. This duty cycle or percentage will indicate if the duty solenoids are active **(see illustration)**. First, use an automotive stethoscope and check the duty solenoids while the engine is running. There should be a definite clicking or vibration. This indicates that the solenoids are receiving power and they are operating. Now observe the dwell meter as the engine idles. It should fluctuate slightly to compensate for the LEAN/RICH command from the

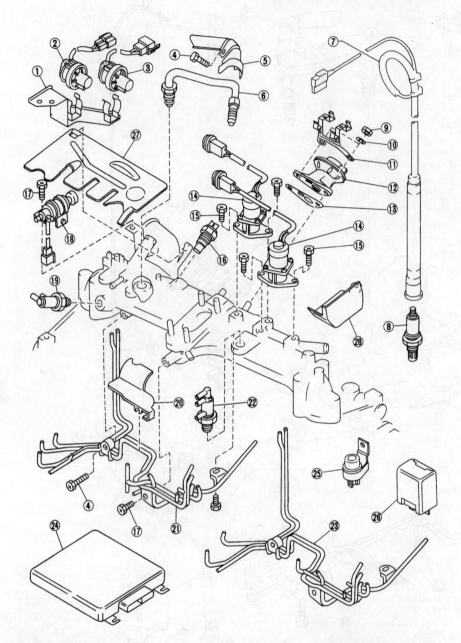

16.1d Exploded view of the emission control components on engines equipped with Hitachi carburetors

1	Bracket	16	Thermosensor
2	Vacuum switch I	17	Bolt and washer
3	Vacuum switch II	18	Solenoid valve I
4	Bolt and washer	19	Thermo vacuum valve II
5	EGR pipe cover	20	Carburetor protector 3
6	EGR pipe	21	Vacuum pipe
7	Oxygen sensor harness	22	Thermo vacuum valve II
8	Oxygen sensor	23	Vacuum pipe (4WD and automatic
9	Nut		transmission)
10	Washer	24	Electronic control module
11	Clamp	25	Ignition relay
12	EGR valve	26	Revolution sensor
13	Gasket	27	Carburetor protector
14	Duty solenoid valve	28	Carburetor protector II
15	Bolt and washer		

17.3 Checking the resistance of the duty solenoids

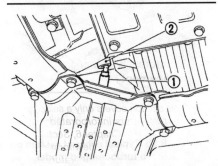

17.13 Location of the oxygen O$_2$ sensor on a feedback system

1   O$_2$ sensor
2   O$_2$ sensor harness

computer. Observe the duty cycle (percentage) as the vacuum hoses to the duty solenoid(s) and the thermosensor electrical connector are disconnected and plugged. It should read approximately 40 percent. This indicates that the system has gone RICH to compensate for the lack of intake air. By changing the amount of intake air, the duty solenoids should compensate for the imbalance by trying to add additional intake air.
3   Another quick check on the duty solenoid(s) is to measure the resistance on the electrical connector terminals **(see illustration)**. The resistance should be approximately 30 to 50 ohms. If all the tests are correct but the duty solenoids are not responding correctly, have the computer and the circuit checked by a dealer service department.

Replacement

4   Disconnect the cable from the negative battery terminal.
5   Remove the air cleaner assembly (see Section 9).
6   Disconnect the electrical connectors from the duty solenoids **(see illustrations 16.1a and 16.1b)**.
7   Remove the mounting bolts for the solenoid.
8   If equipped, install a new grommet onto the solenoid and apply silicon grease.
9   Tighten the mounting bolts.
10   If equipped, install new O-rings.

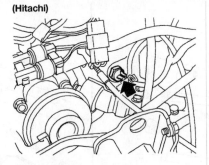

(Hitachi)

(Carter/Weber)

17.12a Location of the vacuum sensors on feedback systems

11   The remainder of installation is the reverse of removal.

Vacuum sensor and vacuum switches

Refer to illustrations 17.12a and 17.12b
12   The vacuum sensor and vacuum switches monitor the intake manifold pressure changes resulting from changes in engine load and speed. This system uses two vacuum switches to control low speed and high speed applications **(see illustrations)**. Have the vacuum sensor and switches diagnosed by a dealer service department.

Oxygen sensor

Refer to illustration 17.13
13   The oxygen sensor is located in the exhaust system, upstream to the catalytic converter **(see illustration)**. This sensor monitors the presence of oxygen and relays the RICH/LEAN signal to the computer. The computer uses this information to alter the amount of air into the carburetor thereby trimming the air/fuel mixture to the correct value for emissions. Refer to Chapter 6 for the checking and replacement procedures.

Thermosensor

Refer to illustration 17.14
14   The thermosensor is located in the intake manifold **(see illustration)**. This sensor detects the temperature of the engine coolant and relays this information to the computer. The computer uses this information to alter the amount of air into the carburetor thereby trimming the air/fuel mixture to the correct value for emissions. Refer to Chapter 6 for the checking and replacement procedures.

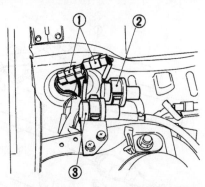

17.12b Locations of the vacuum switches

1   Connectors
2   Vacuum switch II
3   Vacuum switch I

17.14 Checking the resistance of the coolant temperature sensor on a feedback system

High Altitude Compensator

15   The High Altitude Compensator adjusts the air/fuel ratio in response to changing elevation by adding extra air to the main and secondary passages in the carburetor. At high altitude, the bellows expand thereby allowing more air to bypass the needle valve into the carburetor. Have the HAC diagnosed by a dealer service department in the event of failure.

18   Exhaust system - servicing and general information

Refer to illustrations 18.1a, 18.1b and 18.4
Warning: *Inspection and repair of exhaust system components should be done only after enough time has elapsed after driving the vehicle to allow the system components to cool completely. Also, when working under the vehicle, make sure it is securely supported on jackstands.*
1   The exhaust system consists of the exhaust manifold(s), the catalytic converter(s), the muffler, the tailpipe and all connecting pipes, brackets, hangers and clamps **(see illustrations)**. The exhaust system is attached to the body with mounting brackets

4A

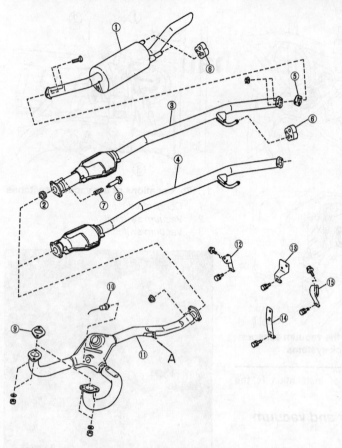

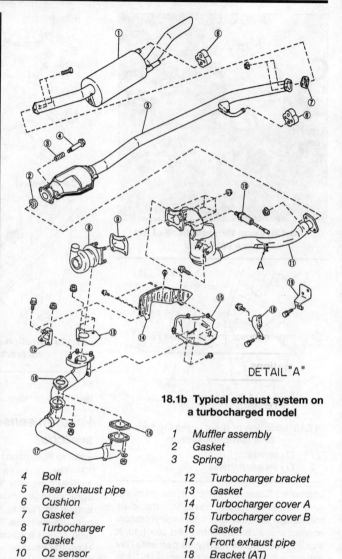

18.1a Typical exhaust system on a non-turbocharged model

1	Muffler assembly	9	Gasket	
2	Gasket	10	O2 sensor	
3	Rear exhaust pipe (2WD)	11	Front exhaust pipe	
4	Rear exhaust pipe (4WD)	12	Bracket (2WD MT)	
5	Gasket	13	Bracket (4WD MT)	
6	Cushion	14	Bracket (2WD AT)	
7	Spring	15	Bracket (4WD AT)	
8	Bolt			

DETAIL "A"

18.1b Typical exhaust system on a turbocharged model

1	Muffler assembly			
2	Gasket			
3	Spring			
4	Bolt	12	Turbocharger bracket	
5	Rear exhaust pipe	13	Gasket	
6	Cushion	14	Turbocharger cover A	
7	Gasket	15	Turbocharger cover B	
8	Turbocharger	16	Gasket	
9	Gasket	17	Front exhaust pipe	
10	O2 sensor	18	Bracket (AT)	
11	Center exhaust pipe	19	Bracket (MT)	

18.4 Apply penetrating lubricant to the exhaust nuts and studs before attempting to remove them. The exhaust pipe attaches directly to the aluminum cylinder head, so be very careful not to damage the delicate aluminum of the cylinder head when disconnecting or attaching the pipe

and rubber hangers. If any of the parts are improperly installed, excessive noise and vibration will be transmitted to the body.
2   Conduct regular inspections of the exhaust system to keep it safe and quiet. Look for any damaged or bent parts, open seams, holes, loose connections, excessive corrosion or other defects which could allow exhaust fumes to enter the vehicle. Deteriorated exhaust system components should not be repaired; they should be replaced with new parts.
3   If the exhaust system components are extremely corroded or rusted together, welding equipment will probably be required to remove them. The convenient way to accomplish this is to have a muffler repair shop remove the corroded sections with a cutting torch. If, however, you want to save money by doing it yourself (and you don't have a welding outfit with a cutting torch), simply cut off the old components with a hacksaw. If you have compressed air, special pneumatic cutting chisels can also be used. If you do

decide to tackle the job at home, be sure to wear safety goggles to protect your eyes from metal chips and work gloves to protect your hands.
4   Here are some simple guidelines to follow when repairing the exhaust system:

a) *Work from the back to the front when removing exhaust system components.*
b) *Apply penetrating oil to the exhaust system component fasteners to make them easier to remove* **(see illustration).**
c) *Use new gaskets, hangers and clamps when installing exhaust system components.*
d) *Apply anti-seize compound to the threads of all exhaust system fasteners during reassembly.*
e) *Be sure to allow sufficient clearance between newly installed parts and all points on the underbody to avoid overheating the floor pan and possibly damaging the interior carpet and insulation. Pay particularly close attention to the catalytic converter and heat shield.*

Chapter 4 Part B Fuel and exhaust systems - fuel-injected engines

Contents

Specifications

Injector resistance
TBI	0.5 to 2 ohms
MPFI	2 to 3 ohms

Torque specifications
Ft-lbs (unless otherwise indicated)

Throttle body mounting bolts	
TBI systems	18 to 22
MPFI systems	15 to 18
Injector cover mounting screws (TBI)	36 to 43 in-lbs
EGR valve-to-throttle body (MPFI)	72 to 108 in-lbs
Fuel rail mounting bolts (MPFI)	70 to 105 in-lbs
Turbocharger-to-exhaust manifold	18 to 28
Exhaust pipe-to-exhaust manifold bolts	15 to 25

4B

1 General information

The fuel system on fuel-injected engines consists of a fuel tank, an electric fuel pump (located under the chassis toward the rear of the vehicle near the fuel tank), a fuel pump relay, fuel injector(s), an air filter assembly and a throttle body unit. Fuel-injected engines appeared in 1984 with Multi Port Fuel (MPFI) Injection on turbocharged models. 1986 and 1987 models are equipped with either the feedback carburetor, MPFI or Throttle Body Injection (TBI). 1988 through 1994 models are equipped with either the Throttle Body Injection (TBI) system or the Multi Port Fuel Injection (MPFI) system. The two systems are easily distinguished. The TBI system uses a large throttle body unit with a single injector, mounted on the intake manifold just like a carburetor, while MPFI uses separate injectors positioned over the intake valves, mounted in the intake manifold. All turbocharged engines

are equipped with the MPFI system. **Note:** *Pre-1984 turbocharged engines mount the fuel injectors in the cylinder heads but 1985 and later turbo models incorporate the fuel injectors into the intake manifold assembly for improved fuel distribution.*

Throttle Body Injection (TBI) system

The Throttle Body Injection system incorporates a single injector mounted in a throttle body similar to that of a conventional carburetor. This system produces greatly improved fuel metering in all running conditions and since most of the control mechanism is electronic, TBI reduces maintenance and minor repair problems.

The Electronic Control Module (ECM) automatically adjusts the air/fuel mixture according to engine load and performance. A fuel pressure regulator mounted in the fuel charging assembly regulates the electric pump-generated fuel pressure at a constant

value. The injector consists of a solenoid activated pintle valve and a small inline fuel filter. It is energized by time-modulated electronic pulses from the ECM (computer).

Multi Port Fuel Injection (MPFI) system

Multi Port Fuel Injection uses timed impulses to inject the fuel directly into the intake port of each cylinder. The injectors are controlled by the Electronic Control Module (ECM). The ECM monitors various engine parameters and delivers the exact amount of fuel required into the intake ports. The throttle body serves only to control the amount of air passing into the system. Because each cylinder is equipped with its own injector, much better control of the fuel/air mixture ratio is possible.

Fuel pump and lines

Fuel is circulated from the fuel tank to the fuel injection system, and back to the fuel

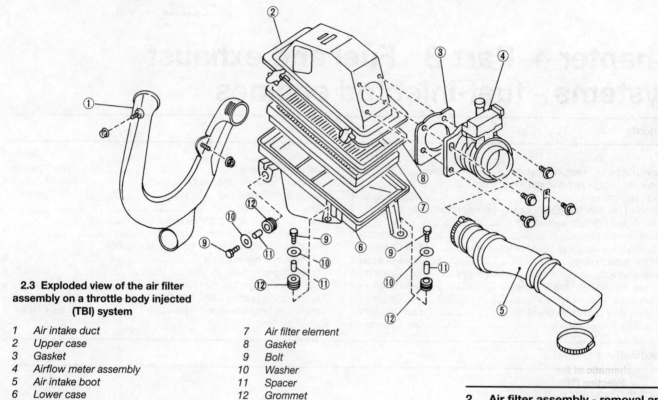

2.3 Exploded view of the air filter assembly on a throttle body injected (TBI) system

1	Air intake duct	7	Air filter element
2	Upper case	8	Gasket
3	Gasket	9	Bolt
4	Airflow meter assembly	10	Washer
5	Air intake boot	11	Spacer
6	Lower case	12	Grommet

tank, through a pair of metal lines running along the underside of the vehicle. An electric fuel pump is located outside of the fuel tank near the rear of the vehicle underbody. A vapor return system routes all vapors back to the fuel tank through a separate return line.

The fuel pump will operate as long as the engine is cranking or running and the ECM is receiving ignition reference pulses from the electronic ignition system. If there are no reference pulses, the fuel pump will shut off after two or three seconds.

Exhaust system

The exhaust system includes an exhaust manifold fitted with an exhaust oxygen sensor, a catalytic converter, an exhaust pipe, and a muffler.

The catalytic converter is an emission control device added to the exhaust system to reduce pollutants. A single-bed converter is used in combination with a three-way (reduction) catalyst. Refer to Chapter 6 for more information regarding the catalytic converter.

2   Air filter assembly - removal and installation

Refer to illustrations 2.3 and 2.4

1   Detach the cable from the negative terminal of the battery.
2   Remove the air filter from the air filter housing (see Chapter 1).
3   Loosen the clamp on the air intake duct **(see illustration)** and separate the duct from the air filter housing.
4   Unclip the upper half of the air filter housing assembly and remove it **(see illustration)**. Leave the airflow meter and air

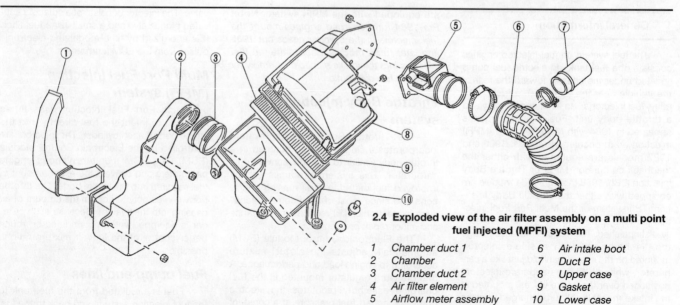

2.4 Exploded view of the air filter assembly on a multi point fuel injected (MPFI) system

1	Chamber duct 1	6	Air intake boot
2	Chamber	7	Duct B
3	Chamber duct 2	8	Upper case
4	Air filter element	9	Gasket
5	Airflow meter assembly	10	Lower case

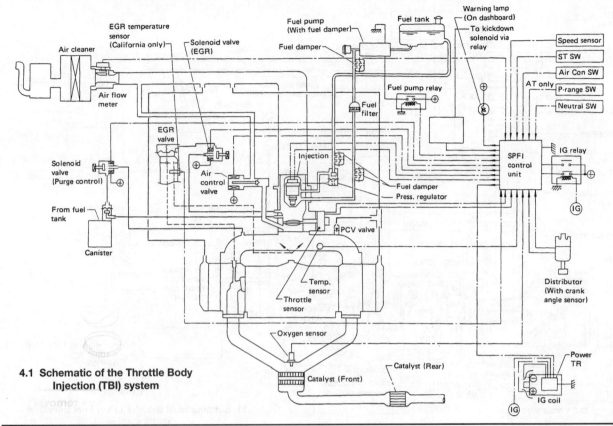

4.1 Schematic of the Throttle Body Injection (TBI) system

intake duct attached to the upper assembly.
5   Remove the mounting bolts from the air filter housing.
6   Remove the air filter housing from the engine compartment.
7   Installation is the reverse of removal.

3   Accelerator cable - removal, installation and adjustment

Removal

1   Remove the air filter assembly (see Section 2).
2   Detach the accelerator cable from the throttle lever.
3   If equipped, remove the cruise control cable from the cable bracket.
4   Separate the accelerator cable from the cable bracket.
5   Detach the nylon collar from the upper end of the accelerator pedal arm.
6   Remove the cable through the firewall from the engine compartment side.

Installation

7   Installation is the reverse of removal. Be sure the cable is routed correctly.
8   If necessary, at the engine compartment side of the firewall, apply sealant around the accelerator cable to prevent water from entering the passenger compartment.

Adjustment

9   To adjust the cable:

a)   Lift up on the cable to remove any slack.
b)   Turn the adjusting nut until it is 1/8-inch away from the cable bracket.
c)   Tighten the locknut and check cable deflection at the throttle linkage. Deflection should be 3/8 to 1/2-inch. If deflection is not within specifications, loosen the locknut and turn the adjusting nut until the deflection is as specified.
d)   After you have adjusted the throttle cable, have an assistant help you verify that the throttle valve opens all the way when you depress the accelerator pedal to the floor and that it returns to the idle position when you release the accelerator. Verify the cable operates smoothly. It must not bind or stick.
e)   If the vehicle is equipped with an automatic transmission, adjust the transmission throttle valve cable (see Chapter 7B).

4   Electronic fuel injection system - general information

Throttle Body Injection (TBI)

Refer to illustration 4.1

The Throttle Body Injection (TBI) system **(see illustration)** uses a single point, pulse time modulated injection system. Fuel is metered into the air intake stream in accordance with engine demands by a single solenoid injection valve mounted in a throttle body on the intake manifold.

Fuel is supplied from the fuel tank by a low pressure, electric fuel pump mounted externally near the fuel tank. The fuel is filtered and sent to the throttle body, where a regulator maintains the fuel delivery pressure at 14 psi (early) or 21 psi (late). An injector nozzle is mounted horizontally above the throttle plate and connected in series with the fuel pressure regulator. Excess fuel supplied by the pump but not needed by the engine is returned to the fuel tank by a steel fuel return line.

The fuel charging assembly consists of five individual components which perform the fuel and air metering function. The throttle body assembly is attached to the conventional carburetor mounting flange on the intake manifold and houses the air control system, fuel injector, fuel pressure regulator, airflow meter, air control valve and throttle sensor.

Air-flow to the engine is controlled by a single butterfly valve mounted in a two piece, die-cast aluminum housing called a throttle body. The butterfly valve is identical in configuration to the throttle plates of a conventional carburetor and is actuated by a similar pedal and linkage arrangement.

The fuel injector is mounted vertically above the throttle plate and is an electro-mechanical device which meters and atomizes the fuel delivered to the engine. The injector valve body consists of a solenoid actuated ball and seat valve assembly.

An electric control signal from the ECM (computer) activates the solenoid, causing

4B

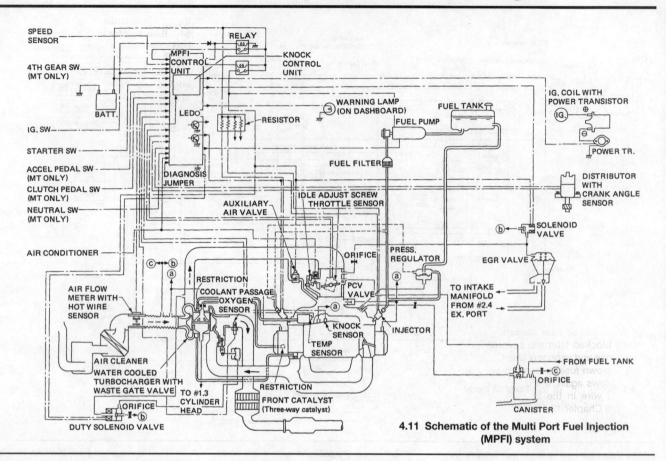

4.11 Schematic of the Multi Port Fuel Injection (MPFI) system

the ball to move off the seat and allowing fuel to flow. The injector flow orifice is fixed and the fuel supply is constant. Therefore, fuel flow to the engine is controlled by how long the solenoid is energized.

The pressure regulator is integral to the fuel charging main body. The regulator is located so as to nullify the effects of the supply line pressure drops. Its design is such that it is not sensitive to back pressure in the return line to the tank.

A second function of the pressure regulator is to maintain fuel supply pressure upon fuel pump shutdown. The regulator functions as a downstream check valve and traps the fuel between itself and the fuel pump. The constant fuel pressure level after engine shutdown precludes fuel line vapor formation and allows for rapid restarts and stable idle operation immediately thereafter.

The air control valve is a rotary solenoid valve. It receives a pulse signal from the ECM and adjusts the bypass air quantity by opening or closing a slider (door) within the air control valve. The air control valve operates in conjunction with other systems to control idle speed. During cold start, feedback control, air conditioning and power steering changes and deceleration vacuum control.

The throttle switch and sensor has two functions. It contains an idle switch and a throttle sensor. The idle switch closes when the throttle valve is at idle and is open at all other positions. The throttle sensor is a potentiometer that transforms throttle posi-

tion into a output voltage and feeds the signals into the ECM. The throttle switch also determines when the throttle lever has contacted the actuator, signaling the need to control engine rpm.

Multi Port Fuel Injection (MPFI)

Refer to illustration 4.11

The Multi Port Fuel Injection (MPFI) system **(see illustration)** is a multi-point, pulse timed, speed density controlled fuel injection system. On the MPFI system, fuel is metered into each intake port in accordance with engine demand through injectors mounted on the intake manifold.

This system incorporates an on-board Electronic Control Module (ECM) computer that accepts inputs from various engine sensors to compute the required fuel flow rate necessary to maintain a prescribed air/fuel ratio throughout the entire engine operational range. The computer then outputs a command to the fuel injectors to meter the approximate quantity of fuel. The system automatically senses and compensates for changes in altitude, load and speed.

The fuel delivery system includes an electric fuel pump mounted externally near the fuel tank which forces pressurized fuel through a series of metal and plastic lines and an inline fuel filter to the fuel charging manifold assembly.

A constant fuel pressure drop is main-

tained across the injector nozzles by a pressure regulator. The regulator is positioned downstream from the fuel injectors. Excess fuel passes through the regulator and returns to the fuel tank through a fuel return line.

5   Electronic fuel injection system - check

Warning: *Gasoline is extremely flammable, so take extra precautions when you work on any part of the fuel system. Don't smoke or allow open flames or bare light bulbs near the work area, and don't work in a garage where a natural gas-type appliance (such as a water heater or a clothes dryer) with a pilot light is present. Since gasoline is carcinogenic, wear latex gloves when there's a possibility of being exposed to fuel, and, if you spill any fuel on your skin, rinse it off immediately with soap and water. Mop up any spills immediately and do not store fuel-soaked rags where they could ignite. The fuel system is under constant pressure, so, if any fuel lines are to be disconnected, the fuel pressure in the system must be relieved first (see Section 2 of Chapter 4A for more information). When you perform any kind of work on the fuel system, wear safety glasses and have a Class B type fire extinguisher on hand.*
Note: *The following procedure is based on the assumption that the fuel pump is working and the fuel pressure is adequate (see Chapter 4A).*

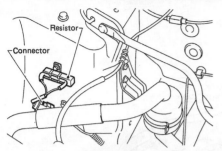

5.8 Location of the TBI resistor

Preliminary checks

1   Check all electrical connectors that are related to the system. Loose electrical connectors and poor grounds can cause many problems that resemble more serious malfunctions.

2   Check to see that the battery is fully charged, as the control unit and sensors depend on an accurate supply voltage in order to properly meter the fuel.

3   Check the air filter element - a dirty or partially blocked filter will severely impede performance and economy (see Chapter 1).

4   If a blown fuse is found, replace it and see if it blows again. If it does, search for a grounded wire in the harness to the fuel pump (see Chapter 12).

System checks

5   Check the condition of the vacuum hoses connected to the intake manifold.

Throttle Body Injection (TBI) systems

Refer to illustration 5.8

6   First, purchase a special injector test light (sometimes called a noid light) and install it into the injector electrical connector. Crank the engine and check to see if the noid light flashes. If it does, the injector is receiving proper voltage. If it doesn't flash, further diagnosis should be performed by a dealer service department or other repair shop.

7   Install a timing light, according to the tool manufacturer's instructions, and point the light into the TBI unit while the engine is running. Watch the conical shaped spray pattern from the injector. Make sure it is even and constant. Vary the idle speed and watch also. There should not be any intermittent breaks or weak spray patterns. **Caution:** *Make sure all timing light wires are carefully tucked away to avoid any accidental contact with the drivebelts or fan blades during testing.*

8   Check the fuel injector resistor. Disconnect the wires from the resistor and using an ohmmeter, check the resistance **(see illustration)**. It should be 38 to 42 ohms. Replace if necessary.

Multi Port Fuel Injection (MPFI) systems

Refer to illustration 5.13

9   Remove the air intake duct from the throttle body and check for dirt, carbon or other residue build-up in the throttle body, particularly around the throttle plate. If it's dirty, clean it with aerosol carburetor cleaner, a rag and a toothbrush, if necessary.

10   With the engine running, place an automotive stethoscope against each injector, one at a time, and listen for a clicking sound, indicating operation. If you don't have a stethoscope, you can place the tip of a long screwdriver against the injector and listen through the handle.

11   If an injector isn't functioning (not clicking), purchase a special injector test light (sometimes called a noid light) and install it into the injector electrical connector. Start the engine and check to see if the noid light flashes. If it does, the injector is receiving proper voltage. If it doesn't flash, further diagnosis should be performed by a dealer service department or other repair shop.

12   With the engine OFF and the fuel injector electrical connectors disconnected, measure the resistance of each injector. Compare your measurements with the injector resistance listed in this Chapter's Specifications. If any injector is open or has an abnormally high resistance, replace it with a new one.

13   Check the fuel injector(s) resistor. Disconnect the harness connector and measure the resistance across terminals W and B **(see illustration)**. It should be 5.8 to 6.5 ohms. If the resistance is incorrect, replace the resistor.

---

6   Throttle Body Injection (TBI) system - component check and replacement

Warning: *Gasoline is extremely flammable, so take extra precautions when you work on any part of the fuel system. Don't smoke or allow open flames or bare light bulbs near the work area, and don't work in a garage where a natural gas-type appliance (such as a water heater or a clothes dryer) with a pilot light is present. Since gasoline is carcinogenic, wear latex gloves when there's a possibility of being exposed to fuel, and, if you spill any*

4B

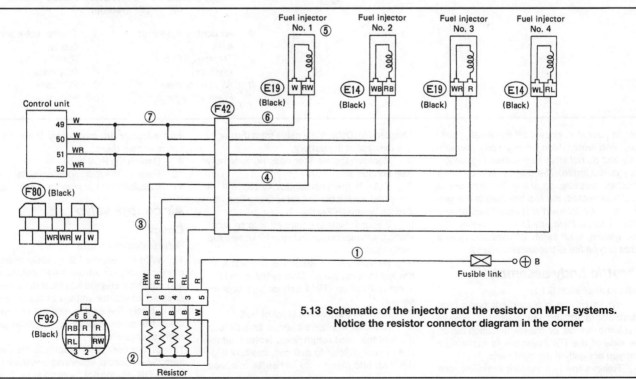

5.13 Schematic of the injector and the resistor on MPFI systems. Notice the resistor connector diagram in the corner

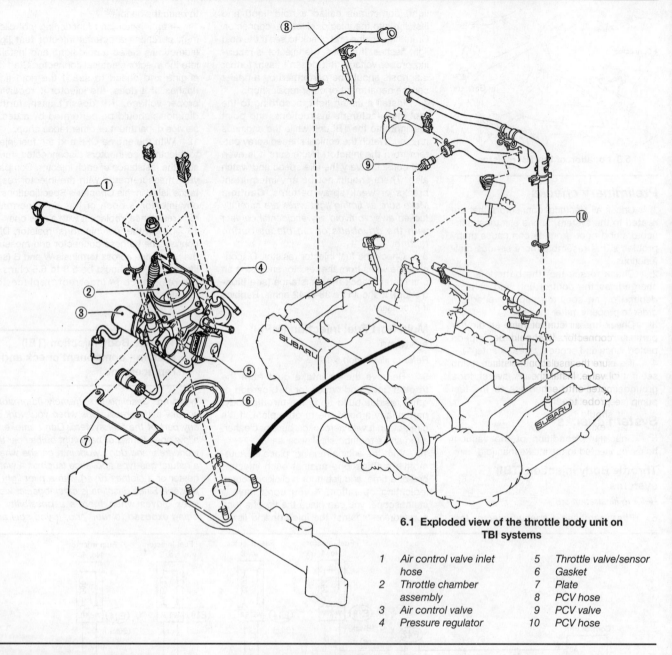

6.1 Exploded view of the throttle body unit on TBI systems

1	Air control valve inlet hose	5	Throttle valve/sensor
2	Throttle chamber assembly	6	Gasket
3	Air control valve	7	Plate
4	Pressure regulator	8	PCV hose
		9	PCV valve
		10	PCV hose

fuel on your skin, rinse it off immediately with soap and water. Mop up any spills immediately and do not store fuel-soaked rags where they could ignite. The fuel system is under constant pressure, so, if any fuel lines are to be disconnected, the fuel pressure in the system must be relieved first (see Chapter 4A). When you perform any kind of work on the fuel system, wear safety glasses and have a Class B type fire extinguisher on hand.

Throttle body assembly

Refer to illustration 6.1

1   When buying replacement parts **(see illustration)** for the TBI assembly, always check the number on the identification tag on the side of the TBI assembly to make sure that you are getting the right parts.

2   Relieve the fuel system pressure (see

Chapter 4A). Detach the cable from the negative terminal of the battery.

3   Remove the air filter housing assembly (see Section 2).

4   Detach the accelerator cable and, if equipped, cruise control cable fitting from the throttle lever (see Section 3).

5   If your vehicle is equipped with an automatic transmission, detach the kickdown rod (early models).

6   Disconnect the electrical connector to the fuel injector, the Air Control Valve and the Throttle Position (TPS) Sensor and coolant sensor.

7   Remove the fuel line bracket bolt.

8   Remove the hose clamps and detach the fuel feed and return lines. **Note:** *If either line proves difficult to pull out, carefully wiggle it up and down - do not strike the lines*

with a tool or attempt to pry them loose or you may dent them.

9   Detach the PCV hose.

10   Remove the four mounting nuts.

11   Installation is the reverse of removal.

Air control valve

Check

Refer to illustration 6.18

12   With the engine idling, disconnect the electrical connector from the air control valve and confirm a change in rpm. If the idle is not affected, check for voltage to the air control valve. **Note:** *The engine rpm will vary greatly when the air control valve is disconnected with the engine cold.*

13   Disconnect the electrical connector from the air control valve and turn the ignition switch ON (engine not running).

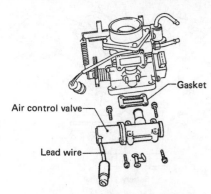

6.18 Remove the air control valve mounting bolts and separate the assembly from the throttle body

14   Install the voltmeter positive probe (+) to the BW terminal. There should be 10 volts or more available.
15   Disconnect the air control valve electrical connector and measure the resistance working on the air control valve side of the harness connector. It should be 7 to 13 ohms.
16   Measure the insulation resistance of the air control valve. Install the positive probe of the ohmmeter onto each terminal with the negative probe touching the body control valve. It should be 1M ohms or greater. If continuity exists, then the internal coils are shorted to the air control valve body.

Replacement

17   Detach the cable from the negative terminal of the battery and disconnect the electrical connector from the air control valve.
18   Remove the two mounting bolts and detach the air control valve **(see illustration)**.
19   Installation is the reverse of removal.

Throttle valve switch/sensor

General description

20   The throttle valve switch and sensor has two functions. It contains an idle switch and a throttle sensor. The idle switch closes when the throttle valve is at idle and is open at all other positions. The throttle sensor is a potentiometer that transforms throttle position into an output voltage and feeds the signals into the ECM. The throttle switch also determines when the throttle lever has contacted the actuator, signaling the need to control engine rpm.

Check

Refer to illustrations 6.23 and 6.25
21   To check the throttle valve switch, warm the engine to normal operating temperature.
22   Check the idle speed and adjust it if necessary (see Chapter 1). Also, check the ignition timing (see Chapter 1).
23   Turn the ignition key OFF and disconnect the throttle valve switch/sensor connector and connect the probes of an ohmmeter to the throttle valve switch terminals A and B **(see illustration)**.

6.23 Check for continuity between the throttle switch/sensor terminals A and B with the throttle closed

24   With the throttle completely closed, continuity should exist. With the throttle valve fully open, continuity should not exist.
25   Insert a 0.0122 inch (0.31 mm) feeler gauge between the throttle lever and the throttle stop screw and see if that continuity exists **(see illustration)**.
26   Now insert a slightly larger feeler gauge 0.0311 inch (0.79 mm) and confirm that continuity does not exist.
27   If the throttle valve switch opens before or after the correct specification, adjust the throttle valve switch (see Steps 34 and 35).
28   To check the throttle sensor, first disconnect the electrical connector to the sensor and check for REFERENCE voltage to the TPS harness connector with the key On (engine not running).It should be 5.0 volts. Refer to the wiring diagrams at the end of Chapter 12 for additional information on wire colors, etc. If REFERENCE voltage is not present, check the harness between the throttle sensor and the ECM for opens or shorts. If the circuits are good, have the ECM diagnosed by a dealer service department or other qualified repair facility.
29   Connect the electrical connector to the throttle sensor and backprobe terminal D (SIGNAL wire) with the positive probe of the voltmeter. Connect the negative probe to a good body ground. With the key On (engine not running), check the voltage as you rotate the throttle by hand from closed to open throttle. The voltage should read approximately 0.5 volt at closed throttle to 5.0 volts at wide-open throttle. If the readings are not as specified or if there isn't a smooth transition from closed to wide-open throttle, replace the throttle switch/sensor. Refer to

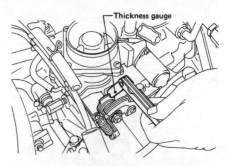

6.25 Checking the throttle switch/sensor operation with a feeler gauge

the wiring diagrams at the end of Chapter 12 for additional information on wire colors, designations, etc.

Replacement

30   Detach the cable from the negative terminal of the battery.
31   Disconnect the wire harness electrical connector from the throttle valve connector.
32   Remove the throttle valve retaining screws.
33   Slide the throttle position sensor off the throttle shaft. Installation is the reverse of removal.

Adjustment

34   With the throttle valve bolts in place and slightly loose, rotate the throttle valve until the switch indicates continuity between terminals A and B with the smaller size feeler gauge 0.0122 inch (0.31 mm) **(see illustration 6.23)**.
35   Tighten the adjustment bolts.

Fuel injector

Check

36   See Section 7 for the fuel injector operational check. If the injector is receiving adequate voltage but doesn't spray fuel, unplug the electrical connector and measure the resistance across the terminals of the injector. Compare your reading with the value listed in this Chapter's Specifications.

Replacement

Refer to illustrations 6.38, 6.39 and 6.40
37   Relieve the fuel pressure (see Chapter 4A).
38   Remove the cap and gasket cover

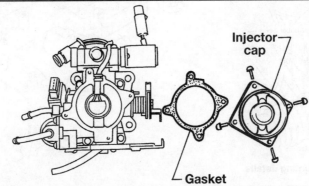

6.38 Be sure to install a new gasket between the injector cap and the throttle body

4B

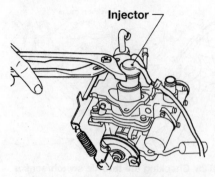

6.39 Lift the injector from the throttle body by carefully wiggling the assembly out of the mounting recess with a pair of pliers

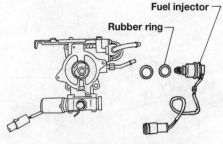

6.40 Install the injector into the throttle body using new O-rings

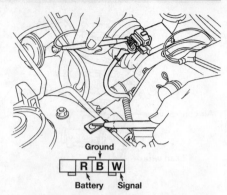

6.45 Check the resistance between the body ground (-) and terminal B (+) on the airflow meter harness connector. It should not be more than 10 ohms

assembly from the top of the throttle body **(see illustration)**.

39   Place a rag on the injector and pull the injector straight up **(see illustration)**.

40   Discard the old O-rings and replace them with new ones. Use a light grade oil to lubricate the new O-rings before installing them **(see illustration)**.

41   Installation is the reverse of removal.

42   Push the injector evenly into the recess using a large socket.

43   Install the injector cover and tighten the screws to torque listed in this Chapter's Specifications.

Airflow meter

Check

Refer to illustrations 6.45 and 6.48

44   Peel back the rubber cover from the harness electrical connector from the airflow meter.

45   With the negative probe on ground and the positive probe backprobed into terminal B, measure resistance between the body ground (-) and terminal B (+) on the airflow meter **(see illustration)**. It should not be more than 10 ohms.

46   Check for voltage at terminal R (battery +) and body ground (-). It should be at least 10 volts.

47   Backprobe terminals W (signal +) and terminal B (ground -) and check the signal voltage with the ignition key ON (engine not running). It should be 0.1 to 0.5 volts.

48   Remove the airflow sensor from the throttle body and using compressed air, apply a steady stream of air across the sensor element. The signal voltage should increase **(see illustration)**.

49   If the voltage does not increase, replace the sensor.

Replacement

Refer to illustration 6.52

50   Detach the cable from the negative battery terminal.

51   Disconnect the harness electrical connector.

52   Remove the mounting bolts and lift the airflow meter from the throttle body **(see illustration)**.

Fuel pressure regulator

Note: *Refer to Chapter 4A, for the fuel pressure checking procedure.*

Replacement

53   Relieve the fuel pressure (see Chapter 4A).

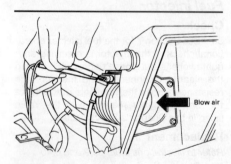

6.48 Blow air through the intake system and see if the signal voltage increases

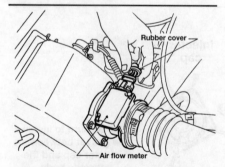

6.52 Airflow meter mounting details

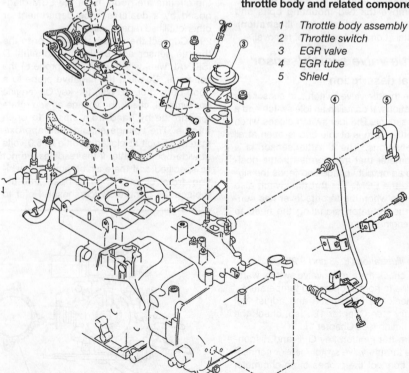

7.5 Exploded view of the Multi Port throttle body and related components

1   *Throttle body assembly*
2   *Throttle switch*
3   *EGR valve*
4   *EGR tube*
5   *Shield*

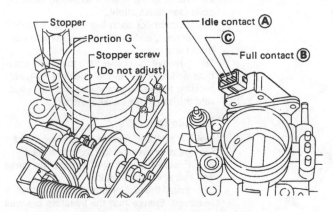

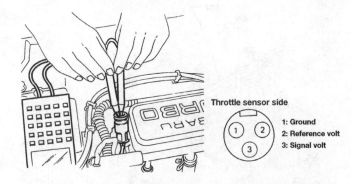

7.11 Details of the throttle switch on MPFI systems

7.16 Checking the REFERENCE voltage on the throttle sensor harness connector on MPFI systems. It should be approximately 5.0 volts with the ignition key ON (engine not running)

4B

54   Remove the bolts that retain the pressure regulator to the venturi chamber of the TBI unit.
55   Installation is the reverse of removal. Be sure to use new O-rings.

7   Multi Port Fuel Injection (MPFI) system - component check and replacement

Throttle body

Removal

Refer to illustration 7.5

1   Detach the cable from the negative terminal of the battery.
2   Detach the throttle switch/sensor connector.
3   Disconnect the accelerator cable (see Section 3) from the throttle body.
4   Carefully mark and remove the vacuum hoses from the throttle body.
5   Remove the four throttle body mounting nuts **(see illustration)**.
6   Remove and discard the gasket between the throttle body air intake plenum.

Installation

7   Clean the gasket mating surfaces. If scraping is necessary, be careful not to damage the gasket surfaces or allow material to drop into the manifold. Installation is the reverse of removal. Be sure to tighten the throttle body mounting nuts to the torque listed in this Chapter's Specifications.

Throttle valve switch/sensor

General description

8   The throttle valve switch and sensor has two functions. It contains an idle switch (three pin rectangular connector) and a throttle sensor (three pin round connector). The idle switch closes when the throttle valve is at idle and is open at all other positions. The throttle sensor is a potentiometer that transforms throttle position into an output voltage and feeds the signals into the ECM. The throttle switch also determines when the throttle lever has contacted the actuator, signaling the need to control engine rpm. On turbo models, the switch actuates at 45-degree throttle angle. These two components are separate and located on different areas on the throttle body.

Check

Refer to illustrations 7.11 and 7.16

9   To check the throttle valve switch, warm the engine to normal operating temperature.
10   Check the idle speed and adjust it if necessary (see Chapter 1). Also, check the ignition timing (see Chapter 1).
11   Turn the ignition key OFF and disconnect the throttle valve switch connector and the throttle sensor connector and connect the probes of an ohmmeter to the throttle valve switch terminals A and C **(see illustration)**.
12   With the throttle completely closed, continuity should exist. With the throttle valve fully open, continuity should not exist.
13   Insert a 0.0217 inch (0.55 mm) feeler gauge between the throttle lever and the throttle stop screw and make sure continuity exists.
14   Now insert a slightly larger feeler gauge 0.0362 inch (0.92 mm) and make sure continuity does not exist.
15   If the throttle valve switch opens before or after the correct specification, adjust the throttle valve switch (see Steps 22 and 23).
16   To check the throttle sensor, first disconnect the electrical connector to the sensor and check for REFERENCE voltage to the TPS harness connector with the key On (engine not running) **(see illustration)**. It should be 5.0 volts. Refer to the wiring diagrams at the end of Chapter 12 for additional information on wire colors, etc. If REFERENCE voltage is not present, check the harness between the throttle sensor and the ECM for opens or shorts. If the circuits are good, have the ECM diagnosed by a dealer service department or other qualified repair facility.
17   Connect the electrical connector to the throttle sensor and backprobe terminal 3 (SIGNAL wire) with the positive probe of the voltmeter. Connect the negative probe to a good body ground. With the key On (engine not running), check the voltage as you rotate the throttle by hand from closed to open throttle. The voltage should read approximately 0.5 volt at closed throttle to 5.0 volts at wide-open throttle. If the readings are not as specified or if there isn't a smooth transition from closed to wide-open throttle, replace the throttle switch/sensor. Refer to the wiring diagrams at the end of Chapter 12 for additional information on wire colors, designations, etc.

Replacement

18   Detach the cable from the negative terminal of the battery.
19   Disconnect the wire harness electrical connector from the throttle valve/sensor connector.
20   Remove the throttle valve retaining screws.
21   Slide the throttle position sensor off the throttle shaft. Installation is the reverse of removal.

Throttle switch adjustment

22   With the throttle valve bolts in place and slightly loose, rotate the throttle valve until the switch indicates continuity between terminals A and B with the smaller size feeler gauge 0.0217 inch (0.55 mm) **(see illustration 7.11)**.
23   Tighten the adjustment bolts.

Fuel rail assembly

Removal

Refer to illustration 7.28

24   Relieve the fuel pressure (see Chapter 4A).
25   Detach the cable from the negative terminal of the battery.
26   Remove the throttle body assembly (see Steps 1 through 9).
27   Disconnect the fuel feed and return lines from the fuel pipe assembly.

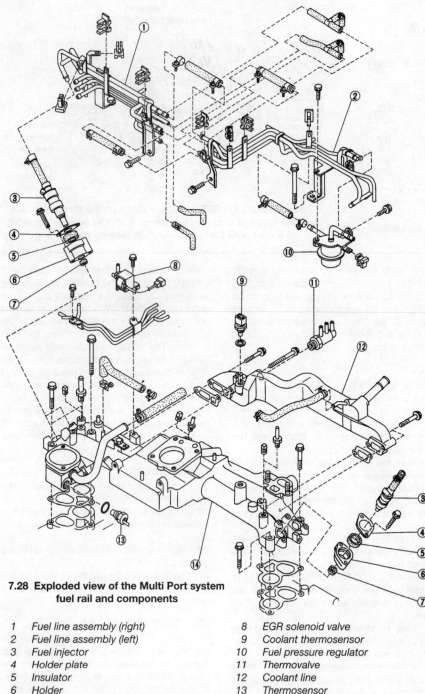

7.28 Exploded view of the Multi Port system fuel rail and components

1	Fuel line assembly (right)	8	EGR solenoid valve
2	Fuel line assembly (left)	9	Coolant thermosensor
3	Fuel injector	10	Fuel pressure regulator
4	Holder plate	11	Thermovalve
5	Insulator	12	Coolant line
6	Holder	13	Thermosensor
7	Seal	14	Intake manifold

7.42 Location of the fuel pressure regulator

28   Remove the fuel rail assembly retaining bolts **(see illustration)**.

29   Disconnect each fuel injector electrical connector. Carefully lift the fuel rail assembly from the engine.

30   Remove the holder from the intake manifold and remove the fuel injectors by gently twisting the fuel injector assembly to separate them from the intake manifold.

Installation

Note: *It's a good idea to replace the injector O-rings whenever the fuel rail is removed.*

31   Ensure that the injector caps are clean and free of contamination.

32   Install the fuel injectors on the fuel rail, if removed. Ensure that the injectors are well seated in the fuel rail assembly.

33   Install the fuel rail and injector assembly onto the engine and secure the fuel rail assembly with the retaining bolts. Tighten the bolts to the torque listed in this Chapter's Specifications.

34   The remainder of installation is the reverse of removal.

Fuel pressure regulator

Check

Note: *This procedure assumes the fuel filter is in good condition.*

35   Check the fuel pressure and perform the necessary steps to diagnose problems with the pressure regulator (see Chapter 4A).

36   Start the engine and check for leakage around the fuel rail, fuel lines and the fuel pressure regulator.

37   If the fuel pressure regulator is faulty or leaking, replace it with a new part.

Replacement

Refer to illustration 7.42

38   Relieve the fuel pressure from the system (see Chapter 4A).

39   Disconnect the cable from the negative terminal of the battery.

40   Remove the fuel rail from the engine (see Steps 24 through 30).

41   Clean any dirt from around the fuel pressure regulator.

42   Loosen the hose clamp and remove the bolts from the fuel pressure regulator **(see illustration)**. Detach the regulator from the fuel rail.

43   Install new O-rings on the pressure regulator and lubricate them with a light coat of oil.

44   Installation is the reverse of removal. Tighten the pressure regulator mounting bolts and the hose clamp securely.

Fuel injectors

Removal

Refer to illustration 7.49

45   Relieve the system fuel pressure (see Chapter 4A).

46   Remove the fuel rail assembly (see Steps 24 through 30).

47   Remove the bolts that retain the injectors to the intake manifold.

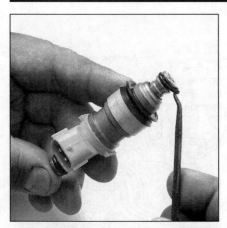

7.49 If you plan to reinstall the original injectors, remove and discard the O-rings and the grommets, and replace them with new ones

48 Grasping the injector body, pull up while gently rocking the injector from side-to-side.
49 Inspect the injector O-rings (two per injector) for signs of deterioration **(see illustration)**. Replace as required. **Note:** As long as you have the fuel rail off it's a good idea to replace the O-rings.
50 If equipped, inspect the injector plastic 'hat' (covering the injector pintle) and washer for signs of deterioration. Replace as required. If the hat is missing, look for it in the intake manifold.

Installation

51 Lubricate the new O-rings with light grade oil and install two on each injector. **Caution:** Do not use silicone grease. It will clog the injectors.
52 Using a light twisting motion, install the injector(s).

53 The remainder of installation is the reverse of removal.

Auxiliary Air Control (AAC) Valve

Refer to illustrations 7.54a, 7.54b and 7.57

General information

54 The AAC valve provides air bypass when the engine is cold for fast idle. It consists of a bimetal heater and rotary shutter. When the temperature of the bimetal is low, the shutter opens and allows air to bypass from the air intake duct into the intake manifold. As the engine warms, the shutter closes and does not allow any air to circulate into the intake manifold. This condition continues until the engine is stopped and the temperature of the engine block cools down **(see illustrations)**.

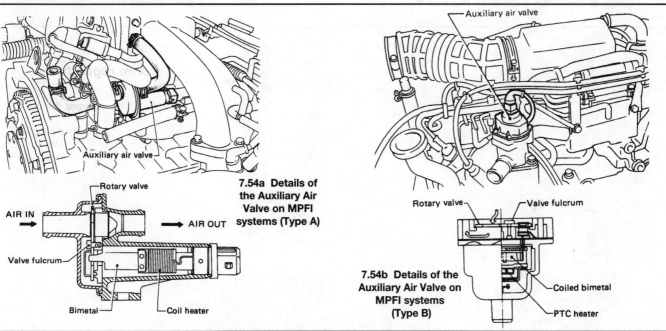

7.54a Details of the Auxiliary Air Valve on MPFI systems (Type A)

7.54b Details of the Auxiliary Air Valve on MPFI systems (Type B)

Check

55 With the engine completely cold, start the engine and check for the presence of battery voltage on the AAC valve harness electrical connector. Battery voltage should be present.

56 Allow the engine to warm up to normal operating temperature, turn the ignition key OFF and remove the AAC valve. Check to make sure the shutter has been activated and is completely closed (no air flow). If the shutter is open, replace the AAC valve.

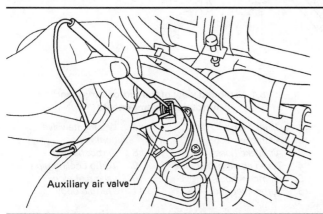

7.57 Checking the resistance of the AAV (Type B shown)

57 Check the AAC valve resistance **(see illustration)**. It should be more than 0 but less than infinity. If the resistance indicates a short or open, replace the AAC valve with a new part.

Replacement

58 Detach the air regulator electrical connector and disconnect the two hoses.
59 Remove the air regulator mounting bolts.
60 Lift the assembly from the intake manifold.
61 Installation is the reverse of removal.

Airflow meter

Check

Refer to illustration 7.63

62 Peel back the rubber cover from the airflow meter electrical connector.
63 With the negative probe on ground and the positive probe backprobed into terminal

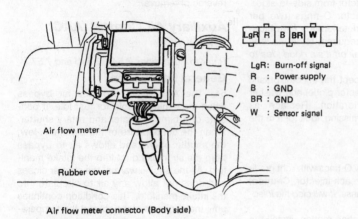

LgR | R | B | BR | W

LgR : Burn-off signal
R : Power supply
B : GND
BR : GND
W : Sensor signal

Air flow meter

Rubber cover

Air flow meter connector (Body side)

7.63 Check the resistance between ground (-) and terminal BR (+) with an ohmmeter. It should be less than 10 ohms

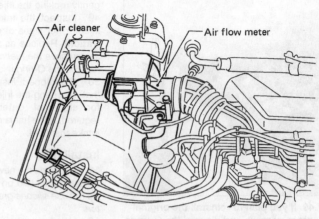

Air cleaner

Air flow meter

7.70 Airflow mounting details on a MPFI system

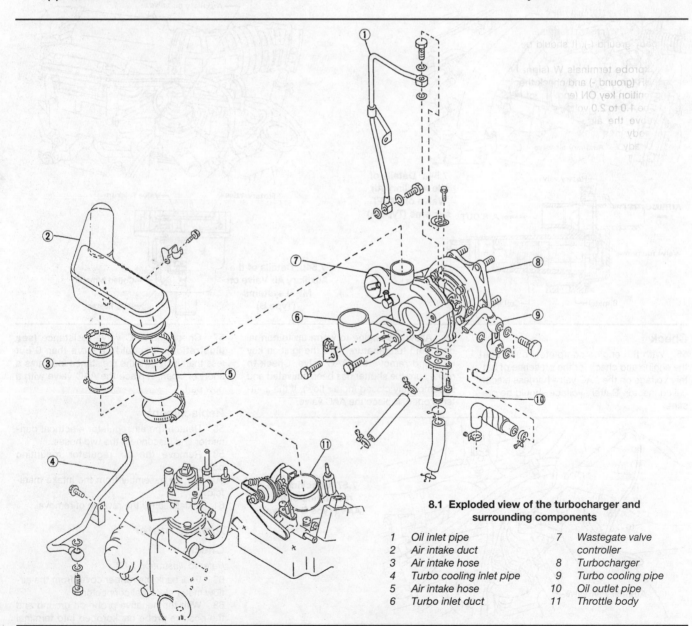

8.1 Exploded view of the turbocharger and surrounding components

1	Oil inlet pipe	7	Wastegate valve
2	Air intake duct		controller
3	Air intake hose	8	Turbocharger
4	Turbo cooling inlet pipe	9	Turbo cooling pipe
5	Air intake hose	10	Oil outlet pipe
6	Turbo inlet duct	11	Throttle body

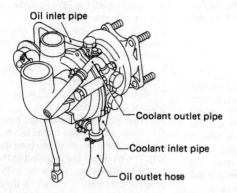

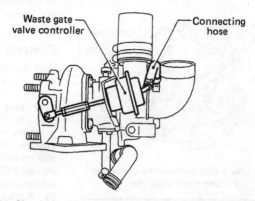

9.8 This turbocharger is equipped with both liquid (coolant) cooling system and the oiling system

9.11 Check the wastegate solenoid for proper operation

B, measure resistance between the body ground (-) and terminal BR (+) on the airflow meter **(see illustration)**. It should not be more than 10 ohms.

64 Check for voltage at terminal R (battery +) and body ground (-). It should be at least 10 volts.

65 Backprobe terminals W (signal +) and terminal BR (ground -) and check the voltage with the ignition key ON (engine not running). It should be 1.0 to 2.0 volts.

66 Remove the airflow sensor from the throttle body and using compressed air, apply a steady stream of air across the sensor element. The voltage should increase.

67 If the voltage does not increase, replace the sensor.

Replacement

Refer to illustration 7.70

68 Detach the cable from the negative battery terminal.

69 Disconnect the harness electrical connector.

70 Remove the mounting bolts and lift the airflow meter from the throttle body **(see illustration)**.

8   Turbocharger - general information

Refer to illustration 8.1

The turbocharger increases power by using an exhaust gas-driven turbine to pressurize the air entering the combustion chambers **(see illustration)**. The amount of boost (intake manifold pressure) is controlled by the wastegate (exhaust bypass valve). The wastegate is operated by a spring-loaded actuator assembly which controls the maximum boost level by allowing some of the exhaust gas to bypass the turbine.

In 1985, all turbocharged systems became water cooled. This design allows for better turbocharger cooling through all driving conditions. The intake manifold channels incorporate separate runners to each cylinder. The injectors are relocated from the cylinder head into the intake manifold for improved fuel distribution. **Note:** *Some models are equipped with both the liquid cooling system and the oil cooling system turbochargers.*

The boost pressure switch has been redesigned after 1985. There are two boost pressure switches; one signals the dash light and the other signals the EGI control light. If excessive boost occurs, the second pressure switch signals the injectors to cut fuel. This design eliminates the air relief valve from previous years.

Also after 1985, the fuel pressure regulator has been moved from the front of the intake manifold to a position above the intake manifold to improve access and cooling. The fuel pump relay has been moved from under the driver's front seat to the dash near the passenger's footwell.

9   Turbocharger - check

Turbocharger check

Refer to illustration 9.8

1 While it is a relatively simple device, the turbocharger is also a precision component which can be severely damaged by an interrupted oil or coolant supply or loose or damaged ducts.

2 Due to the special techniques and equipment required, checking and diagnosis of suspected problems dealing with the turbocharger should be left to a dealer service department or other qualified repair shop. The home mechanic can, however, check the connections and linkages for security, damage and other obvious problems. Also, the home mechanic can check components that govern the turbocharger such as the wastegate solenoid and wastegate actuator. Refer to the checks later in this Section.

3 Because each turbocharger has its own distinctive sound, a change in the noise level can be a sign of potential problems.

4 A high-pitched or whistling sound is a symptom of an inlet air or exhaust gas leak.

5 If an unusual sound comes from the vicinity of the turbine, the turbocharger can be removed and the turbine wheel inspected. **Caution:** *All checks must be made with the engine off and cool to the touch and the turbocharger stopped or personal injury could result. Operating the engine without all the turbocharger ducts and filters installed is also dangerous and can result in damage to the turbine wheel blades.*

6 With the engine OFF, reach inside the housing and turn the turbine wheel to make sure it spins freely. If it doesn't, it's possible the oil has sludged or coked from overheating. Push in on the turbine wheel and check for binding. The turbine should rotate freely with no binding or rubbing on the housing. If it does the turbine bearing is worn out.

7 Check the exhaust manifold for cracks and loose connections.

8 Because the turbine wheel rotates at speeds up to 140,000 rpm, severe damage can result from the interruption of coolant or contamination of the oil supply to the turbine bearings. Check for leaks in the coolant **(see illustration)** and oil inlet lines and obstructions in the oil drain-back line, as this can cause severe oil loss through the turbocharger seals. Burned oil on the turbine housing is a sign of this. **Caution:** *Whenever a major engine bearing such as a main, connecting rod or camshaft bearing is replaced, the turbocharger should be flushed with clean oil.*

Wastegate actuator check

Refer to illustration 9.11

9 The turbocharger wastegate provides additional low speed boost without overboost at high speeds. This increases low speed torque and better driveability. It is important that the wastegate assembly is properly adjusted. The wastegate actuator (solenoid) is controlled by the pressure signal produced by the release of warm, compressed air from the turbocharger.

10 Remove the pressure hose from the wastegate actuator (solenoid).

11 Connect a hand-held pressure pump to the hose and apply approximately 9 to 10 psi (59 to 69 kPa) pressure to the actuator **(see illustration)** and make sure the actuator rod

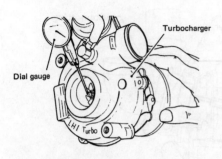

9.17 Use a dial indicator to check the turbine shaft axial play

moves. **Caution:** *Do not apply more than the specified pressure to avoid damaging the actuator.*

12   The control rod should move slightly and hold its position. Make sure the wastegate lever and wastegate are not binding.

13   If the test results are incorrect, replace the wastegate actuator (solenoid).

14   Check the boost pressure. If the boost is too high, the engine may knock and air will be released through the air relief valve. Overboost is usually caused by the wastegate actuator being faulty or stuck closed. Too little boost causes a lack of engine power, poor acceleration or increased fuel consumption. Too little boost is often caused by leaks in the turbo system hoses. With the engine at operating temperatures, connect a T-fitting to the intake pipe pressure hose and install a pressure gauge.

15   With the clutch pressed down (manual transmission), raise the engine rpm to 2,400 and check the boost pressure. It should be 6 to 7 psi (42 to 50 kPa). If the pressure is less than required, check the intake and exhaust system for leaks. Also, check the air relief valve (if equipped) for hissing sounds. Replace if necessary. If there are no leaks, replace the turbocharger.

16   If the boost pressure is more than specified, check for a possible damaged wastegate valve.

General checks

Refer to illustration 9.17

17   If oil leakage is detected inside the intake system, check for a loose or damaged turbine shaft **(see illustration)**. Although slight amounts of oil does not necessarily indicate problems with the turbocharger, it is best to examine the unit carefully. Install a dial gauge and confirm that the axial play does not exceed 0.0035 inch (0.09 mm). Replace the turbocharger if the axial play is excessive.

18   If the system checks out correctly but the TURBO light on the dash remains on or illuminates at the incorrect rpm range, check the pressure switch and other sensors directly involved with the fuel and emissions system. Refer to Chapter 6 for the testing and replacement procedures.

19   Also, check the knock control system. This system detects excessive engine knocking and retards the ignition timing to prevent excessive detonation. Refer to Chapter 6 for checking procedures.

10   Turbocharger - removal and installation

Caution: *The turbocharger is a high-speed component, assembled and balanced to very fine tolerances. Do not disassemble it or try to repair it. Turbochargers should only be overhauled or repaired by authorized turbocharger repair shops or damage could result to the turbocharger and/or the engine.*

Removal

1   Disconnect the negative battery cable from the battery.

2   Drain the engine coolant from the radiator and engine block (see Chapter 1).

3   Disconnect the PCV from the intake system (see Chapter 6).

4   Disconnect the air hose and the intake air connector and remove the assembly from the top of the engine.

5   Disconnect the hose from the coolant inlet pipe **(see illustration 8.1)**.

6   Remove the turbocharger mounting bracket **(see illustration 8.1)**.

7   Remove the coolant outlet pipe.

8   Remove the bolts that retain the oil supply line and the oil return line **(see illustration 8.1)**. The oil return line is bolted to the bottom of the turbocharger. Be ready with a rag to catch any oil from the lines as they are disconnected.

9   Remove the nuts that retain the turbocharger to the exhaust manifold, being careful not to damage the wastegate actuator rod, line or bracket. **Note:** *The wastegate actuator is precisely adjusted. Be careful when laying the complete turbocharger unit on the bench, so as not to disturb wastegate actuator alignment.*

Installation

10   Use a die to clean the studs in the turbocharger mounting portion of the exhaust manifold and coat them with anti-seize compound. Bolt the turbocharger onto the exhaust manifold, using a new gasket. Torque the bolts to the Specifications listed in this Chapter.

11   Reinstall the oil drain line fitting and line with a new gasket.

12   Prime the center bearing of the turbocharger with oil by squirting some clean engine oil into the oil supply hole on top, while turning the compressor wheel, then install the supply line. **Warning:** *The turbine or compressor wheels have very sharp blades; do not turn the blades with your fingers. Use a plastic pen.*

13   The remainder of installation is the reverse of removal.

Chapter 5
Engine electrical systems

Contents

Specifications

Battery voltage
Engine off 12-volts
Engine running .... 14-to-15 volts

Firing order .... See Chapter 2

Spark plug/coil wire resistance (maximum) .... Approximately 1,000 ohms per inch of length, but not more than 30,000 ohms regardless of length

External resistor resistance
1980 breaker points ignition systems
    2WD models .... 0.9 ohms
    4WD models .... Not applicable
1980 breakerless ignition systems
    2WD models .... 1.1 to 1.3 ohms
    4WD models .... Not applicable
1981 and 1982 breakerless ignition systems
    2WD models .... 1.4 to 1.6 ohms
    4WD models .... Not applicable

Ignition coil resistance
1980
  Nippondenso
    Primary resistance .... 1.33 to 1.63 ohms
    Secondary resistance .... 12.6 to 15.4 K-ohms
  Hitachi
    Primary resistance .... 1.17 to 1.43 ohms
    Secondary resistance .... 7.8 to 11.6 K-ohms
1981 and 1982
  Nippondenso
    Primary resistance .... 1.06 to 1.30 ohms
    Secondary resistance .... 12.1 to 14.9 K-ohms
  Hitachi (non-turbocharged engines)
    Primary resistance .... 1.04 to 1.27 ohms
    Secondary resistance .... 7.4 to 11.0 K-ohms
1983 through 1986
  Nippondenso
    Primary resistance .... 1.13 to 1.38 ohms
    Secondary resistance .... 10.8 to 14.6 K-ohms
  Hitachi (non-turbocharged engines)
    Primary resistance .... 1.04 to 1.27 ohms
    Secondary resistance .... 7.4 to 11.0 K-ohms

5

Ignition coil resistance (continued)

Hitachi (turbocharged engines)
- Primary resistance .... 0.84 to 1.02 ohms
- Secondary resistance .... 8.0 to 12.0 K-ohms

1987 through 1994

Nippondenso (MPFI)
- Primary resistance .... 1.13 to 1.38 ohms
- Secondary resistance .... 10.8 to 14.6 K-ohms

Hitachi (TBI)
- Primary resistance .... 0.84 to 1.02 ohms
- Secondary resistance .... 8.0 to 12.0 K-ohms

Hitachi (MPFI turbocharged)
- Primary resistance .... 0.93 to 1.02 ohms
- Secondary resistance .... 8.0 to 12.0 K-ohms

Ignition coil primary winding-to-case resistance .... 10 M-ohms

Distributor

Ignition points
- Point gap .... 0.018 inch
- Point dwell .... 49 to 55-degrees

Pick-up coil resistance

1980
- Nippondenso distributor .... 130 to 190 ohms
- Hitachi distributor .... 600 to 850 ohms

1981 through 1987

Hitachi distributor
- Carbureted engine .... Not measurable
- TBI and MPFI engine .... Not applicable

Nippondenso distributor .... 130 to 190 ohms

1988 through 1994 .... Not applicable

Air gap

1980 through 1983
- 2WD models .... 0.008 to 0.016 inch
- 4WD models .... 0.012 to 0.016 inch

1984
- Hitachi distributor .... 0.012 to 0.020 inch
- Nippondenso distributor .... 0.008 to 0.016 inch

1985

Carbureted engines
- California models .... 0.008 to 0.016 inch
- Federal, Canada 2WD .... 0.008 to 0.016 inch
- Federal, Canada 4WD .... 0.012 to 0.020 inch

Fuel injected engines
- Non-turbocharged .... 0.008 to 0.016 inch
- Turbocharged .... 0.012 to 0.020 inch

1986
- California models with manual transaxle .... 0.008 to 0.016 inch
- California 4WD models with automatic transaxle .... 0.008 to 0.016 inch
- Federal, Canada 2WD models with manual transaxle .... 0.008 to 0.016 inch
- Federal, Canada 4WD models .... 0.012 to 0.020 inch
- Canadian models .... 0.012 to 0.020 inch

1987
- Carbureted engines .... 0.008 to 0.016 inch
- MPFI turbocharged engines .... 0.012 to 0.020 inch
- TBI and MPFI engines... Not applicable

1988 through 1994 .... Not applicable

Alternator brush length

New.. 0.70 inch
Minimum... 0.25 inch

Voltage regulator settings (external regulator)

Standard core gap
- Voltage coil... 0.024 to 0.039 in
- Charge relay .... 0.031 to 0.039 in

Standard point gap
- Voltage coil... 0.014 to 0.018 in
- Charge relay .... 0.016 to 0.024 in

2.1 Detach the battery cables (negative first) then remove the nuts from the battery hold-down clamp

1   General information

The engine electrical systems include all ignition, charging and starting components. Because of their engine-related functions, these components are considered separately from chassis electrical devices like the lights, instruments, etc.

Be very careful when working on the engine electrical components. They are easily damaged if checked, connected or handled improperly. The alternator is driven by an engine drivebelt which could cause serious injury if your hands, hair or clothes become entangled in it with the engine running. Both the starter and alternator are connected directly to the battery and could arc or even cause a fire if mishandled, overloaded or shorted out.

Never leave the ignition switch on for long periods of time with the engine off. Do not disconnect the battery cables while the engine is running. Correct polarity must be maintained when connecting battery cables from another source, such as another vehicle, during jump starting. Always disconnect the negative cable first and hook it up last or the battery may be shorted by the tool being used to loosen the cable clamps.

Additional safety related information on the engine electrical systems can be found in *Safety first* near the front of this manual. It should be referred to before beginning any operation included in this Chapter.

2   Battery - removal and installation

Refer to illustration 2.1

1   Disconnect both cables from the battery terminals **(see illustration). Caution:** *Always disconnect the negative cable first and hook it up last or the battery may be shorted by the tool being used to loosen the cable clamps.*

2   Locate the battery hold-down clamp straddling the top of the battery. Remove the nuts and the hold-down clamp.

3   Lift out the battery. Use the special straps that attach to the battery posts - lifting and moving the battery is much easier if you use one.

4   Installation is the reverse of removal.

3   Battery - emergency jump starting

Refer to the *Booster battery (jump) starting* procedure at the front of this manual.

4   Battery cables - check and replacement

1   Periodically inspect the entire length of each battery cable for damage, cracked or burned insulation and corrosion. Poor battery cable connections can cause starting problems and decreased engine performance.

2   Check the cable-to-terminal connections at the ends of the cables for cracks, loose wire strands and corrosion. The presence of white, fluffy deposits under the insulation at the cable terminal connection is a sign that the cable is corroded and should be replaced. Check the terminals for distortion, missing mounting bolts and corrosion.

3   When replacing the cables, always disconnect the negative cable first and hook it up last or the battery may be shorted by the tool used to loosen the cable clamps. Even if only the positive cable is being replaced, be sure to disconnect the negative cable from the battery first.

4   Disconnect and remove the cable. Make sure the replacement cable is the same length and diameter.

5   Clean the threads of the starter solenoid or ground connection with a wire brush to remove rust and corrosion. Apply a light coat of petroleum jelly to the threads to prevent future corrosion.

6   Attach the cable to the relay or ground connection and tighten the mounting nut/bolt securely.

7   Before connecting the new cable to the battery, make sure that it reaches the battery post without having to be stretched. Clean the battery posts thoroughly (see Chapter 1) and apply a light coat of petroleum jelly to prevent corrosion.

8   Connect the positive cable first, followed by the negative cable.

5   Ignition system - general information

1   The ignition system is designed to ignite the fuel/air charge entering each cylinder at just the right moment. It does this by producing a high-voltage spark between the electrodes of each spark plug.

2   The types of ignition systems installed on these vehicles evolved through the years to accommodate increasingly strict emissions standards. Some of the changes in the ignition systems overlapped in certain years and others changed with certain models depending upon geographical location (Canada, California, etc.). Here is a general listing of the various systems.

Breaker points ignition systems

3   This system controls the ignition spark using the conventional points and condenser arrangement and timing is controlled by mechanical advance components. Depending upon geographical location, model, engine size, etc. only a few of the early carbureted engines are equipped with the breaker points systems.

Breakerless ignition systems

Refer to illustrations 5.4a, 5.4b, 5.4c and 5.4d

4   Early electronic (breakerless) ignition systems **(see illustrations)** were installed on many 1980 and 1982 models and virtually all 1983 through 1987 models. These ignition systems are a solid state electronic design

5

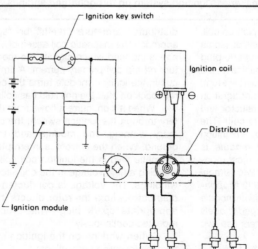

5.4a Diagram of the breakerless type ignition system with an externally mounted ignition module

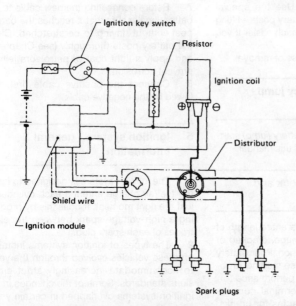

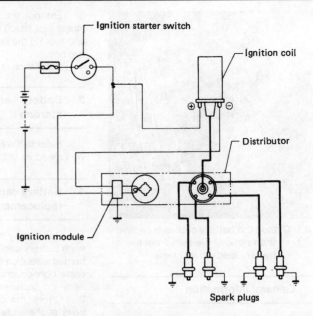

5.4b Diagram of the breakerless ignition system on 4WD models with a resistor in the primary circuit

5.4c Diagram of the breakerless ignition system with the ignition module housed within the distributor

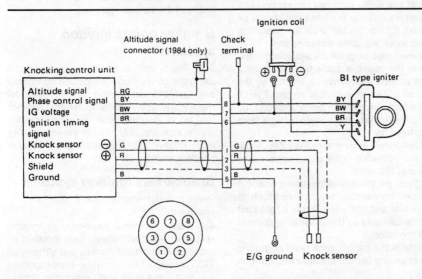

5.4d Diagram of the breakerless ignition system on turbocharged engines

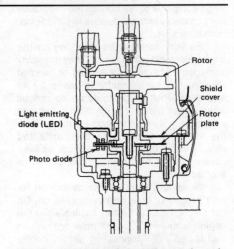

5.8 Cross-sectional view of a crank angle sensor distributor

a) *Do not keep the ignition switch on for more than 10 seconds if the engine will not start.*
b) *Always connect a tachometer in accordance with the tool manufacturer's instructions. Some tachometers may be incompatible with this ignition system.*
c) *Never allow the ignition coil terminals to touch ground. Grounding the coil could result in damage to the igniter and/or the ignition coil.*
d) *Do not disconnect the battery when the engine is running.*
e) *Make sure the igniter is properly grounded.*

Crank angle sensor systems
Refer to illustrations 5.8 and 5.10

8   On this system, installed on 1987 through 1994 models with TBI and MPFI fuel

consisting of an ignition module, pick-up coil, reluctor, ignition coil, external resistor (some early models), distributor, the spark plug wires and the spark plugs. Mechanically, the system is similar to a breaker point system, except that the distributor cam and ignition points have been replaced by a reluctor and a magnetic pick-up unit (pick-up coil). The coil primary circuit is controlled by an ignition module. **Note 1:** *The ignition module is mounted within the distributor on most models. The exceptions being the 1980 Hitachi system and the 1980 through 1982 Nippon-denso systems.* **Note 2:** *The ignition module harness connector on turbocharged models has a four pin connector. All others use two pin module connectors.*
5   When the ignition is switched on, the ignition primary circuit is energized. When the

distributor armature "teeth" or "spokes" approach the magnetic coil assembly, a voltage is induced which signals the module to turn off the coil primary current. A timing circuit in the ignition module turns the coil current back on after the coil field has collapsed.
6   When it's on, current flows from the battery through the ignition switch, the coil primary winding, the module and then to ground. When the current is interrupted, the magnetic field in the ignition coil collapses, inducing a high voltage in the coil secondary windings. The voltage is conducted to the distributor where the rotor directs it to the appropriate spark plug. This process is repeated continuously.
7   When working on the ignition system, take the following precautions:

6.1 To use a calibrated ignition tester, simply disconnect a spark plug wire and connect it to the tester, clip the tester to a convenient ground and operate the starter - if there is enough power to fire the plug, sparks will be visible between the electrode tip and the tester body

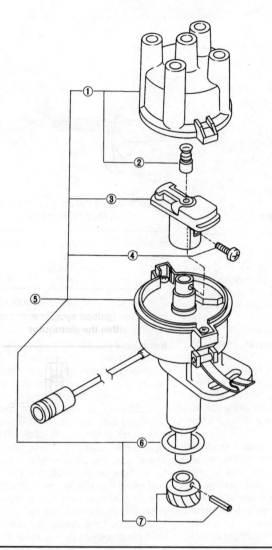

5.10 Exploded view of a crank angle sensor distributor

1   *Cap assembly*
2   *Carbon point*
3   *Rotor head*
4   *Screw*
5   *Distributor assembly*
6   *O-ring*
7   *Pinion set*

systems, the computer and the crank angle sensor located inside the distributor controls the spark timing advance characteristics **(see illustration)**. The vacuum advance unit has been eliminated from this design.

9   The crank angle sensor is the basis of this computer-controlled system. It monitors engine speed and piston position and relays this data to the computer which in turn controls the fuel injection duration (fuel injector on/off time) and ignition timing. The crank angle sensor has a rotor plate and a wave forming circuit. The rotor plate has 360 slits for each degree or one percent signal (engine speed signal) and four slits for the 90-degree crank angle signal. Light Emitting Diodes (LED) and photo diodes are built into the wave forming circuit. When the rotor plate passes the space between the LED and the photo diode, the slits on the rotor plate continually cut the beam of light sent to the photo diode from the LED. They are then converted into on-off pulses by the wave forming circuit and then sent to the ECM (computer).

10   The crank angle sensor type distributor

must be replaced as a complete unit. There are no replacement parts available for the distributor except the cap, rotor and seal cover **(see illustration)**.

6   Ignition system - check

Warning: *Because of the high voltage generated by the ignition system, extreme care should be taken whenever an operation is performed involving ignition components. This not only includes the igniter, coil, distributor and spark plug wires, but related components such as plug connectors, tachometer and other test equipment also.*

All ignition systems

Refer to illustration 6.1

1   If the engine turns over but won't start, disconnect the spark plug wire from any spark plug and attach it to a calibrated tester (available at most auto parts stores) **(see illustration)**. Connect the clip on the tester to a bolt or metal bracket on the engine. If you're unable to obtain a calibrated ignition

tester, remove the wire from one of the spark plugs and, using an insulated tool, pull back the boot and hold the end of the wire about 1/4-inch from a good ground.

2   Crank the engine and watch the end of the tester or spark plug wire to see if bright blue, well-defined sparks occur.

3   If sparks occur, sufficient voltage is reaching the plug to fire it (repeat the check at the remaining plug wires to verify that the distributor cap and rotor are OK). However, the plugs themselves may be fouled, so remove and check them as described in Chapter 1.

4   If no sparks or intermittent sparks occur, remove the distributor cap and check the cap and rotor as described in Chapter 1. If moisture is present, dry out the cap and rotor, then reinstall the cap and repeat the spark test.

5   If there's still no spark, detach the coil secondary wire from the distributor cap and hook it up to the tester (reattach the plug wire to the spark plug), then repeat the spark check. Again, if you don't have a tester, hold the end of the wire about 1/4-inch from a good ground.

6   If sparks now occur, the distributor cap, rotor or plug wire(s) may be defective.

7   If no sparks occur, check the primary wire connections at the coil to make sure they're clean and tight. Check for voltage to the coil on the primary circuit from the ignition switch. Check the ignition coil (see Section 8) and the ignition points (see Chapter 1) or distributor pick-up coil (see Section 11). Make any necessary repairs, then repeat the check again.

8   If there's still no spark, the coil-to-cap wire may be bad (check the resistance with an ohmmeter and compare it to the spark plug wire resistance Specifications found in Chapter 1. If a known good wire doesn't make any difference in the test results, the igniter may be defective.

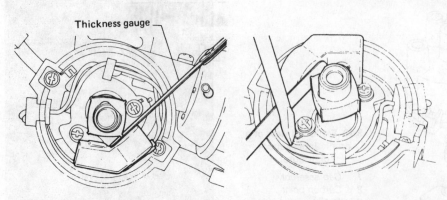

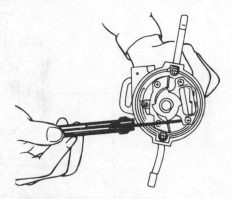

7.2b Checking the air gap on a late model Hitachi distributor

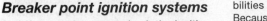

7.2a Adjusting the air gap on an early Nippondenso distributor

Breaker point ignition systems

9   If no sparks occur, check the ignition resistor. The ignition resistor is a ceramic block located near the ignition coil. The ignition resistor stabilizes primary voltage and current for uniform secondary voltage capabilities during all engine speed conditions. Because current varies during cranking (low voltage, high current) and high speed (high voltage, low current), the resistor allows smooth transition and constant secondary voltage to the spark plugs.

10   Disconnect the ignition leads from the resistor and, using an ohmmeter, check the resistance. Refer to the Specifications listed in this Chapter for the correct value.

11   Check for battery voltage to the positive (+) terminal of the ignition resistor with the ignition key ON (engine not running). Battery voltage should be available.

12   Inspect the ignition points (see Chapter 1). If the points appear to be in good shape (no pitting or burn spots), check the point gap or dwell.

13   Measure the voltage at the points with a voltmeter. With the ignition ON (engine not running), the points should produce a voltmeter reading of approximately 10.5 volts. If not, the battery must be recharged or replaced. If the voltage exceeds 10.5 volts, record the voltage reading for future reference.

14   Check for a ground or open in the distributor points circuit. There may be a damaged points terminal that is causing the ignition voltage to be shorted or diminished.

15   Check the condition of the vacuum advance system. Disconnect the vacuum hose and connect a vacuum pump. Apply vacuum and check that the vacuum advance diaphragm moves the plate and allows the points to advance ignition timing. Refer to Section 10 for additional information.

Breakerless ignition systems

16   If no sparks occur, check the ignition resistor. The ignition resistor is a ceramic block located near the ignition coil. The ignition resistor stabilizes primary voltage and current for uniform secondary voltage capa-

bilities during all engine speed conditions. Because current varies during cranking (low voltage, high current) and high speed (high voltage, low current), the resistor allows smooth transition and constant secondary voltage to the spark plugs.

17   Disconnect the ignition leads from the resistor and using an ohmmeter, check the resistance. Refer to the Specifications listed in this Chapter for the correct reading.

18   Check for battery voltage to the pick-up coil with the ignition key ON, engine not running. If voltage is available and there is still no spark, replace the pick-up coil (see Section 11).

19   Check the air gap (see Section 7). Make any necessary repairs, then repeat the check.

20   If there's still no spark, the coil-to-cap wire may be bad (check the resistance with an ohmmeter and compare it to the ignition coil-to-distributor cap wire resistance found in this Chapter's Specifications.

21   If the coil-to-cap wire is good and there is still no spark, the ignition module may be defective (see Section 11).

Crank angle sensor ignition systems

22   Check for battery voltage to the ignition module (power transistor) (see Section 11), with the ignition key ON, engine not running. If voltage is available and there is still no spark, test the ignition module (see Section 11).

23   If there's still no spark, the coil-to-cap wire may be bad (check the resistance with an ohmmeter and compare it to the ignition coil-to-distributor cap wire resistance found in this Chapter's Specifications.

24   If the coil-to-cap wire is good and there is still no spark, follow the checks described in Section 11. These checks include the crankshaft sensor and harness checks and the self diagnostic checks for the ignition and fuel injection system. Many of these checks are described in Chapter 6 so it may be necessary to perform multiple tests to narrow down the source of the problem.

25   If there still is no spark, have the crank angle sensor distributor checked and

replaced, if necessary, by a dealer service department.

---

7   Air gap - check and adjustment

Refer to illustrations 7.2a and 7.2b
Note: *Early models are equipped with breakerless ignition systems with externally mounted ignition modules while later systems incorporate the ignition module within the distributor, mounted opposite to the pick-up coil. Starting in 1987, some models are equipped with the crank angle sensor type distributor (photo optic type) that is not replaceable except as a complete assembly. The air gap, the distance between the reluctor and the pick-up coil, must be adjusted periodically on breakerless ignition distributors. This procedure does not apply to crank angle sensor type distributors.*

1   Remove the distributor cap and rotor from the distributor (see Chapter 1).

2   Position a brass feeler gauge between the reluctor and pick-up coil **(see illustrations)** and measure the distance. Refer to the Specifications listed in this Chapter.

3   If the measurement is incorrect, loosen the pick-up coil mounting screws and adjust the air gap. Refer to Section 11 and the distributor exploded views in Section 10 for the location of the pick-up coil mounting screws.

---

8   Ignition coil - check and replacement

Check

Primary and secondary resistance
Refer to illustrations 8.1 and 8.2
Caution: *On engines equipped with breakerless ignition systems, if the coil terminals touch a ground source, the coil and/or pick-up coil could be damaged.*

1   With the ignition off, disconnect the wires from the coil. Connect an ohmmeter across the coil primary (small wire) terminals **(see illustration)**. The resistance should be

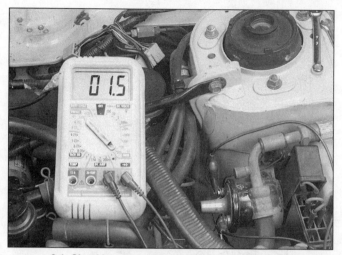

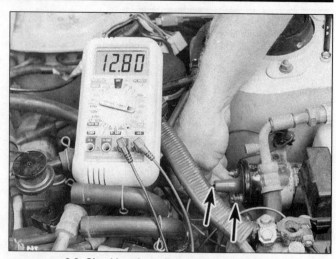

8.1 Checking the ignition coil primary resistance

8.2 Checking the coil secondary resistance

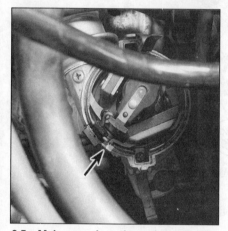

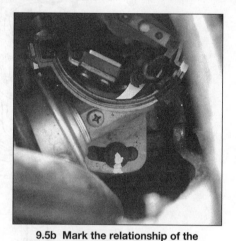

9.5a Make a mark on the perimeter of the distributor body that marks the position of the rotor (arrow)

9.5b Mark the relationship of the distributor body to the engine block or hold-down bolt

as listed in this Chapter's Specifications for the primary resistance. If not, replace the coil.

2   Connect an ohmmeter between the negative primary terminal and the secondary terminal **(see illustration)** (the one that the distributor cap wire connects to). The resistance should be as listed in this Chapter's Specifications for the secondary resistance. If not, replace the coil.

Primary winding-to-case resistance

3   Measure the resistance from the positive primary terminal to the case of the ignition coil. **Note:** *This measurement checks for the possibility of the interior windings (coil) grounding against the case of the coil assembly.*

4   If the indicated resistance is less than the resistance listed in this Chapter's Specifications, replace the ignition coil.

5   Reconnect the ignition coil wires.

Replacement

6   Detach the cable from the negative terminal of the battery.

7   Detach the wires from the primary terminals on the coil (some coils have a single

electrical connector for the primary wires).

8   Disconnect the coil secondary lead.

9   Remove both bracket bolts and detach the coil.

10   Installation is the reverse of removal.

9   Distributor - removal and installation

Removal

Refer to illustrations 9.5a and 9.5b

1   Disconnect the cable from the negative terminal of the battery. On models with breaker point ignition, disconnect the primary lead from the coil.

2   On models with a breakerless ignition system, disconnect the electrical connector for the module. Follow the wires as they exit the distributor to find the connector.

3   Note the raised "1" on the distributor cap. This marks the location for the number one cylinder spark plug wire terminal. Make a mark on the distributor body directly under the number one spark plug wire terminal. **Note:** *Some distributor caps may have been*

replaced with aftermarket units that are not marked.

4   Position the engine at Top Dead Center (TDC) on the compression stroke for cylinder no. 1 (see Chapter 2 Part A). Remove the distributor cap (see Chapter 1). The rotor should be pointing towards the mark made in Step 3.

5   Make a mark on the edge of the distributor base directly below the rotor tip and in line with it **(see illustration)**. Also, mark the distributor base and the engine block **(see illustration)**.

6   Remove the distributor hold-down bolt and clamp, then pull the distributor straight up to remove it. **Caution:** *DO NOT turn the engine while the distributor is removed, or the alignment marks will be useless.*

Installation

7   Insert the distributor into the engine in exactly the same relationship to the block that it was in when removed.

8   To mesh the helical gears on the camshaft and the distributor, it may be necessary to turn the rotor slightly. If the distributor doesn't seat completely. Recheck the alignment marks between the distributor base and the block to verify that the distributor is in the same position it was in before removal. Also check the rotor to see if it's aligned with the mark you made on the edge of the distributor base. **Note:** *If the crankshaft has been moved while the distributor is out, locate Top Dead Center (TDC) for the number one piston (see Chapter 2) and position the distributor and rotor accordingly.*

9   Install the hold-down bolt finger tight.

10   Install the distributor cap.

11   Plug in the distributor electrical connector or attach the negative lead to the coil (as applicable).

12   Reattach the spark plug wires to the plugs (if removed).

13   Connect the cable to the negative terminal of the battery.

14   Check and, if necessary, adjust the ignition timing (refer to Chapter 1), then tighten the distributor hold-down bolt securely.

5

10.4 Point the timing light at the timing scale in the flywheel bellhousing and confirm that the timing marks advance with rpm increase

10 Distributor advance systems - check

General information

1   To provide the proper spark advance or retard during different speeds and throttle openings, breakerless type distributors are equipped with a vacuum advance and a centrifugal advance mechanism in the distributor. These parts may stick, wear out or become defective after years of service. **Note:** *The vacuum advance unit governs ignition timing according to engine load, while the centrifugal advance unit governs ignition timing according to engine speed. Some models are equipped with dual-diaphragm vacuum advance units that provide additional timing retard during engine cranking to aid in starting and also reduce emissions during idle and during coast down.*

2   Both the vacuum advance and the centrifugal advance systems can be tested using the timing light method.

Timing light test

Refer to illustration 10.4

3   Connect a timing light in accordance with the tool manufacturer's instructions. Disconnect the vacuum hose from the vacuum advance unit, plug the hose and run the engine at approximately 1,200 rpm.

4   Point the timing light at the timing scale and observe the paint mark on the flywheel while slowly raising the engine speed to 4,000 rpm **(see illustration)**. The timing mark should move smoothly and without any hesitations or sudden movements. If the timing mark jumps around, it will be necessary to remove the distributor cap and check the centrifugal weights for binding, missing parts or defective parts (refer to Section 11).

5   Next, check the operation of the vacuum advance unit. Run the engine at a steady 1,200 rpm and point the timing light at the timing mark.

6   Note the exact position of the timing mark and raise the rpm while observing the

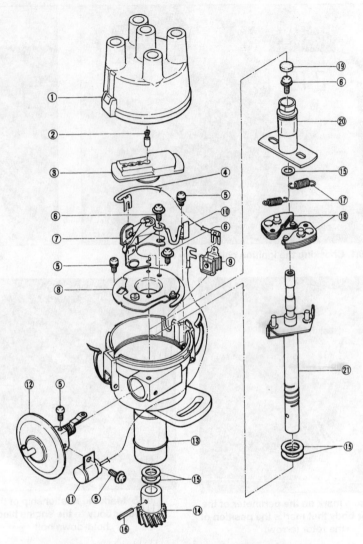

10.8a Distributor components on a breaker point system

1	Distributor cap	12	Vacuum advance unit
2	Carbon contact	13	O-ring
3	Rotor	14	Drive gear
4	Wire lead	15	Washer
5	Screw	16	Roll pin
6	Contact point mounting screw	17	Advance spring
7	Contact point set	18	Advance weight
8	Contact point breaker plate	19	Felt washer
9	Terminal	20	Point cam
10	Ground wire	21	Distributor shaft
11	Condenser		

mark. Connect the vacuum hose to the vacuum advance unit, when the vacuum hose is connected the timing mark should advance noticeably. Most systems will advance the timing approximately 35-degrees when opened to wide open throttle.

Centrifugal advance mechanism check

Refer to illustrations 10.8a, 10.8b, 10.8c, 10.8d, 10.8e and 10.8f

7   With the engine OFF and the distributor cap removed from the distributor, turn the rotor then let go. It should snap back to its original position very quickly and without hesitation. Try oiling the weights and springs with a spray lubricant (WD-40) and repeat the test several times to loosen the springs and weights if they show signs of sticking or binding.

8   Repeat the test several more times until the timing can be advanced without trouble **(see illustrations)**.

Vacuum advance unit check

Refer to illustration 10.11

9   The advance unit is attached to the dis-

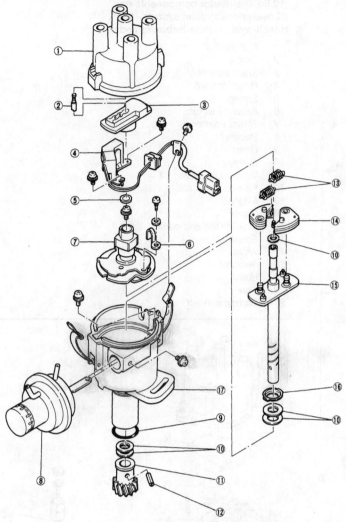

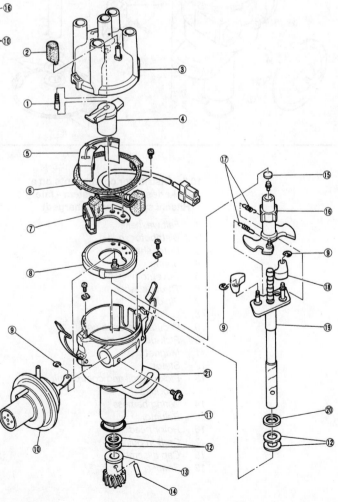

10.8b Distributor components on a breakerless ignition system - early Hitachi system

1   Distributor cap
2   Carbon contact
3   Rotor
4   Pick-up coil
5   Felt washer
6   Clip
7   Reluctor
8   Vacuum advance unit
9   O-ring
10 Thrust washer
11 Distributor drive gear
12 Roll pin
13 Spring
14 Advance weight
15 Distributor shaft
16 Thrust washer
17 Housing

10.8c Distributor components on a breakerless ignition system - early Nippondenso system

1   Carbon contact
2   Rubber cap
3   Cap
4   Rotor
5   Cover
6   Dust proof packing
7   Pick-up coil
8   Pick-up coil base plate
9   Circlip
10 Vacuum advance unit
11 O-ring
12 Thrust washer
13 Distributor drive gear
14 Roll pin
15 Felt washer
16 Signal rotor
17 Spring
18 Advance weight
19 Distributor shaft
20 Washer
21 Housing

5

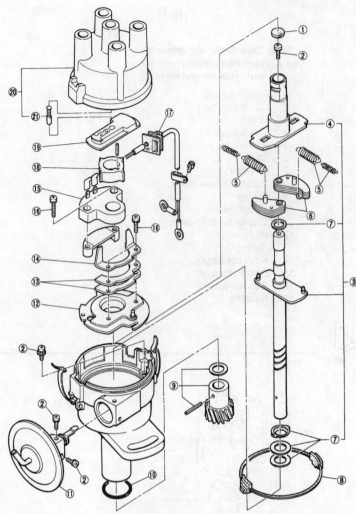

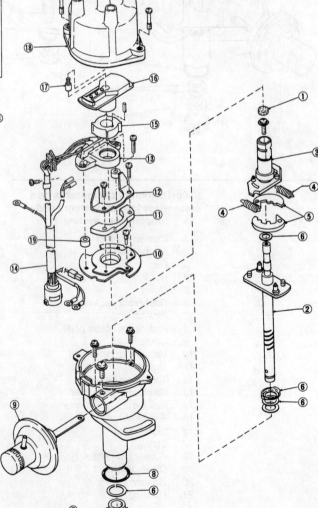

10.8d   Distributor components on a breakerless ignition system - late Hitachi system (non-turbocharged)

1   Felt washer
2   Screw
3   Shaft assembly
4   Reluctor shaft
5   Spring
6   Advance weight
7   Thrust washer
8   Packing
9   Gear
10   O-ring
11   Vacuum advance unit
12   Pick-up coil plate
13   Magnet
14   Stator
15   Pick-up coil and control unit
16   Screw
17   Wires
18   Reluctor
19   Rotor
20   Cap
21   Carbon contact

10.8e   Distributor components on a breakerless ignition system - late Hitachi system (turbocharged)

1   Felt washer
2   Distributor shaft
3   Rotor shaft
4   Spring
5   Governor weight
6   Thrust washer
7   Pinion
8   O-ring
9   Vacuum advance unit
10   Pick-up coil plate
11   Magnet
12   Stator
13   Pick-up coil and control unit (module)
14   Wiring harness
15   Reluctor
16   Rotor head
17   Carbon point
18   Cap assembly
19   Spacer

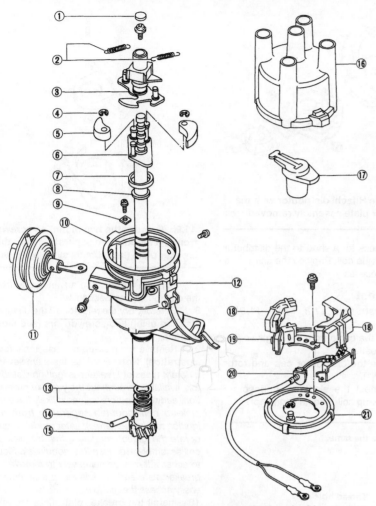

10.11 Apply vacuum to the vacuum advance unit and make sure the breaker plate moves and the unit doesn't bleed down

11.1 Check the pick-up coil resistance on the harness leads after they are disconnected from the ignition coil (late Nippondenso system shown)

5

10.8f Distributor components on a breakerless ignition system - late Nippondenso system

1	Felt washer	12	Housing
2	Governor spring	13	Plate washer
3	Signal rotor	14	Straight pin
4	Snap washer	15	Gear
5	Flyweight	16	Cap
6	Governor shaft	17	Rotor
7	Oil seal	18	Dust proof cover
8	Plate washer	19	Pick-up coil
9	Screw plate	20	Module
10	Dust proof packing	21	Breaker plate
11	Vacuum advance unit		

tributor breaker plate. A vacuum line attaches the diaphragm housing to a ported vacuum source. As vacuum changes from idle to acceleration through deceleration and back to idle, the timing changes accordingly.

10 With the engine OFF check the condition of the vacuum hose from the distributor to the vacuum source. Make sure the hose is connected, doesn't have any holes, and the ends fit tightly.

11 Disconnect the vacuum hose from the advance unit. Connect a hand-held vacuum pump to the port on the advance unit and apply vacuum **(see illustration)**.

12 Make sure the breaker plate moves and the vacuum advance diaphragm holds vac-

uum. If the vacuum bleeds down, replace the advance unit.

Vacuum advance unit replacement

13 Remove the distributor cap and the vacuum hose to the advance unit.

14 Remove the two screws that retain the vacuum advance unit to the distributor body **(see illustrations 10.8a through 10.8f)**.

15 Remove the clip that holds the vacuum advance plate to the vacuum advance link. Be careful not to drop it into the distributor.

16 Remove the old vacuum advance unit and replace it with a new part.

17 Installation is the reverse of removal.

11 Ignition pick-up coil and module - check and replacement

Caution: *The ignition module is a delicate and relatively expensive electronic component. Failure to follow the step-by-step procedures could result in damage to the module and/or other electronic devices, including the ECM microprocessor itself. Additionally, all devices under computer control are protected by a Federally mandated extended warranty. Check with your dealer concerning this warranty before attempting to diagnose and replace the unit yourself.*

Note: *Early breakerless ignition systems are equipped with externally mounted ignition modules, while later systems incorporate the ignition module within the distributor, mounted opposite the pick-up coil. Starting in 1987, some models are equipped with the crank angle sensor type distributor (photo optic type)f which is not serviceable except as a complete assembly.*

Pick-up coil
Check
Refer to illustration 11.1

1 Disconnect the pick-up coil leads from

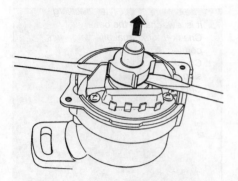

11.8 Pry the reluctor off the distributor shaft using two screwdrivers (late Hitachi system shown)

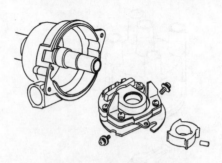

11.9a Late Hitachi distributor with the breaker plate assembly removed

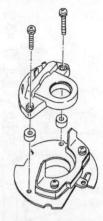

11.9b Remove the two mounting screws from the module and separate it from the breaker plate (late Hitachi system shown)

the ignition module (external ignition modules) or from the ignition coil (internal ignition modules). Connect the probes of an ohmmeter to the terminals and check the pick-up coil resistance **(see illustration)**.

2   Refer to the Specifications listed in this Chapter for the correct readings. If the pick-up coil specifications are incorrect, replace it with a new part.

3   Next, connect one probe of the ohmmeter to the distributor body and the other to one of the pick-up coil terminals and check the resistance. It should be infinite. If continu-

ity exists, check for a short to the distributor from the pick-up coil. Replace the unit with a new part if necessary.

Replacement
Refer to illustrations 11.8, 11.9a, 11.9b and 11.10

4   Detach the cable from the negative terminal of the battery.

5   Remove the distributor cap and rotor (see Chapter 1).

6   Disconnect the electrical connectors from the pick-up coil/module connector.

7   Remove the vacuum advance unit from the distributor (see Section 10).

8   Carefully pry the reluctor off the distributor shaft using two screwdrivers **(see illustration)**.

9   Remove the pick-up coil assembly **(see illustration)**. **Note:** *Because there are several different types of breakerless ignition distributors available throughout the years of production, early distributors will most likely have the pick-up coil mounted separately from the ignition module (external). Later models incorporate the ignition module within the pick-up coil assembly. Because the module is difficult to access, it may be necessary to remove the breaker plate and module as an assembly to easily access the module.*

10   Install the breaker plate (late models) with the ignition module and check the alignment **(see illustration)**.

11   Installation is the reverse of removal.

Module
Check
12   The easiest and quickest way to diagnose a defective module is by process of elimination. Check the ignition coil (see Section 8) and the pick-up coil (on models that can be checked) (see Steps 1 through 3). If these components are functioning properly, replace the module. **Note:** *On models with an internal module/pick-up coil assembly, if the coil checks out OK but there is still no spark, replace the pick-up coil/module unit.*

Replacement
Refer to illustration 11.15
13   Detach the cable from the negative terminal of the battery.

14   Disconnect the electrical connector from the ignition module (externally mounted modules) or the distributor (internally mounted modules).

15   On externally mounted modules, remove the screws that retain the ignition module to the coil **(see illustration)** or fire-

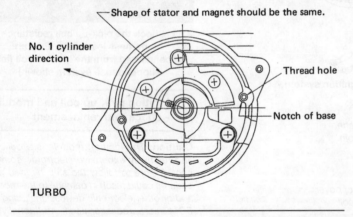

—Shape of stator and magnet should be the same.

No. 1 cylinder direction

Thread hole

Notch of base

TURBO

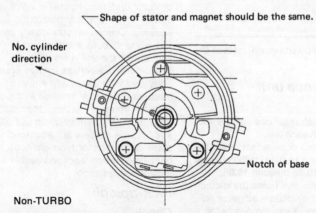

—Shape of stator and magnet should be the same.

No. cylinder direction

Notch of base

Non-TURBO

11.10 Be sure the breaker plate is aligned correctly after it has been installed in the distributor body (late Hitachi systems shown)

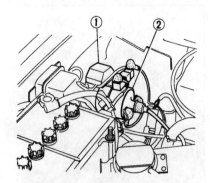

11.15 Ignition coil and module (1980 Hitachi ignition system shown)

1   *Ignition module*
2   *Ignition coil*

wall. **Note:** *Later models incorporate the ignition module within the distributor - on these models, follow the removal procedure for the pickup coil as described earlier in this Section (because the module screws are difficult to access, it may be necessary to remove the breaker plate).*

16   Installation is the reverse of removal.

12   Charging system - general information and precautions

Refer to illustration 12.1

The charging system includes the alternator **(see illustration)**, an external voltage regulator (early models) or internal voltage regulator (late models), a charge indicator or warning light, the battery, a fusible link and the wiring between all the components. The charging system supplies electrical power for the ignition system, the lights, the radio, etc. The alternator is driven by a drivebelt at the front of the engine.

The purpose of the voltage regulator is to limit the alternator's voltage to a preset value. This prevents power surges, circuit overloads, etc., during peak voltage output.

The fusible link is a short length of insulated wire integral with the engine compartment wiring harness. The link is several wire gauges smaller in diameter than the circuit it protects. Production fusible links and their identification flags are identified by the flag color. Refer to Chapter 12 for additional information on fusible links.

The charging system doesn't ordinarily require periodic maintenance. However, the drivebelt, battery and wires and connections should be inspected at the intervals outlined in Chapter 1.

Be very careful when making electrical circuit connections to a vehicle equipped with an alternator and note the following:

a) *When reconnecting wires to the alternator from the battery, be sure to note the polarity.*
b) *Before using arc welding equipment to repair any part of the vehicle, disconnect the wires from the alternator and the battery terminals.*
c) *Never start the engine with a battery charger connected.*
d) *Always disconnect both battery cables before using a battery charger (negative cable first, positive cable last).*

13   Charging system - check

1   If a malfunction occurs in the charging circuit, do not immediately assume that the alternator is causing the problem. First check the following items:

a) *The battery cables where they connect to the battery. Make sure the connections are clean and tight.*

b) *The battery electrolyte specific gravity. If it is low, charge the battery.*
c) *Check the external alternator wiring and connections.*
d) *Check the drivebelt condition and tension (see Chapter 1).*
e) *Check the alternator mounting bolts for tightness.*
f) *Run the engine and check the alternator for abnormal noise.*

2   Using a voltmeter, check the battery voltage with the engine off. It should be approximately 12-volts.

3   Start the engine and check the battery voltage again. It should now be approximately 14 to 15-volts.

4   If the indicated voltage reading is less or more than the specified charging voltage, the problem may be within the alternator.

5   Due to the special equipment necessary to test or service the alternator, it is recommended that if a fault is suspected the vehicle be taken to a repair shop with the proper equipment. But if the home mechanic feels confident in the use of an ohmmeter, and in some cases a soldering iron, the component check and replacement procedures for the most common alternator type are included in Section 15.

6   Some models are equipped with an ammeter on the instrument panel that indicates charge or discharge - current passing in or out of the battery. With all electrical equipment switched ON, and the engine idling, the gauge needle may show a discharge condition. At fast idle or normal driving speeds the needle should stay on the charge side of the gauge, with the charged state of the battery determining just how far over (the lower the battery state of charge, the farther the needle should swing toward the charge side).

7   Some models are equipped with a voltmeter on the instrument panel that indicates

5

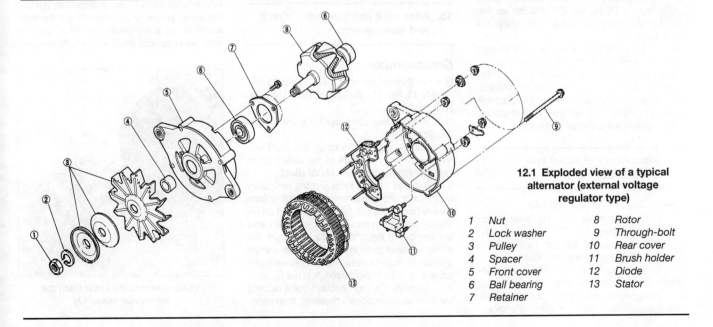

12.1 Exploded view of a typical alternator (external voltage regulator type)

1	Nut	8	Rotor
2	Lock washer	9	Through-bolt
3	Pulley	10	Rear cover
4	Spacer	11	Brush holder
5	Front cover	12	Diode
6	Ball bearing	13	Stator
7	Retainer		

14.2 Disconnect the electrical connectors (arrows) from the rear of the alternator

14.3 Location of the alternator pivot bolt (upper arrow) and adjustment bolt (lower arrow, not visible)

15.2 Make a mark across the front cover, pick-up coil and rear cover to aid in reassembly

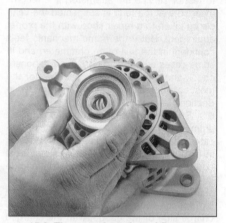

15.3 The use of an air tool (impact wrench) is the easiest way to remove the pulley nut

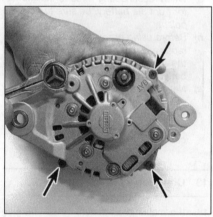
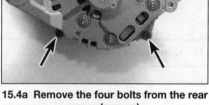

15.4a Remove the four bolts from the rear cover (arrows)

15.4b Separate the front cover from the alternator body

battery voltage with the key ON (engine not running), and alternator output when the engine is running.

8   The charge light on the instrument panel illuminates with the key ON and the engine not running, and should go out when the engine runs.

9   If the gauge does not show a charge when it should or the alternator light (if equipped) remains on, there is a fault in the system. Before inspecting the brushes or replacing the alternator, the battery condition, alternator belt tension and electrical cable connections should be checked.

14 Alternator - removal and installation

Refer to illustrations 14.2 and 14.3

1   Detach the cable from the negative terminal of the battery.

2   Disconnect the electrical connectors from the alternator **(see illustration)**.

3   Loosen the alternator bolts **(see illustration)** and detach the drivebelt.

4   Remove the adjustment and pivot bolts and separate the alternator from the engine.

5   Installation is the reverse of removal.

6   After the alternator is installed, adjust the drivebelt tension (see Chapter 1).

15 Alternator components - check and replacement

Disassembly

Refer to illustrations 15.2, 15.3, 15.4a, 15.4b, 15.4c, 15.5a, 15.5b, 15.6a, 15.6b, 15.6c and 15.7

1   Remove the alternator from the vehicle (Section 14).

2   Scribe or paint marks on the front and rear end-frame housings of the alternator to facilitate reassembly **(see illustration)**.

3   Remove the nut retaining the fan pulley to the rotor shaft and remove the pulley **(see illustration)**. This can be done with an pneumatic impact wrench or with a socket and breaker bar. If the latter method is used, the pulley will have to be immobilized with a strap wrench (in some cases this may have to be done even if an impact wrench is used).

4   Remove the four through-bolts holding the front and rear covers together, then sepa-

rate the rear cover assembly from the front cover. Remove the rotor **(see illustrations)**.

5   Remove the nuts, then detach end frame **(see illustrations)**. **Note:** *On some Hitachi alternators it will necessary to remove the diode assembly and the voltage regulator assembly as a complete unit. First, disconnect the stator coil leads with a soldering iron*

15.4c Remove the rotor from the alternator assembly

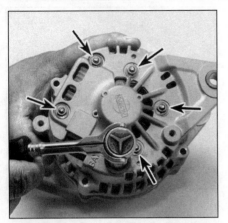

15.5a Remove the mounting nuts (arrows)

15.5b Separate the rear cover from the stator and diode assembly

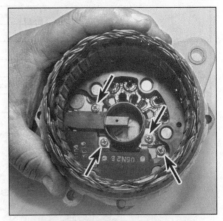

15.6a Remove the diode assembly mounting screws (arrows)

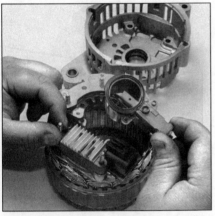

15.6b Remove the brush holder from the diode assembly

15.6c Remove the voltage regulator

15.7 Remove the four set screws and lift the diode from the pick-up coil

5

and be sure to attach a heat sink to avoid damaging the diodes. Then, disconnect the diode assembly from the voltage regulator by melting the L-connection with a soldering iron. Here again, use a heat sink to avoid damaging the diodes.

6   Remove the screws attaching the brush holder and regulator to the diode and remove the brush holder **(see illustrations)**.

7   Remove the diode from the pick-up coil **(see illustration)**. On some types of alterna-

tors it will be necessary to use a soldering iron and heat sink to melt the solder joints that connect the pick-up coil leads to the diode.

Component checks

Refer to illustrations 15.8a, 15.8b, 15.9 and 15.10

8   Check the rotor for an open between the two slip rings **(see illustration)**. There should be continuity between the slip rings. Check

for grounds between each slip ring and the rotor shaft **(see illustration)**. There should be no continuity (infinite resistance) between the rotor shaft and either slip ring. If the rotor fails either test, or if the slip rings are excessively worn, the rotor is defective.

9   Check for opens between the center terminal and each end terminal of the stator windings **(see illustration)**. If either reading is

15.8a Continuity should exist between the rotor slip rings

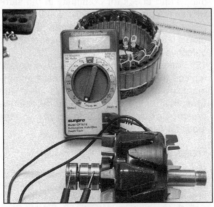

15.8b No continuity should exist between the slip ring(s) and rotor shaft

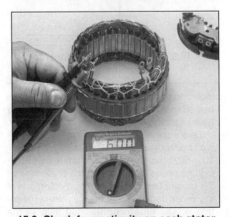

15.9 Check for continuity on each stator lead. There should be no breaks in the windings; therefore, continuity should exist between each terminal

	Ohmmeter probes		Continuity
	Positive ⊕	Negative ⊖	
Diodes check (Positive side)	Positive diode plate	Diode terminals	Yes
	Diode terminals	Positive diode plate	No
Diodes check (Negative side)	Negative diode plate	Diode terminals	No
	Diode terminals	Negative diode plate	Yes

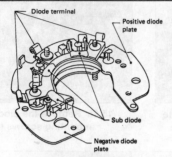

15.10 Check each diode to make sure continuity exists only in ONE direction (typical diode assembly shown)

15.14 Insert a paper clip into the backside of the alternator to hold the brushes in place - after the alternator has been assembled, pull the paper clip out

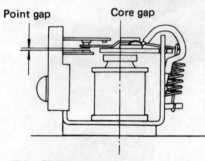

16.2a Charge relay core gap and point gap measurements

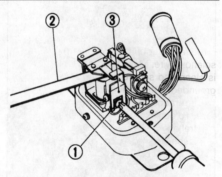

16.2b Adjustment of the voltage coil core gap

1   *Adjusting screw*
2   *Feeler gauge*
3   *Contact set*

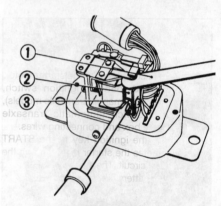

16.2c Adjustment of the voltage coil point gap

1   *Feeler gauge*
2   *Upper contact*
3   *Adjusting screw*

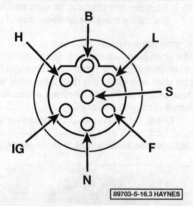

89703-5-16.3 HAYNES

16.3 Voltage regulator connector terminal guide

high (infinite resistance), the stator is defective. Check for a grounded stator winding between each stator terminal and the frame. If there's continuity between any stator winding and the frame, the stator is defective.

10   Start the checks on the diode by touching one probe (positive +) of the ohmmeter on the diode plate and the other probe on one of the other designated diode terminals (negative -) **(see illustration)**. Then reverse the probes and check again. Follow the chart carefully. The diode should have continuity with the ohmmeter one way and no continuity when the probes are reversed. Check each of

the terminals in this manner. If any of the diodes fail the test, the diode is defective. **Note:** *Because there are so many different Hitachi alternators installed on these models, many of the diode assemblies are slightly different in construction but not in operation. Follow the same terminal checks for each type of diode assembly.*

11   To check the sub diodes, connect the probes of the ohmmeter to the sub diode terminals and check for continuity in the same way as the previous diode checks. Be sure to probe only the sub diode terminals. If any sub diode fails the test, the diode assembly is defective.

12   Measure the length of the brushes and replace them if they are at or near the minimum brush length found in this Chapter's Specifications. **Note:** *On some models the brush leads are soldered onto the voltage regulator assembly.*

Reassembly

Refer to illustration 15.14

13   Install the components in the reverse order of removal, noting the following:

14   Before installing the brush holder, push the brushes into the holder and slip a

straightened paper clip or other suitable pin through the hole in the brush holder to hold the brushes in a retracted position. After the front and rear end frames have been bolted together, remove the paper clip **(see illustration)**.

16   Voltage regulator (external) - check and replacement

Check

Refer to illustrations 16.2a, 16.2b, 16.2c and 16.3

1   Remove the regulator from the side wall of the engine compartment for checking and repair. Remove the cover mounting screws and the cover from the regulator. Inspect the points and polish them with light emery cloth if they are burnt or dirty. Replace the voltage regulator with a new one if they are damaged.

2   Use a feeler gauge and check the core gap **(see illustration)** and then the points gap. Refer to the Specifications listed in this Chapter. If the settings are incorrect, adjust them to the correct specifications **(see illustrations)**.

3   Disconnect the voltage regulator har-

ness connector and measure the resistance between terminals IG and F **(see illustration)**. It should be 0 ohms.

4   Measure the resistance between the L terminal and the ground terminal (E terminal). It should be 0 ohms.

5   Measure the resistance between N terminal and ground (E terminal). It should be 32.0 ohms.

6   Measure the resistance between the B terminal and the ground (E terminal). It should be infinity. This checks the charge relay points in OFF position (static). They should be open indicating infinite resistance.

7   Replace the voltage regulator if the test results are incorrect.

17   Starting system - general information and precautions

1   The function of the starting system is to crank the engine quickly enough to start it. The system is composed of the starter motor, starter solenoid, battery, ignition switch, clutch start switch (manual transaxle models), neutral start switch (automatic transaxle models), diode box and connecting wires.

2   Turning the ignition key to the START position actuates the starter relay through the starter control circuit. The starter solenoid then connects the battery to the starter. The battery supplies the electrical energy to the starter motor, which does the actual work of cranking the engine.

3   All models are equipped with a starter/solenoid assembly that is mounted to the transaxle bellhousing.

4   All vehicles are equipped with a clutch start switch or a neutral start switch in the starter control circuit, which prevents operation of the starter unless the shift lever is in Neutral or Park (automatic) or the clutch is depressed (manual).

5   Never operate the starter motor for more than 15 seconds at a time without pausing to allow it to cool for at least two minutes. Excessive cranking can cause overheating, which can seriously damage the starter.

6   These models are equipped with either the direct starter type or the gear reduction type starter assemblies. Direct starters position the solenoid (magnetic switch) integral to the body of the starter (conventional). Gear reduction type starter assemblies incorporate the gear assembly and the solenoid as a combined unit. Consult an automotive parts department for the exact brand and type of starter on your vehicle.

18   Starter motor and circuit - in-vehicle check

Note: *Before diagnosing starter problems, make sure the battery is fully charged.*

General check

1   If the starter motor doesn't turn at all

when the switch is operated, make sure the shift lever is in Neutral or Park or the clutch is fully depressed.

2   Make sure the battery is charged and that all cables at the battery and starter solenoid terminals are secure.

3   If the starter motor spins but the engine doesn't turn over, then the drive assembly in the starter motor is slipping and the starter motor must be replaced (see Section 19).

4   If, when the switch is actuated, the starter motor doesn't operate at all but the starter solenoid operates (clicks), then the problem lies with either the battery, the starter solenoid contacts or the starter motor connections.

5   If the starter solenoid doesn't click when the ignition switch is actuated, either the starter solenoid circuit is open or the solenoid itself is defective. Check the starter solenoid circuit (see the wiring diagrams at the end of this book) or replace the solenoid (see Section 20).

6   To check the starter solenoid circuit, remove the push-on connector from the solenoid wire. Make sure that the connection is clean and secure and the relay bracket is grounded. If the connections are good, check the operation of the solenoid with a jumper wire. To do this, place the transaxle in Park or Neutral and apply the parking brake. Remove the push-on connector from the solenoid. Connect a jumper wire between the battery positive terminal and the exposed terminal on the solenoid. If the starter motor now operates, the starter solenoid is okay. The problem is in the ignition switch, Neutral start switch or in the starting circuit wiring (look for open or loose connections).

7   If the starter motor still doesn't operate, replace the starter solenoid (see Section 20).

8   If the starter motor cranks the engine at an abnormally slow speed, first make sure the battery is fully charged and all terminal connections are clean and tight. Also check the connections at the starter solenoid and battery ground. Eyelet terminals should not be easily rotated by hand. Also check for a short to ground. If the engine is partially seized, or has the wrong viscosity oil in it, it will crank slowly.

Starter cranking circuit test

Note: *To determine the location of excessive resistance in the starter circuit, perform the following simple series of tests.*

9   Disconnect the ignition coil wire from the distributor cap and ground it on the engine.

10   Connect a remote control starter switch from the battery terminal of the starter solenoid to the S terminal of the solenoid.

11   Connect a voltmeter positive lead to the starter motor terminal of the starter solenoid, then connect the negative lead to ground.

12   Actuate the ignition switch and take the voltmeter readings as soon as a steady figure is indicated. Do not allow the starter motor to turn for more than 15 seconds at a time. A

reading of 9-volts or more, with the starter motor turning at normal cranking speed, is normal. If the reading is 9-volts or more but the cranking speed is slow, the motor is faulty. If the reading is less than 9-volts and the cranking speed is slow, the solenoid contacts are probably burned.

19   Starter motor - removal and installation

Refer to illustration 19.4

1   Detach the cable from the negative terminal of the battery.

2   Raise the vehicle and support it securely on jackstands.

3   Disconnect the wire and the large cable from the terminals on the starter solenoid.

4   Remove the starter motor mounting bolts **(see illustration)** and detach the starter from the engine. Depending upon the year and engine type, the starter/solenoid assembly may be mounted above the transaxle or below the intake manifold.

5   If necessary, turn the wheels to one side to provide removal access.

6   Installation is the reverse of removal.

20   Starter solenoid - replacement

Note: *These models are equipped with either the direct starter type or the gear reduction type starter assemblies. Direct starters position the solenoid (magnetic switch) integral to the body of the starter (conventional). Gear reduction type starter assemblies incorporate the gear assembly and the solenoid as a combined unit. Replace the gear reduction starters as a complete unit in the event of solenoid trouble. Consult an automotive parts department for the exact brand and type of starter on your vehicle.*

1   Remove the nut and disconnect the lead wire from the solenoid electrical terminal.

2   Remove the two bolts from the solenoid and separate the solenoid from the starter assembly.

3   Installation is the reverse of removal.

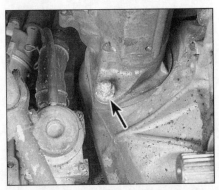

19.4 The lower starter bolt (arrow) can be reached from under the vehicle (the upper bolt is reached from the engine compartment)

5

Notes

Chapter 6
Emissions and engine control systems

Contents

1 General information

Refer to illustrations 1.1a, 1.1b, 1.7a and 1.7b

To prevent pollution of the atmosphere from incompletely burned and evaporating gases, and to maintain good driveability and fuel economy, a number of emission control systems are incorporated **(see illustrations)**.

They include the:

Anti Afterburning system (AAV)
Spark Timing Control (TCS) system
Air Induction system
Air Injection (AIR) system
Coasting Bypass system
High Altitude Compensation (HAC) system
Exhaust Gas Recirculation (EGR) system

Automatic choke system
Heated Air Inlet (HAI) system
Feedback carburetor (Hitachi and Carter/Weber) system
Evaporative Emission Control (EVAP) system
Throttle Body Injection (TBI) system
Multi Port Fuel Injection (MPFI) system
Crankcase Ventilation (PCV) system

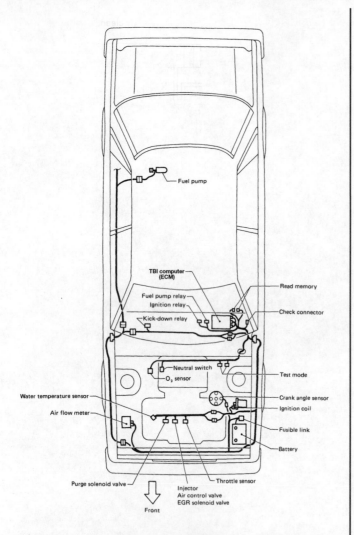

1.1a Emission and engine control system component locations on a typical Throttle Body Injected (TBI) engine

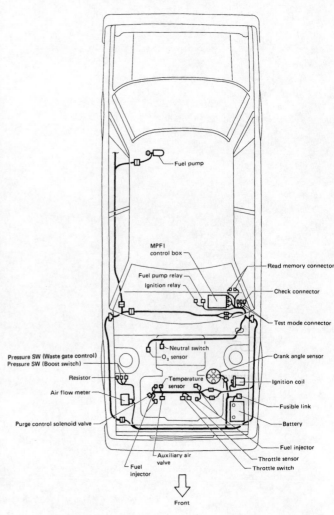

1.1b Emission and engine control system component locations on a typical Multi-Port Fuel Injected (MPFI) engine

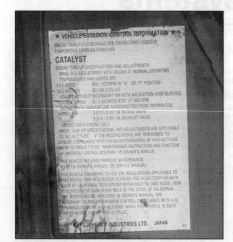

1.7a The Vehicle Emission Control Information (VECI) label on some models is located in the engine compartment under the hood and contains information on the emission devices on your vehicle, vacuum line routing, etc.

Exhaust Gas Recirculation (EGR) system (electronic)
Catalytic converter
Secondary throttle valve system
Shift-up control system

All of these systems are linked, directly or indirectly, to the emission control system.

The Sections in this Chapter include general descriptions, checking procedures within the scope of the home mechanic and component replacement procedures (when possible) for each of the systems listed above.

Before assuming that an emissions control system is malfunctioning, check the fuel and ignition systems carefully. The diagnosis of some emission control devices requires specialized tools, equipment and training. If checking and servicing become too difficult or if a procedure is beyond your ability, consult a dealer service department or other qualified repair facility. Remember, the most frequent cause of emissions problems is simply a loose or broken vacuum hose or wire,

so always check the hose and wiring connections first.

This doesn't mean, however, that emission control systems are particularly difficult

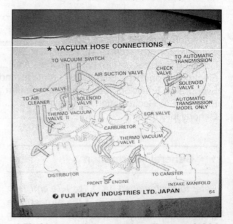

1.7b Vacuum hose routing diagram (1984 feedback carburetor model shown)

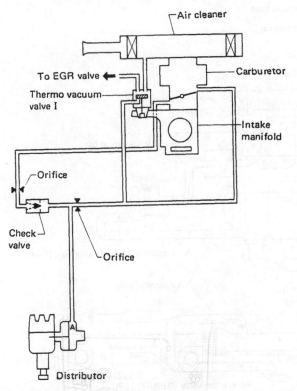

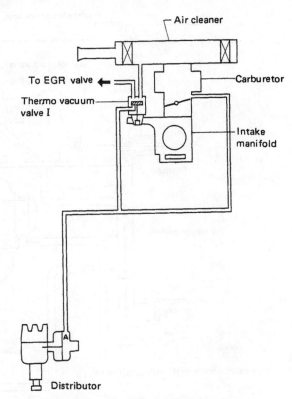

Below-throttle port vacuum   **Above-throttle port vacuum**

2.1a Schematic of the Spark Timing Control (TCS) system

to maintain and repair. You can quickly and easily perform many checks and do most of the regular maintenance at home with common tune-up and hand tools. **Note:** *Because of a Federally mandated extended warranty which covers the emission control system components, check with your dealer about*

warranty coverage before working on any emissions-related systems. Once the warranty has expired, you may wish to perform some of the component checks and/or replacement procedures in this Chapter to save money.

Pay close attention to any special pre-

cautions outlined in this Chapter. It should be noted that the illustrations of the various systems may not exactly match the system installed on the vehicle you're working on because of changes made by the manufacturer during production or from year-to-year.

A Vehicle Emissions Control Information (VECI) label is located in the engine compartment. This label contains important emissions specifications and adjustment information. A vacuum hose schematic with emissions components identified should also be present **(see illustrations)**. When servicing the engine or emissions systems, the VECI label in your particular vehicle should always be checked for up-to-date information.

2   Spark Timing Control (TCS) system

General information

Refer to illustrations 2.1a and 2.1b

1   The spark timing control (TCS) system is designed to control the vacuum advance on the distributor during varying engine load and speed conditions **(see illustrations)**. This system ultimately controls the HC and NOx emissions output. This system consists of a thermal vacuum valve (TVV) which controls vacuum to the distributor according to temperature and a vacuum delay valve which prevents rapid vacuum change in the vacuum

2.1b Typical distributor and vacuum routing diagram on a 1980 carbureted engine

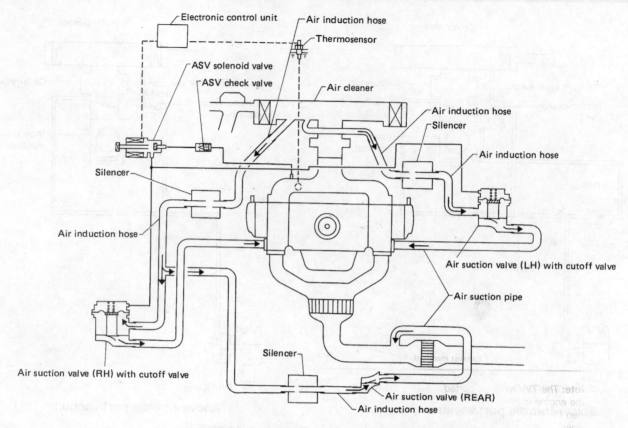

3.1a Typical Air Injection system on 2WD models

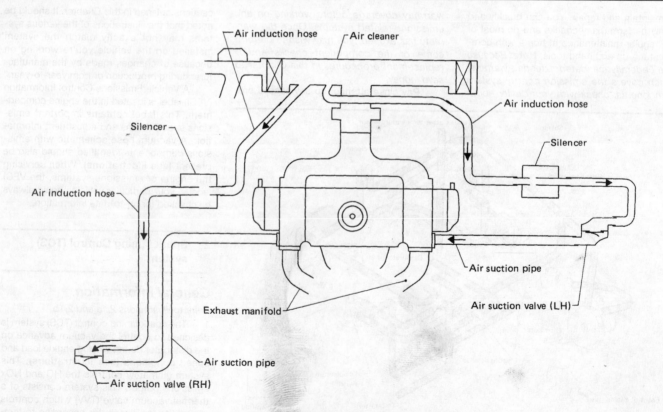

3.1b Typical Air Injection system on 4WD models

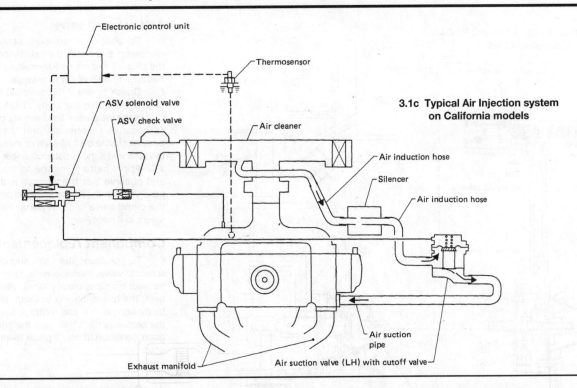

3.1c Typical Air Injection system on California models

advance line. **Note:** *The TVV receives ported vacuum when the engine is idling and manifold vacuum when the throttle is opened up only after the engine has warmed to a specified temperature.* **Note:** *The Spark Timing Control (TCS) system varies depending upon the years, models and geographical locations. Emission standards regulate the amount of ignition timing advance at idle and full load thereby changing timing settings and vacuum advance application. It is best to consult the VECI label and the dealer service department for the correct information regarding your TCS specifications.* **Note:** *Refer to Chapter 5 for additional information regarding checking the distributor vacuum advance unit and the centrifugal weights that regulate the amount of ignition timing advance.*

Check

Thermal vacuum valve (TVV)
Warning: *Wait until the engine is completely cool before beginning this procedure.*

2   Remove the thermal vacuum valve (TVV) from the intake manifold. Be sure to drain approximately two quarts of coolant from the radiator (see Chapter 1) before removing the valve.
3   Place the TVV in a pan of heated water and closely monitor the temperature using a thermometer. Use a hand-held vacuum pump to apply vacuum to the top (intake) port of the TVV and note the operation at the indicated temperatures:

**Temperature below
59-degrees F**   *Valve closed*
(15-degrees C)

**Temperature between   *Valve open*
59 to 95-degrees F**
(15 to 35-degrees C)

**Temperature above   *Valve closed*
95-degrees F**
(35-degrees C)

4   If the TVV valve does not respond correctly, replace it with a new part.

Vacuum delay valve

5   The vacuum delay valve (check valve) is designed for one-way operation. Blow air from the intake manifold side of the valve and observe that the air flows through the valve and can be detected at the distributor side of the vacuum line.
6   Reverse the position and blow from the distributor side. No air pressure should pass through the valve.
7   If the vacuum delay valve tests are incorrect, replace the valve with a new part.

3   Air Injection (AIR) system

General description
Refer to illustrations 3.1a, 3.1b, 3.1c and 3.2
1   The Air Injection system **(see illustrations)** reduces carbon monoxide and hydrocarbon content in the exhaust gases by directing fresh air (intake air) into the hot exhaust gases leaving the exhaust ports during cold engine operation. When fresh air is mixed with hot exhaust gases, oxidation is increased, reducing the concentration of hydrocarbons and carbon monoxide and converting them into harmless carbon dioxide and water.
2   The Air Injection system consists of an air suction valve (ASV), a cutoff valve, an air suction pipe, an air introduction hose, an air filter, a thermosensor, a solenoid valve, check valve(s) and the ECM. The air filter is built into the air cleaner while the cutoff valve is built into the suction valve **(see illustration)**. Early and late systems are basically the same. The operating principle of the air injection system is that the exhaust gas pulsation is transmitted to the air suction valve through

6

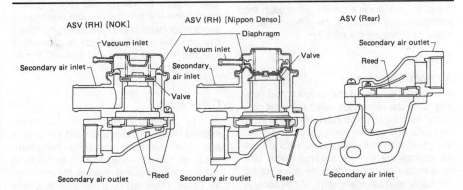

3.2 Cross-sectional view of three different types of air suction valves

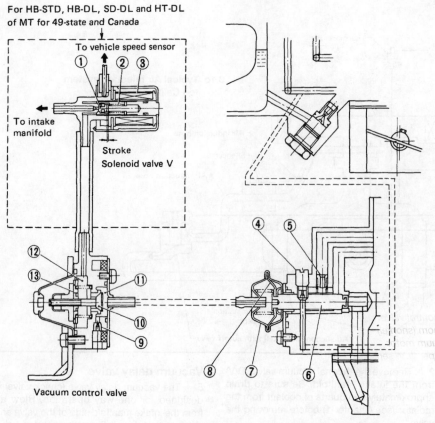

For HB-STD, HB-DL, SD-DL and HT-DL of MT for 49-state and Canada

To vehicle speed sensor

To intake manifold

Stroke
Solenoid valve V

Vacuum control valve

4.1 Schematic of the Coasting By-pass system

1	Plunger	8	Diaphragm
2	Spring	9	Orifice
3	Solenoid	10	Poppet valve
4	By-pass jet	11	Chamber B
5	By-pass air bleed	12	Chamber A
6	By-pass valve	13	Diaphragm
7	Servo diaphragm		

the air suction pipe. When the negative pulsation pressure is transferred to the ASV, the reeds of the valve are opened and simultaneously, fresh air from the air cleaner is sucked into the exhaust passage. When the positive pressure reaches the ASV, the reeds are closed to prevent the reverse flow of exhaust gas. **Note:** *There are three different types of air suction valves equipped on these models. On California models, the air suction valve (ASV-I) is also equipped with a cut-off valve. Federal models with 2WD have two air suction valves (ASV-I), one with two cut-off valves and the other without cut-off valves (ASV-II). Federal models with 4WD are equipped with an air suction valve (ASV-III) without a cut-off valve.*

3   The air injection system is controlled by both the ECM and the coolant temperature sensor (thermosensor). When the coolant temperature is below 95-degrees F (35-degrees C), the ECM gives a command to open the intake manifold passage of the solenoid valve for 123 seconds. This action causes the cutoff valve to be opened by the

diaphragm vacuum actuator to operate the ASV. Under driving conditions such as wide open throttle acceleration, the check valve closes the vacuum circuit to confine the vacuum to hold the cutoff valve open for that period. After this period, the ECM gives a command to close the vacuum passage of the solenoid valve and open the atmospheric pressure passage. The vacuum in the chamber of the cutoff valve bleeds off through the solenoid valve, allowing the cutoff valve to close, deactivating the ASV.

Check

Air suction valve

4   Apply vacuum to the vacuum inlet pipe and see if the air suction valve operates correctly. Air should flow through the secondary inlet pipe and out the secondary outlet pipe, but not in the reverse direction. Replace the air suction valve if necessary. **Note:** *Use compressed air to blow into the valve but do not apply excessive amounts of pressure. A hand-held pressure pump will work but will be less noticeable.*

ASV solenoid valve

5   To check the solenoid valve, use an ohmmeter and check the resistance between the plus (+) and minus (-) terminals to see if it has 32.7 to 39.9 ohms resistance.
6   Check to see if the solenoid is shorted to ground within the body of the solenoid. Check the resistance between the positive (+) or negative (-) terminal and the solenoid body. It should be 1 M-ohm or more. Replace the solenoid if the resistance is less.
7   Apply battery voltage to the solenoid and observe that the vacuum is allowed to pass through the intake manifold port and out the cutoff valve or ECM ports. Replace the solenoid if necessary.

Component replacement

8   To replace the air suction valve, solenoid valve, thermosensor, check valve or air suction pipe, clearly label, then disconnect, the hoses leading to them, replace the faulty component and reattach the hoses to the proper ports. Make sure the hoses are in good condition. If not, replace them with new ones.

4   Coasting by-pass system (1980 models only)

General Information

Refer to illustration 4.1
1   The coasting by-pass system **(see illustration)** controls the HC emission levels by supplying an additional amount of air and fuel mixture to the carburetor through a bypass in the side of the carburetor body for the purpose of improving combustion in the cylinders during deceleration. During deceleration, air/fuel mixture in the engine (manifold and combustion chambers) is RICH and consequently large amounts of unburned HC are emitted from the tailpipe. The coasting bypass system allows more air to be drawn through the carburetor while coasting or decelerating thereby creating a leaner air/fuel mixture and less emissions problems. The coasting bypass system consists of a vacuum control valve and a servo diaphragm.
2   When the vehicle is decelerating, manifold vacuum builds up due to the closed throttle valve. When the vacuum reaches the servo diaphragm of the carburetor, it forces a bypass valve in the carburetor to open. Air is injected into the carburetor through the air horn, changing the air/fuel mixture making it LEAN.

Checks

3   To check the vacuum control valve, remove the air cleaner top, start the engine and allow it to reach normal operating temperature, raise the engine rpm to 3,000 to 4,000 rpm, then quickly release the accelerator pedal. There will be a slight delay then a distinct fizzing (high-pitch whine) sound will resonate from the carburetor when the

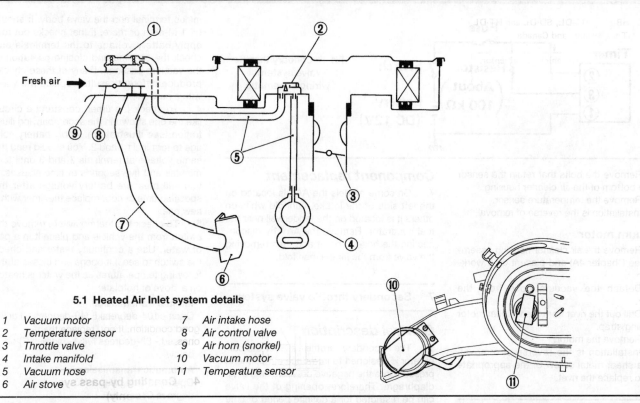

5.1 Heated Air Inlet system details

1	Vacuum motor	7	Air intake hose
2	Temperature sensor	8	Air control valve
3	Throttle valve	9	Air horn (snorkel)
4	Intake manifold	10	Vacuum motor
5	Vacuum hose	11	Temperature sensor
6	Air stove		

engine is decelerating. If there is no fizzing sound, adjust the vacuum control valve.

4   Pry the rubber cap off the vacuum control valve and turn the small screw inside the valve clockwise 1/4 turn until the sound becomes audible. Do not turn the screw more than two complete turns. The fizzing sound should be audible only during deceleration. If there still is no sound from the air control valve, replace it with a new part.

5   To check the servo diaphragm, attach a separate hose to the outside port and apply vacuum. If the diaphragm retracts and is held in place while the vacuum is applied, the servo diaphragm is OK. If the vacuum pump leaks down and dissipates immediately, the servo diaphragm must be replaced with a new part.

Component replacement

6   To replace the vacuum control valve, remove and label the vacuum hoses and remove the mounting hardware holding it in place on its bracket.

7   To replace the servo diaphragm, simply remove the mounting screws from the carburetor and replace it with a new part.

5   Heated Air Inlet (HAI) system

General description

Refer to illustration 5.1

1   The Heated Air Inlet (HAI) system (carbureted models) **(see illustration)** provides heated intake air during warm-up, then maintains the inlet air temperature within a 100-

degrees F to 130-degrees F operating range by mixing warm and cool air. This allows leaner fuel/air mixture settings for the carburetor system, which reduces emissions and improves driveability.

2   Two fresh air inlets - one warm and one cold - are used. The balance between the two is controlled by intake manifold vacuum, a temperature sensor and a vacuum motor. A vacuum motor, which operates a heat duct valve in the air cleaner, is controlled by the temperature sensor.

3   When the underhood temperature is cold, warm air radiating off the exhaust manifold is routed by a shroud which fits over the manifold up through a hot air inlet tube and into the air cleaner. This provides warm air for the carburetor, resulting in better driveability and faster warm-up. As the underhood temperature rises, a heat duct valve is gradually closed by a vacuum motor and the air cleaner draws air through a cold air duct instead. The result is a consistent intake air temperature.

4   A temperature vacuum switch **(see illustration 5.1)**, mounted on the air cleaner housing, monitors the temperature of the inlet air heated by the exhaust manifold.

5   The vacuum motor regulates the duct valve allowing warm air to pass through when the engine is cold and reversely shuts the flow of warm air and opens the cold air duct after the engine has reached operating temperature.

Check

Note: *Make sure that the engine is cold before beginning this test.*

6   Check the vacuum source and the integrity of all vacuum hoses between the

source and the vacuum motor before beginning the test. Do not proceed until they're okay.

7   Apply the parking brake and block the wheels.

8   Remove the air filter (see Chapter 1).

9   Use a hand-held vacuum pump and apply vacuum to the vacuum motor. The duct valve should move. Watch carefully, it may be binding or sticking. Make sure that it's not rusted in an open or closed position by attempting to move it by hand. If it's rusted, it can usually be freed by cleaning and oiling the hinge. If it fails to work properly after servicing, replace it.

10   If the vacuum motor door is okay but the motor still fails to operate correctly, check carefully for a leak in the hose leading to it. Check the vacuum source to and from the sensor and the vacuum motor as well. If no leak is found, replace the vacuum motor.

11   Check the temperature sensor. Monitor the vacuum using a vacuum gauge first, when the engine is cold (start-up) and then finally when the engine has reached operating temperature. There should be vacuum when the engine is cold and then gradually shut down when the engine warms up.

Component replacement

Temperature sensor

12   Clearly label, then detach both vacuum hoses from the temperature sensor (one is coming from the vacuum source at the manifold and the other is going to the vacuum motor underneath the air cleaner housing).

13   Remove the air cleaner housing cover assembly (see Chapter 4A).

6

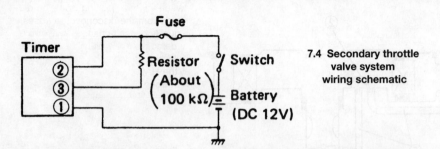

7.4 Secondary throttle valve system wiring schematic

14 Remove the bolts that retain the sensor to the bottom of the air cleaner housing.
15 Remove the temperature sensor.
16 Installation is the reverse of removal.

Vacuum motor

17 Remove the air cleaner housing assembly (see Chapter 4A) and place it on a workbench.
18 Detach the vacuum hose from the motor.
19 Drill out the rivet from the vacuum motor retaining strap.
20 Remove the motor.
21 Installation is the reverse of removal. Use a sheet metal screw of the appropriate size to replace the rivet.

6 Anti-Afterburning (AAV) system

General description

1 During rapid deceleration, the fuel/air mixture becomes heavily concentrated for a short period of time. As the vacuum in the intake manifold increases, it causes the fuel residue on the inside wall of the manifold to vaporize and to enter the combustion chamber.
2 The anti-backfire system prevents this heavy concentration from occurring by introducing air into the intake manifold during this time. This action prevents afterburning in the exhaust system.
3 The main components of this system are the anti-afterburning valve (AAV), the intake manifold and the EGR valve.

Check

4 Check the air passage hose for leaks and looseness and replace it with a new one if necessary. Compare the vacuum hose arrangement to the vacuum schematic located near the VECI label. All vacuum hoses should be intact and installed on the correct vacuum port.
5 Check the vacuum line for leaks and looseness. Disconnect the vacuum hose from the AAV and then run the engine. If air is not sucked into the hose, the AAV is defective and should be replaced with a new one.
6 To check the AAV, hold a piece of paper under the AAV and run the engine up to 3,000 rpm. Then, close the throttle valve quickly. If the paper is not immediately sucked in, the AAV is defective and should be replaced with a new one.

Component replacement

7 On some models the AAV is located on the left side of the intake manifold while on others it is located on the fenderwell near the fuel separator. Remove the AAV by disconnecting the hoses from it and then removing the valve from the intake manifold.

7 Secondary throttle valve system

General description

1 The secondary throttle valve of the carburetor is designed to introduce atmospheric pressure into the negative pressure side of its diaphragm. Therefore, opening of the valve can be restricted for a definite period of time after starting the engine at low temperatures. This is done not only to reduce CO emissions, but also to enhance the driveability of the vehicle in cold weather.
2 The components of the secondary throttle valve system include the carburetor secondary diaphragm, the solenoid switch, a timer and a thermoswitch.

Check

Refer to illustrations 7.4, 7.5a and 7.5b
3 To check the solenoid valve you'll need an ohmmeter. See if the resistance between the plus (+) and minus (-) terminals of the valve
is 32.7 to 39.9 ohms. If it checks out, measure the resistance between the plus or

minus terminal and the valve body. It should be 1 M-ohm or more. If that checks out too, apply battery voltage to the terminals and check the opening and closing operation of the vacuum passage. If any of these checks produce different results, replace the valve with a new one.
4 To check the timer, construct a circuit like the one shown in the accompanying illustration **(see illustration)**. Apply battery voltage to terminals 1 and 2. You should read the same voltage at terminals 2 and 3 until four minutes and five seconds of time elapses. If you still measure battery voltage after the specified time period, replace the timer with a new one.
5 To check the thermoswitch, remove the switch from the vehicle and place it in a pan of water. Use a continuity tester and check the switch to see if it opens and closes at the following temperatures as the water is heated on a stove or hotplate:

Manual transmission
Open - 104-degrees F (40-degrees C) or over
Closed - 88-degrees F (31-degrees C) or below
Automatic transmission
Open - 114-degrees F (45-degrees C) or over
Closed - 97-degrees F (36-degrees C) or below
If the switch does not meet these specifications, replace it with a new one **(see illustrations)**.

Component replacement

6 To replace the timer, pull the electrical connector off and remove the timer mounting hardware.
7 To replace the solenoid valve, pull the vacuum hoses off and mark them along with the solenoid ports.
8 To replace the thermoswitch, pull the connectors off, mark them and then remove the switch.

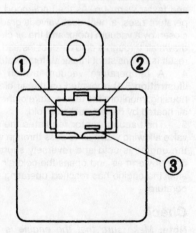

7.5a Timer terminal identification (manual transmission) for secondary throttle valve system

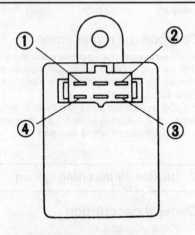

7.5b Timer terminal identification on automatic transmission models on the secondary throttle valve and shift-up control system

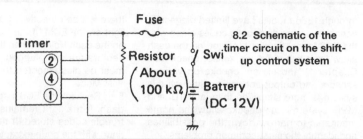

8.2 Schematic of the timer circuit on the shift-up control system

8 Shift-up control system

General description

1   The shift-up control system is provided on automatic transmission vehicles only. It is used to reduce CO emissions due to rapid warm-up. When the coolant temperature is lower than the thermoswitch calls for, the transmission is kept in a kick-down status until the temperature rises. The components of the system are a solenoid valve, a timer and a thermoswitch.

Check

Refer to illustration 8.2

2   To check the timer, construct a circuit like the one shown **(see illustration)**. Apply battery voltage to terminals 1 and 3 and after a time lapse of 65 seconds, there should be no voltage at terminals 2 and 4. If there is, replace the timer with a new one.
3   To check the thermoswitch, refer to Step 3 of the Secondary throttle valve system Section.

Component replacement

4   To replace the solenoid valve, refer to Section 7.
5   To replace the thermoswitch, refer to Section 7.
6   To replace the timer, remove the electrical connector and the mounting hardware.

9 Air induction system

General description

1   This system reduces CO emissions by introducing air from the air cleaner to the intake manifold through the thermo vacuum valve. This function is performed during the choke valve operation so the fuel/air ratio shifts slightly toward 'lean'.

Check

2   Check the hoses for cracks, kinks and correct installation.
3   Remove the thermo valve from the intake manifold and attach hoses to the ports. Submerge the valve in a pan of water. Blow into the valve while heating the water on a stove or hotplate and check to see if the valve opens at 64-degrees F (18-degrees C) to 114-degrees F (45-degrees C) and closes at 50-degrees F (10-degrees C) or below and 130-degrees F (54-degrees C) or above.

4   If the valve does not meet the specifications, replace it with a new one.

Component replacement

5   Mark the hoses, then remove them from the valve.
6   Remove the valve from the intake manifold with a wrench, then thread the new one into the manifold, tighten it securely and hook up the hoses.

10 High-Altitude Compensation (HAC) system

General Information

1   Vehicles that are operated at high altitude, where the air is thinner (and the air/fuel mixture ratio and manifold vacuum boost vary and the amount of emissions increase) require a special system to compensate for the atmospheric changes.
2   The altitude compensator is located in the corner of the engine compartment. Three rubber hoses attach to the unit.

Check

3   Check all the vacuum hoses and fittings for leaks, cuts or damage that would hinder the proper amount of engine vacuum to reach the components.
4   The primary symptom of a defective HAC valve at lower altitudes (below approximately 5,000 feet) is a rough idle condition caused by an excessively lean fuel mixture (the result of the HAC valve allowing air to pass through when it shouldn't; it's actually a vacuum leak). To check the valve at low altitudes, detach the three hoses from the HAC valve **(see illustration 13.1)** and note the idle quality (don't plug the hoses). If the HAC valve is defective, the idle quality won't change (it'll still be rough, as there is no difference

between vacuum leaking from the defective valve or from the disconnected hoses). If the idle quality doesn't change, the valve is probably defective. Now plug the hoses - the idle should smooth out. If it does, this indicates that the HAC valve was allowing extra air to pass through when it shouldn't. Replace the valve.
5   If the vehicle runs rough and emits black exhaust (caused by an overly rich air/fuel ratio) at high altitudes (above approximately 6,000 feet), disconnect all the hoses from the HAC valve and *plug* the hoses (this simulates a HAC valve that *won't* allow the extra air to pass through). If the idle doesn't change, the HAC valve is probably defective. Now unplug the hoses - if the idle smoothes out, this indicates that the HAC valve wasn't allowing the additional air to pass through to lean-out the fuel mixture. Replace the valve.
6   If the test results are incorrect, replace the high altitude compensator.
7   Another way to check the HAC valve is to remove the two bottom hoses from the altitude compensator and blow into the hose. At low altitudes the air should be fairly difficult to force into the compensator. At high altitudes (above approximately 6,000 feet), air should flow into the valve easily. If the altitude compensator bellows do not open up at high altitude, replace the compensator with a new part.
8   Check the EGR system to make sure it is functioning properly (see Section 12).

11 Electronic Control Module (ECM) - removal and installation

Refer to illustration 11.4

1   The Electronic Control Module (ECM) is located inside the passenger compartment. The retaining bracket and bolts must be removed from inside the driver's compartment.
2   Disconnect the negative battery cable from the battery.
3   Working in the driver's side passenger compartment, remove the bolt that retains the lower dash panels and trim panels that surround the area below the steering wheel (see Chapter 11).
4   Disconnect the ECM harness connectors and remove the retaining nuts **(see illustration)** from the ECM.

6

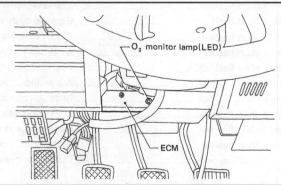

11.4 Location of the ECM

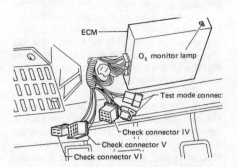

12.2 Location of the TEST MODE Connectors on feedback carburetor systems

5   Carefully slide the ECM out far enough to clear the kick panel. **Caution:** *The ignition switch must be turned OFF when pulling out or plugging in the electrical connectors to prevent damage to the ECM.* **Note:** *Avoid any static electricity damage to the computer by using gloves and a special anti-static pad to store the ECM on once it is removed.*

12   On Board Diagnosis (OBD) system and trouble codes

Feedback carburetor systems

General information

1   Feedback carburetor systems on 1983 through 1986 models have limited diagnostic capabilities. The diagnostic codes along with the ECS inspection light located on the dash allow for a basic oxygen sensor check (see Chapter 1) and simple checks on various sensors and output actuators. Although this system is more simplified than later TBI and MPFI systems, the checks allow the home mechanic to narrow down the possibilities and identify the most common problems.

Self diagnosis

Refer to illustration 12.2

2   Make sure the TEST MODE harness connector for the ECS system is disconnected **(see illustration)**. **Note:** *Models with feedback carburetors are equipped with two modes - Regular Mode and Test Mode. Home mechanics use the Regular Mode access while professional mechanics will use the Test Mode. The Test Mode connectors must be disconnected (male and female) to access the Regular Mode. It will be necessary to partially remove the driver's side trim panels (see Chapter 11) to expose the connectors and the ECM to observe the O2 monitor light.*

3   Turn the ignition key ON (engine not running) and make sure the ECS inspection light on the instrument panel is on. If the light is off, replace the bulb.

4   Observe the O2 monitor light on the ECM. It will flash the trouble codes that have been stored within the ECS computer. If there are no trouble codes stored, the ECS inspection light on the dash will not illuminate and there will be no activity from the O2 monitor light on the ECM. If the ECS inspection light on the dash flickers, then the Test Mode connectors are still plugged together and they must be disconnected to enter the Regular Test Mode.

5   Recheck the ECS inspection light on the dash. If the light remains off, there are no trouble codes stored. If the light is on, continue with the code extraction process.

6   Observe the O2 monitor light on the ECM. It will flash the trouble codes in a clear and distinct manner. The first long flash will represent the first digit of the code designation. Next, the computer will flash the second digit of the code using short flashes. For example, four long flashes will represent the first digit, 4, followed by two short flashes is code 42. Record all the trouble codes on a notepad and observe the computer codes once again to double-check the accuracy as the ECM repeats the list of trouble codes after all the codes have been displayed one time. **Note:** *Many of the diagnostic procedures for the feedback carburetor systems are located in Chapter 4A.*

Canceling the stored trouble codes

7   After the trouble codes have been recorded and the defective components and/or circuits have been repaired, cancel the stored trouble codes from the ECM. Remove the negative battery cable, wait 10 seconds and reconnect the cable. This action will erase the stored trouble codes.

Trouble code chart - feedback carburetor models

Trouble codes	Circuit or system
Code 11 (1 long flash, 1 short flash)	Model designation (5MT, FF, 49 States vehicle)
Code 12 (1 long flash, 2 short flashes)	Model designation (AT, FF, 49 States vehicle)
Code 15 (1 long flash, 5 short flashes)	Model designation (4MT, FF, 49 States vehicle)
Code 71 (7 long flashes, 1 short flash)	Model designation (5MT, FF, California vehicle)
Code 72 (7 long flashes, 2 short flashes)	Model designation (AT, FF, California vehicle)
Code 73 (7 long flashes, 3 short flashes)	Model designation (5MT, 4WD, California vehicle)
Code 74 (7 long flashes, 4 short flashes)	Model designation (AT, 4WD, California vehicle)
Code 22 (2 long flashes, 2 short flashes)	Vehicle speed sensor system
Code 23 (2 long flashes, 3 short flashes)	Oxygen sensor system
Code 24 (2 long flashes, 4 short flashes)	Coolant temperature sensor
Code 25 (2 long flashes, 5 short flashes)	Pressure sensor system)
Code 32 (3 long flashes, 2 short flashes)	Duty solenoid valve system
Code 33 (3 long flashes, 3 short flashes)	Main system in feedback system (TEST MODE only)
Code 34 (3 long flashes, 4 short flashes)	Back-up system
Code 42 (4 long flashes, 2 short flashes)	Clutch switch system (Excluding automatic transmission and 4WD)
Code 52 (5 long flashes, 2 short flashes)	Air suction valve (ASV) control system
Code 53 (5 long flashes, 3 short flashes)	Fuel pump control system
Code 54 (5 long flashes, 4 short flashes)	Automatic choke control system
Code 55 (5 long flashes, 5 short flashes)	Shift-up control system (Automatic transmission only)
Code 62 (6 long flashes, 2 short flashes)	EGR solenoid valve control system
Code 63 (6 long flashes, 3 short flashes)	Canister purge solenoid control system
Code 64 (6 long flashes, 4 short flashes)	Vacuum line control system
Code 65 (6 long flashes, 5 short flashes)	Float chamber vent valve control system

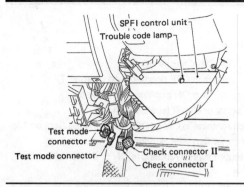

12.19 Location of the TEST MODE Connectors on the TBI and MPFI systems

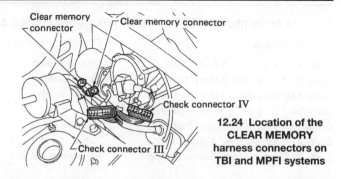

12.24 Location of the CLEAR MEMORY harness connectors on TBI and MPFI systems

Electronic fuel injection systems (TBI and MPFI)

General information

8   The electronic fuel Injection (TBI and MPFI) system controls the fuel injectors, the spark advance system, the self-diagnosis system, the cooling fans, etc. by means of the Electronic Control Module (ECM).

9   The ECM receives signals from various sensors which monitor changing engine operations such as intake air volume, intake air temperature, coolant temperature, engine RPM, acceleration/deceleration, exhaust temperature, etc. These signals are utilized by the ECM to determine the correct injection duration and ignition timing.

10   The Sections in this Chapter include general descriptions and checking procedures, within the scope of the home mechanic and component replacement procedures (when possible). Before assuming the fuel and ignition systems are malfunctioning check the emission control system thoroughly. The emission system and the fuel system are closely interrelated but can be checked separately. The diagnosis of some of the fuel and emission control devices requires specialized tools, equipment and training. If checking and servicing become too difficult or if a procedure is beyond your ability, consult a dealer service department or other qualified repair facility. Remember, the most frequent cause of fuel and emissions problems is simply a loose or broken vacuum hose or wire, so always check the hose and wiring connections first. **Note:** *Because of a federally mandated extended warranty which covers the emission control system components (and any other components which have a primary purpose other than emission control but have significant effects on emissions), check with your dealer about warranty coverage before working on any emission related systems. Once the warranty has expired, you may wish to perform some of the component checks and/or replacement procedures in this Chapter to save you money.*

Precautions

11   Always disconnect the power by either turning off the ignition switch or disconnecting the battery terminals before disconnecting EFI wiring connectors.

12   When installing a battery, be particularly careful to avoid reversing the positive and negative cables.

13   Do not subject EFI or emission related components to severe impact during removal or installation.

14   Do not be careless during troubleshooting. Even slight terminal contact can invalidate a testing procedure and even damage one of the numerous transistor circuits.

15   Never attempt to work on the ECM or open the ECM cover. The ECM is protected by a government mandated extended warranty that will be nullified if you tamper with it.

16   If you are inspecting electronic control system components during rainy weather, make sure water does not enter any part. When washing the engine compartment, do not spray these parts or their connectors with water.

Self diagnosis

Refer to illustration 12.19

17   The self diagnosis mode is useful to diagnose malfunctions in major sensors and actuators of the Electronic Fuel Injection system. There are four different modes available for diagnosing driveability problems. Only the first mode, U-check Mode, is used by home mechanics. The other Modes are used by professional mechanics for self diagnosis. It is important to know that these other modes are used to detect driveability problems that store trouble codes because of random faults that may not be easily detected. The U-check Mode covers malfunctions that are constant or easily detected. Sometimes it will be necessary to double-check the symptoms before proceeding with the actual self diagnostics.

18   There are four modes in the self diagnosis system. The computer will illuminate the ECS light when it detects a problem in U-check Mode but not in D-check Mode. Therefore, it is also important to remember that there may be a problem in the system despite the fact that the ECS light is OFF. This level of diagnostics is difficult and is best handled by a professional.

   U-check Mode - user friendly self-diagnosis mode easily accessed by the home mechanic.

   Read Memory Mode - dealer service department mode for checking stored fault codes that detect past problems.

   D-check Mode - dealer service department mode for checking faulty parts.

   Clear memory Mode - selected mode for canceling stored trouble codes from the computer (ECM).

19   Make sure the TEST MODE connector for the TBI system or the MPFI system is disconnected **(see illustration)**. **Note:** *It will be necessary to partially remove the driver's side trim panels under the dash (see Chapter 11) to expose the connectors and the ECM to observe the O2 monitor light.*

20   Turn the ignition key ON (engine not running) and make sure the CHECK ENGINE inspection light on the instrument panel is on. If the light is off, replace the bulb.

21   Observe the O2 monitor light on the ECM. It will flash the trouble codes that have been stored within the TBI or MPFI computer. If there are no trouble codes stored, the CHECK ENGINE inspection light on the dash will not illuminate and there will be no activity from the O2 monitor light on the ECM. If the CHECK ENGINE inspection light on the dash flickers, then the Test Mode connectors are still plugged together and they must be disconnected to enter the U-check Mode.

22   Recheck the CHECK ENGINE inspection light on the dash. If the light remains off, there are no trouble codes stored. If the light is on, continue with the code extraction process.

23   Observe the O2 monitor light on the ECM. It will flash the trouble codes in a clear and distinct manner. The first long flash will represent the first digit of the code designation. Next, the computer will flash the second digit of the code using short flashes.

For example, four long flashes will represent the first digit, 4, followed by two short flashes is code 42. Record all the trouble codes onto a notepad and observe the computer codes once again to double-check the accuracy as the ECM repeats the list of trouble codes after all the codes have been displayed one time.

Clearing codes

Refer to illustration 12.24

24   The easiest method and most popular method for clearing trouble codes is simply disconnecting the negative battery terminal and waiting 30 seconds. Be sure to write the radio presets for easy reprogramming. There is an alternative method for clearing the codes to avoid cutting power to the radio, clock, accessories, etc. Simply connect the Clear Memory connectors **(see illustration)** while the engine is running. This action will cancel all diagnostic codes only.

6

Trouble code chart - 1983 through 1986 fuel-injected engines

Trouble codes	Circuit or system	Probable cause
Code 11 (1 long flash, 1 short flash)	Ignition system	No reference pulse (see Chapter 5)
Code 12 (1 long flash, 2 short flashes)	Starter switch	Starter switch remains in OFF position (see Chapter 7)
Code 13 (1 long flash, 3 short flashes)	Starter switch	Starter switch remains in ON position (see Chapter 7)
Code 14 (1 long flash, 4 short flashes)	Airflow meter	Airflow meter signal or circuit (see Section 13)
Code 15 (1 long flash, 5 short flashes)	Pressure switch	Pressure switch remains in ON or OFF position (see Section 13)
Code 21 (2 long flashes, 1 short flash)	Airflow meter	Seized airflow meter flap (see Section 13)
Code 22 (2 long flashes, 2 short flashes)	Pressure or vacuum switch	Pressure or vacuum switch remains in ON or OFF position (see Section 13)
Code 23 (2 long flashes, 3 short flashes)	Idle switch	Idle switch remains in the ON or OFF position (see Chapter 4B)
Code 24 (2 long flashes, 4 short flashes)	WOT switch	WOT switch remains in the ON or OFF position (see Chapter 4B)
Code 31 (3 long flashes, 1 short flash)	Vehicle speed sensor	Abnormal signal from the vehicle speed sensor (see Section 13).
Code 32 (3 long flashes, 2 short flashes)	Oxygen sensor	The oxygen sensor circuit is open (see Section 13).
Code 33 (3 long flashes, 3 short flashes)	Coolant temperature sensor	Coolant temperature sensor signal abnormal (see Section 13)
Code 34 (3 long flashes, 4 short flashes)	Air temperature sensor	Air temp sensor signal failure. Check sensor circuit and sensor operation (see Section 13)
Code 35 (3 long flashes, 5 short flashes)	EGR solenoid	EGR solenoid remains in the ON or OFF mode during operation (see Section 14)
Code 41 (4 long flashes, 1 short flash)	Pressure sensor	Pressure sensor circuit signal abnormal (see Section 13)
Code 42 (4 long flashes, 2 short flashes)	Fuel injector	Fuel injector remains in the ON or OFF position (see Chapter 4B)
Code 43 (4 long flashes, 3 short flashes)	KDLH (kickdown low hold) relay	KDLH relay remains in the ON or OFF position (see Chapter 7)

Trouble code chart - 1987 through 1994 fuel-injected engines

Trouble codes	Circuit or system	
Designation codes MPFI systems		
Code 01 (0 long flash, 1 short flash)	Model designation (MT, 49 States and Canada vehicle)	
Code 02 (0 long flash, 2 short flashes)	Model designation (MT, California vehicle)	
Code 03 (0 long flash, 3 short flashes)	Model designation (AT, 49 States and Canada vehicle)	
Code 04 (0 long flash, 4 short flashes)	Model designation (AT, California vehicle)	
Designation codes TBI systems		
Code 05 (0 long flash, 5 short flashes)	Model designation (MT, 49 States and Canada vehicle)	
Code 06 (0 long flash, 6 short flashes)	Model designation (MT, California vehicle)	
Code 07 (0 long flash, 7 short flashes)	Model designation (AT, 49 States and Canada vehicle)	
Code 08 (0 long flash, 8 short flashes)	Model designation (AT, California vehicle)	

All systems

Trouble codes	Circuit or system	Probable cause
Code 11 (1 long flash, 1 short flash)	Crank angle sensor/circuit	No reference pulse (see Chapter 5)
Code 12 (1 long flash, 2 short flashes)	Starter switch	Starter switch remains in ON or OFF position (see Chapter 12)
Code 13 (1 long flash, 3 short flashes)	Crank angle sensor	No position pulse (see Chapter 5)
Code 14** (1 long flash, 4 short flashes)	Fuel injector #1, #2	Abnormal injector output (see Chapter 4A)
Code 15** (1 long flash, 5 short flashes)	Fuel injector #3, #4	Abnormal injector output (see Chapter 4A)
Code 21 (2 long flashes, 1 short flash)	Coolant temperature sensor	Sensor circuit or sensor malfunctioning (see Section 13)
Code 22 (2 long flashes, 2 short flashes)	Knock sensor (MPFI)	Open or shorted knock sensor circuit (see Section 13)
Code 23 (2 long flashes, 3 short flashes)	Airflow meter	Open or shorted airflow meter circuit (see Section 13)

Trouble code chart - 1987 through 1994 fuel-injected engines (continued)

Trouble codes	Circuit or system	Probable cause
Code 24 (2 long flashes, 4 short flashes)	Air control valve	Open or shorted airflow meter circuit (see Section 13)
Code 31 (3 long flashes, 1 short flash)	Throttle Position sensor	TPS sensor circuit is open or shorted (see Section 13).
Code 32 (3 long flashes, 2 short flashes)	Oxygen sensor	The oxygen sensor circuit is open (see Section 13).
Code 33 (3 long flashes, 3 short flashes)	Vehicle speed sensor	No speed sensor signal during operation (see Section 13).
Code 34 (3 long flashes, 4 short flashes)	EGR solenoid (TBI)	EGR solenoid remains in the ON or OFF mode during operation (see Section 14)
Code 35 (3 long flashes, 5 short flashes)	Purge control solenoid valve	Purge control solenoid remains in the ON or OFF position during operation (see Section 15)
Code 41 (4 long flashes, 1 short flash)	Fuel mixture LEAN (MPFI)	Computer detects LEAN air/fuel ratio (see Chapter 4B)
Code 42 (4 long flashes, 2 short flashes)	Idle switch	Idle switch signal incorrect (see Chapter 4B)
Code 44 (4 long flashes, 4 short flashes)	Turbocharger duty solenoid	Duty solenoid circuit (see Chapter 4B)
Code 45 (4 long flashes, 5 short flashes)	Kick down control relay	Kickdown control relay remains in the ON or OFF position during operation (see Chapter 7)
Code 51 (5 long flashes, 1 short flash)	Neutral switch	Neutral switch remains in the ON position during operation (see Chapter 7)
Code 55 (5 long flashes, 5 short flashes)	EGR gas temperature sensor	EGR gas temperature sensor circuit open or shorted (see Section 14)
Code 61 (6 long flashes, 1 short flash)	Parking switch	Parking switch remains in the ON position during operation (see Chapter 7)

** These codes may indicate #1, #2, #3 or #4 injectors on early MPFI models

13 Information sensors

Coolant temperature sensor

General description

1   The coolant temperature sensor is a thermistor (a resistor which varies the value of its voltage output in accordance with temperature changes). The change in the resistance values will directly affect the voltage signal from the coolant sensor. As the sensor temperature DECREASES, the resistance values will INCREASE. As the sensor temperature INCREASES, the resistance values will DECREASE. A failure in the coolant sensor circuit should set a Code 21. This code indicates a failure in the coolant temperature circuit, so in most cases the appropriate solution to the problem will be either repair of a wire or replacement of the sensor.

Check

Refer to illustrations 13.2
2   Check the resistance value of the coolant temperature sensor while it is completely cold (68-degrees F [20-degrees C] = 2,000 to 3,000 ohms). Next, start the engine and warm it up until it reaches operating temperature **(see illustration)**. The resistance should be lower (122-degrees F [50-degrees C] = 700 to 1,000 ohms). **Note:** *Access to the coolant temperature sensor makes it difficult to position electrical probes on the terminals. If necessary, remove the sensor and perform the tests in a pan of heated water to simulate the conditions.*
3   If the resistance values on the sensor are correct, check the signal voltage to the sensor from the ECM. It should be approxi-

mately 5.0 volts. Refer to the wiring diagrams at the end of Chapter 12 for the exact wire color and designations.

Replacement

4   Before installing the new sensor, wrap the threads with Teflon sealing tape to prevent leakage and thread corrosion.
5   Disconnect the electrical connector and remove the sensor. **Caution:** *Handle the*

coolant sensor with care. Damage to this sensor will affect the operation of the entire fuel injection system. Install the sensor and tighten it securely.

Oxygen sensor

General information

6   The oxygen sensor, located in the exhaust manifold, monitors the oxygen content of the exhaust gas stream. The oxygen

6

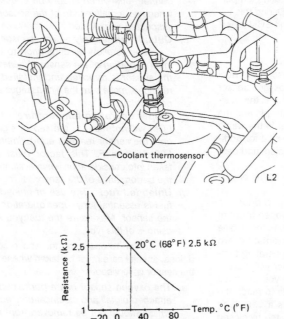

13.2 Check the resistance of the coolant temperature sensor with the engine completely cold and then with the engine at operating temperature. Resistance should decrease as temperature increases

13.19 Remove the oxygen sensor using an open end wrench

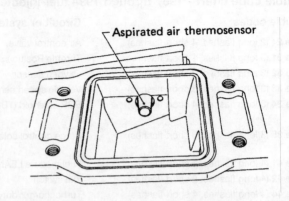

13.31 The air temperature sensor is located in the air duct integral with the airflow meter assembly

content in the exhaust reacts with the oxygen sensor to produce a voltage output which varies from 0.1-volt (high oxygen, lean mixture) to 0.9-volts (low oxygen, rich mixture). The ECM constantly monitors this variable voltage output to determine the ratio of oxygen to fuel in the mixture. The ECM alters the air/fuel mixture ratio by controlling the pulse width (open time) of the fuel injector(s). A mixture ratio of 14.7 parts air to 1 part fuel is the ideal mixture ratio for minimizing exhaust emissions, thus allowing the catalytic converter to operate at maximum efficiency. It is this ratio of 14.7 to 1 which the ECM and the oxygen sensor attempt to maintain at all times. **Note:** *Most models are equipped with a single wire oxygen sensor but California MPFI engines are equipped with the heated oxygen sensor (three wire) type.*

7   The oxygen sensor produces no voltage when it is below its normal operating temperature of about 600-degrees F. During this initial period before warm-up, the ECM operates in open loop mode.

Check

8   Locate the oxygen sensor electrical connector and backprobe the oxygen sensor connector with a straight-pin. Install the positive probe of a voltmeter onto the pin and the negative probe to ground. Refer to the wiring diagrams at the end of Chapter 12 for additional information on the wire colors and designations.

9   Monitor the voltage signal as the engine goes from cold to warm.

10   The oxygen sensor will produce a steady voltage signal at first (open loop) of approximately 0.1 to 0.2 volts with the engine cold. After a period of approximately two minutes, the engine will reach operating temperature and the oxygen sensor will start to fluctuate between 0.1 to 0.9 volts (closed loop). If the oxygen sensor fails to reach the closed loop mode or there is a very long period of time until it does switch to closed loop mode, replace the oxygen sensor with a new part.

11   Also inspect the oxygen sensor heater

on California MPFI models. Disconnect the oxygen sensor electrical connector and connect an ohmmeter to the correct terminals and check for continuity. Refer to the wiring diagrams at the end of Chapter 12 for additional information on the wire colors and terminal designations.

12   Check for proper supply voltage to the heater. Measure the voltage on the harness side of the oxygen sensor electrical connector. There should be battery voltage with the ignition key ON (engine not running). If there is no voltage, check the circuit. Refer to the wiring diagrams at the end of Chapter 12 for additional information on the wire colors and the designations.

13   The proper operation of the oxygen sensor depends on four conditions:

a) **Electrical** - *The low voltages generated by the sensor depend upon good, clean connections which should be checked whenever a malfunction of the sensor is suspected or indicated.*

b) **Outside air supply** - *The sensor is designed to allow air circulation to the internal portion of the sensor. Whenever the sensor is removed and installed or replaced, make sure the air passages are not restricted.*

c) **Proper operating temperature** - *The ECM will not react to the sensor signal until the sensor reaches approximately 600-degrees F. This factor must be taken into consideration when evaluating the performance of the sensor.*

d) **Unleaded fuel** - *The use of unleaded fuel is essential for proper operation of the sensor. Make sure the fuel you are using is of this type.*

14   In addition to observing the above conditions, special care must be taken whenever the sensor is serviced.

a) *The oxygen sensor has a permanently attached pigtail and electrical connector which should not be removed from the sensor. Damage or removal of the pigtail or electrical connector can adversely affect operation of the sensor.*

b) *Grease, dirt and other contaminants*

should be kept away from the electrical connector and the louvered end of the sensor.

c) *Do not use cleaning solvents of any kind on the oxygen sensor.*

d) *Do not drop or roughly handle the sensor.*

e) *The silicone boot must be installed in the correct position to prevent the boot from being melted and to allow the sensor to operate properly.*

15   If the oxygen sensor fails any of these tests, replace it with a new part.

Replacement

Refer to illustration 13.19

Note: *Because it is installed in the exhaust manifold or pipe, which contracts when cool, the oxygen sensor may be very difficult to loosen when the engine is cold. Rather than risk damage to the sensor (assuming you are planning to reuse it in another manifold or pipe), start and run the engine for a minute or two, then shut it off. Be careful not to burn yourself during the following procedure.*

16   Disconnect the cable from the negative terminal of the battery.

17   Raise the vehicle and place it securely on jackstands.

18   Disconnect the electrical connector from the sensor.

19   Carefully unscrew the sensor from the exhaust manifold **(see illustration)**. **Caution:** *Excessive force may damage the threads.*

20   Anti-seize compound must be used on the threads of the sensor to facilitate future removal. The threads of new sensors will already be coated with this compound, but if an old sensor is removed and reinstalled, recoat the threads.

21   Install the sensor and tighten it securely.

22   Reconnect the electrical connector of the pigtail lead to the main engine wiring harness.

23   Lower the vehicle and reconnect the cable to the negative terminal of the battery.

Throttle valve switch/sensor

24   The throttle valve switch/sensor is

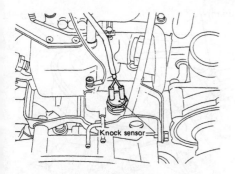

13.33a The knock sensor is located in the engine block

located on the end of the throttle shaft on the throttle body. By monitoring the output voltage from the TPS, the ECM can determine fuel delivery based on throttle valve angle (driver demand). Refer to Chapter 4B (TBI or MPFI) for the checking, adjustment and replacement procedures for the throttle switch and sensor.

Airflow meter

25   The airflow meter is located in the air intake duct. Two different types of airflow meters are used, depending on model year and the type of fuel injection system. The first is the potentiometer type, which uses a flap that is moved in accordance with the amount of air passing through the meter. The angle of the flap is measured by a potentiometer (a variable resistor) and this information is used by the ECM to regulate injector pulse width. The second type is the air mass meter or mass airflow sensor. This sensor uses a hot wire sensing element to measure the amount of air entering the engine. The air passing over the hot wire causes it to cool. Consequently, this change in temperature can be converted into an analog voltage signal to the ECM which in turn calculates the required fuel injector pulse width. Refer to Chapter 4B (TBI or MPFI) for the checking and replacement procedures.

Speed sensor

General description
Note: *The speed sensor is sometimes referred to as the Vehicle Speed Sensor (VSS).*
26   The speed sensor is located in the combination meter. The speed switch transforms vehicle speed into a pulsing voltage signal that is translated by the ECM and provided as information for other systems for fuel and transmission shift control. Any problems with the speed sensor will usually set a Code 33.

Check
27   Because the speed sensor is difficult to access, have the sensor and combination meter checked by a dealer service department or other qualified repair shop.

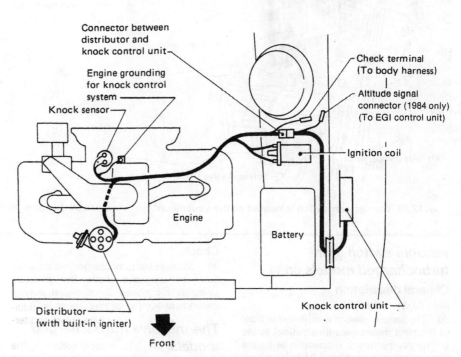

13.33b Schematic of the knock control system on turbocharged engines

Revolution sensor

General description
28   The revolution sensor is an electronic device that calculates the engine rpm and converts it into a pulsing voltage signal that is translated by the ECM and provided as information for other systems for fuel and transmission shift control.
29   The revolution sensor is an early speed sensor device.

Check
30   Because the revolution sensor is difficult to access, have the sensor checked by a dealer service department or other qualified repair shop.

Air temperature sensor

General description
Refer to illustration 13.31
31   The air temperature sensor is located inside the air intake duct near the airflow meter **(see illustration)**. This sensor acts as a resistor which changes value according to the temperature of the air entering the engine. Low temperatures produce a high resistance value. The ECM supplies approximately 5-volts (reference voltage) to the air temperature sensor. The voltage will change according to the temperature of the incoming air. The voltage will be high when the air temperature is cold and low when the air temperature is warm. Any problems with the air temperature sensor will usually set a code 34.

Check
32   Because the air temperature sensor is housed within the airflow meter, it must be checked by a dealer service department or other qualified repair facility. If the air temperature sensor is defective, the airflow meter must be replaced as an assembly.

Knock sensor (turbocharged models only)
Refer to illustrations 13.33a and 13.33b

General description
33   The knock sensor is located in the engine block **(see illustration)**. The knock sensor detects abnormal vibration in the engine. The sensor produces an AC output voltage which increases with the severity of the knock. The signal is fed into the knock control module **(see illustration)** and the timing is retarded up to 5-degrees and the idle speed lowers to compensate for severe detonation.

Check
34   Connect a timing light according to the tool manufacturer's instructions (see Chapter 1) and observe the ignition timing while tapping on the engine block near the knock sensor with a bar or screwdriver. The timing should retard slightly to compensate for the excess detonation (tapping).
35   If ignition timing is not affected by the tapping, have the knock sensor system diagnosed by a dealer service department or other qualified repair facility.

6

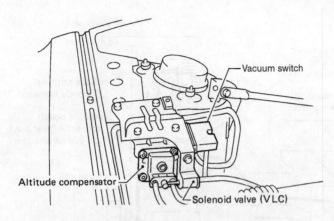

13.36 The vacuum switch is located on the strut mount

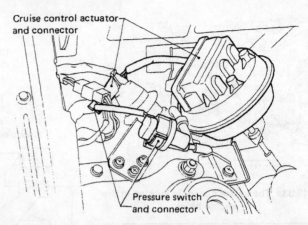

13.38 Location of the pressure switch on turbocharged models

Vacuum switch (non-turbocharged models only)

General description

Refer to illustration 13.36

36   The vacuum switch is mounted in front of the strut mount **(see illustration)** in the engine compartment. It operates when the vacuum reaches negative 3.94 in-Hg (negative 13.3 kPa) pressure. This load signal is transferred to the ECM which in turn richens the fuel mixture to compensate for the large volume of air entering the engine. Trouble with the vacuum switch will set a code 22.

Check

37   Disconnect the vacuum line to the vacuum switch and check for a vacuum signal from the engine at idle and full throttle. The gauge should fluctuate from high vacuum at idle to low vacuum (negative pressure) at high rpm. If the vacuum switch is receiving the proper signals, have the switch checked by a dealer service department or other qualified repair facility.

Pressure switches (turbocharged models)

General description

Refer to illustration 3.38

38   The boost pressure switches are mounted in front of the suspension strut mount **(see illustration)**. There are two boost pressure switches; one activates the light on the instrument panel and the other sends a signal to the ECM. The first pressure switch signals the BOOST light on the dash to indicate that the turbocharger is in operation. If excessive boost occurs, the second pressure switch signals the injectors to cut fuel when an abnormal rise in boost pressure, due to a failed turbocharger wastegate or other similar problem, is detected. This design eliminates the air relief valve installed on previous models. The air relief valve is a cylindrical shaped device mounted on the intake manifold on early models.

Check

39   Because the turbocharger system is difficult to diagnose, have the pressure switches diagnosed by a dealer service department or other qualified repair facility.

Thermovalve (turbocharged models)

General description

40   The thermovalve is mounted on the base of the engine near the oil pump. Its purpose is to divert oil to the turbocharger (below 155-degrees F) or to the oil cooler then to the turbocharger (above 156-degrees F). The thermovalve will close completely diverting the oil to the oil cooler lines.

14 Exhaust Gas Recirculation (EGR) system

General description

Refer to illustrations 14.2a, 14.2b and 14.2c

1   The EGR system is used to lower NOx (oxides of nitrogen) emission levels caused by high combustion temperatures. The EGR recirculates a small amount of exhaust gases into the intake manifold. The additional mixture lowers the temperature of combustion thereby reducing the formation of NOx compounds.

2   Early EGR systems are equipped with either the orifice controlled vacuum modulation **(see illustration)**, thermo vacuum valve controlled vacuum modulation **(see illustra-**

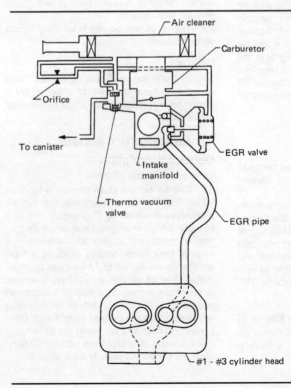

14.2a Schematic of an orifice controlled vacuum modulated EGR system (1985 49 State and Canada, 4WD with manual transaxle)

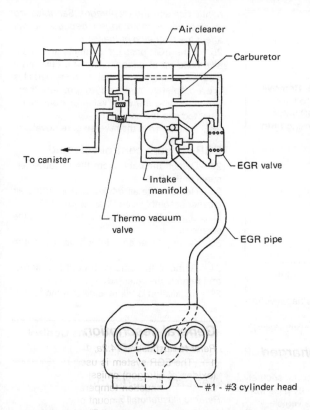

14.2b Schematic of a thermo vacuum valve controlled EGR system (1985 49 State and Canada, 4WD with automatic transaxle)

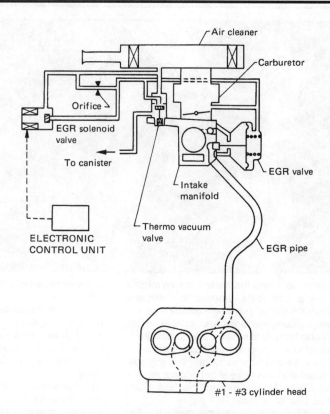

14.2c Schematic of an ECM-controlled EGR system (1985 2WD with manual transaxle)

tion) or the ECM controlled vacuum modulation **(see illustration)**. There are different configurations of these systems so it is important to check the VECI label and the vacuum schematic on your vehicle for the exact type of system. The ported vacuum control system uses a slot in the carburetor body which is exposed to an increasing percentage of manifold vacuum as the throttle valve is opened up during acceleration.

3   On later models, the TBI fuel injection system uses the venturi vacuum signal with the EGR solenoid to activate the EGR valve while the MPFI fuel injection system uses the ECM to activate the EGR valve. The MPFI with turbochargers route the exhaust gas from cylinders 2 and 4 while the TBI systems route the exhaust gas from cylinders 1 and 3. The TBI system is simple and can be checked more readily. The MPFI system relies on sensor signals to relay information to the ECM for correct EGR activation. Refer to Section 13 for additional information on checking the information sensors and output actuators in the fuel injection system.

Check

Refer to illustration 14.6

4   Check all hoses for cracks, kinks, broken sections and proper connection. Inspect all system connections for damage, cracks and leaks.

5   To check the EGR system operation, bring the engine up to operating temperature

and, with the transmission in Neutral (parking brake set and tires blocked to prevent movement), allow it to idle for 70 seconds. Open the throttle abruptly so the engine speed is between 2,000 and 3,000 rpm and then allow it to close. The EGR valve stem should move if the control system is working properly. The test should be repeated several times. Movement of the stem indicates the control system is functioning correctly.

6   If the EGR valve stem does not move, check all of the hose connections to make sure they are not leaking or clogged. Disconnect the vacuum hose and apply ten inches

of vacuum with a hand-held pump **(see illustration)**. If the stem still does not move, replace the EGR valve with a new one. If the valve does open, measure the valve travel to make sure it is approximately 1/8-inch. Also, the engine should run roughly or even stall when the valve is open. If it doesn't, the passages are probably clogged.

7   Apply vacuum with the pump and then clamp the hose shut. The valve should stay open for 30 seconds or longer. If it does not, the diaphragm is leaking and the valve should be replaced with a new one.

8   If the EGR valve is not receiving port or

14.6 Use a hand-held vacuum pump to apply vacuum to the EGR valve

6

14.22 Remove the two EGR valve mounting nuts

venturi vacuum, the carburetor or throttle body unit must be removed to check and clean the slotted port in the throttle bore and the vacuum passages and orifices in the throttle body. Use solvent to remove deposits and check for flow with light air pressure.

9   If the engine idles roughly and it is suspected the EGR valve is not closing, remove the EGR valve and inspect the poppet and seat area for deposits.

10   If the deposits are more than a thin film of carbon, the valve should be cleaned. To clean the valve, apply solvent and allow it to penetrate and soften the deposits, making sure that none gets on the valve diaphragm, as it could be damaged.

11   Use a vacuum pump to hold the valve open and carefully scrape the deposits from the seat and poppet area with a tool. Inspect the poppet and stem for wear and replace the valve with a new one if wear is found.

12   Locate the thermo-vacuum valve and plug one of the ports with a finger. Use a hand held vacuum pump and apply vacuum to the valve. Check for any sign of leaks.

13   With the engine running, check for a vacuum signal from the intake manifold. This test will determine if manifold vacuum is reaching the various valves and components of the EGR system.

14   Also apply vacuum to the port (vacuum hose) that is routed to the EGR valve. The gauge should hold vacuum. If not, check for broken hoses or ruptured diaphragms in the EGR valve.

15   Check the EGR solenoid (if equipped). Using a hand-held vacuum pump, apply vacuum and, using jumper wires, apply battery voltage. The solenoid should activate and allow vacuum to pass through the solenoid.

16   Also remove the vacuum hose(s) from the solenoid and check for vacuum to the EGR solenoid valve.

Component replacement

EGR valve

Refer to illustration 14.22

17   When replacing an EGR valve, make sure that you obtain the correct part. Use the

stamped code located on the top of the EGR valve.

18   Detach the cable from the negative terminal of the battery.

19   Remove the air cleaner housing assembly (see Chapter 4A and 4B).

20   Detach the vacuum line from the EGR valve.

21   Raise the vehicle and support it securely on jackstands. Remove the EGR pipe from the exhaust manifold. Lower the vehicle.

22   Remove the EGR valve mounting bolts **(see illustration)**.

23   Remove the EGR valve and gasket from the manifold. Discard the gasket.

24   Remove all exhaust deposits from the EGR valve mounting surface on the manifold and, if you plan to use the same valve, the mounting surface of the valve itself. Look for exhaust deposits in the valve outlet. Remove deposit build-up with a scraper or screwdriver. **Caution:** *Never wash the valve in solvents or degreaser - both agents will perma-*

nently damage the diaphragm. Sandblasting is also not recommended because it will affect the operation of the valve.

25   If the EGR passage contains an excessive build-up of deposits, clean it out with a wire wheel. Make sure that all loose particles are completely removed to prevent them from clogging the EGR valve or from being ingested into the engine.

26   Installation is the reverse of removal.

EGR vacuum control solenoid

27   Detach the cable from the negative terminal of the battery.

28   Remove the air intake duct from the air cleaner assembly (see Chapter 4A or 4B).

29   Unplug the electrical connector from the solenoid.

30   Clearly label and detach both vacuum hoses.

31   Remove the solenoid mounting screw and remove the solenoid.

32   Installation is the reverse of removal.

15   Evaporative Emissions Control System (EVAP)

General description

Refer to illustration 15.2

1   This system is designed to trap and store fuel vapors that evaporate from the fuel tank, throttle body and intake manifold.

2   The Evaporative Emission Control System (EVAP) consists of a charcoal-filled canister and the lines connecting the canister to the fuel tank, ported vacuum and intake manifold vacuum **(see illustration)**.

3   Fuel vapors are transferred from the fuel tank, throttle body and intake manifold to a canister where they are stored when the engine is not operating. When the engine is

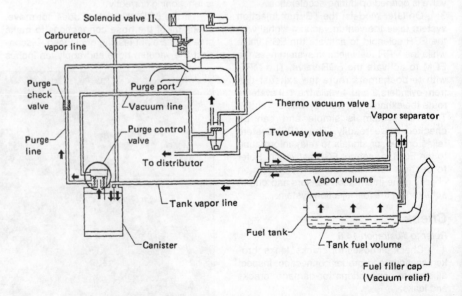

15.2 Schematic of the EVAP system on early models

running, the fuel vapors are purged from the canister by a purge control solenoid and consumed in the normal combustion process.

Check

4   Poor idle, stalling and poor driveability can be caused by an inoperative purge control solenoid, a damaged canister, split or cracked hoses or hoses connected to the wrong tubes.

5   Evidence of fuel loss or fuel odor can be caused by fuel leaking from fuel lines or the throttle body (TBI and MPFI systems, a cracked or damaged canister, an inoperative bowl vent valve, an inoperative purge valve, disconnected, misrouted, kinked, deteriorated or damaged vapor or control hoses or an improperly seated air cleaner or air cleaner gasket.

6   Inspect each hose attached to the canister for kinks, leaks and breaks along its entire length. Repair or replace as necessary.

7   Inspect the canister. If it is cracked or damaged, replace it.

8   Look for fuel leaking from the bottom of the canister. If fuel is leaking, replace the canister and check the hoses and hose routing.

9   Apply a short length of hose to the lower tube of the purge control valve and attempt to blow through it. Little or no air should pass into the canister (a small amount of air will pass because the canister has a constant purge hole).

10   With a hand-held vacuum pump, apply vacuum through the control vacuum signal tube near the throttle body to the EGR and canister control solenoid valve.

11   If the purge control solenoid does not hold vacuum for at least 20 seconds, the purge control solenoid is leaking and must be replaced.

12   If the diaphragm holds vacuum, apply battery voltage to the canister control solenoid and observe that vacuum (vapors) are allowed to pass through to the intake system.

Component replacement

13   Clearly label, then detach, all vacuum lines from the canister.

14   Loosen the canister mounting clamp bolt(s) and pull the canister out.

15   Installation is the reverse of removal.

16 Positive Crankcase Ventilation (PCV) system

Refer to illustration 16.1

1   The Positive Crankcase Ventilation (PCV) system reduces hydrocarbon emissions by scavenging crankcase vapors. It does this by circulating fresh air from the air cleaner through the crankcase, where it mixes with blow-by gases and is then rerouted through a PCV valve to the intake manifold (see illustration).

2   The main components of the PCV system are the PCV valve, a fresh air filtered inlet and the vacuum hoses connecting these two components with the engine.

3   To maintain idle quality, the PCV valve restricts the flow when the intake manifold vacuum is high. If abnormal operating conditions arise, the system is designed to allow excessive amounts of blow-by gases to flow back through the crankcase vent tube into the air cleaner to be consumed by normal combustion.

4   Checking and replacement of the PCV valve and filter is covered in Chapter 1.

17 Catalytic Converter (CAT)

General description

1   The catalytic converter is an emission control device added to the exhaust system to reduce pollutants from the exhaust gas stream. A single-bed converter design is used in combination with a three-way (reduction) catalyst. The coating on the three-way catalyst media contains platinum and rhodium, which lowers the levels of oxides of nitrogen (NOx) as well as hydrocarbons (HC) and carbon monoxide (CO). Refer to Chapter 4A for additional information on the exhaust system.

Check

2   The test equipment for a catalytic converter is expensive and highly sophisticated. If you suspect that the converter on your vehicle is malfunctioning, take it to a dealer service department or an authorized emissions inspection facility for diagnosis and repair.

3   Whenever the vehicle is raised for servicing of underbody components, check the converter for leaks, corrosion and other damage. If damage is discovered, the converter should be replaced.

Replacement

4   Because the converter part of the exhaust system, converter replacement requires removal of the exhaust pipe assembly (see Chapter 4A). Take the vehicle, or the exhaust system, to a muffler shop or other qualified repair facility.

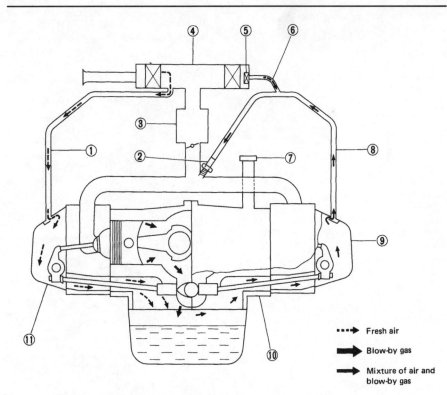

16.1 Cross-sectional view of the PCV system on an OHV engine

1	Connecting hose	6	Connecting hose	10	Crankcase
2	PCV valve	7	Oil filler cap	11	Valve cover on
3	Carburetor	8	Connecting hose		cylinders 1-3 side
4	Air cleaner	9	Valve cover on		
5	Air filter		cylinders 2-4 side		

····► Fresh air

➡ Blow-by gas

➡ Mixture of air and blow-by gas

6

Notes

Chapter 7 Part A
Manual transaxle

Contents

7A

Specifications

Pitching stopper cushion-to-washer clearance (adjustable type) .... 0.031 to 0.047 inch (0.8 to 1.2 mm)

Torque specifications

	Ft-lbs
Back-up light/neutral start switch	12 to 15
Transaxle-to-engine fasteners	
Lower nuts	34 to 40
Upper bolts/nuts	34 to 40
Pitching stopper (non-adjustable type)	
Rear (firewall bracket) nut/bolt	27 to 42
Front (engine side) nut/bolt	32 to 40

1 General information

The manual transaxle is a fully-synchronized four- or five-speed unit. The "transaxle" is actually several components bolted together into a single assembly: the clutch housing; the main case, which houses the differential and transmission; and the rear case. On 2WD models, the rear case is sim-ply a one-piece extension housing; on 4WD models, the rear case consists of a transfer case/transfer control system and an extension housing. However, the transaxle is removed and installed as a single assembly; do not try to separate any of these components from the transaxle. If the transaxle must be replaced, obtain a complete new, rebuilt or used assembly.

2 Shift lever - removal and installation

2WD models

Refer to illustrations 2.1a, 2.1b and 2.4

1   Remove the shift lever knob **(see illus-trations)**.

2   Raise the vehicle and place it securely on jackstands.

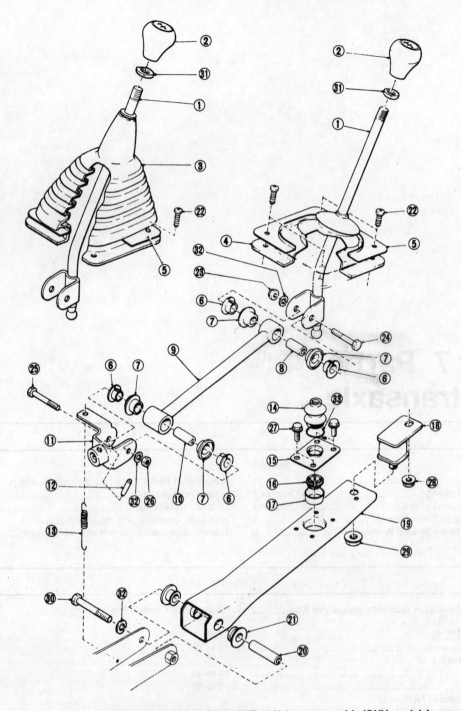

2.1a An exploded view of a typical 2WD shift lever assembly (OHV models)

1	Shift lever	12	Spring pin	23	Nut
2	Knob	13	Neutral set spring	24	Bolt
3	Boot	14	Dust seal	25	Bolt
4	Soot	15	Plate	26	Nut
5	Plate	16	Bushing	27	Flange bolt
6	Bushing (resin)	17	Cushion	28	Flange nut
7	Bushing (rubber)	18	Cushion rubber	29	Flange nut
8	Spacer	19	Stay	30	Bolt
9	Rod	20	Spacer	31	Nut
10	Spacer	21	Bushing (rubber)	32	Spring washer
11	Joint	22	Screw	33	Lock ring

2.1b An exploded view of a typical 2WD shift lever assembly (OHC models)

1	Knob	13	Rod
2	Boot plate	14	Spacer
3	Boot	15	Rubber bushing
4	Shift lever	16	Spacer
5	Dust seal	17	Spring
6	Plate	18	Bracket
7	Shift lever bushing	19	Bracket mount
8	Cushion	20	Spacer
9	Cushion rubber	21	Joint
10	Stay	22	Rubber bushing
11	Nylon bushing	23	Boss
12	Rubber bushing	24	Spring pin

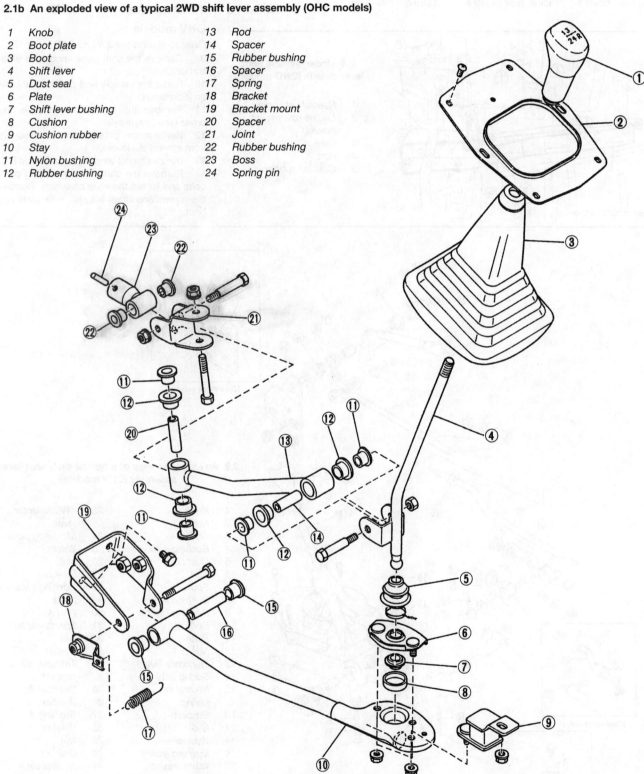

3   Remove the front exhaust pipe and cover (see Chapter 4).

4   Remove the Neutral set spring and unbolt the front end of the stay from the engine rear mounting bracket **(see illustration)**.

5   Disconnect the front end of the rod from the joint and remove the cushion rubber from the underside of the body.

6   To remove the shift lever assembly, pull it straight down.

7   Installation is the reverse of removal. Make sure that all fasteners are tight.

8   Remove the jackstands and lower the vehicle.

4WD models

OHV models

Refer to illustrations 2.9 and 2.23

9   Remove the shift lever knob **(see illustration)**.

10   Raise the vehicle and place it securely on jackstands.

11   Remove the front exhaust pipe and cover (see Chapter 4).

12   Remove the plastic shift lever covers from around the levers.

13   Remove the nut connecting rod A to rod B.

14   Remove the shift lever mounting plate bolts and lift out the lever assembly. Remove the screws and lift off the shift lever plate and boot.

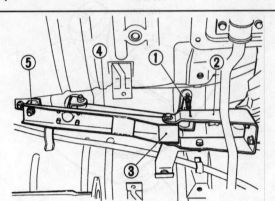

2.4 Under-vehicle shift lever details (2WD models)

1   *Neutral set spring*
2   *Engine rear mount bracket*
3   *Stay*
4   *Rod*
5   *Cushion rubber*

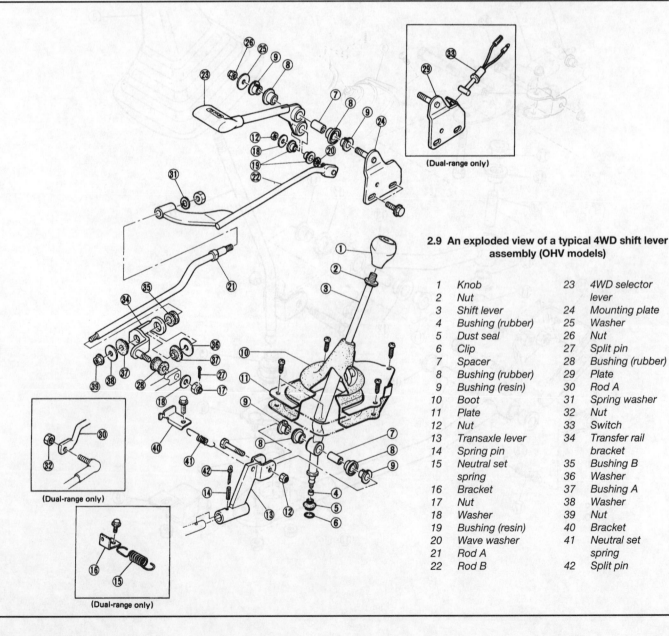

2.9 An exploded view of a typical 4WD shift lever assembly (OHV models)

1	*Knob*	23	*4WD selector lever*
2	*Nut*		
3	*Shift lever*	24	*Mounting plate*
4	*Bushing (rubber)*	25	*Washer*
5	*Dust seal*	26	*Nut*
6	*Clip*	27	*Split pin*
7	*Spacer*	28	*Bushing (rubber)*
8	*Bushing (rubber)*	29	*Plate*
9	*Bushing (resin)*	30	*Rod A*
10	*Boot*	31	*Spring washer*
11	*Plate*	32	*Nut*
12	*Nut*	33	*Switch*
13	*Transaxle lever*	34	*Transfer rail bracket*
14	*Spring pin*		
15	*Neutral set spring*	35	*Bushing B*
16	*Bracket*	36	*Washer*
17	*Nut*	37	*Bushing A*
18	*Washer*	38	*Washer*
19	*Bushing (resin)*	39	*Nut*
20	*Wave washer*	40	*Bracket*
21	*Rod A*	41	*Neutral set spring*
22	*Rod B*	42	*Split pin*

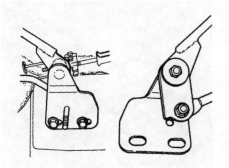

2.23 Use an 8 mm bolt or drill bit to align the notch in the selector lever with the hole in the mounting plate

2.27 On 4WD models, unplug the electrical connector from the 4WD indicator light switch, remove the switch retaining nut (arrow) and remove the switch

15 Disconnect the Neutral set spring and separate rod A from the transfer rail or bracket. Be careful not to lose the bushings (if equipped).
16 Disconnect the shift lever from the transaxle lever.
17 Now, remove the shift lever assembly by pulling it up.
18 Attach the shift lever to the transaxle lever.
19 Install the Neutral set spring and then attach rod A to the transfer rail or bracket. Make sure that the bushings (if equipped) are installed correctly.
20 Insert the shift lever into the boot, then attach the boot and plate to the body (make sure rod A protrudes through the boot) and tighten the screws.
21 Install the jam nut and knob on the shift lever.
22 Connect rod A to rod B with the nut while holding rod A with a wrench.
23 Attach the 4WD selector lever mounting to the body. Make sure that the transfer rail is set at the forward position. Use a 0.3 inch (8 mm) diameter rod to align the selector lever notch with the hole in the plate **(see illustration)**, then remove the pin.
24 Install the shift lever covers.

OHC models

Refer to illustrations 2.27, 2.28 and 2.31
25 Unscrew the shift lever knob.
26 If the vehicle is equipped with a center console, remove the console (see Chapter 11).
27 On 4WD models, remove the 4WD indicator light switch **(see illustration)**.
28 Remove the shift lever boot **(see illustration)**.
29 Unbolt the shift lever from the shift lever rod **(see illustration 2.28)**. Remove the nylon and rubber bushings and the spacer, inspect them for wear and damage and replace parts as necessary.
30 Raise the vehicle and place it securely on jackstands.
31 Remove the two nuts that attach the shift lever plate to the stay rod **(see illustration)**.
32 Pull the shift lever straight up. Inspect the dust seal, plate, shift lever bushing and

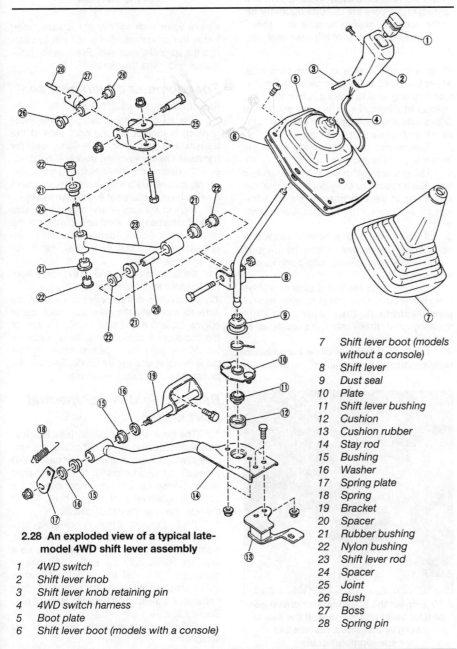

2.28 An exploded view of a typical late-model 4WD shift lever assembly

1 4WD switch
2 Shift lever knob
3 Shift lever knob retaining pin
4 4WD switch harness
5 Boot plate
6 Shift lever boot (models with a console)
7 Shift lever boot (models without a console)
8 Shift lever
9 Dust seal
10 Plate
11 Shift lever bushing
12 Cushion
13 Cushion rubber
14 Stay rod
15 Bushing
16 Washer
17 Spring plate
18 Spring
19 Bracket
20 Spacer
21 Rubber bushing
22 Nylon bushing
23 Shift lever rod
24 Spacer
25 Joint
26 Bush
27 Boss
28 Spring pin

7A

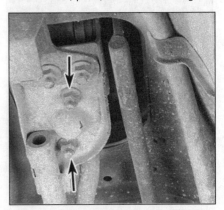

2.31 To detach the lower end of the shift lever from the stay rod, remove these two nuts (arrows)

3.4 Remove the extension housing seal with a seal removal tool (shown) or a large screwdriver; make sure you don't damage the splines on the output shaft

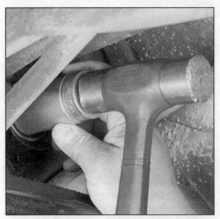

3.6 Make sure the seal is square to the bore, then use a hammer and large socket to tap the new extension housing seal into place; make sure the outside diameter of the socket is slightly smaller than the outside diameter of the new seal

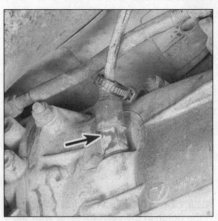

3.8 The speedometer driven gear (arrow) is located on the right side of the transaxle

cushion for wear and damage and replace parts as necessary **(see illustration 2.28)**.

33   Installation is the reverse of removal. Lube the shift lever rod-to-shift lever bolt and bushing, and the shift lever bushing at the lower end of the shift lever, with multipurpose grease. Tighten all fasteners securely.

3   Oil seal - replacement

1   Oil leaks frequently occur as a result of a worn extension housing oil seal, or a worn seal at the speedometer driven gear, back-up light switch or neutral start switch. Replacement of these seals is relatively easy, since the repairs can be performed without removing the transaxle from the vehicle. If you see puddles of lubricant under the transaxle, raise the vehicle and place it securely on jackstands. First, try to determine where the leak is coming from.

Extension housing seal

Refer to illustrations 3.4 and 3.6

2   The extension housing oil seal is located

at the extreme rear end of the transaxle, where the driveshaft is attached. If the extension housing seal is leaking, there will be a buildup of lubricant on the front end of the driveshaft, and lubricant may even be dripping from the rear of the transaxle.

3   Disconnect the driveshaft from transaxle (see Chapter 8).

4   Using a seal removal tool or screwdriver **(see illustration)**, carefully pry the oil seal out of the rear of the transmission. Do not damage the splines on the transmission output shaft.

5   If the oil seal cannot be removed with a screwdriver or prybar, a special oil seal removal tool (available at auto parts stores) will be required.

6   Using a large section of pipe or a large deep socket as a drift, install the new oil seal **(see illustration)**. Drive it into the bore squarely and make sure it's completely seated.

7   Lubricate the splines of the transmission output shaft and the outside of the driveshaft

sleeve yoke with lightweight grease, then install the driveshaft. Be careful not to damage the lip of the new seal. Remove the jackstands and lower the vehicle.

Speedometer driven gear seal

Refer to illustrations 3.8, 3.9 and 3.10

8   The speedometer driven gear **(see illustration)** is located on the right side of the transaxle. If you think it's leaking, look for transaxle lubricant around the cable housing.

9   To detach the cable from the transaxle, simply loosen the plastic cable housing with a wrench and unscrew it **(see illustration)**.

10   Inspect the seal on the end of the cable **(see illustration)** for wear and damage. If the cable seal is worn or damaged, replace the speedometer cable (the seal can't be replaced separately).

11   Detach the upper end of the cable from the speedometer (see Chapter 12).

12   Installation is the reverse of removal. Be sure to lubricate the new seal with clean engine oil, and make sure the square end of the cable seats properly into the speedometer driven gear shaft before screwing the cable housing into the transaxle. Remove the jackstands and lower the vehicle.

Back-up light switch/neutral start switch

13   The back-up light switch **(see illustration 5.2)** is located on the left side of the rear case (2WD models) or the transfer case (4WD models); on some models, the neutral start switch is also located here, right behind the back-up light switch (if it's not here, it's on the upper end of the clutch pedal).

14   If you suspect a leak in this area, look for a build-up of lubricant on the switch(es). Neither switch uses O-rings or seals, so a leak will result only if a switch is loose or damaged. Wipe off the switch(es) with a clean shop rag and look for cracks or other damage. If a switch is damaged, renew it (see Section 5).

15   Remove the jackstands and lower the vehicle.

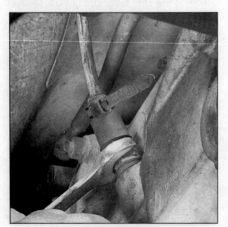

3.9 To detach the speedometer cable from the transaxle, unscrew it with a wrench

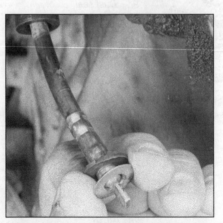

3.10 Inspect the speedometer driven gear seal for wear and damage; if the seal is worn or damaged, replace the speedometer cable

4.2 To check the transaxle mounts, insert a large prybar between the transaxle and the crossmember and try to pry the transaxle up; if it moves much, one or both of the rubber mounts is torn, cracked or damaged

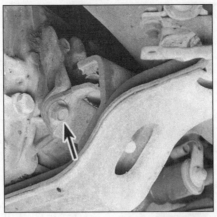

4.3a To unbolt the left transaxle mount from the transaxle, remove this bolt (arrow) . . .

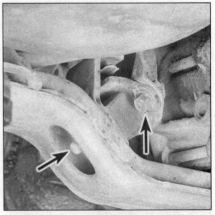

4.3b . . . and this one (right arrow), then remove the nut from this stud (left arrow); once the mount is unbolted, simply raise the transaxle slightly with a jack and remove the mount

4 Transmission mount - check and replacement

Refer to illustrations 4.2, 4.3a, 4.3b and 4.3c

1 Raise the vehicle and place it securely on jackstands.
2 Insert a large screwdriver or prybar into the space between the transaxle and the crossmember and try to pry the transmission up slightly **(see illustration)**. The transmission should move very little. If it moves a lot, inspect the rubber portions of the two mounts. If either mount is damaged, replace it.
3 To replace a mount, remove the bolts attaching the mount to the crossmember and to the transaxle **(see illustrations)**.
4 Raise the transaxle slightly with a jack and remove the mount.
5 Installation is the reverse of the removal procedure. Be sure to tighten the bolts securely.

6 Remove the jackstands and lower the vehicle.

5 Neutral start switch/back-up light switch - check and replacement

Check

Refer to illustrations 5.2, 5.3 and 5.4

1 Raise the vehicle and place it securely on jackstands.
2 The back-up light switch **(see illustration)** is located on the left side of the rear case (2WD models) or the transfer case (4WD models); on some models, the neutral start switch is also located here, right behind the back-up light switch (if it's not here, it's on the upper end of the clutch pedal).
3 To check either switch, trace the electrical lead back to its connector **(see illustration)** and hook up an ohmmeter.

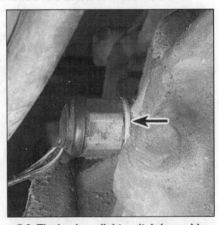

5.2 The back-up light switch (arrow) is located on the left side of the rear case (2WD models) or the transfer case (4WD models); on some models, the neutral start switch is also located here, right behind the back-up light switch (if it's not here, it's on the upper end of the clutch pedal)

7A

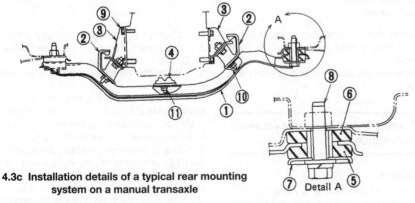

4.3c Installation details of a typical rear mounting system on a manual transaxle

1 Rear crossmember
2 Rear cushion rubber
3 Bracket
4 Stopper
5 Cushion A
6 Cushion B
7 Plate
8 Bolt
9 Flange bolt
10 Flange nut
11 Flange nut

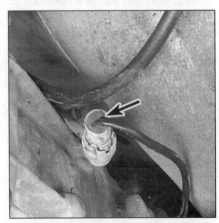

5.3 To check either switch, trace the electrical lead back to its connector (arrow), unplug the connector and hook up an ohmmeter to the connector terminals

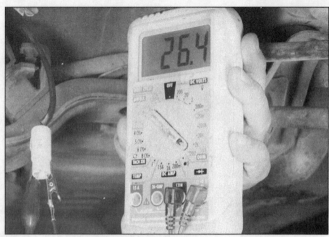

5.4 To check the back-up light switch, put the transaxle into reverse and verify that there's continuity (low resistance), then put the transaxle in any other gear and verify that there's no continuity (high resistance); to check the neutral start switch, put the transaxle in Neutral and verify that there's continuity (low resistance), then put the transaxle in any other gear and verify that there's no continuity (high resistance)

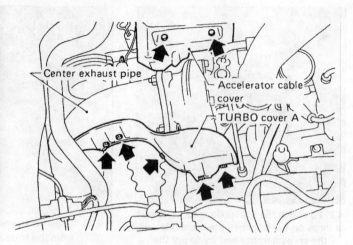

6.5 On turbocharged models, remove the accelerator cable cover and turbo cover A by removing the indicated cover screws

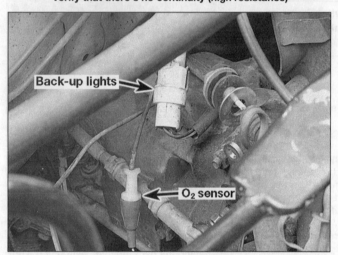

6.7a Unplug the electrical connector for the back-up light switch (upper arrow) and for the oxygen sensor (lower arrow) (on some models, there may also be a connector for the neutral start switch - if it's located on the transaxle instead of the clutch pedal)

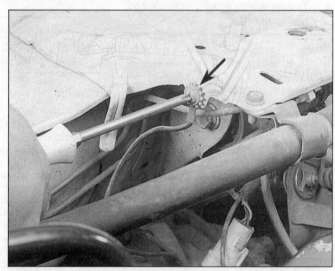

6.7b Locate and detach all ground wire connectors (this one is to the right of the bracket for the engine pitching stopper bracket)

4   To check the back-up light switch, put the transaxle into reverse and verify that there's continuity (low resistance) **(see illustration)**. Then put the transaxle in any other gear and verify that there's no continuity (high or infinite resistance).

5   To check the neutral start switch, put the transaxle in Neutral and verify that there's continuity (low resistance). Then put the transaxle in any other gear and verify that there's no continuity (high or infinite resistance).

6   If either switch fails to operate as described, replace it.

Replacement

7   Simply unscrew the old switch, install the new switch (make sure the washer is installed) and tighten it to the torque listed in this Chapter's Specifications.

8   Verify that the new switch works properly (see above), then plug in the electrical connector.

9   Remove the jackstands and lower the vehicle.

6   Manual transaxle - removal and installation

Removal

Refer to illustrations 6.5, 6.7a, 6.7b, 6.9a, 6.9b, 6.9c, 6.9d, 6.11a, 6.11b, 6.12,, 6.14a, 6.14b, 6.14c, 6.14d, 6.16, 6.17, 6.18a and 6.18b

1   Open the hood and hold it securely in place with the hood stay. Remove the spare tire and the spare tire support.

2   Disconnect the negative battery cable.

3   Disconnect the clutch cable (see Chapter 8).

4   Raise the vehicle and place it securely on jackstands.

5   Remove the front part of the exhaust system (see Chapter 4). On turbo models, you'll have to remove the throttle cable cover and turbo cover "A" **(see illustration)**.

6   The speedometer cable **(see illustration 3.8)** is located on the right side of the transaxle. To disconnect it from the transaxle, simply unscrew it **(see illustration 3.9)** and pull it straight up. If the cable is attached to the transaxle by a clip, detach it.

7   Clearly label, then unplug, the electrical connectors for the oxygen sensor, the back-up light switch **(see illustration)**, the neutral start switch (if it's located on the transaxle; some are located on the clutch pedal) and

6.9a On earlier models with an adjustable engine pitching stopper, loosen and reposition the nuts (arrows) at the stopper bracket to tilt the rear of the engine down slightly

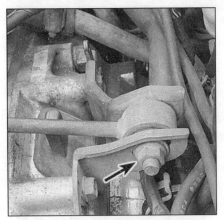

6.9b On newer models with a non-adjustable engine pitching stopper, remove the stopper-to-engine bolt and nut (arrow), . . .

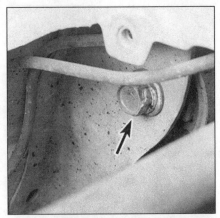

6.9c . . . the stopper-to-firewall bracket bolt (arrow) and nut, . . .

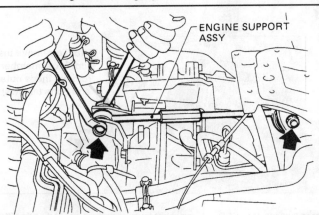

ENGINE SUPPORT ASSY

6.9d . . . and install an engine support assembly; if you don't have access to engine support, you can use an engine hoist to support the engine and tilt it to the best angle for removing and installing the transaxle

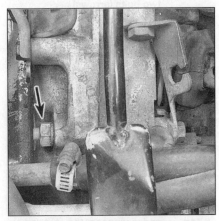

6.11a To detach the upper part of the transaxle from the engine, remove this nut and bolt (arrow) from the left side . . .

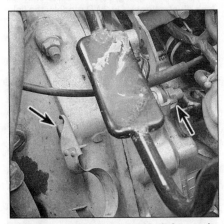

6.11b . . . and this nut and bolt (arrows) from the right

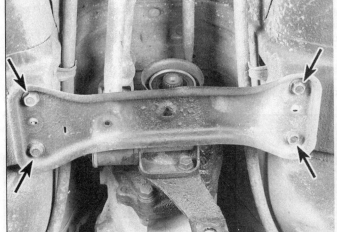

6.12 To remove the rear crossmember, remove these bolts (arrows)

the starter (see Chapter 5). Disconnect any ground wires (see illustration).

8   On 4WD models, unplug the connector for the 4WD indicator light switch, and detach the vacuum hose.

9   On earlier models, loosen the adjusting nut on the *transaxle* side of the pitching stopper and tighten the adjusting nut on the *engine* side until you have moved the nuts

about 3/8-inch (see illustration). On later models with a non-adjustable pitching stopper, remove the rod (see illustrations) and install an engine support in place of the pitching stopper (see illustration). The purpose of repositioning the pitching stopper nuts on older models, or replacing the stopper with the engine support on newer models, is to allow the engine to be tilted backwards slightly, which facilitates removal and installation of the transaxle. You can also achieve

the desired angle by simply removing the stopper and using an extra jack or engine hoist to slightly raise the front of the engine.

10   Remove the starter motor (see Chapter 5).

11   Remove the upper nuts and bolts which attach the transaxle to the engine (see illustrations).

12   Remove the rear crossmember (see illustration).

13   On 4WD vehicles, remove the driveshaft (see Chapter 8).

7A

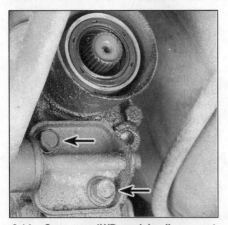

6.14a On newer 4WD models, disconnect the stay rod by removing these two bolts (arrows) . . .

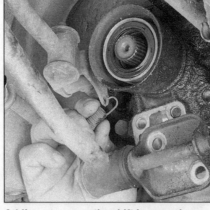

6.14b . . . remove the shift lever spring . . .

6.14c . . . remove this split pin and disconnect the select rod . . .

6.14d . . . and disconnect the shift rod by removing this nut and bolt (2WD models use a similar linkage setup, but have no select rod)

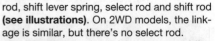

6.16 To remove the front crossmember, remove these nuts and bolts (arrows)

14   On older 4WD vehicles (with shift linkage similar to that shown in **illustration 2.9**), separate the 4WD selector and gearshift system as follows:

a) Remove the parking brake cover and tray.
b) Remove the rod cover.

c) Set the drive selector lever in the 4WD position.
d) Remove the nut connecting rod B to rod A (see illustration 2.9).
e) Separate rod B and the drive selector lever from the plate by removing the nuts.
f) Remove the boot mounting screws.
g) Remove the bolt connecting the gearshift lever to the transaxle lever and pull up on the gearshift lever and the boot.

On newer 4WD models, disconnect the stay

rod, shift lever spring, select rod and shift rod **(see illustrations)**. On 2WD models, the linkage is similar, but there's no select rod.
15   Disconnect the driveaxle assemblies from the transaxle (see Chapter 8).
16   Remove the front crossmember **(see illustration)**.
17   Place a transmission jack or a floor jack under the transaxle **(see illustration)**. As a safety measure, secure the transaxle to the jack head with a tie-down as shown, or a piece of chain or rope.
18   Remove the lower transaxle-to-engine

6.17 Place a transmission jack (shown) or floor jack underneath the transaxle and secure the transaxle to the jack head with a tie-down, or a piece of rope or chain

6.18a To detach the lower left side of the transaxle from the engine, remove this nut (arrow)

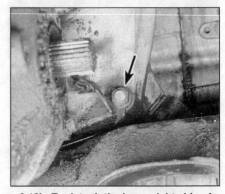

6.18b To detach the lower right side of the transaxle from the engine, remove this nut (arrow)

bolts or nuts **(see illustrations)**.

19   Move the jack to the rear slightly to disengage the transaxle input shaft from the clutch hub, then slowly lower the transaxle assembly.

20   While the transaxle is separated from the engine, inspect the clutch assembly and replace any worn or damaged parts (see Chapter 8).

Installation

21   Support the transaxle on the floor jack then raise it into alignment with the engine. Apply a little multipurpose grease to the input shaft splines.

22   Slowly and carefully slide the transaxle forward and insert the input shaft into the clutch hub. If the input shaft hangs up, rotate the crankshaft or the transaxle output shaft until the input shaft splines are aligned with the clutch hub splines. Shove the transaxle forward until the transaxle and engine are fully engaged, then install the lower transaxle-to-engine mounting bolts or nuts and tighten them to the torque listed in this Chapter's Specifications.

23   Install the front crossmember. Be sure to align the left and right rubber cushion guides for the transaxle mounts with the guides of the crossmember. Holding the crossmember in place, tighten the rubber cushion mounting nuts, then the crossmember-to-body nuts, securely.

24   Remove the jack supporting the transaxle.

25   Reattach the driveaxles (see Chapter 8).

26   Install the shift linkage and tighten all fasteners securely. On 4WD models, use a new split pin to secure the select rod.

27   On 4WD vehicles, install the driveshaft (see Chapter 8).

28   Install the rear crossmember and tighten the fasteners securely.

29   Install the front exhaust pipe assembly

(see Chapter 4).

30   Remove the jackstands and lower the vehicle.

31   Install the starter motor (see Chapter 5).

32   Plug in the electrical connectors for the back-up light switch, the neutral start switch (if applicable) and the oxygen sensor. Reattach all grounds.

33   On models with an adjustable pitching stopper, adjust the stopper as follows:

a) *Loosen the front (engine-side) stopper nut until it turns freely.*

b) *Tighten the rear (transaxle-side) stopper nut until the rubber cushion-to-washer clearance is within the dimension listed in this Chapter's Specifications.*

c) *Hold the rear nut with a backup spanner and tighten the front nut securely.*

On models with a non-adjustable pitching stopper, install the stopper and tighten the bolts and nuts to the torque listed in this Chapter's Specifications.

34   Connect the speedometer cable to the transaxle and tighten it securely with your fingers. Then, using a wrench, turn it another 30 degrees.

35   Connect the clutch cable and adjust the cable freeplay (see Chapter 8).

36   Connect the battery ground cable to the battery.

37   Add fluid to the transaxle by referring to the appropriate Section in Chapter 1.

38   Start the engine and check the exhaust system for any leaks or noise.

39   Check the clutch cable and shift linkage for smooth operation.

40   Install the spare tire support and the spare tire.

7   Manual transmission overhaul - general information

Overhauling a manual transmission is a

difficult job for the do-it-yourselfer. It involves the disassembly and reassembly of many small parts. Numerous clearances must be precisely measured and, if necessary, changed with select fit spacers and snap-rings. If transmission problems arise, you can remove and install the transmission yourself, but overhaul should be left to a transmission repair shop. Rebuilt transmissions may be available - check with your dealer parts department and auto parts stores. At any rate, the time and money involved in an overhaul is almost sure to exceed the cost of a rebuilt unit.

Nevertheless, it's not impossible for an inexperienced mechanic to rebuild a transmission if the special tools are available and the job is done in a deliberate step-by-step manner so nothing is overlooked.

The tools necessary for an overhaul include internal and external snap-ring pliers, a bearing puller, a slide hammer, a set of pin punches, a dial indicator and possibly a hydraulic press. In addition, a large, sturdy workbench and a vise or transmission stand will be required.

During disassembly of the transmission, make careful notes of how each piece comes off, where it fits in relation to other pieces and what holds it in place. Be sure to note how the parts are installed as you remove them; this will make it much easier to get the transmission back together.

Before taking the transmission apart for repair, it will help if you have some idea what area of the transmission is malfunctioning. Certain problems can be closely tied to specific areas in the transmission, which can make component examination and replacement easier. Refer to the *Troubleshooting* section at the front of this manual for information regarding possible sources of trouble.

7A

Notes

Chapter 7 Part B
Automatic transaxle

Contents

Specifications

Pitching stopper cushion-to-washer clearance	0.031 to 0.047 inch (0.8 to 1.2 mm)

Torque specifications

	Ft-lb
Brake band adjusting screw	
Screw	6
Locknut	18 to 21
Torque converter mounting bolts	17 to 19
Transaxle-to-engine nuts/bolts	
Lower transaxle-to-engine nuts	34 to 40
Upper nuts/bolts	34 to 40
Pitching stopper (non-adjustable type)	
Rear (firewall bracket) nut/bolt	27 to 42
Front (engine side) nut/bolt	32 to 40

1 General information

All vehicles covered in this manual are equipped with either a four- or five-speed manual transaxle or a three- or four-speed automatic transaxle. All information on the automatic transaxle is included in this Part of Chapter 7. Information for the manual transaxle can be found in Part A.

Special tools and equipment are needed to service automatic transaxles because of their complexity. This Chapter is restricted to routine maintenance, general diagnosis and transaxle replacement.

If the transaxle requires major repair work, it should be left to a dealer service department or an automotive transaxle repair shop. You can, however, save money by removing and installing the transaxle yourself.

2 Diagnosis - general

Note: *Automatic transaxle malfunctions may be caused by five general conditions: poor engine performance, improper adjustments, hydraulic malfunctions, mechanical malfunctions or computer malfunctions. Diagnosis of these problems should always begin with a check of the easily repaired items: fluid level and condition (Chapter 1), and shift linkage adjustment. Next, perform a road test to*

determine if the problem has been corrected or if more diagnosis is necessary. If the problem persists after the preliminary tests and corrections are completed, additional diagnosis should be done by a dealer service department or transaxle repair shop. Refer to the Troubleshooting Section at the front of this manual for information on symptoms of transaxle problems.

Preliminary checks

1   Drive the vehicle to warm the transaxle to normal operating temperature.
2   Check the fluid level as described in Chapter 1:
  a) If the fluid level is unusually low, add enough fluid to bring the level within the designated area of the dipstick, then check for external leaks (see below).
  b) If the fluid level is abnormally high, drain off the excess, then check the drained fluid for contamination by coolant. The presence of engine coolant in the automatic transaxle fluid indicates that a failure has occurred in the internal radiator walls that separate the coolant from the transaxle fluid (see Chapter 3).
  c) If the fluid is foaming, drain it and refill the transaxle, then check for coolant in the fluid or a high fluid level.
3   Check the engine idle speed. **Note:** *If the engine is malfunctioning, do not proceed with the preliminary checks until it has been repaired and runs normally.*

4   Inspect the shift linkage (see Section 4). Make sure that it's properly adjusted and that the linkage operates smoothly.

Fluid leak diagnosis

5   Most fluid leaks are easy to locate visually. Repair usually consists of replacing a seal or gasket. If a leak is difficult to find, the following procedure may help.
6   Identify the fluid. Make sure it's transaxle fluid and not engine oil or brake fluid (automatic transaxle fluid is a deep red color).
7   Try to pinpoint the source of the leak. Drive the vehicle several miles, then park it over a large sheet of cardboard. After a minute or two, you should be able to locate the leak by determining the source of the fluid dripping onto the cardboard.
8   Make a careful visual inspection of the suspected component and the area immediately around it. Pay particular attention to gasket mating surfaces. A mirror is often helpful for finding leaks in areas that are hard to see.
9   If the leak still cannot be found, clean the suspected area thoroughly with a degreaser or solvent, then dry it.
10   Drive the vehicle for several miles at normal operating temperature and varying speeds. After driving the vehicle, visually inspect the suspected component again.
11   Once the leak has been located, the cause must be determined before it can be

7B

properly repaired. If a gasket is replaced but the sealing flange is bent, the new gasket will not stop the leak. The bent flange must be straightened.

12   Before attempting to repair a leak, check to make sure that the following conditions are corrected or they may cause another leak. **Note:** *Some of the following conditions cannot be fixed without highly specialized tools and expertise. Such problems must be referred to a transaxle repair shop or a dealer service department.*

Gasket leaks

13   Check the pan periodically. Make sure the bolts are tight, no bolts are missing, the gasket is in good condition and the pan is flat (dents in the pan may indicate damage to the valve body inside).

14   If the pan gasket is leaking, the fluid level or the fluid pressure may be too high, the vent may be plugged, the pan bolts may be too tight, the pan sealing flange may be warped, the sealing surface of the transaxle housing may be damaged, the gasket may be damaged or the transaxle casting may be

cracked or porous. If sealant instead of gasket material has been used to form a seal between the pan and the transaxle housing, it may be the wrong sealant.

Seal leaks

15   If a transaxle seal is leaking, the fluid level or pressure may be too high, the vent may be plugged, the seal bore may be damaged, the seal itself may be damaged or improperly installed, the surface of the shaft protruding through the seal may be damaged or a loose bearing may be causing excessive shaft movement.

16   Make sure the dipstick tube seal is in good condition and the tube is properly seated. Periodically check the area around the speedometer gear or sensor for leakage. If transaxle fluid is evident, check the O-ring for damage.

Case leaks

17   If the case itself appears to be leaking, the casting is porous and will have to be repaired or replaced.

18   Make sure the oil cooler hose fittings are tight and in good condition.

Fluid comes out vent pipe or fill tube

19   If this condition occurs, the transaxle is overfilled, there is coolant in the fluid, the case is porous, the dipstick is incorrect, the vent is plugged or the drain back holes are plugged.

---

3   Shift lever - removal and installation

Rod-type

Refer to illustrations 3.1a, 3.1b, 3.1c, 3.2, 3.4 and 3.6

1   Remove the shift lever grip **(see illustrations).**

2   Pry off the trim piece surrounding the gear position indicator panel (see Chapter 11), then remove the gear position indicator panel **(see illustration)**. Unplug the electrical connector for the gear position indicator panel illumination bulb.

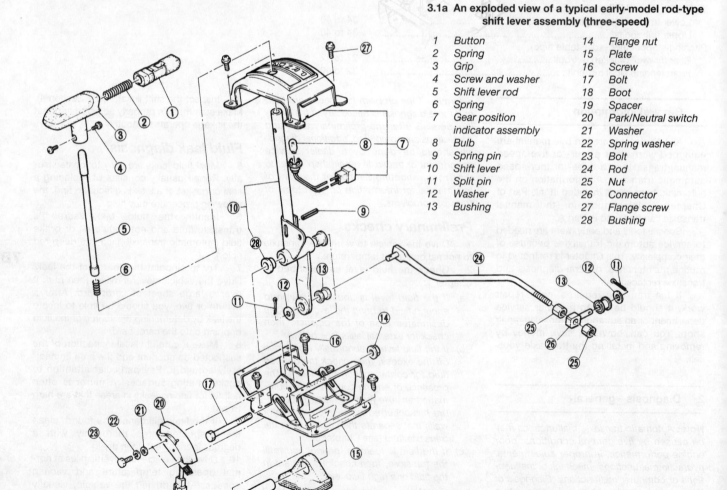

3.1a An exploded view of a typical early-model rod-type shift lever assembly (three-speed)

1	Button	14	Flange nut
2	Spring	15	Plate
3	Grip	16	Screw
4	Screw and washer	17	Bolt
5	Shift lever rod	18	Boot
6	Spring	19	Spacer
7	Gear position indicator assembly	20	Park/Neutral switch
8	Bulb	21	Washer
9	Spring pin	22	Spring washer
10	Shift lever	23	Bolt
11	Split pin	24	Rod
12	Washer	25	Nut
13	Bushing	26	Connector
		27	Flange screw
		28	Bushing

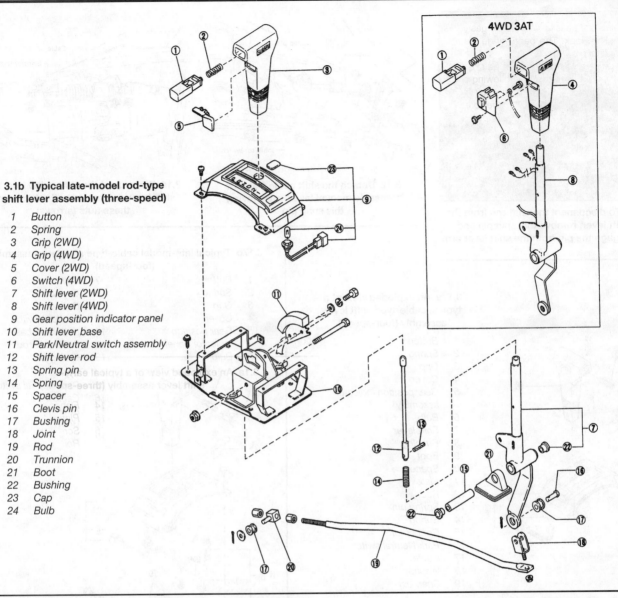

4WD 3AT

3.1b Typical late-model rod-type shift lever assembly (three-speed)

1   Button
2   Spring
3   Grip (2WD)
4   Grip (4WD)
5   Cover (2WD)
6   Switch (4WD)
7   Shift lever (2WD)
8   Shift lever (4WD)
9   Gear position indicator panel
10 Shift lever base
11 Park/Neutral switch assembly
12 Shift lever rod
13 Spring pin
14 Spring
15 Spacer
16 Clevis pin
17 Bushing
18 Joint
19 Rod
20 Trunnion
21 Boot
22 Bushing
23 Cap
24 Bulb

3   Unplug the electrical connector for the Park/Neutral and back-up light switch and remove the switch (see Section 5).

4   Set the shift lever to the Neutral position, then remove the shift lever assembly mounting screws **(see illustration)** and remove the shift lever assembly.

5   Raise the vehicle and place it securely on jackstands.

3.1c To release the grip from the shift lever, remove this screw, pull out the button and the spring, then lift off the grip

3.2 To remove the gear position indicator panel, remove these screws (arrows)

3.4 To detach the shift lever assembly from the floorpan, remove these mounting screws (arrows) (right front screw not visible in this photo)

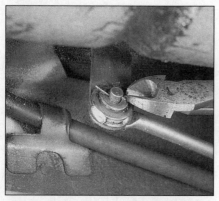

3.6 To disconnect the shift rod from the shift lever, remove this split pin and disengage the pin from the shift lever arm

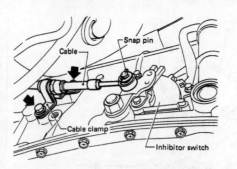

3.12 Detach the shift cable from the transaxle manual lever by removing this snap pin

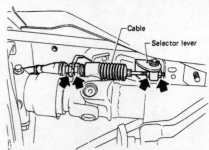

3.14 Disconnect the shift cable from the shift lever and bracket after loosening these nuts (arrows)

3.17b Typical late-model cable-type shift lever assembly (four-speed)

1	Button	7	Shift lever
2	Spring	8	Connector
3	Grip	9	Bulb
4	Cover	10	1st hold switch
5	Gear position	11	Shift lever base
	indicator panel	12	Shift lever rod
6	Bulb	13	Spring pin
		14	Spring
		15	Park/Neutral switch
		16	Cable
		17	Bushing
		18	Boot
		19	Spacer

3.17a An exploded view of a typical cable-type shift lever assembly (four-speed)

1	Button
2	Spring
3	Grip
4	Cover
5	Gear position indicator assembly
6	Bulb
7	Shift lever
8	Bushing
9	Boot
10	Spacer
11	Plate
12	Rod
13	Spring pin
14	Spring
15	Connector
16	Park/Neutral switch
17	Cable
18	Washer
19	Snap pin

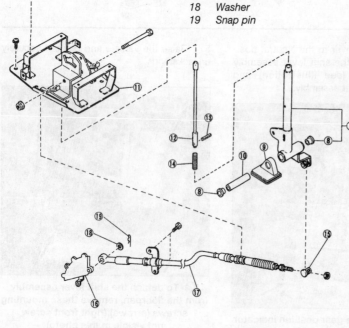

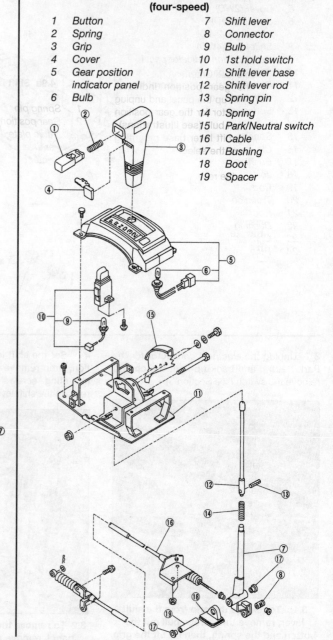

6   Disconnect the shift rod from the shift lever **(see illustration)**.

7   Installation is the reverse of removal.

8   Adjust the shift linkage (see Section 4) and the Park/Neutral and back-up light switch (see Section 5) when you're done.

9   Remove the jackstands and lower the vehicle.

Cable-type

Refer to illustrations 3.12, 3.14, 3.17a and 3.17b

10   Raise the vehicle and place it securely on jackstands.

11   Place the transaxle in Neutral.

12   Disconnect the shift cable from the transaxle lever **(see illustration)**.

13   Detach the cable clamp from the transaxle case.

14   Disconnect the shift cable from the shift lever **(see illustration)**.

15   Remove the mounting nuts and detach the cable assembly from the bracket.

16   Remove the parking brake cover and the center console (see Chapter 11).

17   Remove the gear position indicator retaining screws, lift up the panel and unplug the electrical connector for the gear position indicator illumination bulb **(see illustrations)**.

18   Remove the shift lever base mounting screws and remove the select lever assembly.

19   Installation is the reverse of the removal procedure.

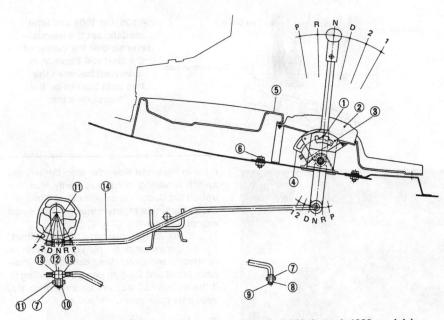

4.9a Shift linkage assembly adjustment details (1979 through 1983 models)

1	Spring pin	8	Washer
2	Gear position indicator	9	Split pin
3	Guide plate	10	Split pin
4	Park/Neutral and back-up light switch	11	Shift lever
5	Center console	12	Trunnion block
6	Shift lever assembly retaining bolt	13	Trunnion block adjusting nuts
7	Bushing	14	Shift rod

4   Shift linkage - check and adjustment

Check

1   As you move the shift lever (inside the vehicle) from the Park to the 1st gear position, you should hear an audible "click" in each gear as the manual valve (in the transaxle) is brought into each detent position. Verify that the shift lever position corresponds to the indicated gear on the gear position indicator, and that it's properly aligned with the corresponding notch in the guide plate, in each gear.

2   Verify that the shift lever cannot be moved from Neutral to Reverse unless the release button in the grip is pushed.

3   Verify that the engine cannot be started in any gear other than Neutral or Park.

4   Verify that the back-up light comes on only in the Reverse position.

5   Verify that the vehicle remains stationary on a slope when the shift lever is in the Park position.

6   If the shift linkage fails any part of this check, adjust it.

Adjustment

1979 through 1983 models

Refer to illustrations 4.9a and 4.9b

7   First, verify that the shift lever cannot be

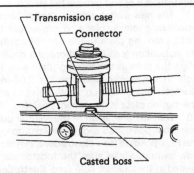

4.9b On 1979 through 1983 models, set the manual lever arm so that the center of the shift rod trunnion is aligned with the cast boss on the transaxle case

moved past the 1st gear position.

8   Raise the vehicle and place it securely on jackstands.

9   Return the shift lever to the Neutral position and adjust the linkage position so that the Neutral position in the guide plate and the detent position of the manual valve inside the transaxle are correctly aligned **(see illustration)**. To set the manual lever (the small shift lever arm at the transaxle end of the shift rod) to the Neutral position, align the arm-to-shift rod trunnion block with the cast boss on the transaxle **(see illustration)**.

10   After adjustment, if the guide plate position doesn't correspond with the indicated gear on the gear position indicator, remove

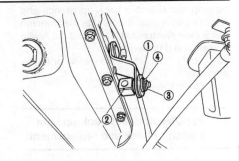

4.13a Shift rod-to-shift lever assembly details (1984 and later models)

1	Bushing	3	Washer
2	Trunnion	4	Split pin

the console (see Chapter 11), loosen the four indicator retaining screws, move the indicator to bring the indicator into alignment with the guide plate, then retighten the screws.

11   Lower the vehicle.

1984 and later models

Refer to illustrations 4.13a, 4.13b and 4.14

12   Raise the vehicle and place it securely on jackstands.

13   Put the shift lever in the Neutral position. Set the manual lever (the small shift lever arm at the transaxle end of the shift rod) to the Neutral position by aligning the arm-to-shift rod trunnion block with the cast bosses on the transaxle **(see illustrations)**.

7B

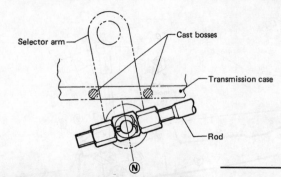

4.13b On 1984 and later models, set the manual lever so that the center of the shift rod trunnion is centered between the two cast bosses on the transaxle case

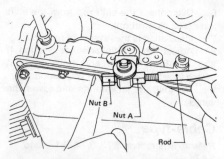

4.14 On 1984 and later models, hold nut B with a back-up wrench and tighten nut A until it lightly contacts the trunnion block; then hold nut A with a back-up wrench and tighten nut B securely

5.5 To adjust the Park/Neutral and back-up light switch, loosen the switch retaining bolts (arrows); to detach the switch from the shift lever assembly, remove the bolts

nuity in Park and Reverse, then tighten the switch retaining bolts and verify that the switch produces no continuity at the indicated terminals in any other gear position except Reverse

7   If the switch operates as described, tighten the switch bolts, plug in the electrical connector and install the gear position indicator panel and the trim panel surrounding it. If the switch still doesn't operate properly, even after adjustment, replace it.

Replacement

Refer to illustrations 5.11, 5.12a and 5.12b

8   Remove the trim piece surrounding the gear position indicator panel and remove the panel **(see illustration 3.2)**, if you haven't already done so.
9   Unplug the electric connector for the switch.
10   Remove the switch retaining bolts **(see illustration 5.5)** and remove the switch.
11   The new switch should already have a positioning pin in place to pre-adjust the switch moving plate to the correct position for installation **(see illustration)**. If it doesn't, align the hole in the moving plate with the hole in the switch and insert a 0.08-inch diameter drill bit through both holes to hold the moving plate in the correct position.
12   With the shift lever in the Neutral position - but positioned slightly forward, toward the Park position **(see illustration)**, install the new switch. Make sure the locator pin is seated in the bracket hole **(see illustration)**. Tighten the switch bolts.

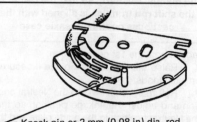

← Knock pin or 2 mm (0.08 in) dia. rod

5.11 The new switch should already have a positioning pin in place to pre-adjust the switch moving plate to the correct position for installation; if not, align the hole in the moving plate with the hole in the switch and insert a 0.08-inch diameter drill bit through both holes to hold the moving plate in the correct position

PIN NO. / CODE / POSITION	2	1	6	5	4	3	10	8	9	7	11
	G	B	YB	YW	YL	Br	GW	BY	BW	GR	G
P	O—O							O—O			
R		O								O	O
N		O			O			O—O			
D		O			O						
3	O—O										
2		O								O	

5.6 To check/adjust the Park/Neutral and back-up light switch, hook up an ohmmeter to the indicated switch connector terminals and move the switch to produce continuity in Park and Reverse, then tighten the switch retaining bolts and verify that the switch produces no continuity at the indicated terminals in any other gear position except Reverse

13   Remove the positioning pin or drill bit.
14   Plug in the switch electrical connector.
15   Install the gear position indicator panel and the trim piece surrounding it.

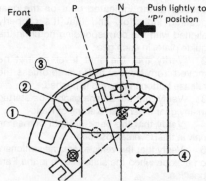

5.12a With the shift lever in the Neutral position - but positioned slightly forward, toward the Park position, install the new switch

1	Locator	3	Spring pin
2	Moving plate		position
	pin	4	Guide plate

14   Adjust the length of the shift rod by holding Nut B with a back-up wrench and turning Nut A until it contacts the trunnion block **(see illustration)**. Then hold nut A with a wrench and tighten nut B.
15   Verify that the shift lever operates smoothly.
16   Lower the vehicle.

5   Park/Neutral and back-up light switch - check and replacement

Check

1   Verify that the engine can only be started in the Park or Neutral position, and that the back-up lights work only when the shift lever is in the Reverse position.
2   If the Park/Neutral and back-up light switch doesn't operate as described, adjust it.

Adjustment

Refer to illustrations 5.5 and 5.6

3   Remove the trim piece surrounding the gear position indicator panel and remove the panel **(see illustration 3.2)**.
4   Unplug the electrical connector for the switch.
5   Loosen the switch retaining bolts **(see illustration)**.
6   Hook up an ohmmeter to the indicated switch connector terminals **(see illustration)** and move the switch until it produces conti-

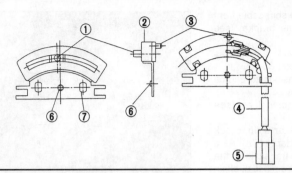

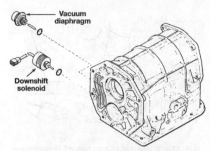

5.12b Make sure the locator pin is seated in the bracket hole

1 Moving plate
2 Case
3 Pin
4 Harness
5 Electrical connector
6 Locator
7 Bolt hole

6.2 The downshift solenoid (arrow) is located on the right side of the transaxle; to replace it, simply unplug the electrical connector and unscrew the solenoid; be sure to install a new O-ring with the new solenoid

6 Downshift switch and solenoid - check and replacement

Refer to illustration 6.2

1 Driving the vehicle, depress the accelerator pedal to the floor and verify that the transaxle downshifts. If it doesn't, check the downshift switch and solenoid.

2 With the vehicle parked inside the garage (it must be quiet for this test), open the hood and locate the downshift solenoid on the side of the transaxle **(see illustration)**. Have a helper turn the ignition switch to the On position and depress the accelerator pedal to the floor while you listen to the solenoid, which should emit an audible "click" when the switch at the accelerator pedal closes the downshift circuit and energizes the solenoid.

3 If you don't hear the solenoid click, either the switch at the pedal, the solenoid on the transaxle, or the circuit, is defective. Using an ohmmeter, verify that the switch and the solenoid both work. If the switch or the solenoid is defective, replace it and retest. If the switch and solenoid are both okay, troubleshoot the circuit for a short or open.

7 Vacuum diaphragm and hose - check and replacement

1 A loose, torn or disconnected vacuum hose will cause a rough idle and abrupt shifting, even under light-load conditions.

2 Locate the vacuum diaphragm on the side of the transaxle **(see illustration 6.2)** and verify that the hose is connected. Inspect the hose and make sure that it's a tight fit and is in good condition.

3 Extremely rough shifting and the emission of white exhaust smoke may indicate a broken vacuum diaphragm.

4 If either of the above conditions occurs, loosen the two bolts securing the vacuum pipe to the governor cover and the engine/transaxle, rotate the vacuum pipe up, disengage the vacuum pipe from the diaphragm bracket, pull the vacuum hose and pipe toward you and drain the remaining ATF.

5 Unscrew the diaphragm assembly and install a new unit. Don't forget to use a new O-ring.

6 Reattach the vacuum hose to the diaphragm and the vacuum pipe to its retaining brackets.

7 Add the type and amount of ATF listed in the Chapter 1 Specifications.

8 Brake band - adjustment

Refer to illustration 8.2

1 Road test the vehicle and note the following:

a) If engine rpm increases significantly when the transaxle shifts up from 2nd to 3rd gear, or there's more than a 0.7 second delay when the transaxle is downshifted from 3rd to 2nd, there's too much clearance between the reverse clutch drum and the brake band. Raise the vehicle and place it securely on jackstands, then tighten the brake band adjusting screw slightly by turning it clockwise (see Step 3). Lower the vehicle and retest.

b) If the transaxle shifts from 1st into 2nd gear with little noticeable "shock," or if you notice a "braking" effect when the transaxle upshifts from 2nd to 3rd, the brake band clearance is too small. Raise the vehicle and place it securely on jackstands, then loosen the brake band adjusting screw slightly by turning it counterclockwise (see Step 3).

c) If the transaxle goes directly from 1st to 3rd during upshifts, or tire slip occurs when shifting up from 2nd to 3rd, go to Step 4.

2 To adjust the brake band, locate the

band adjusting screw on the left side of the transaxle, hold the end of the screw with a wrench and loosen the locknut with a wrench **(see illustration)**. Proceed to Step 3 or 4 as indicated.

3 If one of the problems described in Step 1a or 1b occurred, tighten or loosen the adjusting screw as indicated, in slight increments, retesting after each adjustment. Do NOT exceed 3/4-turn total. **Caution:** *Do NOT loosen the adjusting screw excessively, or the band strut on the servo piston will fall off.*

4 If either of the problems described in Step 1c occurred, tighten the adjusting screw to the torque listed in this Chapter's Specifications, then back it off two turns. Hold the adjusting screw with a wrench and tighten the locknut to the torque listed in this Chapter's Specifications.

9 Automatic transaxle - removal and installation

Removal

Refer to illustrations 9.3, 9.8, 9.18 and 9.20

1 Open the hood and hold it securely in place with the stay. Remove the spare tire and the spare tire support.

2 Disconnect the battery ground cable.

3 The speedometer cable **(see illustration)** is located on top of the transaxle. To disconnect it from the transaxle, simply

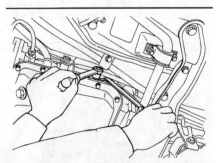

8.2 The band adjustment screw is located on the left side of the transaxle; to loosen the locknut, hold the screw with a wrench and break the nut loose with an offset-head wrench

9.3 To disconnect the speedometer cable housing (arrow), simply unscrew it with a wrench

7B

9.8 Mark the relationship of the torque converter to the driveplate, then remove the four torque converter-to-driveplate bolts (arrow)

unscrew it (see Chapter 7A) and pull it straight up. If the cable is attached to the transaxle by a clip, detach it.

4   Clearly label, then unplug, the electrical connector for the oxygen sensor. On three-speed models, label and unplug the electrical connectors for the transaxle fluid temperature switch, the downshift solenoid valve and, if equipped, the 4WD solenoid valve. On four-speed models, label and unplug the electrical connectors for the transaxle harness, the Park/Neutral and back-up light switch and the vehicle speed sensor.

5   Detach the diaphragm vacuum hose.

6   On earlier models, loosen the adjusting nut on the *transaxle* side of the pitching stopper and tighten the adjusting nut on the *engine* side until you have moved the nuts about 3/8-inch (see Chapter 7A). On later models with a non-adjustable pitching stopper, remove the rod (see Chapter 7A).

7   Remove the starter motor (see Chapter 5).

8   Remove the timing hole plug, mark the relationship of the torque converter to the driveplate and remove the four bolts which attach the torque converter to the driveplate **(see illustration)**.

9   Install an engine support in place of the pitching stopper (see Chapter 7A). The purpose of repositioning the pitching stopper nuts on older models, or replacing the stopper with the engine support on newer models, is to allow the engine to be tilted backwards slightly, which facilitates removal and installation of the transaxle. You can also achieve the desired angle by simply removing the stopper and using an extra jack or engine hoist to slightly raise the front of the engine.

10   Remove the upper nuts and bolts which attach the transaxle to the engine (see Chapter 7A).

11   Raise the vehicle and place it securely on jackstands.

12   Remove the front part of the exhaust system (see Chapter 4). On turbo models, you'll have to remove the throttle cable cover and turbo cover "A" (see Chapter 7A).

13   Remove the rear crossmember (see Chapter 7A).

14   On 4WD vehicles, remove the driveshaft (see Chapter 8).

15   On three-speeds, disconnect the shift rod from the shift lever (see Chapter 7A). On

four-speeds, disconnect the shift cable from the shift lever and from the bracket (see Chapter 7A).

16   Disconnect the driveaxle assemblies from the transaxle (see Chapter 8).

17   Remove the lower transaxle-to-engine bolts or nuts (see Chapter 7A).

18   Disconnect the oil cooler lines **(see illustration)**.

19   Place a transaxle jack or a floor jack under the transaxle (see Chapter 7A). As a safety measure, secure the transaxle to the jack head with a tie-down, or a piece of chain or rope.

20   Remove the rear crossmember **(see illustration)**.

21   Move the jack to the rear slightly to disengage the torque converter from the engine, then slowly lower the transaxle and torque converter assembly.

Installation

22   Support the transaxle on the floor jack then raise it into alignment with the engine.

23   Slowly and carefully slide the transaxle forward until the engine and transaxle are fully engaged, then install the lower transaxle-to-engine mounting nuts and tighten them to the torque listed in this Chapter's Specifications.

24   Install the rear crossmember. Be sure to align the left and right rubber cushion guides for the transaxle mounts with the guides of the crossmember. Holding the crossmember in place, tighten the rubber cushion mounting nuts, then the crossmember-to-body nuts, securely.

25   Remove the jack supporting the transaxle.

26   Reattach the driveaxles (see Chapter 8).

27   Attach the shift rod or cable and tighten all fasteners securely.

28   On 4WD vehicles, install the driveshaft (see Chapter 8).

29   Install the front crossmember and tighten the fasteners securely.

30   Install the front exhaust pipe assembly (see Chapter 4).

31   Remove the jackstands and lower the vehicle.

32   Install the starter motor (see Chapter 5).

33   On three-speeds, plug in the electrical connectors for the oxygen sensor, ATF tem-

9.18 To disconnect the oil cooler lines from the transaxle, unscrew these tube nut fittings (arrow) (other fitting not visible in this photo)

perature switch, downshift solenoid valve, and 4WD solenoid valve; on four-speeds, plug in the connectors for the oxygen sensor, transaxle harness, Park/Neutral and back-up light switch, and vehicle speed sensor. Reattach all ground connections.

34   On models with an adjustable pitching stopper, adjust the stopper as follows:

a) *Loosen the front (engine-side) stopper nut until it turns freely.*

b) *Tighten the rear (transaxle-side) stopper nut until the rubber cushion-to-washer clearance is within the dimension listed in this Chapter's Specifications.*

c) *Hold the rear nut with a backup spanner and tighten the front nut securely.*

On models with a non-adjustable pitching stopper, install the stopper and tighten the bolts and nuts to the torque listed in this Chapter's Specifications.

35   Connect the speedometer cable to the transaxle and tighten it securely with your fingers. Then, using a wrench, turn it another 30 degrees.

36   Connect the ground cable to the battery.

37   Add fluid to the transaxle by referring to the appropriate Section in Chapter 1.

38   Start the engine and check the exhaust system for any leaks or noise.

39   Check the shift rod or cable for smooth operation.

40   Install the spare tire support and the spare tire.

9.20 To detach the rear crossmember from the vehicle floorpan, remove these bolts (arrows)

Chapter 8
Clutch and driveline

Contents

Specifications

Clutch

Clutch cable adjustment	
Clutch pedal freeplay	25/64 to 51/64 inch
Release lever freeplay	
2WD	5/64 to 1/8 inch
4WD	43/64 to 45/64 inch
Release lever full stroke	
2WD	1/8 to 5/32 inch
4WD	1 to 1-1/16 inches

Torque specifications

	Ft-lb
Center bearing retaining bolts	25 to 33
Center bearing flange nut	180 to 220
Clutch pressure plate bolts	132 to 144 in-lbs
Driveshaft-to-pinion flange nuts/bolts	
1984 and earlier	13 to 18
1985 on	17 to 24
Front driveaxle nut	145
Rear differential pinion flange nut	123 to 145
Side-gear bearing retainer bolts	78 to 104 in-lbs

1   General information

The Sections in this Chapter deal with the components from the rear of the engine to the rear wheels (except for the transaxle, which is covered in Chapter 7B) and, on four-wheel drive (4WD) models, to the front wheels. In this Chapter, the components are grouped into three categories: clutch, drive-shaft and driveaxles. Separate Sections in this Chapter cover checks and repair procedures for components in each group.

Since nearly all these procedures involve working under the vehicle, make sure it's safely supported on sturdy jackstands or a hoist where the vehicle can be safely raised and lowered.

2   Clutch - description and check

1   Vehicles with a manual transaxle use a single dry-plate diaphragm spring type clutch. The clutch disc has a splined hub which allows it to slide along the splines of the transaxle input shaft. The clutch and pressure plate are held in contact by spring pressure exerted by the diaphragm in the pressure plate.

2   The clutch release system is cable-operated. The release system consists of the clutch pedal, the clutch cable, a release lever and a release bearing which rides on the transaxle input shaft.

3   When pressure is applied to the clutch pedal, the clutch cable pulls the outer end of the release lever. When the lever pivots at its fulcrum point on a ball stud, the inner end of

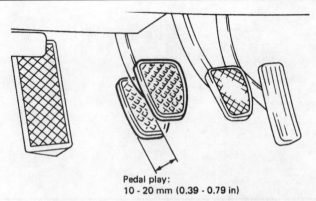

Pedal play:
10 - 20 mm (0.39 - 0.79 in)

3.1 To check clutch cable adjustment, measure clutch pedal freeplay, which is the distance the pedal travels from its fully released (up) position to the point at which you first feel resistance (the point at which the cable begins to pull the clutch release lever)

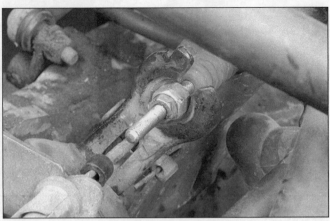

3.2a There are two nuts on the forward end of the clutch cable; the front (smaller) nut is the locknut and the rear (larger) nut is the adjusting nut

the lever pushes against the release bearing, which slides forward on the transaxle input shaft against the diaphragm fingers, releasing the pressure plate from the clutch disc.

4   Terminology can be a problem when discussing the clutch components because common names are in some cases different from those used by the manufacturer. For example, the driven plate is also called the clutch plate or disc, the clutch release bearing is sometimes called a throwout bearing, and so on.

5   Unless you're replacing parts with obvious damage, you can use the following preliminary checks to determine the condition of the clutch components:

a) *First, always check the clutch cable adjustment* (see Section 3).
b) *Check clutch "spin-down time": Run the engine at normal idle speed with the transaxle in Neutral (pedal released, clutch engaged). Disengage the clutch (depress the pedal), wait several seconds and shift the transaxle into Reverse. You should not hear any grinding noises. Assuming the transaxle is in good condition, the most likely cause of a grinding noise is a defective pressure*

plate or clutch disc.
c) *Verify that the clutch is releasing completely: With the parking brake applied to prevent the vehicle from moving, run the engine and hold the clutch pedal about 1/2-inch from the floor. Shift the transaxle between 1st gear and Reverse several times. If the shift is rough, the clutch assembly is defective.*
d) *Visually inspect the pivot bushing at the top of the clutch pedal to make sure there is no binding or excessive play.*

3   Clutch cable - check, adjustment and replacement

Check

Refer to illustration 3.1

1   To check the adjustment of the clutch cable, check clutch pedal freeplay. Push down on the pedal until you feel a slight resistance. This is the point at which the pedal begins to pull on the cable, which in turn pulls on the upper end of the clutch release lever. Measure the distance that the pedal travels, from its fully released position (all the way up), to the point at which you feel resistance **(see illustration)**. Jot down this dimension

and compare it to the pedal freeplay listed in this Chapter's Specifications. If the freeplay isn't with the allowable range, adjust the clutch cable.

Adjustment

Refer to illustrations 3.2a and 3.2b

2   Disengage the release lever return spring from the release lever. There are two nuts on the end of the clutch cable at the release lever **(see illustration)**. Back off the locknut (the smaller nut), then turn the adjusting nut (the nut closer to the release lever) to bring release lever freeplay and full stroke **(see illustration)** within the dimensions listed in this Chapter's Specifications.
3   Tighten the locknut securely.
4   Install the release lever return spring.

Replacement

Refer to illustrations 3.7, 3.8 and 3.9

5   Remove the release lever return spring.
6   Remove both the locknut and the adjusting nut from the end of the clutch cable.
7   Remove the U-clip which attaches the cable to the bracket **(see illustration)**.
8   Detach the cable from the release lever **(see illustration)**.
9   Working inside the vehicle, locate the

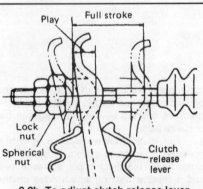

Full stroke

Play

Lock nut

Spherical nut

Clutch release lever

3.2b To adjust clutch release lever freeplay and stroke, back off the locknut, then turn the adjusting nut to produce the lever freeplay and full stroke dimensions listed in this Chapter's Specifications

3.7 Remove this U-clip with a pair of pliers, . . .

3.8 . . . then detach the clutch cable from its bracket

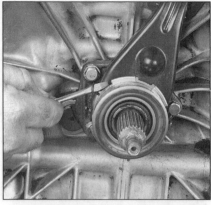

4.2a Disengage the retaining clips from the release bearing . . .

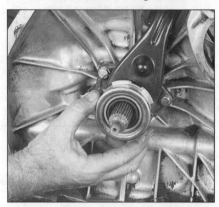

4.2b . . . and slide the release bearing off the input shaft; note which end of the bearing faces toward the clutch pressure plate diaphragm fingers - this is the bearing surface, and the bearing must be installed this way

To clutch release fork

SUBARU 1800

SUBARU 1600

Brake booster (Master-Vac)

Clutch pedal

*Apply grease

Release fork

Stroke

3.9 Typical clutch cable installation details

1 Lock nut
2 Adjusting nut
3 Clutch cable
4 U-clip

other end of the clutch cable at the top of the clutch pedal **(see illustration)**.
10   Remove the cotter pin from the clevis pin connected to the clutch pedal.
11   Pull the cable, from the engine compartment side, through the rubber grommet in the firewall.
12   Install the new cable by inserting the correct end through the grommet and into the passenger compartment. Be sure to route the cable correctly, so that there are no sharp bends or kinks.
13   Lightly grease the clevis pin, then attach the cable to the clutch pedal with the clevis pin and secure it with the cotter pin (use a new cotter if the old one is deformed or weak).
14   Lightly grease the cable "pocket" on the

end of the release lever, then attach the cable to the release lever with the adjusting nut, adjust the lever freeplay (see Step 2), then tighten the locknut securely.
15   Install the release lever return spring.

4   Clutch release bearing - removal, inspection and installation

Removal

Refer to illustrations 4.2a, 4.2b, 4.3a and 4.3b
1   Remove the transaxle (see Chapter 7A).
2   Remove the release bearing retaining clips (or springs) from the bearing and remove the bearing from the input shaft **(see illustrations)**.
3   Pry off the release lever from the ball stud and remove the lever and the rubber

sealing boot from the transaxle **(see illustrations)**.

Inspection

Refer to illustration 4.4
4   Hold the bearing and rotate the outer portion while applying pressure. If the bearing

4.4 To check the release bearing, hold it one hand and turn it with the other, pushing on it at the same time; the bearing should rotate smoothly and quietly; if it's rough or noisy, replace it

8

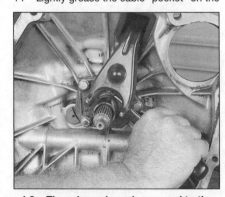

4.3a The release lever is secured to the ball stud by a wire retainer spring on the backside of the lever; to disengage the lever from the ball stud, insert a screwdriver behind the lever and carefully but firmly pry it off . . .

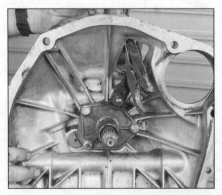

4.3b . . . then pull the release lever and the old rubber dust boot out through the hole in the bellhousing

4.6a Lubricate the bearing surface of the bearing holder (arrow) and the end of the ballstud (arrow) with high-temperature grease

4.6b Lubricate the lever-to-bearing contact points of the two release lever fingers . . .

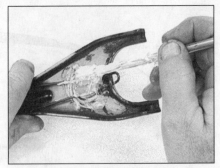

4.6c . . . then turn over the lever and lubricate the pocket for the ball stud and the retainer spring

doesn't turn smoothly or if it's noisy, replace it. Wipe the bearing with a clean shop rag and inspect it for cracks, wear and other damage. Do NOT immerse the bearing in solvent; it a sealed unit, so putting it into solvent will ruin it **(see illustration).**

Installation

Refer to illustrations 4.6a, 4.6b, 4.6c, 4.7a and 4.7b

5   Replace the release bearing retaining clips, or the release bearing/ballstud retainer spring, if they're deformed or weak

6   Apply a light coat of grease to the bearing surface of the release bearing holder and the input shaft splines **(see illustration)**, and to the contact surfaces of the release lever

(see illustrations).

7   Installation is essentially the reverse of removal **(see illustrations)**. Make sure the release lever is properly positioned on the ball stud, then push it firmly until the ball stud pops into place between the two sides of the retainer spring.

8   Install the release bearing and secure it with the retaining clips.

9   Install the transaxle (see Chapter 7A).

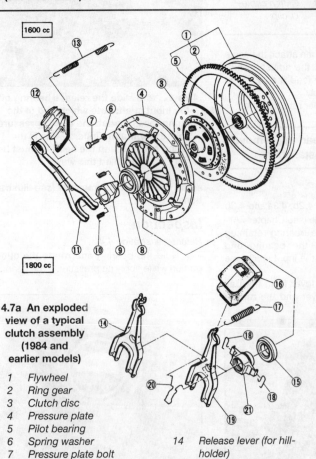

4.7a An exploded view of a typical clutch assembly (1984 and earlier models)

1   Flywheel
2   Ring gear
3   Clutch disc
4   Pressure plate
5   Pilot bearing
6   Spring washer
7   Pressure plate bolt
8   Release bearing
9   Release bearing holder
10   Spring
11   Release lever
12   Release lever dust boot
13   Spring

14   Release lever (for hill-holder)
15   Release bearing
16   Release lever dust boot
17   Release lever return spring
18   Retaining clip
19   Release fork
20   Retainer spring
21   Release bearing holder

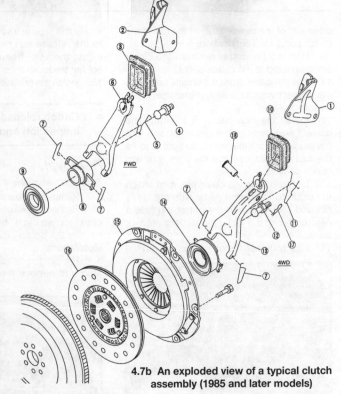

4.7b An exploded view of a typical clutch assembly (1985 and later models)

1   Clutch cable bracket
2   Clutch cable bracket
3   Clutch release lever dust boot
4   Ball stud (lever fulcrum)
5   Retainer spring
6   Clutch release lever
7   Clip
8   Release bearing holder
9   Release bearing
10   Release lever dust boot

11   Retainer spring
12   Ball stud (lever fulcrum)
13   Clutch release lever
14   Clutch release bearing assembly (no separate bearing holder on this type)
15   Clutch pressure plate
16   Clutch disc
17   Cotter pin
18   Clevis pin

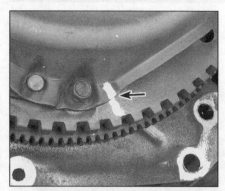

5.4 If you're planning to re-use the same pressure plate, mark its relationship to the flywheel (arrow)

5.7 Inspect the surface of the flywheel for cracks, dark-colored areas (signs of overheating) and other obvious defects; resurfacing will correct minor defects (the surface of this flywheel is in fairly good condition, but resurfacing is always a good idea)

5.5a Jam a large screwdriver between the flywheel ring gear and the flywheel housing to lock the flywheel while you break loose the six clutch pressure plate bolts (arrows)

5.9 Inspect the clutch plate lining, springs, and splines (arrows) for wear

5.5b If you don't have a helper, use a clutch alignment tool to support the pressure plate so it doesn't fall off when the bolts are removed; you'll also need this tool to center the clutch disc during installation

5   Clutch components - removal and installation

Warning: *Dust produced by clutch wear and deposited on clutch components may contain asbestos, which is hazardous to your health. DO NOT blow it out with compressed air and DO NOT inhale it. DO NOT use gasoline or petroleum-based solvents to remove the dust. Brake system cleaner should be used to flush the dust into a drain pan. After the clutch components are wiped clean with a rag, dispose of the contaminated rags and cleaner in a covered, marked container.*

Removal

Refer to illustrations 5.4, 5.5a and 5.5b
1   Access to the clutch components is normally accomplished by removing the transaxle, leaving the engine in the vehicle. However, if the engine is being removed for major overhaul, then check the clutch for wear and replace worn components as necessary. The relatively low cost of the clutch components compared to the time and trou-

ble spent gaining access to them warrants their replacement anytime the engine or transaxle is removed, unless they are new or in near-perfect condition. The following procedures are based on the assumption the engine will stay in place.
2   Disconnect the clutch cable from the release lever (see Section 3).
3   Remove the transaxle (see Chapter 7A). Support the engine while the transaxle is out. An engine hoist should be used to support it from above. If you use a jack underneath the engine instead, make sure a piece of wood is positioned between the jack and oil pan to spread the load. **Caution:** *The pick-up for the oil pump is very close to the bottom of the oil pan. If the pan is bent or distorted in any way, engine oil starvation could occur.*
4   Carefully inspect the flywheel and pressure plate for indexing marks. The marks are usually an X, an O or a white letter. If they cannot be found, paint a mark so the pressure plate and the flywheel will be in the same alignment during installation **(see illustration).**
5   Using a screwdriver jammed between the ring gear and the clutch housing **(see**

illustration), loosen the pressure plate-to-flywheel bolts in 1/4-turn increments until they can be removed by hand. Work in a criss-cross pattern until all spring pressure is relieved, then hold the pressure plate securely and completely remove the bolts, followed by the pressure plate and clutch disc. If you don't have someone to hold the clutch pressure plate and disc while you're loosening the bolts, use an alignment tool to support them **(see illustrations).**

Inspection

Refer to illustrations 5.7, 5.9, 5.11a and 5.11b
6   Ordinarily, when a clutch problem occurs, it's caused by clutch disc wear. Nevertheless, it's a good idea to inspect all clutch components at this time. If the clutch components are contaminated with oil, there will be shiny, black glazed spots on the clutch disc lining, which will cause the clutch to slip. Replacing clutch components won't completely solve the problem - be sure to check the crankshaft rear oil seal and the transaxle input shaft seal for leaks. If it looks like a seal is leaking, be sure to install a new one to avoid the same problem with the new clutch.
7   Check the flywheel for cracks, heat checking, grooves and other obvious defects **(see illustration).** If the imperfections are slight, a machine shop can machine the surface flat and smooth, which is highly recommended regardless of the surface appearance. Refer to Chapter 2, Part A, for the flywheel removal and installation procedure.
8   Inspect the pilot bearing (see Section 6).
9   Check the lining on the clutch disc. There should be at least 1/16-inch of lining above the rivet heads. Check for loose rivets, distortion, cracks, broken springs and other obvious damage **(see illustration).** As mentioned above, ordinarily the clutch disc is routinely replaced, so if you're in doubt about its condition, replace it.
10   The release bearing should also be

8

NORMAL FINGER WEAR

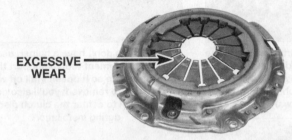

EXCESSIVE —
WEAR

EXCESSIVE FINGER WEAR

BROKEN OR BENT FINGERS

5.11a Replace the pressure plate if excessive wear is noted

5.11b Examine the pressure plate friction surface for score marks, cracks and evidence of overheating

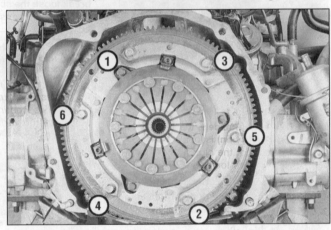

5.15 Tighten the clutch pressure plate bolts in a criss-cross pattern as shown, gradually and evenly tightening them to the torque listed in this Chapter's Specifications

replaced along with the clutch disc (see Section 4).

11   Check the machined surfaces and the diaphragm spring fingers of the pressure plate **(see illustrations)**. If the surface is grooved or otherwise damaged, replace the pressure plate. Also check for obvious damage, distortion, cracks, etc. Light glazing can be removed with medium-grit emery cloth. If a new pressure plate is required, new and factory-rebuilt units are available.

Installation

Refer to illustration 5.15

12   Before installation, clean the machined surfaces of the flywheel and pressure plate with lacquer thinner or acetone. It's vital that these surfaces and the clutch disc lining be free of all grease and oil. Be sure to wash your hands before handling these parts.

13   Position the clutch disc and pressure plate against the flywheel with the clutch held in place with an alignment tool **(see illustration 5.5b)**. Make sure the clutch disc is correctly installed (most replacement clutch plates will be marked "flywheel side" or something similar.

14   Tighten the pressure plate-to-flywheel bolts only finger-tight, working around the pressure plate.

15   Center the clutch disc by ensuring the alignment tool extends through the splined hub and into the pilot bearing in the crankshaft. Wiggle the tool up, down or from side-to-side as needed to bottom the tool in the pilot bearing. Working in a criss-cross pattern **(see illustration)**, tighten the pressure plate-to-flywheel bolts a little at a time, to prevent distorting the cover. After all the bolts are snug, tighten them to the torque listed in this Chapter's Specifications. Remove the alignment tool.

16   Lubricate the friction surfaces and contact points of the release lever and release bearing and install them, if removed (see Section 4).

17   Install the transaxle (see Chapter 7A).

6   Pilot bearing - inspection and replacement

Refer to illustrations 6.5, 6.9 and 6.10

1   The clutch pilot bearing is a needle roller

type bearing which is pressed into the rear of the crankshaft. It's greased at the factory and does not require additional lubrication. Its primary purpose is to support the front of the transaxle input shaft. The pilot bearing should be inspected whenever the clutch components are removed from the engine, and replaced, if you have any doubt about its condition. **Note:** *If the engine has been removed from the vehicle, disregard the following Steps which don't apply.*

2   Remove the transaxle (see Chapter 7A).

3   Remove the clutch components (see Section 5).

4   Using a flashlight, inspect the bearing for excessive wear, scoring, dryness, roughness and any other obvious damage. If any of these conditions are noted, replace the bearing.

5   Removal can be accomplished with a special puller available at most auto parts stores **(see illustration)**, but an alternative method also works very well.

6   Find a solid steel bar which is slightly smaller in diameter than the bearing. Alternatives to a solid bar would be a wood dowel or a socket with a bolt fixed in place to make it solid.

7   Check the bar for fit - it should just slip into the bearing with very little clearance.

8   Pack the bearing and the area behind it (in the crankshaft recess) with heavy grease. Pack it tightly to eliminate as much air as possible.

9   Insert the bar into the bearing bore and strike the bar sharply with a hammer, which will force the grease to the back side of the bearing and push it out **(see illustration)**. Remove the bearing and clean all grease from the crankshaft recess.

10   To install the new bearing, lightly lubricate the outside surface with grease, then drive it into the recess with a soft-face hammer **(see illustration)**. Some bearings have an O-ring seal, which must face out.

11   Install the clutch components, transaxle and all other components removed previously. Tighten all fasteners to the recommended torque.

---

7   Neutral start switch - check and replacement

Check

Refer to illustration 7.1

1   On carbureted models, the neutral start switch **(see illustration)** is located under the dash, at the top of the clutch pedal (you'll need a flashlight to locate it). Remove the lower trim panel from the dash to provide more room to work (see Chapter 11).

2   On fuel-injected models, the neutral start switch is located on the left side of the transaxle, right behind the back-up light switch (Chapter 7A). If the vehicle is equipped with air suspension, make sure that the vehicle is in the normal (low) position, the height control switch is turned off, and the battery ground cable is disconnected. Raise the vehicle and place it securely on jackstands.

3   Unplug the electrical connector for the

6.5 One way to remove the pilot bearing is with a special puller designed for the job

neutral start switch, hook up an ohmmeter to the switch connector terminals, then test the switch as follows:

a) *If the switch is at the clutch pedal, depress the clutch pedal and verify that there is continuity, then release the pedal and verify that there's no continuity.*

b) *If the switch is on the transaxle, put the transaxle in Neutral and verify that there is continuity, then put the transaxle in gear and verify that there's no continuity.*

4   If the switch doesn't operate as described, replace it.

Replacement

5   Unplug the electrical connector from the switch.

6   If the switch is at the clutch pedal, remove the adjustment nut on the underside of the pedal bracket (the nut that's NOT next to the switch) and pull the switch out of the

6.9 You can also remove the pilot bearing by packing the recess behind the bearing with heavy grease and forcing it out hydraulically with a steel rod slightly smaller than the bore in the bearing - when the hammer strikes the rod, the bearing will pop out of the crankshaft

clutch pedal bracket. Note the position of the upper adjustment nut (the one next to the switch) on the old switch, turn the upper nut to the same position on the threaded barrel of the new switch, insert the switch barrel through the pedal bracket, install the lower adjustment nut and adjust the switch with an ohmmeter by verifying that it's open when the pedal is released and closed when the pedal is depressed. When the switch is satisfactorily adjusted, tighten the lower nut securely.

7   If the switch is on the transaxle, simply unscrew the old switch and screw in the new one. Don't forget to install the washer. Tighten the switch to the torque listed in this Chapter's Specifications.

8   Plug in the electrical connector.

9   Install the under-dash trim panel, if you removed it.

10   Lower the vehicle, if you raised it.

6.10 Tap the bearing into place with a bushing driver or a socket slightly smaller than the outside diameter of the bearing

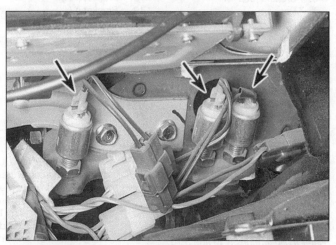

7.1 On carbureted models, the neutral start switch (left arrow), which is located above the clutch pedal, is attached to the pedal bracket by a couple of adjusting nuts; the two switches on the right (arrows) are the brake light and cruise control switches

8

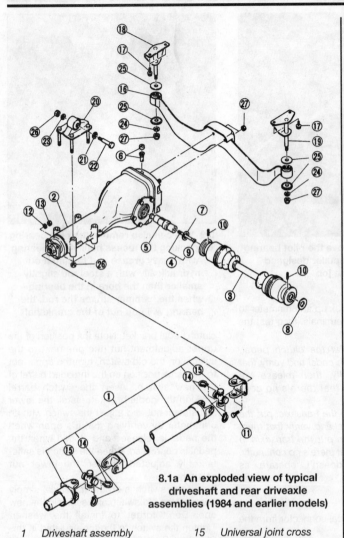

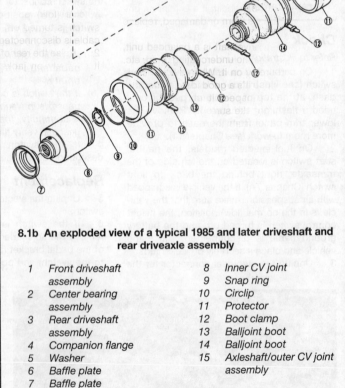

8.1a An exploded view of typical driveshaft and rear driveaxle assemblies (1984 and earlier models)

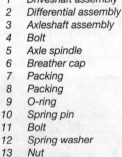

1	Driveshaft assembly	15	Universal joint cross
2	Differential assembly		assembly
3	Axleshaft assembly	16	Differential mount
4	Bolt		assembly
5	Axle spindle	17	Bolt
6	Breather cap	18	Bracket (RH)
7	Packing	19	Bracket (LH)
8	Packing	20	Bracket assembly
9	O-ring	21	Washer
10	Spring pin	22	Differential mount bolt
11	Bolt	23	Washer
12	Spring washer	24	Washer
13	Nut	25	Stopper
14	Snap-ring	26	Locknut
		27	Locknut

8.1b An exploded view of a typical 1985 and later driveshaft and rear driveaxle assembly

1	Front driveshaft	8	Inner CV joint
	assembly	9	Snap ring
2	Center bearing	10	Circlip
	assembly	11	Protector
3	Rear driveshaft	12	Boot clamp
	assembly	13	Balljoint boot
4	Companion flange	14	Balljoint boot
5	Washer	15	Axleshaft/outer CV joint
6	Baffle plate		assembly
7	Baffle plate		

8   Driveshafts, universal joints and driveaxles - general information

Driveshafts and universal joints

Refer to illustrations 8.1a and 8.1b

1   The driveshaft **(see illustrations)** is a tube, or pair of tubes, that transmits power between the transaxle/transfer case assembly and the rear differential. Universal joints are located at either end of the driveshaft; on 1985 and later models with a two-piece driveshaft, a third U-joint is installed right behind the center bearing.

2   The driveshaft employs a splined sleeve yoke at the front end, which slips into the extension housing. This arrangement allows the driveshaft to slide back-and-forth within the extension housing during vehicle operation. An oil seal prevents fluid from leaking out of the extension housing and keeps dirt from entering the transaxle. If leakage is evident at the front of the driveshaft, replace the oil seal (see Chapter 7A).

3   The rear end of the driveshaft is bolted to the differential pinion flange.

4   A center bearing supports the two-piece driveshaft used on 1985 and later models. The center bearing is a ball-type bearing mounted in a rubber cushion attached to the vehicle pan. The bearing is pre-lubricated and sealed at the factory.

5   The driveshaft assembly requires very little service. The universal joints are lubricated for life and must be replaced if problems develop. The driveshaft must be removed from the vehicle for this procedure.

10.2 Before disconnecting the driveshaft from the differential, be sure to mark the relationship of the rear U-joint yoke to the differential pinion flange

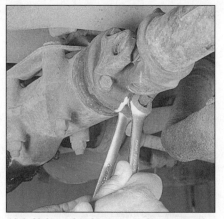

10.3 Using a back-up wrench, remove the four yoke-to-flange nuts and bolts

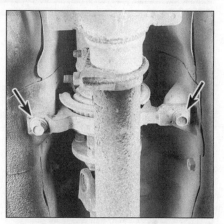

10.4 On 1985 and later models, remove the center bearing retaining bolts (arrows)

On 1984 and earlier models, the U-joints can be overhauled. On 1985 and later models, the U-joints cannot be rebuilt; if a U-joint on one of these models is worn or damaged, replace the driveshaft.

6   Since the driveshaft is a balanced unit, it's important that no undercoating, mud, etc. be allowed to stay on it. When the vehicle is raised for service it's a good idea to clean the driveshaft and inspect it for any obvious damage. Also, make sure the small weights used to originally balance the driveshaft are in place and securely attached. Whenever the driveshaft is removed it must be reinstalled in the same relative position to preserve the balance.

7   Problems with the driveshaft are usually indicated by a noise or vibration while driving the vehicle. A road test should verify if the problem is the driveshaft or another vehicle component. Refer to the *Troubleshooting* Section at the front of this manual. If you suspect trouble, inspect the driveline (see the next Section).

Driveaxles

8   All models are equipped with a pair of front driveaxles; 4WD models also have two rear driveaxles. The front and rear driveaxle assemblies are identical in design. All driveaxles consist of an inner and outer ball-and-cage type CV joint connected by an axleshaft. On 1984 and earlier models, the inner and outer CV joints are both rebuild-able. On 1985 and later models, the inner CV joint can be rebuilt, but the axleshaft and outer CV joint are a single assembly and cannot be disassembled; they can, however, be cleaned and inspected, and the boots can be replaced. Before you can service the front driveaxle CV joints and/or boots, however, the outer end of the driveaxle must be separated from the steering knuckle/hub assembly by an automotive machine shop; it's pressed into the hub and cannot be separated at home unless you have a hydraulic press and the appropriate adapters.

9   Driveline inspection

1   If the vehicle is equipped with air suspension, make sure that the vehicle is in the normal (low) position, the height control switch is turned off, and the battery ground cable is disconnected.

2   Raise the rear of the vehicle and support it securely on jackstands. Block the front wheels to keep the vehicle from rolling off the stands.

3   Crawl under the vehicle and visually inspect the driveshaft. Look for any dents or cracks in the tubing. If any are found, the driveshaft must be replaced.

4   Check for oil leakage at the front and rear of the driveshaft. Leakage where the driveshaft enters the transaxle indicates a defective transaxle/transfer case seal (see Chapter 7A). Leakage where the driveshaft joins the differential indicates a defective pinion seal (see Section 13).

5   While under the vehicle, have an assistant rotate a rear wheel so the driveshaft will rotate. As it does, make sure the universal joints are operating properly without binding, noise or looseness. Listen for any noise from the center bearing (if equipped), indicating it's worn or damaged. Also check the rubber portion of the center bearing for cracking or separation, which will necessitate replacement.

6   The universal joint can also be checked with the driveshaft motionless, by gripping your hands on either side of the joint and attempting to twist the joint. Any movement at all in the joint is a sign of considerable wear. Lifting up on the shaft will also indicate movement in the universal joints.

7   Check all driveshaft U-joint mounting bolts; make sure they're tight.

8   Finally, check for looseness in the CV joints of the front and rear driveaxles. Also check for grease or oil leakage from around the driveaxles by inspecting the rubber boots and both ends of each axle. Leakage at the wheel end of a driveaxle indicates a torn or damaged rubber boot (see Section 14 or 15). (If the tear is serious, the surface of the wheel

housing will be splattered with oil.) Oil leakage at the differential end of a driveaxle could also indicate a damaged boot (again, look for signs of oil being thrown onto the surrounding components), or it could indicate a defective side gear oil seal. The rear differential side gear seals can be replaced at home (see Section 16); the front side gear seals must be replaced by a professional.

10   Driveshaft (4WD models) - removal and installation

Removal

Refer to illustrations 10.2, 10.3 and 10.4

1   If the vehicle is equipped with air suspension, make sure that the vehicle is in the normal (low) position, the height control switch is turned off, and the battery ground cable is disconnected. Raise the vehicle and place it securely on jackstands.

2   Place match marks on the rear U-joint yoke and the differential pinion flange **(see illustration)**.

3   Remove the bolts and nuts which attach the yoke to the pinion flange **(see illustration)**.

4   On 1985 and later models, remove the center bearing retaining bolts **(see illustration)**.

5   Pull the sleeve yoke out of the extension housing and remove the driveshaft. Plug the extension housing to prevent transaxle lubricant from leaking out.

6   If you're replacing the universal joints on a 1984 and earlier model, refer to Section 11. If you're replacing the center bearing on a 1985 or later model, refer to Section 12.

Installation

7   Lubricate the sleeve yoke splines, then remove the extension housing plug and carefully insert the sleeve yoke into the extension housing. Make sure you don't damage the extension housing seal or the splines of the transaxle output shaft.

8   On 1984 and later models, raise the

8

11.2 Use needle-nose pliers to remove the U-joint snap rings

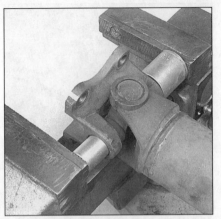

11.4 To press the U-joint out of the driveshaft yoke, set it up in a vise with the small socket pushing the joint and bearing cap into the large socket

11.8 If a snap ring won't seat in its groove, strike the yoke with a brass hammer - this will slightly spring the yoke ears and relieve tension in the yoke (this is also a good method for relieving tension if the joint feels tight when assembled)

center bearing into place, install the center bearing retaining bolts and tighten them to the torque listed in this Chapter's Specifications.

9   Align the match marks you made on the rear U-joint yoke and the pinion flange, connect the yoke to the flange with the nuts and bolts and tighten them to the torque listed in this Chapter's Specifications.

10   Remove the jackstands and lower the vehicle.

11   Universal joints (4WD) - replacement

Refer to illustrations 11.2, 11.4 and 11.8

Note: *This procedure applies to 1984 and earlier models; the U-joints on later models are not rebuildable.*

1   Remove the driveshaft (see Section 10).

2   Clean away all dirt from the ends of the bearings on the yokes so the snap-rings can be removed with a pair of long-nose pliers or a screwdriver **(see illustration)**.

3   Supporting the driveshaft, place it in a

bench vise.

4   Place a piece of pipe or a large socket with the same inside diameter over one end of the bearing caps. Position a socket of slightly smaller diameter than the cap on the opposite bearing cap **(see illustration)** and use the vise or press to force the cap out (inside the pipe or large socket, stopping just before it comes completely out of the yoke. Use the vise or large pliers to work the cap the rest of the way out.

5   Transfer the sockets to the other side and press the opposite bearing cap out in the same manner.

6   Pack the new U-joint bearings with grease. Ordinarily, specific instructions for lubrication will be included with the U-joint servicing kit and should be followed carefully.

7   Position the spider into the bearing cap, then partially install the other cap. Align the spider and press the bearing caps into position, being careful not to damage the dust seals.

8   Install the snap rings. If the snap rings are difficult to seat, strike the driveshaft yoke sharply with a hammer **(see illustration)**. This

will spring the yoke ears slightly, allowing the snap rings to seat in their grooves.

9   Install the grease fitting and fill the joint with grease. Be careful not to overfill the joint, as this could blow out the grease seals.

10   Install the driveshaft, tightening the companion flange bolts to the torque listed in this Chapter's Specifications.

12   Center bearing - replacement

Refer to illustrations 12.3, 12.4, 12.5, 12.6 and 12.7

1   Remove the driveshaft assembly (see Section 10).

2   Put the driveshaft assembly in a bench vise.

3   Mark the relationship of the center U-joint to the front driveshaft flange, then unbolt the U-joint from the flange **(see illustration)** and remove the rear driveshaft.

4   Mark the relationship of the flange to the

12.3 Mark the relationship of the center U-joint to the front driveshaft flange, then remove the nuts and bolts that attach the U-joint to the flange

12.4 Mark the relationship of the flange to the front driveshaft, then unstake the nut and remove it

12.5 Remove the flange with a puller (if you don't have a suitable puller, have it pressed off at an automotive machine shop)

12.6 To separate the front driveshaft from the center bearing, lightly tap the threaded nose with a brass hammer, then remove the flange and the large washer behind it (be sure to hold the front driveshaft with one hand while striking it so that it doesn't fall on the floor when it breaks free)

front driveshaft, then unstake the nut **(see illustration)** and remove it.

5   Remove the flange with a puller **(see illustration)**, or have it pressed off at an automotive machine shop.

6   To separate the front driveshaft from the center bearing, lightly tap the threaded nose with a brass hammer **(see illustration)**. Remove the flange and the washer.

7   Inspect the center bearing. Make sure it rotates smoothly and quietly **(see illustration)**. If you detect any sign of roughness, noise or excessive play, replace the center bearing.

8   Install the center bearing on the front

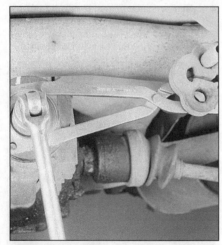

13.4 Holding the flange with a suitable tool (such as this pin spanner braced by an exhaust hanger bracket), remove the retaining nut (if you don't have a pin spanner, try a pair of large water pump pliers or a plumber's wrench)

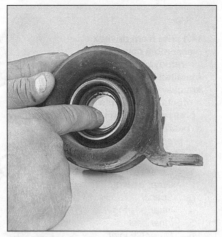

12.7 Make sure the center bearing rotates smoothly and quietly; if it doesn't, replace it

driveshaft. If you have trouble getting the center bearing onto the front driveshaft, take the front driveshaft and center bearing to an automotive machine shop and have the center bearing installed.

9   Coat both sides of the large washer with moly grease, then install the washer and the flange. Make sure the marks you made on the flange and the front driveshaft are aligned. Tighten the flange nut to the torque listed in this Chapter's Specifications, then stake it with a hammer and punch. Again, if the flange is difficult to install, take the front driveshaft and flange to an automotive machine shop and have the flange installed.

10   Make sure the marks you made on the flange and the U-joint are aligned, then attach the rear driveshaft. Tighten the U-joint-to-flange bolts and nuts to the torque listed in this Chapter's Specifications.

11   Install the driveshaft assembly (see Section 10).

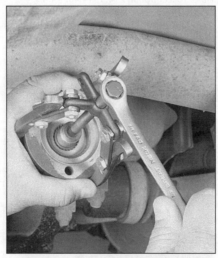

13.5 Sometimes, you can remove the pinion flange by simply pulling it off; if not, use a smaller puller

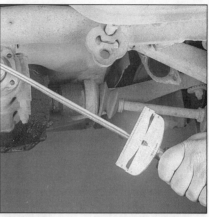

13.3 Using an inch-pound torque wrench, measure the turning torque of the pinion flange, jot down this number and save it for reassembly; if you don't have an inch-pound torque wrench, mark the relationship of the flange nut to the pinion shaft

13 Rear differential pinion gear seal - replacement

Refer to illustrations 13.3, 13.4, 13.5, 13.6 and 13.7

1   If the vehicle is equipped with air suspension, make sure that the vehicle is in the normal (low) position, the height control switch is turned off, and the battery ground cable is disconnected. Raise the vehicle and place it securely on jackstands.

2   Remove the driveshaft (see Section 10).

3   Using an inch-pound torque wrench, measure the turning torque of the pinion flange **(see illustration)**. Jot down this figure and save it for reassembly. If you don't have an inch-pound torque wrench, mark the relationship of the flange nut to the shaft.

4   Holding the flange with a suitable tool, remove the retaining nut **(see illustration)**.

5   Remove the pinion flange; use a puller if necessary **(see illustration)**.

6   Remove the old seal **(see illustration)**.

8

13.6 Remove the old seal with a seal removal tool (shown) or with a large screwdriver

13.7 Install the new seal with a large socket; make sure the seal is square to the bore, then carefully tap it into place until it's fully seated

14.1 The front driveaxle assembly cannot be removed from or installed in the steering knuckle without special tools because it's pressed into a pair of bearings which are pressed into the steering knuckle

1 Outer seal
2 Outer bearing
3 Spacer
4 Inner bearing
5 Inner seal
6 Outer CV joint

7   Install a new seal **(see illustration)**.
8   Installation is the reverse of removal. Gradually tighten the pinion flange retaining

14.4a To remove the hub, remove the cotter pin from the castellated nut . . .

nut to the minimum torque listed in this Chapter's Specifications; as you're tightening the nut, use the figure you recorded prior to disassembly to periodically check the pinion flange turning torque. By the time the retaining nut's minimum specified torque is reached, the turning torque of the pinion flange should be the same as it was before disassembly. When this figure is attained, add another five inch-pounds of turning torque.
9   Install the driveshaft (see Section 10).
10   Lower the vehicle.

14   Driveaxles - removal and installation

Front driveaxle

Refer to illustrations 14.1, 14.4a, 14.4b, 14.4c, 14.4d, 14.7 and 14.8
1   The outer ends of the front driveaxles

are pressed into inner and outer bearings in the steering knuckles **(see illustration)**; they can't be disengaged from the knuckles without a special puller, nor can they be installed without another special tool. Instead, the driveaxle and the steering knuckle must be removed as a single assembly, then separated by a dealer service department or an automotive machine shop with the proper tools.
2   If the vehicle is equipped with air suspension, make sure that the vehicle is in the normal (low) position, the height control switch is turned off, and the battery ground cable is disconnected. Loosen the wheel lug nuts, raise the vehicle and place it securely on jackstands. Remove the wheel.
3   Disconnect the parking brake cable, remove the brake caliper, the brake pads, and the caliper support bracket.
4   Remove the hub **(see illustrations)**.
5   Remove the brake disc (see Chapter 9).
6   Remove the brake disc splash shield from the steering knuckle (see Chapter 10).

14.4b . . . immobilize the hub with a prybar as shown, remove the castellated nut . . .

14.4c . . . remove the washer and centering piece . . .

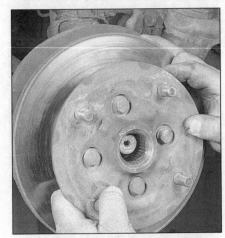

14.4d . . . and pull off the hub; if the hub is stuck, use a small puller to remove it

14.7 To disconnect a front driveaxle inner CV joint from the differential, knock out the spring pin with a hammer and punch

14.8 Remove the driveaxle and steering knuckle together, then have them separated by a dealer service department or an automotive machine shop

14.12a Mark the relationship of the CV joints to the rear differential (shown) and to the trailing arm to ensure that the spring pin holes are correctly aligned during reassembly

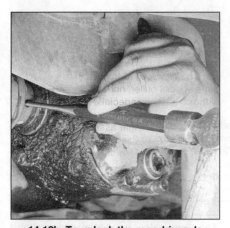

14.12b To unlock the rear driveaxle assembly from the differential, knock out this spring pin . . .

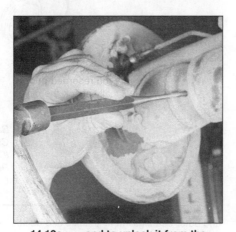

14.12c . . . and to unlock it from the spindle, remove this pin

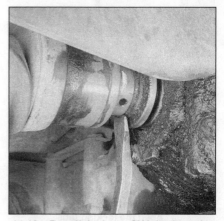

14.13a Pry off the inner CV joint from the rear differential side-gear shaft . . .

7   Locate the spring pin that locks the inner CV joint to the differential. Rotate the driveaxle and note that one end of the pin - and the pin hole - is smaller, and the other end is larger. You must knock out the spring pin *from the small end* **(see illustration)**. It's a good idea to mark the relationship of the CV joint to the differential side-gear preload adjuster, not to preserve driveaxle balance but to ensure that the spring pin holes in either side of the CV joint housing are correctly matched with the tapered hole in the splined stub shaft. When the driveaxle is installed, the big hole in the CV joint housing must be matched with the big end of the tapered hole in the stub shaft; the small hole in the CV joint must be matched with the small end of the tapered hole. Failure to do so will make it impossible to install a spring pin.

8   Disconnect the tie-rod end from the steering knuckle (see Chapter 10), disconnect the knuckle from the strut assembly and from the lower control arm (see Chapter 10), then remove the steering knuckle / driveaxle assembly **(see illustration)**.

9   If you're planning to replace an inner and/or outer CV joint boot, or overhaul

an inner CV joint, take the steering knuckle/driveaxle assembly to a dealer service department or an automotive machine shop and have the two components separated. Then proceed to the next section to replace the CV joint boot(s) or overhaul the inner CV joint. This is also a good time to inspect the inner and outer bearings in the knuckle and decide whether to reuse them or install new ones (see Chapter 10).

10   Installation is the reverse of removal. Be sure to use a new spring pin to lock the inner CV joint to the differential side-gear stub shaft. And don't forget that those holes in the CV joint and the stub shaft must be correctly matched before installing the new spring pin. After the vehicle has been lowered to the ground, tighten the driveaxle nut to the torque listed in this Chapter's Specifications.

Rear driveaxle (4WD models)

Refer to illustrations 14.12a, 14.12b, 14.12c, 14.13a and 14.13b

11   If the vehicle is equipped with air suspension, make sure that the vehicle is in the normal (low) position, the height control switch is turned off, and the battery ground cable is disconnected. Loosen the rear wheel

lug nuts, raise the vehicle and place it securely on jackstands. Remove the rear wheel.

12   Locate the spring pins that lock the inner CV joint to the differential and the outer CV joint to the spindle/wheel bearing assembly. Rotate the driveaxle and note that one end of the pins - and the pin holes - is smaller, and the other end is larger. Mark the relationship of the CV joints to the differential **(see illustration)** and spindle, not to preserve driveaxle balance, but to ensure that the spring pin holes in either side of the CV joint housings are correctly matched with the tapered holes in the splined stub shafts. Knock out the spring pins *from the small ends* **(see illustrations)**. When the driveaxle is installed, the big hole in the CV joint housing must be matched with the big end of the tapered hole in the stub shaft; the small hole in the CV joint must be matched with the small end of the tapered hole. Failure to do so will make it impossible to install a spring pin.

13   Disengage the driveaxle shaft from the splined stub shafts of the rear differential and the wheel spindle/bearing assembly **(see illustrations)**. Don't lose the spacer washer between the outer CV joint and the

8

14.13b . . . then disengage the outer CV joint from the splined spindle shaft

15.3b To remove the boot clamps, pry open the locking tabs

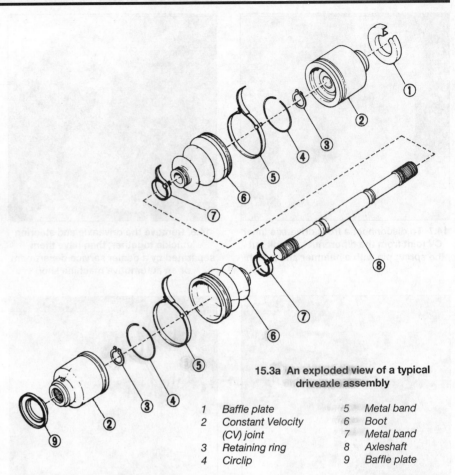

15.3a An exploded view of a typical driveaxle assembly

1	Baffle plate	5	Metal band
2	Constant Velocity (CV) joint	6	Boot
3	Retaining ring	7	Metal band
4	Circlip	8	Axleshaft
		9	Baffle plate

spindle/bearing assembly ring nut. This washer should be cleaned, inspected for wear, replaced if necessary, greased and installed prior to installing the driveaxle assembly.

14   If you're planning to replace an inner and/or outer CV joint boot, or overhaul an inner CV joint, proceed to the next section. This is also a good time to inspect the inner

15.4 Pry the wire retainer ring from the CV joint housing with a small screwdriver

and outer bearings in the knuckle and decide whether to reuse them or install new ones (see Chapter 10).

15   Installation is the reverse of removal. Be sure to use new spring pins to lock the inner CV joint to the differential side-gear stub shaft and the outer CV joint to the spindle/wheel bearing assembly. And don't forget that those holes in the CV joint and the stub shafts must be correctly matched before installing the new spring pin.

15.5 With the retainer removed, the outer race can be pulled off the bearing assembly

15   Driveaxle - boot replacement and constant velocity (CV) joint overhaul

Note: *If the CV joints exhibit signs of wear indicating need for an overhaul (usually due to torn boots), explore all options before beginning the job. Complete rebuilt driveaxles are available on an exchange basis, which eliminates much time and work. Whichever route you choose to take, check on the cost and availability of parts before disassembling the vehicle.*

Inner CV joint

Disassembly

Refer to illustrations 15.3a, 15.3b, 15.4, 15.5, 15.7, 15.9, 15.10 and 15.11

1   Remove the driveaxle (see Section 14).

2   Mount the driveaxle in a vise. The jaws of the vise should be lined with wood or rags to prevent damage to the axleshaft.

3   Cut the boot clamps from the boot and discard them **(see illustrations)**.

4   Slide the boot back on the axleshaft and pry the wire ring ball retainer from the outer race **(see illustration)**.

5   Pull the outer race off the inner bearing assembly **(see illustration)**.

6   Wipe as much grease as possible off the inner bearing.

15.7 Remove the snap ring from the end of the axleshaft

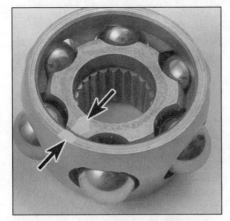

15.9 Make index marks on the inner race and cage so they'll both be facing the same direction when reassembled

15.10 Pry the balls from the cage with a screwdriver (be careful not to nick or scratch them)

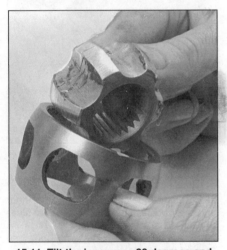

15.11 Tilt the inner race 90 degrees and rotate it out of the cage

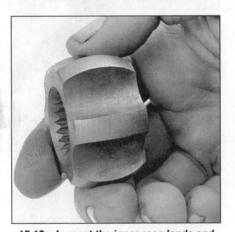

15.12a Inspect the inner race lands and grooves for pitting and score marks

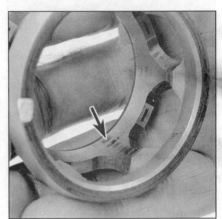

15.12b Inspect the cage for cracks, pitting and score marks (shiny spots are normal and don't affect operation)

7   Remove the snap ring from the end of the axleshaft **(see illustration)**.

8   Slide the inner bearing assembly off the axleshaft.

9   Mark the inner race and cage to ensure that they are reassembled with the correct sides facing out **(see illustration)**.

10   Using a screwdriver or piece of wood, pry the balls from the cage **(see illustration)**. Be careful not to scratch the inner race, the balls or the cage.

11   Rotate the inner race 90-degrees, align the inner race lands with the cage windows and rotate the race out of the cage **(see illustration)**.

Inspection

Refer to illustrations 15.12a and 15.12b

12   Clean the components with solvent to remove all traces of grease. Inspect the cage and races for pitting, score marks, cracks and other signs of wear and damage. Shiny, polished spots are normal and will not adversely affect CV joint performance **(see illustrations)**.

Reassembly

Refer to illustrations 15.14, 15.16, 15.17, 15.20, 15.23, 15.24a, 15.24b, 15.24c and 15.24d

13   Insert the inner race into the cage. Verify that the matchmarks are on the same side. However, it's not necessary for them to be in direct alignment with each other.

15.14 Press the balls into the cage through the windows

14   Press the balls into the cage windows with your thumbs **(see illustration)**.

15   Wrap the axleshaft splines with tape to avoid damaging the boot.

16   Slide the small boot clamp and boot onto the axleshaft, then remove the tape **(see illustration)**.

8

15.16 Wrap the splined area of the axle with tape to prevent damage to the boot

15.17 Install the inner race and cage assembly with the large diameter end toward the splined end of the axleshaft

15.20 Pack grease into the bearing until it's completely full

15.23 Equalize the pressure inside the boot by inserting a small screwdriver between the boot and the outer race

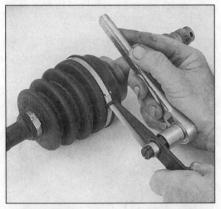

15.24b . . . peen over the locking tabs, . . .

15.24c . . . and cut off the excess

15.24a Secure the boot clamps with a special banding tool such as the one shown here (available at most auto parts stores): install the clamp, thread it onto the tool, pull the clamp tight, . . .

17   Install the inner race and cage assembly on the axleshaft with the larger diameter side or "bulge" of the cage facing the axleshaft end **(see illustration)**.
18   Install the snap ring **(see illustration 15.7)**.
19   Fill the boot with CV joint grease (normally included with the new boot kit).
20   Pack the inner race and cage assembly with grease, by hand, until grease is worked completely into the assembly **(see illustration)**.
21   Slide the outer race down onto the inner race and install the wire ring retainer.
22   Wipe any excess grease from the axle boot groove on the outer race. Seat the small diameter of the boot in the recessed area on the axleshaft and install the clamp. Push the other end of the boot onto the outer CV joint housing, seat it into the recessed area on the housing and move the race in-or-out so that the pleats of the boot are neither kinked nor stretched out.
23   With the axle set to the proper length, equalize the pressure in the boot by inserting a dull screwdriver between the boot and the outer race **(see illustration)**. Don't damage the boot with the tool.
24   Install the boot clamps **(see illustrations)**. A special clamp installation tool is

needed. The tool is available at most auto parts stores.
25   Install the driveaxle (see Section 14).

Outer CV joint and boot

Refer to illustration 15.30
Note: *The outer CV joint is a non-serviceable item and is permanently retained to the driveaxle. If any damage or excessive wear occurs to the axle or the outer CV joint, the entire driveaxle assembly must be replaced (excluding the inner CV joint). Service to the outer CV joints is limited to boot replacement and grease repacking only.*
26   Remove the driveaxle (see Section 14).
27   Mount the driveaxle in a vise. The jaws of the vise should be lined with wood or rags

15.24d Install the rubber protector over the big boot clamp (if equipped) when you're done

to prevent damage to the axleshaft.
28   Cut the boot clamps from both inner and outer boots and discard them **(see illustration 15.3a)**.
29   Remove inner CV joint and boot (see Steps 4 through 11).
30   Remove the outer CV joint boot. Wash the outer CV joint assembly in solvent and inspect it **(see illustration)** as described in

15.30 After the old grease has been rinsed away and the cleaning solvent has been blown out with compressed air, rotate the outer joint housing through its full range of motion and inspect the bearing surfaces for wear or damage - if any of the balls, the race or cage look damaged, replace the driveaxle and outer joint

16.1 If your rear differential looks like this, it's time to change the side-gear seals!

Step 12. Replace the axle assembly if any CV joint components are excessively worn. Install the new, outer boot and clamp onto the axleshaft **(see illustration 15.16)**.

31　Repack the outer CV joint with CV joint grease and spread grease inside the new boot as well.

32　Position the outer boot on the CV joint and install new boot clamps, using boot clamp pliers **(see illustration 15.24)**.

33　Reassemble the inner CV joint and boot (see Steps 13 through 24).

34　Install the driveaxle (see Section 14).

16　Rear differential side-gear seals (4WD models) - replacement

Refer to illustrations 16.1, 16.5, 16.6, 16.7, 16.8 and 16.10

Note: *The side oil seals can be replaced with the differential in the vehicle, even though this procedure shows it being done with the differential removed.*

1　The rear differential side-gear seals can become worn and leak gear lubricant onto the differential housing and inner CV joint **(see illustration)**. If your differential is covered with gear lube, replace the seals.

16.5 Remove the side bearing retainer bolts, then remove the retainer; don't lose the big washer on the stub shaft - it's a critical spacer that must be installed before installing the driveaxle assembly

2　If the vehicle is equipped with air suspension, make sure that the vehicle is in the normal (low) position, the height control switch is turned off, and the battery ground cable is disconnected. Loosen the rear wheel lug nuts, block the front wheels, raise the rear of the vehicle and support it securely on jack stands. Remove the rear wheel(s).

3　Drain the gear lubricant from the differential (see Chapter 1).

4　Remove the rear driveaxle(s) (see Section 14).

5　Remove the side-gear bearing retainer bolts **(see illustration)**, then remove the side-gear bearing retainer and bearing spacer (washer). Note the position of the retainer notch; the retainer must be installed with the notch in the same position. **Caution:** *When you remove the retainer from the differential, be careful not to move any of the internal parts, or you might change the bearing preload.*

6　With the retainer removed, replace the retainer O-ring **(see illustration)**. Also remove the metal shims.

7　To remove the oil seal from the retainer,

16.6 Remove and discard the retainer O-ring; a new O-ring must be installed before installing the retainer

place the retainer on two blocks of wood as shown, then, using a socket with the same outside diameter as the outside diameter of the seal, drive the seal out of the retainer **(see illustration)**.

8　To install a new seal, use the same socket and one block of wood and carefully drive the new seal into position **(see illustration)**. Make sure that the seal is installed *flush* with the surface of the retainer.

9　Install the metal shims. If using new shims, they must be the same thicknesses as the ones that were removed. Install a new O-ring on the retainer.

10　Install the bearing retainer onto the differential, making sure that the notch is in the same place as when it was removed **(see illustration)**.

11　Install the bearing retainer bolts and tighten them to the torque listed in this Chapter's Specifications. Install the side bearing spacer washer.

12　Install the rear driveaxle.

13　Fill the rear differential with the type and quantity of lubricant specified in Chapter 1.

14　Install the wheel, lower the vehicle.

15　Drive the vehicle, then inspect for leaks around the seal and retainer.

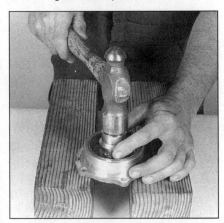

16.7 Use a socket to drive the old oil seal out of the retainer

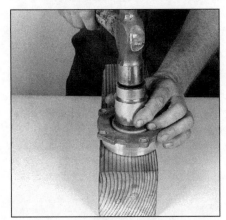

16.8 Carefully install the new seal flush with the retainer

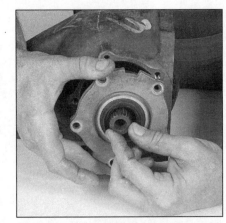

16.10 Install the side bearing retainer with the notch in the upper position

8

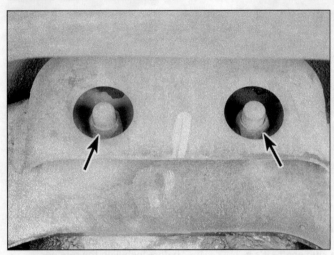

17.6 To detach the differential from the rear crossmember, remove these two nuts (arrows)

17.7 To detach the differential from its mounting bracket, remove these four nuts (arrows), or simply remove the nut and bolt up top (shown) and detach the bracket itself (you can separate the bracket from the differential after lowering the differential)

17 Rear differential (4WD models) - removal and installation

Refer to illustrations 17.6 and 17.7

1   If the vehicle is equipped with air suspension, make sure that the vehicle is in the normal (low) position, the height control switch is turned off, and the battery ground cable is disconnected. Loosen the rear wheel lug nuts, block the front wheels and raise the rear of the vehicle. Support it securely on jack stands. Remove the rear wheels.

2   Drain the lubricant from the differential (see Chapter 1).

3   Disconnect the driveshaft from the rear differential (see Section 10).

4   Disconnect the driveaxles from the rear differential (see Section 14).

5   Support the rear of the differential with a floorjack.

6   Remove the mounting nuts that attach the differential to the rear crossmember **(see illustration)**.

7   Remove the four mounting nuts which attach the front of the differential to the mounting bracket **(see illustration 8.1a)**, or simply remove the nut and bolt that attach the mounting bracket to the vehicle pan **(see illustration)**.

8   Carefully lower the differential and remove it from under the vehicle.

9   With the differential removed from the vehicle, now would be a good time to check or replace the rubber mounts for the differen-

tial mounting brackets and/or the rear crossmember **(see illustration 8.1a)**.

10   Place the differential on the jack head and position it directly underneath the mounting bracket and crossmember.

11   Raise the differential into position and install the rear mounting nuts loosely. Then install the front mounting nuts. Tighten all mounting fasteners securely.

12   Install the driveaxles and the driveshaft.

13   If it was drained, fill the differential with the type and amount of lubricant specified in Chapter 1.

14   Install the wheels, remove the jack and lower the vehicle to the ground. Tighten the wheel lug nuts to the torque listed in Chapter 1 Specifications.

Chapter 9   Brakes

Contents

Specifications

General

Brake fluid type	See Chapter 1
Brake pedal adjustments	
Pedal freeplay	1/64 to 3/32 inch
Pedal height	5-1/8 inch

Disc brakes (front and rear)

Minimum brake pad thickness	See Chapter 1
Disc minimum thickness	Refer to the dimension marked on the disc
Disc runout limit	0.0039 inch

Rear drum brake

Minimum brake shoe lining thickness	See Chapter 1
Brake drum maximum diameter	Refer to the dimensions marked on the drum

Torque specifications

	Ft-lbs (unless otherwise indicated)
Brake booster-to-firewall	108 to 204 in-lbs
Brake hose-to-front caliper banjo bolt	132 to 180 in-lbs
Front caliper	
Caliper lock pin	33 to 54
Caliper mounting bolt	36 to 51
Rear caliper bolts	16 to 23
Caliper support bracket bolts	
Front caliper bracket	36 to 51
Rear caliper bracket	34 to 43
Master cylinder check valve cap	18 to 25
Master cylinder stopper screw	24 in-lbs
Master cylinder mounting nut	84 to 144 in-lbs
Front hub-to-disc bolts	33 to 43
Rear brake disc/hub-to-spindle nut	145
Rear hub-to-brake disc bolt/nut	58 to 72
Rear brake drum or disc-to-spindle nut (4WD models)	145
Wheel cylinder mounting nuts	72 to 84 in-lbs

2.4a   Remove the U-clip which attaches the parking brake cable to its bracket

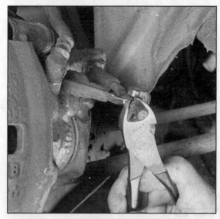

2.4b   Disconnect the parking brake cable from the lever, pull it through the bracket and set it aside

2.4c   Remove the caliper lock pin (some calipers are equipped with a small bolt that locks the pin in place; this bolt must be removed before the lock pin can be unscrewed)

1   General information

The vehicles covered by this manual are equipped with hydraulically operated front and rear brake systems. The front brakes are disc-type. The rear brakes are either drums or discs.

These models are equipped with a dual-circuit hydraulic system with a primary and secondary circuit. The primary circuit serves the right front and the left rear brakes; the secondary circuit serves the left front and the right rear brakes. Thus, if one circuit should fail, the other circuit will still enable the vehicle to stop.

The brake hydraulic system also employs a proportioning valve which limits pressure to the rear brakes under heavy braking to prevent rear wheel lock-up.

All models are equipped with a power brake booster which uses engine vacuum to amplify braking force.

The parking brake system uses a parking brake lever to apply the front brakes through cables to each front brake caliper.

Later models with a manual transaxle feature a "hill-holder" system. This device, which is connected to the clutch release lever, is activated when the clutch pedal is depressed. The hill-holder activates the brakes on a steep incline so that the clutch does not wear out and also makes it easier to start the vehicle in motion when on a hill. The hill-holder is deactivated when the clutch pedal is released.

There are some notes and cautions involving the brake system on this vehicle:

a) *Use only DOT 3 brake fluid in this system.*

b) *The brake pads and linings contain asbestos fibers which are hazardous to your health if inhaled. Whenever you work on the brake system components, carefully clean all parts with brake cleaner. Do not allow the fine asbestos dust to become airborne.*

c) *Safety should be paramount whenever any servicing of the brake components is performed. Do not use parts or fasten-* ers which are not in perfect condition, and be sure that all clearances and torque specifications are adhered to. If you are at all unsure about a certain procedure, seek professional advice. Upon completion of any brake system work, test the brakes carefully in a controlled area before putting the vehicle into normal service. If a problem is suspected in the brake system, do not drive the vehicle until the fault is corrected.*

d) *Tires, load and front end alignment are factors which also affect braking performance.*

2   Disc brake pads - replacement

Warning: *Disc brake pads must be replaced on both wheels at the same time - never replace the pads on only one wheel. Also, brake system dust may contain asbestos, which is hazardous to your health. DO NOT blow it out with compressed air and DO NOT inhale it. An approved filtering mask should be worn when working on the brakes. DO NOT use gasoline or petroleum-based solvents to remove the dust. Use brake system cleaner only!*

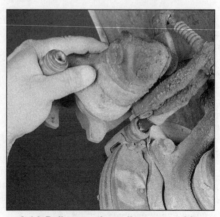

2.4d   Pull up on the caliper assembly, pivot it upward, . . .

1   Before replacing the pads, measure them to make sure they need to be replaced (see Chapter 1). Make sure you have the correct pad replacements for your vehicle.

2   If the vehicle is equipped with air suspension, make sure that the vehicle is in the normal (low) position, the height control switch is turned off, and the battery ground cable is disconnected. Block the wheels opposite the end to be worked on, loosen the wheel lugs nuts, raise the vehicle and place it securely on jackstands. Remove the wheels. Release the parking brake lever if you're working on the front brakes.

3   Remove about two-thirds of the fluid from the master cylinder reservoir and discard it; when the pistons are depressed to allow the caliper to fit over the disc with the new pads installed, fluid will be forced back into the reservoir. Position a drain pan under the brake assembly and clean the caliper and surrounding area with brake system cleaner.

Front brake pads

Refer to illustrations 2.4a through 2.4s

4   Before beginning, wash down the entire

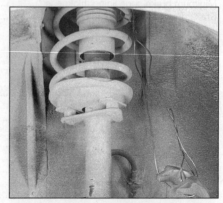

2.4e   . . . and hang it from the front strut with a piece of stiff wire or a straightened coat hanger (it's not necessary to disconnect the brake hose from the caliper)

2.4f Remove the outer brake pad, . . .

2.4g . . . then remove the shim from the outer pad and inspect it for wear or warpage; replace it if necessary

2.4h Remove the inner brake pad; if necessary, the pads can now be thoroughly inspected and the lining thickness accurately measured (don't depress the brake pedal while the pads are removed)

2.4i Remove the anti-rattle clips and inspect them for wear or breakage (upper clip shown); replace them with new ones if necessary

2.4j Remove the boot from the upper pin and inspect it for tears or other damage; replace it if necessary

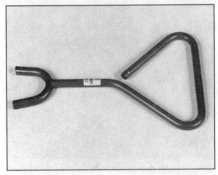

2.4k This is a special tool, available at most auto parts stores, used to turn the piston back into the caliper bore

brake assembly with brake system cleaner. To replace the brake pads, follow the accompanying photos, beginning with **illustration 2.4a**. Be sure to stay in order and read the caption under each illustration. Work on one brake assembly at a time so that you'll have something to refer to if you get in trouble.

5   While the pads are removed, inspect the caliper for brake fluid leaks and ruptures in the piston boot. Overhaul or replace the caliper as necessary (see Section 3). Also inspect the brake disc carefully (see Section 4). If machining is necessary, follow the information in that Section to remove the disc.

6   Before installing the caliper mounting pins and/or bolts, clean them and check them for corrosion and damage. If they're obviously corroded or damaged, replace them. Be sure to tighten the caliper mounting bolts to the torque listed in this Chapter's Specifications.

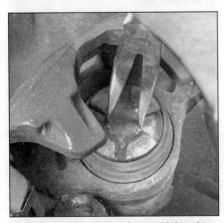

2.4l If you don't have the special tool to turn the piston, use a pair of needle-nosed pliers; turn the piston in until it bottoms in the bore

2.4m If the face of the piston doesn't line up as shown, back it out until it is

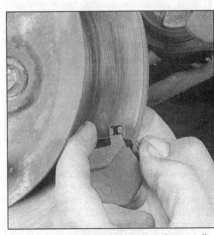

2.4n Install the anti-rattle clips (lower clip shown); make sure they're both fully seated onto the caliper support bracket

9

2.4o Install the shim on the outer pad, then install the outer pad and shim

2.4p Make sure that the outer pad is properly seated in the caliper support bracket, between the upper and lower anti-rattle clips, as shown

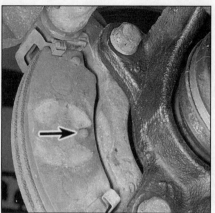

2.4q To install the inner pad, insert the bottom of the pad into the lower anti-rattle clip, press it down and push the upper end into the upper anti-rattle clip; make sure that the pad is fully seated in the caliper support bracket, between the anti-rattle clips, as shown; make sure that the raised pin (arrow); engages one of the notches in the piston face when the caliper is installed

2.4r Install the caliper assembly by sliding it back onto the upper pin (make sure the pin is greased) . . .

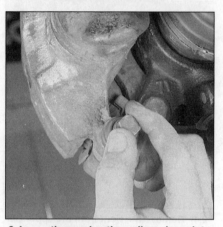

2.4s . . . then swing the caliper down into place, install the caliper lock pin and tighten it to the torque listed in this Chapter's Specifications

7   Install the brake pads on the opposite wheel, then install the wheels and lower the vehicle. Tighten the wheel lug nuts to the torque listed in the Chapter 1 Specifications.
8   Reconnect the parking brake cable to both parking brake levers on the calipers and secure the cables to their brackets with the U-clips. Adjust the parking brake cables, if necessary (see Section 12).
9   Add brake fluid to the reservoir until it's full (see Chapter 1). Pump the brakes several times to seat the pads against the discs, then check the fluid level again.
10   Check the operation of the brakes before driving the vehicle in traffic. Try to avoid heavy brake applications until the brakes have been applied lightly several times to seat the pads.

Rear brake pads

11   The rear brake pad replacement procedure is virtually identical to the front pad procedure, except that the caliper pistons should be depressed with a large C-clamp, *before* removing the caliper. Also, there is no parking brake cable to disconnect; so it's not necessary to retract the piston into the caliper with a special tool. Be sure to tighten

the rear caliper bolts to the torque listed in this Chapter's Specifications when you're done.

All models

12   Firmly depress the brake pedal a few times to bring the pads into contact with the disc. Check the fluid level in the master cylinder, topping it up if necessary.
13   Road test the vehicle carefully before placing it into normal use.

---

3   Brake caliper - removal, overhaul and installation

Removal

1   If the vehicle is equipped with air suspension, make sure that the vehicle is in the normal (low) position, the height control switch is turned off, and the battery ground cable is disconnected. Block the wheels opposite the end being worked on. Release the parking brake lever if you're working on

the front brakes. Raise the vehicle and place it securely on jackstands. Initially follow the instructions in the previous Section and remove the disc brake pads.
2   Place a container under the caliper and have some rags handy to catch any spilled brake fluid. If you're removing a front caliper, remove the brake hose-to-caliper banjo bolt (the bolt that connects the brake hose to the caliper). Plug the hose to prevent contaminants from entering the brake hydraulic system and to prevent fluid from leaking out the hose. If you're removing a rear caliper, proceed to Step 32.
3   Remove the caliper assembly (the caliper bracket need not be removed for this procedure).

Overhaul

Front caliper

Refer to illustrations 3.5a, 3.5b, 3.5c, 3.6, 3.7, 3.8, 3.9a, 3.9b, 3.11a, 3.11b, 3.12, 3.13, 3.14a, 3.14b, 3.20, 3.21, 3.24, 3.25, 3.27, 3.29

Note: *If an overhaul is indicated (usually because of fluid leaks, a stuck piston or broken bleeder screw) explore all options before beginning this procedure. New and factory rebuilt calipers are available on an exchange basis, which makes this job quite easy. If it's decided to rebuild the calipers, make sure rebuild kits are available before proceeding. Always rebuild or replace the calipers in pairs - never rebuild just one of them.*
4   Thoroughly clean the outside of the caliper assembly with brake fluid or brake cleaning solution. Place the caliper assembly on a suitable workbench and prepare to disassemble it by referring to the following Section.

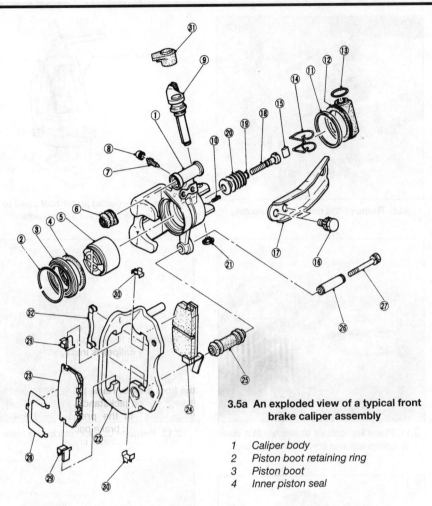

3.5b Remove the cylinder boot retaining ring

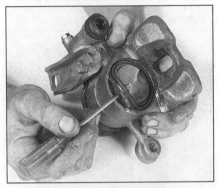

3.5c Remove the cylinder boot

3.5a An exploded view of a typical front brake caliper assembly

1   Caliper body
2   Piston boot retaining ring
3   Piston boot
4   Inner piston seal

5	Piston	15	Connecting link	25	Lock pin boot
6	Guide pin boot	16	Bolt assembly	26	Sleeve
7	Bleeder screw	17	Bracket	27	Lock pin
8	Bleeder cap	18	Spindle	28	Pad shim
9	Lever and shaft	19	O-ring	29	Outer pad clip
10	Spring pin	20	Conical springs	30	Inner pad clip
11	Cap ring	21	Snap-ring	31	Upper lever cap
12	Lever cap	22	Pad support	32	Inner pad clip
13	Cap spring	23	Outer pad		Installation
14	Return spring	24	Inner pad		

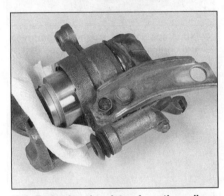

3.6 Removing the piston from the caliper assembly (note the rag, which acts as a cushion)

5   Remove the piston boot retaining ring **(see illustrations)** with a small screwdriver. Remove the piston boot **(see illustration)**

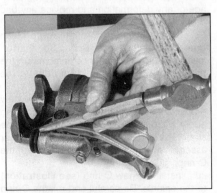

3.7 Remove the guide pin boot and metal retainer

and discard it. A new boot will be supplied in the rebuild kit to be used upon reassembly.
6   To remove the piston, try tapping on the

3.8 Use a non-metallic tool to remove the piston seal from the groove in the bore

caliper housing with a soft-faced hammer. If that doesn't work (it usually doesn't), it will be necessary to dislodge the piston with compressed air directed into the brake fluid inlet. Put a rag between the piston face and the caliper frame to protect the piston face **(see illustration)**. **Warning:** *Be careful not to place your fingers between the piston and caliper frame, as the piston may come out with some force.*
7   Remove the guide pin boot **(see illustration)** from the caliper by evenly tapping both metal tabs that hold the boot in place with a hammer and a chisel. Discard the boot; a new one should be included in the rebuild kit.
8   Remove the piston seal **(see illustration)** with a wood or plastic tool. Metal tools

9

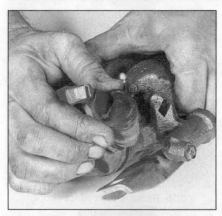

3.9a Remove the upper parking brake lever cap

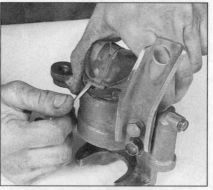

3.9b Remove the main lever cap ring

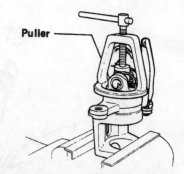

Puller

3.11a The special puller tool used to remove the lever and spindle

3.11b A special tool is used to compress the conical spring washers (see text for dimensions)

3.12 Place the caliper assembly in a vise to compress the conical springs and remove the lever

3.13 Remove the parking brake lever

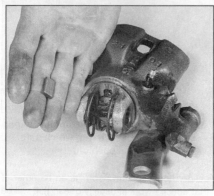

3.14a Remove the connecting link . . .

3.14b . . . and the return spring from the caliper body

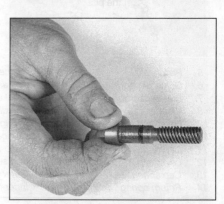

3.20 Install the new O-ring on the spindle

may cause bore damage.

9   Remove the rubber cap from the parking brake lever **(see illustration)**, remove the garter spring **(see illustration)**, then turn the cap inside out and push it aside.

10   Remove the snap ring holding the lever in position.

11   To disassemble the rest of the caliper assembly, you will need a special puller **(see illustration)**, available at most auto parts stores, or you can make a tool as shown **(see illustration)**, with the following dimensions: outside diameter - 1.06 inches (26.9 mm); inside diameter - 0.8125 inch (20.6 mm); total

height - 1.50 inches (38.1 mm); notch depth - 1.25 inches (31.7 mm); and notch width - 0.62 inch (15.7 mm).

12   Insert the caliper assembly into a vise as shown and compress the conical springs in order to remove the lever **(see illustration)**.

13   Carefully and slowly remove the lever **(see illustration)** from the assembly. Remove the assembly from the vise.

14   Remove the connecting link **(see illustration)** and the return spring **(see illustration)** from the caliper assembly.

15   Pull the spindle, with the conical washers, out of the caliper assembly.

16   Remove the springs and the O-ring from the spindle.

17   Inspect all parts for wear, scoring, damage or any deformation and replace any bad parts with new ones.

18   Clean all parts thoroughly with clean brake fluid before reassembly. See the following Section for seal replacements on the pad support which should be done at the same time as caliper overhaul.

19   Apply silicone compound to the new rubber O-ring that goes on the spindle. Also apply silicone to the O-ring groove of the spindle and to the area inside the caliper assembly where it comes in contact with the O-ring.

20   Install the new O-ring **(see illustration)** to the spindle. Be careful and roll the O-ring onto the spindle slowly so that you do not damage it.

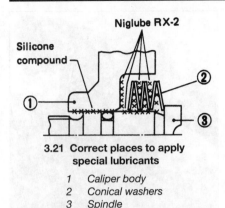

3.21 Correct places to apply
special lubricants

1 Caliper body
2 Conical washers
3 Spindle

3.24 Install the piston with your fingers

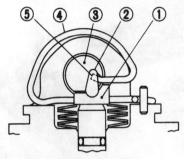

**3.25 Parking brake lever
installation details**

1	Spindle	4	Return
2	Connecting		spring
	link	5	Hooked
3	Lever and		portion of
	shaft		return spring

21   Install the conical spring washers as shown **(see illustration)**. Install the springs, one at a time, applying a thick coat of silicone-base grease between each of the springs.
22   Apply clean brake fluid to the cylinder walls of the caliper assembly. Then, apply a coat of silicone to the groove inside the cylinder.
23   Apply silicone to the complete exterior of the rubber seal which mounts into the groove of the cylinder wall. Carefully install the rubber seal into this groove.
24   Install the piston into the caliper assembly. To do this, start the back side of the piston into the caliper assembly and then carefully push (squeeze) the piston into place with your fingers **(see illustration)**.
25   Install the spindle, with the conical

washers attached, into the caliper **(see illustration)**. Make sure the groove on top of the spindle is in line with the holes that retain the lever shaft.
26   Apply plenty of silicone-base grease to the top of the spindle. This will also help hold the connecting link and spring in place.
27   Install the connecting link as shown **(see illustration)**, with the large round end facing down. Place the spring in position over the spindle (it only fits one way).
28   Place the caliper assembly in a vise and, using your special tool, compress the conical springs and spindle until you can install the lever handle. Apply a heavy coat of silicone-base grease to the lever shaft before you install it.
29   When you have the lever handle installed correctly, install the retaining snap-ring **(see illustration)** on the end of the lever shaft. Fully pack the interior of the main lever handle boot with silicone-base grease and then position the boot as you install the cap ring.
30   Install a new guide pin boot by using a

socket with the same inside diameter as the outside diameter of the new rubber boot. Place the boot (and its metal retainer) into position.
31   Install the rubber boot on the lever handle.

Rear caliper

Refer to illustrations 3.33, 3.35, 3.37a, 3.37b, 3.39, 3.40a and 3.40b
32   Loosen the brake hose fitting where it joins the metal line and pull out the U-clip **(see illustrations 8.3 and 8.4)**. The brake hose can now be unscrewed from the caliper. Wrap a plastic bag around the end of the hose to prevent fluid loss and contamination.
33   Remove the caliper mounting bolts **(see illustration)**.

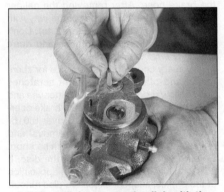

**3.27 Install the connecting link with the
large round end down**

**3.29 Install the retaining ring onto the end
of the parking brake lever shaft**

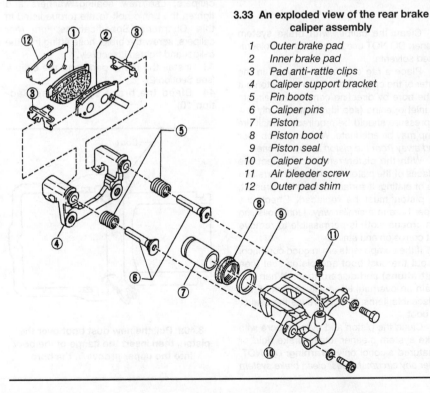

**3.33 An exploded view of the rear brake
caliper assembly**

1 Outer brake pad
2 Inner brake pad
3 Pad anti-rattle clips
4 Caliper support bracket
5 Pin boots
6 Caliper pins
7 Piston
8 Piston boot
9 Piston seal
10 Caliper body
11 Air bleeder screw
12 Outer pad shim

9

3.35 Use compressed air to pop the piston out of the caliper bore (use a wood block as a cushion

3.37a Pry out the dust boot out of the caliper bore

3.37b Remove the piston seal from its groove in the caliper bore

3.39 Lubricate the new piston seal with clean brake fluid and position the seal in the cylinder groove using your *fingers*

34   Clean the caliper with brake system cleaner. DO NOT use kerosene or petroleum-based solvents.

35   Place a rag or a block of wood in the center of the caliper, then force the piston out of the bore by directing compressed air into the inlet opening **(see illustration)**. Only low air pressure should be required; a small tire pump may be adequate. **Warning:** *Keep your hand away from the piston as this is done!*

36   With the piston removed, inspect the surfaces of the piston for nicks and burrs and loss of plating. If surface defects are present, the piston must be replaced. Check the caliper bore in a similar way. Light polishing with crocus cloth is permissible to remove light corrosion and stains.

37   If the components are in good condition, pry out the dust boot and piston seal **(see illustrations)** and discard them. When you obtain an overhaul kit, it will contain all the replaceable items. Do NOT reuse the seal or the boot.

38   Clean the piston and cylinder bore with brake system cleaner, clean brake fluid or denatured alcohol only. **Warning:** *DO NOT, under any circumstances, clean brake system*

parts with gasoline or petroleum-based solvents.

39   Lubricate the new piston seal with clean brake fluid and position the seal in the cylinder groove using your *fingers* **(see illustration)**.

40   Dip the piston in clean brake fluid, then pull the new dust boot over the open end of the piston. Place the flange of the boot in the upper groove in the caliper bore, then depress the piston into the bore and seat the lip of the boot in the piston **(see illustrations)**.

Installation

41   Before installing the caliper assembly back onto the caliper support, apply silicone-base grease, to the caliper mounting pivot.

42   Install the caliper assembly and reconnect the brake line to the caliper. On front calipers, use new sealing washers and tighten the banjo bolt to the torque listed in this Chapter's Specifications; on rear calipers, screw the brake hose fitting into the caliper and tighten it securely.

43   Install the brake pads and the caliper (see Section 2).

44   Bleed the brake system (see Section 10).

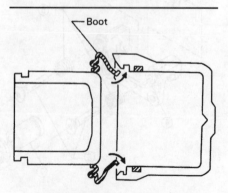

3.40a Pull the new dust boot over the piston, then insert the flange of the boot into the upper groove in the bore

4   Brake disc - inspection, removal and installation

Inspection

Refer to illustrations 4.4a, 4.4b, 4.5a and 4.5b

1   If the vehicle is equipped with air suspension, make sure that the vehicle is in the normal (low) position, the height control switch is turned off, and the battery ground cable is disconnected. Loosen the wheel lug nuts, raise the vehicle and support it securely on jackstands. Remove the wheel.

2   Unbolt the brake caliper **(see illustration 2.4c)**. It's not necessary to disconnect the brake hose. After removing the caliper bolt, suspend the caliper out of the way with a piece of wire **(see illustration 2.4e)**. Don't let the caliper hang by the hose and don't stretch or twist the hose.

3   Visually check the disc surface for score marks and other damage. Light scratches and shallow grooves are normal after use and may not always be detrimental to brake operation, but deep score marks - over 0.015-inch (0.38 mm) - require disc removal and refinishing by an automotive machine shop. Be sure to check both sides of the disc. If pulsating has been noticed during application of the brakes, suspect excessive disc runout.

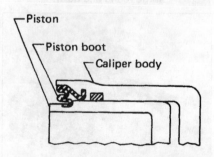

3.40b Depress the piston and seat the boot in the groove near the outer end of the piston

4.4a Check brake disc runout with a dial indicator; check both sides of the disc

4.4b Using a swirling motion, remove the glaze from the disc with sandpaper or emery cloth

4.5a The minimum thickness of the disc should be cast into the hub area

4.5b Measure the thickness of the disc and compare it to the Specifications

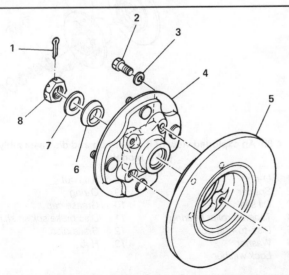

4.6 To remove the front caliper support bracket, remove these bolts (arrows) (rear bracket similar)

4   To check disc runout, place a dial indicator at a point about 1/2-inch from the outer edge of the disc **(see illustration)**. Set the indicator to zero and turn the disc. The indicator reading should not exceed the specified allowable runout limit. If it does, the disc should be refinished by an automotive machine shop. Measure runout on both the

outside and inside faces of the disc. **Note:** *Professionals recommend resurfacing of brake discs regardless of the dial indicator reading (to produce a smooth, flat surface, that will eliminate brake pedal pulsations and other undesirable symptoms related to questionable discs). At the very least, if you elect*

not to have the discs resurfaced, deglaze the brake pad surface with sandpaper or emery cloth (use a swirling motion to ensure a non-directional finish) **(see illustration).**

5   The disc must not be machined to a thickness less than the specified minimum refinish thickness. The minimum wear thickness is cast into the inside of the disc **(see illustration)**. Disc thickness can be checked with a micrometer **(see illustration)**. Measure the thickness at several different points around the disc. If the disc has worn down below the minimum thickness, replace it. Slight imperfections can be removed by resurfacing the disc at a machine shop.

Removal

Refer to illustrations 4.6, 4.7a, 4.7b, 4.7c, 4.8a and 4.8b

6   Remove the caliper support bracket bolts **(see illustration)** and remove the brackets.

7   If you're removing the front discs, loosen the driveaxle hub nut, washer and spacer **(see illustration)**; also *refer to Chapter 8*. Use a puller, if necessary, to remove the hub and disc assembly **(see illustrations)**. Once the hub/disc assembly has been removed from the vehicle, simply unbolt the hub from the disc.

4.7a An exploded view of the front hub and disc assembly

1   Cotter pin
2   Bolt
3   Washer
4   Hub
5   Disc
6   Conical spacer
7   Washer
8   Driveaxle/hub nut

4.7b If the hub and disc assembly is seized on the end of the driveaxle, use a puller to separate it from the driveaxle

9

4.7c   Note the order in which the washer and conical spacer are installed; don't forget the spacer when you install the hub and disc assembly

8   Rear discs on 4WD models are removed the same way **(see illustration)**. On 2WD models, remove the grease cap, O-ring, axle nut and lock washer, then remove the disc **(see illustration)**. Once the disc and hub assembly has been removed, simply unbolt the two parts and separate them.

9   If the rear disc on a 2WD model is removed, now is a good time to repack the bearings (see Chapter 1).

Installation

10   Reattach the disc and hub, if separated, and tighten the hub-to-disc bolts to the torque listed in this Chapter's Specifications.

11   Thoroughly clean all parts, then lubricate the driveaxle, or spindle, and the bearings with wheel bearing grease. Install the hub/disc assembly. Be sure to install any spacers, washers or lock washers that were removed. Tighten the front driveaxle nut to the torque listed in the Chapter 8 Specifications; tighten the rear driveaxle nut to the torque listed in this Chapter's Specifications (4WD models). Install a new cotter pin. If you're installing a rear disc on a 2WD model, install the hub, disc and wheel bearings. Adjust the rear wheel bearings following the procedure in Chapter 1.

12   Install the caliper support bracket and tighten the bracket bolts to the torque listed in this Chapter's Specifications.

13   Install the brake pads and caliper (see Sections 2 and 3) and tighten the caliper pins to the torque listed in this Chapter's Specifications.

14   Install the wheels, then lower the vehicle to the ground. Depress the brake pedal a few times to bring the brake pads into contact with the disc. Bleeding of the system will not be necessary unless the brake hose was disconnected from the caliper. Check the operation of the brakes carefully before placing the vehicle into normal service.

5   Drum brake shoes - replacement

Refer to illustrations 5.3a through 5.3i and 5.4a through 5.4cc

Warning: *Brake shoes must be replaced on both wheels at the same time - never replace the shoes on only one wheel. Also, brake system dust often contains asbestos, which is hazardous to your health. DO NOT blow it out with compressed air and DO NOT inhale it. An approved filtering mask should be worn when working on the brakes. DO NOT use gasoline or petroleum-based solvent to remove the dust. Use brake system cleaner or denatured alcohol only.*

1   If the vehicle is equipped with air suspension, make sure that the vehicle is in the normal (low) posiÒion, the height control switch is turned off, and the battery ground cable is disconnected. Loosen the wheel lug nuts, raise the rear of the vehicle and support it securely on jackstands. Block the front wheels to keep the vehicle from rolling off the stands. Remove the rear wheels.

2   Remove the axle nut and pull off the brake drum. It may also be necessary to back off the adjuster if the shoes have worn the brake drum excessively.

3   On models with a cam-type (manual) adjuster clean the brake assembly with brake system cleaner before beginning work, then follow **illustrations 5.3a through 5.3i.**

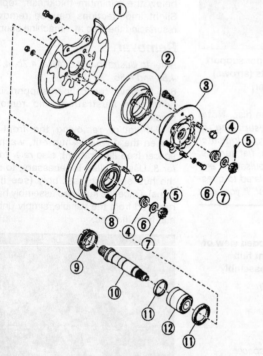

4.8a   An exploded view of the rear hub and disc or drum assembly (4WD models)

1	Disc brake splash shield	7	Castellated nut
2	Brake disc	8	Brake drum
3	Hub	9	Ring nut
4	Conical spacer	10	Spindle
5	Cotter pin	11	Oil seal
6	Spring washer	12	Bearing assembly

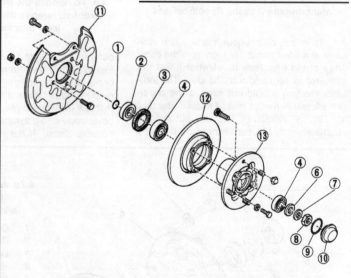

4.8b   An exploded view of the rear hub and disc assembly (2WD models)

1	O-ring	8	Axle nut
2	Spacer	9	O-ring
3	Oil seal	10	Grease cap
4	Tapered roller bearing	11	Disc brake splash shield
5	Disc-to-hub bolt	12	Brake disc
6	Washer	13	Hub
7	Lock washer		

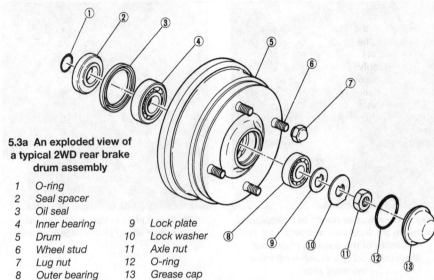

5.3a An exploded view of a typical 2WD rear brake drum assembly

1 O-ring
2 Seal spacer
3 Oil seal
4 Inner bearing
5 Drum
6 Wheel stud
7 Lug nut
8 Outer bearing

9 Lock plate
10 Lock washer
11 Axle nut
12 O-ring
13 Grease cap

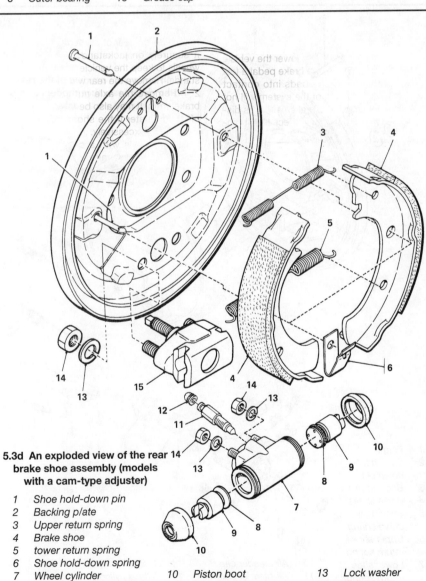

5.3d An exploded view of the rear brake shoe assembly (models with a cam-type adjuster)

1 Shoe hold-down pin
2 Backing plate
3 Upper return spring
4 Brake shoe
5 tower return spring
6 Shoe hold-down spring
7 Wheel cylinder
8 Piston cup
9 Piston

10 Piston boot
11 Bleeder screw
12 Bleeder cap

13 Lock washer
14 Nut
15 Adjuster

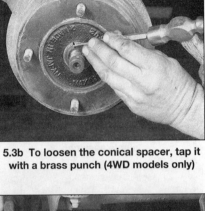

5.3b To loosen the conical spacer, tap it with a brass punch (4WD models only)

5.3c When you remove the brake drum, be sure to save the washer and conical spacer (4WD models only); the drum cannot be properly installed without them

5.3e Back-off the adjuster screw

9

5.3f Remove the shoes and springs as a single assembly

5.3g If the adjuster needs to be replaced, remove the nuts and washers from the backside of the backing plate (see illustration 5.3d) and pull it off from the front side

5.3h Apply high-temperature grease to the raised areas of the backing plate

5.3i Here's how it should look if you've assembled it correctly; now do the other side

5.4a Wash down the brake shoe assembly with brake system cleaner; do **NOT** use compressed air to blow off the brake assembly

4   On models with a strut-type (automatic) adjuster, follow **illustrations 5.4a through 5.4cc.** Be sure to stay in order and read the caption under each illustration.

5   Clean the brake drum and check it for score marks, deep grooves, hard spots (which will appear as small discolored areas) and cracks. If the drum is worn, scored or out-of-round, it can be resurfaced by an

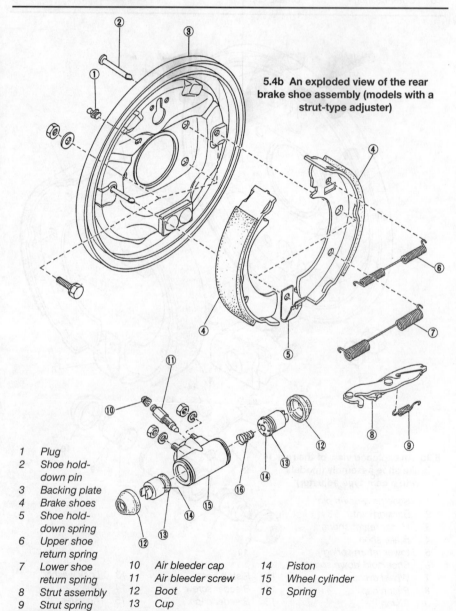

5.4b An exploded view of the rear brake shoe assembly (models with a strut-type adjuster)

1	Plug
2	Shoe hold-down pin
3	Backing plate
4	Brake shoes
5	Shoe hold-down spring
6	Upper shoe return spring
7	Lower shoe return spring
8	Strut assembly
9	Strut spring

10	Air bleeder cap	14	Piston
11	Air bleeder screw	15	Wheel cylinder
12	Boot	16	Spring
13	Cup		

5.4c Remove the rear shoe
hold-down clip

5.4d Remove the front shoe
hold-down clip

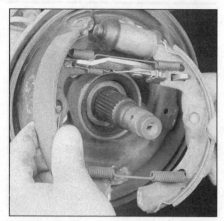

5.4e Remove the brake shoes and springs
as a single assembly

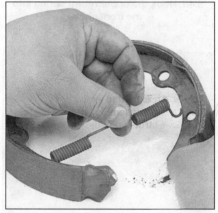

5.4f Unhook the lower return spring from
the rear shoe . . .

5.4g . . . and from the front shoe

5.4h Note how the strut assembly is
engaged with the rear shoe, disengage
the rear shoe from the strut . . .

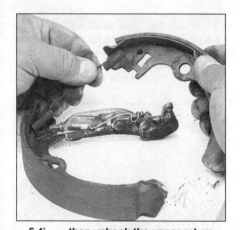

5.4i . . . then unhook the upper return
spring from the rear shoe . . .

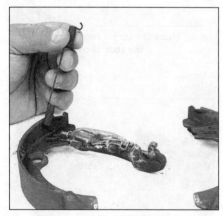

5.4j . . . and from the front shoe

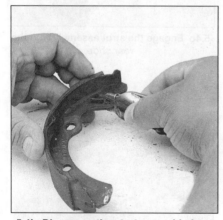

5.4k Disengage the strut assembly from
the front shoe

9

automotive machine shop. **Note:** *Professionals recommend resurfacing the drums whenever a brake job is done. Resurfacing will eliminate the possibility of out-of-round drums. If the drums are worn so much they can't be resurfaced without exceeding the maximum allowable diameter (stamped into the drum), new ones will be required. At the*

very least, if you elect not to have the drums resurfaced, remove the glazing from the surface with sandpaper or emery cloth using a swirling motion.

6   Repeat this procedure for the other rear brake assembly.

7   Install the brake drums. To adjust the brake shoes on models with a cam-type adjuster, turn the adjuster **(see illustration**

5.3e) until the wheel stops turning, then back off the adjuster a half-turn. The wheel should now turn freely; if it doesn't, back off the adjuster a tiny bit more. To adjust the brake shoes on models with a strut-type adjuster, simply pump the brake pedal several times; the shoes will be adjusted automatically.

8   Install the rear wheels, install the lug nuts, lower the vehicle and tighten the wheel

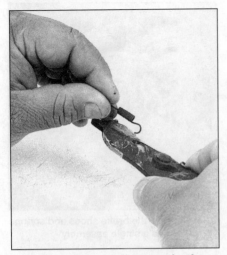

5.4l   Remove the small strut spring from the strut assembly

5.4m   Using high-temperature grease, lubricate the shoe contact points on the brake backing plate

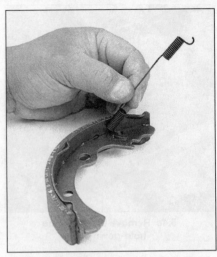

5.4n   Hook the upper return spring into the front shoe

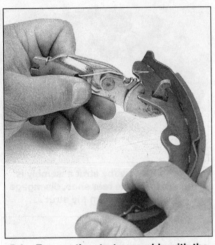

5.4o   Engage the strut assembly with the rear shoe

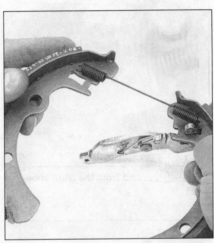

5.4p   Hook the upper return spring into the rear shoe

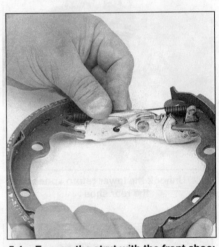

5.4q   Engage the strut with the front shoe; again, if you're not sure whether the two parts are correctly engaged, refer to the other rear brake

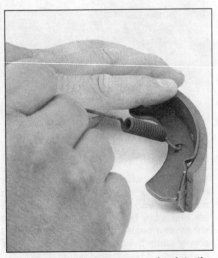

5.4r   Hook the lower return spring into the rear shoe

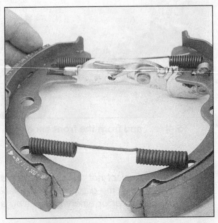

5.4s   At this point, stop and make sure that the strut assembly and the upper and lower return springs are engaged with the front and rear shoes exactly as shown

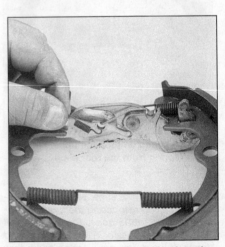

5.4t   Hook the small strut spring into the strut assembly . . .

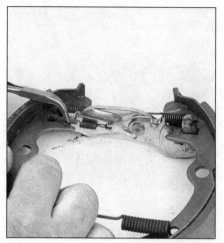

5.4u . . . then hook it into the front shoe

5.4v Insert the front shoe hold-down pin through its hole in the backing plate . . .

5.4w . . . and the rear shoe hold-down pin (arrow) through its hole

5.4x Carefully install the shoes, springs and strut onto the brake backing plate . . .

5.4y . . . pull the lower ends of the brake shoes apart and seat them behind the flange on the anchor

5.4z Install the front shoe hold-down clip . . .

5.4aa . . . and give the hold-down pin a twist to lock the clip into place

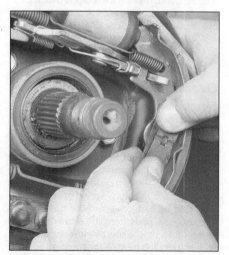

5.4bb Install the rear shoe hold-down clip . . .

5.4cc . . . and give the hold-down pin a twist to lock the clip into place

9

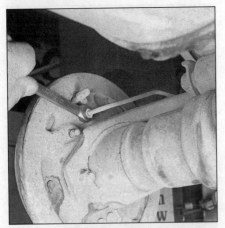

6.2 To remove the wheel cylinder, disconnect the brake line fitting with a flare-nut wrench (to protect the corners of the nut), then remove the two wheel cylinder retaining nuts and washers

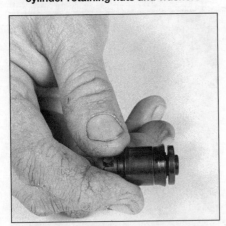

6.12 Install new rubber cups on the pistons; make sure the cups are facing in (toward each other) when the pistons are installed

6.6 Remove the bleeder screw and clean it with new brake fluid; make sure the hole is clean before installing the bleeder

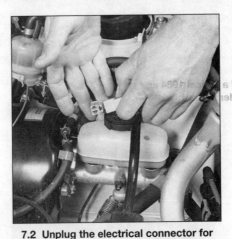

7.2 Unplug the electrical connector for the brake fluid level indicator

6.7 Remove both rubber dust boots from the wheel cylinder

lug nuts to the torque listed in the Chapter 1 Specifications. Test the brakes for proper operation before driving the vehicle in traffic.

6   Wheel cylinder - removal, overhaul and installation

Note: *If an overhaul is indicated (usually because of fluid leakage or sticky operation) explore all options before beginning the job. New wheel cylinders are available, which makes this job quite easy. If you decide to rebuild the wheel cylinder, make sure a rebuild kit is available before proceeding. Never overhaul only one wheel cylinder. Always rebuild both of them at the same time.*

Removal

Refer to illustration 6.2

1   Remove the brake drum and brake shoes (see Section 5).
2   Unscrew the brake line fitting from the rear of the wheel cylinder **(see illustration)**. If

available, use a flare-nut wrench to avoid rounding off the corners on the fitting. Don't pull the metal line out of the wheel cylinder - it could bend, making installation difficult.
3   Remove the two nuts securing the wheel cylinder to the brake backing plate.
4   Remove the wheel cylinder.
5   Plug the end of the brake line to prevent the loss of brake fluid and the entry of dirt.

Overhaul

Refer to illustrations 6.6, 6.7 and 6.12

6   Remove the bleeder screw **(see illustration)**. Make sure the screw and the hole are clean.
7   Remove the rubber boot from each end of the cylinder **(see illustration)**.
8   Push out the two pistons and cups, then remove the cup return spring **(see illustration 5.3d or 5.4b)**. Discard the rubber parts and use new ones from the rebuild kit when reassembling the wheel cylinder.
9   Inspect the pistons for scoring and scuff marks. If present, the pistons should be replaced with new ones.
10   Examine the inside of the cylinder bore for score marks and corrosion. If these condi-

tions exist, the cylinder can be honed slightly to restore it, but replacement is recommended.
11   If the cylinder is in good condition, clean it with brake system cleaner or denatured alcohol. **Warning:** *DO NOT, under any circumstances, use gasoline or petroleum-based solvents to clean brake parts!*
12   Install new rubber cups on the pistons **(see illustration)**. Make sure the cup lips face the inner ends of the piston.
13   Lubricate the cylinder bore with clean brake fluid, then insert one of the pistons into the bore.
14   Place the spring in the opposite end of the bore and push it in.
15   Install the remaining piston in the cylinder bore.

Installation

16   Installation is the reverse of removal. Attach the brake line to the wheel cylinder *before* installing the wheel cylinder mounting bolts, but don't *tighten* the tube nut fitting until *after* the wheel cylinder mountings bolts have been tightened. If available, use a flare-nut wrench to tighten the tube nut fitting. Be sure to tighten the wheel cylinder mounting nuts to the torque listed in this Chapter's Specifications.
17   Bleed the brakes (see Section 10). Don't drive the vehicle in traffic until the operation of the brakes has been thoroughly tested.

7   Master cylinder - removal, overhaul and installation

Removal

Refer to illustration 7.2
Note: *Make sure you have the correct rebuild kit for your vehicle before starting.*
1   Place some shop rags underneath the master cylinder to catch spilled brake fluid, then siphon the brake fluid from the reservoir.
2   Unplug the electrical connector **(see illustration)** for the brake fluid level indicator.

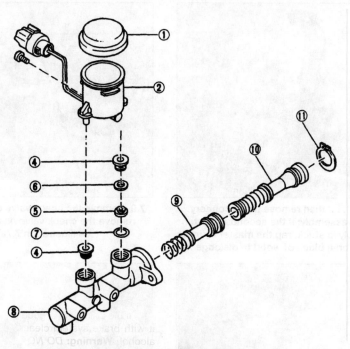

7.6 An exploded view of a typical 1984 and later master cylinder assembly

1	Reservoir cap	7	O-ring
2	Reservoir	8	Master cylinder body
3	Float (not shown)	9	Secondary piston assembly
4	Grommet	10	Primary piston assembly
5	Valve	11	Snap-ring
6	C-ring		

7.7a An exploded view of a typical pre-1984 master cylinder assembly (reservoir assembly already removed)

1	Master cylinder	6	Stopper screw
2	Check valve spring	7	Secondary piston assembly
3	Check valve	8	Primary piston assembly
4	Tube seat	9	Stopper washer
5	Check valve cap	10	Stopper ring

3   Place some shop rags under the brake line fittings. Using a flare-nut wrench, unscrew the brake line tube nuts and allow any residual fluid to drain onto the rags. Remove the rags and mop up any spilled fluid immediately.

4   Remove the nuts which attach the master cylinder to the power brake booster. Place the hose clamp up and out of your way.

5   Wrap the master cylinder in shop rags, then remove it.

Overhaul

Refer to illustrations 7.6, 7.7a, 7.7b, 7.7c, 7.8a, 7.8b, 7.9, 7.10 and 7.14

6   Place the master cylinder in a bench vise and pry off the reservoir(s) **(see illustration)**. 1984 and later units have a single reservoir, as shown here. Earlier models used a pair of smaller reservoirs. But they're removed the same way. Be sure to discard any rubber grommets, seals and/or O-rings used to seal the connections between the reservoir(s) and the master cylinder; these parts should be replaced.

7   On older (pre-1984) units, push in on the primary piston with a punch and remove the stopper screw **(see illustrations)**. On all units,

7.7b To remove the piston stopper screw, depress the primary piston with a punch, then unscrew the stopper

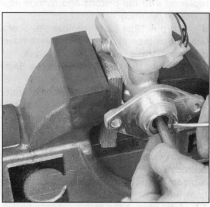

7.7c To remove the piston stopper ring, depress the primary piston with a punch and pry out the ring; then remove the stopper washer (1984 and later units have a snap ring instead)

9

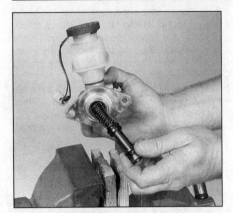

7.8a   Remove the primary piston assembly, . . .

7.8b   . . . then remove the secondary piston assembly; if the secondary piston assembly is stuck, rap the master cylinder body on a block of wood to dislodge it

7.9   Remove the check valve caps, then remove the check valve assemblies (see illustration 7.7a)

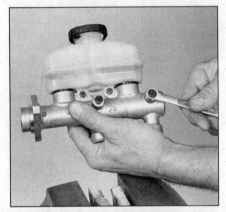

7.10   Remove both of the bleeder valves

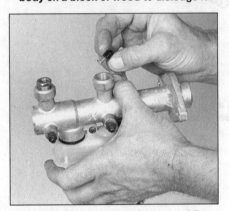

7.14   Install the check valve assemblies (see illustration 7.7a)

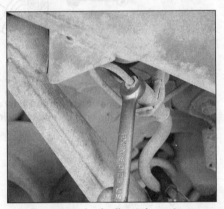

8.3   To protect brake line tube nuts, use a flare-nut wrench so the corners of the nut don't become rounded off (if they do - and you're unable to tighten the nut - you'll have to replace that particular section of metal line!)

push in on the primary piston and (on pre-1984 units) pry out the stopper ring **(see illustration)** and stopper washer, or (on 1984 and later units) remove the snap-ring **(see illustration 7.6)** with a pair of snap-ring pliers.

8   Remove the primary piston assembly and the secondary piston assembly **(see illustrations)**. **Note:** *Do not bother to disassemble either piston assembly. If the rubber cups must be replaced, they must be replaced with the pistons and springs as a complete assembly.*

9   On pre-1984 units, remove the check valve caps **(see illustration)**, then remove, disassemble and clean the check valves.

10   Remove the bleeder valves **(see illustration)**, if equipped.

11   Thoroughly clean the master cylinder and all parts with rubbing alcohol, brake system cleaner or brake fluid. Do not use petroleum-based solvents.

12   Inspect the inside walls of the cylinder for any scoring or other damage. If the bore is scored, feels rough or is otherwise damaged, replace the master cylinder. Do not try to hone it out.

13   After coating the piston assemblies with clean brake fluid, install them, secondary piston first, into the master cylinder **(see illustration 7.6 or 7.7a)**.

14   On pre-1984 units, install the check valve assemblies **(see illustration)**.

15   Push in on the primary piston with a punch and install the stopper washer and stopper ring (pre-1984) or the snap-ring (1984 and later units).

16   On pre-1984 units, push in on the primary piston again and install the stopper screw. Tighten it to the torque listed in this Chapter's Specifications.

Installation

17   Install the master cylinder onto the power brake booster. Tighten the mounting nuts to the torque listed in this Chapter's Specifications.

18   Connect the brake lines to the master cylinder and tighten the tube nuts securely.

19   Plug in the electrical connector for the fluid level indicator.

20   Bleed the brake system (see Section 10).

8   Brake hoses and lines - check and replacement

1   If the vehicle is equipped with air suspension, make sure that the vehicle is in the normal (low) position, the height control switch is turned off, and the battery ground cable is disconnected. Raise the vehicle and

place it securely on jackstands.

2   About every six months, inspect the flexible hoses which connect the steel brake lines with the front and rear brake assemblies for cracks, chafing of the outer cover, leaks, blisters and other damage. These are important and vulnerable parts of the brake system and your inspection should be thorough. You'll need a light and mirror. If a hose exhibits any of the above defects, replace it with a new one.

Flexible hoses

Refer to illustrations 8.3 and 8.4

3   Clean all dirt away from the ends of the hose. Using a flare-nut wrench, disconnect the brake line from the hose fitting **(see illustration)**. Be careful not to bend the frame bracket or kink the metal line. If necessary, soak the connections with penetrating oil.

4   Remove the U-clip **(see illustration)** and separate the hose from the bracket.

5   Disconnect the hose from the caliper. On calipers with a banjo-type fitting, discard the copper washers on either side of the banjo fitting.

6   Screw the new hose into the caliper, or

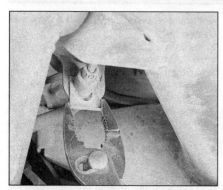

8.4 Before you can separate the flexible brake hose from the metal brake line tube nut, you must remove this U-clip from the bracket

9.2 To replace the proportioning valve, loosen all four tube nuts (rear two shown, other two, not visible in this photo, on front side of valve), then remove the two mounting bracket bolts (arrows)

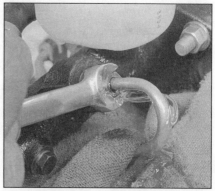

10.1 Have an assistant depress the brake pedal and hold it down, then loosen the fitting nut, allowing the air and fluid to escape. Repeat this procedure on both fittings until the fluid is clear of air bubbles

attach it to the caliper with the banjo bolt. On banjo fittings, be sure to use new copper sealing washers. Tighten non-banjo type hoses securely; don't tighten banjo-type fittings until the other end of the hose has been connected.

7   Route the hose so that it doesn't touch any suspension components. Make sure there are no kinks or twists, then attach the hose to the metal line at the bracket by loosely tightening the tube nut.

8   Install the U-clip.

9   Tighten the brake line tube nut securely. Make sure that the hose doesn't turn, and the metal line doesn't kink, as you tighten the tube nut.

10   Make sure no suspension or steering components contact the hose. Have an assistant push down on the vehicle and also turn the steering wheel lock-to-lock during inspection.

11   Bleed the brake system (see Section 10).

Metal brake lines

12   When replacing metal brake lines, be sure to use the correct parts. Don't use copper tubing for any brake system components. Purchase steel brake lines from a dealer parts department or auto parts store.

13   Prefabricated brake line, with the tube ends already flared and fittings installed, is available at auto parts stores and dealer parts departments. If pre-bent lines are not available, remove the defective line and purchase a straight section of brake line (with the ends already flared and the fittings attached) that measures as close as possible to the length of the original line (including the bends). Using the proper tubing bending tools, bend the new line to resemble the original.

14   When installing the new line make sure it's well supported by all clips and brackets, and has plenty of clearance between moving or hot components.

15   After installation, check the master cylinder fluid level and add fluid as necessary. Bleed the brake system as outlined in the next Section and test the brakes carefully before placing the vehicle into normal operation.

9   Proportioning valve - replacement

Refer to illustration 9.2

1   If the vehicle is equipped with air suspension, make sure that the vehicle is in the normal (low) position, the height control switch is turned off, and the battery ground cable is disconnected. Raise the vehicle and place it securely on jackstands.

2   Unscrew all four metal brake line tube nuts **(see illustration)**.

3   Unbolt the proportioning valve mounting bracket from the body.

4   Installation is the reverse of removal. Be sure to bleed the brake system (see Section 10) when you're done.

10   Brake hydraulic system - bleeding

Refer to illustrations 10.1 and 10.8
Warning: *Wear eye protection when bleeding the brake system. If the fluid comes in contact with your eyes, immediately rinse them with water and seek medical attention.*
Note: *Bleeding the brake system is necessary to remove any air that's trapped in the system when it's opened during removal and installation of a hose, line, caliper, wheel cylinder or master cylinder.*

1   It will probably be necessary to bleed the system at all four brakes if air has entered the system due to low fluid level, or if the brake lines have been disconnected at the master cylinder. **Note:** *If the master cylinder has run dry (due to a leak in the system) or has been rebuilt or replaced, begin by bleeding the master cylinder* **(see illustration)**.

2   If a brake line was disconnected only at a wheel, then only that caliper or wheel cylinder must be bled.

3   If a brake line is disconnected at a fitting located between the master cylinder and any of the brakes, that part of the system served by the disconnected line must be bled.

4   Remove any residual vacuum (or

hydraulic pressure) from the brake power booster by applying the brake several times with the engine off.

5   Remove the master cylinder reservoir cover and fill the reservoir with brake fluid. Reinstall the cover. **Note:** *Check the fluid level often during the bleeding operation and add fluid as necessary to prevent the fluid level from falling low enough to allow air bubbles into the master cylinder.*

6   Have an assistant on hand, as well as a supply of new brake fluid, an empty clear plastic container, a length of plastic, rubber or vinyl tubing to fit over the bleeder valve and a wrench to open and close the bleeder valve.

7   Beginning at the right rear wheel, loosen the bleeder screw slightly, then tighten it to a point where it's snug but can still be loosened quickly and easily.

8   Place one end of the tubing over the bleeder screw fitting and submerge the other end in brake fluid in the container **(see illustration)**.

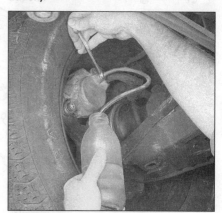

10.8 When bleeding the brakes, a hose is connected to the bleed screw at the caliper or wheel cylinder and then submerged in brake fluid - air will be seen as bubbles in the tube and container (all air must be expelled before moving to the next wheel)

9

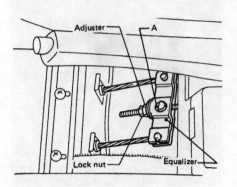

11.5 Adjust the parking brake cable tension at the equalizer, which is located in the center console, right in front of the parking brake lever base

9   Have the assistant push down on the brake pedal and hold the pedal firmly depressed.

10   While the pedal is held depressed, open the bleeder screw just enough to allow a flow of fluid to leave the valve. Watch for air bubbles to exit the submerged end of the tube. When the fluid flow slows after a couple of seconds, tighten the screw and have your assistant release the pedal.

11   Repeat Steps 9 and 10 until no more air is seen leaving the tube, then tighten the bleeder screw and proceed to the left front wheel, the left rear wheel and the right front wheel, in that order, and perform the same procedure. Be sure to check the fluid in the master cylinder reservoir frequently.

12   Never use old brake fluid. It contains moisture which can boil, rendering the brakes useless.

13   Refill the master cylinder with fluid at the end of the operation.

14   Check the operation of the brakes. The pedal should feel solid when depressed, with no sponginess. If necessary, repeat the entire process. **Warning:** *Do not operate the vehicle if you are in doubt about the effectiveness of the brake system.*

11   Parking brake - adjustment

Refer to illustration 11.5

1   Before adjusting the parking brake, make sure that the brake hydraulic system is free of all air (see Section 10) and that the rear brakes have been adjusted properly (see Section 5).

2   Firmly apply the parking brake lever three to five times.

3   Count how many clicks the brake lever travels before it becomes fully engaged. The correct number is three or four clicks. If the parking brake lever needs more than this before it's fully applied, adjust the parking brake as follows.

4   Remove the parking brake cover screws and the cover from the center console (see Chapter 11).

5   Back off the locknut **(see illustration)**, then turn the adjuster nut clockwise to tighten the cable.

6   Apply the parking brake lever again and count how many clicks it takes to fully apply the parking brake system. Repeat this procedure until the lever is fully applied in three to four clicks.

7   After the adjustment is made, tighten the locknut against the adjuster nut.

8   If it is impossible to achieve the correct adjustment, the cables are stretched beyond adjustment. Replace them (see Section 12).

9   Install the parking brake cover and tighten its mounting screws.

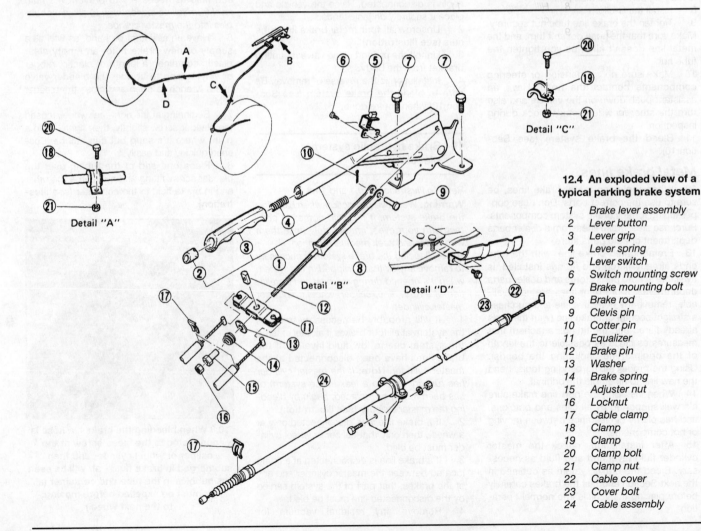

12.4 An exploded view of a typical parking brake system

1   Brake lever assembly
2   Lever button
3   Lever grip
4   Lever spring
5   Lever switch
6   Switch mounting screw
7   Brake mounting bolt
8   Brake rod
9   Clevis pin
10   Cotter pin
11   Equalizer
12   Brake pin
13   Washer
14   Brake spring
15   Adjuster nut
16   Locknut
17   Cable clamp
18   Clamp
19   Clamp
20   Clamp bolt
21   Clamp nut
22   Cable cover
23   Cover bolt
24   Cable assembly

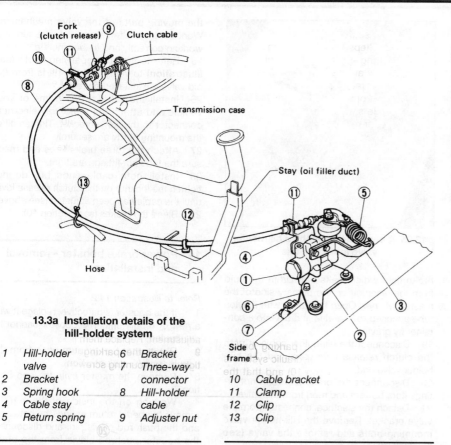

13.3a Installation details of the hill-holder system

1	Hill-holder valve	6	Bracket
2	Bracket	7	Three-way connector
3	Spring hook	8	Hill-holder cable
4	Cable stay	10	Cable bracket
5	Return spring	9	Adjuster nut	11	Clamp
		12	Clip
		13	Clip

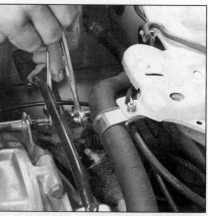

13.3b Turn this adjusting nut to tighten or loosen the hill-holder cable

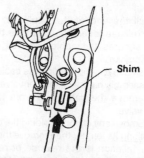

13.9 The hill-holder can be fine-tuned by placing one or two adjustment shims (available at the dealer) between the bracket and the frame

12 Parking brake cables - replacement

Refer to illustration 12.4

1   Inside the vehicle, remove the parking brake cover from the center console (see Chapter 11).

2   If the vehicle is equipped with air suspension, make sure that the vehicle is in the normal (low) position, the height control switch is turned off, and the battery ground cable is disconnected. Loosen the front wheel lug nuts, raise the front of the vehicle and place it securely on jackstands. Remove the front wheels.

3   Loosen the cable equalizer locknut and adjuster nut **(see illustration 11.5)** and disengage the cable ends from the equalizer.

4   Trace the routing of each cable and remove all clamps and/or clips attaching the cables to the vehicle body **(see illustration)**.

5   Remove the clips holding the cables to the brackets at the front brake calipers, detach the cables from the brackets and disengage the cables from the levers on the calipers **(see illustrations 2.4a and 2.4b)**.

6   Installation is the reverse of removal. Make sure that the cables are routed so that they're not kinked and so that nothing interferes with them.

7   Adjust the new cables (see Section 11).

8   Tighten the locknut up against the adjuster nut and install the parking brake cable cover (see Chapter 11).

13 Hill-holder system - adjustment and component replacement

Adjustment

Refer to illustrations 13.3a, 13.3b and 13.9

1   Check the clutch cable adjustment (see Chapter 8). If necessary, adjust it. The clutch and hill-holder valve work hand in hand - when one is engaged, the other isn't, and vice versa.

2   Find a hill with at least three degrees of incline (the valve doesn't engage on a hill with less than three degrees of slope).

3   Start the vehicle up the hill, stop, then depress the clutch pedal. If the vehicle starts to roll backward, the cable is too loose. Locate the adjusting nut and tighten it **(see illustrations)**.

4   Repeat the test: start up the hill, stop, depress the clutch pedal, and note whether the vehicle remains in place or rolls backward. If it still rolls, tighten the adjusting nut a little more.

5   Follow this procedure until the hill-holder operates properly. Do not tighten the cable any more than necessary.

6   It's the brakes that actually hold the vehicle in place when the valve is actuated (the hill-holder valve is connected directly to the master cylinder).

7   If the brakes are still applied, preventing the vehicle from rolling freely, the hill-holder cable is probably adjusted too tightly. Take the vehicle to a three-degree or steeper hill

and loosen the cable adjuster nut until the vehicle rolls freely under power.

8   If the brakes will not release your vehicle at all, check the hill-holder return spring and note whether it's broken. If it is, replace the hill-holder mechanism immediately. You can get the vehicle home by removing the hill-holder cable adjusting nuts, disconnecting the cable from the clutch release lever and manually retracting the hill-holder valve lever until the brakes are released.

9   You can also fine-tune the hill-holder to activate on smaller or larger hills by inserting shims (available at Subaru dealers) between the valve mounting bracket and the frame **(see illustration)**.

a)   If you want the valve to be activated only on steeper hills, insert the shim under the rear of the valve.

b)   If you want the valve to be activated on smaller hills, insert the shim under the front of the valve.

Note: *Use only Subaru-approved shims and never add more than two shims to the valve.*

Replacement

Hill-holder cable

10   Loosen and remove the locknut from the end of the hill-holder cable.

11   Loosen the adjuster nut for the hill-holder cable enough to release it from the clutch release lever.

9

13.21 Remove the hill-holder valve from the frame

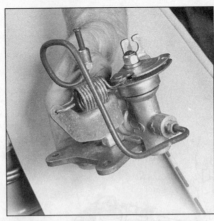

13.25 A correctly assembled hill-holder valve looks like this

the moving parts of the valve mechanism. Work the lever a few times to make sure it is working correctly and to loosen it up.

25   Refer to the accompanying photo **(see illustration)** to verify that the parts from the old valve are installed correctly.

26   Install the valve to the frame of your vehicle and attach the three-way electrical connector to the valve bracket. Tighten all of the mounting hardware securely.

27   Attach the three brake lines and make sure the tube nut fittings are tight.

28   Install both cable ends but do not tighten the locknut on the clutch release lever until the cable has been adjusted (see above).

29   Bleed the brakes (see Section 10).

---

12   Pull the end of the cable out of the clutch release lever, then remove the clip which secures the cable in place on the engine bracket.

13   Remove the clip holding the cable to the lever assembly on the hill-holder valve.

14   Remove the cable end from the hill-holder valve.

15   Remove any clamps holding the cable in place along its length, then remove the cable.

16   Installation is the reverse of removal. Make sure that the cable is installed correctly at both ends. Do not tighten the adjusting nut at the clutch release lever until the cable has been adjusted.

17   Adjust the hill-holder cable (see above).

Hill-holder valve

Refer to illustrations 13.21 and 13.25

18   Place shop rags underneath the master cylinder and the hill-holder valve to catch any

brake fluid which leaks out. Drain the fluid from the reservoir on the primary side of the master cylinder. Open the valve, with a nylon tube attached to it, and let it drain into a container by gravity.

19   Disconnect the hill-holder cable at both the clutch release lever end and the hill-holder valve end.

20   Disconnect the brake line tube nut fittings (top, bottom and rear) from the valve.

21   Detach the electrical connector from the valve bracket. Remove the Hill-holder valve mounting bolts and remove the valve **(see illustration)**.

22   Inspect the return spring. If it's worn or damaged, replace it.

23   To inspect the valve, rotate it back and forth in your hands. If the sound of a rolling ball is heard, then the valve is probably still good.

24   Apply a lithium-based grease to all of

14   Power brake booster - removal and installation

Refer to illustration 14.2

1   If the booster is defective, replace it with a new or rebuilt unit. The booster cannot be overhauled.

2   Disconnect the vacuum hose from the booster unit **(see illustration)**.

3   Remove the master cylinder (see Section 7).

4   Working on the inside of the vehicle, remove the pedal return spring, the cotter pin and the push rod clevis pin, and disconnect the booster pushrod clevis from the brake pedal.

5   Remove the four booster-to-firewall nuts, then remove the booster from the vehicle. Discard the old seals.

6   Installation is the reverse of removal. Be sure to install new seals on both sides of the engine firewall before installing the booster assembly. Tighten the booster-to-firewall

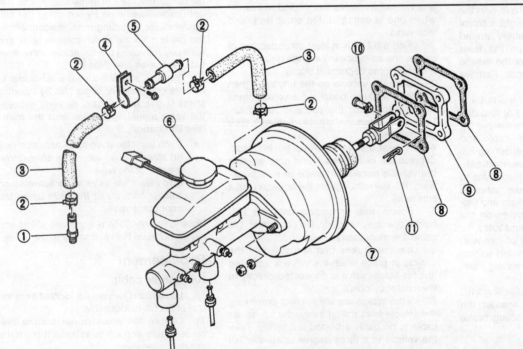

14.2 An exploded view of a typical power brake booster assembly

1   *Vacuum hose joint bolt*
2   *Clip*
3   *Vacuum hose*
4   *Clamp*
5   *Check valve*
6   *Master cylinder assembly*
7   *Brake booster*
8   *Seal*
9   *Spacer*
10 *Clevis pin*
11 *Snap-ring*

15.1 The brake light switch and cruise control switch (arrows), if equipped, are located at the top of the brake pedal; although both switches look alike, they work in just the opposite fashion, so make sure you have the right switch before testing, adjusting or replacing it!

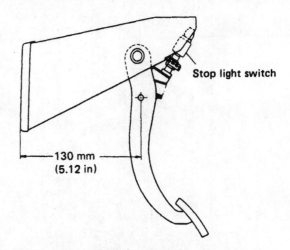

15.5 Brake pedal height is measured from the pedal to the firewall as shown

nuts to the torque listed in this Chapter's Specifications.
7 Bleed the brake system (see Section 10).

15 Brake light switch - check, adjustment and replacement

Check

Refer to illustration 15.1

1 The brake light switch **(see illustration)** is located at the top of the brake pedal. You'll need a flashlight to locate it. If the vehicle is equipped with cruise control, you will see *two* switches which look exactly alike; the other switch is for the cruise-control system. But they work exactly the opposite way: the brake light switch is normally open, and is closed when the brake pedal is depressed; the cruise switch is normally closed, and is opened when the brake pedal is depressed.
2 To check the switch, trace the switch lead to the electrical connector, unplug the connector and hook up an ohmmeter to the terminals on the switch side of the connector.
3 With the brake pedal released, the switch should have no continuity; when the pedal is depressed, there should be continuity. If the switch doesn't operate as described, adjust it and retest. (If the switch operates exactly opposite to this, you're checking the cruise control switch.)
Refer to illustrations 15.5, 15.7 and 15.9

Adjustment

4 First, make sure that the brake pedal height and freeplay are adjusted correctly.
5 To adjust brake pedal height, unplug the electrical connector for the brake light switch. Loosen the switch locknut and turn the brake light switch until the pedal height **(see illustration)** listed in this Chapter's Specifications is obtained.
6 Tighten the locknut, plug in the electrical connector and check the brake lights for proper operation. They should come on when the brake pedal is depressed, and go out when it is released.
7 To check pedal freeplay (the distance the pedal travels before it begins to move the power brake pushrod), loosen the locknut on the power brake pushrod (at the clevis that attaches the pushrod to the brake pedal) and turn the pushrod (pliers may be necessary) until the proper amount of freeplay **(see illustration)** is obtained. Tighten the locknut securely.
8 Depress the pedal as far as possible and make sure that the pedal-to-floor clearance is as specified. If the pedal has an excessively long stroke, check the brake shoe lining-to-drum clearance (see Chapter 1).
9 Adjust the switch by loosening the locknut and turning the switch threaded switch barrel up or down until the stroke of the switch plunger is within the correct dimension **(see illustration)**.

Replacement

10 Unplug the switch electrical connector.
11 Remove the switch locknut and remove the switch from its bracket.
12 Installation is the reverse of removal. Be sure to adjust the switch, then check it to verify that it operates properly.

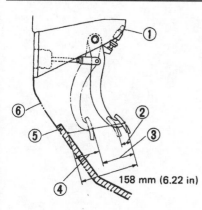

15.7 Brake pedal freeplay and reserve clearance (the distance between the pedal and the floor mat) are measured between the indicated points

1 Brake light switch
2 Brake pedal freeplay
3 Brake pedal stroke
4 Reserve clearance
5 Floor mat
6 Toe board (firewall)

158 mm (6.22 in)

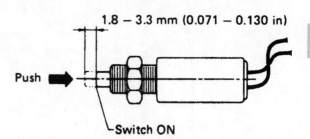

15.9 Adjust the brake light switch so that the plunger stroke is within the indicated dimension

9

Notes

Chapter 10
Suspension and steering systems

Contents

Specifications

Ground clearance

1979 through 1983 models

Front

Hatchback (std)	10-7/16 to 11-27/64 inches
Hatchback (GL)	10-5/8 to 11-39/64 inches
Station wagon (DL)	10-7/16 to 11-27/64 inches
Station wagon (GL)	10-5/8 to 11-39/64 inches
Maximum additional height (all)	63/64 inch

Rear

Hatchback (std)	12-19/32 to 13-25/64 inches
Hatchback (GL)	12-51/64 to 13-37/64 inches
Station wagon (DL)	13-3/16 to 13-63/64 inches
Station wagon (GL)	13-25/64 to 14-11/64 inches
Maximum additional height (all)	1-3/16 inches

1984 4WD models

Front

Sedan	9-21/32 11-1/64 inches
Station wagon	9-27/32 to 11-7/32 inches

Rear

Sedan	9-21/32 to 10-53/64 inches
Station wagon	10-15/64 to 11-27/64 inches

1985 through 1988 4WD models

Front

Sedan and hatchback	9-19/32 to 10-15/16 inches
Station wagon	9-3/4 to 11-7/64 inches

Rear

Sedan and hatchback	9-41/64 to 10-53/64 inches
Station wagon	10-3/16 to 11-3/8 inches

1989 4WD models

Front

All models	9-11/64 to 10-1/2 inches

Rear

All models	9-3/64 to 10-15/64 inches

10

Ground clearance (continued)

1990 and later models

Front

Sedan and hatchback (2WD)	8-27/64 to 9-3/4 inches
Station wagon (2WD)	8-21/32 to 10 inches
Sedan and hatchback (4WD)	9-39/64 to 10-15/16 inches
Station wagon (4WD)	9-3/4 to 11-7/64 inches

Rear

Sedan and hatchback (2WD)	7-3/4 to 8-15/16 inches
Station wagon (2WD)	8-1/2 to 9-3/4 inches
Sedan and hatchback (4WD)	9-41/64 to 10-53/64 inches
Station wagon (4WD)	10-3/16 to 11-3/8 inches

Torque specifications

Ft-lbs (unless otherwise indicated)

Front suspension

Leading rod	
Leading rod-to-bracket nut	
1984 and earlier	
Metal self-locking nut	27 to 31
Nylon self-locking nut	43 to 51
1985 and later	58 to 72
Leading rod-to-lower control arm nuts/bolts	
1983 and earlier	27 to 31
1984 and later	
Metal self-locking nut	49 to 55
Nylon self-locking nut	83 to 98
Stabilizer bar (1984 and earlier)	
Stabilizer-to-leading rod clamp nut/bolt	13 to 23
Stabilizer bushing clamp nuts	13 to 16
Stabilizer bar (1985 and later)	
Stabilizer bushing clamp bolt	15 to 21
Stabilizer-to-lower control arm plate nut/bolt	14 to 22
Plate-to-lower control arm nut/bolt	14 to 22
Steering knuckle-to-balljoint pinch bolt	28 to 37
Strut assembly	
Strut upper mounting nuts	22 to 27
Steering knuckle pinch bolt and strut-to-knuckle bolt	
1984 and earlier	22 to 29
1985 and later	28 to 37
Strut damper rod-to-mount nut	
1984 and earlier	43 to 54
1985 and later	38 to 49
Lower control arm	
Lower arm-to-crossmember pivot bolt/nut	43 to 51
Lower arm-to-ballstud nut	29

Rear suspension

Shock absorber	
Lower mounting bolt/nut	65 to 87
Upper mounting bolts	65 to 94
Lower damper shaft nut	7 to 14
Upper damper shaft nut	13 to 19
Stabilizer bar bushing clamp bolts	13 to 16
Inner suspension arm pivot bolt/nut	80 to 101
Outer bushing locking bolt (1984 and earlier)	23 to 29
Outer suspension arm-to-inner suspension arm bolts	87 to 108
Outer suspension arm-to-crossmember bolt/nut (1985 and later)	108 to 130
Wheel bearing ring nut	127 to 163

Steering

Idler pulley lock bolt	18 to 25
Tie-rod balljoint nut	18 to 22
Steering gear mounting bolts	
1984 and earlier	33 to 40
1985 and later	35 to 52
Steering shaft U-joint pinch bolt	16 to 19
Steering wheel nut	22 to 29

1.1a Typical front suspension components (1984 and earlier models)

1	Stabilizer bar	6	Lower control arms	11	Steering gear boots
2	Stabilizer bar bushing clamps	7	Steering knuckles	12	Lower control arm pivot bolts/nuts
3	Leading rod	8	Tie-rod ends	13	Steering gear brackets
4	Leading rod bracket	9	Tie rods	14	Steering gear
5	Stabilizer bar-to-leading rod clamps	10	Strut/coil spring assemblies		

1.1b Typical front suspension components (1985 and later models)

1	Stabilizer bar	5	Steering gear boots	9	Balljoint nuts
2	Stabilizer bar bushing clamps	6	Tie rods	10	Lower control arms
3	Steering gear	7	Tie-rod ends	11	Leading rods
4	Steering gear brackets	8	Stabilizer bar-to-lower control arm plates		

10

1 General information

Suspension

Refer to illustrations 1.1a, 1.1b, 1.2a and 1.2b

The front suspension is fully independent. It consists of MacPherson strut/coil spring assemblies, lower control arms, steering knuckles and a stabilizer bar. The upper end of each strut is attached to the body and the lower end is bolted to the steering knuckle. The lower end of the knuckle is attached to the lower control arm by a balljoint. The inner end of the lower control arm is bolted to a crossmember. The stabilizer bar is attached to the crossmember by a pair of clamps and is connected to the lower control arms by a pair of plates at each end. The lower control arms are positioned by a pair of leading rods. The front end of each leading rod is attached to a bracket bolted to the vehicle; the rear end of each rod is bolted to the lower control arm **(see illustrations)**.

The rear suspension is also fully independent. It consists of a pair of two-piece trailing arm assemblies bolted to a crossmember.

1984 and earlier models use a torsion bar set-up and shock absorbers; on these models, the outer suspension arms are splined onto the ends of the torsion bars, which are housed inside the crossmember. The rear suspension assembly on 1985 and later models uses coil springs instead of torsion bars, and is equipped with a stabilizer bar, but is otherwise identical in design to earlier models **(see illustrations)**.

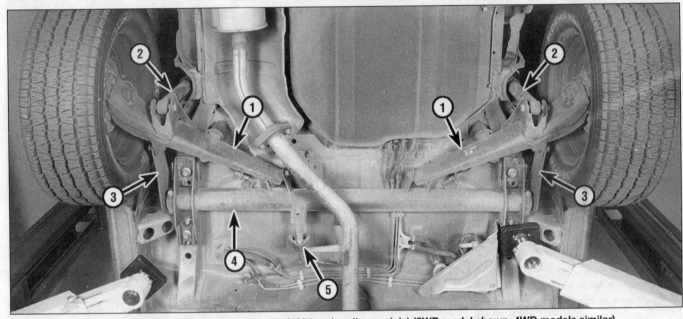

1.2a Typical rear suspension components (1984 and earlier models) (2WD model shown, 4WD models similar)

1	Inner suspension arms	3	Outer suspension arms	5	Center arm
2	Shock absorbers	4	Crossmember (torsion bars inside)		

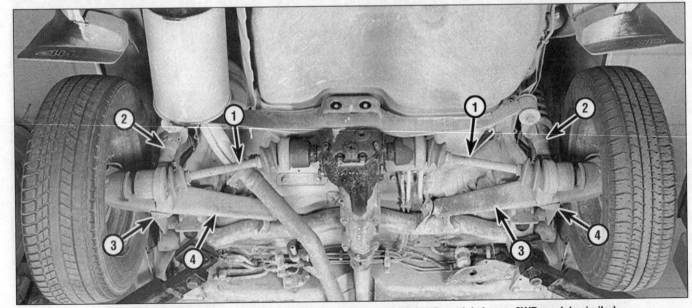

1.2b Typical rear suspension components (1985 and later models) (4WD model shown, 2WD models similar)

1	Driveaxle assemblies	3	Inner suspension arms
2	Shock absorber/coil spring assemblies	4	Outer suspension arms

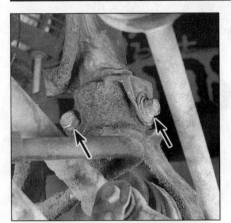

2.3a To detach the lower end of the strut/coil spring assembly from the steering knuckle, remove the knuckle pinch bolt (left arrow) and the strut-to-knuckle bolt (right arrow)

2.3b To disengage the steering knuckle from the strut, grasp the knuckle and try to wiggle it back and forth while pushing down

2.3c If the steering knuckle is frozen to the strut assembly, pry it down with a prybar or large screwdriver as shown

Steering

All vehicles use a rack-and-pinion type steering gear. Some units are manual; most are power-assisted. The steering gear is connected to the steering knuckles by a pair of tie-rods. Front wheel toe-in is adjusted by screwing the tie-rod ends in or out.

2   Strut/coil spring assembly - removal and installation

Removal

Refer to illustrations 2.3a, 2.3b, 2.3c, 2.4a, 2.4b and 2.4c

1   If the vehicle is equipped with air suspension, make sure that the vehicle is in the normal (low) position, the height control switch is turned off, and the battery ground cable is disconnected.

2   Loosen the front wheel lug nuts, block the rear wheels, raise the front of the vehicle and place it securely on jackstands. Remove the front wheels.

3   Detach the clips holding the flexible brake hose to the strut. Remove the two bolts - steering knuckle pinch bolt and strut-to-knuckle bolt - securing the lower end of the strut to the steering knuckle **(see illustration)**, then grasp the knuckle with your hands and turn it back and forth while simultaneously pushing down **(see illustration)** to disengage the knuckle from the strut. If the knuckle is stuck, pry it off with a large screwdriver or prybar **(see illustration)**.

4   From the engine compartment, remove the mounting nuts which attach the top of the strut to the strut tower **(see illustrations)**.

5   Remove the strut assembly. If you're planning to replace either the strut or the coil spring, refer to Section 3.

Installation

Refer to illustration 2.6

6   Place the strut assembly in position. On

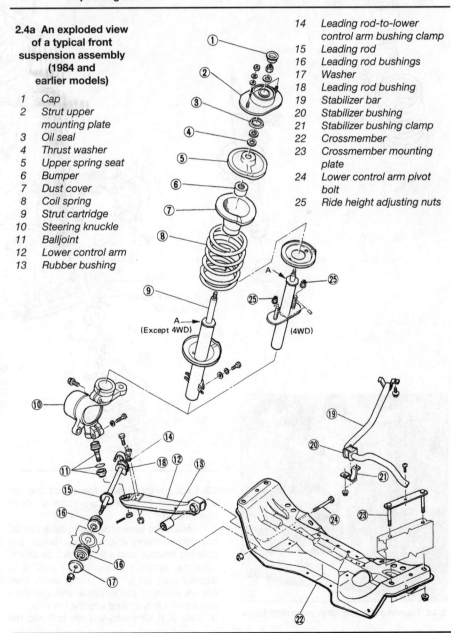

2.4a An exploded view of a typical front suspension assembly (1984 and earlier models)

1   Cap
2   Strut upper mounting plate
3   Oil seal
4   Thrust washer
5   Upper spring seat
6   Bumper
7   Dust cover
8   Coil spring
9   Strut cartridge
10   Steering knuckle
11   Balljoint
12   Lower control arm
13   Rubber bushing
14   Leading rod-to-lower control arm bushing clamp
15   Leading rod
16   Leading rod bushings
17   Washer
18   Leading rod bushing
19   Stabilizer bar
20   Stabilizer bushing
21   Stabilizer bushing clamp
22   Crossmember
23   Crossmember mounting plate
24   Lower control arm pivot bolt
25   Ride height adjusting nuts

10

2.4b An exploded view of a typical front suspension assembly (1985 and later models)

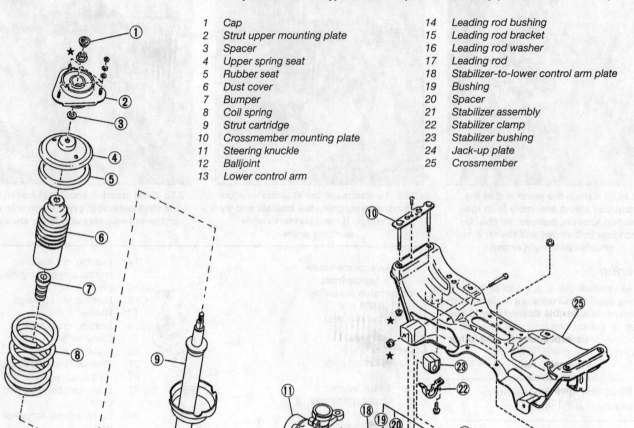

1	Cap	14	Leading rod bushing
2	Strut upper mounting plate	15	Leading rod bracket
3	Spacer	16	Leading rod washer
4	Upper spring seat	17	Leading rod
5	Rubber seat	18	Stabilizer-to-lower control arm plate
6	Dust cover	19	Bushing
7	Bumper	20	Spacer
8	Coil spring	21	Stabilizer assembly
9	Strut cartridge	22	Stabilizer clamp
10	Crossmember mounting plate	23	Stabilizer bushing
11	Steering knuckle	24	Jack-up plate
12	Balljoint	25	Crossmember
13	Lower control arm		

Tighten further within 60°

★: Self-locking nuts are coated with special wax to provide proper torque setting. Discard old self-locking nut after removal. Replace with a new one.

2.4c Remove the top strut mounting bolts

1984 and earlier models, make sure that the strut assembly is oriented correctly **(see illustration)**.

7   Install the upper mounting nuts but do not tighten them. Place a jack under the steering knuckle and use the jack to slowly raise the knuckle into position until it is aligned with the bottom of the strut, then continue raising the knuckle until the strut assembly is fully seated into the knuckle.

8   Install the strut-to-knuckle bolt and the

Front →   ← Front

VAN 4WD PS   SEDAN

(Station Wagon, 4WD vehicle and vehicle with power steering)   (Hatchback, Sedan and Hardtop)

2.6 On 1984 and earlier models, make sure that the upper strut mounting plate is oriented correctly

3.3 Install the spring compressor in accordance with the manufacturer's instructions and compress the spring until all pressure is relieved from the upper spring seat

3.4 Remove the damper shaft nut

3.5 Remove the upper mount from the damper shaft

3.6 Remove the upper spring seat from the damper shaft

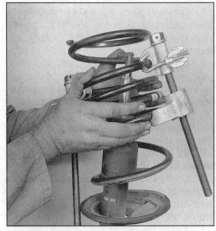

3.7 Remove the compressed spring assembly; keep the ends of the spring pointed away from your body

knuckle pinch bolt and tighten them to the torque listed in this Chapter's Specifications.

9   Attach the flexible brake hose to the strut with the clip.

10   Repeat this procedure for the other strut.

11   Install the wheels, remove the jackstands and lower the vehicle.

12   Tighten the wheel lug nuts to the torque listed in the Chapter 1 Specifications. Tighten the upper strut mounting nuts to the torque listed in this Chapter's Specifications.

13   Have the front end aligned at an alignment shop.

3   Strut/coil spring - replacement

1   If the struts or coil springs exhibit the telltale signs of wear (leaking fluid, loss of damping capability, chipped, sagging or cracked coil springs) explore all options before beginning any work. The strut/shock absorber assemblies are not serviceable and must be replaced if a problem develops. However, strut assemblies complete with springs may be available on an exchange basis, which eliminates much time and work. Whichever route you choose to take, check on the cost and availability of parts before disassembling your vehicle. **Warning:** *Disassembling a strut assembly is a potentially dangerous undertaking and utmost attention must be directed to the job at hand, or serious bodily injury may result. Use only a high quality spring compressor and carefully follow the manufacturer's instructions furnished with the tool. After removing the coil spring from the strut assembly, set it aside in a safe, isolated area (a steel cabinet is preferred).*

Disassembly

Refer to illustrations 3.3, 3.4, 3.5, 3.6 and 3.7

2   Remove the strut and spring assembly (see Section 2).

3   Mount the strut assembly in a vise. Line the vise jaws with wood or rags to prevent damage to the unit and don't tighten the vise excessively. Following the tool manufacturer's instructions, install the spring compressor (which can be obtained at most auto parts stores or equipment yards on a daily rental basis) on the spring and compress it sufficiently to relieve all pressure from the upper spring seat **(see illustration)**. This can be verified by wiggling the spring.

4   Loosen the self-locking damper shaft nut with a socket wrench **(see illustration)**.

5   Remove the self-locking nut and discard it. Remove the upper strut mount **(see illustration)**. Inspect the bearing in the suspension support for smooth operation. If it doesn't turn smoothly, replace the strut mount. Check the rubber portion of the strut mount for cracking and general deterioration. If there is any separation of the rubber, replace it.

6   On 1984 and earlier models, remove the oil seal, the thrust washer, the upper spring seat, the bumper and the dust cover. On 1985 and later models, remove the upper spring seat **(see illustration)**, the rubber

seat, the dust cover and the bumper. On 1984 and earlier models, inspect the condition of the upper seat, the bumper and the dust cover and replace any damaged parts as necessary. On 1985 and later models, inspect the spring seat, rubber seat, dust cover and bumper for cracking and hardness, replacing the damaged parts as necessary.

7   Carefully lift the compressed spring from the assembly **(see illustration)** and set it in a safe place, such as a steel cabinet. **Warning:** *Never place your head near the end of the spring!*

8   Slide the rubber bumper off the damper shaft.

9   Check the lower insulator (if equipped) for wear, cracking and hardness and replace it if necessary.

Reassembly

Refer to illustrations 3.11 and 3.12

10   If the lower insulator is being replaced, set it into position with the dropped portion seated in the lowest part of the seat. Extend the damper rod to its full length and install the rubber bumper.

10

3.11 When installing the spring, make sure the end fits into the recessed portion of the lower seat (arrow)

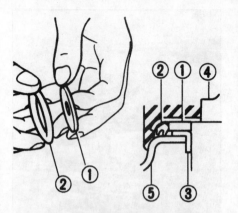

3.12 Installation details for the strut oil seal and thrust washer (1984 and earlier models)

1   Washer
2   Oil seal
3   Thrust washer
4   Piston rod
5   Upper spring seat

4.2a To disconnect the stabilizer bar from the leading rods on 1984 and earlier models, remove these bushing clamp bolts (arrow) (left end clamping bolt shown)

11   Carefully place the coil spring onto the lower insulator, with the end of the spring resting in the lowest part of the insulator **(see illustration).**
12   On 1984 and earlier models, install the dust cover, the rubber bumper, the upper spring seat and the thrust washer **(see illustration 2.4a).** Install the ground surface of the washer facing the lip side of the oil seal. Then install the oil seal and washer assembly over the thrust washer. Install them with the oil seal lip facing the upper spring seat **(see illustration).**
13   On 1985 and later models, install the rubber bumper, the dust cover, the rubber seat and the upper spring seat **(see illustration 2.4b).**
14   Install the upper strut mount. Install a new self-locking nut and tighten it to the torque listed in this Chapter's Specifications.
15   Install the strut/coil spring assembly (see Section 2).

4   Stabilizer bar (front) - removal and installation

Refer to illustrations 4.2a, 4.2b, 4.3a and 4.3b
1   If the vehicle is equipped with air suspension, make sure that the vehicle is in the normal (low) position, the height control switch is turned off, and the battery ground cable is disconnected. Loosen the wheel lug nuts. Block the rear wheels, raise the front of the vehicle and place it securely on jackstands. Remove the front wheels.
2   On 1984 and earlier models, remove the bolts **(see illustration)** which attach the stabilizer bar to the leading rod. On 1985 and later models, unbolt the stabilizer bar from the plates that connect it to the lower control arms **(see illustration).**
3   Remove the stabilizer bar bushing clamps **(see illustrations).** Remove the stabilizer.
4   Remove the bushings from the stabilizer and inspect them for cracks or deterioration.

Inspect the stabilizer bar for cracks in the curved portions and deformation. Replace any parts, as necessary.
5   Installation is the reverse of removal. Don't fully tighten the mounting nuts and bolts until the vehicle is lowered to the ground.
6   Install the wheels, remove the jackstands and lower the vehicle.
7   Tighten the wheel lug nuts to the torque listed in the Chapter 1 Specifications. Tighten the stabilizer bar nuts and bolts to the torque listed in this Chapter's Specifications.

5   Leading rod - removal and installation

Refer to illustrations 5.2 and 5.3
1   If the vehicle is equipped with air suspension, make sure that the vehicle is in the normal (low) position, the height control switch is turned off, and the battery ground cable is disconnected. Loosen the wheel lug nuts, block the rear wheels, raise the front of the vehicle and place it securely on jackstands. Remove the front wheel.

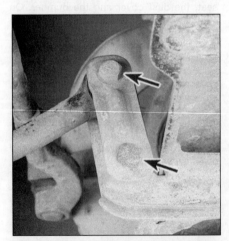

4.2b To disconnect the stabilizer bar from the lower control arms on 1985 and later models, remove the upper plate bolts (upper arrow) and nuts; to disconnect the plates themselves, remove the lower bolts (lower arrow) and nuts (right end plates/bolts shown)

4.3a To detach the stabilizer bar bushing clamps from 1984 and earlier models, remove these nuts (arrows) (left clamp shown)

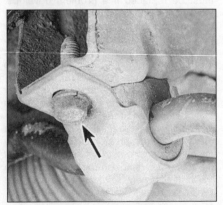

4.3b To detach the stabilizer bar bushing clamps from 1985 and later models, remove this bolt (arrow) from each clamp (right clamp/bolt shown)

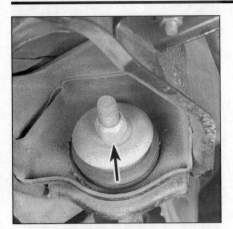

5.2 To disconnect the rear end of the leading rod from its bracket, remove this nut (arrow)

5.3 To disconnect the front end of the leading rod from the lower control arm, remove these two bolts

6.4a If you have a suitable puller, remove the cotter pin from the castellated nut . . .

2   Remove the nut which attaches the rear end of the leading rod to its bracket **(see illustration)**. Remove the washer and bushing.
3   Remove the bolts which attaches the front end of the leading rod to the lower control arm **(see illustration)**.
4   Remove the leading rod from the vehi-

cle, then remove the other bushing from the rod.
5   Inspect the bushings for cracks or deterioration. Inspect the leading rod for cracks and deformation. Replace any damaged parts as necessary.
6   Installation is the reverse of removal. Do not fully tighten the leading rod nut and bolts until the vehicle is on the ground.
7   Install the wheel, remove the jackstands and lower the vehicle.
8   Tighten the wheel lug nuts to the torque listed in the Chapter 1 Specifications. Tighten the leading rod nut and bolts to the torque listed in this Chapter's Specifications.
9   Have the front end aligned at an alignment shop.

6   Lower control arm - removal and installation

Refer to illustrations 6.4a, 6.4b, 6.4c, 6.5a, 6.5b and 6.8
1   If the vehicle is equipped with air suspension, make sure that the vehicle is in the normal (low) position, the height control switch is turned off, and the battery ground cable is disconnected.

2   Loosen the wheel lug nuts, block the rear wheels, raise the front of the vehicle and place it securely on jackstands. Remove the front wheel.
3   Detach the parking brake cable bracket from the suspension arm.
4   There are two ways to disconnect the outer end of the control arm from the steering knuckle. Neither method is better. Which method you use depends on whether you have a suitable puller. If you have a suitable puller, remove the cotter pin, loosen the balljoint mounting nut about halfway, then attach a puller to separate the balljoint stud from the lower control arm **(see illustrations)**.
5   If you don't have a suitable puller, remove the balljoint pinch bolt from the steering knuckle and use a large prybar to lever the balljoint from the knuckle **(see illustrations)**.
6   On 1985 and later models, disconnect the stabilizer bar from the lower control arm (see Section 4).
7   Disconnect the forward end of the leading rod from the lower control arm (see Section 5).

6.4b . . . loosen - but don't remove - the nut . . .

6.4c . . . install a puller and separate the ballstud from the lower control arm; remove the nut and disengage the arm from the ballstud

6.5a If you don't have a suitable puller, remove the balljoint pinch bolt from the steering knuckle . . .

6.5b . . . then insert a large prybar between the lower control arm and the steering knuckle and lever the balljoint out of the knuckle

10

6.8 Using a backup wrench, remove the pivot bolt and nut that attach the inner end of the lower control arm to the crossmember

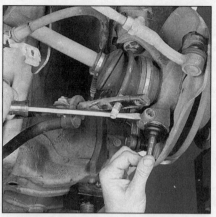

7.9 Use a screwdriver to pry open the slot in the steering knuckle to facilitate removal of the balljoint from the knuckle

7.10 Carefully pry the boot ring from the balljoint with a small screwdriver

8   Remove the lower control arm pivot bolt and nut **(see illustration)**.
9   Remove the lower control arm.
10   Inspect the control arm bushings for cracks or deterioration. Inspect the control arm for cracks and deformations. Replace any damaged parts.
11   Installation is the reverse of removal. Do not fully tighten the suspension fasteners until the vehicle is on the ground.
12   Install the wheel, remove the jackstands and lower the vehicle.
13   Tighten the wheel lug nuts to the torque listed in this Chapter's Specifications. Tighten all suspension fasteners to the torque listed in this Chapter's Specifications.
14   Have the front end aligned at an alignment shop.

7   Balljoints - check and replacement

Check

1   Inspect the control arm balljoints for looseness anytime either of them is separated from the lower control arm. See if you can turn the ballstud in its socket with your fingers. If the balljoint is loose, or if the ballstud can be turned, replace the balljoint. You can also check the balljoints with the suspension assembled as follows.
2   If the vehicle is equipped with air suspension, make sure that the vehicle is in the normal (low) position, the height control switch is turned off, and the battery ground cable is disconnected. Loosen the wheel lug nuts, raise the front of the vehicle and support it securely on jackstands. Remove the wheels.
3   Place jackstands under the lower control arms. Position the stands as close to each balljoint as possible. Make sure the vehicle is stable. It should not rock on the stands.
4   Wipe each balljoint clean and inspect the seal for cuts and tears. If the seal is damaged, replace the balljoint.

5   Position a dial indicator against the wheel rim and insert a prybar between the lower control arm and the steering knuckle. As you lever the prybar, the needle should not deflect more than 0.125-inch. If it does, replace the balljoint.

Replacement

Refer to illustrations 7.9 and 7.10
6   If the vehicle is equipped with air suspension, make sure that the vehicle is in the normal (low) position, the height control switch is turned off, and the battery ground cable is disconnected. Loosen the wheel lug nuts. Block the rear wheels, raise the front of the vehicle and place it on jackstands. Remove the front wheel.
7   Disconnect the lower control arm from the balljoint (see Section 6). **Note:** *The following procedure does not apply if you use the alternative (no-puller) method to separate the lower arm from the steering knuckle described in Section 6. If you're using that method, you'll have to remove the lower control arm and have the balljoint separated from the arm by an automotive machine shop.*
8   Remove the balljoint pinch bolt from the steering knuckle **(see illustration 6.5a)**.
9   Use a large screwdriver to pry open the slot in the steering knuckle **(see illustration)**, then install the castle nut onto the end of the ballstud and use it as a handle to pull the balljoint out of the knuckle.
10   Remove the boot ring from the balljoint **(see illustration)** and remove the rubber boot.
11   Inspect the boot for cracks or deterioration. Check the balljoint for rust, pitting and abnormal wear. Replace any parts, if necessary, with new ones.
12   Apply wheel bearing grease to the balljoint and pack the inside of the rubber boot. Also apply a thin coat of oil to the part of the balljoint that fits into the steering knuckle.
13   Install the balljoint into the knuckle and tighten the pinch bolt to the torque listed in this Chapter's Specifications.

14   Reattach the lower control arm to the steering knuckle (see Section 6).
15   Have the front end aligned at an alignment shop.

8   Hub (front) - removal and installation

1   The front hub is bolted to the front disc, but cannot be unbolted from the disc until the disc has been removed. Refer to Chapter 9 for the disc removal and installation procedure.
2   Once the hub/disc assembly is removed, separate the two components.
3   Installation is the reverse of removal. Be sure to tighten the hub-to-disc bolts to the torque listed in the Chapter 9 Specifications.

9   Steering knuckle/driveaxle assembly - removal and installation

Refer to illustrations 9.4 and 9.8
1   The outer ends of the front driveaxles are pressed into inner and outer bearings in the steering knuckles (see Chapter 8); they can't be disengaged from the knuckles without a special puller, nor can they be installed without another special tool. Instead, the driveaxle and the steering knuckle must be removed as a single assembly, then separated by a dealer service department or an automotive machine shop with the proper tools.
2   If the vehicle is equipped with air suspension, make sure that the vehicle is in the normal (low) position, the height control switch is turned off, and the battery ground cable is disconnected. Loosen the wheel lug nuts, block the rear wheels, raise the front of the vehicle and place it securely on jackstands. Remove the front wheel.
3   Remove the brake caliper, the brake pads, the caliper support bracket and the hub/disc assembly (see Chapter 9).

9.4 To detach the brake backing plate from the steering knuckle, remove these bolts (arrows)

4 Remove the brake backing plate from the steering knuckle **(see illustration)**.
5 Disconnect the tie-rod end from the steering knuckle (see Section 21).
6 Remove the spring pin from the transaxle end of the driveaxle assembly (see Chapter 8).
7 Disconnect the lower end of the strut from the steering knuckle (see Section 2).
8 Remove the steering knuckle and driveaxle assembly from the vehicle **(see illustration)**.
9 Take the steering knuckle and driveaxle assembly to a dealer service department or to an automotive machine shop to have the two components separated.
10 While the driveaxle is removed, have the shop check and, if necessary, replace the front wheel bearings (they're pressed into the steering knuckle). If either CV joint boot is damaged, now is the time to disassemble the driveaxle, clean and repack the joint, install a new boot and reassemble the driveaxle (see Chapter 8).
11 While the suspension is disassembled, inspect and, if necessary, replace the lower control arm balljoint (see Section 7).
12 Installation is the reverse of removal. Be sure to use a new spring pin to connect the inner end of the driveaxle assembly to the transaxle. Don't torque any suspension fasteners until the vehicle is on the ground.
13 Install the wheel, remove the jackstands and lower the vehicle.
14 Tighten the wheel lug nuts to the torque listed in the Chapter 1 Specifications. Tighten all suspension fasteners to the torque listed in this Chapter's Specifications.
15 Have the front end aligned at an alignment shop.

10 Wheel bearings (front) - replacement

Refer to illustration 10.2
1 Remove the steering knuckle and

driveaxle assembly (see Section 9). Have a dealer service department or an automotive machine shop separate the driveaxle from the steering knuckle, then have it inspect and, if necessary, replace the front wheel bearings.
2 The bearings **(see illustration)** are pressed onto the driveaxle assembly and into the steering knuckle, and therefore cannot be removed and installed at home without a hydraulic press and the right adapters.
3 Install the steering knuckle and driveaxle assembly (see Section 9). After the drive-axle/steering knuckle assembly has been reassembled, make sure that the outer bearing is packed with grease before installing the brake/hub assembly (see Chapter 1). (The shop must pack the inner bearing before installing the driveaxle.)

11 Shock absorber/coil spring - removal and installation

Refer to illustrations 11.3a, 11.3b and 11.4
Note: *1984 and earlier models, which use torsion bars, do not have coil springs. However, the procedure for removing shock absorbers on those models is identical to the procedure outlined below.*
1 If the vehicle is equipped with air sus-

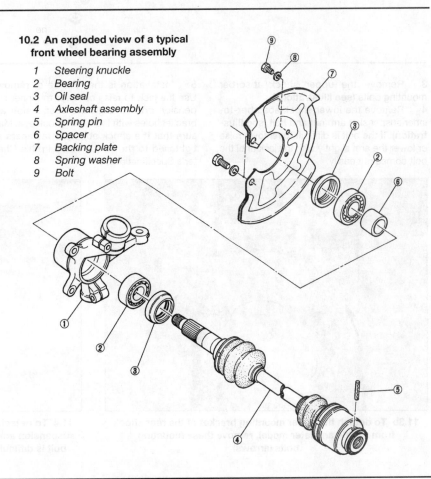

10.2 An exploded view of a typical front wheel bearing assembly

1 Steering knuckle
2 Bearing
3 Oil seal
4 Axleshaft assembly
5 Spring pin
6 Spacer
7 Backing plate
8 Spring washer
9 Bolt

9.8 Remove the steering knuckle and driveaxle as a single assembly

pension, make sure that the vehicle is in the normal (low) position, the height control switch is turned off, and the battery ground cable is disconnected. Loosen the rear wheel lug nuts, block the front wheels, raise the rear of the vehicle and place it on jackstands. Remove the rear wheels.
2 Place a floor jack under the inner suspension arm and raise the jack just enough so that the arm is supported.

10

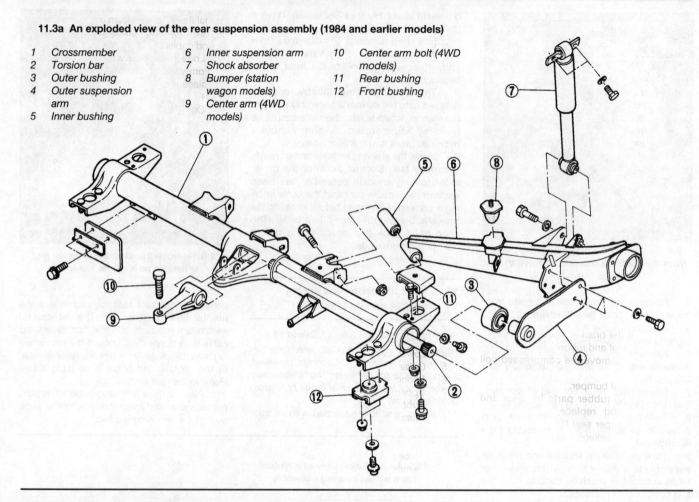

11.3a An exploded view of the rear suspension assembly (1984 and earlier models)

1 Crossmember	6 Inner suspension arm	10 Center arm bolt (4WD
2 Torsion bar	7 Shock absorber	models)
3 Outer bushing	8 Bumper (station	11 Rear bushing
4 Outer suspension	wagon models)	12 Front bushing
arm	9 Center arm (4WD	
5 Inner bushing	models)	

3   Remove the upper shock absorber mounting bolts **(see illustrations)**.

4   Remove the lower shock absorber-to-inner suspension arm nut and bolt **(see illustration)**. If the bolt is difficult to remove, raise or lower the arm slightly with the jack until the bolt comes out easily.

5   Installation is the reverse of removal. Use the jack to raise or lower the inner suspension arm to align the suspension arm bracket holes with the lower shock eye. Make sure that the shock absorber fasteners are tightened to the torque listed in this Chapter's Specifications.

6   Repeat this procedure for the other shock absorber.

7   Install the wheels, remove the jackstands and lower the vehicle.

8   Tighten the wheel lug nuts to the torque listed in this Chapter's Specifications.

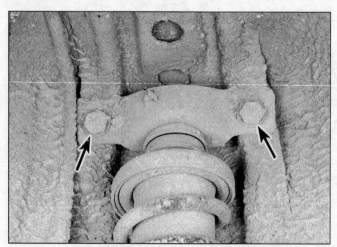

11.3b To detach the upper mounting bracket of the rear shock from a 1984 and later model, remove these mounting bolts (arrows)

11.4 To detach the lower end of the rear shocks from the inner suspension arm bracket, remove this nut (arrow) and bolt; if the bolt is difficult to pull out, raise or lower the suspension arm slightly with a floor jack

12 Shock absorber/coil spring - replacement

Refer to illustration 12.3

Note: *This procedure applies to 1985 and later models only; earlier models, which use torsion bars, do not have coil springs.*

1   Remove the shock absorber/coil spring assembly (see Section 11).

2   Mount the shock absorber/coil spring assembly in a vise. Line the vise jaws with wood or rags to prevent damage to the unit and don't tighten the vise excessively. Following the tool manufacturer's instructions, install a spring compressor (which can be obtained at most auto parts stores or equipment yards on a daily rental basis) on the spring and compress it sufficiently to relieve all pressure from the upper spring seat **(see illustration 3.3)**. This can be verified by wiggling the spring.

3   Remove both damper shaft nuts **(see illustration)**.

4   Remove the bracket, spring seat plate, upper spring seat and rubber seat.

5   Carefully remove the compressed coil spring.

6   Remove the bumper.

7   Inspect all rubber parts for wear and deformation and replace as necessary. Inspect the damper seal for leaks; if there's evidence of any leakage more obvious than a light coating on the damper shaft (oil sprayed on the coil spring, or dripping down the side of the shock body, for example), replace the shock. Inspect the lower rubber bushing for cracks and deterioration and replace as necessary. Push the damper shaft in and out of the shock; the stroke should be smooth and firm. If it isn't, replace the shock.

8   Reassembly is the reverse of disassembly. Make sure that the coil spring is mounted with the flat end facing down (toward the shock body). Tighten the two damper shaft nuts to the torque listed in this Chapter's Specifications (note that the torque values for the nuts are different).

9   Install the shock absorber/coil spring assembly (see Section 11).

13 Stabilizer bar (rear) - removal and installation

Note: *This procedure applies to models with air suspension and a few other models.*

1   If the vehicle is equipped with air suspension, make sure that the vehicle is in the normal (low) position, the height control switch is turned off, and the battery ground cable is disconnected.

2   Loosen the rear wheel lug nuts, block the front wheels, raise the rear of the vehicle and place it on jackstands. Remove the rear wheels.

3   Remove the stabilizer bar bushing clamp bolts **(see illustration 12.3)**.

4   Remove the stabilizer bar.

5   Inspect the rubber bushings for cracks and deterioration and replace as necessary.

6   Installation is the reverse of removal. Be sure to tighten the bushing clamp bolts to the torque listed in this Chapter's Specifications.

7   Install the wheels, remove the jackstands and lower the vehicle.

14 Inner suspension arm (rear) - removal and installation

Refer to illustrations 14.5a, 14.5b, 14.8 and 14.9

1   If the vehicle is equipped with air suspension, make sure that the vehicle is in the normal (low) position, turn off the height control switch, and disconnect the battery ground cable.

2   Loosen the rear wheel lug nuts, block the front wheels, raise the rear of the vehicle and place it on jackstands. Remove the rear wheel.

3   On 4WD models, remove the rear driveaxle assembly (see Chapter 8).

4   Locate the flexible brake hose that connects the metal lines attached to the vehicle pan and the inner suspension arm. Disconnect this hose from the metal brake line on the arm (see Chapter 9). Plug the hose to prevent brake fluid from leaking and to protect it from contamination.

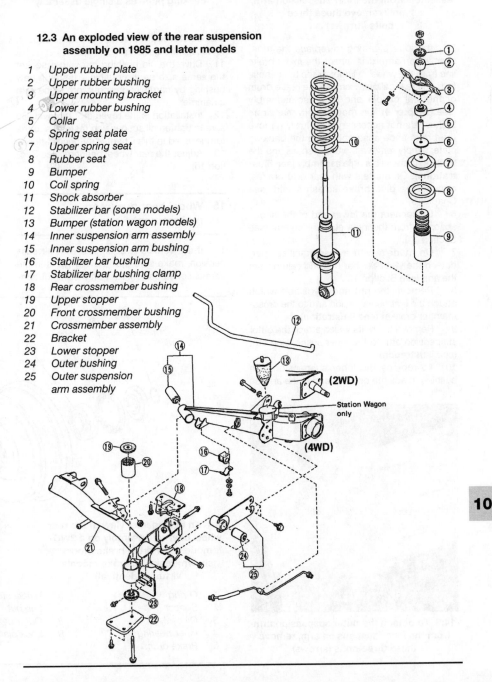

12.3 An exploded view of the rear suspension assembly on 1985 and later models

1   Upper rubber plate
2   Upper rubber bushing
3   Upper mounting bracket
4   Lower rubber bushing
5   Collar
6   Spring seat plate
7   Upper spring seat
8   Rubber seat
9   Bumper
10 Coil spring
11 Shock absorber
12 Stabilizer bar (some models)
13 Bumper (station wagon models)
14 Inner suspension arm assembly
15 Inner suspension arm bushing
16 Stabilizer bar bushing
17 Stabilizer bar bushing clamp
18 Rear crossmember bushing
19 Upper stopper
20 Front crossmember bushing
21 Crossmember assembly
22 Bracket
23 Lower stopper
24 Outer bushing
25 Outer suspension arm assembly

10

14.5a To remove the rear brake shoe assembly from the inner suspension arm, simply remove these three bolts (arrows) . . .

14.5b . . . and lift off the brake shoes and backing plate as a single assembly

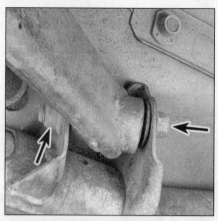

14.8 To detach the inner suspension arm from the crossmember bracket, remove this pivot bolt and nut (arrows)

5   If you're planning to *replace* the inner suspension arm, disconnect the metal brake line from the wheel cylinder or the brake hose from the rear caliper. Remove the brake drum or the rear caliper and hub/disc assembly (see Chapter 9). On models with rear drum brakes, it's not necessary to actually remove the brake shoe assembly from the backing plate; simply remove the brake shoes and the backing plate as a single assembly **(see illustrations)**. On models with rear disc brakes, remove the disc brake splash shield (see Chapter 9).

6   Disconnect the lower end of the shock absorber from the inner suspension arm (see Section 11).

7   On models with a rear stabilizer bar, detach the stabilizer bar bushing clamp from the arm (see Section 13).

8   Remove the nut and pivot bolt which attach the inner suspension arm to the crossmember bracket **(see illustration)**.

9   Remove the bolts which attach the outer suspension arm to the inner suspension arm **(see illustration)**.

10   To replace the inner suspension arm bushing, place the bushing end of the arm on

a block of wood with a hole in it large enough to accept the bushing.

11   Drive the old bushing out with a socket the same size as the bushing. Install a new bushing by carefully driving it into place with a hammer.

12   Installation is the reverse of removal. Be sure to tighten all suspension fasteners to the torque listed in this Chapter's Specifications.

13   Adjust the rear wheel bearings (see Section 15).

15 Wheel bearings (rear) - replacement

1   If the vehicle is equipped with air suspension, make sure that the vehicle is in the normal (low) position, turn off the height con-

trol switch, and disconnect the battery ground cable.

2   Loosen the rear wheel lug nuts, block the front wheels, raise the rear of the vehicle and place it on jackstands. Remove the rear wheel.

2WD models

Refer to illustration 15.4

3   On 4WD models, remove the rear driveaxle assembly (see Chapter 8).

4   Remove the rear brake drum or disc (see Chapter 9) **(see illustration)**. The outer bearing will come off with the brake drum or disc, but the inner bearing may remain on the spindle. Use a puller to remove the inner bearing and spacer from the spindle, if necessary.

5   Check the bearings for grease. Make sure that they are packed full of grease.

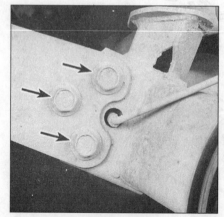

14.9 To detach the outer suspension arm from the inner suspension arm, remove these three bolts (arrows)

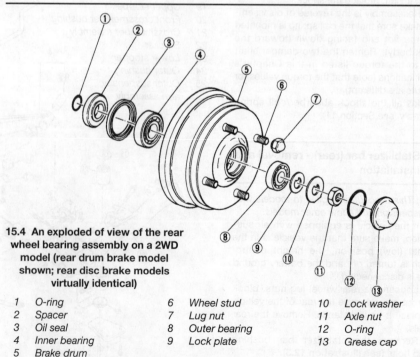

15.4 An exploded of view of the rear wheel bearing assembly on a 2WD model (rear drum brake model shown; rear disc brake models virtually identical)

1	O-ring	6	Wheel stud	10	Lock washer
2	Spacer	7	Lug nut	11	Axle nut
3	Oil seal	8	Outer bearing	12	O-ring
4	Inner bearing	9	Lock plate	13	Grease cap
5	Brake drum				

6 If they do not have a lot of grease around them, clean the bearings thoroughly with solvent, and dry them with compressed air. Inspect the bearings for scoring or burn (blue or yellow) spots. Replace the bearings if they're scored, burned or excessively worn.

7 Pack the bearings with wheel bearing grease. Install the spacer with a new O-ring and the inner bearing onto the spindle. Install the outer bearing along with the brake drum (see Chapter 9).

8 Install the lock plate and new lock washer, then tighten the axle nut to 30 ft-lb. Turn the drum back and forth a few times to make sure that the bearings seat properly. Loosen thee nut 1/4 turn, then tighten it snugly (hand-tight).

9 Make sure that the drum turns easily and smoothly. Bend the locking washer into place. Install a new O-ring on the grease cap, then install the grease cap with a soft-faced hammer.

4WD models

Refer to illustrations 15.10a, 15.10b, 15.11a, 15.11b, 15.13, 15.14, 15.15, 15.16a and 15.16b

Note: For the sake of clarity, the inner suspension arm is removed from the vehicle in most of the photos accompanying this section. However, it's not really necessary to remove the arm to replace the rear wheel bearings (although the procedure is a little easier!). Also, the photos depict a bearing assembly consisting of two tapered roller bearings; many rear bearing assemblies, however, have a single large sealed bearing instead.

10 Remove the rear driveaxle assembly (see Chapter 8). Remove the rear brake drum or disc (see Chapter 9). Remove the spacer washer between the outer CV joint and the ring nut **(see illustrations)**.

11 Loosen the ring nut with a hammer and punch **(see illustration)**, then unscrew and remove the ring nut **(see illustration)**.

12 To remove the spindle, seals and bearings, gently tap on the outer end of the spindle with a dead blow hammer.

13 Dig out and discard the outer seal. Remove the outer tapered roller bearing **(see illustration)**.

14 Pull out the spindle, inner bearing and spacer **(see illustration)**.

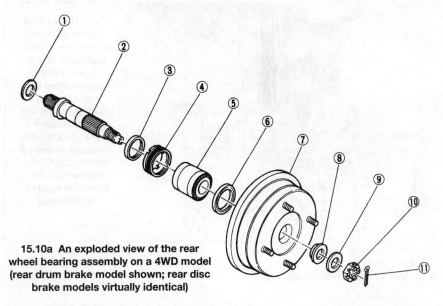

15.10a An exploded view of the rear wheel bearing assembly on a 4WD model (rear drum brake model shown; rear disc brake models virtually identical)

1	Packing	4	Ring nut	8	Centering piece
2	Rear spindle	5	Bearing assembly	9	Spring washer
3	Inner oil seal (fits inside ring nut)	6	Outer oil seal	10	Axle nut
		7	Brake drum	11	Cotter pin

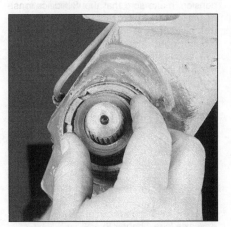

15.10b After disconnecting the outer CV joint from the spindle, remove this spacer washer

15.11a Use a hammer and punch to unstake and loosen the ring nut . . .

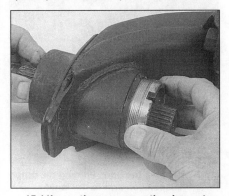

15.11b . . . then unscrew the ring nut

15.13 Pull off the outer tapered roller bearing . . .

15.14 . . . then remove the spindle, inner taper roller and spacer

10

15.15 Here's how the rear wheel bearing assembly looks out of the suspension arm (keep in mind that not all wheel bearing setups use tapered rollers - some units have a single large sealed bearing that goes right where the spacer is located on this unit)

1   Ring nut (inner seal inside ring nut)
2   Outer seal
3   Outer tapered roller bearing
4   Spacer
5   Inner tapered roller bearing
6   Spindle

15   Thoroughly wash all the parts in clean solvent, blow them dry with compressed air and lay them out for inspection **(see illustration)**. Inspect the bearings for scoring and burn (blue and yellow) spots. If the bearings are damaged or worn, replace them.
16   Installation is the reverse of removal. Be sure to grease the bearings liberally with wheel bearing grease and use new seals **(see illustrations)**. The inner seal fits *inside the ring nut*. Tighten the ring nut securely (see this Chapter's Specifications), then stake the axle housing to the ring nut. Make sure that the spindle and bearings can turn freely without any play.
17   Install the driveaxle assembly (see Chapter 8). Install the rear brake drum or disc (see Chapter 9).

All models

18   Install the rear wheels, remove the jackstands and lower the vehicle. Tighten the wheel lug nuts to the torque listed in this Chapter's Specifications.
19   Turn on the air suspension system, if equipped.

16   Outer suspension arm (rear) - removal and installation

1   If the vehicle is equipped with air suspension, make sure that the vehicle is in the normal (low) position, turn off the height control switch, and disconnect the battery ground cable.
2   Loosen the rear wheel lug nuts, block the front wheels, raise the rear of the vehicle and place it on jackstands. Remove the rear wheel.

1984 and earlier models

Refer to illustration 16.9, 16.11, 16.12, 16.13, 16.15 and 16.16

3   Remove the rear shock absorber (see Section 11).
4   On 4WD models, remove the driveshaft (see Chapter 8).
5   On 4WD models, remove the rear driveaxle (see Chapter 8).
6   On 4WD models, remove the rear differential (see Chapter 8).
7   Remove the front and rear exhaust pipe sections (see Chapter 4).

15.16a Place the outer seal square to the bore . . .

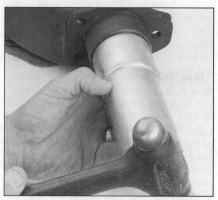

15.16b . . . and tap it into the bore with a large socket

8   Disconnect the brake line fitting attached to the arm. Plug the brake line with the bleeder cap off of the rear brake to keep brake fluid from leaking.
9   Support the crossmember with a floor jack, then remove the crossmember mounting bolts **(see illustration)**.
10   Lower the crossmember assembly to the floor and remove it from the floor jack.
11   Mark the relationship of the torsion bar to the outer suspension arm and the outer suspension arm to the crossmember **(see illustration)** to ensure proper reassembly.
12   Remove the bolts holding the outer suspension arm to the inner suspension arm bracket **(see illustration)**.

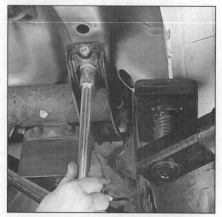

16.9 Remove the bolts holding the crossmember to the frame

16.11 Match mark the torsion bar to the outer suspension arm and then to the crossmember

16.12 Remove the bolts holding the outer suspension arm to the inner suspension arm

16.13 Remove the outer bushing locking bolt

16.15 Remove the torsion bar from the outer suspension arm with a puller

16.16 Remove the outer bushing from the outer suspension arm with a puller on a level surface

13   Remove the outer bushing locking bolt **(see illustration)**.
14   Remove the outer suspension arm and with the torsion bar from the crossmember.
15   Remove the torsion bar from the outer suspension arm with a gear puller **(see illustration)**.
16   Use a puller to remove the bushing **(see illustration)**. Inspect and, if necessary, replace the outer bushing. Apply grease to the exterior of the bushing before installing it.
17   Apply grease to the splines of the torsion bar. Install the outer suspension arm and torsion bar into the crossmember; make sure the marks you made are aligned and make sure that the inner splined end of the torsion bar is properly engaged with the center arm (see Section
17). Install - but don't fully tighten - the outer bushing locking bolt.
18   Install the crossmember and tighten the mounting bolts securely.
19   Install the shock absorbers (see Section 11).
20   Install the front and rear exhaust pipes (see Chapter 4).
21   On 4WD vehicles, install the rear differential, the driveshaft and the rear driveaxles (see Chapter 8).
22   Make sure that all suspension fasteners except the outer bushing locking bolt are tightened to the torque listed in this Chapter's Specifications.

23   Install the wheels, remove the jackstands and lower the vehicle. Now tighten the outer bushing locking bolt to the torque listed in this Chapter's Specifications.

1985 and later models

Refer to illustration 16.25
24   Disconnect the brake line fitting attached to the arm. Plug the brake line with the bleeder cap off of the rear brake to keep brake fluid from leaking.
25   Remove the pivot bolt and nut that connect the outer suspension arm to the crossmember bracket **(see illustration)**.
26   Detach the outer suspension arm from the inner suspension arm **(see illustration 14.9)**.
27   Installation is the reverse of removal. Be sure to tighten all suspension fasteners to the torque listed in this Chapter's Specifications.

17 Center arm (1984 and earlier models) - removal and installation

1   Remove the outer suspension arm and torsion bar assemblies (see Section 16).
2   Remove the center arm height adjustment bolt **(see illustration 11.3a)**, then remove the center arm.
3   Make sure that grease is applied to the

inside of the center arm and also to the splines on both of the torsion bars.
4   Place the center arm in position.
5   Install the outer suspension arm and torsion bar assemblies (see Section 16).

18 Ground clearance (4WD models) - check and adjustment

1   Before checking and adjusting vehicle ground clearance, make sure that the tire pressure is correct, then place the vehicle - unloaded - on a level surface.

1984 and earlier models

Front

Refer to illustrations 18.2 and 18.3
2   Check the ground clearance by measuring the distance between the centerline of the lower control arm pivot bolt and the ground **(see illustration)**. Compare your measurement with the ground clearance listed in this Chapter's Specifications.
3   To adjust the ground clearance, turn the two 21 mm adjusting nuts **(see illustration)** on each strut the same number of turns.

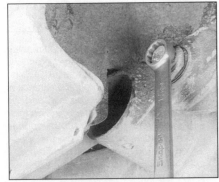

16.25 To disconnect the forward end of the outer suspension arm from the crossmember bracket on a 1984 or later model, remove this pivot bolt and nut

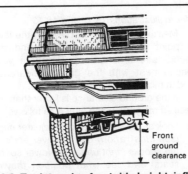

18.2 To determine front ride height, inflate the tires to their correct pressure, place the vehicle on flat ground, and measure the distance between the centerline of the lower control arm pivot bolt and the ground as shown

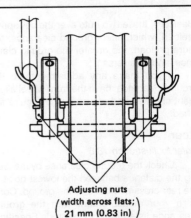

Adjusting nuts
(width across flats;
21 mm (0.83 in)

18.3 The two 21 mm adjusting nuts on each strut, right below the lower spring seat, can be turned to increase or decrease spring preload, which alters ground clearance

10

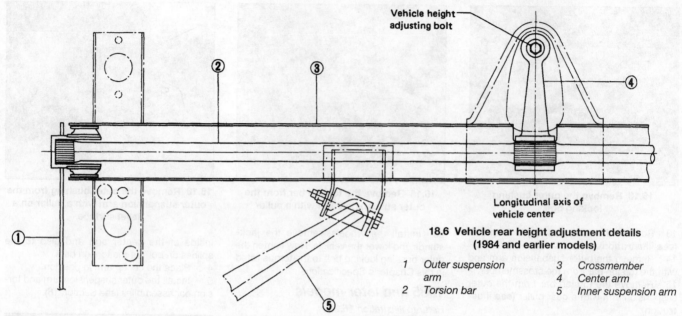

18.6 Vehicle rear height adjustment details (1984 and earlier models)

1	Outer suspension arm	3	Crossmember
2	Torsion bar	4	Center arm
		5	Inner suspension arm

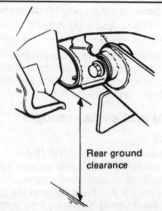

18.12 To determine the rear ground clearance on 1985 and later models, measure the distance from the lowest point on the rear crossmember to the ground

(Basically, these two nuts alter the coil spring preload, which alters ground clearance; the more preload, the greater the ground clearance, and vice versa.)

4   If you make any adjustments to the ground clearance, have the front wheel alignment checked and adjusted when you're finished.

Rear

Refer to illustration 18.6

5   Check the ground clearance by measuring the distance between the lowest point of the rear crossmember and the ground. Compare your measurement with the ground clearance listed in this Chapter's Specifications.

6   To adjust the ground clearance, turn the height adjustment bolt on the center arm **(see illustration)**. An access hole in the floor allows easy access to the adjustment bolt.

7   Turning the bolt clockwise increases

vehicle ground clearance; turning it counterclockwise decreases clearance.

1985 and later models

Front

8   Measure the distance between the centerline of the lower control arm pivot bolt and the ground **(see illustration 18.2)**. Compare your measurement with the ground clearance listed in this Chapter's Specifications.

9   If the ground clearance is out of the specified range on 1985 and 1986 models, the coil spring preload can be adjusted in the same manner as earlier models (see Step 3).

10   If the ground clearance is out of the specified range on 1987 and later models, replace the coil springs (see Sections 2 and 3).

11   If you make any adjustments to ground clearance on a 1985 and 1986 model, or replace the coil springs on a 1987 or later model, have the front wheel alignment checked and adjusted when you're done.

Rear

Refer to illustrations 18.12 and 18.13

12   Measure the distance between the lowest point on the crossmember and the ground **(see illustration)**. Compare your measurement with the ground clearance listed in this Chapter's Specifications.

13   If the ground clearance is lower than the specified range, you can alter it as follows:

a) *Look at the spring preload adjuster rings* **(see illustration)** *on the lower ends of the shocks (right under the lower spring seats) and see what position they're already at. If the preload adjuster rings are set at the highest notch (least amount of spring preload), they can be rotated to produce a total of 1.18 inches more ground clearance (moving from position b to position c produces 0.59-*

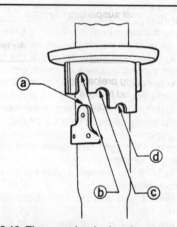

18.13 The rear shock absorbers on 1985 and later models have spring preload adjusters that can be rotated to produce more preload and, therefore, more ground clearance: moving the preload adjuster from position b to position c produces 0.59-inch more ground clearance, and moving it from c to d produces another 0.59-inch, so there's a total of 1.18-inch more ground clearance available (after that, buy new coil springs!)

inch more ground clearance, moving from position c to position d produces another 0.59-inch of clearance).

b) *If the vehicle's rear ground clearance is less than 1.18 inches too low, and the spring preload adjusters are at their highest notch (position b), the springs can be adjusted to produce the specified ground clearance (see Steps 14 through).*

c) *If the ground clearance is greater than 1.18 inches, you won't be able to bring it within the specified range. Replace the rear coil springs (see Sections 11 and 12).*

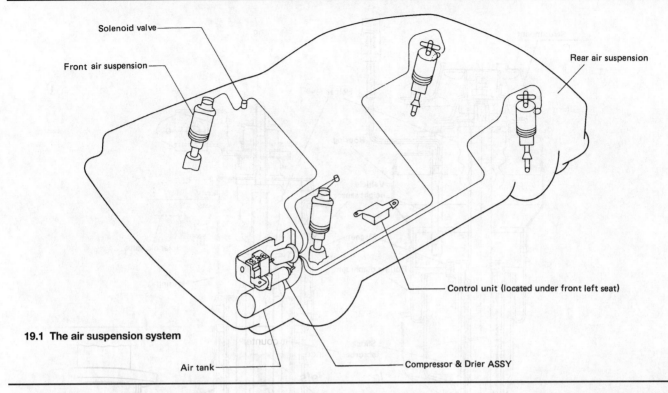

19.1 The air suspension system

d) *If the spring preload adjuster has already been moved to position c, you only have 0.59 inch of adjustment to work with. Whether this will be sufficient to bring the ground clearance within the specified clearance depends on how low it is. If it's more than 0.59-inch too low, replace the coil springs (see Sections 11 and 12).*

e) *If the spring preload adjuster is already at position d, there is no further adjustment available. If the ground clearance is less than the specified clearance, replace the coil springs (see Sections 11 and 12).*

14 Remove the rear shock absorbers (see Section 11), then disassemble them (see Section 12).

15 Rotate the lower spring seat **(see illustration 18.13)** as necessary. Remember: moving the seat from position b to position c increases ground clearance about 0.59 inch; moving the seat from position c to position d increases ground clearance another 0.59 inch.

16 Reassemble the shocks (see Section 12), install them (see Section 11) and re-measure the rear ground clearance to verify that it's now within the specified clearance.

19 Air suspension system - general information and component replacement

General information

Refer to illustrations 19.1, 19.3 and 19.7

1 Some models are equipped with an air suspension system **(see illustration)** which controls vehicle ground clearance. A height control switch allows selection of either of two levels of ground clearance - Normal or High. The difference in height between high and normal is 1.18 inches for the front and 1.38 inches for the rear.

2 The system also maintains a constant ground clearance by altering the clearance in response to vehicle load. This is accomplished by altering the air volume in each air spring in response to a signal from a vehicle height sensor installed in each spring.

3 The system **(see illustration)** consists of four shock absorber/air springs, an air compressor, an air tank and the air lines connecting these components. When the height sensors inside each shock indicate that the

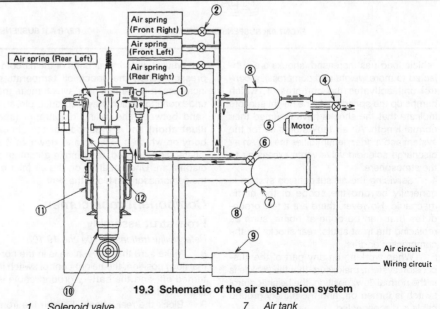

19.3 Schematic of the air suspension system

1	Solenoid valve	7	Air tank
2	Solenoid valve	8	Pressure switch
3	Drier	9	Control unit
4	Air discharge solenoid valve	10	Shock absorber
5	Compressor	11	Rolling diaphragm
6	Air charge solenoid valve	12	Vehicle height sensor

10

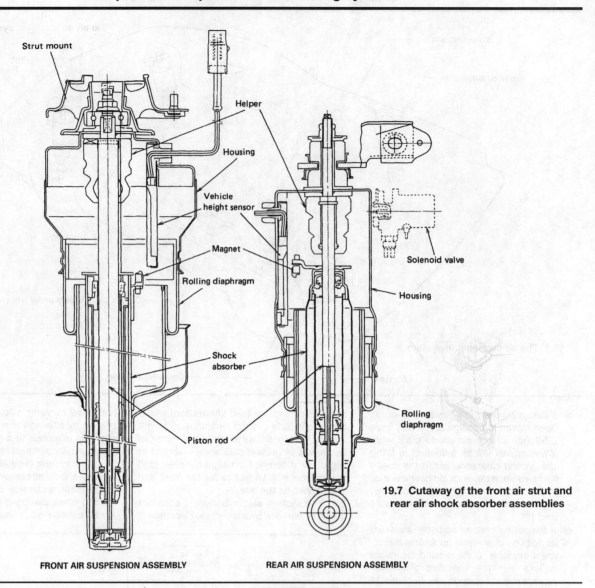

FRONT AIR SUSPENSION ASSEMBLY   **REAR AIR SUSPENSION ASSEMBLY**

19.7 Cutaway of the front air strut and rear air shock absorber assemblies

vehicle load has increased (shocks are subjected to more weight and compress), a control unit activates the compressor, which pumps up the springs until the height sensors indicate that the shocks have resumed their normal length. An air tank stores air for the system and a drier dehumidifies the air. An air discharge solenoid valve vents excess air to the atmosphere.

4   Servicing the air suspension system is generally beyond the scope of the home mechanic. However, there are a few procedures that can be done at home, such as replacing the front struts, rear shocks, or the compressor or drier.

5   When working on any part of the suspension system, make sure that the vehicle is in the normal (low) position, the height control switch is turned off, and the battery ground cable is disconnected.

6   When installing components, do not reuse old O-rings. Apply grease to all O-rings and make sure you don't damage the grooves for the O-rings.

7   Do not apply an undercoating for local rust prevention to the air bags or the air compressor. When the shock oil temperature increases, it generates heat, which melts the undercoating, which may trap dust, dirt and sand between the rolling diaphragm **(see illustration)** and the surface of the shock body on which it rolls up and down as it's inflated and deflated, resulting in a damaged diaphragm. Undercoating on the air inlet of the compressor can block the vent.

Component replacement

Front strut assembly

Refer to illustrations 19.10a and 19.10b

8   Make sure that the vehicle is in the normal (low) position, the height control switch is turned off, and the battery ground cable is disconnected.

9   Block the rear wheels. Loosen the front wheel lug nuts, raise the front of the vehicle and support it securely on jackstands. Remove the front wheels.

10   Disconnect the air pipe **(see illustrations)**.

11   Detach the vehicle height sensor harness from the clip and unplug the harness electrical connector.

12   The rest of the procedure is similar to removing a conventional strut assembly (see Section 2).

13   Installation is the reverse of removal.

Rear shock absorber

14   Make sure that the vehicle is in the normal (low) position, the height control switch is turned off, and the battery ground cable is disconnected.

15   Apply the parking brake. Loosen the rear wheel lug nuts, raise the rear of the vehicle and support it securely on jackstands. Remove the rear wheels.

16   Remove the solenoid valve from the rear air suspension assembly **(see illustration 19.10b)**. If you're going to replace the solenoid valve, disconnect the air pipe from the solenoid valve.

17   Pull out the vehicle height sensor harness from the access hole in the shock body and unplug the harness electrical connector.

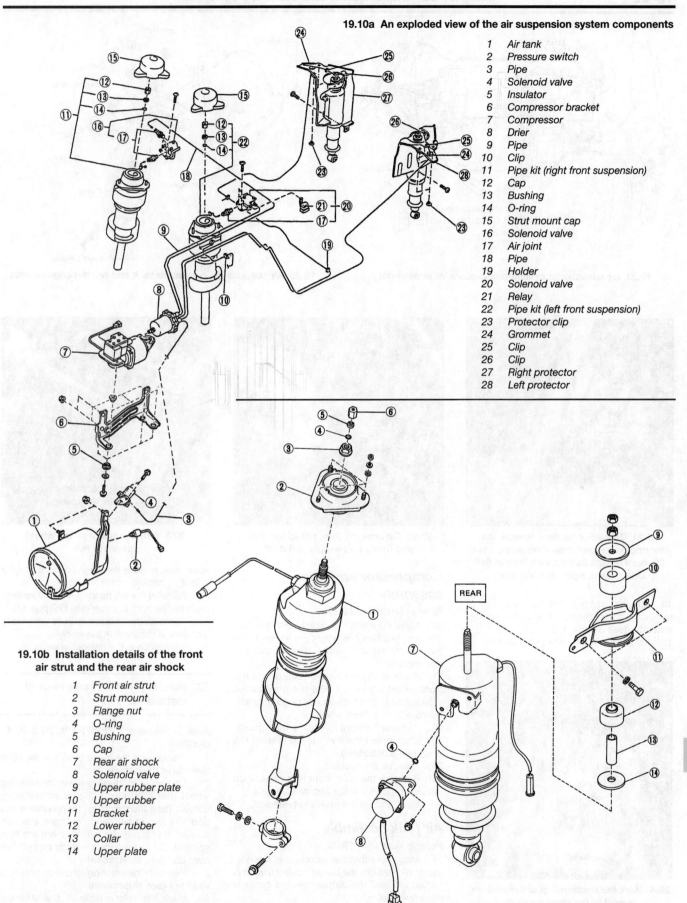

19.10a An exploded view of the air suspension system components

1   Air tank
2   Pressure switch
3   Pipe
4   Solenoid valve
5   Insulator
6   Compressor bracket
7   Compressor
8   Drier
9   Pipe
10 Clip
11 Pipe kit (right front suspension)
12 Cap
13 Bushing
14 O-ring
15 Strut mount cap
16 Solenoid valve
17 Air joint
18 Pipe
19 Holder
20 Solenoid valve
21 Relay
22 Pipe kit (left front suspension)
23 Protector clip
24 Grommet
25 Clip
26 Clip
27 Right protector
28 Left protector

19.10b Installation details of the front air strut and the rear air shock

1   Front air strut
2   Strut mount
3   Flange nut
4   O-ring
5   Bushing
6   Cap
7   Rear air shock
8   Solenoid valve
9   Upper rubber plate
10 Upper rubber
11 Bracket
12 Lower rubber
13 Collar
14 Upper plate

10

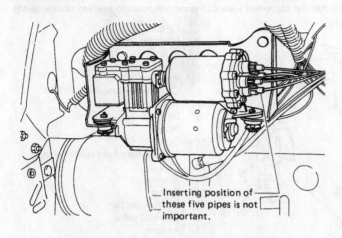

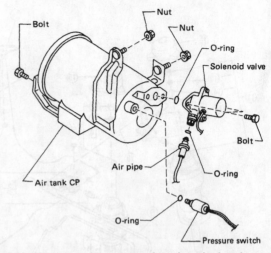

19.23 Air suspension system compressor/drier assembly

19.28 Air suspension system air tank and related components

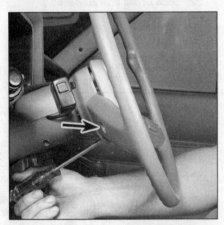

20.2a On earlier models, remove the steering wheel pad mounting screws and the horn button pad screws (arrow) (left side shown, right side identical)

20.2b On later models, grasp the horn pad firmly and simply pull it off

20.3 Remove the steering wheel retaining nut

18   The rest of the procedure is similar to removing a conventional shock absorber assembly (see Section 11).
19   Installation is the reverse of removal.

20.4 Mark the relationship of the steering wheel to the steering shaft

Compressor and drier assembly

Refer to illustration 19.23
20   Make sure that the vehicle is in the normal (low) position, the height control switch is turned off, and the battery ground cable is disconnected.
21   Block the rear wheels. Loosen the left front wheel lug nuts. Raise the front of the vehicle and support it securely on jackstands. Remove the left front wheel.
22   Remove the front half of the mud guard.
23   Disconnect the five air pipes from the drier **(see illustration)**.
24   Remove the coupler.
25   Remove the four mounting nuts, then remove the compressor and drier assembly.
26   Installation is the reverse of removal.

Air tank assembly

Refer to illustration 19.28
27   Make sure that the vehicle is in the normal (low) position, the height control switch is turned off, and the battery ground cable is disconnected.
28   Detach the air pipe from the solenoid

valve, then remove the solenoid valve coupler **(see illustration)**.
29   Remove the left hand turn signal assembly from the front bumper (see Chapter 11).
30   Remove the mounting nuts and bolts and detach the air tank assembly.
31   Installation is the reverse of removal.

20   Steering wheel - removal and installation

Refer to illustrations 20.2a, 20.2b, 20.3, 20.4 and 20.5
1   Disconnect the cable from the negative terminal of the battery.
2   On earlier models, remove the steering wheel pad and horn button pad retaining screws **(see illustration)**, then remove the pad (on two-spoke wheels, there are two screws; on four-spoke wheels there are four screws). On later models, simply pull off the horn pad **(see illustration)**.
3   Remove the steering wheel-to-steering shaft nut **(see illustration)**.
4   Mark the relationship of the steering wheel to the steering shaft **(see illustration)**.

20.5 If the steering wheel doesn't come right off the shaft, install a steering wheel puller to separate the wheel from the shaft

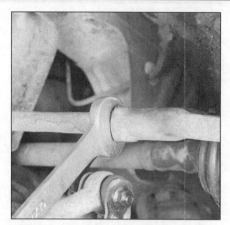

21.3a Loosen and back off the jam nut from the tie-rod end . . .

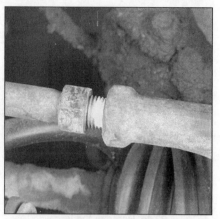

21.3b . . . and paint the threads adjacent to the tie-rod end to mark its position

21.4a Remove the cotter pin from the castellated nut . . .

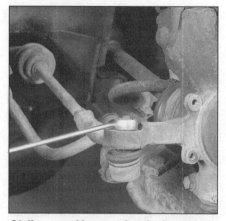

21.4b . . . and loosen - but don't remove - the nut (leaving the nut on the ballstud prevent the tie-rod end from jumping out of the steering knuckle when it's forced out by the puller)

21.5 Install a suitable small puller or tie-rod removal tool such as the one shown to force the tie-rod end ballstud out of the steering knuckle

5   Remove the steering wheel from the steering shaft; a steering wheel puller is not usually needed for earlier models. On later models, if the steering wheel is difficult to remove, install a steering wheel puller **(see illustration)** to separate the wheel from the shaft.

6   Installation is the reverse of removal. Be sure to tighten the steering wheel nut to the torque listed in this Chapter's Specifications.

21 Tie-rod ends - replacement

Refer to illustrations 21.3a, 21.3b, 21.4a, 21.4b, 21.5 and 21.7

1   If the vehicle is equipped with air suspension, make sure that the vehicle is in the normal (low) position, the height control switch is turned off, and the battery ground cable is disconnected.

2   Loosen the wheel lug nuts. Block the rear wheels. Raise the front of the vehicle and support it securely. Remove the front wheel.

3   Loosen the jam nut enough to mark the position of the tie-rod end in relation to the threads **(see illustrations)**.

4   Remove the cotter pin and loosen - but

don't remove - the nut on the tie-rod end stud **(see illustrations)**.

5   Disconnect the tie-rod end from the steering knuckle with a puller **(see illustration)**. Remove the nut and separate the tie-rod from the steering knuckle.

6   Unscrew the tie-rod end from the tie-rod.

7   Even if you're planning to install the old tie-rod end, you should inspect the tie-rod end boot for cracks or tears. If it's damaged, simply remove the boot ring **(see illustration)**, slide off the old boot, wipe off the balljoint with a clean rag, grease it with a suitable waterproof multipurpose grease, slide on a new boot and install the boot ring.

8   Thread the tie-rod end on to the marked position and insert the tie-rod stud into the steering knuckle. Tighten the jam nut securely.

9   Install a new nut on the stud and tighten it to the torque listed in this Chapter's Specifications. Install a new cotter pin.

10   Install the wheel and lug nuts. Lower the vehicle and tighten the wheel lug nuts to the torque listed in this Chapter's Specifications.

Reactivate the air suspension system, if equipped.

11   Have the alignment checked by a dealer service department or an alignment shop.

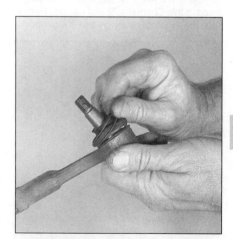

21.7 To replace the old boot on the tie-rod end, remove the boot retaining ring

10

22.4a Remove the large boot retaining spring . . .

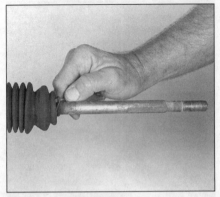

22.4b . . . and the small boot retaining ring

23.7 On newer models, mark the relationship of the steering shaft U-joint to the steering gear input shaft, then remove the pinch bolt (arrow)

22 Steering gear boots - replacement

Refer to illustrations 22.4a and 22.4b

1   If the vehicle is equipped with air suspension, make sure that the vehicle is in the normal (low) position, the height control switch is turned off, and the battery ground cable is disconnected.

2   Loosen the front wheel lug nuts, raise the vehicle and support it securely on jackstands. Remove the wheel.

3   Remove the tie-rod end (see Section 21).

4   Remove the steering gear boot clamps **(see illustrations)** and slide off the boot.

5   Before installing the new boot, wrap the threads and serrations on the end of the inner tie rod with a layer of tape so the small end of the new boot isn't damaged.

6   Slide the new boot into position on the steering gear until it seats in the groove in the steering gear and install new clamps.

7   Remove the tape from the inner tie rod and install the tie-rod end (see Section 21).

8   Install the wheel and lug nuts. Lower the vehicle and tighten the lug nuts to the torque listed in this Chapter's Specifications. Reactivate the air suspension system, if equipped.

9   Have the alignment checked by a dealer service department or an alignment shop.

23 Steering gear - removal and installation

Refer to illustrations 23.7, 23.8, 23.9a and 23.9b

1   If the vehicle is equipped with air suspension, make sure that the vehicle is in the normal (low) position, the height control switch is turned off, and the battery ground cable is disconnected.

2   Loosen the wheel lug nuts. Block the rear wheels, raise the front of the vehicle and place it securely on jackstands. Remove the front wheels.

3   Disconnect the tie-rod ends from the steering knuckles (see Section 21).

4   Remove the front exhaust pipes, if necessary (see Chapter 4).

5   Remove the small skid plate that protects the steering gear.

6   Disconnect the power steering fluid lines from the steering gear.

7   Mark the relationship of the U-joint, if equipped, that connects the steering shaft to the steering gear input shaft **(see illustration)**.

8   On older models, unbolt the coupling

(see illustration). On newer models, remove the steering shaft U-joint pinch bolt **(see illustration 23.7)**.

9   Remove the steering gear mounting bolts **(see illustrations)** and then remove the steering gear from the vehicle.

10   Installation is the reverse of removal. Be sure to tighten the steering gear mounting bolts, the U-joint pinch bolt (if equipped), and the tie-rod end-to-steering knuckle nuts to the torque listed in this Chapter's Specifications.

11   Install the front wheels, remove the jackstands and lower the vehicle. Reactivate the air suspension system, if equipped.

12   Fill the steering system with the recommended fluid and then check for leaks. Bleed the system (see Section 25).

13   Have the front end alignment checked by a dealer service department.

24 Power steering pump - removal and installation

1   If the vehicle is equipped with air suspension, make sure that the vehicle is in the

23.8 On older models, remove the two bolts that attach the steering shaft coupling to the steering gear input shaft

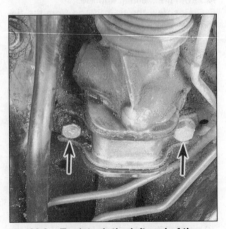

23.9a To detach the left end of the steering gear from the vehicle, remove these bolts (arrows)

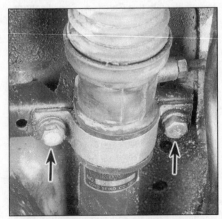

23.9b To detach the right end of the steering gear from the vehicle, remove these bolts (arrows)

normal (low) position, the height control switch is turned off, and the battery ground cable is disconnected.

2   Loosen the wheel lug nuts, block the rear wheels, raise the front of the vehicle and place it securely on jackstands. Remove the front wheels.

3   Remove the power steering fluid from the system. To do this disconnect the hydraulic fittings attached directly to the tube of the gearbox. Attach vinyl hoses to these fittings and plug the ports of the gearbox.

4   Place the other end of the vinyl hoses in a container, start the engine and turn the steering wheel from lock to lock several times until the fluid is completely pumped out of the system.

1984 and earlier models

Refer to illustrations 24.5, 24.10 and 24.12

5   Grab the brim of the idler cap **(see illustration)** with pliers and remove it.

6   Loosen the lock bolt by turning it about two turns.

7   Turn the adjustment bolt counterclockwise and take out the drive pump belt (after turning the adjustment bolt, the idler pulley will move up due to the tension of the drivebelt, which will allow the belt to be removed easily).

8   Disconnect the hoses to the air cleaner assembly. Remove the air cleaner assembly. Place a rag inside the carburetor after the air cleaner is removed to avoid getting dirt inside.

9   Remove the hoses on the backside of the power steering pump and plug them to keep dirt out.

10   Remove the oil pump stay **(see illustration)** by removing its mounting bolts.

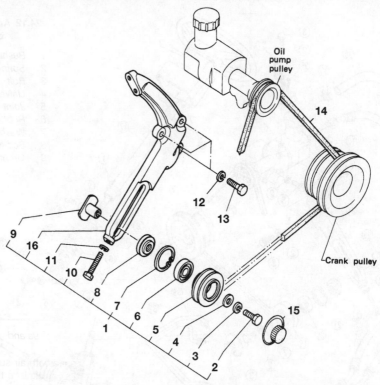

24.5 An exploded view of the power steering idler pulley assembly (1984 and earlier models)

1	Front bracket assembly	9	Shaft
2	Lock bolt	10	Adjustment bolt
3	Spring washer	11	Washer
4	Plain washer	12	Washer
5	Idler pulley	13	Bolt
6	Ball bearing	14	Drivebelt
7	Snap-ring	15	Idler cap
8	Dust seal	16	Beltline bracket

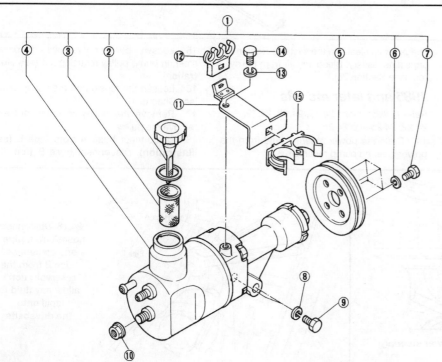

24.10 An exploded view of the power steering p;ump assembly (1984 and earlier models)

1	Pump assembly
2	Cap
3	Strainer
4	Oil pump
5	Pulley
6	Spring washer
7	Bolt
8	Spring washer
9	Bolt
10	Flange nut
11	Stay
12	Supporter
13	Spring washer
14	Bolt
15	Hose clamp

10

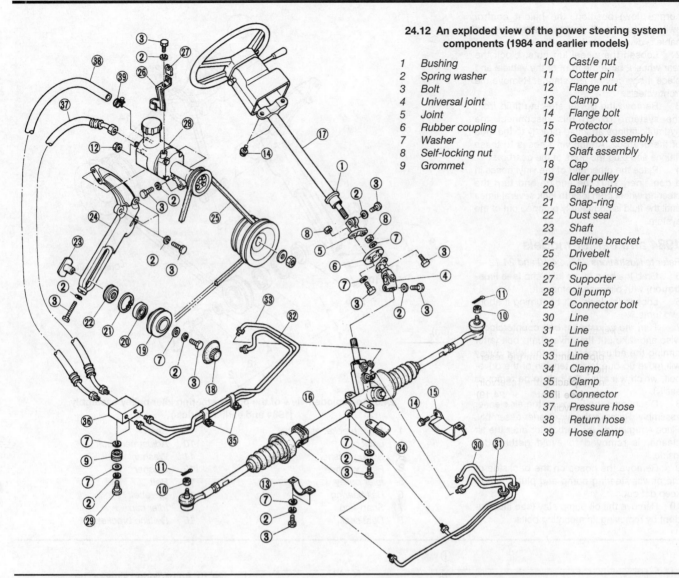

24.12 An exploded view of the power steering system components (1984 and earlier models)

1	Bushing	10	Cast/e nut
2	Spring washer	11	Cotter pin
3	Bolt	12	Flange nut
4	Universal joint	13	Clamp
5	Joint	14	Flange bolt
6	Rubber coupling	15	Protector
7	Washer	16	Gearbox assembly
8	Self-locking nut	17	Shaft assembly
9	Grommet	18	Cap
		19	Idler pulley
		20	Ball bearing
		21	Snap-ring
		22	Dust seal
		23	Shaft
		24	Beltline bracket
		25	Drivebelt
		26	Clip
		27	Supporter
		28	Oil pump
		29	Connector bolt
		30	Line
		31	Line
		32	Line
		33	Line
		34	Clamp
		35	Clamp
		36	Connector
		37	Pressure hose
		38	Return hose
		39	Hose clamp

11   Remove the mounting bolts holding the pump in position, then lift out the pump.
12   Installation is the reverse of removal **(see illustration)**. Be sure to tighten the pump lock bolt and adjustment bolt securely. Refer to Chapter 1 to adjust the drivebelt tension. Don't forget to install the idler cap in its correct position.
13   Install new power steering fluid and

check for any leaks in the system. Tighten fittings if necessary. Bleed any air from the system (see Section 25).

1985 and later models

Refer to illustrations 24.15, 24.18, 24.19, 24.22, 24.25 and 24.26
14   Drain the power steering fluid from the power steering pump reservoir.

15   Loosen - but do not remove - the power steering pump pulley retaining nut **(see illustration)**.
16   Loosen the tension on the pulley belt(s) (see Chapter 1).
17   Remove the pulley retaining nut and remove the pulley.
18   Disconnect hose A from pipe E **(see illustration)**. Disconnect hose B from the

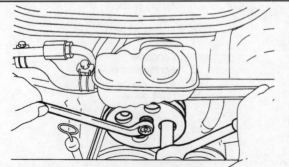

24.15 Loosen - but do not remove - the power steering pump pulley retaining nut

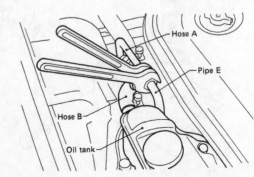

24.18 Disconnect hose A from pipe E and disconnect hose B from the reservoir; don't allow any fluid to spill onto the drivebelts

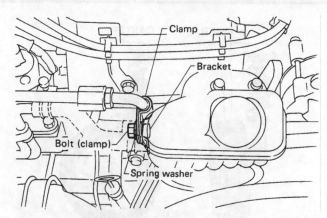

24.19 To detach this clamp from the reservoir, unbolt it and pull it away

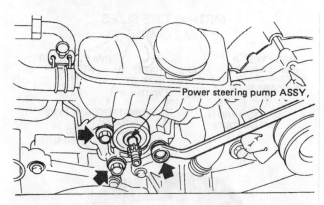

24.22 To remove the power steering pump, remove these three bolts (arrows)

reservoir. Use a bunch of shop rags to soak up spilled fluid. Do not allow any fluid to spill onto the drivebelts. Plug the ends of the hoses to prevent fluid from leaking out and to protect the power steering system from contamination.

19 Detach the pipe clamp from the reservoir **(see illustration)**.

20 If you are only replacing the reservoir, loosen the two bolts **(see illustration 24.19)** from the top of the reservoir. When the bolts are loosened, fluid will run out of the reservoir. To minimize the amount of fluid lost, press the reservoir against the power steering pump, then quickly remove the bolts and the reservoir. Wipe up any spilled fluid.

21 If you're replacing the pump, don't detach the reservoir right now. You can separate the two later, on the bench, without making such a mess.

22 Remove the three bolts from the front of the power steering pump **(see illustration)** and remove the pump.

23 The power steering pump bracket doesn't need to be removed, but if you wish to do so, it's bolted to the engine by three bolts.

24 If you haven't yet removed the reservoir from the power steering pump, do so now. Put the pump in a bench vise and remove the two bolts from the top of the reservoir. Protect the pump by placing wood or plastic jaw liners between the vise and the pump. Don't

over tighten the vise! The pump can be easily distorted.

25 Also, if you're replacing the pump, remove the pipe from the pump **(see illustration)**.

26 Installation is the reverse of removal **(see illustration)**. Be sure to tighten all fasteners securely. Refer to Chapter 1 to adjust the drivebelt tension.

27 Install new power steering fluid and

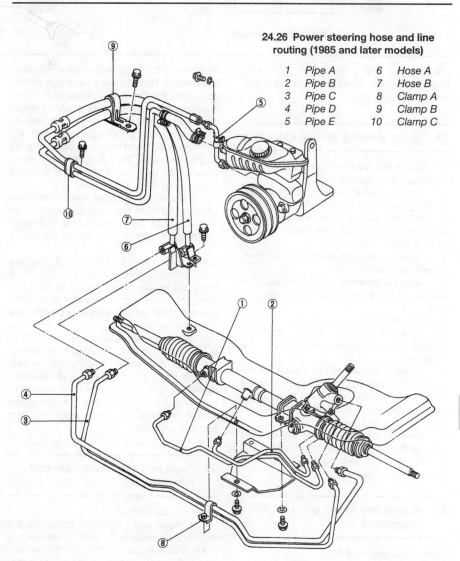

24.26 Power steering hose and line routing (1985 and later models)

1	Pipe A	6	Hose A
2	Pipe B	7	Hose B
3	Pipe C	8	Clamp A
4	Pipe D	9	Clamp B
5	Pipe E	10	Clamp C

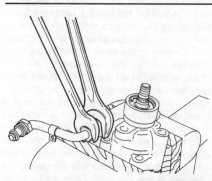

24.25 Also, if you're replacing the pump, remove this pipe from the pump as shown

10

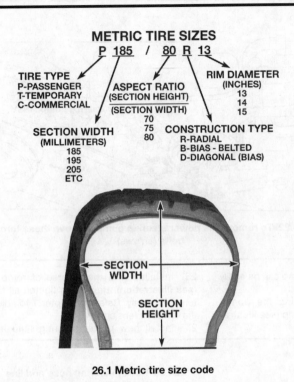

METRIC TIRE SIZES

P 185 / 80 R 13

TIRE TYPE
P-PASSENGER
T-TEMPORARY
C-COMMERCIAL

ASPECT RATIO
(SECTION HEIGHT)
―――――――――――
(SECTION WIDTH)
70
75
80

RIM DIAMETER
(INCHES)
13
14
15

SECTION WIDTH
(MILLIMETERS)
185
195
205
ETC

CONSTRUCTION TYPE
R-RADIAL
B-BIAS - BELTED
D-DIAGONAL (BIAS)

SECTION
WIDTH

SECTION
HEIGHT

26.1 Metric tire size code

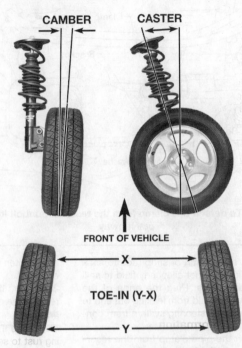

CAMBER   CASTER

FRONT OF VEHICLE

X

TOE-IN (Y-X)

Y

27.1 Camber, caster and toe-in angles

check for any leaks in the system. Tighten fittings if necessary. Bleed any air from the system (see Section 25).

25 Power steering system - bleeding

1   Check the fluid level and add fluid as necessary (see Chapter 1).
2   If the vehicle is equipped with air suspension, make sure that the vehicle is in the normal (low) position, the height control switch is turned off, and the battery ground cable is disconnected.
3   Raise and support the front of the vehicle with jackstands.
4   Turn the steering wheel from lock-to-lock two or three times and recheck the fluid level.
5   Start the engine and let it idle. Turn the steering wheel from lock- to-lock again (two or three times) and recheck the fluid level one more time.
6   Lower the front of the vehicle to the ground. Run the engine and again turn the wheel from lock-to-lock two or three times. Recheck the fluid level. Position the wheels in the straight-ahead position.
7   Bleeding is complete if the fluid level did not rise, from the Full mark, more than 0.200 in (5 mm) and if no foaming is observed when the engine is stopped.

26 Wheels and tires - general information

Refer to illustration 26.1
All models covered by this manual are

equipped with metric-sized radial tires **(see illustration)**. Use of other size or type of tires may affect the ride and handling of the vehicle. Don't mix different types of tires, such as radials and bias belted, on the same vehicle as handling may be seriously affected. It's recommended that tires be replaced in pairs on the same axle, but if only one tire is being replaced, be sure it's the same size, structure and tread design as the other.

Because tire pressure has a substantial effect on handling and wear, the pressure on all tires should be checked at least once a month or before any extended trips (see Chapter 1).

Wheels must be replaced if they are bent, dented, leak air, have elongated bolt holes, are heavily rusted, out of vertical symmetry or if the lug nuts won't stay tight. Wheel repairs that use welding or peening are not recommended.

Tire and wheel balance is important to the overall handling, braking and performance of the vehicle. Unbalanced wheels can adversely affect handling and ride characteristics as well as tire life. Whenever a tire is installed on a wheel, the tire and wheel should be balanced by a shop with the proper equipment.

27 Front end alignment - general information

Refer to illustration 27.1
A front end alignment refers to the adjustments made to the front wheels so they are in proper angular relationship to the suspension and the ground. Front wheels that

are out of proper alignment not only affect steering control, but also increase tire wear **(see illustration)**.

Getting the proper front wheel alignment is a very exacting process, one in which complicated and expensive machines are necessary to perform the job properly. Because of this, you should have a technician with the proper equipment perform these tasks. We will, however, use this space to give you a basic idea of what is involved with front end alignment so you can better understand the process and deal intelligently with the shop that does the work.

Toe-in is the turning in of the front wheels. The purpose of a toe specification is to ensure parallel rolling of the front wheels. In a vehicle with zero toe-in, the distance between the front edges of the wheels will be the same as the distance between the rear edges of the wheels. The actual amount of toe-in is normally only a fraction of an inch. Toe-in adjustment is controlled by the tie-rod end position on the tie-rod. Incorrect toe-in will cause the tires to wear improperly by making them scrub against the road surface.

Camber is the tilting of the front wheels from the vertical when viewed from the front of the vehicle. When the wheels tilt out at the top, the camber is said to be positive (+). When the wheels tilt in at the top the camber is negative (-). The amount of tilt is measured in degrees from the vertical and this measurement is called the camber angle. This angle affects the amount of tire tread which contacts the road and compensates for changes in the suspension geometry when the vehicle is cornering or traveling over an undulating surface.

Chapter 11 Body

Contents

1   General information

These models feature a "unibody" construction, using a floor pan with front and rear frame side rails which support the body components, front and rear suspension systems and other mechanical components. Certain components are particularly vulnerable to accident damage and can be unbolted and repaired or replaced. Among these parts are the body moldings, bumpers, hood, doors, trunk lid and all glass.

Only general body maintenance practices and body panel repair procedures within the scope of the do-it-yourselfer are included in this Chapter.

2   Body - maintenance

1   The condition of your vehicle's body is very important, because the resale value depends a great deal on it. It's much more difficult to repair a neglected or damaged body than it is to repair mechanical components. The hidden areas of the body, such as the wheel wells, the frame and the engine compartment, are equally important, although they don't require as frequent attention as the rest of the body.

2   Once a year, or every 12,000 miles, it's a good idea to have the underside of the body steam cleaned. All traces of dirt and oil will be removed and the area can then be inspected carefully for rust, damaged brake lines, frayed electrical wires, damaged cables and other problems. The front suspension components should be greased after completion of this job.

3   At the same time, clean the engine and the engine compartment with a steam cleaner or water-soluble degreaser.

4   The wheel wells should be given close attention, since undercoating can peel away and stones and dirt thrown up by the tires can cause the paint to chip and flake, allowing rust to set in. If rust is found, clean down to the bare metal and apply an anti-rust paint.

5   The body should be washed about once a week. Wet the vehicle thoroughly to soften the dirt, then wash it down with a soft sponge and plenty of clean soapy water. If the surplus dirt is not washed off very carefully, it can wear down the paint.

6   Spots of tar or asphalt thrown up from the road should be removed with a cloth soaked in solvent.

7   Once every six months, wax the body and chrome trim. If a chrome cleaner is used to remove rust from any of the vehicle's plated parts, remember that the cleaner also removes part of the chrome, so use it sparingly.

3   Vinyl trim - maintenance

Don't clean vinyl trim with detergents, caustic soap or petroleum-based cleaners. Plain soap and water works just fine, with a soft brush to clean dirt that may be ingrained. Wash the vinyl as frequently as the rest of the vehicle. After cleaning, application of a high-quality rubber and vinyl protectant will help prevent oxidation and cracks. The protectant can also be applied to weatherstripping, vacuum lines and rubber hoses, which often fail as a result of chemical degradation, and to the tires.

4   Upholstery and carpets - maintenance

1   Every three months remove the floormats and clean the interior of the vehicle (more frequently if necessary). Use a stiff whisk broom to brush the carpeting and loosen dirt and dust, then vacuum the upholstery and carpets thoroughly, especially along seams and crevices.

2   Dirt and stains can be removed from carpeting with basic household or automotive carpet shampoos available in spray cans. Follow the directions and vacuum again, then use a stiff brush to bring back the "nap" of the carpet.

3   Most interiors have cloth or vinyl upholstery, either of which can be cleaned and maintained with a number of material-specific cleaners or shampoos available in auto supply stores. Follow the directions on the product for usage, and always spot-test any upholstery cleaner on an inconspicuous area (bottom edge of a back seat cushion) to ensure that it doesn't cause a color shift in the material.

4   After cleaning, vinyl upholstery should be treated with a protectant. **Note:** *Make sure the protectant container indicates the product can be used on seats - some products may make a seat too slippery.* **Caution:** *Do not use protectant on vinyl-covered steering wheels.*

5   Leather upholstery requires special care. It should be cleaned regularly with saddlesoap or leather cleaner. Never use alcohol, gasoline, nail polish remover or thinner to clean leather upholstery.

6   After cleaning, regularly treat leather upholstery with a leather conditioner, rubbed in with a soft cotton cloth. Never use car wax on leather upholstery.

7   In areas where the interior of the vehicle is subject to bright sunlight, cover leather seating areas of the seats with a sheet if the vehicle is to be left out for any length of time.

5   Body repair - minor damage

Repair of scratches

1   If the scratch is superficial and does not penetrate to the metal of the body, repair is

11

These photos illustrate a method of repairing simple dents. They are intended to supplement *Body repair - minor damage* in this Chapter and should not be used as the sole instructions for body repair on these vehicles.

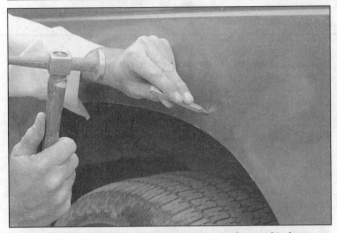

1   If you can't access the backside of the body panel to hammer out the dent, pull it out with a slide-hammer-type dent puller. In the deepest portion of the dent or along the crease line, drill or punch hole(s) at least one inch apart . . .

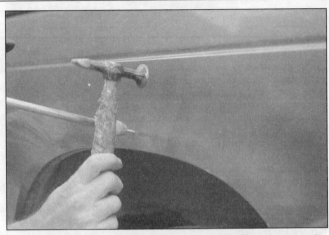

2   . . . then screw the slide-hammer into the hole and operate it. Tap with a hammer near the edge of the dent to help 'pop' the metal back to its original shape. When you're finished, the dent area should be close to its original contour and about 1/8-inch below the surface of the surrounding metal

3   Using coarse-grit sandpaper, remove the paint down to the bare metal. Hand sanding works fine, but the disc sander shown here makes the job faster. Use finer (about 320-grit) sandpaper to feather-edge the paint at least one inch around the dent area

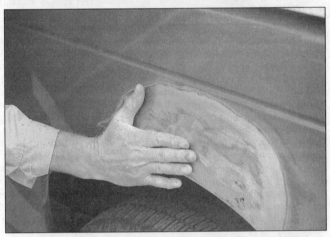

4   When the paint is removed, touch will probably be more helpful than sight for telling if the metal is straight. Hammer down the high spots or raise the low spots as necessary. Clean the repair area with wax/silicone remover

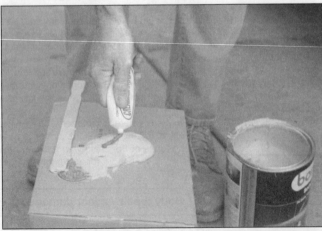

5   Following label instructions, mix up a batch of plastic filler and hardener. The ratio of filler to hardener is critical, and, if you mix it incorrectly, it will either not cure properly or cure too quickly (you won't have time to file and sand it into shape)

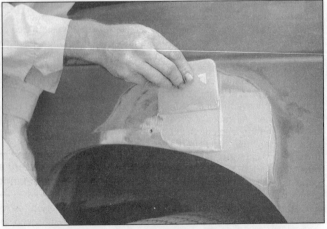

6   Working quickly so the filler doesn't harden, use a plastic applicator to press the body filler firmly into the metal, assuring it bonds completely. Work the filler until it matches the original contour and is slightly above the surrounding metal

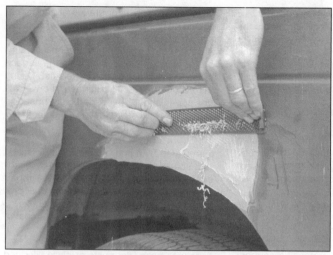

7   Let the filler harden until you can just dent it with your fingernail. Use a body file or Surform tool (shown here) to rough-shape the filler

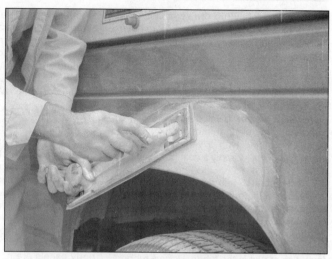

8   Use coarse-grit sandpaper and a sanding board or block to work the filler down until it's smooth and even. Work down to finer grits of sandpaper - always using a board or block - ending up with 360 or 400 grit

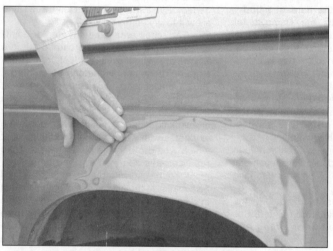

9   You shouldn't be able to feel any ridge at the transition from the filler to the bare metal or from the bare metal to the old paint. As soon as the repair is flat and uniform, remove the dust and mask off the adjacent panels or trim pieces

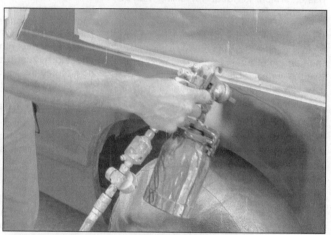

10   Apply several layers of primer to the area. Don't spray the primer on too heavy, so it sags or runs, and make sure each coat is dry before you spray on the next one. A professional-type spray gun is being used here, but aerosol spray primer is available inexpensively from auto parts stores

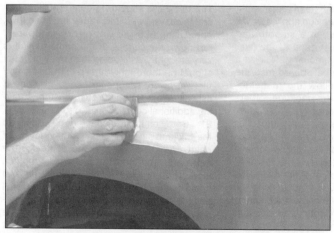

11   The primer will help reveal imperfections or scratches. Fill these with glazing compound. Follow the label instructions and sand it with 360 or 400-grit sandpaper until it's smooth. Repeat the glazing, sanding and respraying until the primer reveals a perfectly smooth surface

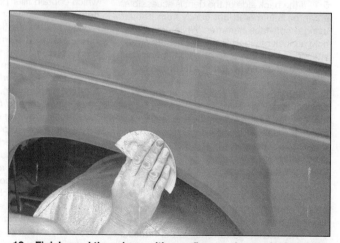

12   Finish sand the primer with very fine sandpaper (400 or 600-grit) to remove the primer overspray. Clean the area with water and allow it to dry. Use a tack rag to remove any dust, then apply the finish coat. Don't attempt to rub out or wax the repair area until the paint has dried completely (at least two weeks)

very simple. Lightly rub the scratched area with a fine rubbing compound to remove loose paint and built-up wax. Rinse the area with clean water.

2   Apply touch-up paint to the scratch, using a small brush. Continue to apply thin layers of paint until the surface of the paint in the scratch is level with the surrounding paint. Allow the new paint at least two weeks to harden, then blend it into the surrounding paint by rubbing with a very fine rubbing compound. Finally, apply a coat of wax to the scratch area.

3   If the scratch has penetrated the paint and exposed the metal of the body, causing the metal to rust, a different repair technique is required. Remove all loose rust from the bottom of the scratch with a pocket knife, then apply rust inhibiting paint to prevent the formation of rust in the future. Using a rubber or nylon applicator, coat the scratched area with glaze-type filler. If required, the filler can be mixed with thinner to provide a very thin paste, which is ideal for filling narrow scratches. Before the glaze filler in the scratch hardens, wrap a piece of smooth cotton cloth around the tip of a finger. Dip the cloth in thinner and then quickly wipe it along the surface of the scratch. This will ensure that the surface of the filler is slightly hollow. The scratch can now be painted over as described earlier in this Section.

Repair of dents

See photo sequence

4   When repairing dents, the first job is to pull the dent out until the affected area is as close as possible to its original shape. There is no point in trying to restore the original shape completely as the metal in the damaged area will have stretched on impact and cannot be restored to its original contours. It is better to bring the level of the dent up to a point which is about 1/8-inch below the level of the surrounding metal. In cases where the dent is very shallow, it is not worth trying to pull it out at all.

5   If the back side of the dent is accessible, it can be hammered out gently from behind using a soft-face hammer. While doing this, hold a block of wood firmly against the opposite side of the metal to absorb the hammer blows and prevent the metal from being stretched.

6   If the dent is in a section of the body which has double layers, or some other factor makes it inaccessible from behind, a different technique is required. Drill several small holes through the metal inside the damaged area, particularly in the deeper sections. Screw long, self tapping screws into the holes just enough for them to get a good grip in the metal. Now the dent can be pulled out by pulling on the protruding heads of the screws with locking pliers.

7   The next stage of repair is the removal of paint from the damaged area and from an inch or so of the surrounding metal. This is easily done with a wire brush or sanding disk in a drill motor, although it can be done just

as effectively by hand with sandpaper. To complete the preparation for filling, score the surface of the bare metal with a screwdriver or the tang of a file or drill small holes in the affected area. This will provide a good grip for the filler material. To complete the repair, see the Section on *filling and painting*.

Repair of rust holes or gashes

8   Remove all paint from the affected area and from an inch or so of the surrounding metal using a sanding disk or wire brush mounted in a drill motor. If these are not available, a few sheets of sandpaper will do the job just as effectively.

9   With the paint removed, you will be able to determine the severity of the corrosion and decide whether to replace the whole panel, if possible, or repair the affected area. New body panels are not as expensive as most people think and it is often quicker to install a new panel than to repair large areas of rust.

10   Remove all trim pieces from the affected area except those which will act as a guide to the original shape of the damaged body, such as headlight shells, etc. Using metal snips or a hacksaw blade, remove all loose metal and any other metal that is badly affected by rust. Hammer the edges of the hole on the inside to create a slight depression for the filler material.

11   Wire brush the affected area to remove the powdery rust from the surface of the metal. If the back of the rusted area is accessible, treat it with rust inhibiting paint.

12   Before filling is done, block the hole in some way. This can be done with sheet metal riveted or screwed into place, or by stuffing the hole with wire mesh.

13   Once the hole is blocked off, the affected area can be filled and painted. See the following subsection on *filling and painting*.

Filling and painting

14   Many types of body fillers are available, but generally speaking, body repair kits which contain filler paste and a tube of resin hardener are best for this type of repair work. A wide, flexible plastic or nylon applicator will be necessary for imparting a smooth and contoured finish to the surface of the filler material. Mix up a small amount of filler on a clean piece of wood or cardboard (use the hardener sparingly). Follow the manufacturer's instructions on the package, otherwise the filler will set incorrectly.

15   Using the applicator, apply the filler paste to the prepared area. Draw the applicator across the surface of the filler to achieve the desired contour and to level the filler surface. As soon as a contour that approximates the original one is achieved, stop working the paste. If you continue, the paste will begin to stick to the applicator. Continue to add thin layers of paste at 20-minute intervals until the level of the filler is just above the surrounding metal.

16   Once the filler has hardened, the excess can be removed with a body file. From then

on, progressively finer grades of sandpaper should be used, starting with a 180-grit paper and finishing with 600-grit wet-or-dry paper. Always wrap the sandpaper around a flat rubber or wooden block, otherwise the surface of the filler will not be completely flat. During the sanding of the filler surface, the wet-or-dry paper should be periodically rinsed in water. This will ensure that a very smooth finish is produced in the final stage.

17   At this point, the repair area should be surrounded by a ring of bare metal, which in turn should be encircled by the finely feathered edge of good paint. Rinse the repair area with clean water until all of the dust produced by the sanding operation is gone.

18   Spray the entire area with a light coat of primer. This will reveal any imperfections in the surface of the filler. Repair the imperfections with fresh filler paste or glaze filler and once more smooth the surface with sandpaper. Repeat this spray-and-repair procedure until you are satisfied that the surface of the filler and the feathered edge of the paint are perfect. Rinse the area with clean water and allow it to dry completely.

19   The repair area is now ready for painting. Spray painting must be carried out in a warm, dry, windless and dust free atmosphere. These conditions can be created if you have access to a large indoor work area, but if you are forced to work in the open, you will have to pick the day very carefully. If you are working indoors, dousing the floor in the work area with water will help settle the dust which would otherwise be in the air. If the repair area is confined to one body panel, mask off the surrounding panels. This will help minimize the effects of a slight mismatch in paint color. Trim pieces such as chrome strips, door handles, etc., will also need to be masked off or removed. Use masking tape and several thickness of newspaper for the masking operations.

20   Before spraying, shake the paint can thoroughly, then spray a test area until the spray painting technique is mastered. Cover the repair area with a thick coat of primer. The thickness should be built up using several thin layers of primer rather than one thick one. Using 600-grit wet-or-dry sandpaper, rub down the surface of the primer until it is very smooth. While doing this, the work area should be thoroughly rinsed with water and the wet-or-dry sandpaper periodically rinsed as well. Allow the primer to dry before spraying additional coats.

21   Spray on the top coat, again building up the thickness by using several thin layers of paint. Begin spraying in the center of the repair area and then, using a circular motion, work out until the whole repair area and about two inches of the surrounding original paint is covered. Remove all masking material 10 to 15 minutes after spraying on the final coat of paint. Allow the new paint at least two weeks to harden, then use a very fine rubbing compound to blend the edges of the new paint into the existing paint. Finally, apply a coat of wax.

6   Body repair - major damage

1   Major damage must be repaired by an auto body shop specifically equipped to perform body and frame repairs. These shops have the specialized equipment required to do the job properly.

2   If the damage is extensive, the body must be checked for proper alignment or the vehicle's handling characteristics may be adversely affected and other components may wear at an accelerated rate.

3   Due to the fact that all of the major body components (hood, fenders, etc.) are separate and replaceable units, any seriously damaged components should be replaced rather than repaired. Sometimes the components can be found in a wrecking yard that specializes in used vehicle components, often at considerable savings over the cost of new parts.

7   Hinges and locks - maintenance

Once every 3000 miles, or every three months, the hinges and latch assemblies on the doors, hood and trunk should be given a few drops of light oil or lock lubricant. The door latch strikers should also be lubricated with a thin coat of grease to reduce wear and ensure free movement. Lubricate the door and trunk locks with spray-on graphite lubricant.

8   Windshield and fixed glass - replacement

Replacement of the windshield and fixed glass requires the use of special fast-setting adhesive/caulk materials and some specialized tools and techniques. These operations should be left to a dealer service department or a shop specializing in glass work.

9   Hood - removal, installation and adjustment

Note: *The hood is heavy and somewhat awkward to remove and install - at least two people should perform this procedure.*

Removal and installation

Refer to illustrations 9.2, 9.4a and 9.4b

1   Use blankets or pads to cover the cowl area of the body and fenders. This will protect the body and paint as the hood is lifted off.

2   Make marks or scribe a line around the hood hinge to ensure proper alignment during installation **(see illustration)**.

3   Disconnect any cables or wires that will interfere with removal.

4   Have an assistant support the hood and remove the hinge-to-hood nuts or bolts **(see illustrations)**.

9.2 Before removing the hood, draw a line around the hinge plate

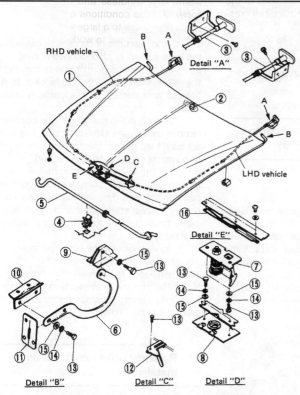

9.4a Hood mounting details (Early model)

1	Hood	9	Hinge bracket
2	Grommet	10	Hood bracket
3	Hood release cable	11	Rubber plate
4	Hood stay clip	12	Clip
5	Hood stay	13	Bolt
6	Hinge	14	Spring washer
7	Striker	15	Washer
8	Hood lock		

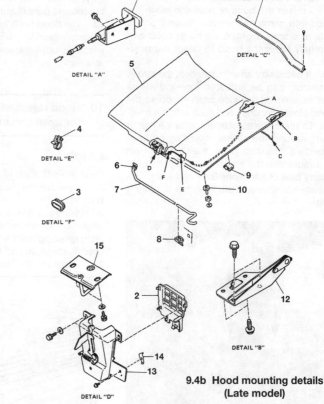

9.4b Hood mounting details (Late model)

1	Front hood cable assembly	7	Hood stay	12	Hinge
2	Lock cover	8	Clamp	13	Hood lock assembly
3	Grommet	9	Buffer	14	Clamp
4	Clip	10	Hood buffer assembly	15	Striker assembly
5	Hood	11	Front panel seal		
6	Grommet				

11

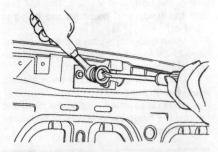

9.11 Adjust the position of the hood striker by loosening the lock nut at the bottom, then adjust the height of the hood striker by turning it in or out with a screwdriver (Early model)

5   Lift off the hood.
6   Installation is the reverse of removal.

Adjustment

Refer to illustrations 9.11 and 9.12

7   Fore-and-aft and side-to-side adjustment of the hood is done by moving the hinge plate slot after loosening the bolts or nuts.
8   Scribe a line around the entire hinge plate so you can determine the amount of movement **(see illustration 9.2)**.
9   Loosen the bolts or nuts and move the hood into correct alignment. Move it only a little at a time. Tighten the hinge bolts and carefully lower the hood to check the position.
10   If necessary after installation, the striker assembly can be adjusted fore-and-aft as well as from side-to-side on the hood so the hood closes securely and flush with the fenders. To make the adjustment, scribe a line or mark around the striker mounting bolts to provide a reference point, then loosen them and reposition the striker assembly, as necessary **(see illustrations 9.4a and 9.4b)**. Following adjustment, retighten the mounting bolts.

10.7 After removing the driver's side kick panel, detach the hood release lever retaining screws (arrows) and pull the cable rearward into the passenger compartment

9.12 Adjust the hood closing height by turning the hood bumpers in or out (Late model)

11   On early models, after the hood is aligned properly with the cowl and front fenders, the height and position of the hood striker assembly should be adjusted to provide positive engagement with the latch assembly **(see illustration)**.
12   On later models, adjust the hood bumpers on the radiator support (if necessary) so the hood, when closed, is flush with the fenders **(see illustration)**.
13   The hood latch assembly, as well as the hinges, should be periodically lubricated with white, lithium-base grease to prevent binding and wear.

10   Hood release latch and cable - removal and installation

Latch

Refer to illustration 10.2

1   Remove the radiator grille (see Section 11).
2   Scribe a line around the latch to aid alignment when installing, then detach the latch retaining bolts from the radiator support **(see illustration)** and remove the latch.
3   Remove the cable retaining nut or

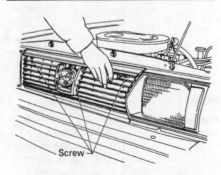

11.1a Radiator grille mounting details (Early model)

— Screw

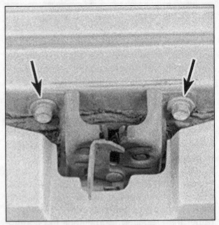

10.2 Detach the hood latch retaining bolts (arrows), remove the cable retaining bolt from the backside of the hood latch assembly, then disengage the cable

screw, then disconnect the hood release cable by disengaging the cable from the latch assembly.
4   Installation is the reverse of the removal procedure.

Cable

Refer to illustration 10.7

5   Disconnect the hood release cable from the latch assembly as described above.
6   Attach a piece of stiff wire to the end of the cable, then follow the cable back to the firewall and detach all the cable retaining clips.
7   Working in the passenger compartment, remove the driver's side kick panel (late models only) then detach the screws securing the hood release lever **(see illustration)**.
8   Pull the cable and grommet rearward into the passenger compartment until you can see the wire. Ensure that the new cable has a grommet attached, then remove the old cable from the wire and replace it with the new cable.
9   Working from engine compartment pull the wire back through the firewall.
10   Installation is the reverse of the removal
Note: *Push on the grommet with your fingers from the passenger compartment to seat the grommet in the firewall correctly.*

11   Radiator grille - removal and installation

Refer to illustrations 11.1a and 11.1b

1   The radiator grille is held in place by clips and screws. Remove any screws, then disengage the grille retaining clips with a small screwdriver **(see illustrations)**.
2   Once all the retaining screws and clips are disengaged, pull the grille out and remove it.
3   Installation is the reverse of removal.

(SEDAN and STATION WAGON)   **(3-Door)**

11.1b Radiator grille mounting details (Late model)

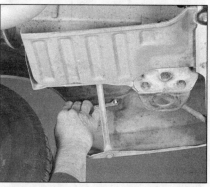

12.1 Remove the lower splash shields (arrows) (if equipped)

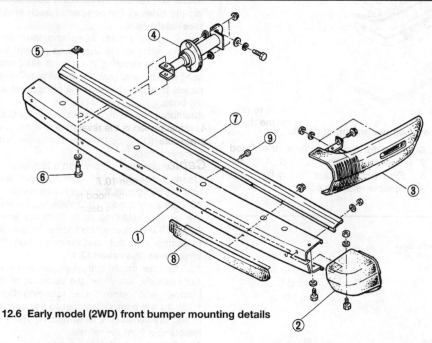

12.6 Early model (2WD) front bumper mounting details

1	Bumper center	6	Bumper retaining bolt
2	Bumper end molding	7	Front bumper cover
3	Bumper side molding	8	Bumper protector
4	Damper assembly	9	Rivet
5	Stop nut		

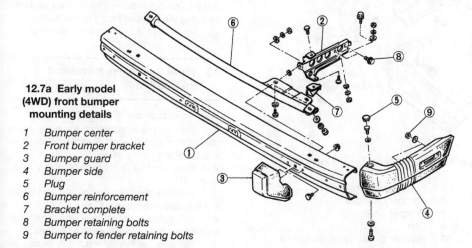

12.7a Early model (4WD) front bumper mounting details

1 Bumper center
2 Front bumper bracket
3 Bumper guard
4 Bumper side
5 Plug
6 Bumper reinforcement
7 Bracket complete
8 Bumper retaining bolts
9 Bumper to fender retaining bolts

12.2 On early models remove the bumper to fender retaining nuts

12 Bumpers - removal and installation

Front bumper

Refer to illustrations 12.1, 12.2, 12.6, 12.7a and 12.7b

1 Working below the bumper assembly, remove any lower splash shields (if equipped) that would interfere with bumper removal **(see illustration)**.

2 On early models, reach up behind the fender and remove the retaining bolts securing the sides of the bumper to each fender **(see illustration)**.

3 On later models, reposition the air conditioning and the automatic transaxle cooler lines away from the bumper assembly (if equipped).

4 Disconnect any electrical connections such as the side marker light or front turn signal assemblies and wiring harness retaining clips that would interfere with bumper removal.

5 Support the bumper with a jack or jackstands. Alternatively, have an assistant support the bumper as the bolts are removed.

6 On early models, remove the bumper retaining bolts from the lower edge of the bumper which secure the bumper to damper assembly and remove it from the vehicle **(see illustration)**.

7 On later models and early 4WD models,

11

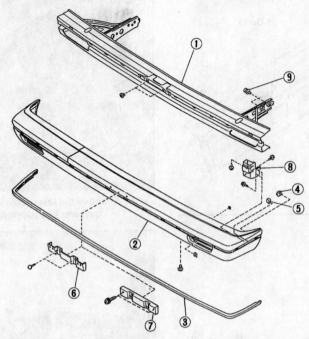

12.7b   Late model (2WD and 4WD) front bumper mounting details

1 Front bumper	6 Base (for Australia)
2 Front fascia	7 Base (for export)
3 Bumper molding	8 Front beam bracket
4 Bumper molding clamp	9 Bumper retaining bolts
5 Front bumper side clamp	

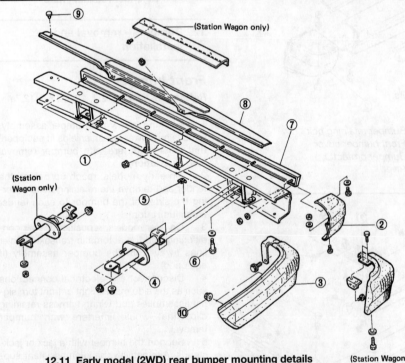

12.11   Early model (2WD) rear bumper mounting details

(Station Wagon only)

1 Bumper center	6 Bumper retaining bolt
2 Bumper end molding	7 Bumper protector
3 Bumper side molding	8 Bumper cover
4 Damper assembly	9 Clip
5 Stop nut	10 Bumper to fender retaining nuts

work from the backside of the bumper and remove the retaining bolts securing the bumper bracket to the outside of each frame rail **(see illustrations)**. Remove the bumper from the vehicle.

8   If replacing the bumper fascia on a late model vehicle remove the screws or clips securing the bumper fascia to the bumper.

9   Installation is the reverse of removal.

Rear bumper

Refer to illustrations 12.11, 12.16a, 12.16b and 12.17

10   Apply the parking brake, raise the vehicle and support it securely on jackstands.

11   On early models, reach up behind the fender and remove the retaining bolts securing the sides of the bumper to each fender **(see illustration)**.

12   On later model three and four door sedans, work in the trunk and pry out the plastic clips securing the drivers side, passenger side, and rear inside trunk finishing panels to allow access to the bumper retaining bolts.

13   Disconnect any electrical connections such as the license plate light and wiring harness retaining clips that would interfere with bumper removal.

14   Support the bumper with a jack or jackstands. Alternatively, have an assistant support the bumper as the bolts are removed.

15   On early model 2WD vehicles, remove the bumper retaining bolts from the lower edge of the bumper which secure the bumper to damper assembly and remove it from the vehicle **(see illustration 12.11)**.

16   On later model station wagon and early 4WD models, work from the backside of the bumper and remove the retaining bolts securing the bumper bracket to the outside of each frame rail **(see illustrations)**. Remove the bumper from the vehicle.

17   On later model three and four door sedans, work in the trunk and remove the bumper retaining nuts **(see illustration)** then pull the bumper assembly out and away from the vehicle.

18   If replacing the bumper fascia on a late model vehicle remove the screws or clips securing the bumper fascia to the bumper.

19   Installation is the reverse of removal.

13   Front fender - removal and installation

Refer to illustrations 13.4 and 13.5

1   Loosen the front wheel lug nuts, raise the vehicle and support it securely on jackstands. Remove the wheel.

2   Remove the front bumper (see Section 12).

3   Remove the front turn signal and parking light assemblies (see Chapter 12).

4   Detach the inner fenderwell splash shield from the fender **(see illustration)**.

5   Remove the fender mounting bolts and nuts **(see illustration)**.

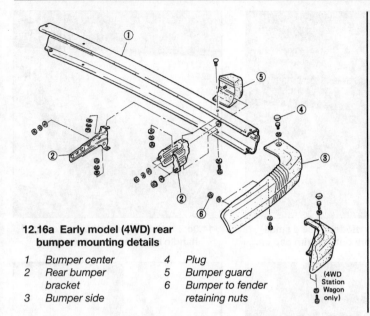

12.16a Early model (4WD) rear bumper mounting details

1	Bumper center	4	Plug
2	Rear bumper bracket	5	Bumper guard
3	Bumper side	6	Bumper to fender retaining nuts

(4WD Station Wagon only)

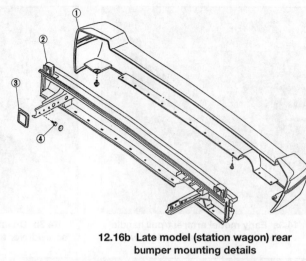

12.16b Late model (station wagon) rear bumper mounting details

1	Rear bumper fascia	3	Bumper stay grommet
2	Rear beam	4	Bumper retaining bolt

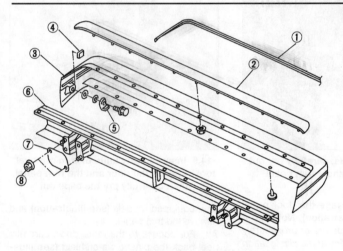

12.17 Late model (three and four door sedan) rear bumper mounting details

1	Bumper molding	6	Rear bumper beam
2	Rear bumper fascia	7	Rear bumper bracket spacer
3	Rear PP bumper	8	Bumper retaining nuts
4	Bumper molding clamp		
5	Trunk board bracket		

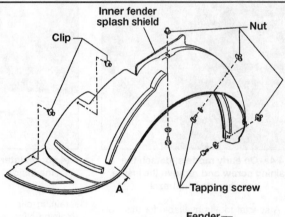

13.4 Front fender inner splash shield mounting details

6   Detach the fender. It's a good idea to have an assistant support the fender while it's being moved away from the vehicle to prevent damage to the surrounding body panels.

7   Installation is the reverse of removal.

14 Door trim panel - removal and installation

Refer to illustrations 14.2, 14.3a, 14.3b, 14.3c, 14.4a, 14.4b, 14.5, 14.6 and 14.7

1   Disconnect the negative cable from the battery.

2   On manual window equipped models, remove the window crank, using a hooked tool to remove the retainer clip (see illustra-

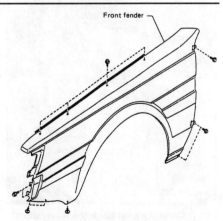

13.5 Front fender mounting details

Front fender

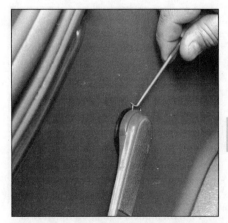

14.2 Use a hooked tool like this to remove the window crank retaining clip

11

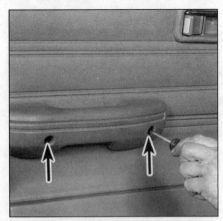

14.3a Early model armrest/pull handle retaining screw locations (arrows)

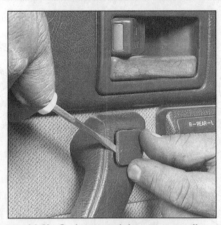

14.3b On later models, use a small screwdriver to pry out the trim cap . . .

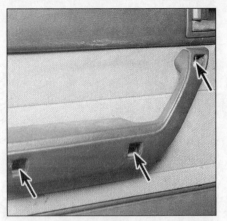

14.3c . . . then remove the armrest/pull handle retaining screws (arrows)

14.4a On early models, detach the retaining screw and remove the inside door handle trim bezel

14.4b On later models, carefully pry out the inside door handle trim bezel

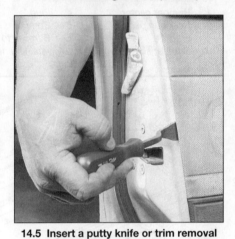

14.5 Insert a putty knife or trim removal tool between the door and the trim panel, then carefully pry the clips out

tion). A special tool is available for this purpose, but it's not essential. With the clip removed, pull off the handle.

3   Detach the armrest pull handle retaining screws **(see illustrations)**.

4   Remove the inside door handle trim bezel **(see illustrations)**.

5   Insert a wide putty knife, a thin screwdriver or a special trim panel removal tool between the trim panel and the head of the

retaining clip to disengage the door panel retaining clips **(see illustration)**. **Note:** *Door trim panel retaining clips are approximately five to six inches apart. Pry at the clip location only. Prying in between clips will result in distorted or damaged door trim panels.*

6   Once all of the clips and screws are disengaged, detach the trim panel from the door by gently pulling it up and out, then disconnect any electrical connectors on power win-

dow equipped models **(see illustration)** and remove the trim panel.

7   For access to the inner door, carefully peel back the plastic watershield **(see illustration)**.

8   Prior to installation of the door panel, be sure to reinstall any clips in the panel which may have come out during the removal procedure and remain in the door itself.

9   Installation is the reverse of the removal procedure. **Note:** *When installing door trim panel retaining clips, make sure the clips are lined up with their mating holes first, then gently tap the clips in with the palm of your hand.*

15   Door latch, lock cylinder and handles - removal and installation

Door latch

Refer to illustrations 15.2 and 15.4

1   Raise the window then remove the door trim panel and watershield as described in Section 14.

2   Working through the large access hole, remove the inside lock to latch rod and the inside handle to latch rod **(see illustration)**.

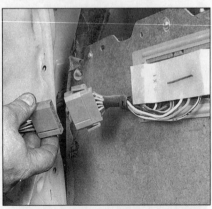

14.6 On models equipped with power windows, disconnect the electrical connector from the switch control plate

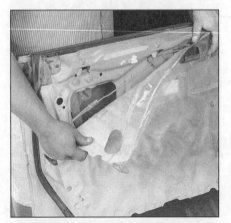

14.7 Carefully peel back the watershield to access the inside of the door

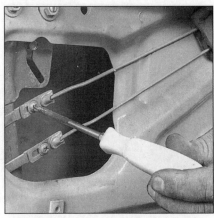

15.2 Detach the inside handle actuating rods from the latch assembly

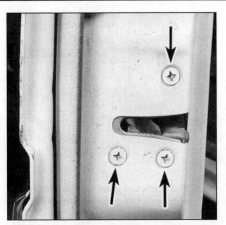

15.4 Remove the latch screws from the end of the door and pull the latch assembly through the access hole

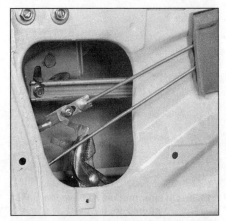

15.8 To remove the lock cylinder on early models, detach the plastic clip securing the lock rod, then pry off the lock cylinder retaining clip

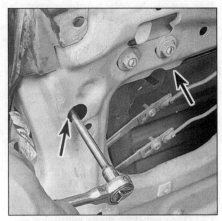

15.10 The outside handle retaining nuts (arrows) can be reached through the access holes in the door frame

15.19 Inside door handle retaining screw locations (arrows)

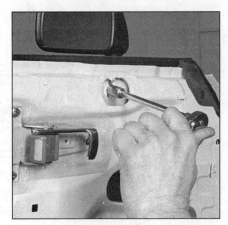

16.3a On early models remove both door stops

Then disengage the outside door handle-to-latch rod, the outside door lock cylinder-to-latch rod and the door lock solenoid (if equipped) from the latch assembly.

3 Door locking rods are usually attached by plastic clips. The plastic clips can be removed by unsnapping the portion engaging the connecting rod and then by pulling the rod out of its locating hole.

4 Remove the screws securing the latch to the door **(see illustration)**, then remove the latch assembly from the door.

5 Installation is the reverse of removal.

Door lock cylinder and outside handle

Early models

Refer to illustrations 15.8 and 15.10

6 To remove the lock cylinder, raise the window and remove the door trim panel and watershield as described in Section 14.

7 Working through the large access hole, disengage the plastic clip that secures the lock cylinder to latch rod.

8 Using a pair of pliers, slide the lock cylinder retaining clip out of engagement and remove the lock cylinder from the door **(see illustration)**.

9 To remove the outside handle, work through the access hole and disengage the plastic clip that secures the outside handle-to-latch rod.

10 Remove the outside handle retaining nuts **(see illustration)** and pull the handle from the door.

11 Installation is the reverse of removal.

Late models

12 To remove the outside handle and lock cylinder assembly, raise the window then remove the door trim panel and watershield as described in Section 14.

13 Working through the access hole, disengage the plastic clips that secure the outside door lock to latch rod.

14 Detach the handle retaining bolts, then remove the handle and lock cylinder assembly from the door **(see illustration 15.10)**.

15 The lock cylinder can now be removed from the rear of the handle by removing the lock cylinder retaining bolt.

16 Installation is the reverse of removal.

Inside handle

Refer to illustration 15.19

17 Remove the door trim panel as described in Section 14 and peel away the watershield.

18 Detach the actuating rods from the latch assembly **(see illustration 15.2)**.

19 Unclip the door actuating rod guide, then remove the door handle retaining screws **(see illustration)**.

20 Pull the handle free from the door and remove it from the vehicle.

21 Installation is the reverse of removal.

---

16 Door window glass - removal and installation

Refer to illustrations 16.3a, 16.3b, 16.4, 16.5 and 16.8

1 Remove the door trim panel and the plastic watershield (see Section 14).

2 Lower the window glass all the way down into the door.

3 On early models, remove both upper window stops **(see illustration)**. On later

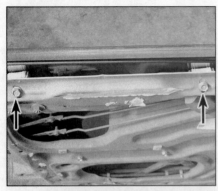

16.3b On later models remove the glass stabilizers (arrows)

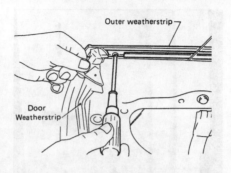

16.4 Pull back the door weather stripping to access the outer weatherstrip retaining screws

16.5 Raise the window just enough to access the glass retaining bolts (arrow) through the hole in the door frame

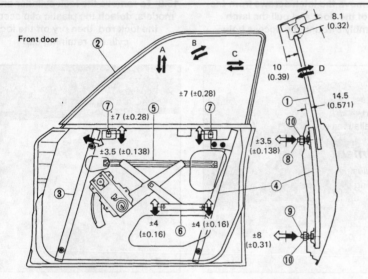

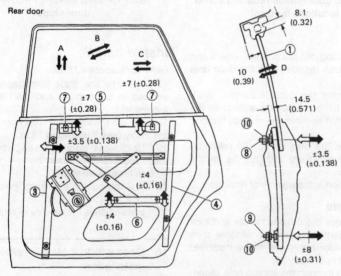

16.8 Door glass adjustment details

A	Vertical adjustment	4	Rear sash
B	Inclination adjustment	5	Regulator channel A
C	Front/back adjustment	6	Regulator channel B
D	Fitting pressure adjustment	7	Upper stoppers
1	Glass	8	Upper adjuster bolts
2	Retainer	9	Lower adjuster bolts
3	Front sash	10	Nuts with conical with spring washers

models, remove the glass inner stabilizers **(see illustration).**

4   Remove the screws securing each edge of the outer weatherstrip **(see illustration).** Then remove the outer weatherstripping by carefully prying it out of the door window opening.

5   Raise the window just enough to access the window retaining bolts through the hole in the door frame **(see illustration).**

6   Place a rag over the glass to help prevent scratching the glass and remove the two glass mounting bolts.

7   Remove the glass by pulling it up and out.

8   Installation of the window glass is the reverse of removal. Adjust the window glass as necessary to make it operate smoothly and seal properly **(see illustration).**

17   Door window glass regulator - removal and installation

Refer to illustration 17.4

1   Remove the door trim panel and the plastic watershield (see Section 14).

2   Remove the window glass assembly (see Section 16).

3   On power operated windows, disconnect the electrical connector from the window regulator motor.

4   Remove the equalizer arm bracket and the regulator mounting bolts **(see illustration).**

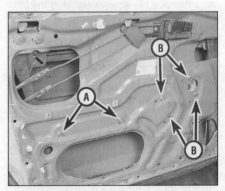

17.4 Detach the window equalizer (A) and the window regulator (B) mounting bolts

18.1 On later models, Insert a wide putty knife, a thin screwdriver or a special trim panel removal tool and pry off the trim cover

5   Pull the equalizer arm and regulator assemblies through the service hole in the door frame to remove it.
6   Installation is the reverse of removal.

18 Outside mirrors - removal and installation

Refer to illustrations 18.1, 18.2a and 18.2b

1   On later model vehicles pry off the mirror trim cover **(see illustration)**.
2   Remove the mirror retaining screws and detach the mirror from the vehicle **(see illustrations)**.
3   Disconnect the electrical connector from the mirror (if equipped).
4   Installation is the reverse of removal.

19 Door - removal, installation and adjustment

Note: *The door is heavy and somewhat awkward to remove and install - at least two people should perform this procedure.*

Removal and installation

Refer to illustrations 19.6, 19.8a and 19.8b

1   Raise the window completely in the door and then disconnect the negative cable from the battery.
2   Open the door all the way and support it on jacks or blocks covered with rags to prevent damaging the paint.
3   Remove the door trim panel and water deflector as described in Section 14.
4   Disconnect all electrical connections, ground wires and harness retaining clips from the door. **Note:** *It is a good idea to label all connections to aid the reassembly process.*
5   From the door side, detach the rubber conduit between the body and the door. Then pull the wiring harness through conduit hole and remove from the door.
6   Remove the door stop strut center pin **(see illustration)**.

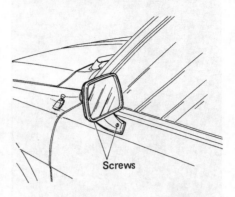

18.2a Outside mirror retaining screw locations (Early model)

7   Mark around the door hinges with a pen or a scribe to facilitate realignment during reassembly.
8   With an assistant holding the door, remove the hinge to door bolts **(see illustrations)** and lift the door off.
9   Installation is the reverse of removal.

Adjustment

Refer to illustration 19.13

10   Having proper door to body alignment is a critical part of a well functioning door assembly. First check the door hinge pins for excessive play. Fully open the door and lift up and down on the door without lifting the body. If a door has 1/16-inch or more excessive play, the hinges should be replaced.
11   Door-to-body alignment adjustments are made by loosening the hinge-to-body bolts or hinge-to-door bolts and moving the door. Proper body alignment is achieved when the top of the doors are parallel with the roof section, the front door is flush with the fender, the rear door is flush with the rear quarter panel and the bottom of the doors are aligned with the lower rocker panel. If these goals can't be reached by adjusting the hinge-to-body or hinge-to-door bolts, body

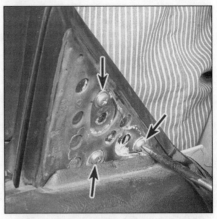

18.2b Outside mirror retaining screw locations (Late model)

19.6 Gently tap the pin for the door stop strut in the direction shown

alignment shims may have to be purchased and inserted behind the hinges to achieve correct alignment.
12   To adjust the door closed position, scribe a line or mark around the striker plate to provide a reference point, then check that the door latch is contacting the center of the latch striker. If not adjust the up and down position first.

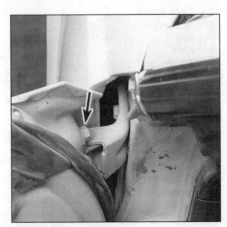

19.8a Before loosening the door retaining bolts (arrow), draw a line around the hinge plate for a reinstallation reference

19.8b Open the front door to access the rear door hinge-to-body mounting bolts (arrows)

11

19.13 Adjust the door lock striker by loosening the mounting screws and gently tapping the striker in the desired direction (arrows)

20.3 Scribe a mark around the hinge plate (arrow) for realignment of the trunk lid on installation

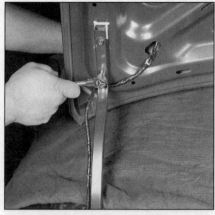

20.4 With an assistant holding the trunk lid - remove the retaining bolts from each hinge and lift off the trunk lid

13   Finally adjust the latch striker sideways position, so that the door panel is flush with the center pillar or rear quarter panel and provides positive engagement with the latch mechanism **(see illustration)**.

20   Trunk lid - removal, installation and adjustment

Note: *The trunk lid is heavy and somewhat awkward to remove and install - at least two people should perform this procedure.*

Removal and installation

Refer to illustrations 20.3 and 20.4

1   Open the trunk lid and cover the edges of the trunk compartment with pads or cloths to protect the painted surfaces when the lid is removed.
2   Disconnect any cables or wire harness connectors attached to the trunk lid that would interfere with removal.
3   Make alignment marks around the hinge mounting bolts with a marking pen **(see illustration)**.
4   While an assistant supports the trunk lid, remove the lid-to-hinge bolts **(see illustration)**.
on both sides and lift it off.
5   Installation is the reverse of removal.
Note: *When reinstalling the trunk lid, align the lid-to-hinge bolts with the marks made during removal.*

Adjustment

6   Fore-and-aft and side-to-side adjustment of the trunk lid is accomplished by moving the lid in relation to the hinge after loosening the bolts or nuts.
7   Scribe a line around the entire hinge plate as described earlier in this Section so you can determine the amount of movement.
8   Loosen the bolts or nuts and move the trunk lid into correct alignment. Move it only a little at a time. Tighten the hinge bolts or nuts and carefully lower the trunk lid to check the alignment.

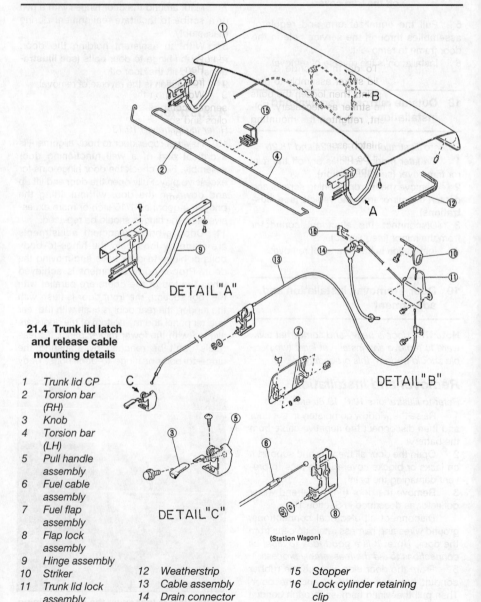

21.4 Trunk lid latch and release cable mounting details

1	Trunk lid CP
2	Torsion bar (RH)
3	Knob
4	Torsion bar (LH)
5	Pull handle assembly
6	Fuel cable assembly
7	Fuel flap assembly
8	Flap lock assembly
9	Hinge assembly
10	Striker
11	Trunk lid lock assembly
12	Weatherstrip
13	Cable assembly
14	Drain connector
15	Stopper
16	Lock cylinder retaining clip

(Station Wagon)

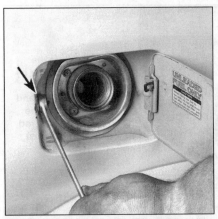

21.7 Open the fuel door and remove the opening mechanism retaining nut (arrow)

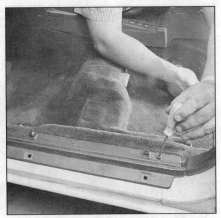

21.9 Detach the clips and screws securing the driver's side door sill plates

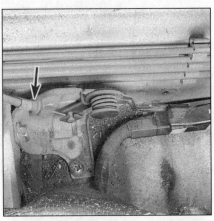

21.11 Use a screwdriver to pry out the cable from the lever retaining bracket (arrow), then disengage the cable from the lever assembly

9 If necessary after installation, the entire trunk lid striker assembly **(see illustration 21.4)** can be adjusted up and down as well as from side to side on the trunk lid so the lid closes securely and is flush with the rear quarter panels. To do this, scribe a line around the trunk lid striker assembly to provide a reference point. Then loosen the bolts and reposition the striker as necessary. Following adjustment, retighten the mounting bolts.

10 The trunk lid latch assembly, as well as the hinges, should be periodically lubricated with white lithium-base grease to prevent sticking and wear.

21 Trunk lid latch, release cable, and lock cylinder - removal and installation

Note: *This procedure applies to all sedan and three door (hatchback) models.*

Trunk lid latch

Refer to illustration 21.4

1 Open the trunk and remove the rear finishing panels (if equipped). Then scribe a line around the trunk lid latch assembly for a reference point to aid the installation procedure.

2 Detach the latch-to-lock cylinder rod from the lock cylinder.

3 Remove the bolt securing the trunk lid release cable to the body.

4 The trunk lid latch is retained by two bolts **(see illustration)**. Detach the two retaining bolts, then disengage the release cable from the latch assembly and remove the latch.

5 Installation is the reverse of removal.

Trunk and fuel door release cable

Refer to illustrations 21.7, 21.9 and 21.11

6 Working in the trunk, remove the latch assembly as described above in Steps 1 through 4.

7 Open the fuel door and remove the opening mechanism retaining nut **(see illus-**

tration). **Note:** *If the cable is broken the fuel door can be opened manually by reaching between the inner fender support and rear quarter panel and pulling upward on the fuel door opening mechanism.*

8 Remove the driver's seat and the rear seat from the vehicle (see Section 31).

9 Working on the drivers side of the passenger compartment, remove the plastic clips and screws securing the front and rear door sill plates at the bottom of the door openings **(see illustration)**.

10 Peel back the carpeting to access the release cable and lever.

11 Disengage the cable from the release lever assembly **(see illustration)** and the remaining cable retaining clips. Attach a piece of thin wire to the end of the cable to aid in installation.

12 Working in the trunk compartment, pull the cable towards the rear of the vehicle until you can see the wire. Attach the new cable to the wire and pull it back into the passenger compartment.

13 Installation is the reverse of removal.

Trunk lock cylinder

14 Open the trunk and remove the rear finishing panels (if equipped).

15 Detach the latch to lock cylinder rod and

the drain connector (if equipped) from the lock cylinder.

16 Using a pair of pliers remove the lock cylinder retaining clip **(see illustration 21.4)**.

17 Working from the outside of the trunk lid, grasp the lock cylinder and pull it outward to remove it.

18 Installation is the reverse of removal.

22 Liftgate support struts - removal and installation

Refer to illustrations 22.4a and 22.4b

Note: *The rear liftgate is heavy and somewhat awkward to hold - at least two people should perform this procedure.*

1 Open the rear liftgate and support it securely.

2 Remove any interior trim panels which would interfere with the removal of the support strut.

3 Disconnect the electrical connector from the support strut (if equipped).

4 Remove the retaining bolts at both ends of the support strut and detach it from the vehicle **(see illustrations)**.

5 Installation is the reverse of removal.

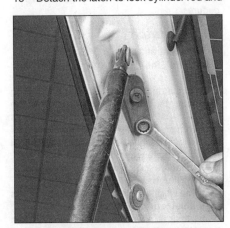

22.4a Remove the mounting bracket retaining bolts from both ends of the strut

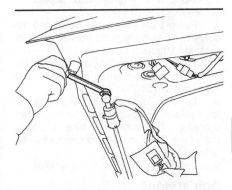

22.4b On some models it will be necessary to disconnect the electrical connector and unscrew the stud on the upper end of the support strut

11

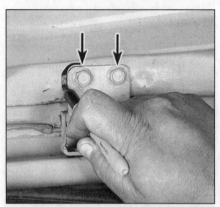

23.4 Before loosening the liftgate retaining bolts (arrows), draw a line around the hinge plate for a reinstallation reference

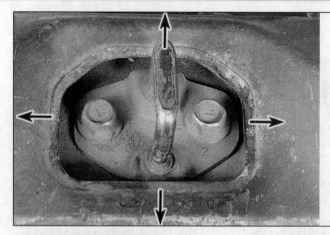

23.7 Adjust the liftgate lock striker by loosening the mounting screws and gently tapping the striker in the desired direction (arrows)

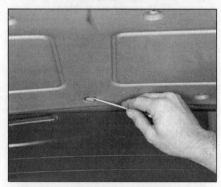

24.2 Pry out the retaining clips securing the liftgate interior trim panel

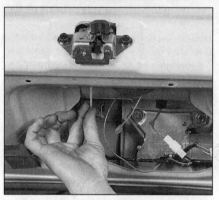

24.3 Disconnect the latch rod from the lock cylinder

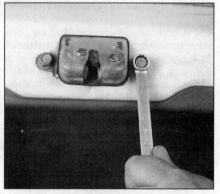

24.4 Remove the liftgate latch retaining bolts

23   Liftgate - removal, installation and adjustment

Note: *This procedure applies to all station wagon and three door (hatchback) models. The liftgate is heavy and somewhat awkward to hold - at least two people should perform this procedure.*

Removal and installation

Refer to illustration 23.4

1   Open the liftgate and support it securely.

2   Remove the liftgate trim panels and disconnect all wiring harness connectors leading to the liftgate.

3   While an assistant supports the liftgate, detach the support struts from the liftgate assembly (see Section 22).

4   Scribe a line around the liftgate hinges for a reference point to aid the installation procedure. Then detach the hinge to liftgate bolts **(see illustration)**. and remove the liftgate from the vehicle.

5   Installation is the reverse of removal.

Adjustment

Refer to illustration 23.7

6   Adjustments are made by loosening the hinge-to liftgate bolts and moving the liftgate. Proper alignment is achieved when the edges

of the liftgate are parallel with the rear quarter panel and the top of the tailgate.

7   Finally, adjust the latch striker assembly as necessary to provide positive engagement with the latch mechanism **(see illustration)**.

24   Liftgate latch, outside handle and lock cylinder (station wagon only) - removal and installation

Note: *All three door (hatchback) models refer to Section 21 for removal and installation procedures.*

Liftgate latch

Refer to illustrations 24.2, 24.3 and 24.4

1   Open the liftgate and support it securely.

2   To gain access to most of the following components, the interior trim panel on the liftgate must be removed. Using a small screwdriver, carefully pry out the trim panel retaining clips and remove the trim panel from the liftgate **(see illustration)**.

3   Detach the latch rod from the lock cylinder **(see illustration)**.

4   The liftgate latch is retained by two bolts **(see illustration)**. Detach the two retaining bolts, then remove the latch assembly from the vehicle.

5   Installation is the reverse of removal.

Outside handle and lock cylinder

Refer to illustrations 24.8a, 24.8b, 24.8c, 24.9a and 24.9b

6   Remove the interior trim panel and latch rod on as described above in Step 2 and 3.

7   Disconnect both license plate bulb connectors from the outside handle.

8   Detach the nuts and bolts securing the outside handle **(see illustrations)**. Then remove the handle from the liftgate.

9   On early models, the lock cylinder can

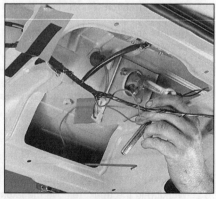

24.8a On early models, work through the large access hole and detach the outside handle retaining nuts from inside the liftgate . . .

24.8b . . . then detach the retaining bolts on the outside of the liftgate and remove the handle

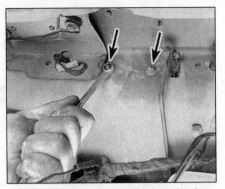

24.8c On late model vehicles, simply detach the outside handle retaining nuts (arrows) and the latch rod from inside the liftgate to remove the handle

24.9a On early models, turn the handle over to access the lock cylinder retaining screws

24.9b On late model vehicles, simply detach the lock cylinder retaining clip (A) and the latch rod (B) from inside the liftgate

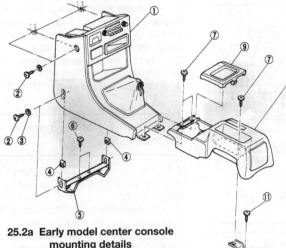

25.2a Early model center console mounting details

1	Console box	7	Screw
2	Screw	8	Parking brake cover
3	Washer	9	Cover tray
4	Spring nut	10	Bracket
5	Bracket	11	Screw
6	Screw		

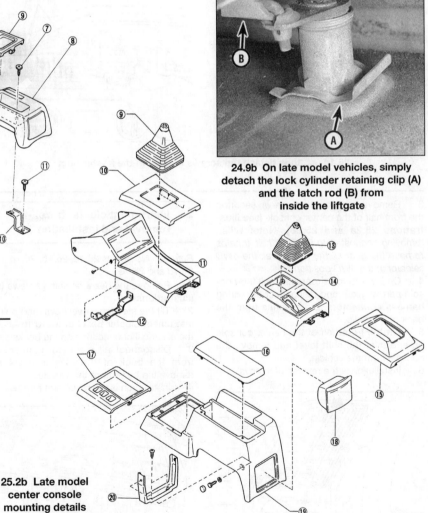

25.2b Late model center console mounting details

9	Boot (2WD-MT and 4WD S/R)	15	Indicator panel (AT)
10	Boot panel (2WD-MT and 4WD	16	Pocket lid
11	Console box	17	Parking bracket cover tray
12	Console box bracket	18	Ash tray
13	Boot (4WD-D/R)	19	Parking brake cover
14	Boot panel (4WD-D/r)	20	Cover bracket

now be removed from the handle by removing its mounting screws (see illustration). On late model vehicles , simply detach the lock cylinder retaining clip and remove it from the vehicle (see illustration).

10   Installation is the reverse of removal.

25   Center console - removal and installation

Refer to illustrations 25.2a and 25.2b

1   Unscrew the shift knob(s) on manual transmission or 4WD shift levers. On early models, loosen the cord on the 4WD selector boot and or the manual transaxle shift lever boot.

2   Position the parking brake lever in the full upward (ON) position, then detach the parking brake panel cover screws and then remove the cover (see illustrations).

11

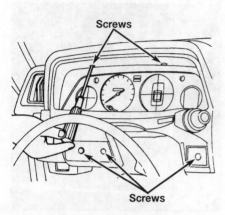

26.1a   Early DL model instrument cluster bezel mounting details

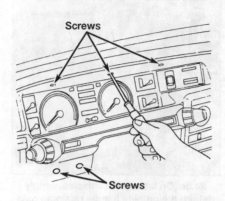

26.1b   On early GL models, detach the screws securing the top and bottom edge of the bezel . . .

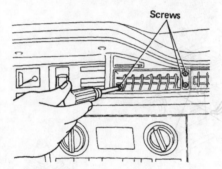

26.1c   . . . then detach the screws located in the heater duct

3   Remove the mounting screws securing the front half of the center console **(see illustrations 25.2a and 25.2b)**. **Note:** *When removing and installing the front half, it helps to have the gear shifter in Neutral, the 4WD selector in the 4WD position.*
4   On early models, carefully pull the console part way out and disconnect the wiring harness connectors and antenna from the back of the radio.
5   Lift the front half of the center console up and over the shift lever and remove the console from the vehicle.
6   Installation is the reverse of removal.

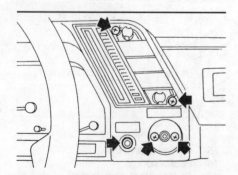

26.1d   On late model vehicles, remove the plastic trim caps and knobs to access the retaining screws at each corner . . .

26   Instrument cluster bezel - removal and installation

Refer to illustrations 26.1a, 26.1b, 26.1c, 26.1d and 26.1e
1   Remove the bezel retaining screws **(see illustrations)**.
2   Tilt the steering wheel down and pull the instrument cluster bezel outward to access the electrical connections on the backside.
3   Disconnect all electrical connections from the back of the cluster bezel and remove the bezel from the vehicle.
4   Installation is the reverse of removal.

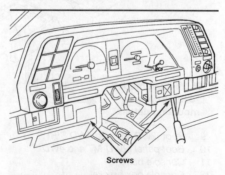

26.1e   . . . and along the lower edge of the instrument cluster bezel

27   Steering column cover - removal and installation

Refer to illustration 27.3
1   Remove the steering wheel (see Chapter 10).
2   Remove the steering column cover screws.
3   Separate the cover halves and detach them from the steering column **(see illustration)**.
4   Installation is the reverse of removal.

28   Dashboard trim panels - removal and installation

Refer to illustrations 28.1a and 28.1b
1   All of the dashboard trim panels are held in place by clips and screws. Remove any screws or clips and disengage the trim panels as necessary **(see illustrations)**.
2   Disconnect any wiring harness connectors which would interfere with removal.
3   Installation is the reverse of removal.

29   Instrument panel - removal and installation

1   Disconnect the negative battery cable.
2   Remove the steering wheel (see Chapter 10).
3   Remove the center floor console (see Section 25).
4   Remove all the dashboard trim panels such as the glove box, instrument cluster bezel, radio trim bezel and the driver side lower trim panel.
5   Remove the radio and instrument cluster (see Chapter 12).
6   On early models, remove the heater control panel (see Chapter 3). On later models, remove the temperature control cables from the control levers.
7   Detach the nuts and bolts securing the fuse box, and the hood release handle (see

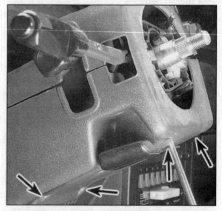

27.3   The steering column cover screws (arrows) are accessible from the bottom of the lower cover

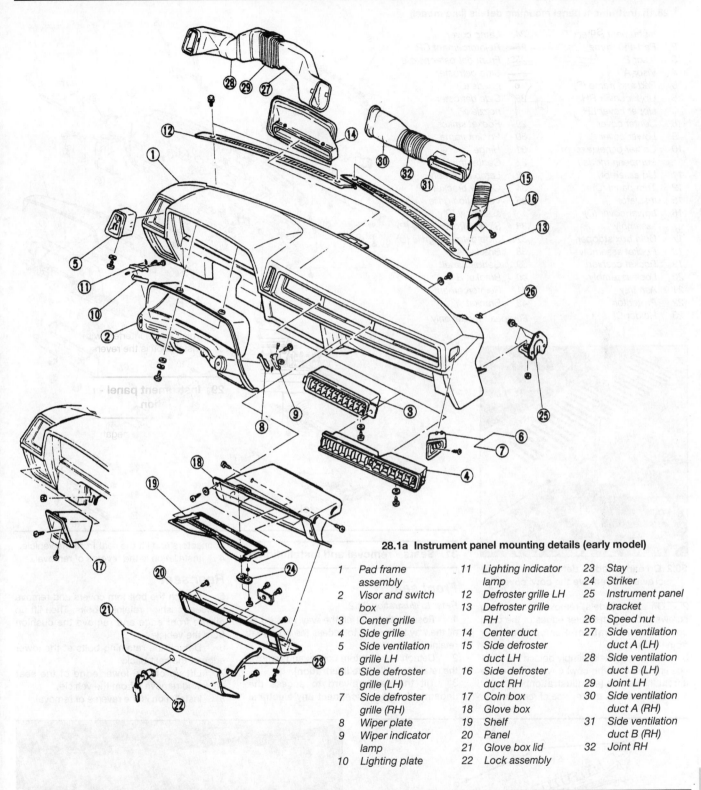

28.1a Instrument panel mounting details (early model)

1	Pad frame assembly	11	Lighting indicator lamp	23	Stay
2	Visor and switch box	12	Defroster grille LH	24	Striker
3	Center grille	13	Defroster grille RH	25	Instrument panel bracket
4	Side grille	14	Center duct	26	Speed nut
5	Side ventilation grille LH	15	Side defroster duct LH	27	Side ventilation duct A (LH)
6	Side defroster grille (LH)	16	Side defroster duct RH	28	Side ventilation duct B (LH)
7	Side defroster grille (RH)	17	Coin box	29	Joint LH
8	Wiper plate	18	Glove box	30	Side ventilation duct A (RH)
9	Wiper indicator lamp	19	Shelf	31	Side ventilation duct B (RH)
10	Lighting plate	20	Panel	32	Joint RH
		21	Glove box lid		
		22	Lock assembly		

Section 10).

8   Remove the steering column mounting bolts and lower the steering column to the floor.

9   Remove the bolts securing the instrument panel **(see illustrations 28.1a and 28.1b)**.

10   Pull the instrument panel towards the rear of the vehicle and detach any electrical connectors and vacuum lines interfering with removal.

11   Lift the instrument panel up and out to remove it from the vehicle.

12   Installation is the reverse of removal.

30 Cowl cover - removal and installation

Refer to illustrations 30.2 and 30.3

1   Remove the windshield wiper arms (see Chapter 12).

11

28.1b Instrument panel mounting details (late model)

1	Instrument panel CP	24	Lamp cover
2	Pad and frame (P)	25	Reinforcement CP
3	Visor B	26	Front defroster nozzle
4	Visor A	27	Side defroster
5	Pad and frame (D)		nozzle (D)
6	Upper cover RH	28	Side defroster
7	Upper cover LH		nozzle (P)
8	Center cover	29	Pocket striker
9	Lower cover	30	Pocket frame
10	Center panel (except	31	Hinge
	European model)	32	Center tray
11	Lid assembly	33	Lamp assembly
12	Trim panel (D)	34	Center bracket CP
15	Insulator	35	Ventilation grille
16	Lower cover (D)		assembly (P)
	assembly	36	Side defroster grille (P)
17	Coin box stopper	37	Side defroster grille (D)
18	Pocket assembly	38	Bracket A*
19	Pocket cushion	39	Center panel*
20	Lock assembly	40	Bracket B*
21	Ash tray	41	Reinforcement
22	Protector	42	Bracket
23	Holder CP		*European model only

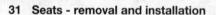

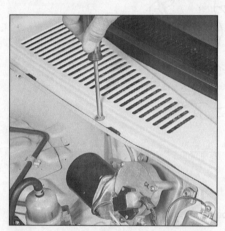

30.2 On early models detach the retaining screws and remove the cowl cover

2   On early models, remove the retaining screws securing the outer edges of the cowl cover **(see illustration)**. Remove the cover from the vehicle.

3   On later models, simply detach the plastic clips securing the cowl cover and remove it from the vehicle **(see illustration)**.

4   Installation is the reverse of removal.

---

31 Seats - removal and installation

Front seat

Refer to illustration 31.2

1   Position the seat all the way forward or all the way to the rear to access the front seat retaining bolts.

2   Detach any bolt trim covers and remove the retaining bolts **(see illustration)**.

3   Tilt the seat upward to access the underneath, then disconnect any electrical connectors and lift the seat from the vehicle.

4   Installation is the reverse of removal.

Rear seat

5   Detach the bolt trim covers and remove the seat cushion retaining bolts. Then lift up on the front edge and remove the cushion from the vehicle.

6   Detach the retaining bolts at the lower edge of the seat back.

7   Lift up on the lower edge of the seat back and remove it from the vehicle.

8   Installation is the reverse of removal.

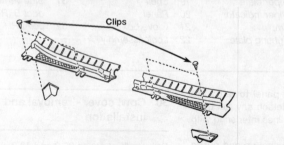

30.3 On later models pry out the plastic clips and remove the cowl cover

31.2 Detach the trim covers to access the seat retaining bolts (arrows)

Chapter 12
Chassis electrical system

Contents

1   General information

The electrical system is a 12-volt, negative ground type. Power for the lights and all electrical accessories is supplied by a lead/acid-type battery which is charged by the alternator.

This Chapter covers repair and service procedures for the various electrical components not associated with the engine. Information on the battery, alternator, distributor and starter motor can be found in Chapter 5.

It should be noted that when portions of the electrical system are serviced, the cable should be disconnected from the negative battery terminal to prevent electrical shorts and/or fires.

2   Electrical troubleshooting - general information

A typical electrical circuit consists of an electrical component, any switches, relays, motors, fuses, fusible links or circuit breakers related to that component and the wiring and electrical connectors that link the component to both the battery and the chassis. To help you pinpoint an electrical circuit problem, wiring diagrams are included at the end of this Chapter.

Before tackling any troublesome electrical circuit, first study the appropriate wiring diagrams to get a complete understanding of what makes up that individual circuit. Trouble spots, for instance, can often be narrowed down by noting if other components related to the circuit are operating properly. If several components or circuits fail at one time, chances are the problem is in a fuse or ground connection, because several circuits are often routed through the same fuse and ground connections.

Electrical problems usually stem from simple causes, such as loose or corroded connections, a blown fuse, a melted fusible link or a bad relay. Visually inspect the condition of all fuses, wires and connections in a problem circuit before troubleshooting it.

If testing instruments are going to be utilized, use the diagrams to plan ahead of time where you will make the necessary connections in order to accurately pinpoint the trouble spot.

The basic tools needed for electrical troubleshooting include a circuit tester or voltmeter (a 12-volt bulb with a set of test leads can also be used), a continuity tester, which includes a bulb, battery and set of test leads, and a jumper wire, preferably with a circuit breaker incorporated, which can be used to bypass electrical components. Before attempting to locate a problem with test instruments, use the wiring diagram(s) to decide where to make the connections.

Voltage checks

Voltage checks should be performed if a circuit is not functioning properly. Connect one lead of a circuit tester to either the negative battery terminal or a known good ground. Connect the other lead to a electrical connector in the circuit being tested, preferably nearest to the battery or fuse. If the bulb of the tester lights, voltage is present, which means that the part of the circuit between the electrical connector and the battery is problem free. Continue checking the rest of the circuit in the same fashion. When you reach a point at which no voltage is present, the problem lies between that point and the last test point with voltage. Most of the time the problem can be traced to a loose connection. **Note:** *Keep in mind that some circuits receive voltage only when the ignition key is in the Accessory or Run position.*

Finding a short

One method of finding shorts in a circuit is to remove the fuse and connect a test light or voltmeter in its place. There should be no voltage present in the circuit. Move the wiring harness from side to side while watching the test light. If the bulb goes on, there is a short to ground somewhere in that area, probably where the insulation has rubbed through. The same test can be performed on each component in the circuit, even a switch.

Ground check

Perform a ground test to check whether a component is properly grounded. Disconnect the battery and connect one lead of a self-powered test light, known as a continuity tester, to a known good ground. Connect the other lead to the wire or ground connection being tested. If the bulb goes on, the ground is good. If the bulb does not go on, the ground is not good.

Continuity check

A continuity check is done to determine if there are any breaks in a circuit - if it is passing electricity properly. With the circuit off (no power in the circuit), a self-powered continuity tester can be used to check the circuit. Connect the test leads to both ends of the circuit (or to the "power" end and a good ground), and if the test light comes on the circuit is passing current properly. If the light doesn't come on, there is a break somewhere in the circuit. The same procedure can be used to test a switch, by connecting the continuity tester to the power in and power out sides of the switch. With the switch turned On, the test light should come on.

Finding an open circuit

When diagnosing for possible open circuits, it is often difficult to locate them by sight because oxidation or terminal misalignment are hidden by the electrical connectors. Merely wiggling an electrical connector on a sensor or in the wiring harness may correct the open circuit condition. Remember this when an open circuit is indicated when troubleshooting a circuit. Intermittent problems may also be caused by oxidized or loose connections.

3.1a The fuse box is located on the driver's side of the instrument panel, behind the fuse panel cover

Electrical troubleshooting is simple if you keep in mind that all electrical circuits are basically electricity running from the battery, through the wires, switches, relays, fuses and fusible links to each electrical component (light bulb, motor, etc.) and to ground, from which it is passed back to the battery. Any electrical problem is an interruption in the flow of electricity to and from the battery.

3 Fuses - general information

Refer to illustrations 3.1a, 3.1b, 3.3a and 3.3b

The electrical circuits of the vehicle are protected by a combination of fuses, circuit breakers and fusible links. The fuse block is located under the instrument panel on the driver's side of the dashboard and in the engine compartment **(see illustrations)**. Access is gained by simply unsnapping the plastic cover.

Each of the fuses is designed to protect a specific circuit, as identified on the fuse cover. Spare fuses and a special removal tool are included in the fuse box cover.

If an electrical component fails, always check the fuse first. A blown fuse is easily identified by inspecting the metal element inside the housing **(see illustrations)**. If this element is broken, the fuse is inoperable and should be replaced with a new one.

Fuses are replaced by simply pulling out the old one and pushing in the new one.

Be sure to replace blown fuses with the correct type. Fuses of different ratings are physically interchangeable, but only fuses of

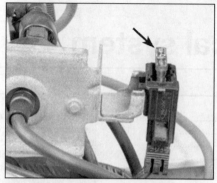

3.1b Some circuits are protected by inline fuses (arrow) - consult the wiring diagrams for the specific circuits

the proper rating should be used. Replacing a fuse with one of a higher or lower value than specified is not recommended. Each electrical circuit needs a specific amount of protection. The amperage value of each fuse is molded into the fuse body.

If the replacement fuse immediately fails, don't replace it again until the cause of the problem is isolated and corrected. In most cases, this will be a short circuit in the wiring caused by a broken or deteriorated wire.

4 Fusible links - general information

Refer to illustrations 4.2 and 4.3

Some circuits are protected by fusible links. The links are used in circuits which are not ordinarily fused, such as the ignition circuit.

On early models the fusible link is located near the positive battery terminal and is easily removed by unplugging the connectors at either end **(see illustration)**.

On late models the fusible links are located in the engine compartment fuse block **(see illustration)**. To replace a fusible link, first disconnect the negative cable from the battery. Unplug the burned-out link from

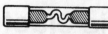
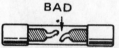
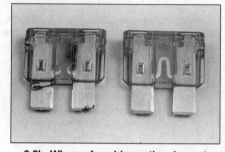

3.3a Early model fuses are cylindrical in shape with a glass tube covering the filament

3.3b When a fuse blows, the element between the terminals melts - the fuse on the left is blown, the fuse on the right is good

the fuse block and replace it with a new one (available from your dealer or auto parts store). Always determine the cause for the overload which melted the fusible link before installing a new one.

5 Circuit breakers - general information

Refer to illustration 5.2

Circuit breakers protect components such as, power windows, power door locks and headlights.

On some models the circuit breaker resets itself automatically, so an electrical overload in a circuit breaker protected system will cause the circuit to fail momentarily, then come back on. If the circuit doesn't come back on, check it immediately **(see illustration)**. Once the condition is corrected, the circuit breaker will resume its normal function. Some circuit breakers must be reset manually.

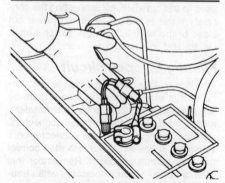

4.2 On early models, the fusible links are located at the positive battery post

4.3 On late models, the fusible links (arrow) are located next to the coolant reserve tank and are easily accessible after removing the cover

5.2 Perform a continuity test with an ohmmeter to check a circuit breaker - no reading indicates a bad circuit breaker

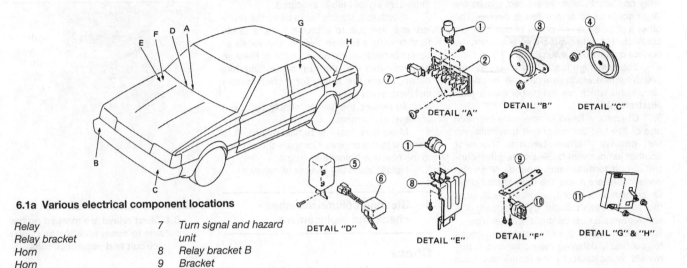

6.1a Various electrical component locations

1	Relay	7	Turn signal and hazard unit
2	Relay bracket	8	Relay bracket B
3	Horn	9	Bracket
4	Horn	10	Relay set
5	4WD-AT checker unit	11	AT control unit (4AT only)
6	Chime		

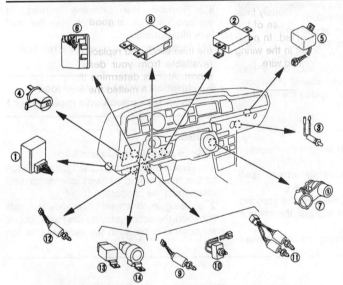

6.1b Various instrument panel electrical component locations

1	Fuel pump control unit	10	Kick-down switch (A/T)
2	Cruise control unit	11	Stop and brake switch (cruise control)
3	Glove box light switch	12	Clutch switch (cruise control)
4	Intermittent wiper unit	13	Turn signal and hazard flasher
5	Chime	14	Kick-down relay (A/T)
6	Timer		
7	Ignition and key warning		
8	ECM		
9	Stoplight switch		

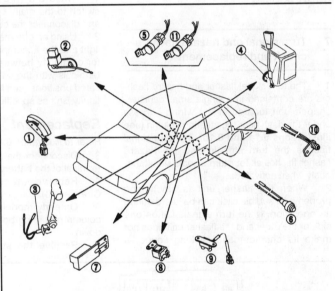

6.1c Various interior electrical component locations

1	Inhibitor switch	7	Power window control unit
2	Parking brake switch	8	Power window relay
3	4WD switch (dual range)	9	Power window circuit breaker
4	Seat belt switch	10	Door switch (rear)
5	Ignition relay	11	Automatic choke relay
6	Door switch (front)		

6 Relays - general information and testing

General information

Refer to illustrations 6.1a, 6.1b and 6.1c

1 Several electrical accessories in the vehicle, such as the fuel injection system, horns, starter, and fog lamps use relays to transmit the electrical signal to the compo-

nent. Relays use a low-current circuit (the control circuit) to open and close a high-current circuit (the power circuit). If the relay is defective, that component will not operate properly. The various relays are mounted in instrument panel **(see illustrations)** and several locations throughout the vehicle . If a faulty relay is suspected, it can be removed and tested using the procedure below or by a dealer service department or a repair shop. Defective relays must be replaced as a unit.

Testing

Refer to illustration 6.4

2 It's best to refer to the wiring diagram for the circuit to determine the proper hook-ups for the relay you're testing. However, if you're not able to determine the correct hook-up from the wiring diagrams, you may be able to determine the test hook-ups from the information that follows.

3 On most relays, two of the terminals are the relay's control circuit (they connect to the

12

relay coil which, when energized, closes the large contacts to complete the circuit). The other terminals are the power circuit (they are connected together within the relay when the control-circuit coil is energized).

4　The relays are marked as an aid to help you determine which terminals are the control circuit and which are the power circuit **(see illustration)**.

5　Connect a fused jumper wire between one of the two control circuit terminals and the positive battery terminal. Connect another jumper wire between the other control circuit terminal and ground. When the connections are made, the relay should click. On some relays, polarity may be critical, so, if the relay doesn't click, try swapping the jumper wires on the control circuit terminals.

6　With the jumper wires connected, check for continuity between the power circuit terminals as indicated by the markings on the relay.

7　If the relay fails any of the above tests, replace it.

7　Turn signal and hazard flashers - check and replacement

1　The turn signal flasher and hazard flashers are contained in a single small canister-shaped unit located in the wiring harness under the dash near the steering column **(see illustrations 6.1a and 6.1b)**. The turn signal flashes the turn signals and the hazard flasher flashes all four turn signals simultaneously when activated.

2　When the flasher unit is functioning properly, an audible click can be heard during its operation. If the turn signals fail on one side or the other and the flasher unit does not make its characteristic clicking sound, a

faulty turn signal bulb is indicated.

3　If both turn signals fail to blink, the problem may be due to a blown fuse, a faulty flasher unit, a broken switch or a loose or open connection. If a quick check of the fuse box indicates that the turn signal fuse has blown, check the wiring for a short before installing a new fuse.

4　To replace the flasher, simply pull it out of the wiring harness.

5　Make sure that the replacement unit is identical to the original. Compare the old one to the new one before installing it.

6　Installation is the reverse of removal.

8　Steering column switches - check and replacement

Check

Refer to illustrations 8.2a, 8.2b, 8.2c and 8.2d

1　Trace the wire from the combination switch to the main wiring harness connector and disconnect the connectors.

2　Using an ohmmeter or self-powered test light and the accompanying diagrams, check for continuity between the indicated switch terminals with the switch in each of the indicated positions **(see illustrations)**. If the continuity isn't as specified, replace the switch.

Replacement

Refer to illustration 8.8

3　Disconnect the cable from the negative terminal of the battery.

4　Remove the steering wheel (see Chapter 10).

5　On early models, remove the steering column mounting bolts and pull the column down.

6　Remove the steering column covers

6.4 Most relays are marked on the outside to easily identify the power circuit and control circuits

(see Chapter 11).

7　Unplug the electrical connectors from the combination switch.

8　Remove the retaining screws (If equipped) and pull the switch from the shaft **(see illustration)**.

9　Installation is the reverse the removal.

9　Ignition switch and key lock cylinder - check and replacement

Check

Refer to illustrations 9.2a and 9.2b

1　Trace the wire from the ignition switch to the main wiring harness connector and disconnect the connector.

2　Using an ohmmeter or self-powered test light and the accompanying diagrams, check for continuity between the indicated switch

Body Electrical System

Switch position	Terminal	B	BH	HL	HU	FU	R	L	FH
Dimmer switch	Low beam	o—	—o						
	High beam	o—		—o				
	Headlight flasher			o—	—o				
Turn signal switch	Left turn						o—	—o	
	Neutral								
	Right turn						o—	—o	
Hazard warning light switch	OFF								
	ON						o—	—o—	—o

8.2a Early model combination switch terminal guide and continuity chart equipped with a ten pin connector

Switch position	Terminal	EP	E	HU	HL	TB	HB	FUB	FU	L	R
Dimmer switch	Low beam		o—		—o						
	High beam		o—	—o							
	Headlight flasher		o—		—o						
Turn signal switch	Left turn						o—	—o		o—	—o	
	Neutral						o—				
	Right turn						o—	—o			o—	—o
Hazard warning light switch	OFF										
	ON								o—	—o—	—o

8.2b Early model combination switch terminal guide and continuity chart equipped with a seven pin and four pin connector

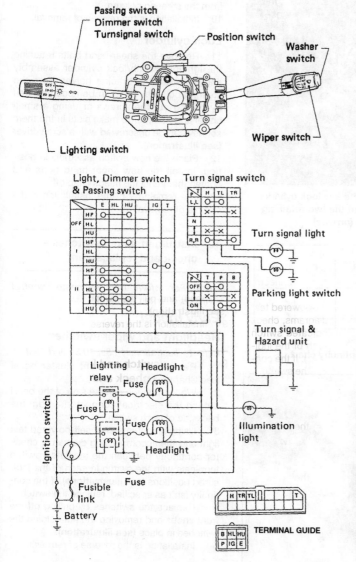

8.2c Late model combination switch identification, terminal guide and continuity chart

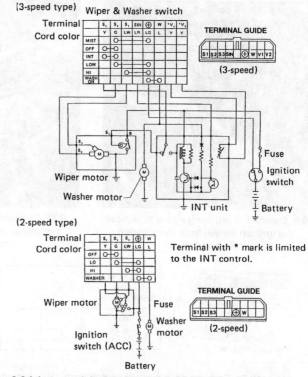

8.2d Late model wiper/washer switch terminal guide and continuity chart

Terminal with * mark is limited to the INT control.

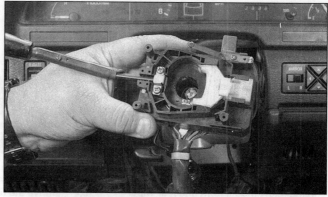

8.8 Pull the combination switch over the steering shaft to remove it

terminals with the switch in each of the indicated positions **(see illustrations)**. If the continuity isn't as specified, replace the switch.

Replacement

Refer to illustrations 9.9 and 9.11

3   Disconnect the cable from the negative terminal of the battery.

4   Place the ignition key in the OFF position.
5   Remove the steering wheel (see Chapter 10).
6   Remove the steering column cover (see Chapter 11).
7   Remove the combination switch from the steering column (see Section 8).

Ignition switch

8   Unplug the ignition switch wiring harness.

9.2a Ignition switch terminal guide

Connector	Switch operation			
Terminal	LOCK	ACC	ON	START
B			○	○
A		○	○	
IG			○	○
S				○
R				○

9.2b Ignition switch continuity chart

12

9.9 Detach the retaining screw to remove the ignition switch from the steering column housing

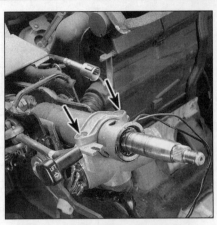

9.11 To remove the key lock cylinder assembly, drill out the two retaining rivets (arrows)

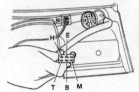

Terminal Switch position	B	T	H	E	M
OFF	o				
1st step	o——o			o—/\/\—o	
2nd step	o——o		o——o	o—/\/\—o	

10.3a Early model headlight switch terminal guide and continuity chart

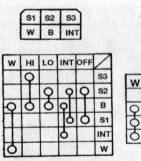

	S1	S2	S3
	W	B	INT

W	HI	LO	INT	OFF	
					S3
					S2
					B
					S1
					INT
					W

	S1	S2
	W	B

W	ON	OFF	
			S1
			S2
			B
			W

10.3b Early model front and rear wiper switch terminal guide and continuity chart

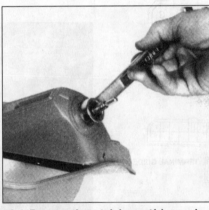

10.4 Remove the retaining nut(s) securing the switches to the instrument cluster bezel

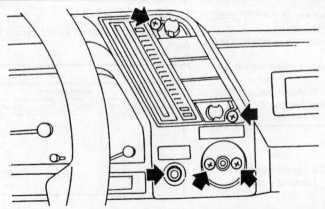

10.6 Carefully pry out the switch control knobs to access the switch control plate mounting screws (arrows)

9   Detach the switch retaining screw (see illustration) remove the switch assembly from the steering column.

10   Installation is the reverse of removal.

Lock cylinder

11   Remove the shear-head bolts retaining the ignition switch/lock cylinder assembly and separate the bracket halves from the steering column. This can be accomplished by drilling out the screws or using a small chisel and hammer to make slots in the them so they can be unscrewed with a screwdriver (see illustration).

12   Place the new switch assembly in position, install the new shear-head bolts and tighten them until the heads snap off.

13   The remainder of the installation is the reverse of removal.

10 Instrument panel switches - check and replacement

Note: *For information on heater control switches refer to Chapter 3.*

Early model

Headlight and wiper switches

Refer to illustrations 10.3a, 10.3b and 10.4

1   Remove the instrument cluster bezel (see Chapter 11).

2   Working on the reverse side of the bezel detach the electrical connector(s) from the backside of each switch.

3   Using an ohmmeter or self-powered test light and the accompanying diagrams, check for continuity between the indicated switch terminals with the switch in each of the indicated positions (see illustrations). If the continuity isn't as specified, replace the switch.

4   Replace the switches by pulling off the front knobs and removing the nut holding the switches in place (see illustration).

5   Installation is the reverse of removal.

Late model

Rear defogger, headlight washer, hazard and illumination control switches

Refer to illustrations 10.6, 10.8a and 10.8b

6   Using a small screwdriver pry off the switch knobs and remove the switch control plate mounting screws (see illustration).

7   Working on the reverse side of the control plate detach the electrical connector(s) from the backside of each switch.

8   Using an ohmmeter or self-powered test light and the accompanying diagrams, check for continuity between the indicated switch terminals with the switch in each of the indicated positions (see illustrations). If the continuity isn't as specified, replace the switch.

9   Replace the switches by unsnapping or unscrewing the switch from the instrument cluster bezel.

10   Installation is the reverse of removal.

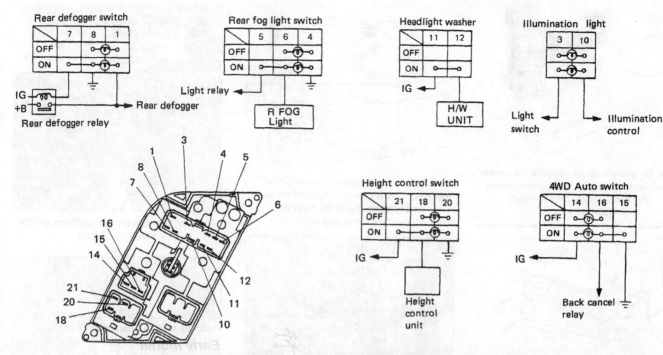

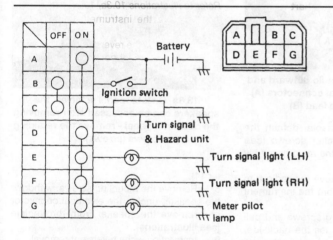

10.8a Late model instrument panel switch control plate terminal guide and continuity chart

10.8b Late model hazard warning switch terminal guide and continuity chart

12.3 Typical instrument cluster retaining screw locations (arrows)

11   Instrument panel gauges - check

Note: *The procedures described below are for use on analog type gauges only (non-digital).*

Fuel, oil and temperature gauges

1   All tests below require the ignition switch to be turned to ON position when testing.

2   If the gauge pointer does not move from the empty, low or cold positions, check the fuse. If the fuse is OK, locate the particular sending unit for the circuit you're working on (see Chapter 4 for fuel sending unit location, Chapter 2 for the oil sending unit location or Chapter 3 for the temperature sending unit location). Connect the sending unit connector to ground. If the pointer goes to the full, high or hot position replace the sending unit. If the pointer stays in same position, use a jumper wire to ground the sending unit terminal on the back of the gauge, if necessary, refer to the wiring diagrams at the end of this Chapter. If the pointer moves, the problem lies in the wire between the gauge and the sending unit. If the pointer does not move with the sending unit terminal on the back of the gauge grounded, check for voltage at the other terminal of the gauge. If voltage is present, replace the gauge.

12   Instrument cluster - removal and installation

Refer to illustration 12.3

1   Disconnect the negative battery cable.

2   Remove the instrument cluster bezel (see Chapter 11).

3   Remove the cluster mounting screws **(see illustration)** and pull the instrument cluster towards the steering wheel.

4   Reach behind the instrument cluster and disconnect the speedometer cable from the backside of the cluster.

5   Disconnect any electrical connectors that would interfere with removal.

6   Cover the steering column with a cloth

12

13.2a On early models, remove the center console, then detach the control knobs and remove the control shaft retaining nuts . . .

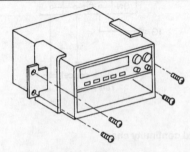

13.4a Remove the radio mounting screws

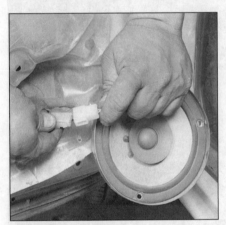

13.8b . . . and disconnect the electrical connector

to protect the trim covers then remove the instrument cluster from the vehicle.

7   Installation is the reverse of removal.

---

13   Radio and speakers - removal and installation

1   Disconnect the negative battery cable.

Radio

Refer to illustration 13.2a, 13.2b, 13.3, 13.4a and 13.4b

2   On early models, remove the center console (see Chapter 11). Detach the radio control knobs and remove the control shaft retaining nuts **(see illustration)**. Working

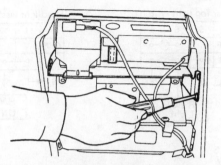

13.2b . . . then detach the bracket retaining screws located behind the radio and remove the radio from the center console

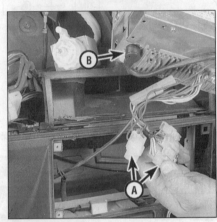

13.4b . . . then pull the radio outward and disconnect the electrical connectors (A) and the antenna lead (B)

from the rear of the console, detach the remaining mounting bracket screws **(see illustration)** and remove the radio assembly from the center console.

3   On late models, remove the radio trim bezel by unsnapping it from the instrument panel **(see illustration)**.

4   Remove the retaining screws and pull the radio outward to access the backside, then disconnect the electrical connectors and the antenna lead and lift the radio out of the vehicle **(see illustrations)**.

5   Installation is the reverse of removal.

Speakers

Instrument panel mounted

6   To remove the left speaker simply pry out the speaker grille and detach the speaker retaining screws. Lift the speaker away from the instrument panel, then disconnect the electrical connector and remove it from the vehicle. To remove the right speaker , first remove the instrument panel glove box (see Chapter 11). Working through the glove box opening detach the speaker retaining nuts, then disconnect the electrical connector and remove it from the vehicle.

Door mounted

Refer to illustrations 13.8a and 13.8b

7   Remove the door trim panel (see Chap-

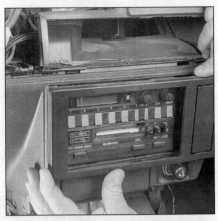

13.3 On late models carefully pry off the radio trim bezel

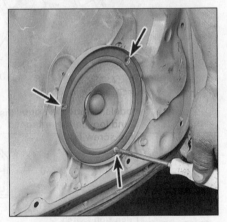

13.8a On late model vehicles, the speakers can be accessed after removing the door trim panel - remove the retaining screws (arrows) . . .

ter 11).

8   Remove the mounting screws, withdraw the speaker, unplug the electrical connector and remove the speaker from the vehicle **(see illustrations)**.

9   Installation is the reverse of removal.

Package shelf mounted

10   Remove the speaker grille mounting screws.

11   Remove the speaker retaining screws, withdraw the speaker, unplug the electrical connector and remove the speaker from the vehicle.

12   Installation is the reverse of removal

---

14   Antenna - removal and installation

1   Detach the radio and disconnect the antenna lead from the backside of the radio (see Section 11). Attach a piece of stiff wire to the end of the antenna lead, then remove any retaining clips under the instrument panel securing the antenna lead.

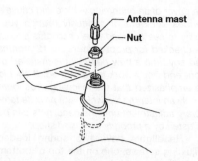

14.2 On early models, detach the antenna mast and the antenna base retaining nut

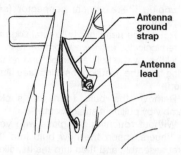

14.4 Remove the bolt securing the antenna ground strap

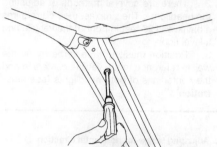

14.8 On late models, remove the door pillar trim panel and loosen the antenna base retaining screw two turns

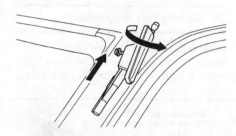

14.9 Lift the antenna base upward then twist it out to dislodge it from the body

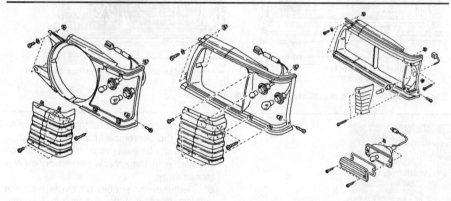

15.2 Early model headlight bezel mounting details

Early model

Refer to illustrations 14.2 and 14.4

2   Working on the outside of the vehicle, use a small wrench to remove the antenna mast and the antenna base retaining nut **(see illustration)**.

3   Remove the right front tire and the right front inner fenderwell as described in the fender removal Section in Chapter 11.

4   Remove the antenna ground strap from the inner fenderwell **(see illustration)**.

5   Pull the antenna base assembly down into the inner fenderwell opening, then pull the remainder of the antenna lead out of the passenger compartment until you can see the wire. then remove the old antenna lead from the wire and replace it with the new antenna lead.

6   Working in the passenger compartment, pull the wire and the antenna lead rearward into the passenger compartment.

7   The remainder of installation is the reverse of removal.

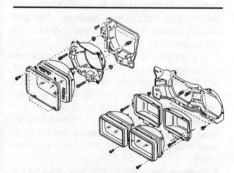

15.3 Early model headlight retaining ring mounting details

Late model

Refer to illustrations 14.8 and 14.9

8   Working in the passenger compartment, remove the front door pillar trim panel then loosen the antenna retaining screw two full turns **(see illustration)**.

9   Working in the door opening, grasp the antenna base with two hands and slowly maneuver it upward until the retaining screw dislodges itself from the outer sheetmetal **(see illustration)**.

10   Pull the antenna up and out to remove it.

11   Installation is the reverse of removal.

15   Headlights - removal and installation

1   Disconnect the negative cable from the battery.

Sealed beam type

Refer to illustrations 15.2 and 15.3

2   Remove the radiator grille (see Chapter 11) and the headlight trim bezel **(see illustration)**.

3   Remove the headlight retainer screws, taking care not to disturb the adjustment screws **(see illustration)**.

4   Remove the retainer and pull the headlight out far enough to unplug the connector.

5   Remove the headlight.

6   To install the headlight, plug the connector in, place the headlight in position and install the retainer and screws. Tighten the screws securely.

7   Install the radiator grille.

Halogen bulb-type

Refer to illustrations 15.8 and 15.10

Warning: *Halogen gas filled bulbs are under pressure and may shatter if the surface is scratched or the bulb is dropped. Wear eye protection and handle the bulbs carefully, grasping only the base whenever possible. Do not touch the surface of the bulb with your fingers because the oil from your skin could cause it to overheat and fail prematurely. If you do touch the bulb surface, clean it with rubbing alcohol.*

8   Reach behind the headlight assembly

15.8 On late models equipped with halogen type bulbs, detach the electrical connector from the rear of head light bulb assembly . . .

12

15.10 . . . then rotate the headlight bulb retaining ring counterclockwise and pull the bulb socket assembly out of the housing - when installing the new bulb, don't touch the surface; clean it with rubbing alcohol if you do

and unplug the electrical connector **(see illustration)**.

9   Rotate the headlight bulb retaining ring counterclockwise as viewed from the rear.

10   Withdraw the bulb assembly and retaining ring from the headlight housing **(see illustration)**.

11   Remove the bulb from the socket assembly by pulling it straight out.

12   Without touching the glass with your bare fingers, insert the new bulb into the socket assembly and then into the headlight housing, install and tighten the retaining ring.

13   Plug in the electrical connector. Test headlight operation, then close the hood.

16 Headlights - adjustment

Refer to illustrations 16.1 and 16.3
Note: *The headlights must be aimed correctly. If adjusted incorrectly they could blind*

the driver of an oncoming vehicle and cause a serious accident or seriously reduce your ability to see the road. The headlights should be checked for proper aim every 12 months and any time a new headlight is installed or front end body work is performed. It should be emphasized that the following procedure is only an interim step which will provide temporary adjustment until the headlights can be adjusted by a properly equipped shop.

1   Headlights have two spring loaded adjusting screws, one on the top or bottom controlling up-and-down movement and one on the side controlling left-and-right movement **(see illustration)**.

2   There are several methods of adjusting the headlights. The simplest method requires a blank wall 25 feet in front of the vehicle and a level floor.

3   Position masking tape vertically on the wall in reference to the vehicle centerline and the centerlines of both headlights **(see illustration)**.

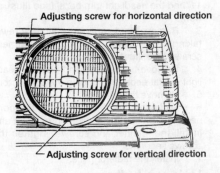

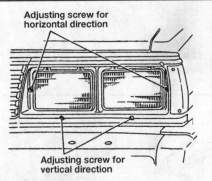

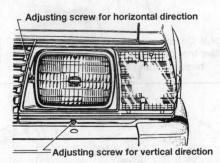

— Adjusting screw for horizontal direction

Adjusting screw for horizontal direction

Adjusting screw for horizontal direction

Adjusting screw for vertical direction

Adjusting screw for vertical direction

Adjusting screw for vertical direction

16.1 Early model headlight adjusting screw locations

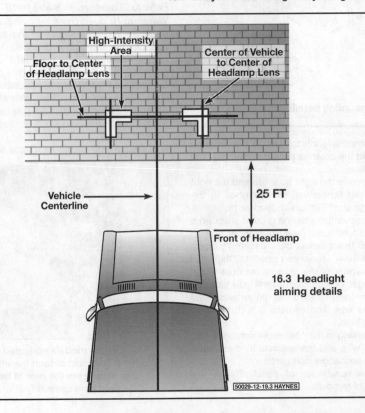

16.3 Headlight aiming details

High-Intensity Area

Floor to Center of Headlamp Lens

Center of Vehicle to Center of Headlamp Lens

Vehicle Centerline

25 FT

Front of Headlamp

50029-12-19.3 HAYNES

4   Position a horizontal tape line in reference to the centerline of all the headlights.
Note: *It may be easier to position the tape on the wall with the vehicle parked only a few inches away.*

5   Adjustment should be made with the vehicle sitting level, the gas tank half-full and no unusually heavy load in the vehicle.

6   Starting with the low beam adjustment, position the high intensity zone so it is two inches below the horizontal line and two inches to the right of the headlight vertical line. Adjustment is made by turning the top or bottom adjusting screw to raise or lower the beam. The adjusting screw on the side should be used in the same manner to move the beam left or right.

7   With the high beams on, the high intensity zone should be vertically centered with the exact center just below the horizontal line. **Note:** *It may not be possible to position the headlight aim exactly for both high and low beams. If a compromise must be made, keep in mind that the low beams are the most used and have the greatest effect on driver safety.*

8   Have the headlights adjusted by a dealer service department or service station at the earliest opportunity.

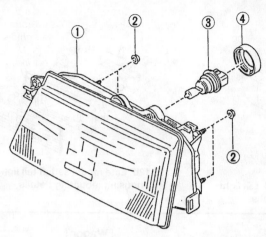

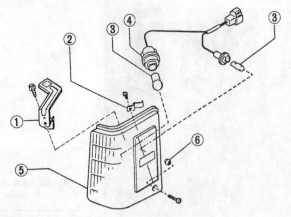

17.3 Late model headlight housing retaining nut locations

1	Lens and body	3	Bulb (Halogen)
2	Nut	4	Cap

18.1a Late model side marker light housing mounting details

1	Bracket	5	Front combination light
2	Spring	6	Lens and body screw
3	Bulb		grommet
4	Socket CP		

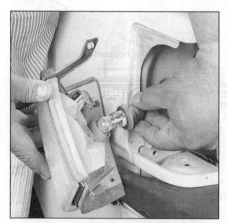

18.1b Rotate the bulb holder counterclockwise to release the bulb from the housing

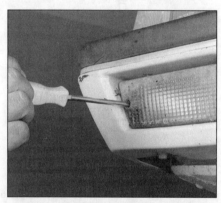

18.3 Remove the lens retaining screws to access the bulb

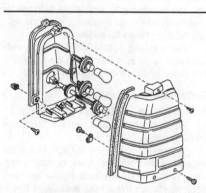

18.6 Early model station wagon tail light housing mounting details

17 Headlight housing - removal and installation

Refer to illustration 17.3

Warning: *These vehicles are equipped with halogen gas-filled headlight bulbs which are under pressure and may shatter if the surface is damaged or the bulb is dropped. Wear eye protection and handle the bulbs carefully, grasping only the base whenever possible. Do not touch the surface of the bulb with your fingers because the oil from your skin could cause it to overheat and fail prematurely. If you do touch the bulb surface, clean it with rubbing alcohol.*

1   Remove the headlight bulb (see Section 15).

2   Remove the radiator grille (see Chapter 11) and the side marker light(s) (see Section 18).

3   Reaching behind the radiator support, remove the retaining nuts. Then detach the housing and withdraw it from the vehicle **(see illustration)**.

4   Installation is the reverse of removal.

18 Bulb replacement

Front side marker lights

Refer to illustrations 18.1a and 18.1b

1   On early models equipped with sealed beam type headlights, remove the screws that secure the side marker light lens **(see illustration 15.2)**. On late models equipped with halogen type bulbs, remove the screws that secure the side marker light housing. Lift the lens or the housing outward, then rotate the bulb (early models) or the bulb holder (late models) counterclockwise and pull the bulb out **(see illustrations)**.

2   Installation is the reverse of removal.

Front turn signal light

Refer to illustration 18.3

Note: *On some early models, the front turn signal bulbs are located in the side marker light assembly. Follow steps 1 and 2 for the removal procedure.*

3   Remove the screws securing the turn signal lens **(see illustration)**.

4   Rotate the bulb counterclockwise to remove it.

5   Installation is the reverse of removal.

Rear tail light/brake light/turn signal

Station wagon

Refer to illustrations 18.6, 18.7a and 18.7b

6   On early station wagon models, remove screws and detach the tail light lens **(see illustration)**. Lift the lens out, then rotate the bulb counterclockwise to remove it.

7   On late model station wagons, open the

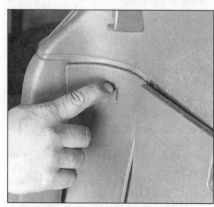

18.7a On late model station wagons, remove the interior trim panel . . .

12

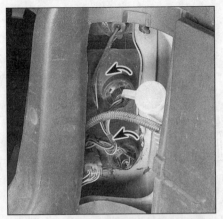

18.7b ... then rotate the bulb holder(s) counterclockwise to remove it from the tail light housing

liftgate and remove the interior trim panel from the affected side. Rotate the bulb holder counterclockwise to remove it from the tail-light housing **(see illustrations)**.

8   Push in and rotate the bulb counter-clockwise to remove them from the holder.

9   Installation is the reverse of removal

Sedan and hatchback

Refer to illustrations 18.12a and 18.12b

10   Open the trunk and remove the trunk finishing panels (if equipped).

11   On some models the tail light bulbs are accessible from the rear trunk compartment. If so, simply rotate the bulb holder counter-clockwise to remove it from the taillight housing, then push in and rotate the bulb counter-clockwise to remove them from the holder(s).

12   On models where the tail light bulbs are not accessible from the rear trunk compartment, detach the retaining nuts **(see illustrations)** securing the rear tail light housing, then pull the tail light assembly outward to access the tail light bulbs.

13   Twist the bulb socket a quarter turn counterclockwise, then remove the bulb assembly from the housing.

14   The defective bulb can then be pulled straight out of the socket and replaced.

15   Installation of the tail light housing is the reverse of removal.

License plate light

Refer to illustration 18.16

16   Remove the screws and detach the lens assembly **(see illustration)**, then remove the bulb from the socket.

17   Installation is the reverse of removal.

Instrument cluster lights

Refer to illustration 18.19

18   To gain access to the instrument cluster illumination bulbs, the instrument cluster will have to be removed (see Section 12). The bulbs can then be removed and replaced from the rear of the cluster.

19   Rotate the bulb counterclockwise to remove it **(see illustration)**.

20   Installation is the reverse of removal.

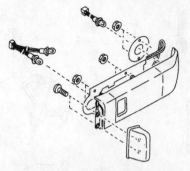

18.12a Late model hatchback tail light housing mounting details

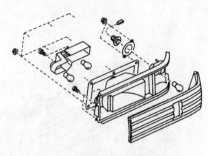

18.12b Late model sedan tail light housing mounting details

[Except Wagon]   **[Wagon]**

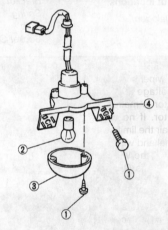

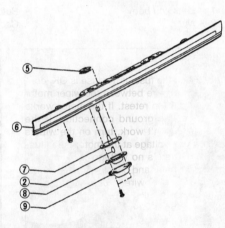

18.16 License plate light mounting details

1 Screw	4 Number plate light	7 Socket
2 Bulb	assembly	8 Lens
3 Lens	5 Packing	9 Cover
	6 Ornament	

Interior light

21   Pry the interior lens off the interior light housing.

22   Detach the bulb from the terminals. It may be necessary to pry the bulb out - if this is the case, pry only on the ends of the bulb (otherwise the glass may shatter).

23   Installation is the reverse of removal.

19 Wiper motor - removal and installation

Wiper motor circuit check

Refer to illustration 19.2

Note: *Refer to the wiring diagrams for wire colors and locations in the following checks. Keep in mind that power wires are generally larger in diameter and brighter colors, where ground wires are usually smaller in diameter and darker colors. When checking for voltage, probe a grounded 12-volt test light to each terminal at a connector until it lights; this verifies voltage (power) at the terminal.*

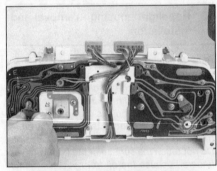

18.19 Remove the instrument cluster bulbs by rotating them 1/4-turn counterclockwise and pulling straight out

1   If the wipers work slowly, make sure the battery is in good condition and has a strong charge (see Chapter 1). If the battery is in good condition, remove the wiper motor (see below) and operate the wiper arms by hand. Check for binding linkage and pivots. Lubricate or repair the linkage or pivots as necessary. Reinstall the wiper motor. If the wipers still operate slowly, check for loose or cor-

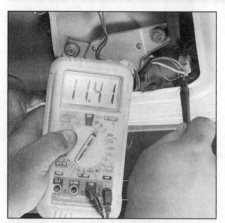

19.2 Use a voltmeter or test light to check for battery power at the wiper motor (rear wiper motor shown)

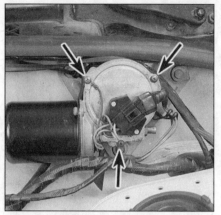

19.10 Front wiper motor retaining bolt locations (arrows)

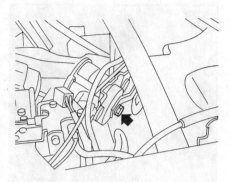

19.11 Pull the front wiper motor outward and unscrew the spindle nut (arrow)

roded connections, especially the ground connection. If all connections look OK, replace the motor.

2   If the wipers fail to operate when activated, check the fuse. If the fuse is OK, connect a jumper wire between the wiper motor and ground, then retest. If the motor works now, repair the ground connection. If the motor still doesn't work, turn on the wipers and check for voltage at the motor **(see illustration)**. If there's no voltage at the motor, remove the motor and check it off the vehicle with fused jumper wires from the battery. If the motor now works, check for binding linkage (see Step 1 above). If the motor still doesn't work, replace it. If there's no voltage at the motor, check for voltage at the switch. If there's no voltage at the switch, check the wiring between the switch and fuse panel for continuity. If the wiring is OK, the switch is probably bad.

3   If the wipers only work on one speed, check the continuity of the wires between the switch and motor. If the wires are OK, replace the switch.

4   If the interval (delay) function is inoperative, check the continuity of all the wiring between the switch and motor. If the wiring is

OK, replace the interval module.

5   If the wipers stop at the position they're in when the switch is turned off (fail to park), check for voltage at the wiper motor when the wiper switch is OFF but the ignition is ON. If voltage is present, the limit switch in the motor is malfunctioning. Replace the wiper motor. If no voltage is present, trace and repair the limit switch wiring between the fuse panel and wiper motor.

6   If the wipers won't shut off unless the ignition is OFF, disconnect the wiring from the wiper control switch. If the wipers stop, replace the switch. If the wipers keep running, there's a defective limit switch in the motor; replace the motor.

7   If the wipers won't retract below the hoodline, check for mechanical obstructions in the wiper linkage or on the vehicle's body which would prevent the wipers from parking. If there are no obstructions, check the wiring between the switch and motor for continuity. If the wiring is OK, replace the wiper motor.

Wiper motor replacement
Front

Refer to illustrations 19.10 and 19.11

8   Remove the cowl cover or the cowl vent

screen depending on the model year of the vehicle (see Chapter 11).

9   Disconnect the electrical connector from the wiper motor.

10   Remove the wiper motor retaining bolts **(see illustration)**.

11   Pull the wiper motor outward slightly and detach the bolt securing the wiper arm linkage to the backside of the motor, then remove the motor from the vehicle **(see illustration)**.

12   Installation is the reverse of removal.

Rear

Refer to illustrations 19.13, 19.14 and 19.17

13   Pull the rear wiper arm cover back to access the wiper arm retaining nut. Detach the nut and pull the wiper arm straight off the shaft to remove it **(see illustration)**.

14   Remove the drive spindle retaining nut **(see illustration)**.

15   Open the liftgate and remove the liftgate trim panel and the liftgate access cover (see Chapter 11).

16   Disconnect the electrical connector from wiper motor.

17   Detach the wiper motor retaining bolts , then remove the motor from the vehicle **(see illustration)**.

18   Installation is the reverse of removal.

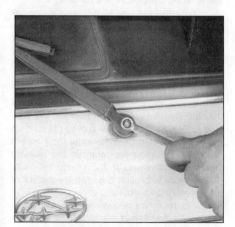

19.13 Pull off the rear wiper arm cover, then remove the nut and pull the arm straight off its splined shaft

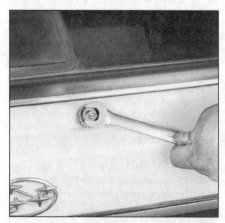

19.14 Remove the drive spindle retaining nut from the outside of the liftgate

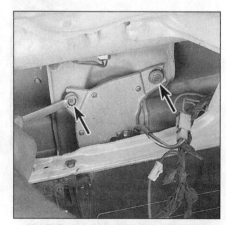

19.17 Rear wiper motor retaining bolt locations (arrows)

12

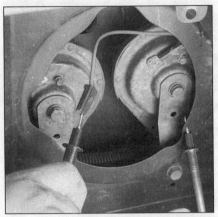

20.3 Check for power at the horn terminal with the horn button depressed

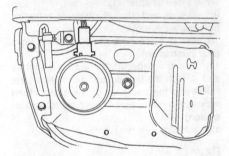

20.9b Late model horn mounting details

20   Horn - check and replacement

Check

Refer to illustration 20.3
Note: *Check the fuses before beginning electrical diagnosis.*
1   Disconnect the electrical connector from the horn.

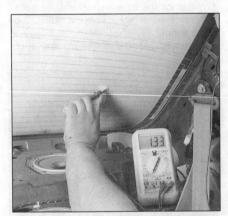

21.7 To find the break, place the voltmeter positive lead against the defogger positive terminal, place the voltmeter negative lead with the foil strip against the heating element at the positive terminal end and slide it toward the negative terminal end - the point at which the voltmeter reading changes abruptly is the point at which the element is broken

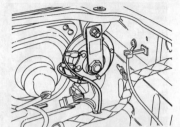

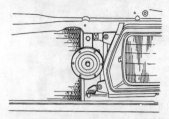

20.9a On early models, the low pitched horn is mounted in the engine compartment and the high pitched horn is mounted behind the radiator grille

21.4 When measuring the voltage at the rear window defogger grid, wrap a piece of aluminum foil around the negative probe of the voltmeter and press the foil against the wire with your finger

2   To test the horn(s), connect battery voltage to the two terminals with a pair of jumper wires. If the horn doesn't sound, replace it.
3   If the horn does sound, check for voltage at the terminal when the horn button is depressed **(see illustration)**. If there's voltage at the terminal, check for a bad ground at the horn.
4   If there's no voltage at the horn, check the relay (see Section 6). Note that most horn relays are either the four-terminal or externally grounded three-terminal type.
5   If the relay is OK, check for voltage to the relay power and control circuits. If either of the circuits is not receiving voltage, inspect the wiring between the relay and the fuse panel.
6   If both relay circuits are receiving voltage, depress the horn button and check the circuit from the relay to the horn button for continuity to ground. If there's no continuity, check the circuit for an open. If there's no open circuit, replace the horn button.
7   If there's continuity to ground through the horn button, check for an open or short in the circuit from the relay to the horn.

Replacement

Refer to illustrations 20.9a and 20.9b
8   Remove the radiator grille (see Chapter 11).
9   To replace the horn(s), disconnect the electrical connector and remove the bracket bolt **(see illustrations)**.
10   Installation is the reverse of removal.

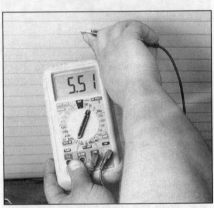

21.5 To determine if a heating element has broken, check the voltage at the center of each element - if the voltage is 6-volts, the element is unbroken - if the voltage is 12-volts, the element is broken between the center and the positive end - if there is no voltage, the element is broken between the center and ground

21   Rear window defogger - check and repair

1   The rear window defogger consists of a number of horizontal elements baked onto the glass surface.
2   Small breaks in the element can be repaired without removing the rear window.

Check

Refer to illustrations 21.4, 21.5 and 21.7
3   Turn the ignition switch and defogger system switches to the ON position.
4   When measuring voltage during the next two tests, wrap a piece of aluminum foil around the tip of the voltmeter negative probe and press the foil against the heating element with your finger **(see illustration)**.
5   Check the voltage at the center of each heating element **(see illustration)**. If the voltage is 6-volts, the element is okay (there is no break). If the voltage is 12-volts, the element is broken between the center of the element and the positive end. If the voltage is 0-volts the element is broken between the center of the element and ground.
6   Connect the negative lead to a good body ground. The reading should stay the same.
7   To find the break, place the voltmeter positive lead against the defogger positive terminal. Place the voltmeter negative lead

with the foil strip against the heating element at the positive terminal end and slide it toward the negative terminal end. The point at which the voltmeter deflects from zero to several volts is the point at which the heating element is broken **(see illustration)**.

Repair

Refer to illustration 21.13

8   Repair the break in the element using a repair kit specifically recommended for this purpose, such as Dupont paste No. 4817 (or equivalent). Included in this kit is plastic conductive epoxy.

9   Prior to repairing a break, turn off the system and allow it to cool off for a few minutes.

10   Lightly buff the element area with fine steel wool, then clean it thoroughly with rubbing alcohol.

11   Use masking tape to mask off the area being repaired.

12   Thoroughly mix the epoxy, following the instructions provided with the repair kit.

13   Apply the epoxy material to the slit in the masking tape, overlapping the undamaged area about 3/4-inch on either end **(see illustration)**.

14   Allow the repair to cure for 24 hours before removing the tape and using the system.

22   Cruise control system - description and check

1   The cruise control system maintains vehicle speed with a vacuum actuated servo located in the engine compartment, which is connected to the accelerator pedal by a cable. The system consists of the cruise control unit, brake switch, control switches, vacuum hose and vehicle speed sensor. Some features of the system require special testers and diagnostic procedures which are beyond the scope of this manual. Listed below are some general procedures that may be used to locate common problems.

2   Locate and check the fuse (see Section 3).

3   Have an assistant operate the brake lights while you check their operation (voltage from the brake light switch deactivates the cruise control.

4   If the brake lights don't come on or don't shut off, correct the problem and retest the cruise control.

5   Visually inspect the control cable between actuator assembly and accelerator pedal for free movement, replace if necessary.

6   The cruise control system uses a speed sensing device. The speed sensor is located in the speedometer. To test the speed sensor (see chapter 6).

7   Test drive the vehicle to determine if the cruise control is now working. If it isn't, take it to a dealer service department or an automotive electrical specialist for further diagnosis.

23   Power window system - description and check

Refer to illustrations 23.10a and 23.10b

1   The power window system operates electric motors, mounted in the doors, which lower and raise the windows. The system consists of the control switches, relays, the motors, regulators, glass mechanisms and associated wiring.

2   The power windows can be lowered and raised from the master control switch by the driver or by remote switches located at the individual windows. Each window has a separate motor which is reversible. The position of the control switch determines the polarity and therefore the direction of operation.

3   The circuit is protected by a fuse and a circuit breaker. Each motor is also equipped with an internal circuit breaker, this prevents one stuck window from disabling the whole system.

4   The power window system will only operate when the ignition switch is ON. In addition, many models have a window lock-

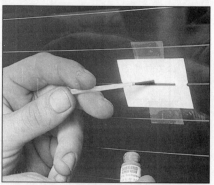

21.13 To use a defogger repair kit, apply masking tape to the inside of the window at the damaged area, then brush on the special conductive coating

out switch at the master control switch which, when activated, disables the switches at the rear windows and, sometimes, the switch at the passenger's window also. Always check these items before troubleshooting a window problem.

5   These procedures are general in nature, so if you can't find the problem using them, take the vehicle to a dealer service department or other properly equipped repair facility.

6   If the power windows won't operate, always check the fuse and circuit breaker first.

7   If only the rear windows are inoperative, or if the windows only operate from the master control switch, check the rear window lockout switch for continuity in the unlocked position. Replace it if it doesn't have continuity.

8   Check the wiring between the switches and fuse panel for continuity. Repair the wiring, if necessary.

9   If only one window is inoperative from the master control switch, try the other control switch at the window. **Note:** *This doesn't apply to the drivers door window.*

10   If the same window works from one switch, but not the other, check the switch

23.10a Late model power window master control switch terminal guide and continuity chart

Terminal	Color	Front (Driver side)					Front (Passenger side)			Rear (RH)			Rear (LH)			Connection
		AU	U	N	D	AD	U	N	D	U	N	D	U	N	D	
1	YW												○	○	○	REAR LH SW
2	GW												○	○	○	REAR LH SW
3	YR									○	○	○				REAR RH SW
4	GR									○	○	○				REAR RH SW
5	WL						○	○								FRONT LH SW
6	LB						○	○								FRONT LH SW
7	R	○	○	○ ○	○	○										C. UNIT (c)
8	Y			○	○ ○											C. UNIT (b)
9	G	○ ○	○ ○	○												C. UNIT (a)
10	RW	○	○		○		○		○	○		○	○		○	IG SW
11	B						○	○ ○		○	○ ○		○	○ ○		○	EARTH

Main switch (LH)

Main switch connector

```
1  2  3  4  5  6
7  8  9 10 11
```

Sub-switch connector

Connector		Switch operation			Connection
Terminal	Color	U	N	D	
Front door sub-switch (RH)					
1	R	O		O	Ignition switch
2	WB		O	O	Main switch
3	LB	O	O		Main switch
4	L	O	O	O	Electric motor (passenger's window)
5	LR	O	O	O	Electric motor (passenger's window)
Rear door sub-switch (LH)					
1	R	O		O	Ignition switch
2	WB		O	O	Main switch
3	LB	O	O		Main switch
4	L	O	O	O	Electric motor (passenger's window)
5	LR	O	O	O	Electric motor (passenger's window)
Rear door sub-switch (RH)					
1	R	O		O	Ignition switch
2	WB		O	O	Main switch
3	LB	O	O		Main switch
4	L	O	O	O	Electric motor (passenger's window)
5	LR	O	O	O	Electric motor (passenger's window)

23.10b Late model power window switch terminal guide and continuity chart

for continuity **(see illustrations)**. If the continuity is not as specified replace the switch.

11 If the switch tests OK, check for a short or open in the circuit between the affected switch and the window motor.

12 If one window is inoperative from both switches, remove the trim panel from the affected door and check for voltage at the switch and at the motor while the switch is operated.

13 If voltage is reaching the motor, disconnect the glass from the regulator (see Chapter 11). Move the window up and down by hand while checking for binding and damage. Also check for binding and damage to the regulator. If the regulator is not damaged and the window moves up and down smoothly, replace the motor. If there's binding or damage, lubricate, repair or replace parts, as necessary.

14 If voltage isn't reaching the motor, check the wiring in the circuit for continuity between the switches and motors. You'll need to consult the wiring diagram for the vehicle. If the circuit is equipped with a relay, check that the relay is grounded properly and receiving voltage.

15 Test the windows after you are done to confirm proper repairs.

24 Power door lock system - description and check

The power door lock system operates the door lock actuators mounted in each door. The system consists of the switches, actuators, a control unit and associated wiring. Diagnosis can usually be limited to simple checks of the wiring connections and actuators for minor faults which can be easily repaired. Since this system uses an electronic control unit in-depth diagnosis should be left to a dealership service department. The door lock control unit is located behind the instrument panel, to the right of the fuse box.

Power door lock systems are operated by bi-directional solenoids located in the doors. The lock switches have two operating positions: Lock and Unlock. When activated, the switch sends a ground signal to the door lock control unit to lock or unlock the doors. Depending on which way the switch is activated, the control unit reverses polarity to the solenoids, allowing the two sides of the circuit to be used alternately as the feed (positive) and ground side.

Some vehicles may have an anti-theft systems incorporated into the power locks. If you are unable to locate the trouble using the following general Steps, consult your a dealer service department.

1 Always check the circuit protection first. Some vehicles use a combination of circuit breakers and fuses.

2 Operate the door lock switches in both directions (Lock and Unlock) with the engine off. Listen for the click of the solenoids operating.

3 Test the switches for continuity. Replace the switch if there's not continuity in both switch positions.

4 Check the wiring between the switches, control unit and solenoids for continuity. Repair the wiring if there's no continuity.

5 Check for a bad ground at the switches or the control unit.

6 If all but one lock solenoids operate, remove the trim panel from the affected door (see Chapter 11) and check for voltage at the solenoid while the lock switch is operated One of the wires should have voltage in the Lock position; the other should have voltage in the Unlock position.

7 If the inoperative solenoid is receiving voltage, replace the solenoid.

8 If the inoperative solenoid isn't receiving voltage, check the relay or for an open or short in the wire between the lock solenoid and the control unit. **Note:** *It's common for wires to break in the portion of the harness between the body and door (opening and closing the door fatigues and eventually breaks the wires).*

25 Electric side view mirrors - description and check

Refer to illustration 25.7

1 Most electric rear view mirrors use two motors to move the glass; one for up and down adjustments and one for left-right adjustments.

2 The control switch has a selector por-

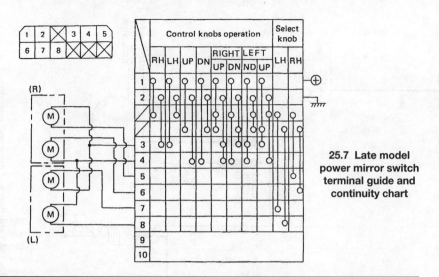

25.7 Late model power mirror switch terminal guide and continuity chart

between this wire and ground. If the mirror works normally with this wire in place, repair the faulty ground connection.

9 If the mirror still doesn't work, remove the mirror and check the wires at the mirror for voltage. Check with ignition ON and the mirror selector switch on the appropriate side. Operate the mirror switch in all its positions. There should be voltage at one of the switch-to-mirror wires in each switch position (except the neutral "off" position).

10 If there's not voltage in each switch position, check the circuit between the mirror and control switch for opens and shorts.

11 If there's voltage, remove the mirror and test it off the vehicle with jumper wires. Replace the mirror if it fails this test.

26 Wiring diagrams - general information

Since it isn't possible to include all wiring diagrams for every year covered by this manual, the following diagrams are those that are typical and most commonly needed.

Prior to troubleshooting any circuits, check the fuse and circuit breakers (if equipped) to make sure they're in good condition. Make sure the battery is properly charged and check the cable connections (see Chapter 1).

When checking a circuit, make sure that all connectors are clean, with no broken or loose terminals. When unplugging a connector, do not pull on the wires. Pull only on the connector housings themselves.

tion which sends voltage to the left or right side mirror. With the ignition ON but the engine OFF, roll down the windows and operate the mirror control switch through all functions (left-right and up-down) for both the left and right side mirrors.

3 Listen carefully for the sound of the electric motors running in the mirrors.

4 If the motors can be heard but the mirror glass doesn't move, there's probably a problem with the drive mechanism inside the mirror. Remove and disassemble the mirror to locate the problem.

5 If the mirrors don't operate and no sound comes from the mirrors, check the fuse (see Chapter 1).

6 If the fuse is OK, remove the mirror control switch from its mounting without disconnecting the wires attached to it. Turn the ignition ON and check for voltage at the switch. There should be voltage at one terminal. If there's no voltage at the switch, check for an open or short in the circuit between the fuse panel and the switch.

7 If there's voltage at the switch, disconnect it. Check the switch for continuity in all its operating positions **(see illustration)**. If the switch does not have continuity, replace it.

8 Re-connect the switch. Locate the wire going from the switch to ground. Leaving the switch connected, connect a jumper wire

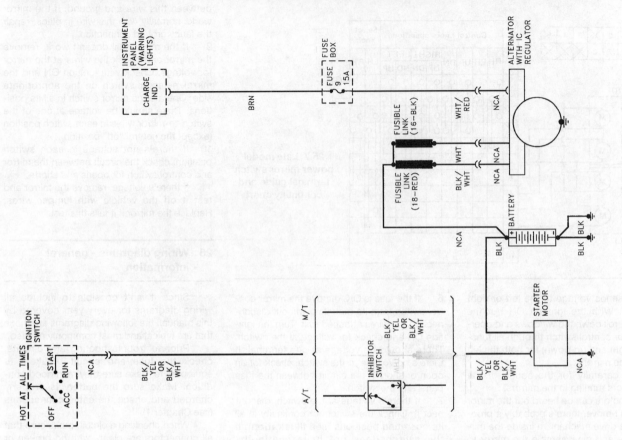

Typical 1984 through 1989 starting and charging system

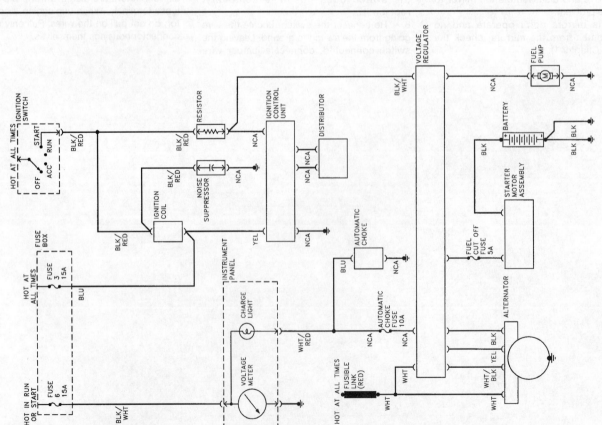

Typical 1980 through 1983 starting and charging system

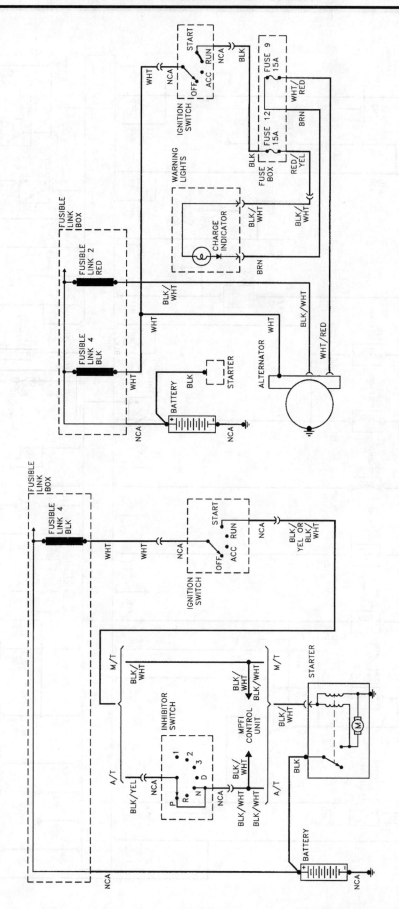

Typical 1990 through 1994 starting and charging system

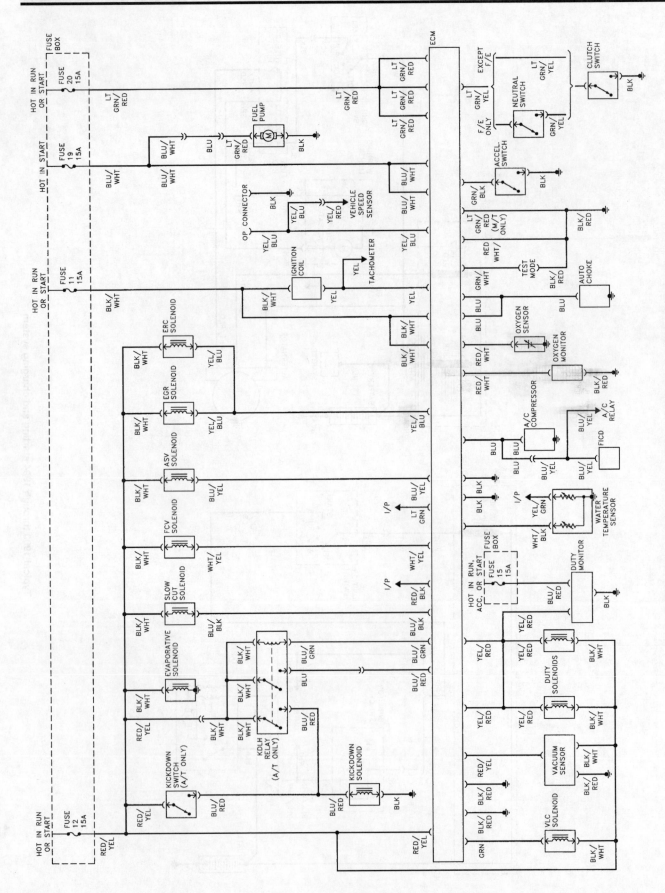

Typical 1980 through 1986 feedback carburetor engine control system

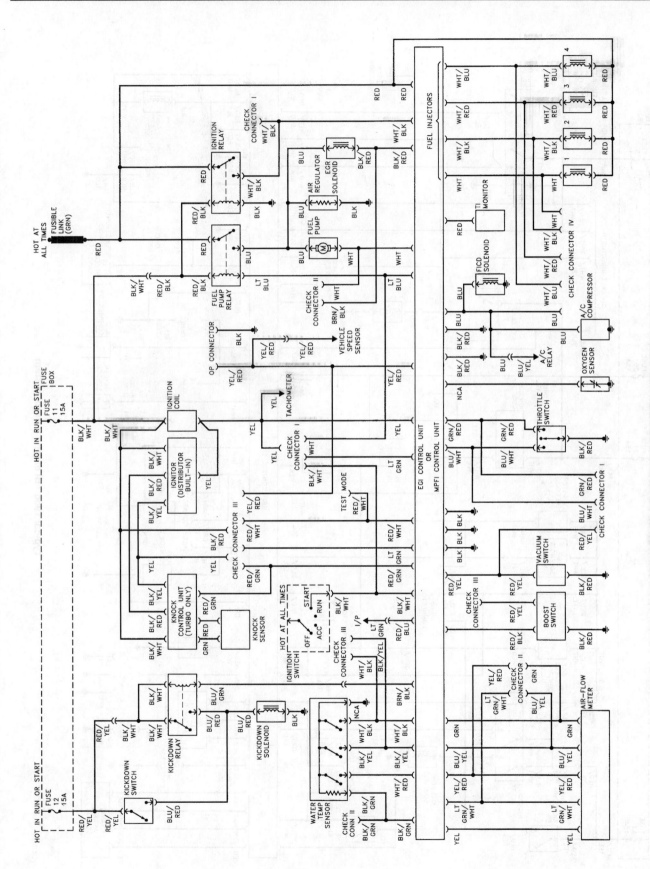

Typical 1984 through 1986 MPFI engine control system

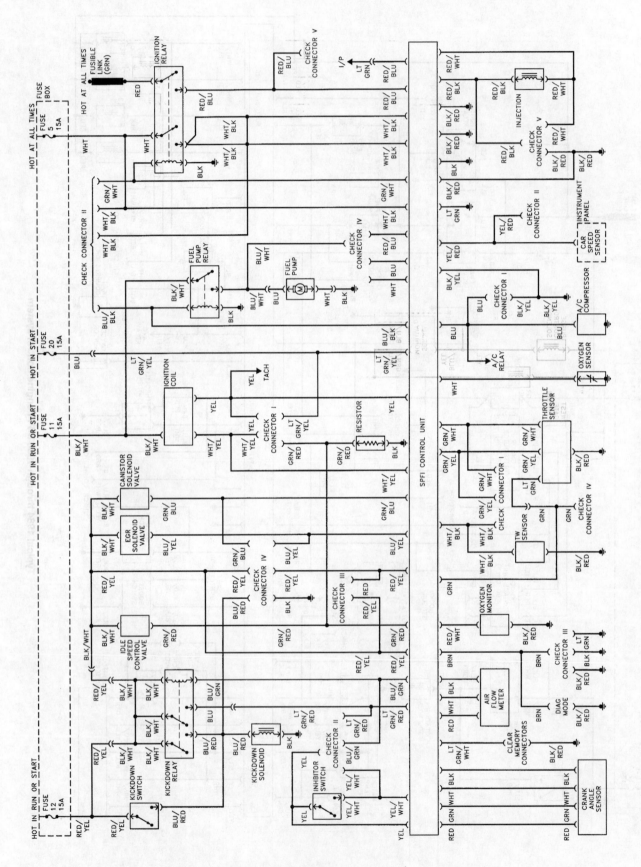

Typical 1986 TBI engine control system

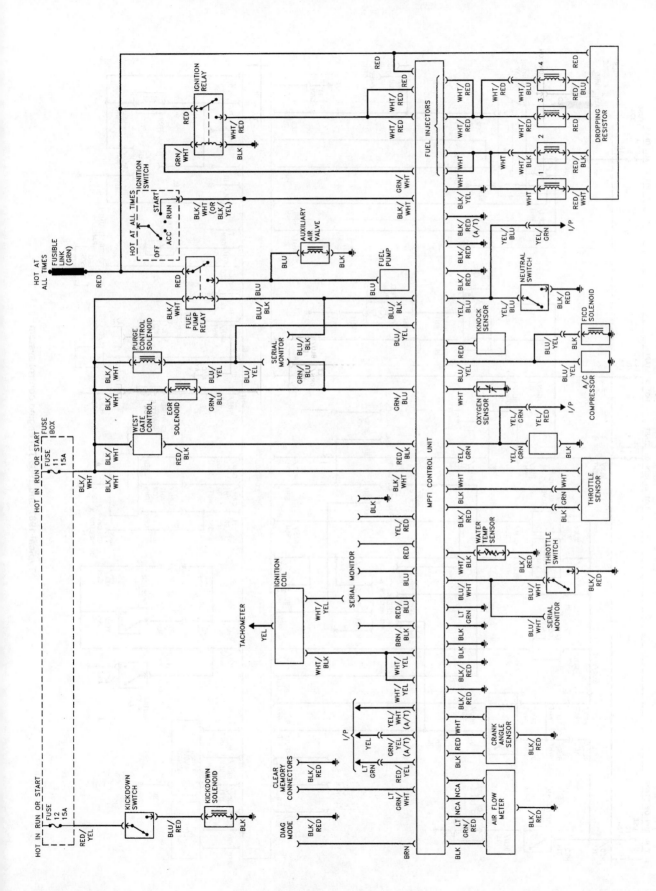

Typical 1987 and 1988 MPFI engine control system

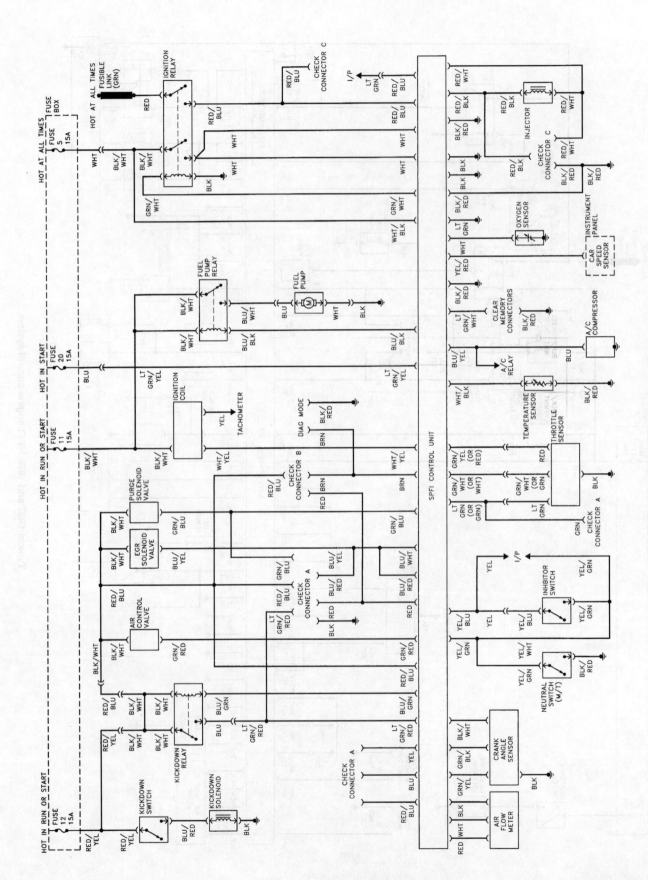

Typical 1987 and 1988 TBI engine control system

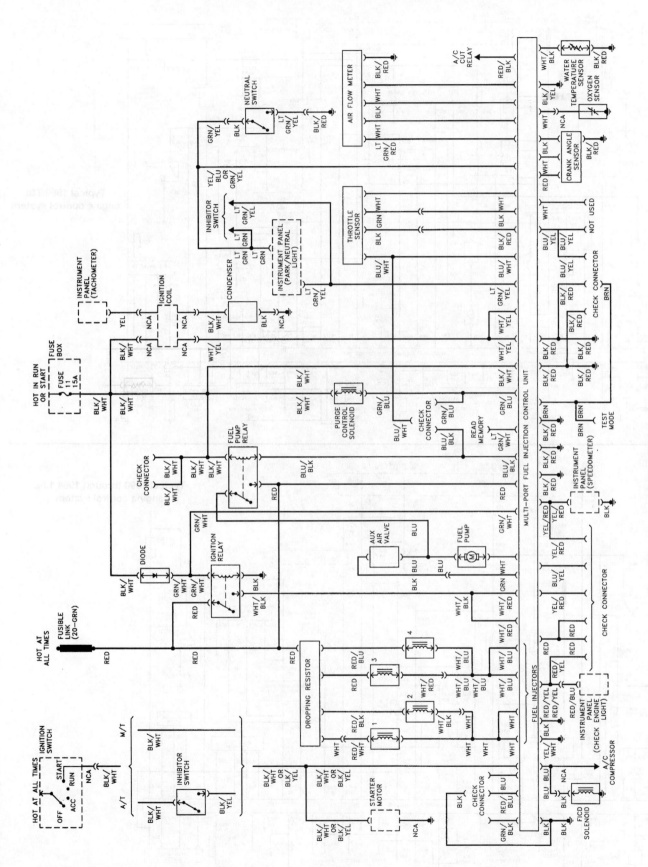

Typical 1989 MPFI engine control system

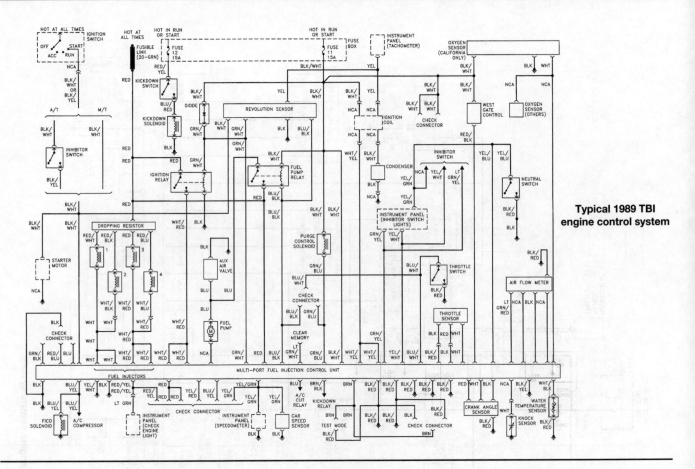

Typical 1989 TBI engine control system

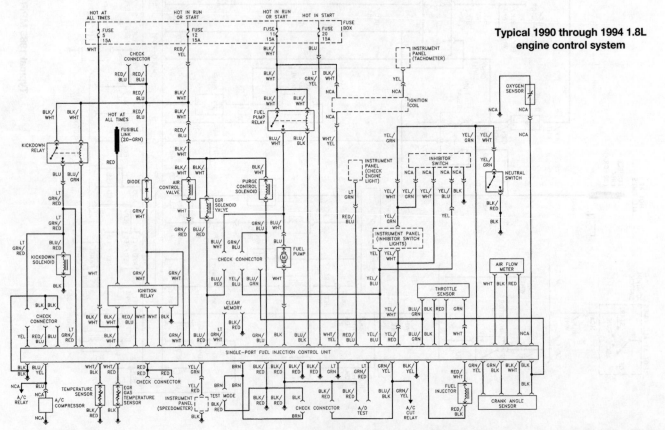

Typical 1990 through 1994 1.8L engine control system

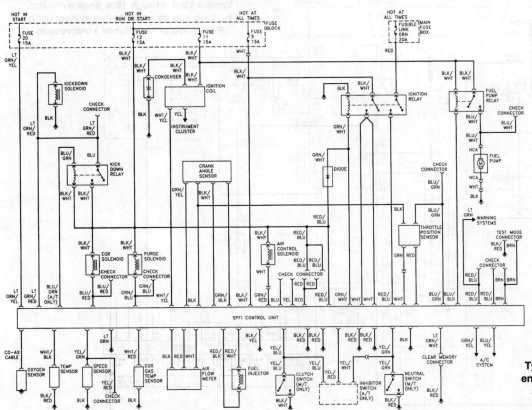

**Typical 1980 through 1984
engine cooling, heating and
air conditioning system**

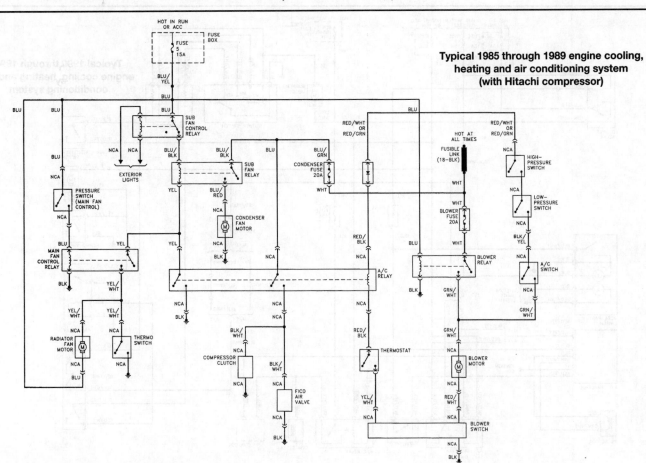

**Typical 1985 through 1989 engine cooling,
heating and air conditioning system
(with Hitachi compressor)**

12

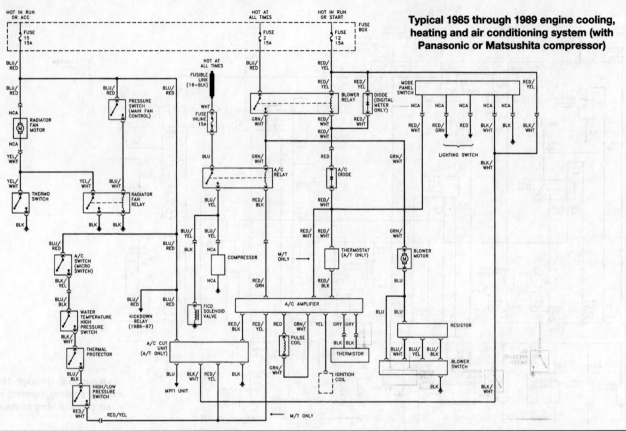

Typical 1985 through 1989 engine cooling, heating and air conditioning system (with Panasonic or Matsushita compressor)

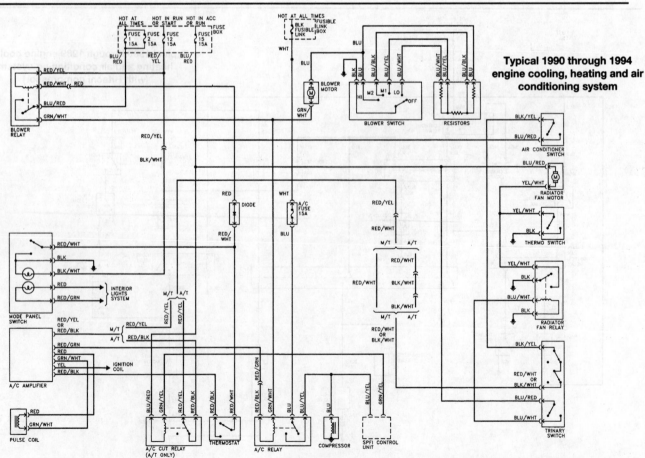

Typical 1990 through 1994 engine cooling, heating and air conditioning system

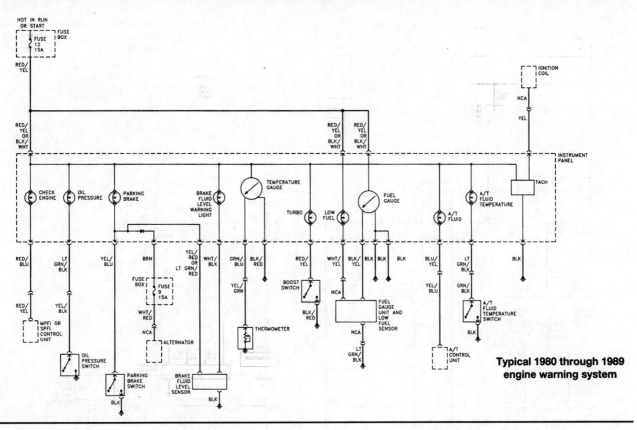

Typical 1980 through 1989 engine warning system

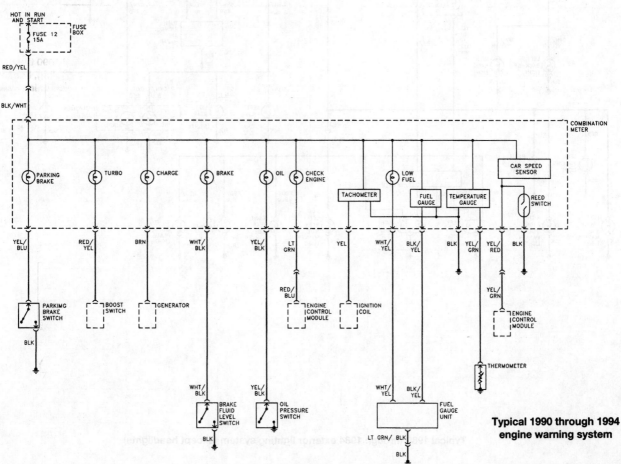

Typical 1990 through 1994 engine warning system

12

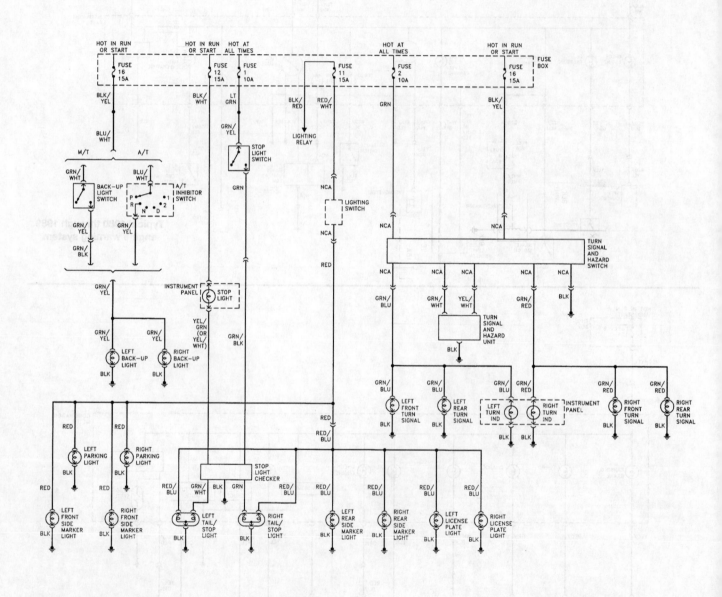

Typical 1980 through 1984 exterior lighting system (except headlights)

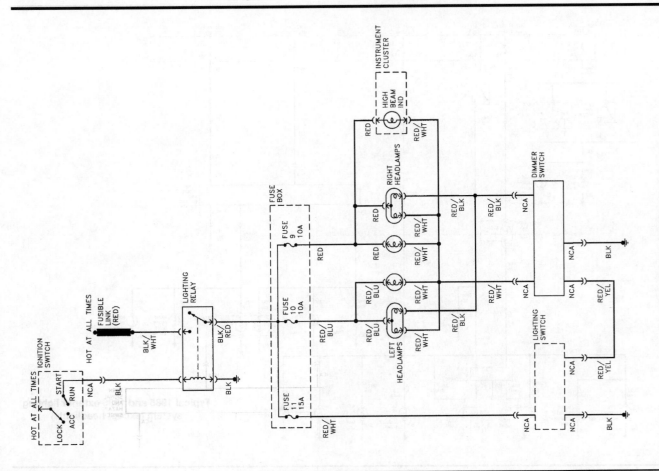

Typical 1980 through 1984 headlight system

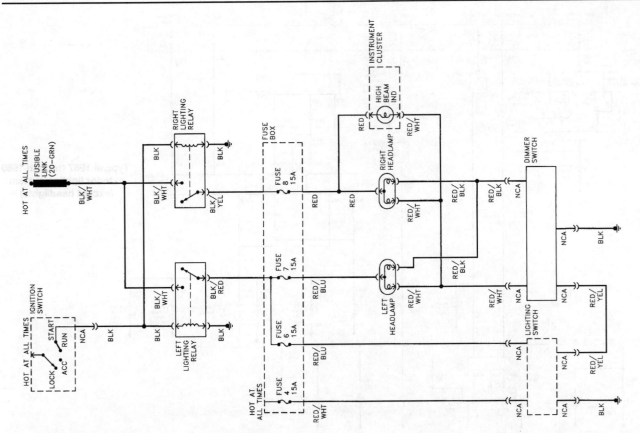

Typical 1985 and 1986 headlight system

12

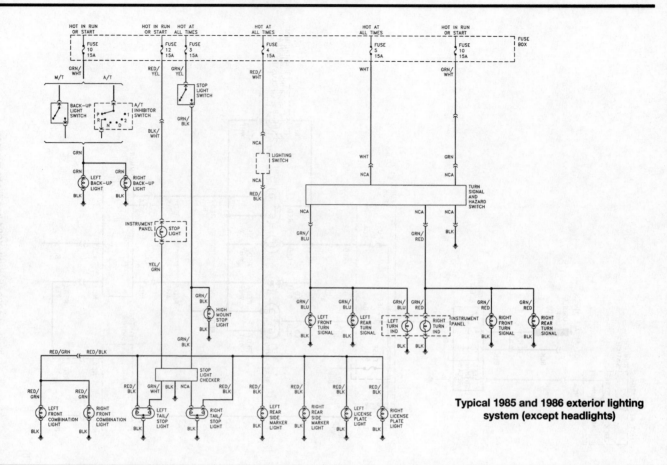

Typical 1985 and 1986 exterior lighting
system (except headlights)

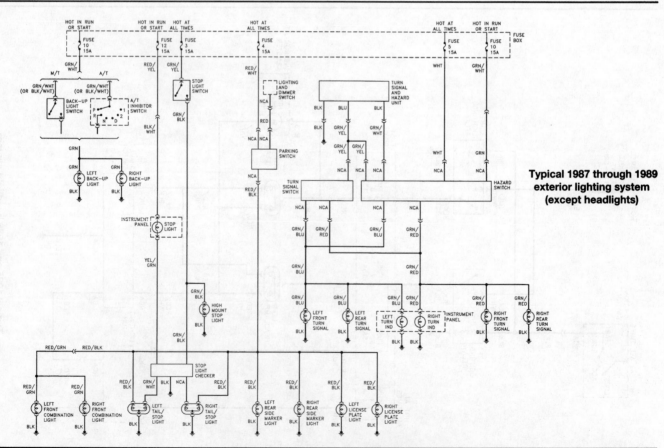

Typical 1987 through 1989
exterior lighting system
(except headlights)

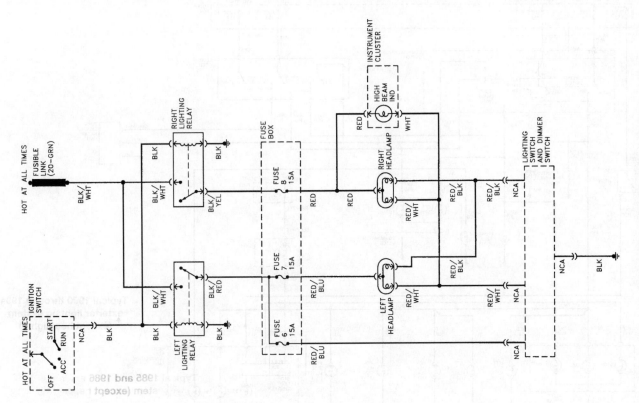

Typical 1987 through 1989 headlight system

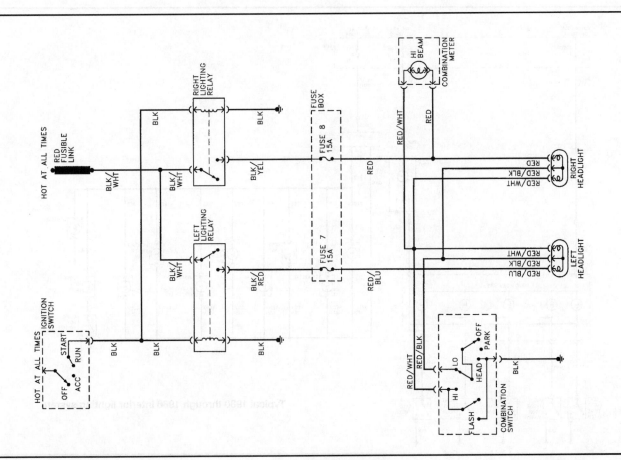

Typical 1990 through 1994 headlight system

12

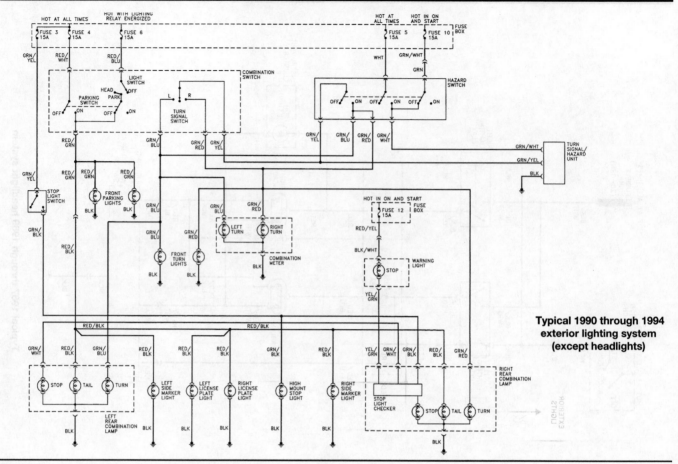

Typical 1990 through 1994 exterior lighting system (except headlights)

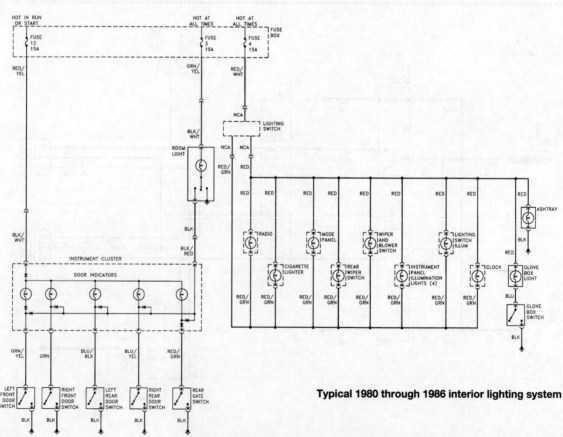

Typical 1980 through 1986 interior lighting system

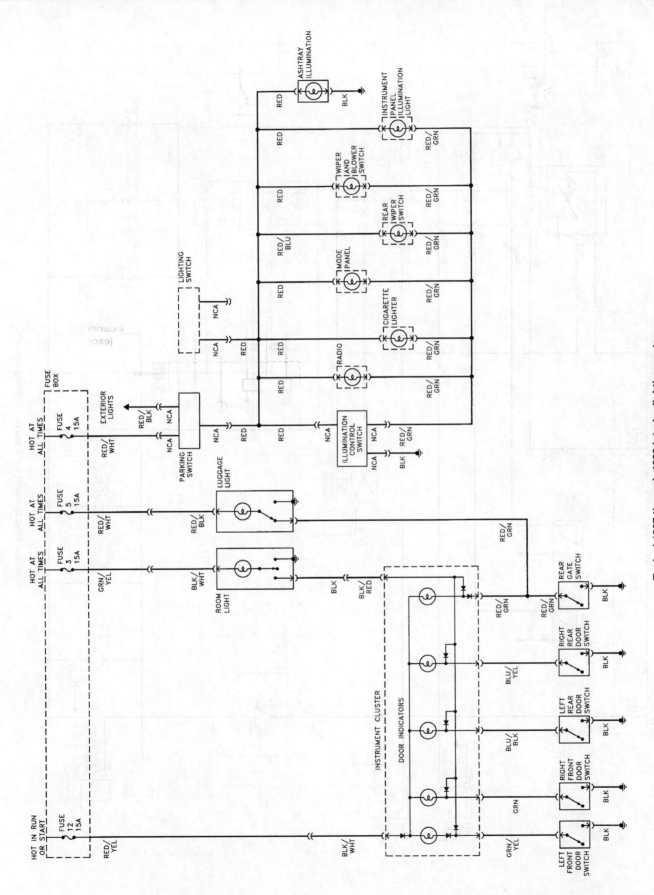

Typical 1987 through 1989 interior lighting system

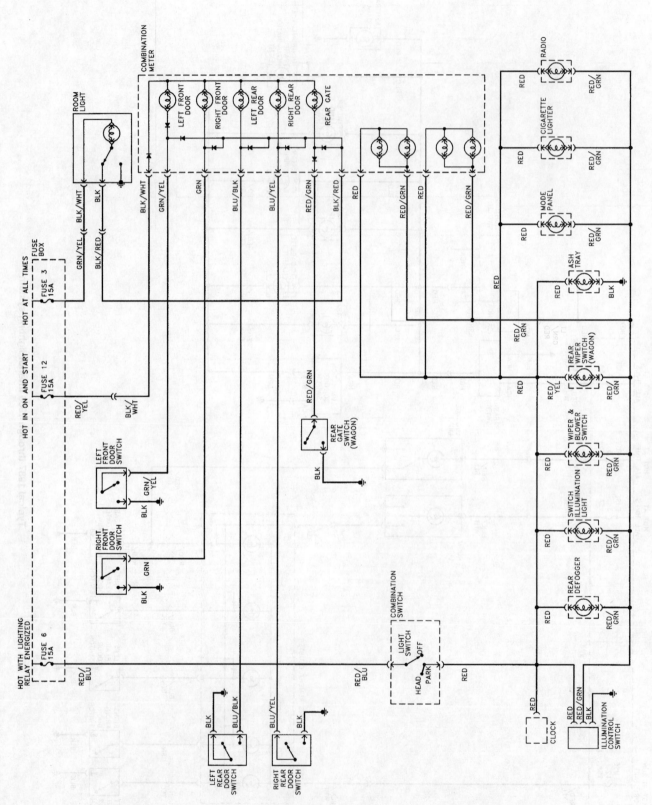

Typical 1990 through 1994 interior lighting system

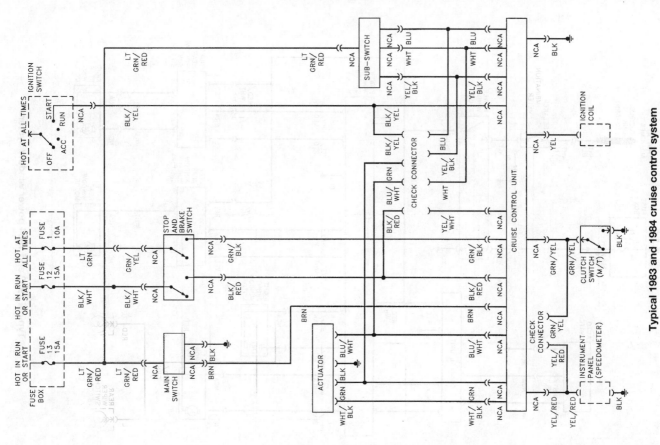

Typical 1983 and 1984 cruise control system

Typical 1985 through 1989 cruise control system

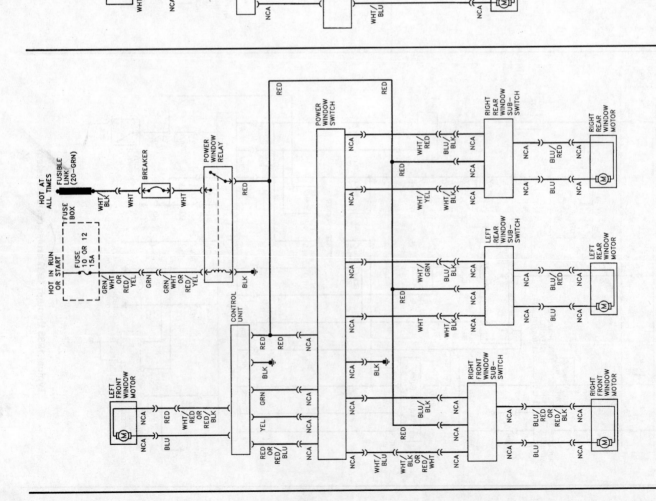

Typical 1983 and 1984 power window system

Typical 1985 through 1989 power window system

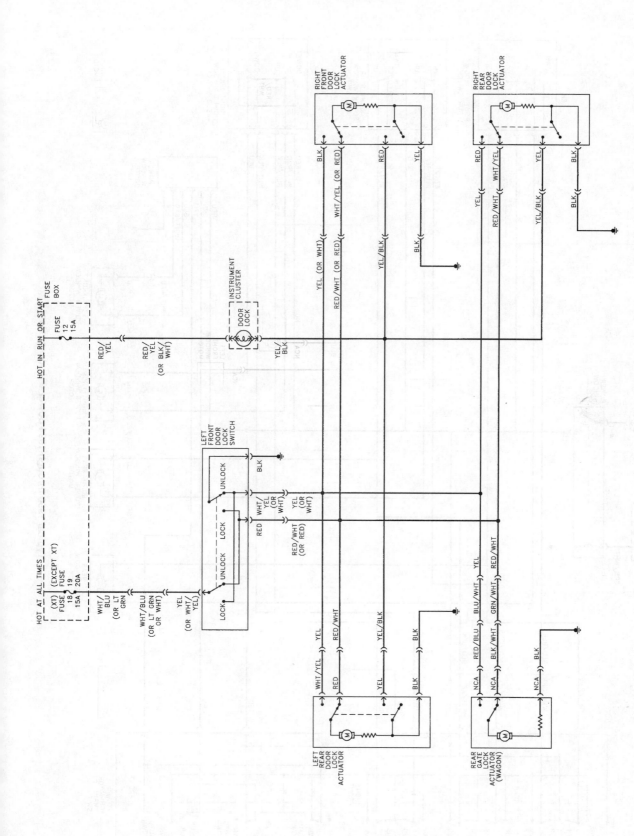

Typical 1985 through 1994 power door lock system

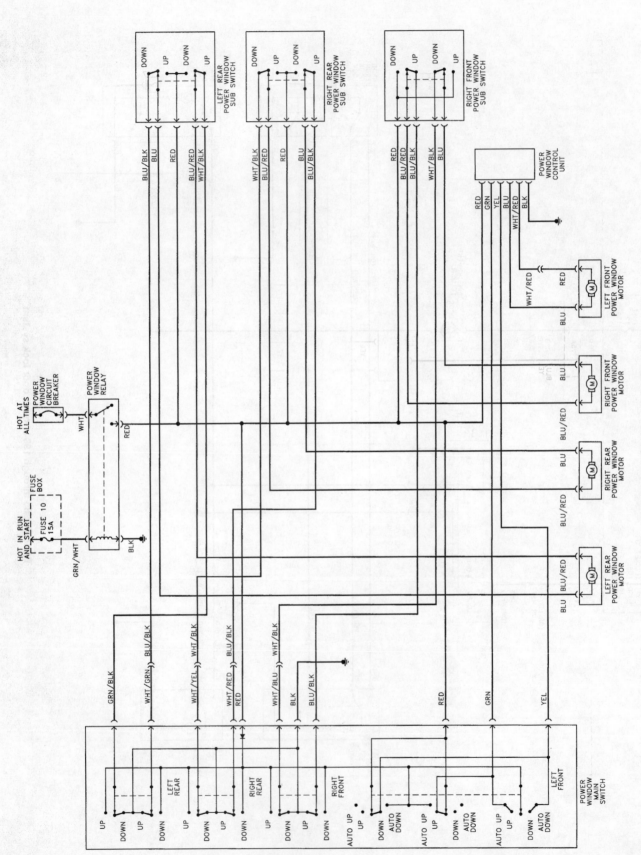

Typical 1990 through 1994 power window system

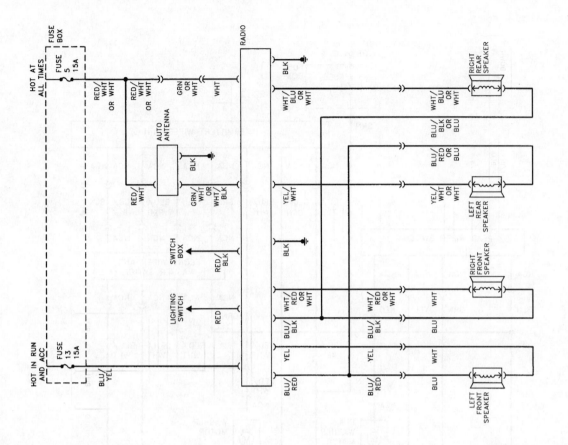

Typical 1980 through 1994 audio system

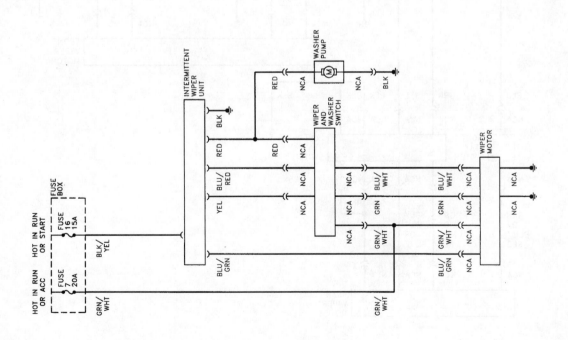

Typical 1980 through 1984 windshield wiper and washer system

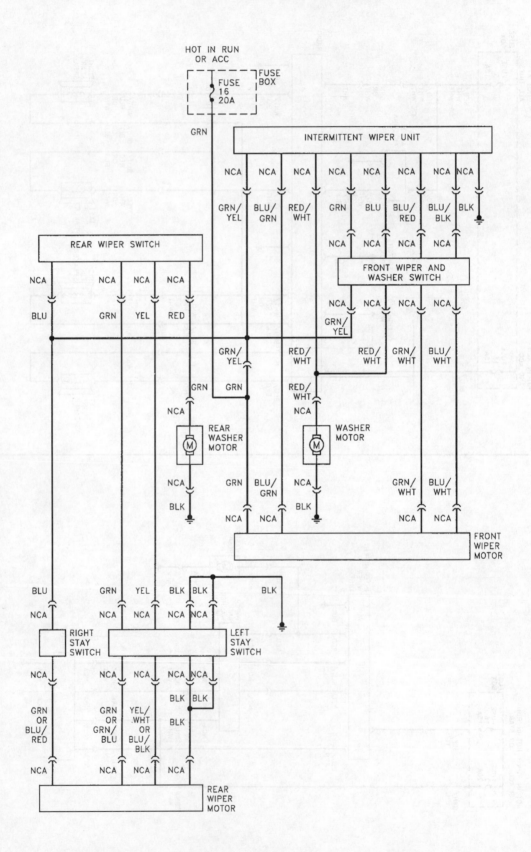

Typical 1985 through 1989 windshield wiper and washer system

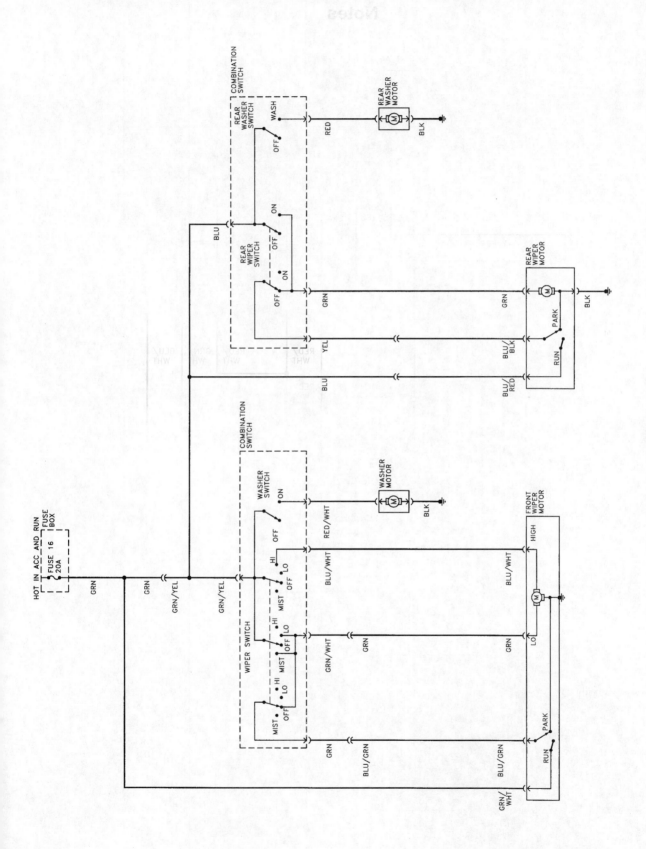

Typical 1990 through 1994 windshield wiper and washer system

Notes

Index

Haynes Automotive Manuals

ACURA
- *12020 Integra '86 thru '89 & Legend '86 thru '90

AMC
- Jeep CJ - see JEEP (50020)
- 14020 Concord/Hornet/Gremlin/Spirit '70 thru '83
- 14025 (Renault) Alliance & Encore '83 thru '87

AUDI
- 15020 4000 all models '80 thru '87
- 15025 5000 all models '77 thru '83
- 15026 5000 all models '84 thru '88

AUSTIN
- Healey Sprite - see MG Midget (66015)

BMW
- *18020 3/5 Series '82 thru '92
- *18021 3 Series except 325iX models '92 thru '97
- 18025 320i all 4 cyl models '75 thru '83
- 18035 528i & 530i all models '75 thru '80
- 18050 1500 thru 2002 except Turbo '59 thru '77

BUICK
- Century (FWD) - see GM (38005)
- *19020 Buick, Oldsmobile & Pontiac Full-size (Front wheel drive) '85 thru '98
  Buick Electra, LeSabre and Park Avenue; Oldsmobile Delta 88 Royale, Ninety Eight and Regency; Pontiac Bonneville
- 19025 Buick Oldsmobile & Pontiac Full-size (Rear wheel drive)
  Buick Estate '70 thru '90, Electra'70 thru '84, LeSabre '70 thru '85, Limited '74 thru '79
  Oldsmobile Custom Cruiser '70 thru '90, Delta 88 '70 thru '85,Ninety-eight '70 thru '84
  Pontiac Bonneville '70 thru '81, Catalina '70 thru '81, Grandville '70 thru '75, Parisienne '83 thru '86
- 19030 Mid-size Regal & Century '74 thru '87
  Regal - see GENERAL MOTORS (38010)
  Skyhawk - see GM (38020, 38025)
  Skylark - see GM (38020, 38025)
  Somerset - see GENERAL MOTORS (38025)

CADILLAC
- *21030 Cadillac Rear Wheel Drive '70 thru '93
  Cimarron, Eldorado & Seville - see GM (38015, 38030)

CHEVROLET
- 10305 Chevrolet Engine Overhaul Manual
- *24010 Astro & GMC Safari Mini-vans '85 thru '93
- 24015 Camaro V8 all models '70 thru '81
- 24016 Camaro all models '82 thru '92
  Cavalier - see GM (38015)
  Celebrity - see GM (38005)
- 24017 Camaro & Firebird '93 thru '97
- 24020 Chevelle, Malibu, El Camino '69 thru '87
- 24024 Chevette & Pontiac T1000 '76 thru '87
  Citation - see GENERAL MOTORS (38020)
- *24032 Corsica/Beretta all models '87 thru '96
- 24040 Corvette all V8 models '68 thru '82
- *24041 Corvette all models '84 thru '96
- 24045 Full-size Sedans Caprice, Impala, Biscayne, Bel Air & Wagons '69 thru '90
- 24046 Impala SS & Caprice and Buick Roadmaster '91 thru '96
  Lumina '90 thru '94 - see GM (38010)
- 24048 Lumina & Monte Carlo '95 thru '98
  Lumina APV - see GM (38036)
- 24050 Luv Pick-up all 2WD & 4WD '72 thru '82
- 24055 Monte Carlo all models '70 thru '88
  Monte Carlo '95 thru '98 - see LUMINA
- 24059 Nova all V8 models '69 thru '79
- *24060 Nova/Geo Prizm '85 thru '92
- 24064 Pick-ups '67 thru '87 - Chevrolet & GMC, all V8 & in-line 6 cyl, 2WD & 4WD '67 thru '87; Suburbans, Blazers & Jimmys '67 thru '91
- *24065 Pick-ups '88 thru '98 - Chevrolet & GMC, all full-size pick-ups '88 thru '98; Blazer & Jimmy '92 thru '94; Suburban '92 thru '98; Tahoe & Yukon '95 thru '98
- *24070 S-10 & GMC S-15 Pick-ups '82 thru '93
- 24071 S-10, Gmc S-15 & Jimmy '94 thru '96
- *24075 Sprint & Geo Metro '85 thru '94
- *24080 Vans - Chevrolet & GMC '68 thru '96

CHRYSLER
- 10310 Chrysler Engine Overhaul Manual
- *25015 Chrysler Cirrus, Dodge Stratus, Plymouth Breeze, '95 thru '98
- *25020 Full-size Front-Wheel Drive '88 thru '93
  K-Cars - see DODGE Aries (30008)
  Laser - see DODGE Daytona (30030)
- 25025 Chrysler LHS, Concorde & New Yorker, Dodge Intrepid, Eagle Vision, '93 thru '97
- *25030 Chrysler/Plym. Mid-size '82 thru '95
  Rear-wheel Drive - see DODGE (30050)

DATSUN
- 28005 200SX all models '80 thru '83
- 28007 B-210 all models '73 thru '78
- 28009 210 all models '78 thru '82
- 28012 240Z, 260Z & 280Z Coupe '70 thru '78
- 28014 280ZX Coupe & 2+2 '79 thru '83
  300ZX - see NISSAN (72010)
- 28016 310 all models '78 thru '82
- 28018 510 & PL521 Pick-up '68 thru '73
- 28020 510 all models '78 thru '81
- 28022 620 Series Pick-up all models '73 thru '79
  720 Series Pick-up - NISSAN (72030)
- 28025 810/Maxima all gas models, '77 thru '84

DODGE
- 400 & 600 - see CHRYSLER (25030)
- *30008 Aries & Plymouth Reliant '81 thru '89
- 30010 Caravan & Ply. Voyager '84 thru '95
- *30011 Caravan & Ply. Voyager '96 thru '98
- 30012 Challenger/Plymouth Saporro '78 thru '83
  Challenger '67-'76 - see DART (30025)
- 30016 Colt/Plymouth Champ '78 thru '87
- *30020 Dakota Pick-ups all models '87 thru '96
- 30025 Dart, Challenger/Plymouth Barracuda & Valiant 6 cyl models '67 thru '76
- *30030 Daytona & Chrysler Laser '84 thru '89
  Intrepid - see Chrysler (25025)
- *30034 Dodge & Plymouth Neon '95 thru '97
- *30035 Omni & Plymouth Horizon '78 thru '90
- 30040 Pick-ups all full-size models '74 thru '93
- 30041 Pick-ups all full-size models '94 thru '96
- *30045 Ram 50/D50 Pick-ups & Raider and Plymouth Arrow Pick-ups '79 thru '93
- 30050 Dodge/Ply./Chrysler RWD '71 thru '89
- *30055 Shadow/Plymouth Sundance '87 thru '94
- *30060 Spirit & Plymouth Acclaim '89 thru '95
- *30065 Vans - Dodge & Plymouth '71 thru '96

EAGLE
- Talon - see MITSUBISHI Eclipse (68030)
- Vision - see CHRYSLER (25025)

FIAT
- 34010 124 Sport Coupe & Spider '68 thru '78
- 34025 X1/9 all models '74 thru '80

FORD
- 10355 Ford Automatic Transmission Overhaul
- 10320 Ford Engine Overhaul Manual
- *36004 Aerostar Mini-vans '86 thru '96
  Aspire - see FORD Festiva (36030)
- *36006 Contour/Mercury Mystique '95 thru '98
- 36008 Courier Pick-up all models '72 thru '82
- 36012 Crown Victoria & Mercury Grand Marquis '88 thru '96
- 36016 Escort/Mercury Lynx '81 thru '90
- *36020 Escort/Mercury Tracer '91 thru '96
  Expedition - see FORD Pick-up (36059)
- *36024 Explorer & Mazda Navajo '91 thru '95
- 36028 Fairmont & Mercury Zephyr '78 thru '83
- 36030 Festiva & Aspire '88 thru '97
- 36032 Fiesta all models '77 thru '80
- 36036 Ford & Mercury Full-size,
  Ford LTD & Mercury Marquis ('75 thru '82); Ford Custom 500,Country Squire, Crown Victoria & Mercury Colony Park ('75 thru '87); Ford LTD Crown Victoria & Mercury Gran Marquis ('83 thru '87)
- 36040 Granada & Mercury Monarch '75 thru '80
- 36044 Ford & Mercury Mid-size,
  Ford Thunderbird & Mercury Cougar ('75 thru '82); Ford LTD & Mercury Marquis ('83 thru '86); Ford Torino,Gran Torino, Elite, Ranchero pick-up, LTD II, Mercury Montego, Comet, XR-7 & Lincoln Versailles ('75 thru '86)
- 36048 Mustang V8 all models '64-1/2 thru '73
- 36049 Mustang II 4 cyl, V6 & V8 '74 thru '78
- 36050 Mustang & Mercury Capri incl. Turbo Mustang, '79 thru '93; Capri, '79 thru '86
- *36051 Mustang all models '94 thru '97
- *36054 Pick-ups and Bronco '73 thru '79
- *36058 Pick-ups and Bronco '80 thru '96
- *36059 Pick-ups, Expedition & Lincoln Navigator '97 thru '98
- 36062 Pinto & Mercury Bobcat '75 thru '80
- 36066 Probe all models '89 thru '92
- *36070 Ranger/Bronco II gas models '83 thru '92
- *36071 Ford Ranger '93 thru '97 & Mazda Pick-ups '94 thru '97
- *36074 Taurus & Mercury Sable '86 thru '95
- 36075 Taurus & Mercury Sable '96 thru '98
- *36078 Tempo & Mercury Topaz '84 thru '94
- 36082 Thunderbird/Mercury Cougar '83 thru '88
- *36086 Thunderbird/Mercury Cougar '89 and '97
- 36090 Vans all V8 Econoline models '69 thru '91
- *36094 Vans full size '92 thru '95
- *36097 Windstar Mini-van '95 thru '98

GENERAL MOTORS
- *10360 GM Automatic Transmission Overhaul
- *38005 Buick Century, Chevrolet Celebrity, Olds Cutlass Ciera & Pontiac 6000 all models '82 thru '96
- *38010 Buick Regal, Chevrolet Lumina, Oldsmobile Cutlass Supreme & Pontiac Grand Prix front wheel drive '88 thru '95
- *38015 Buick Skyhawk, Cadillac Cimarron, Chevrolet Cavalier, Oldsmobile Firenza Pontiac J-2000 & Sunbird '82 thru '94
- *38016 Chevrolet Cavalier & Pontiac Sunfire '95 thru '98
- 38020 Buick Skylark, Chevrolet Citation, Olds Omega, Pontiac Phoenix '80 thru '85
- 38025 Buick Skylark & Somerset, Olds Achieva, Calais & Pontiac Grand Am '85 thru '95
- 38030 Cadillac Eldorado & Oldsmobile Toronado '71 thru '85, Seville '80 thru '85, Buick Riviera '79 thru '85
- *38035 Chevrolet Lumina APV, Oldsmobile Silhouette & Pontiac Trans Sport '90 thru '95
  General Motors Full-size
  Rear-wheel drive - see BUICK (19025)

GEO
- Metro - see CHEVROLET Sprint (24075)
- Prizm - see CHEVROLET (24060) or TOYOTA (92036)
- *40030 Storm all models '90 thru '93
  Tracker - see SUZUKI Samurai (90010)

GMC
- Safari - see CHEVROLET ASTRO (24010)
- Vans & Pick-ups - see CHEVROLET

HONDA
- 42010 Accord CVCC all models '76 thru '83
- 42011 Accord all models '84 thru '89
- 42012 Accord all models '90 thru '93
- *42013 Accord all models '94 thru '95
- 42020 Civic 1200 all models '73 thru '79
- 42021 Civic 1300 & 1500 CVCC '80 thru '83
- 42022 Civic 1500 CVCC all models '75 thru '79
- 42023 Civic all models '84 thru '91
- 42024 Civic & del Sol '92 thru '95
  Passport - see ISUZU Rodeo (47017)
- *42040 Prelude CVCC all models '79 thru '89

HYUNDAI
- *43015 Excel all models '86 thru '94

ISUZU
- Hombre - see CHEVROLET S-10 (24071)
- *47017 Rodeo '91 thru '97, Amigo '89 thru '94, Honda Passport '95 thru '97
- *47020 Trooper '84 thru '91, Pick-up '81 thru '93

JAGUAR
- *49010 XJ6 all 6 cyl models '68 thru '86
- *49011 XJ6 all models '88 thru '94
- *49015 XJ12 & XJS all 12 cyl models '72 thru '85

JEEP
- *50010 Cherokee, Comanche & Wagoneer Limited all models '84 thru '96
- 50020 CJ all models '49 thru '86
- *50025 Grand Cherokee all models '93 thru '98
- *50029 Grand Wagoneer & Pick-up '72 thru '91
- *50030 Wrangler all models '87 thru '95

LINCOLN
- Navigator - see FORD Pick-up (36059)
- 59010 Rear Wheel Drive all models '70 thru '96

MAZDA
- 61010 GLC (rear wheel drive) '77 thru '83
- 61011 GLC (front wheel drive) '81 thru '85
- *61015 323 & Protegé '90 thru '97
- *61016 MX-5 Miata '90 thru '97
- *61020 MPV all models '89 thru '94
  Navajo - see FORD Explorer (36024)
- 61030 Pick-ups '72 thru '93
  Pick-ups '94 on - see Ford (36071)
- *61035 RX-7 all models '79 thru '85
- *61036 RX-7 all models '86 thru '91
- *61040 626 (rear wheel drive) '79 thru '82
- *61041 626 & MX-6 (front wheel drive) '83 thru '91

MERCEDES-BENZ
- 63012 123 Series Diesel '76 thru '85
- *63015 190 Series 4-cyl gas models, '84 thru '88
- 63020 230, 250 & 280 6 cyl sohc '68 thru '72
- 63025 280 123 Series gas models '77 thru '81
- 63030 350 & 450 all models '71 thru '80

MERCURY
- See FORD Listing

MG
- 66010 MGB Roadster & GT Coupe '62 thru '80
- 66015 MG Midget & Austin Healey Sprite Roadster '58 thru '80

MITSUBISHI
- *68020 Cordia, Tredia, Galant, Precis & Mirage '83 thru '93
- *68030 Eclipse, Eagle Talon & Plymouth Laser '90 thru '94
- *68040 Pick-up '83 thru '96, Montero '83 thru '93

NISSAN
- 72010 300ZX all models incl. Turbo '84 thru '89
- *72015 Altima all models '93 thru '97
- *72020 Maxima all models '85 thru '91
- *72030 Pick-ups '80 thru '96, Pathfinder '87 thru '95
- 72040 Pulsar all models '83 thru '86
- 72050 Sentra all models '82 thru '94
- *72051 Sentra & 200SX all models '95 thru '98
- *72060 Stanza all models '82 thru '90

OLDSMOBILE
- *73015 Cutlass '74 thru '88
  For other OLDSMOBILE titles, see BUICK, CHEVROLET or GENERAL MOTORS listing.

PLYMOUTH
- For PLYMOUTH titles, see DODGE.

PONTIAC
- 79008 Fiero all models '84 thru '88
- 79018 Firebird V8 models except Turbo '70 thru '81
- 79019 Firebird all models '82 thru '92
  For other PONTIAC titles, see BUICK, CHEVROLET or GENERAL MOTORS listing.

PORSCHE
- *80020 911 Coupe & Targa models '65 thru '89
- 80025 914 all 4 cyl models '69 thru '76
- 80030 924 all models incl. Turbo '76 thru '82
- *80035 944 all models incl. Turbo '83 thru '89

RENAULT
- Alliance, Encore - see AMC (14020)

SAAB
- *84010 900 including Turbo '79 thru '88

SATURN
- *87010 Saturn all models '91 thru '96

SUBARU
- 89002 1100, 1300, 1400 & 1600 '71 thru '79
- *89003 1600 & 1800 2WD & 4WD '80 thru '94

SUZUKI
- *90010 Samurai/Sidekick/Geo Tracker '86 thru '96

TOYOTA
- 92005 Camry all models '83 thru '91
- *92006 Camry all models '92 thru '96
- 92015 Celica Rear Wheel Drive '71 thru '85
- *92020 Celica Front Wheel Drive '86 thru '93
- 92025 Celica Supra all models '79 thru '92
- 92030 Corolla all models '75 thru '79
- 92032 Corolla rear wheel drive models '80 thru '87
- *92035 Corolla front wheel drive models '84 thru '92
- *92036 Corolla & Geo Prizm '93 thru '97
- 92040 Corolla Tercel all models '80 thru '82
- 92045 Corona all models '74 thru '82
- 92050 Cressida all models '78 thru '82
- 92055 Land Cruiser Series FJ40, 43, 45 & 55 '68 thru '82
- *92056 Land Cruiser Series FJ60, 62, 80 & FZJ80 '68 thru '82
- *92065 MR2 all models '85 thru '87
- 92070 Pick-up all models '69 thru '78
- 92075 Pick-up all models '79 thru '95
- *92076 Tacoma '95 thru '98,
  4Runner '96 thru '98, T100 '93 thru '98
- *92080 Previa all models '91 thru '95
- 92085 Tercel all models '87 thru '94

TRIUMPH
- 94007 Spitfire all models '62 thru '81
- 94010 TR7 all models '75 thru '81

VW
- 96008 Beetle & Karmann Ghia '54 thru '79
- 96012 Dasher all gasoline models '74 thru '81
- *96016 Golf, Jetta, Scirocco, & Pick-up gas models '74 thru '91 & Convertible '80 thru '92
- *96017 Golf & Jetta '93 thru '97
- 96020 Rabbit, Jetta, Pick-up diesel '77 thru '84
- 96030 Transporter 1600 all models '68 thru '79
- 96035 Transporter 1700, 1800, 2000 '72 thru '79
- 96040 Type 3 1500 & 1600 '63 thru '73
- 96045 Vanagon air-cooled models '80 thru '83

VOLVO
- 97010 120, 130 Series & 1800 Sports '61 thru '73
- 97015 140 Series all models '66 thru '74
- *97020 240 Series all models '76 thru '93
- *97025 260 Series all models '75 thru '82
- *97040 740 & 760 Series all models '82 thru '88

TECHBOOK MANUALS
- 10205 Automotive Computer Codes
- 10210 Automotive Emissions Control Manual
- 10215 Fuel Injection Manual, 1978 thru 1985
- 10220 Fuel Injection Manual, 1986 thru 1996
- 10225 Holley Carburetor Manual
- 10230 Rochester Carburetor Manual
- 10240 Weber/Zenith/Stromberg/SU Carburetor
- 10305 Chevrolet Engine Overhaul Manual
- 10310 Chrysler Engine Overhaul Manual
- 10320 Ford Engine Overhaul Manual
- 10330 GM and Ford Diesel Engine Repair
- 10340 Small Engine Repair Manual
- 10345 Suspension, Steering & Driveline
- 10355 Ford Automatic Transmission Overhaul
- 10360 GM Automatic Transmission Overhaul
- 10405 Automotive Body Repair & Painting
- 10410 Automotive Brake Manual
- 10415 Automotive Detailing Manual
- 10420 Automotive Eelectrical Manual
- 10425 Automotive Heating & Air Conditioning
- 10430 Automotive Reference Dictionary
- 10435 Automotive Tools Manual
- 10440 Used Car Buying Guide
- 10445 Welding Manual
- 10450 ATV Basics

SPANISH MANUALS
- 98903 Reparación de Carrocería & Pintura
- 98905 Códigos Automotrices de la Computadora
- 98910 Frenos Automotriz
- 98915 Inyección de Combustible 1986 al 1994
- 99040 Chevrolet & GMC Camionetas '67 al '87
- 99041 Chevrolet & GMC Camionetas '88 al '95
- 99042 Chevrolet Camionetas Cerradas '68 al '95
- 99055 Dodge Caravan/Ply. Voyager '84 al '95
- 99075 Ford Camionetas y Bronco '80 al '94
- 99077 Ford Camionetas Cerradas '69 al '91
- 99083 Ford Modelos de Tamaño Grande '75 al '87
- 99088 Ford Modelos de Tamaño Mediano '75 al '86
- 99091 Ford Taurus & Mercury Sable '75 al '86
- 99095 GM Modelos de Tamaño Grande '70 al '88
- 99100 GM Modelos de Tamaño Mediano '70 al '88
- 99110 Nissan Camionetas '80 al '96, Pathfinder '87 al '95
- 99118 Nissan Sentra '82 al '94
- 99125 Toyota Camionetas y 4-Runner '79 al '95